MATLAB
An Introduction with Applications

MATLAB
An Introduction with Applications

Rao V. Dukkipati
Ph.D., P.E.
Fellow of ASME and CSME
Professor and Chair
Graduate Program Director
Department of Mechanical Engineering
Fairfield University
Fairfield, Connecticut
USA

PUBLISHING FOR ONE WORLD
NEW AGE INTERNATIONAL (P) LIMITED, PUBLISHERS
New Delhi • Bangalore • Chennai • Cochin • Guwahati • Hyderabad
Jalandhar • Kolkata • Lucknow • Mumbai • Ranchi
Visit us at **www.newagepublishers.com**

Published by New Age International (P) Ltd., Publishers
First Edition: 2010
Reprint: 2011

Branches:

- No. 37/10, 8th Cross (Near Hanuman Temple), Azad Nagar, Chamrajpet, **Bangalore** - 560 018. Tel.: (080) 26756823, Telefax: 26756820, E-mail: bangalore@newagepublishers.com
- 26, Damodaran Street, T. Nagar, **Chennai** - 600 017. Tel.: (044) 24353401, Telefax: 24351463 E-mail: chennai@newagepublishers.com
- CC-39/1016, Carrier Station Road, Ernakulam South, **Cochin** - 682 016. Tel.: (0484) 2377004, Telefax: 4051303 E-mail: cochin@newagepublishers.com
- Hemsen Complex, Mohd. Shah Road, Paltan Bazar, Near Starline Hotel, **Guwahati** - 781 008.Tel.: (0361) 2513881 Telefax: 2543669, E-mail: guwahati@newagepublishers.com
- No. 105, 1st Floor, Madhiray Kaveri Tower, 3-2-19, Azam Jahi Road, Nimboliadda, **Hyderabad** - 500 027. Tel.: (040) 24652456, Telefax: 24652457, E-mail:hyderabad@newagepublishers.com
- RDB Chambers (Formerly Lotus Cinema)106A, 1st Floor, S.N. Banerjee Road, **Kolkata** - 700 014. Tel.: (033) 22273773, Telefax: 22275247, E-mail:kolkata@newagepublishers.com
- 16-A, Jopling Road, **Lucknow** - 226 001. Tel.: (0522) 2209578, 4045297, Telefax: 2204098 E-mail: lucknow@newagepublishers.com
- 142C, Victor House, Ground Floor, N.M. Joshi Marg, Lower Parel, **Mumbai** - 400 013. Tel.: (022) 24927869 Telefax: 24915415, E-mail: mumbai@newagepublishers.com
- 22, Golden House, Daryaganj, **New Delhi** - 110 002. Tel.: (011) 23262370, 23262368, Telefax: 43551305 E-mail: sales@newagepublishers.com

---

ISBN : 978-81-224-2698-4

₹ 695.00

C-11-04-5543

Printed in India at Glorious Printers, Delhi.
Typeset at In-house.

PUBLISHING FOR ONE WORLD
NEW AGE INTERNATIONAL (P) LIMITED, PUBLISHERS
4835/24, Ansari Road, Daryaganj, New Delhi-110002
Visit us at **www.newagepublishers.com**

To

Lord Sri Venkateswara

PREFACE

The main objective of this book is to provide the students with the opportunity to improve their programming skills using the MATLAB environment to implement algorithms and to teach the use of MATLAB as a tool in solving problems in engineering. This book includes the coverage of basics of MATLAB and application of MATLAB software to solve problems in electrical circuits, control systems, numerical methods, optimization, direct numerical integration methods in engineering. With this foundation of basic MATLAB applications in engineering problem solving, the book provides opportunities to explore advanced topics in application of MATLAB as a tool.

An introduction to MATLAB basics is presented in Chapter 1. Chapter 1 also presents MATLAB commands. MATLAB is considered as the software of choice. MATLAB can be used interactively and has an inventory of routines, called as functions, which minimize the task of programming even more. Further information on MATLAB can be obtained from: The MathWorks, Inc., 3 Apple Hill Drive, Natick, MA 01760. In the computational aspects, MATLAB has emerged as a very powerful tool for numerical computations involved in engineering problems. The idea of computer-aided design and analysis using MATLAB with the Symbolic Math Tool box, and the Control System Tool box has been incorporated. Chapter 2,3,4,5 and 6 consists of many solved problems that demonstrate the application of MATLAB to the analysis of electrical circuits, control systems, numerical methods, optimization and direct numerical integration methods. In chapter 6, we have briefly reviewed the direct numerical integration methods for the solution of a single or system of differential equations. Many numerical methods are available for the solutions of the response of dynamic systems. We have discussed several widely used step-by-step numerical integration methods for linear dynamic response analysis. A brief description of these integration methods is presented and their application is illustrated. The integration schemes considered were three explicit and four implicit methods. They are the explicit schemes (the central difference method, two-cycle interaction with trapezoidal rule and fourth order Runge-Kutta method) and the implicit schemes (Houbolt method, Wilson Theta method, Newmark Beta method and the Park Stiffly stable method). Application of these direct numerical integration methods is illustrated with a case study of a linear dynamic system.

Presentations are limited to very basic topics to serve as an introduction to advanced topics in those areas of discipline. Chapters 2, 3, 4, 5 and 6 include a great number of worked examples and unsolved exercise problems to guide the student to understand the basic principles, concepts and use of MATLAB in solving a variety of engineering problems.

An extensive references to guide the student to further sources of information on electrical circuits, control systems, numerical methods, optimization and direct numerical integration methods is provided at the end of each chapter. ***All end-of-chapter problems are fully solved in the Solution Manual available only to Instructors.***

I sincerely hope that the final outcome of this book will help the students in developing an appreciation for the topic of solving engineering problems with MATLAB.

Rao V. Dukkipati

ACKNOWLEDGEMENT

I am grateful to all those who have had a direct impact on this work. Many people working in the general areas of engineering have influenced the format of this book. I would also like to thank and recognize all the undergraduate and graduate students in mechanical and electrical engineering programs at Fairfield University over the years with whom I had the good fortune to teach and work and who contributed in some ways and provide feedback to the development of the material of this book. In addition, I greatly owe my indebtedness to all the authors of the articles listed in the bibliography of this book. Finally, I would very much like to acknowledge the encouragement, patience and support provided by my family members: Sudha, Ravi, Madhavi, Anand, Ashwin, Raghav, and Vishwa; who have also shared in all the pain, frustration, and fun of producing a manuscript.

I would appreciate being informed of errors, or receiving other comments about the book. Please write to the authors' address or send e-mail to Professordukkipati@yahoo.com.

Rao V. Dukkipati

CONTENTS

CHAPTER 1

MATLAB BASICS

1.1 INTRODUCTION

This chapter is a brief introduction to **MATLAB** (an abbreviation of **MAT**rix **LAB**oratory) basics, registered trademark of computer software, version 4.0 or later developed by the Math Works Inc. The software is widely used in many of science and engineering fields. MATLAB is an interactive program for numerical computation and data visualization. MATLAB is supported on Unix, Macintosh and Windows environments. For more information on MATLAB, contact **The MathWorks.Com**. A Windows version of MATLAB is assumed here. The syntax is very similar for the DOS version.

MATLAB integrates mathematical computing, visualization, and a powerful language to provide a flexible environment for technical computing. The open architecture makes it easy to use MATLAB and its companion products to explore data, create algorithms and create custom tools, that provide early insights and competitive advantages.

Known for its highly optimized matrix and vector calculations, MATLAB offers an intuitive language for expressing problems and their solutions both mathematically and visually. Typical uses include:

- Numeric computation and algorithm development.
- Symbolic computation (with the built-in Symbolic Math functions).
- Modeling, simulation and prototyping.
- Data analysis and signal processing.
- Engineering graphics and scientific visualization.

In this chapter, we will introduce the MATLAB environment. We will learn how to create, edit, save, run and debug M-files (ASCII files with series of MATLAB statements). We will see how to create arrays (matrices and vectors), and explore the built-in MATLAB linear algebra functions for matrix and vector multiplication, dot and cross products, transpose, determinants and inverses, and for the solution of linear equations. MATLAB is based on the language C, but is generally much easier to use. We will also see how to program logic constructs and loops in MATLAB, how to use subprograms and functions, how to use comments (%) for explaining the programs and tabs for easy readability, and how to print and plot graphics both two and three dimensional. MATLAB's functions for symbolic mathematics are presented. Use of these functions to perform symbolic operations, to develop closed form expressions for solutions to algebraic equations, ordinary differential equations, and system of equations was presented. Symbolic mathematics can also be used to determine analytical expressions for the derivative and integral of an expression.

1.1.1 Starting and Quitting MATLAB

To start MATLAB click on the MATLAB icon or type in MATLAB, followed by pressing the *enter* or *return* key at the system prompt. The screen will produce the MATLAB **prompt** >> (or EDU >>), which indicates that MATLAB is waiting for a command to be entered.

In order to quit MATLAB, type **quit** or **exit** after the prompt, followed by pressing the *enter* or *return* key.

1.1.2 Display Windows

MATLAB has three display windows. They are

1. A *Command Window* which is used to enter commands and data to display plots and graphs.
2. A *Graphics Window* which is used to display plots and graphs.
3. An *Edit Window* which is used to create and modify M-files. M-files are files that contain a program or script of MATLAB commands.

1.1.3 Entering Commands

Every command has to be followed by a carriage return <cr> (enter key) in order that the command can be executed. MATLAB commands are case sensitive and *lower case* letters are used throughout.

To execute an M-file (such as Project_1.m), simply enter the name of the file without its extension (as in Project_1).

1.1.4 MATLAB Expo

In order to see some of the MATLAB capabilities, enter the *demo* command. This will initiate the *MATLAB EXPO. MATLAB EXPO* is a graphical demonstration environment that shows some of the different types of operations which can be conducted with MATLAB.

1.1.5 Abort

In order to *abort* a command in MATLAB, hold down the control key and press *c* to generate a local abort with MATLAB.

1.1.6 The Semicolon (;)

If a semicolon (;) is typed at the end of a command, the output of the command is not displayed.

1.1.7 Typing %

When per cent symbol (%) is typed in the beginning of a line, the line is designated as a comment. When the *enter* key is pressed, the line is not executed.

1.1.8 The clc Command

Typing *clc* command and pressing *enter* cleans the command window. Once the *clc* command is executed, a clear window is displayed.

1.1.9 Help

MATLAB has a host of built-in functions. For a complete list, refer to MATLAB user's guide or refer to the *on-line Help*. To obtain help on a particular topic in the list, *e.g.*, inverse, type *help inv*.

1.1.10 Statements and Variables

Statements have the form

```
>> variable = expression
```

The equals ("=") sign implies the assignment of the expression to the variable. For instance, to enter a 2 × 2 matrix with a variable name *A*, we write

```
>> A == [1 2 ; 3 4] ⟨ret⟩
```

The statement is executed after the carriage return (or enter) key is pressed to display

```
A =
     1    2
     3    4
```

1.2 ARITHMETIC OPERATIONS

The symbols for arithmetic operations with scalars are summarized below in Table 1.1.

Table 1.1

Arithmetic operation	Symbol	Example
Addition	+	6 + 3 = 9
Subtraction	–	6 – 3 = 3
Multiplication	*	6 * 3 = 18
Right division	/	6/3 = 2
Left division	\	6\3 = 3/6 = 1/2
Exponentiation	^	6 ^ 3 = 6^3 = 216

1.3 DISPLAY FORMATS

MATLAB has several different screen output formats for displaying numbers. These formats can be found by typing the help command: help format in the Command Window. A few of these formats are shown in Table 1.2 for 2π.

Table 1.2 Display formats

Command	Description	Example
format short	Fixed-point with 4 decimal digits	>> 351/7 ans = 50.1429
format long	Fixed-point with 14 decimal digits	>> 351/7 ans = 50.14285714285715
format short e	Scientific notation with 4 decimal digits	>> 351/7 ans = 5.0143e + 001
format long e	Scientific notation with 15 decimal digits	>> 351/7 ans = 5.014285714285715e001
format short g	Best of 5 digit fixed or floating point	>> 351/7 ans = 50.143

Contd...

format long g	Best of 15 digit fixed or floating point	>> 351/7 ans = 50.1428571428571
format bank	Two decimal digits	>> 351/7 ans = 50.14
format compact	Eliminates empty lines to allow more lines with information displayed on the screen	
format loose	Adds empty lines (opposite of compact)	

1.4 ELEMENTARY MATH BUILT-IN FUNCTIONS

MATLAB contains a number of functions for performing computations which require the use of logarithms, elementary math functions and trigonometric math functions. List of these commonly used elementary MATLAB mathematical built-in functions are given in Tables 1.3 to 1.8.

Table 1.3 Common math functions

Function	Description
abs(x)	Computes the absolute value of **x**.
sqrt(x)	Computes the square root of **x**.
round(x)	Rounds **x** to the nearest integer.
fix(x)	Rounds (or truncates) **x** to the nearest integer toward 0.
floor(x)	Rounds **x** to the nearest integer toward –∞.
ceil(x)	Rounds **x** to the nearest integer toward ∞.
sign(x)	Returns a value of –1 if **x** is less than 0, a value of 0 if **x** equals 0, and a value of 1 otherwise.
rem(x,y)	Returns the remainder of **x/y**. for example, **rem(25, 4)** is 1, and **rem(100, 21)** is 16. This function is also called a **modulus** function.
exp(x)	Computes e^x, where *e* is the base for natural logarithms, or approximately 2.718282.
log(x)	Computes ln **x**, the natural logarithm of **x** to the base *e*.
log10(x)	Computes $\log_{10}$ **x**, the common logarithm of **x** to the base 10.

Table 1.4 Exponential functions

Function	Description
exp(x)	Exponential (e^x)
log(x)	Natural logarithm
log10(x)	Base 10 logarithm
sqrt(x)	Square root

Table 1.5 Trigonometric and hyperbolic functions

Function	Description
sin(x)	Computes the sine of **x**, where **x** is in radians.
cos(x)	Computes the cosine of **x**, where **x** is in radians.
tan(x)	Computes the tangent of **x**, where **x** is in radians.
asin(x)	Computes the arcsine or inverse sine of **x**, where **x** must be between –1 and 1. The function returns an angle in radians between $-\pi/2$ and $\pi/2$.
acos(x)	Computes the arccosine or inverse cosine of **x**, where **x** must be between –1 and 1. The function returns an angle in radians between 0 and π.
atan(x)	Computes the arctangent or inverse tangent of **x**. The function returns an angle in radians between $-\pi/2$ and $\pi/2$.
atan2(y,x)	Computes the arctangent or inverse tangent of the value *y*/*x*. The function returns an angle in radians that will be between $-\pi$ and π, depending on the signs of **x** and **y**.
sinh(x)	Computes the hyperbolic sine of **x**, which is equal to $\frac{e^{x}-e^{-x}}{2}$.
cosh(x)	Computes the hyperbolic cosine of **x**, which is equal to $\frac{e^{x}+e^{-x}}{2}$.
tanh(x)	Computes the hyperbolic tangent of **x**, which is equal to $\frac{\sinh x}{\cosh x}$.
asinh(x)	Computes the inverse hyperbolic sine of **x**, which is equal to $\ln\left(x+\sqrt{x^2+1}\right)$.
acosh(x)	Computes the inverse hyperbolic cosine of **x**, which is equal to $\ln\left(x+\sqrt{x^2-1}\right)$.
atanh(x)	Computes the inverse hyperbolic tangent of **x**, which is equal to $\ln\sqrt{\frac{1+x}{1-x}}$ for $\lvert x\rvert \le 1$.

Table 1.6 Round-off functions

Function	Description	Example
round(x)	Round to the nearest integer	>> round(20/6) ans = 3
fix(x)	Round towards zero	>> fix(13/6) ans = 2
ceil(x)	Round towards infinity	>> ceil(13/5) ans = 3
floor(x)	Round towards minus infinity	>> floor(–10/4) ans = –3
rem(x,y)	Returns the remainder after **x** is divided by **y**	>> rem(14,3) ans = 2
sign(x,y)	Signum function. Returns 1 if **x** > 0, –1 if **x** < 0, and 0 if **x** = 0.	>> sign(7) ans = 1

Table 1.7 Complex number functions

Function	Description
conj(x)	Computes the complex **conjugate** of the complex number **x**. Thus, if **x** is equal to $a + ib$, then **conj(x)** will be equal to $a - ib$.
angle(x)	Computes the real portion of the complex number **x**.
real(x)	Computes the imaginary portion of the complex number **x**.
imag(x)	Computes the absolute value of **magnitude** of the complex number **x**.
abs(x)	Computes the angle using the value of **atan2(imag(x), real(x))**; thus, the angle value is between $-\pi$ and π.

Table 1.8 Arithmetic operations with complex numbers

Operation	Result
$c_1 + c_2$	$(a_1 + a_2) + i(b_1 + b_2)$
$c_1 + c_2$	$(a_1 - a_2) + i(b_1 - b_2)$
$c_1 \bullet c_2$	$(a_1a_2 - b_1b_2) + i(a_1b_2 - a_2b_1)$
$\frac{c_1}{c_2}$	$\frac{a_1a_2 + b_1b_2}{a_2^2 + b_2^2} + i\,\frac{a_2b_1 + b_2a_1}{a_2^2 + b_2^2}$
$\lvert c_1 \rvert$	$\sqrt{a_1^2 + b_1^2}$ (magnitude or absolute value of c_1)
c_1*	$a_1 - ib_1$ (conjugate of c_1)
(Assume that $c_1 = a_1 + ib_1$ and $c_2 = a_2 + ib_2$.)	

1.5 VARIABLE NAMES

A variable is a name made of a letter or a combination of several letters and digits. Variable names can be up to 63 (in MATLAB 7) characters long (31 characters on MATLAB 6.0). MATLAB is case sensitive. For instance, *XX*, *Xx*, *xX* and *xx* are the names of four different variables. It should be noted here that not to use the names of a built-in functions for a variable. For instance, avoid using: sin, cos, exp, sqrt, ..., etc. Once a function name is used to define a variable, the function cannot be used.

1.6 PREDEFINED VARIABLES

MATLAB includes a number of predefined variables. Some of the predefined variables that are available to use in MATLAB programs are summarized in Table 1.9.

Table 1.9 Predefined variables

Predefined variable in MATLAB	Description
ans	Represents a value computed by an expression but not stored in variable name.
pi	Represents the number π.
eps	Represents the floating-point precision for the computer being used. This is the smallest difference between two numbers.
inf	Represents infinity which for instance occurs as a result of a division by zero. A warning message will be displayed or the value will be printed as ∞.
i	Defined as $\sqrt{-1}$, which is: $0 + 1.0000i$.
j	Same as i.
NaN	Stands for Not a Number. Typically occurs as a result of an expression being undefined, as in the case of division of zero by zero.
clock	Represents the current time in a six-element row vector containing year, month, day, hour, minute, and seconds.
date	Represents the current date in a character string format.

1.7 COMMANDS FOR MANAGING VARIABLES

Table 1.10 lists commands that can be used to eliminate variables or to obtain information about variables that have been created. The procedure is to enter the command in the Command Window and the *Enter* key is to be pressed.

Table 1.10 Commands for managing variables

Command	Description
clear	Removes all variables from the memory.
clear x, y, z	Clears/removes only variables **x, y** and **z** from the memory.
who	Lists the variables currently in the workspace.
whos	Displays a list of the variables currently in the memory and their size together with information about their bytes and class.

1.8 GENERAL COMMANDS

In Tables 1.11 to 1.15 the useful general commands on on-line help, workspace information, directory information and general information are given.

Table 1.11 On-line help

Function	Description
help	Lists topics on which help is available.
helpwin	Opens the interactive help window.
helpdesk	Opens the web browser based help facility.
help *topic*	Provides help on *topic*.
lookfor *string*	Lists help topics containing *string*.
demo	Runs the demo program.

Table 1.12 Workspace information

Function	Description
who	Lists variables currently in the workspace.
whos	Lists variables currently in the workspace with their size.
what	Lists m-, mat- and mex-files on the disk.
clear	Clears the workspace, all variables are removed.
clear *x y z*	Clears only variables *x*, *y*, and *z*.
clear all	Clears all variables and functions from workspace.
mlock *fun*	Locks function *fun* so that **clear** cannot remove it.
munlock *fun*	Unlocks function *fun* so that **clear** can remove it.
clc	Clears command window, command history is lost.
home	Same as **clc**.
clf	Clears figure window.

Table 1.13 Directory information

Function	Description
pwd	Shows the current working directory.
cd	Changes the current working directory.
dir	Lists contents of the current directory.
ls	Lists contents of the current directory, same as **dir**.
path	Gets or sets MATLAB search path.
editpath	Modifies MATLAB search path.
copyfile	Copies a file.
mkdir	Creates a directory.

Table 1.14 General information

Function	Description
computer	Tells you the computer type you are using.
clock	Gives you wall clock time and date as a vector.
date	Tells you the date as a string.
more	Controls the paged output according to the screen size.
ver	Gives the license and the version information about MATLAB installed on your computer.
bench	Benchmarks your computer on running MATLAB compared to other computers.

Table 1.15 Termination

Function	Description
c (Control-c)	Local abort, kills the current command execution.
quit	Quits MATLAB.
exit	Same as **quit**.

1.9 ARRAYS

An array is a list of numbers arranged in rows and/or columns. A one-dimensional array is a row or a column of numbers and a two-dimensional array has a set of numbers arranged in rows and columns. An array operation is performed *element-by-element.*

1.9.1 Row Vector

A vector is a row or column of elements.

In a row vector, the elements are entered with a space or a comma between the elements inside the square brackets. For example, $x = [7\ -1\ 2\ -5\ 8]$.

1.9.2 Column Vector

In a column vector, the elements are entered with a semicolon between the elements inside the square brackets. For example, $x = [7;\ -1;\ 2;\ -5;\ 8]$.

1.9.3 Matrix

A matrix is a two-dimensional array which has numbers in rows and columns. A matrix is entered row-wise with consecutive elements of a row separated by a space or a comma, and the rows separated by semicolons or carriage returns. The entire matrix is enclosed within square brackets. The elements of the matrix may be real numbers or complex numbers. For example, to enter the matrix,

$$A = \begin{bmatrix} 1 & 3 & -4 \\ 0 & -2 & 8 \end{bmatrix}$$

The MATLAB input command is

```
A = [1 3 -4 ; 0 -2 8]
```

Similarly, for complex number elements of a matrix B

$$B = \begin{bmatrix} -5x & \ln 2x + 7\sin 3y \\ 3i & 5 - 13i \end{bmatrix}$$

The MATLAB input command is

```
B = [-5*x  log(2*x) + 7*sin(3*y);  3i  5 - 13i]
```

1.9.4 Addressing Arrays

A colon can be used in MATLAB to address a range of elements in a vector or a matrix.

1.9.4.1 Colon for a vector

Va(:) – refers to all the elements of the vector **Va** (either a row or a column vector).
Va(*m*:*n*) – refers to elements *m* through *n* of the vector **Va**.
For instance,

```
>> V= [2 5 -1 11 8 4 7 -3 11]
>> u = V (2 : 8)
   u = 5 -1 11 8 4 7 -3 11
```

1.9.4.2 Colon for a matrix

Table 1.16 gives the use of a colon in addressing arrays in a matrix.

Table 1.16 Colon use for a matrix

Command	Description
A(:, *n*)	Refers to the elements in all the rows of a column *n* of the matrix *A*.
A(*n*, :)	Refers to the elements in all the columns of row *n* of the matrix *A*.
A(:, *m*:*n*)	Refers to the elements in all the rows between columns *m* and *n* of the matrix *A*.
A(*m*:*n*, :)	Refers to the elements in all the columns between rows *m* and *n* of the matrix *A*.
A(*m*:*n*, *p*:*q*)	Refers to the elements in rows *m* through *n* and columns *p* through *q* of the matrix *A*.

1.9.5 Adding Elements to a Vector or a Matrix

A variable that exists as a vector or a matrix can be changed by adding elements to it. Addition of elements is done by assigning values of the additional elements, or by appending existing variables. Rows and/or columns can be added to an existing matrix by assigning values to the new rows or columns.

1.9.6 Deleting Elements

An element or a range of elements of an existing variable can be deleted by reassigning blanks to these elements. This is done simply by the use of square brackets with nothing typed in between them.

1.9.7 Built-in Functions

Some of the built-in functions available in MATLAB for managing and handling arrays as listed in Table 1.17.

Table 1.17 Built-in functions for handling arrays

Function	Description	Example
length(A)	Returns the number of elements in the vector **A**.	>> *A* = [5 9 2 4]; >> length(*A*) ans = 4
size(A)	Returns a row vector [*m, n*], where *m* and *n* are the size *m* × *n* of the array **A**.	>>*A* = [2 3 0 8 11 ; 6 17 5 7 1] *A* = 2 3 0 8 11 6 17 5 7 1 >> size(*A*) ans = 2 5
reshape(A, m, n)	Rearrange a matrix *A* that has *r* rows and *s* columns to have *m* rows and *n* columns. *r* times *s* must be equal to *m* times *n*.	>> *A* = [3 1 4 ; 9 0 7] *A* = 3 1 4 9 0 7 >> *B* = reshape(*A*, 3, 2) *B* = 3 0 9 4 1 7
diag(v)	When *v* is a vector, creates a square matrix with the elements of *v* in the diagonal	>> *v* = [3 2 1]; >> *A* = diag(*v*) *A* = 3 0 0 0 2 0 0 0 1
diag(A)	When *A* is a matrix, creates a vector from the diagonal elements of *A*.	>> *A* = [1 8 3 ; 4 2 6 ; 7 8 3] *A* = 1 8 3 4 2 6 7 8 3 >> vec = diag(*A*) vec = 1 2 3

1.10 OPERATIONS WITH ARRAYS

We consider here matrices that have more than one row and more than one column.

1.10.1 Addition and Subtraction of Matrices

The addition (the sum) or the subtraction (the difference) of the two arrays is obtained by adding or subtracting their corresponding elements. These operations are performed with arrays of identical size (same number of rows and columns).

For example, if A and B are two arrays (2×3 matrices).

$$A = \begin{bmatrix} a_{11} & a_{12} & a_{13} \\ a_{21} & a_{22} & a_{23} \end{bmatrix} \text{ and } B = \begin{bmatrix} b_{11} & b_{12} & b_{13} \\ b_{21} & b_{22} & b_{23} \end{bmatrix}$$

Then, the matrix addition $(A + B)$ is obtained by adding A and B is

$$\begin{bmatrix} a_{11}+b_{11} & a_{12}+b_{12} & a_{13}+b_{13} \\ a_{21}+b_{21} & a_{22}+b_{22} & a_{23}+b_{23} \end{bmatrix}$$

1.10.2 Dot Product

The dot product is a scalar computed from two vectors of the same size. The scalar is the sum of the products of the values in corresponding positions in the vectors.
For n elements in the vectors A and B:

$$\text{dot product} = A \cdot B = \sum_{i=1}^{n} a_i \, b_i$$

dot(A, B): Computes the dot product of A and B. If A and B are matrices, the dot product is a row vector containing the dot products for the corresponding columns of A and B.

1.10.3 Array Multiplication

The value in position $c_{i,j}$ of the product C of two matrices, A and B, is the dot product of row i of the first matrix and column of the second matrix.

$$c_{i,j} = \sum_{k=1}^{n} a_{i,k} \, b_{k,j}$$

1.10.4 Array Division

The division operation can be explained by means of the identity matrix and the inverse matrix operation.

1.10.5 Identity Matrix

An identity matrix is a square matrix in which all the diagonal elements are 1's, and the remaining elements are 0's. If a matrix A is square, then it can be multiplied by the identity matrix, I, from the left or from the right:

$$AI = IA = A$$

1.10.6 Inverse of a Matrix

The matrix B is the inverse of the matrix A when the two matrices are multiplied and the product is an identity matrix. Both matrices A and B must be square and the order of multiplication can be AB or BA.

$$AB = BA = I$$

1.10.7 Transpose

The transpose of a matrix is a new matrix in which the rows of the original matrix are the columns of the new matrix. The transpose of a given matrix A is denoted by A^T. In MATLAB, the transpose of the matrix A is denoted by A'.

1.10.8 Determinant

A determinant is a scalar computed from the entries in a square matrix. For a 2 × 2 matrix A, the determinant is

$$|A| = a_{11}\,a_{22} - a_{21}\,a_{12}$$

MATLAB will compute the determinant of a matrix using the **det** function:

det(A): Computes the determinant of a square matrix A.

1.10.9 Array Division

MATLAB has two types of array division, which are the left division and the right division.

1.10.10 Left Division

The left division is used to solve the matrix equation $Ax = B$ where x and B are column vectors. Multiplying both sides of this equation by the inverse of A, A^{-1}, we have

$$A^{-1}Ax = A^{-1}\,B$$

or $$Ix = x = A^{-1}\,B$$

Hence $$x = A^{-1}\,B$$

In MATLAB, the above equation is written by using the left division character:

$$x = A \backslash B$$

1.10.11 Right Division

The right division is used to solve the matrix equation $xA = B$ where x and B are row vectors. Multiplying both sides of this equation by the inverse of A, A^{-1}, we have

$$x * AA^{-1} = B * A^{-1}$$

or $$x = B * A^{-1}$$

In MATLAB, this equation is written by using the right division character:

$$x = B/A$$

1.10.12 Eigenvalues and Eigenvectors

Consider the following equation:

$$AX = \lambda X \qquad ...(1.1)$$

where A is an $n \times n$ square matrix, X is a column vector with n rows and λ is a scalar.

The values of λ for which X are non-zero are called the *eigenvalues* of the matrix A, and the corresponding values of X are called the *eigenvectors* of the matrix A.

Equation (1.1) can also be used to find the following equation:

$$(A - \lambda I)X = 0 \qquad ...(1.2)$$

where I is an $n \times n$ identity matrix. Equation (1.2) corresponding to a set of homogeneous equations and has non-trivial solutions only if the determinant is equal to zero, or

$$|A - \lambda I| = 0 \qquad ...(1.3)$$

Equation (1.3) is known as the *characteristic equation* of the matrix A. The solution to Eq.(1.3) gives the eigenvalues of the matrix A.

MATLAB determines both the eigenvalues and eigenvectors for a matrix *A*.

eig(A): Computes a column vector containing the eigenvalues of *A*.

[Q, d] = eig(A): Computes a square matrix *Q* containing the eigenvectors of *A* as columns and a square matrix *d* containing the eigenvlaues (λ) of *A* on the diagonal. The values of *Q* and *d* are such that $Q * Q$ is the identity matrix and $A*X$ equals λ times *X*.

***Triangular factorization or lower-upper factorization*:** Triangular or lower-upper factorization expresses a square matrix as the product of two triangular matrices—a lower triangular matrix and an upper triangular matrix. The **lu** function in MATLAB computes the **LU** factorization.

[L, U] = lu(A): Computes a permuted lower triangular factor in *L* and an upper triangular factor in *U* such that the product of *L* and *U* is equal to *A*.

QR *factorization*: The **QR** factorization method factors a matrix *A* into the product of an orthonormal matrix and an upper-triangular matrix. The **qr** function is used to perform the **QR** factorization in MATLAB.

[Q, R] = qr(A): Computes the values of *Q* and *R* such that $A = QR$. *Q* will be an orthonormal matrix, and *R* will be an upper triangular matrix..

For a matrix *A* of size $m \times n$, the size of *Q* is $m \times m$, and the size of *R* is $m \times n$.

***Singular Value Decomposition (SVD)*:** Singular value decomposition decomposes a matrix *A* (size $m \times n$) into a product of three matrix factors.

$$A = USV$$

where *U* and *V* are orthogonal matrices and *S* is a diagonal matrix. The size of *U* is $m \times m$, the size of *V* is $n \times n$, and the size of *S* is $m \times n$. The values on the diagonal matrix *S* are called singular values. The number of non-zero singular values is equal to the rank of the matrix.

The *SVD* factorization can be obtained using the **svd** function.

[U, S, V] = svd(A): Computes the factorization of *A* into the product of three matrices, *USV*, where *U* and *V* are orthogonal matrices and *S* is a diagonal matrix.

svd(A): Returns the diagonal elements of *S*, which are the singular values of *A*.

1.11 ELEMENT-BY-ELEMENT OPERATIONS

Element-by-element operations can only be done with arrays of the same size. Element-by-element multiplication, division and exponentiation of two vectors or matrices is entered in MATLAB by typing a period in front of the arithmetic operator. Table 1.18 lists these operations.

Table 1.18 Element-by-element operations

Arithmetic operators			
Matrix operators		Array operators	
+	Addition	+	Addition
–	Subtraction	–	Subtraction
*	Multiplication	.*	Array multiplication
^	Exponentiation	.^	Array exponentiation
/	Right division	./	Array right division
\	Left division	.\	Array left division

1.11.1 Built-in Functions for Arrays

Table 1.19 lists some of the many built-in functions available in MATLAB for analysing arrays.

Table 1.19 MATLAB built-in array functions

Function	Description	Example
mean(A)	If *A* is a vector, returns the mean value of the elements	>> *A* = [3 7 2 16]; >> mean(*A*) ans = 7
C = max(A)	If *A* is a vector, *C* is the largest element in *A*. If *A* is a matrix, *C* is a row vector containing the largest element of each column of *A*.	>> *A* = [3 7 2 16 9 5 18 13 0 4]; >> *C* = max(*A*) *C* = 18
[d, n] = max(A)	If *A* is a vector, *d* is the largest element in *A*, *n* is the position of the element (the first if several have the max value).	>> [*d*, *n*] = max(*A*) *d* = 18 *n* = 7
min(A)	The same as **max(A)**, but for the smallest element.	>> *A* = [3 7 2 16]; >> min(*A*) ans = 2
[d, n] = min(A)	The same as **[d, n] = max(A)**, but for the smallest element.	
sum(A)	If *A* is a vector, returns the sum of the elements of the vector.	>> *A* = [3 7 2 16]; >> sum(*A*) ans = 28
sort(A)	If *A* is a vector, arranges the elements of the vector in ascending order.	>> *A* = [3 7 2 16]; >> sort(*A*) ans = 2 3 7 16
median(A)	If *A* is a vector, returns the median value of the elements of the vector.	>> *A* = [3 7 2 16]; >> median(*A*) ans =5
std(A)	If *A* is a vector, returns the standard deviation of the elements of the vector.	>> *A* = [3 7 2 16]; >> std(*A*) ans = 6.3770
det(A)	Returns the determinant of a square matrix *A*.	>> *A* = [1 2 ; 3 4]; >> det(*A*) ans = – 2
dot(a, b)	Calculates the scalar (dot) product of two vectors *a* and *b*. The vector can each be row or column vectors.	>> *a* = [5 6 7]; >> *b* = [4 3 2]; >> dot(*a*,*b*) ans = 52
cross(a, b)	Calculates the cross product of two vectors *a* and *b*, (*a* × *b*). The two vectors must have 3 elements.	>> *a* = [5 6 7]; >> *b* = [4 3 2]; >> cross(*a*, *b*) ans = –9 18 –9

Contd...

inv(A)	Returns the inverse of a square matrix *A*.	>> *a* = [1 2 3; 4 6 8; –1 2 3]; >> inv(*A*) ans = –0.5000 0.0000 –0.5000 –5.0000 1.5000 1.0000 3.5000 –1.0000 –0.5000

1.12 RANDOM NUMBERS GENERATION

There are many physical processes and engineering applications that require the use of *random numbers* in the development of a solution.

MATLAB has two commands *rand* and *rand n* that can be used to assign random numbers to variables.

The *rand* command: The *rand* command generates uniformly distributed over the interval [0, 1]. A *seed value* is used to initiate a random sequence of values. The seed value is initially set to zero. However, it can be changed with the *seed* function.

The command can be used to assign these numbers to a scalar, a vector or a matrix as shown in Table 1.20.

Table 1.20 The *rand* command

Command	Description	Example
rand	Generates a single random number between 0 and 1.	>> rand ans = 0.9501
rand(1, n)	Generates an *n* elements row vector of random numbers between 0 and 1.	>> *a* = rand(1, 3) *a* = 0.4565 0.0185 0.8214
rand(n)	Generates an $n \times n$ matrix with random numbers between 0 and 1.	>> *b* = rand(3) *b* = 0.7382 0.9355 0.8936 0.1763 0.9165 0.0579 0.4057 0.4103 0.3529
rand(m, n)	Generates an $m \times n$ matrix with random numbers between 0 and 1.	>> *c* = rand(2, 3) *c* = 0.2028 0.6038 0.1988 0.1987 0.2722 0.0153
randperm (n)	Generates a row vector with *n* elements that are random permutation of integers 1 through *n*.	>> randperm(7) ans = 5 2 4 7 1 6 3

1.12.1 The Random Command

MATLAB will generate Gaussian values with a mean of zero and a variance of 1.0 if a normal distribution is specified. The MATLAB functions for generating Gaussian values are as follows:

randn(n): Generates an $n \times n$ matrix containing Gaussian (or normal) random numbers with a mean of 0 and a variance of 1.

randn(m, n): Generates an $m \times n$ matrix containing Gaussian (or normal) random numbers with a mean of 0 and a variance of 1.

1.13 POLYNOMIALS

A *polynomial* is a function of a single variable that can be expressed in the following form:

$$f(x) = a_0x^n + a_1x^{n-1} + a_2x^{n-2} + \cdots + a_{n-1}x^1 + a_n$$

where the variable is x and the coefficients of the polynomial are represented by the values a_0, a_1, ... and so on. The *degree* of a polynomial is equal to the largest value used as an exponent.

A vector represents a polynomial in MATLAB. When entering the data in MATLAB, simply enter each coefficient of the polynomial into the vector in descending order. For example, consider the polynomial

$$5s^5 + 7s^4 + 2s^2 - 6s + 10$$

To enter this into MATLAB, we enter this as a vector as

```
>>x = [5 7 0  2 -6 10]
  x =
         5 7 0 2 -6 10
```

It is necessary to enter the coefficients of all the terms.

MATLAB contains functions that perform polynomial multiplication and division, which are listed below:

conv(a, b): Computes a coefficient vector that contains the coefficients of the product of polynomials represented by the coefficients in **a** and **b**. The vectors **a** and **b** do not have to be the same size.

[q, r] = deconv(n, d): Returns two vectors. The first vector contains the coefficients of the quotient and the second vector contains the coefficients of the remainder polynomial.

The MATLAB function for determining the roots of a polynomial is the **roots** function:

root(a): Determines the roots of the polynomial represented by the coefficient vector **a**.

The roots function returns a column vector containing the roots of the polynomial; the number of roots is equal to the degree of the polynomial. When the roots of a polynomial are known, the coefficients of the polynomial are determined. When all the linear terms are multiplied, we can use the **poly** function:

poly(r): Determines the coefficients of the polynomial whose roots are contained in the vector **r**.

The output of the function is a row vector containing the polynomial coefficients.

The value of a polynomial can be computed using the *polyval* function, **polyval (a, x).** It evaluates a polynomial with coefficients **a** for the values in **x**. The result is a matrix the same size as **x**. For instance, to find the value of the above polynomial at $s = 2$,

```
>>x = polyval([5 7 0 2 -6 10], 2)
  x =
     278
```

To find the roots of the above polynomial, we enter the command **roots (a)** which determines the roots of the polynomial represented by the coefficient vector **a**.

```
>>roots([5 7 0  2 -6 10])
ans =
-1.8652
-0.4641 + 1.0832i
-0.4641 - 1.0832i
 0.6967 + 0.5355i
 0.6967 - 0.5355i
```

```
%or
>> x = [5 7 0 2 -6 10]
   x = 5 7 0  2 -6 10
>> r = roots(x)
r =
   -1.8652
   -0.4641 + 1.0832i
   -0.4641 - 1.0832i
    0.6967 + 0.5355i
    0.6967 - 0.5355i
```

To multiply two polynomials together, we enter the command *conv*.
The polynomials are: $x = 2x + 5$ and $y = x^2 + 3x + 7$

```
>>x = [2 5];
>>y = [1 3  7];
>>z = conv(x, y)
  z = 2 11 29 35
```

To divide two polynomials, we use the command *deconv*.

```
z = [2 11 29 35]; x = [2 5]
 >> [g, t] = deconv (z, x)
g = 1   3   7
t = 0   0   0   0
```

1.14 SYSTEM OF LINEAR EQUATIONS

A system of equations is non-singular if the matrix **A** containing the coefficients of the equations is non-singular. A system of non-singular simultaneous linear equations (**AX = B**) can be solved using two methods:

(a) Matrix Division Method.

(b) Matrix Inversion Method.

1.14.1 Matrix Division

The solution to the matrix equation **AX = B** is obtained using matrix division, or **X = A/B.** The vector **X** then contains the values of **x.**

1.14.2 Matrix Inverse

For the solution of the matrix equation **AX = B**, we premultiply both sides of the equation by $\mathbf{A^{-1}}$.

$$\mathbf{A^{-1}AX = A^{-1}B}$$

or $$\mathbf{IX = A^{-1}B}$$

where **I** is the identity matrix.

Hence $$\mathbf{X = A^{-1}B}$$

In MATLAB, we use the command **x** = inv **(A)*B**. Similarly, for **XA = B**, we use the command **x = B** * inv **(A)**.

The basic computational unit in MATLAB is the matrix. A matrix expression is enclosed in square brackets, [ ]. Blanks or commas separate the column elements, and semicolons or carriage returns separate the rows.

```
>>A = [1 2 3 4 ; 5 6 7 8 ; 9 10 11 12]
A =
   1   2   3   4
   5   6   7   8
   9  10  11  12
```

The transpose of a simple matrix or a complex matrix is obtained by using the *apostrophe* key

```
>>B = A'
B =
   1   5   9
   2   6  10
   3   7  11
   4   8  12
```

Matrix multiplication is accomplished as follows:

```
>>C = A*B
C =
    30   70  110
    70  174  278
   110  278  446
>>C = B*A
C =
   107  122  137  152
   122  140  158  176
   137  158  179  200
   152  176  200  224
```

The inverse of a matrix D is obtained as

```
>>D = [1  2 ; 3  4]
D =
   1   2
   3   4
>>E = inv (D)
E =
   -2.0000    1.0000
    1.5000   -0.5000
```

Similarly, its eigenvalue is

```
>>eig (D)
ans =
   -0.3723
    5.3723
```

Matrix operations require that the matrix dimensions be compatible. If A is an $n \times m$ and B is a $p \times r$, then $A \pm B$ is allowed only if $n = p$ and $m = r$. Similarly, matrix product $A * B$ is allowed only if $m = p$.

Example E1.1: Consider the two matrices:

$$\mathbf{A} = \begin{bmatrix} 1 & 0 & 1 \\ 2 & 3 & 4 \\ -1 & 6 & 7 \end{bmatrix} \quad \text{and} \quad \mathbf{B} = \begin{bmatrix} 7 & 4 & 2 \\ 3 & 5 & 6 \\ -1 & 2 & 1 \end{bmatrix}$$

Using MATLAB, determine the following:

(*a*) $\mathbf{A}+\mathbf{B}$

(*b*) $\mathbf{AB}$

(*c*) $\mathbf{A}^2$

(*d*) $\mathbf{A}^T$

(*e*) $\mathbf{B}^{-1}$

(*f*) $\mathbf{B}^T\mathbf{A}^T$

(*g*) $\mathbf{A}^2+\mathbf{B}^2-\mathbf{AB}$

(*h*) determinant of **A**, determinant of **B** and determinant of **AB**.

Solution:

```
>> A = [1 0 1; 2 3 4; -1 6 7]
A =
     1     0     1
     2     3     4
    -1     6     7
>> B = [7 4 2; 3 5 6; -1 2 1]
B =
     7     4     2
     3     5     6
    -1     2     1
```

(*a*)
```
>> C = A + B
C =
     8     4     3
     5     8    10
    -2     8     8
```

(*b*)
```
>> D = A*B
D =
     6     6     3
    19    31    26
     4    40    41
```

(*c*)
```
>> E = A^2 = A²
E =
    0     6     8
    4    33    42
    4    60    72
```

(*d*)
```
>> % Let F = transpose of A
>> F=A'
   F =
        1    2   -1
        0    3    6
        1    4    7
```

(*e*)
```
>> H = inv (B)
H =
    0.1111    0.0000   -0.2222
    0.1429   -0.1429    0.5714
   -0.1746    0.2857   -0.3651
```

(*f*)
```
>> J = B'*A'
   J =
        6   19    4
        6   31   40
        3   26   41
```

(*g*)
```
>> K = A^2 + B^2 - A*B
   K =
       53   52   45
       15   51   58
       -2   28   42
```

(*h*)
```
det  (A) = 12
det  (B) = -63
det(A*B) = -756
```

Example E1.2: Determine the eigenvalues and eigenvectors of *A* and *B* using MATLAB

$$\mathbf{A} = \begin{bmatrix} 4 & 2 & -3 \\ -1 & 1 & 3 \\ 2 & 5 & 7 \end{bmatrix} \quad \text{and} \quad \mathbf{B} = \begin{bmatrix} 1 & 2 & 3 \\ 8 & 7 & 6 \\ 5 & 3 & 1 \end{bmatrix}$$

Solution:

```
% Determine the eigenvalues and eigenvectors
A = [4 2 -3 ; -1 1 3 ; 2 5 7]
   A =
       4    2   -3
      -1    1    3
       2    5    7
eig(A)
  ans = 0.5949
        3.0000
        8.4051
```

```
lamda = eig(A)
lamda = 0.5949
        3.0000
        8.4051
[V, D] = eig (A)
   V =
      -0.6713    0.9163   -0.3905
       0.6713   -0.3984    0.3905
      -0.3144    0.0398    0.8337
   D =
       0.5949    0         0
       0         3.0000    0
       0         0         8.4051
```

Example E1.3: Determine the values of *x*, *y* and *z* for the following set of linear algebraic equations:

$$x_2 - 3x_3 = -5$$
$$2x_1 + 3x_2 - x_3 = 7$$
$$4x_1 + 5x_2 - 2x_3 = 10$$

Solution:

Here

$$\mathbf{A} = \begin{bmatrix} 0 & 1 & -3 \\ 2 & 3 & -1 \\ 4 & 5 & -2 \end{bmatrix}, \mathbf{B} = \begin{bmatrix} 5 \\ 7 \\ 10 \end{bmatrix} \text{ and } \mathbf{X} = \begin{bmatrix} x_1 \\ x_2 \\ x_3 \end{bmatrix}$$

$$\mathbf{AX} = \mathbf{B}$$
$$\mathbf{A}^{-1}\mathbf{AX} = \mathbf{A}^{-1}\mathbf{B}$$
$$\mathbf{IX} = \mathbf{A}^{-1}\mathbf{B}$$

or $$\mathbf{X} = \mathbf{A}^{-1}\mathbf{B}$$

```
>> A = [0 1 -3; 2 3 -1; 4 5 -2];
>> B = [-5; 7; 10]
>> x = inv (A)*B
   x =
       -1.0000
        4.0000
        3.0000
>> check = A*x
check =
       -5
        7
       10
```

% Alternative method

```
>> x = A\B
   x =
      -1
       4
       3
```

1.15 SCRIPT FILES

A *script* is a sequence of ordinary statements and functions used at the command prompt level. A script is invoked the command prompt level by typing the file-name or by using the pull down menu. Scripts can also invoke other scripts.

The commands in the Command Window cannot be saved and executed again. Also, the Command Window is not interactive. To overcome these difficulties, the procedure is first to create a file with a list of commands, save it and then run the file. In this way, the commands contained are executed in the order they are listed when the file is run. In addition, as the need arises, one can change or modify the commands in the file; the file can be saved and run again. The files that are used in this fashion are known as *script files*. Thus, a script file is a text file that contains a sequence of MATLAB commands. Script file can be edited (corrected and/or changed) and executed many times.

1.15.1 Creating and Saving a Script File

Any text editor can be used to create script files. In MATLAB, script files are created and edited in the Editor/Debugger Window. This window can be opened from the Command Window. From the Command Window, select *File*, *New* and then M-file. Once the window is open, the commands of the script file are typed line by line. The commands can also be typed in any text editor or word processor program and then copied and pasted in the Editor/Debugger Window. The second type of M-files is the *function file*. Function file enables the user to extend the basic library functions by adding ones own computational procedures. Function *M*-files are expected to return one or more results. Script files and function files may include reference to other MATLAB toolbox routines.

MATLAB function file begins with a header statement of the form:

function (name of result or results) = name (argument list)

Before a script file can be executed it must be saved. All script files must be saved with the extension ".m". MATLAB refers to them as M-files. When using MATLAB M-files editor, the files will automatically be saved with a ".m" extension. If any other text editor is used, the file must be saved with the ".m" extension, or MATLAB will not be able to find and run the script file. This is done by choosing *Save As*... from the *File* menu, selecting a location, and entering a name for the file. The names of user defined variables, predefined variables, MATLAB commands or functions should not be used to name script files.

1.15.2 Running a Script File

A script file can be executed either by typing its name in the Command Window and then pressing the *Enter* key, directly from the Editor Window by clicking on the *Run* icon. The file is assumed to be in the current directory, or in the search path.

1.15.3 Input to a Script File

There are three ways of assigning a value to a variable in a script file.

1. The variable is defined and assigned value in the script file.
2. The variable is defined and assigned value in the Command Window.
3. The variable is defined in the script file, but a specified value is entered in the Command Window when the script file is executed.

1.15.4 Output Commands

There are two commands that are commonly used to generate output. They are the *disp* and *fprintf* commands.

1. The *disp* command:

The *disp* command displays the elements of a variable without displaying the name of the variable and displays text.

```
disp(name of a variable) or disp('text as string')
        >>A = [1 2 3 ; 4 5 6 ];
        >> disp(A)
              1 2 3
              4 5 6
        >> disp('Solution to the problem.')
          Solution to the problem.
```

2. The *fprintf* command:

The *fprintf* command displays output (text and data) on the screen or saves it to a file. The output can be formatted using this command.

Example E1.4: Write a function file Veccrossprod to compute the cross product of two vectors **a** and **b**, where **a** $= (a_1, a_2, a_3)$, **b** $= (b_1, b_2, b_3)$, and $a \times b = (a_2b_3 - a_3b_2, a_3b_1 - a_1b_3, a_1b_2 - a_2b_1)$. Verify the function by taking the cross products of pairs of unit vectors: (**i**, **j**), (**j**, **k**), etc.

Solution:

```
    function c = Veccrossprod(a, b);
% Veccrossprod : function to compute c = a x b where a and b are 3-D vectors
% call syntax:
% c = Veccrossprod(a, b);
c = [a(2) * b(3) - a(3) * b(2) ; a(3) * b(1) - a(1) * b(3) ; a(1) * b(2) - a(2) * b(1)];
```

1.16 PROGRAMMING IN MATLAB

One most significant feature of MATLAB is its extendibility through user-written programs such as the M-files. M-files are ordinary ASCII text files written in MATLAB language. A function file is a subprogram.

1.16.1 Relational and Logical Operators

A relational operator compares two numbers by finding whether a comparison statement is true or false. A logical operator examines true/false statements and produces a result which is true or false according to the specific operator. Relational and logical operators are used in mathematical expressions and also in combination with other commands to make decision that control the flow of a computer program.

MATLAB has six relational operators as shown in Table 1.21.

Table 1.21 Relational operators

Relational operator	Interpretation
<	Less than
<=	Less than or equal
>	Greater than
>=	Greater than or equal
==	Equal
~=	Not equal

The logical operators in MATLAB are shown in Table 1.22.

Table 1.22 Logical operators

<table>
<tr><th>Logical operator</th><th>Name</th><th>Description</th></tr>
<tr><td>&
Example: A&B</td><td>AND</td><td>Operates on two operands (A and B). If both are true, the result is true (1), otherwise the result is false (0).</td></tr>
<tr><td>|
Example: A|B</td><td>OR</td><td>Operates on two operands (A and B). If either one, or both are true, the result is true (1), otherwise (both are false) the result is false (0).</td></tr>
<tr><td>~
Example: ~A</td><td>NOT</td><td>Operates on one operand (A). Gives the opposite of the operand. True (1) if the operand is false, and false (0) if the operand is true.</td></tr>
</table>

1.16.2 Order of Precedence

The following Table 1.23 shows the order of precedence used by MATLAB.

Table 1.23

<table>
<tr><th>Precedence</th><th>Operation</th></tr>
<tr><td>1 (highest)</td><td>Parentheses (If nested parentheses exist, inner have precedence).</td></tr>
<tr><td>2</td><td>Exponentiation.</td></tr>
<tr><td>3</td><td>Logical NOT (~).</td></tr>
<tr><td>4</td><td>Multiplication, Division.</td></tr>
<tr><td>5</td><td>Addition, Subtraction.</td></tr>
<tr><td>6</td><td>Relational operators (>, <, >=, <=, = =, ~=).</td></tr>
<tr><td>7</td><td>Logical AND (&).</td></tr>
<tr><td>8 (lowest)</td><td>Logical OR (|).</td></tr>
</table>

1.16.3 Built-in Logical Functions

The MATLAB built-in functions which are equivalent to the logical operators are:

and (A, B) Equivalent to *A* & *B*
or (A, B) Equivalent to *A* | *B*
not (A) Equivalent to ~*A*

List the MATLAB logical built-in functions are described in Table 1.24.

Table 1.24 Additional logical built-in functions

Function	Description	Example
xor(a, b)	Exclusive or. Returns true (1) if one operand is true and the other is false.	>>xor(8, –1) ans = 0 >>xor(8, 0) ans = 1
all(A)	Returns 1 (true) if all elements in a vector *A* are true (non-zero). Returns 0 (false) if one or more elements are false (zero). If *A* is a matrix, treats columns of *A* as vectors, returns a vector with 1's and 0's.	>>*A* = [5 3 11 7 8 15] >>all(*A*) ans = 1 >>*B* = [3 6 11 4 0 13] >>all(*B*) ans = 0
any(A)	Returns 1 (true) if any element in a vector *A* is true (non-zero). Returns 0 (false) if all elements are false (zero). If *A* is a matrix, treats columns of *A* as vectors, returns a vector with 1's and 0's.	>>*A* = [5 0 14 0 0 13] >>any(*A*) ans = 1 >>*B* = [0 0 0 0 0 0] >>any(*B*) ans = 0
find(A) **find(A>d)**	If *A* is a vector, returns the indices of the non-zero elements. If *A* is a vector, returns the address of the elements that are larger than *d* (any relational operator can be used).	>>*A* = [0 7 4 2 8 0 0 3 9] >>find(*A*) ans = 2 3 4 5 8 9 >>find(*A* > 4) ans = 4 5 6

The truth table for the operation of the four logical operators, and, or, xor and not are summarized in Table 1.25.

Table 1.25 Truth table

INPUT		OUTPUT				
A	*B*	AND *A*&*B*	OR *A*|*B*	XOR *(A,B)*	NOT *~A*	NOT *~B*
false	false	false	false	false	true	true
false	true	false	true	true	true	false
true	false	false	true	true	false	true
true	true	true	true	false	false	false

1.16.4 Conditional Statements

A conditional statement is a command that allows MATLAB to make a decision on whether to execute a group of commands that follow the conditional statement or to skip these commands.

if conditional expression consists of relational and/or logical operators

```
if a < 30
    count = count + 1
    disp a
    end
```

The general form of a simple **if** statement is as follows:

```
if    logical expression
          statements
end
```

If the logical expression is true, the statements between the **if** statement and the **end** statement are executed. If the logical expression is false, then it goes to the statements following the **end** statement.

1.16.5 Nested if Statements

Following is an example of *nested if* statements:

```
if  a < 30
    count = count + 1;
    disp(a);
    if  b > a
        b = 0;
    end
end
```

1.16.6 else AND elseif Clauses

The else clause allows to execute one set of statements if a logical expression is true, and a different set if the logical expression is false.

```
%   variable name inc
    if  inc < 1
        x_inc = inc/10;
        else
        x_inc = 0.05;
        end
```

When several levels of **if-else** statements are nested, it may be difficult to find which logical expressions must be true (or false) to execute each set of statements. In such cases, the **elseif** clause is used to clarify the program logic.

1.16.7 MATLAB while Structures

There is a structure in MATLAB that combines the for loop with the features of the if block. This is called the *while loop* and has the form:

while *logical expression*

This set of statements is executed repeatedly as long as the logical expressions remain true (equals +1) or if the expression is a matrix rather than a simple scalar variable, as long as, *all* the elements of the matrix remain non-zero.

end

In addition to the normal termination of a loop by means of the **end** statement, there are additional MATLAB commands available to interrupt the calculations. These commands are listed in Table 1.26.

Table 1.26

Command	Description
break	Terminates the execution of MATLAB **for** and **while** loops. In nested loops, **break** will terminate only the innermost loop in which it is placed.
return	Primarily used in MATLAB functions, **return** will cause a normal return from a function from the point at which the **return** statement is executed.
error ('*text*')	Terminates execution and displays the message contained in *text* on the screen. Note, the text must be enclosed in single quotes.

The MATLAB functions used are summarized in Table 1.27 below:

Table 1.27

<table>
<tr><th>Function</th><th>Description</th></tr>
<tr><td>Relational operators</td><td>A MATLAB logical relation is a comparison between two variables x and y of the same size effected by one of the six operators, <, <=, >, >=, = =, ~ =. The comparison involves corresponding elements of x and y, and yields a matrix or scalar of the same size with values of "true" or "false" for each of its elements. In MATLAB, the value of "false" is zero, and "true" has a value of one. Any non-zero quantity is interpreted as "true".</td></tr>
<tr><td>Combinatorial operators</td><td>The operators & (AND) and | (OR) may be used to combine two logical expressions.</td></tr>
<tr><td>all, any</td><td>If x is a vector, all(x) returns a value of one; if all of the elements of x are non-zero, and a value of zero otherwise. When X is a matrix, all(X) returns a row vector of ones or zeros obtained by applying all to each of the columns of X. The function any operates similarly if any of the elements of x are non-zero.</td></tr>
<tr><td>find</td><td>If x is a vector, i = find(x) returns the indices of those elements of x that are non-zero (i.e., true). Thus, replacing all the negative elements of x by zero could be accomplished by
i = find(x < 0);
x(i) = zeros(size(i));
If X is a matrix, [i, j] = find(X)operates similarly and returns the row-column indices of non-zero elements.</td></tr>
<tr><td>if, else, elseif</td><td>The several forms of MATLAB if blocks are as follows:
if variable   if variable 1   if variable 1
block of statements   block of statements   block of statements</td></tr>
</table>

Contd...

	executed if *variable* executed if *variable* 1 executed if *variable* 1 is "true", *i.e.*, non-zero is "true", *i.e.*, Non-zero is "true", **end** **else** **else if** *variable* 2 block of statements block of statements executed if *variable* 1 executed if *variable* 2 is "false", *i.e.*, zero is "true", **end** **else** **end** block of statements executed if neither *variable* is "true"
break	Terminates the execution of a **for** or **while** loop. Only the innermost loop in which **break** is encountered will be terminated.
return	Causes the function to return at that point to the calling routine. MATLAB M-file functions will return normally without this statement.
error (*'text'*)	Within a loop or function, if the statement **error** (*'text'*) is encountered, the loop or function is terminated, and the *text* is displayed.
while	The form of the MATLAB **while** loop is **while** *variable* block of statements executed as long as the value of *variable* is "true"; *i.e.*, non-zero **end** Useful when a function *F* itself calls a second "dummy" function "*f*". For example, the function *F* might find the root of an arbitrary function identified as a generic *f*(*x*). Then, the name of the actual M-file function, say **fname**, is passed as a *character string* to the function *F* either through its argument list or as a global variable, and the function is evaluated within *F* by means of **feval.** The use of **feval(name, x1, x2, ..., xn)**, where **fname** is a variable containing the name of the function as a character string; *i.e.*, enclosed in single quotes, and **x1, x2, ..., xn** are the variables needed in the argument list of function **fname**.

1.17 GRAPHICS

MATLAB has many commands that can be used to create basic 2-D plots, overlay plots, specialized 2-D plots, 3-D plots, mesh and surface plots.

1.17.1 Basic 2-D Plots

The basic command for producing a simple 2-D plot is

plot(*x* values, *y* values, 'style option')

where

x values and *y* values are vectors containing the *x*- and *y*-coordinates of points on the graph.

Style option is an optional argument that specifies the color, line-style and the point-marker style.

The style option in the plot command is a character string that consists of 1, 2 or 3 characters that specify the color and/or the line style. The different color, line-style and marker-style options are summarized in Table 1.28.

Table 1.28 Color, line-style and marker-style options

Color style-option		Line style-option		Marker style-option	
y	yellow	–	solid	+	plus sign
m	magenta	– –	dashed	o	circle
c	cyan	:	dotted	*	asterisk
r	red	–.	dash-dot	x	x-mark
g	green			.	point
b	blue			^	up triangle
w	white			s	square
k	black			d	diamond, etc.

1.17.2 Specialized 2-D Plots

There are several specialized graphics functions available in MATLAB for 2-D plots. The list of functions commonly used in MATLAB for plotting *x-y* data are given in Table 1.29.

Table 1.29 List of functions for plotting x-y data

Function	Description
area	Creates a filled area plot.
bar	Creates a bar graph.
barh	Creates a horizontal bar graph.
comet	Makes an animated 2-D plot.
compass	Creates arrow graph for complex numbers.
contour	Makes contour plots.
contourf	Makes filled contour plots.
errorbar	Plots a graph and puts error bars.
feather	Makes a feather plot.
fill	Draws filled polygons of specified color.
fplot	Plots a function of a single variable.
hist	Makes histograms.
loglog	Creates plot with log scale on both *x* and *y* axes.
pareto	Makes pareto plots.
pcolor	Makes pseudo color plot of matrix.
pie	Creates a pie chart.
plotyy	Makes a double *y*-axis plot.
plotmatrix	Makes a scatter plot of a matrix.
polar	Plots curves in polar coordinates.
quiver	Plots vector fields.
rose	Makes angled histograms.
scatter	Creates a scatter plot.
semilogx	Makes semilog plot with log scale on the *x*-axis.
semilogy	Makes semilog plot with log scale on the *y*-axis.
stairs	Plots a stair graph.
stem	Plots a stem graph.

1.17.2.1 Overlay plots

There are three ways of generating overlay plots in MATLAB. They are:

(*a*) Plot command.
(*b*) Hold command.
(*c*) Line command.

(*a*) *Plot command*

Example E1.5(a) shows the use of plot command used with matrix argument, each column of the second argument matrix plotted against the corresponding column of the first argument matrix.

(*b*) *Hold command*

Invoking hold on at any point during a session freezes the current plot in the graphics window. All the next plots generated by the plot command are added to the exiting plot. See Example E1.5(a).

(*c*) *Line command*

The line command takes a pair of vectors (or a triplet in 3-D) followed by a parameter name/parameter value pairs as argument. For instance, the command: *line (x data, y data, parameter name, parameter value)* adds lines to the existing axes. See Example E1.5(a).

1.17.3 3-D Plots

MATLAB provides various options for displaying three-dimensional data. They include line and wire, surface, mesh plots, among many others. More information can be found in the Help Window under Plotting and Data visualization. Table 1.30 lists commonly used functions.

Table 1.30 Functions used for 3-D graphics

Command	Description
plot3	Plots three-dimensional graph of the trajectory of a set of three parametric equations $x(t)$, $y(t)$, and $z(t)$ can be obtained using **plot3(x,y,z)**.
meshgrid	If **x** and **y** are two vectors containing a range of points for the evaluation of a function, **[X,Y] = meshgrid(x, y)** returns two rectangular matrices containing the x and y values at each point of a two-dimensional grid.
mesh(X,Y,z)	If **X** and **Y** are rectangular arrays containing the values of the x and y coordinates at each point of a rectangular grid , and if **z** is the value of a function evaluated at each of these points, **mesh(X,Y,z)** will produce a three-dimensional perspective graph of the points. The same results can be obtained with **mesh(x,y,z)** can also be used.
meshc, meshz	If the xy grid is rectangular, these two functions are merely variations of the basic plotting program **mesh**, and they operate in an identical fashion. **meshc** will produce a corresponding contour plot drawn on the xy plane below the three-dimensional figure, and **meshz** will add a vertical wall to the outside features of the figures drawn by **mesh**.
surf	Produces a three-dimensional perspective drawing. Its use is usually to draw surfaces, as opposed to plotting functions, although the actual tasks are quite similar. The output of **surf** will be a *shaded* figure. If row vectors of length n are defined by $x = r \cos \theta$ and $y = r \sin \theta$, with $0 \le \theta \le 2\pi$, they correspond to a circle of radius r. If $\vec{r}$ is a *column* vector equal to **r = [0 1 2]'**; then **z = r*ones(size(x))** will be a rectangular, $3 \times n$, arrays of 0's and 2's, and **surf(x, y, z)** will produce a shaded surface bounded by three circles; i.e., a cone.

surfc	This function is related to **surf** in the same way that **meshc** is related to mesh.
Colormap	Used to change the default coloring of a figure. See the MATLAB reference manual or the help file.
Shading	Controls the type of color shading used in drawing figures. See the MATLAB reference manual or the help file.
view	**view(az,el)** controls the perspective view of a three-dimensional plot. The view of the figure is from angle "**el**" above the *xy* plane with the coordinate axes (and the figure) rotated by an angle "**az**" in a clockwise direction about the *z* axis. Both angles are in degrees. The default values are **az** = 37½° and **el** = 30°.
axis	Determines or changes the scaling of a plot. If the coordinate axis limits of a two-dimensional or three-dimensional graph are contained in the row vector $r = [x_{min}, x_{max}, y_{min}, y_{max}, z_{min}, z_{max}]$, **axis** will return the values in this vector, and **axis(r)** can be used to alter them. The coordinate axes can be turned *on* and *off* with **axis('on')** and **axis('off')**. A few other string constant inputs to **axis** and their effects are given below: **axis('equal')** *x* and *y* scaling are forced to be the same. **axis('square')** The box formed by the axes is square. **axis('auto')** Restores the scaling to default settings. **axis('normal')** Restoring the scaling to full size, removing any effects of *square* or *equal* settings. **axis('image')** Alters the aspect ratio and the scaling so the screen pixels are square shaped rather than rectangular.
contour	The use is **contour(x,y,z)**. A default value of *N* = 10 contour lines will be drawn. An optional fourth argument can be used to control the number of contour lines that are drawn. **contour(x,y,z,N)**, if **N** is a positive integer, will draw **N** contour lines, and **contour(x,y,z,V)**, if **V** is a vector containing values in the range of *z* values, will draw contour lines at each value of *z* = *V*.
plot3	Plots lines or curves in three dimensions. If **x, y,** and **z** are vectors of equal length, **plot3(x,y,z)** will draw, on a three-dimensional coordinate axis system, the lines connecting the points. A fourth argument, representing the color and symbols to be used at each point, can be added in exactly the same manner as with **plot**.
grid	**grid on** adds grid lines to a two-dimensional or three-dimensional graph; **grid off** removes them.
slice	Draws "slices" of a volume at a particular location within the volume.

Example E1.5:

(*a*) Generate an overlay plot for plotting three lines

$$y_1 = \sin t$$

$$y_2 = t$$

$$y_3 = t - \frac{t^3}{3!} + \frac{t^5}{5!} + \frac{t^7}{7!}; \qquad 0 \le t \le 2\pi$$

Use (*i*) the plot command
(*ii*) the hold command
(*iii*) the line command

(*b*) Use the functions for plotting *x*-*y* data for plotting the following functions:

(*i*) $f(t) = t\cos t$
$0 \le t \le 10\pi$

(*ii*) $x = e^t$
$y = 100 + e^{3t}$
$0 \le t \le 2\pi$

Solution:

(*a*) Overlay plot

(*i*) % using the plot command

```
t = linspace(0, 2*pi, 100);
y1 = sin(t); y2 = t;
y3 = t -(t.^3)/6 + (t.^5)/120-(t.^7)/5040;
plot(t, y1, t, y2, '-', t, y3, 'o')
axis([0 5 -1 5])
xlabel('t')
ylabel('sin(t) approximation')
title('sin(t) function')
text(3.5,0, 'sin(t)')
gtext('Linear approximation')
gtext('4-term approximation')
```

Output is shown in Fig. E1.5(*a*).

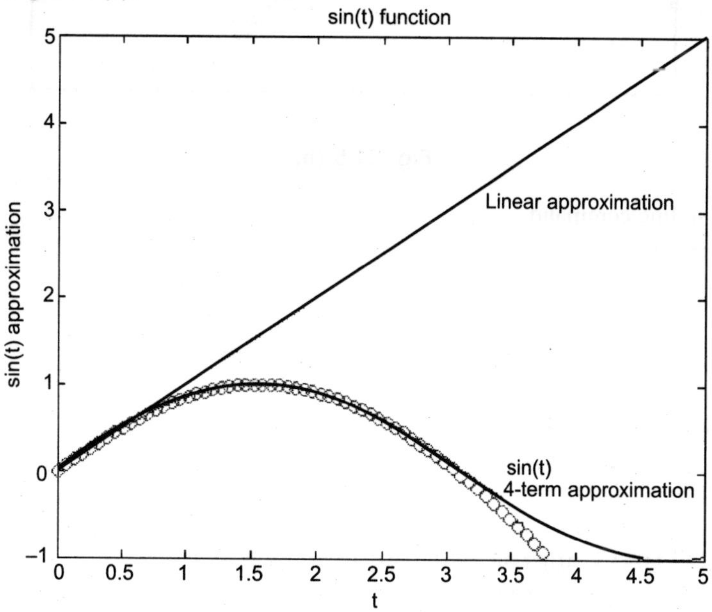

Fig. E1.5 (a)

(*ii*) % using the hold command

```
x = linspace(0, 2*pi, 100); y1=sin(x);
plot(x,y1)
hold on
y2 = x; plot(x, y2, '-' )
y3 = x-(x.^3)/6 + (x.^5)/120-(t.^7)/5040;
plot(x, y3, 'o')
axis([0 5-1 5])
hold off
```

Output is shown in Fig. E1.5(*b*).

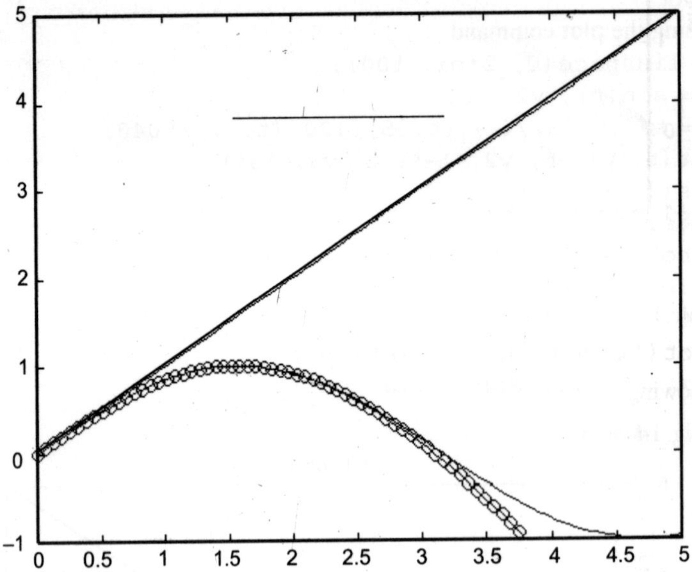

Fig. E1.5 (b)

(*iii*) % using the line command

```
t = linspace(0, 2*pi, 100);
y1 = sin(t);
y2 = t;
y3 = t-(t.^3)/6 + (t.^5)/120 - (t.^7)/5040;
plot(t, y1)
line(t, y2, 'linestyle', '-')
line(t, y3, 'marker', 'o')
axis([0 5 -1 5])
xlabel('t')
ylabel('sin(t) approximation')
title('sin(t) function')
legend('sin(t)', 'linear approx', '7th order approx')
```

Output is shown in Fig. E1.5(*c*).

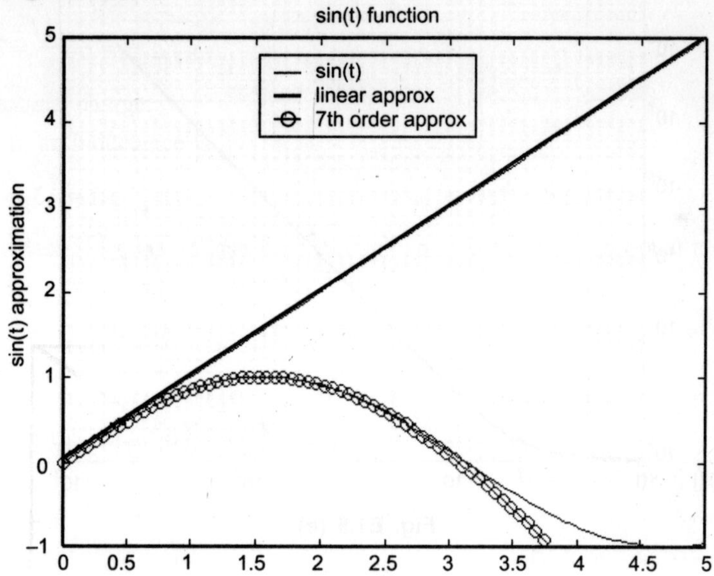

Fig. E1.5 (c)

(*b*) Using Table 1.29, functions

(*i*) `fplot('x*cos(x)', [0 10*pi])`

This will give the following figure (Fig. E1.5 (*d*)).

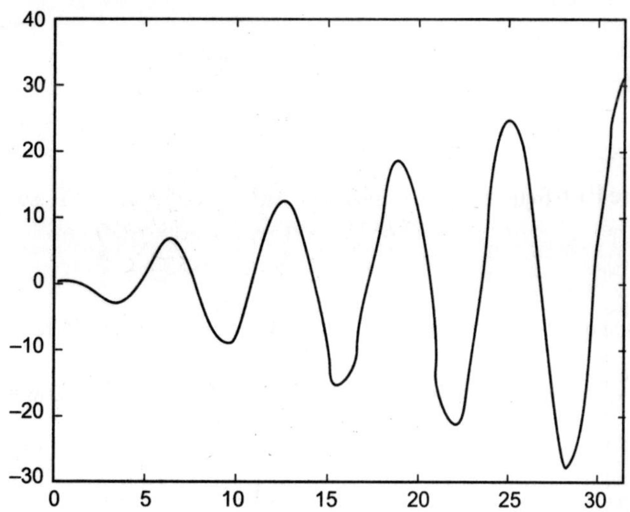

Fig. E1.5 (d)

(*ii*)
```
t = linspace(0, 2*pi, 200);
x = exp(t);
y = 100 + exp(3*t);
loglog(x, y), grid
```

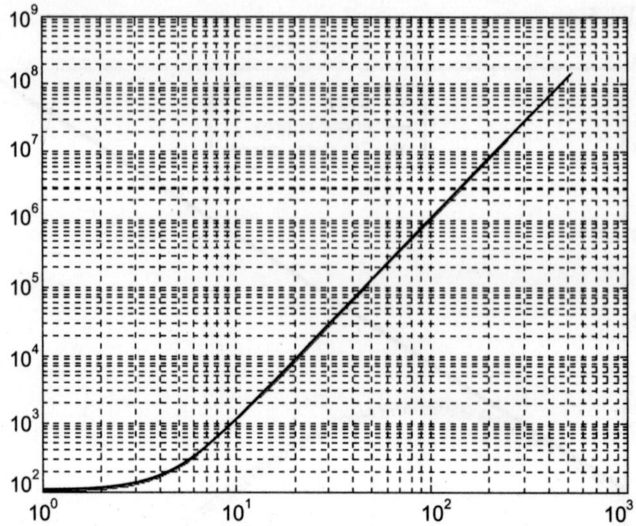

Fig. E1.5 (e)

Example E1.6:

(*a*) Plot the parametric space curve of

$x(t) = t$

$y(t) = t^2$

$z(t) = t^3; \qquad 0 \le t \le 1.0$

(*b*) $z = -7/(1 + x^2 + y^2); \; |x| \le 5, \; |y| \le 5$

Solution:

(*a*)
```
>> t = linspace(0, 2,100);
>> x =t; y = t. ^2; z = t. ^3;
>> plot 3 (x, y, z), grid
```

The plot is shown in figure E1.6 (*a*).

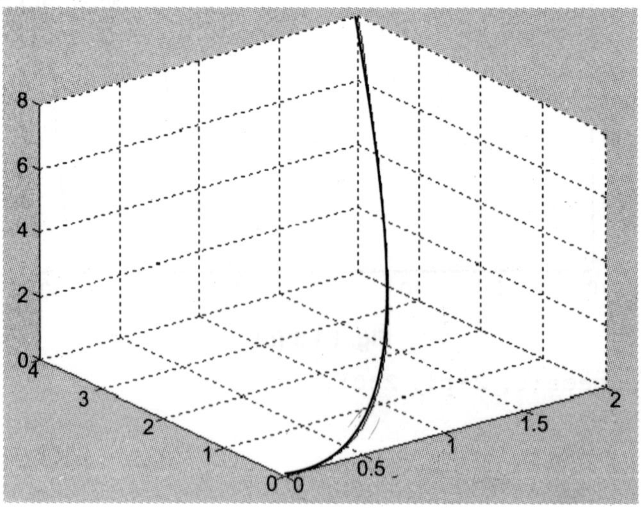

Fig. E1.6 (a)

(*b*)
```
>> t=linspace(0,2,100);
>> x=t; y=t. ^2; z=t.^3;
>> plot3 (x,y,z), grid
>> t=linspace(-5,5,50); y=x;
>> z=-7./(1+x.^2+y.^2);
>> mesh(z)
```

The plot is shown in figure E1.6(*b*).

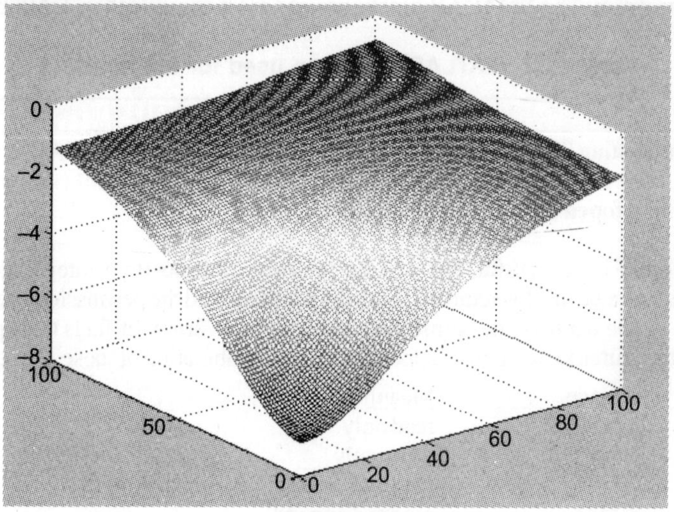

Fig. E1.6(b)

1.17.4 Saving and Printing Graphs

To obtain a hardcopy of a graph, type *print* in the Command Window after the graph appears in the Figure Window. The figure can also be saved into a specified file in the PostScripter or Encapsulated PostScript (EPS) format. The command to save graphics to a file is

print – d devicetype – options filename

where device type for Postscript printers are listed in the following Table 1.31.

Table 1.31 Devicetype for PostScript printers

Devicetype	Description	Devicetype	Description
ps	Black and white PostScript	**eps**	Black and white EPSF
psc	Color PostScript	**epsc**	Color EPSF
ps2	Level 2 BW PostScript	**eps2**	Level 2 black and white EPSF
psc2	Level 2 color PostScript	**epsc2**	Level 2 color EPSF

MATLAB can also generate a graphics file in the following popular formats among others:

–dill : Saves file in Adobe Illustrator format.
–djpeg : Saves file as a JPEG image.
–dtiff : Saves file as a compressed TIFF image.
–dmfile : Saves file as an M-file with graphics handles.

1.18 INPUT/OUTPUT IN MATLAB

In this section, we present some of the many available commands in MATLAB for reading data from an external file into a MATLAB matrix, or writing the numbers computed in MATLAB into such an external file.

1.18.1 The fopen Statement

To have the MATLAB read or write a separate data file of numerical values, we need to *connect* the file to the executing MATLAB program. The MATLAB functions used are summarized in Table 1.32.

Table 1.32 MATLAB functions used for input/output

Function	Description
fopen	Connects an existing file to MATLAB or to create a new file from MATLAB. **fid = fopen** (*'Filename'*, *permission code*); where, if **fopen** is successful, **fid** will be returned as a positive integer greater than 2. When unsuccessful, a value of –1 is returned. Both the file name and the permission code are string constants enclosed in single quotes. The permission code can be a variety of flags that specify whether or not the file can be written to, read from, appended to, or a combination of these. Some common codes are: Code — Meaning **'r'** — read only **'w'** — write only **'r+'** — read and write **'a+'** — read and append The **fopen** statement positions the file at the beginning.
fclose	Disconnects a file from the operating MATLAB program. The use is **fclose(fid)**, where **fid** is the *file identification number* of the file returned by **fopen.fclose('all')** will close all files.
fscanf	Reads opened files. The use is **A = fscanf(fid,** *FORMAT, SIZE***)** where *FORMAT* specifies the types of numbers (integers, reals with or without exponent, character strings) and their arrangement in the data file, and optional *SIZE* determines how many quantities are to be read and how they are to be arranged into the matrix **A**. If *SIZE* is omitted, the entire file is read. The *FORMAT* field is a string (enclosed in single quotes) specifying the form of the numbers in the file. The *type* of each number is characterized by a percent sign (%), followed by a letter (**i** or **d** for integers, **e** or **f** for floating-point numbers with or without exponents). Between the percent sign and the type code, one can insert an integer specifying the maximum width of the field.
fprintf	Writes files previously opened. **fprintf(fid,** *FORMAT*, **A)** where **fid** and *FORMAT* have the same meaning as for **fscanf**, with the exception that for output formats the string must end with **\n**, designating the end of a line of output.

1.19 SYMBOLIC MATHEMATICS

In Secs. 1.1 to 1.18, the capability of MATLAB for numerical computations have been described. In this section some of MATLAB's capabilities for symbolic manipulations will be presented. Specifically, the symbolic expressions, symbolic algebra, simplification of mathematical expressions, operations on symbolic expressions, solution of a single equation or a set of linear algebraic equations, solutions to differential equations, differentiation and integration of functions using MATLAB are presented.

1.19.1 Symbolic Expressions

A symbolic expression is stored in MATLAB as a *character string*. A single quote marks are used to define the symbolic expression. For instance:

'sin(*y*/*x*)'; '*x*^4 + 5 * *x*^3 + 7 * *x*^2 – 7'

The independent variable in many functions is specified as an additional function argument. If an independent variable is not specified, then MATLAB will pick one. When several variables exist, MATLAB will pick the one that is a single lower case letter (except *i* and *j*), which is closest to *x* alphabetically.
The independent variable is returned by the function *symvar*,
symvar(s): Returns the independent variable for the symbolic expression *s*.
For example:

Expression (s)	**symvar(s)**
'5 * c * *d* + 34'	*d*
'sin(*y*/*x*)'	*x*

In MATLAB, a number of functions are available to simplify mathematical expressions by expanding the terms, factoring expressions, collecting coefficients, or simplifying the expression. For instance;
expand(s): Performs an expansion of **s**.

A summary of these expressions is given in Table 1.33. A summary of basic operations is given in Table 1.34. The standard arithmetic operation (Table 1.35) is applied to symbolic expressions using symbolic functions. These symbolic expressions are summarized in Table 1.36.

Table 1.33

Simplification	
collect	Collect common terms
expand	Expand polynomials and elementary functions
factor	Factorization
horner	Nested polynomial representation
numden	Numerator and denominator
simple	Search for shortest form
simplify	Simplification
subexpr	Rewrite in terms of subexprssions

Table 1.34

Basic operations	
ccode	C code representation of a symbolic expression
conj	Complex conjugate
findsym	Determine symbolic variables
fortran	Fortran representation of a symbolic expression
imag	Imaginary part of a complex number
latex	LaTeX representation of a symbolic expression
pretty	Pretty prints a symbolic expression
real	Real part of an imaginary number
sym	Create symbolic object
syms	Shortcut for creating multiple symbolic objects

Table 1.35

Arithmetic operations	
+	Addition
–	Subtraction
*	Multiplication
.*	Array multiplication
/	Right division
./	Array right division
\	Left division
.\	Array left division
^	Matrix or scalar raised to a power
.^	Array raised to a power
‘	Complex conjugate transpose
.‘	Real transpose

Table 1.36

	Symbolic expressions
horner(S)	Transposes S into its Horner, or nested, representation.
numden(S)	Returns two symbolic expressions that represent, respectively, the numerator expression and the denominator expression for the rational representation of **S**.
numeric(S)	Converts **S** to a numeric form (**S** must not contain any symbolic variables).
poly2sym(c)	Converts a polynomial coefficient vector **c** to a symbolic polynomial.
pretty(S)	Prints **S** in an output form that resembles typeset mathematics.
sym2poly(S)	Converts **S** to a polynomial coefficient vector. *
symadd(A,B)	Performs a symbolic addition, **A + B**.
symdiv(A,B)	Performs a symbolic division, **A / B.**
symmul(A,B)	Performs a symbolic multiplication, **A * B.**
sympow(S,p)	Performs a symbolic power, **S^p**.
symsub(A,B)	Performs a symbolic subtraction, **A – B.**

1.19.2 Solution to Differential Equations

Symbolic math functions can be used to solve a single equation, a system of equations and differential equations. For example:

solve(f) : Solves a symbolic equation **f** for its symbolic variable. If **f** is a symbolic expression, this function solves the equation **f** = 0 for its symbolic variable.

solve(f1, ..., fn): Solves the system of equations represented by **f1, ..., fn.**

The symbolic function for solving ordinary differential equation is **dsolve** as shown below:

dsolve('equation', 'condition'): Symbolically solves the ordinary differential equation specified by **'equation'**. The optional argument **'condition'** specifies a boundary or initial condition.

The symbolic equation uses the letter **D** to denote differentiation with respect to the independent variable. **D** followed by a digit denotes repeated differentiation. Thus, **Dy** represents dy/dx, and **D2y** represents d^2y/dx^2. For example, given the ordinary second order differential equation;

$$\frac{d^2x}{dt^2} + 5\frac{dx}{dt} + 3x = 7$$

with the initial conditions $x(0) = 0$ and $\dot{x}(0) = 1$.

The MATLAB statement that determines the symbolic solution for the above differential equation is the following:

```
x = dsolve('D2x = -5*Dx - 3*x + 7', 'x(0) = 0', 'Dx(0) =1')
```

The symbolic functions are summarized in Table 1.37.

Table 1.37 Solution of equations

compose	Functional composition
dsolve	Solution of differential equations
finverse	Functional inverse
solve	Solution of algebraic equations

1.19.3 Calculus

There are four forms by which the symbolic derivative of a symbolic expression is obtained in MATLAB. They are:

diff(f) : Returns the derivative of the expression **f** with respect to the default independent variable.

diff(f, 't') : Returns the derivative of the expression **f** with respect to the variable **t**.

diff(f, n) : Returns the nth derivative of the expression **f** with respect to the default independent variable.

diff(f,'t', n) : Returns the nth derivative of the expression **f** with respect to the variable **t**.

The various forms that are used in MATLAB to find the integral of a symbolic expression **f** are given and summarized in Table 1.38.

int(f) : Returns the integral of the expression **f** with respect to the default independent variable.

int(f, 't') : Returns the integral of the expression **f** with respect to the variable **t**.

int(f, a, b) : Returns the integral of the expression **f** with respect to the default independent variable evaluated over the interval **[a, b]**, where **a** and **b** are numeric expressions.

int(f,'t', a, b): Returns the integral of the expression **f** with respect to the variable **t** evaluated over the interval **[a, b]**, where **a** and **b** are numeric expressions.

int(f, 'm', 'n'): Returns the integral of the expression **f** with respect to the default independent variable evaluated over the interval **[m, n]**, where **m** and **n** are numeric expressions.

The other symbolic functions for pedagogical and graphical applications, conversions, integral transforms, and linear algebra are summarized in Tables 1.38 to 1.42.

Table 1.38

Calculus	
diff	Differentiate
int	Integrate
jacobian	Jacobian matrix
limit	Limit of an expression
symsum	Summation of series
taylor	Taylor series expansion

Table 1.39

Pedagogical and graphical applications	
ezcontour	Contour plotter
ezcontourf	Filled contour plotter
ezmesh	Mesh plotter
ezmeshc	Combined mesh and contour plotter
ezplot	Function plotter
ezplot	Easy-to-use function plotter
ezplot3	Three-dimensional curve plotter
ezpolar	Polar coordinate plotter
ezsurf	Surface plotter
ezsurfc	Combined surface and contour plotter
funtool	Function calculator
rsums	Riemann sums
taylortool	Taylor series calculator

Table 1.40

Conversions	
char	Convert symbolic object to string
double	Convert symbolic matrix to double
poly2sym	Function calculator
sym2poly	Symbolic polynomial to coefficient vector

Table 1.41

Integral transforms	
fourier	Fourier transform
ifourier	Inverse Fourier transform
ilaplace	Inverse Laplace transform
iztrans	Inverse Z-transform
laplace	Laplace transform
ztrans	Z-transform

Table 1.42

	Linear algebra
colspace	Basis for column space
det	Determinant
diag	Create or extract diagonals
eig	Eigenvalues and eigenvectors
expm	Matrix exponential
inv	Matrix inverse
jordan	Jordan canonical form
null	Basis for null space
poly	Characteristic polynomial
rank	Matrix rank
rref	Reduced row echelon form
svd	Singular value decomposition
tril	Lower triangle
triu	Upper triangle

1.20 THE LAPLACE TRANSFORMS

The Laplace transformation method is an operational method that can be used to find the transforms of time functions, the inverse Laplace transformation using the partial-fraction expansion of $B(s)/A(s)$, where $A(s)$ and $B(s)$ are polynomials in s. In this Chapter, we present the computational methods with MATLAB to obtain the partial-fraction expansion of $B(s)/A(s)$ and the zeros and poles of $B(s)/A(s)$.

MATLAB can be used to obtain the partial-fraction expansion of the ratio of two polynomials, $B(s)/A(s)$ as follows:

$$\frac{B(s)}{A(s)} = \frac{\text{num}}{\text{den}} = \frac{b(1)s^n + b(2)s^{n-1} + \cdots + b(n)}{a(1)s^n + a(2)s^{n-1} + \cdots + a(n)}$$

where $a(1) \neq 0$ and num and den are row vectors. The coefficients of the numerator and denominator of $B(s)/A(s)$ are specified by the num and den vectors.

Hence $\quad \text{num} = [b(1) \quad b(2) \quad \ldots \quad b(n)]$
$\quad \text{den} = [a(1) \quad a(2) \quad \ldots \quad a(n)]$

The MATLAB command

r, p, k = residue(num, den)

is used to determine the residues, poles and direct terms of a partial-fraction expansion of the ratio of two polynomials $B(s)$ and $A(s)$ is then given by

$$\frac{B(s)}{A(s)} = k(s) = \frac{r(1)}{s - p(1)} + \frac{r(2)}{s - p(2)} + \cdots + \frac{r(n)}{s - p(n)}$$

The MATLAB command **[num, den] = residue(r, p, k)** where r, p, k are the output from MATLAB converts the partial fraction expansion back to the polynomial ratio $B(s)/A(s)$.
The command **printsys (num, den,'s')** prints the num/den in terms of the ratio of polynomials in s.
The command **ilaplace** will find the inverse Laplace transform of a Laplace function.

1.20.1 Finding Zeros and Poles of B(s)/A(s)

The MATLAB command **[z, p, k] = tf 2zp(num, den)** is used to find the zeros **(z)**, poles **(p)**, and gain **(k)** of *B(s)/A(s)*.

If the zeros **(z)**, poles **(p)** and gain **(k)** are given, the following MATLAB command can be used to find the original num/den:

[num, den] = zp2tf (z,p,k)

1.21 CONTROL SYSTEMS

MATLAB has an extensive set of functions for the analysis and design of control systems. They involve matrix operati7ons, root determination, model conversions and plotting of complex functions. These functions are found in MATLAB's control systems toolbox. The analytical techniques used by MATLAB for the analysis and design of control systems assume the processes that are linear and time invariant. MATLAB uses models in the form of *transfer-functions* or *state-space equations*.

1.21.1 Transfer Functions

The transfer function of a linear time invariant system is expressed as a ratio of two polynomials. The transfer function for a single input and a single output (SISO) system is written as

$$H(s) = \frac{b_0 s^n + b_1 s^{n-1} + ... + b_{n-1}s + b_n}{a_0 s^m + a_1 s^{m-1} + ... + a_{m-1}s + a_m}$$

when the numerator and denominator of a transfer function are factored into the *zero-pole-gain form*, it is given by

$$H(s) = k\frac{(s - z_1)(s - z_2)...(s - z_n)}{(s - p_1)(s - p_2)...(s - p_m)}$$

The *state-space model* representation of a linear control system *s* is written as

$$\dot{x} = Ax + Bu$$

$$y = Cx + Du$$

1.21.2 Model Conversion

There are a number of functions in MATLAB that can be used to convert from one model to another. These conversion functions and their applications are summarized in Table 1.43.

Table 1.43 Model conversion functions

Function	Purpose
C2d	Continuous state-space to discrete state-space
residue	Partial-fraction expansion
ss3tf	State-space to transfer function
ss2zp	State-space to zero-pole-gain
tf2ss	Transfer function to state-space
tf2zp	Transfer function to zero-pole-gain
zp2ss	Zero-pole-gain to state-space
zp2tf	Zero-pole-gain to transfer function

Residue Function: The **residue** function converts the polynomial transfer function

$$H(s)=\frac{b_0s^n+b_1s^{n-1}+...+b_{n-1}s+b_n}{a_0s^m+a_1s^{m-1}+...+a_{m-1}s+a_m}$$

to the partial fraction transfer function

$$H(s)=\frac{r_1}{s-p_1}+\frac{r_2}{s-p_2}+\cdots+\frac{r_n}{s-p_n}+k(s)$$

[r, p, k] = residue(B, *A*) Determine the vectors **r, p** and **k,** which contain the residue values, the poles and the direct terms from the partial-fraction expansion. The inputs are the polynomial coefficients **B** and **A** from the numerator and denominator of the transfer function, respectively.

ss2tf Function: The **ss2tf** function converts the continuous-time, state-space equations

$$x'=Ax+Bu$$

$$y=Cx+Du$$

to the polynomial transfer function

$$H(s)=\frac{b_0s^n+b_1s^{n-1}+...+b_{n-1}s+b_n}{a_0s^m+a_1s^{m-1}+...+a_{m-1}s+a_m}$$

The function has two output matrices:

[num, den] = ss2tf(A, B, C, D,iu) Computes vectors **num** and **den** containing the coefficients, in descending powers of **s,** of the numerator and denominator of the polynomial transfer function for the **iu**[th] input. The input arguments **A, B, C** and **D** are the matrices of the state-space equations corresponding to the **iu**[th] input, where **iu** is the number of the input for a multi-input system. In the case of a single-input system, **iu** is 1.

ss2zp Function: The **ss2zp** function converts the continuous-time, state-space equations

$$x'=Ax+Bu$$

$$y=Cx+Du$$

to the zero-pole-gain transfer function

$$H(s)=k\frac{(s-z_1)(s-z_2)...(s-z_n)}{(s-p_1)(s-p_2)...(s-p_m)}$$

The function has three output matrices:

[z, p, k] = ss2zp(A, B, C, D, iu) Determines the zeros **(z)** and poles **(p)** of the zero-pole-gain transfer function for the **iu**[th] input, along with the associated gain **(k).** The input matrices **A, B, C** and **D** of the state-space equations correspond to the **iu**[th] input, where **iu** is the number of the input for a multi-input system. In the case of a single-input system, **iu** is 1.

tf2ss Function: The **ts2ss** function converts the polynomial transfer function

$$H(s)=\frac{b_0s^n+b_1s^{n-1}+...+b_{n-1}s+b_n}{a_0s^m+a_1s^{m-1}+...+a_{m-1}s+a_m}$$

to the controller-canonical form state-space equations

$$x' = Ax + Bu$$
$$y = Cx + Du$$

The function has four output matrices:

[A, B, C, D] = tf2ss(num,den) Determines the matrices **A, B, C** and **D** of the controller-canonical form state-space equations. The input arguments num and den contain the coefficients, in descending powers of **s**, of the numerator and denominator polynomials of the transfer function that is to be converted.

tf 2zp Function: The **tf 2zp** function converts the polynomial transfer function

$$H(s) = \frac{b_0 s^n + b_1 s^{n-1} + ... + b_{n-1} s + b_n}{a_0 s^m + a_1 s^{m-1} + ... + a_{m-1} s + a_m}$$

to the zero-pole-gain transfer function

$$H(s) = k \frac{(s - z_1)(s - z_2)...(s - z_n)}{(s - p_1)(s - p_2)...(s - p_m)}$$

The function has three output matrices:

[z, p, k] = tf 2zp(num, den) Determines the zeros **(z)**, poles **(p)** and associated gain **(k)** of the zero-pole-gain transfer function using the coefficients, in descending powers of **s**, of the numerator and denominator of the polynomial transfer function that is to be converted.

zp2tf Function: The **zp2tf** function converts the zero-pole-gain transfer function

$$H(s) = k \frac{(s - z_1)(s - z_2)...(s - z_n)}{(s - p_1)(s - p_2)...(s - p_m)}$$

to the polynomial transfer function

$$H(s) = \frac{b_0 s^n + b_1 s^{n-1} + ... + b_{n-1} s + b_n}{a_0 s^m + a_1 s^{m-1} + ... + a_{m-1} s + a_m}$$

The function has two output matrices:

[num, den] = zp2tf(z, p, k) Determines the vectors num and den containing the coefficients, in descending powers of **s**, of the numerator and denominator of the polynomial transfer function. **p** is a column vector of the pole locations of the zero-pole-gain transfer function, **z** is a matrix of the corresponding zero locations, having one column for each output of a multi-output system, **k** is the gain of the zero-pole-gain transfer function. In the case of a single-output system, **z** is a column vector of the zero locations corresponding to the pole locations of vector **p.**

zp2ss Function: The **zp2ss** function converts the zero-pole-gain transfer function

$$H(s) = k \frac{(s - z_1)(s - z_2)...(s - z_n)}{(s - p_1)(s - p_2)...(s - p_m)}$$

to the controller-canonical form state-space equations

$$x' = Ax + Bu$$

$$y = Cx + Du$$

The function has four output matrices:

[A, B, C, D] = zp2ss(z, p, k) Determines the matrices **A, B, C,** and **D** of the control-canonical form state-space equations. **p** is a column vector of the pole locations of the zero-pole-gain transfer function, **z** is a matrix of the corresponding zero locations, having one column for each output of a multi-output system, **k** is the gain of the zero-pole-gain transfer function. In the case of a single-output system, **z** is a column vector of the zero locations corresponding to the pole locations of vector **p.**

Example Problems and Solutions

Example E1.7: Consider the function

$$H(s) = \frac{n(s)}{d(s)}$$

where $n(s) = s^4 + 6s^3 + 5s^2 + 4s + 3$

$$d(s) = s^5 + 7s^4 + 6s^3 + 5s^2 + 4s + 7$$

(*a*) Find $n(-10)$, $n(-5)$, $n(-3)$ and $n(-1)$

(*b*) Find $d(-10)$, $d(-5)$, $d(-3)$ and $d(-1)$

(*c*) Find $H(-10)$, $H(-5)$, $H(-3)$ and $H(-1)$

Solution:

(*a*)
```
>> n=[1 6 5 4 3];    % n=s^4+6s^3+5s^2+4s+3
>> d=[1 7 6 5 4 7]; % d=s^5+7s^4+6s^3+5s^2+4s+7
>> n2=polyval(n,[-10])
n2=4463
>> nn10=polyval(n,[-10])
nn10=4463
>> nn5=polyval(n,[-5])
nn5=-17
>> nn3=polyval(n,[-3])
nn3=-45
>> nn1=polyval(n,[-1])
nn1=-1
```

(*b*)
```
>> dn10=polyval(d,[-10])
dn10=-35533
>> dn5=polyval(d,[-5])
dn5=612
>> dn3=polyval(d,[-3])
```

```
dn3=202
>> dn1=polyval(d,[-1])
dn1=8
```

(c)
```
>> Hn10=nn10/dn10
Hn10=-0.1256
>> Hn5=nn5/dn5
Hn5=-0.0278
>> Hn3=nn3/dn3
Hn3=-0.2228
>> Hn1=nn1/dn1
Hn1=-0.1250
```

Example E1.8: Generate a plot of

$$y(x) = e^{-0.7x} \sin \omega x$$

where $\omega = 15$ rad/s, and $0 \le x \le 15$. Use the colon notation to generate the x vector in increments of 0.1.

Solution:

```
>> x=[0:0.1:15];
>> w=15;
>> y=exp(-0.7*x)*sin(w*x);
>> plot(x,y)
>> title('y(x)=e^-^0^.^7^xsin\omegax')
>> xlabel('x')
>> ylabel('y')
```

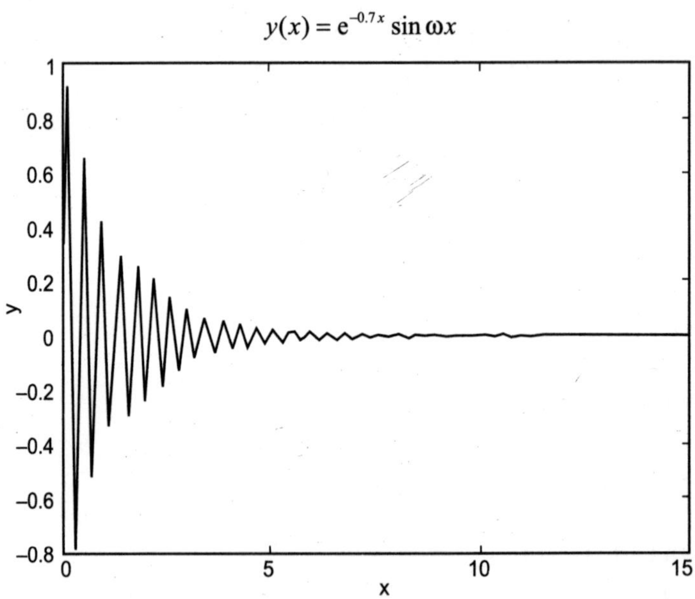

Fig. E1.8

Example E1.9: Generate a plot of

$$y(x) = e^{-0.6x} \cos \omega x$$

where $\omega = 10$ rad/s, and $0 \le x \le 15$. Use the colon notation to generate the x vector in increments of 0.05.

Solution:

```
>> x=[0:0.1:15];
>> w=10;
>> y=exp(-0.6*x)*cos(w*x);
>> plot(x,y)
>> title('y(x)=e^-^0^.^6^xcos\omega x')
>> xlabel('x')
>> ylabel('y')
```

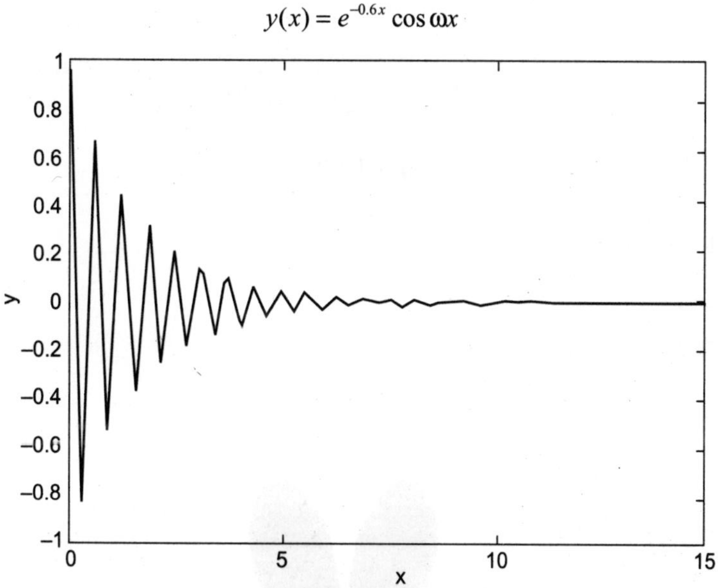

Fig. E1.9

Example E1.10: Using the functions for plotting *x-y* data given in Table 1.29, plot the following functions:

(*a*) $r^2 = 5 \cos 3t;\ 0 \le t \le 2\pi$

(*b*) $r^2 = 5 \cos 3t;\ 0 \le t \le 2\pi$

$x = r \cos t,\ y = r \sin t$

(*c*) $y_1 = e^{-2x} \cos x;\ 0 \le t \le 20$

$y_2 = e^{2x}$

(*d*) $y = \dfrac{\cos(x)}{x};\ -5 \le x \le 5\pi$

(*e*) $f = e^{-3t/5} \cos t;\ 0 \le t \le 2\pi$

(*f*) $z = -\dfrac{1}{3} - x^2 + 2xy + y^2;\ |x| \le 7,\ |y| \le 7$

Solution:

(*a*)
```
t = linspace(0,2*pi,200);
r = sqrt(abs(5*cos(3*t)));
   polar(t,r)
```

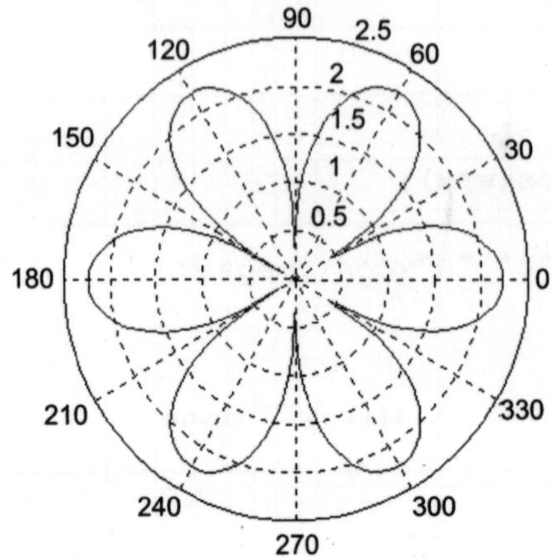

Fig. E1.10(a)

(*b*)
```
t=linspace(0, 2*pi, 200);
r=sqrt(abs(5*cos(3*t)));
x=r*cos(t);
y=r*sin(t);
fill(x, y, 'k'),
axis('square')
```

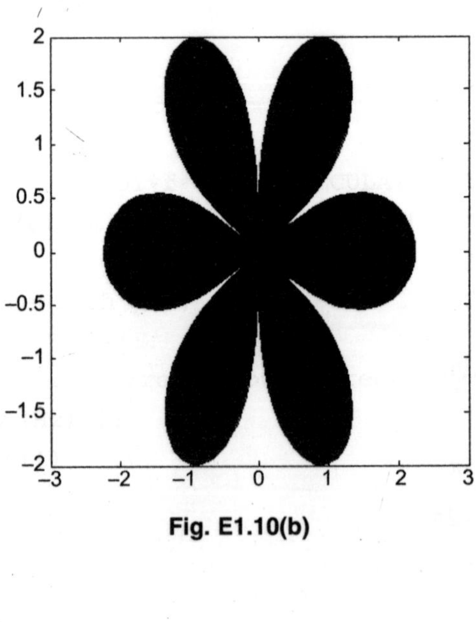

Fig. E1.10(b)

(*c*)

```
x=1:0.1:20;
y1=exp(-2*x)*cos(x);
y2=exp(2*x);
Ax=plotyy(x,y1,x,y2);
hy1=get(Ax(1),'ylabel');
hy2=get(Ax(2),'ylabel');
set(hy1,'string','exp(-2x)·cos(x)')
set(hy2,'string','exp(-2x)');
```

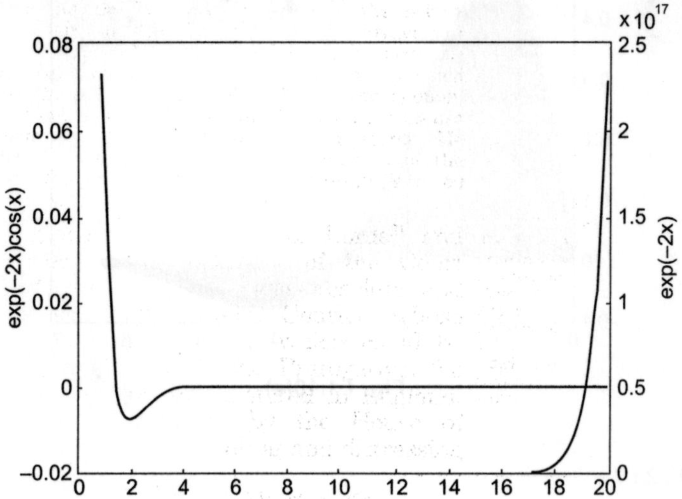

Fig. E1.10(c)

(*d*)

```
x = linspace(-5*pi, 5*pi,100);
y = cos(x)./x;
area(x, y);
xlabel('x (rad)'), ylabel('cos(x)/x')
hold on
```

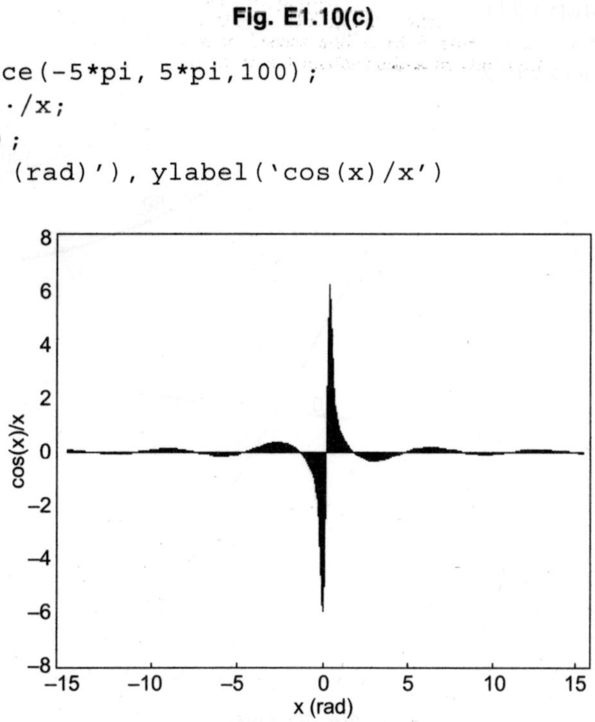

Fig. 1.10(d)

(*e*)
```
t = linspace(0,2*pi,200);
f = exp(-0.6*t)*sin(t);
stem(t, f)
```

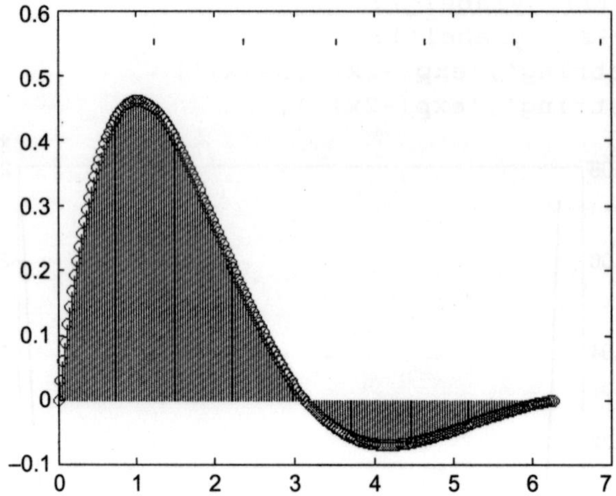

Fig. E1.10(e)

(*f*)
```
r=-7:0.2:7;
[X,Y]=meshgrid(r,r);
Z=-0.333*X.^2+2*X*Y+Y.^2;
cs=contour(X,Y,Z);
label(cs)
```

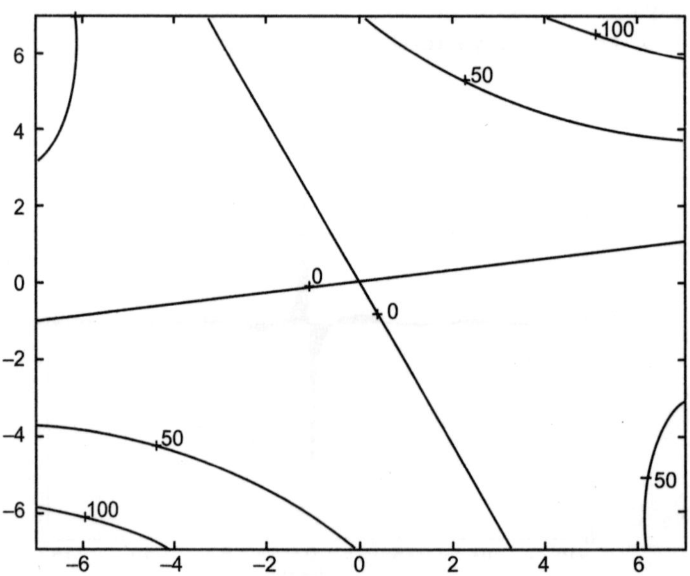

Fig. E1.10(f)

Example E1.11: Use the functions listed in Table 1.30 for plotting 3-D data for the following:

(*a*) $z = \cos x \cos y \, e^{-\frac{\sqrt{x^2+y^2}}{5}}$

$|x| \leq = 7, |y| \leq 7$

(*b*) Discrete data plots with stems

$x = t, y = t\cos(t)$

$z = e^{t/5} - 2; 0 \leq t \leq 5\pi$

(*c*) A cylinder generated by

$r = \sin(5\pi z) + 3$

$0 \leq z \leq 1; 0 \leq \theta \leq 2\pi$

Solution:

(*a*)
```
u=-7:0.2:7;x
[X,Y]=meshgrid(u,u);
Z=cos(X)*cos(Y)*exp(-sqrt(X^2+Y^2)/5);
surf(X,Y,Z)
```

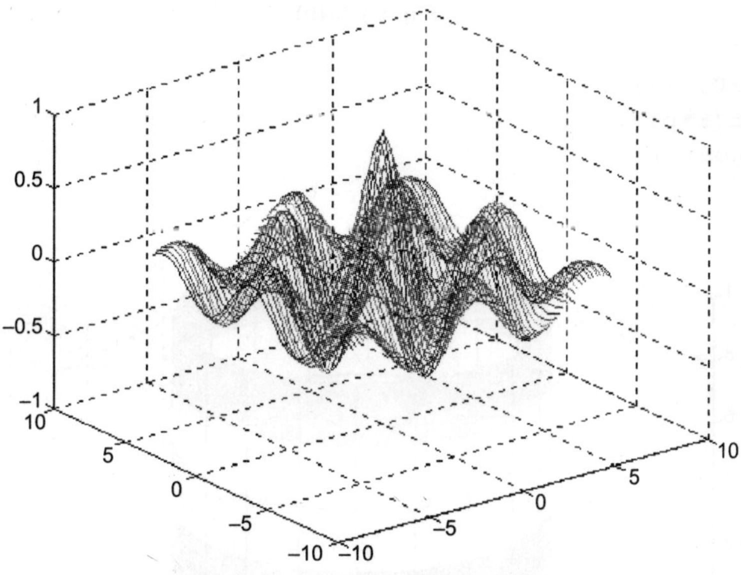

Fig. E1.11(a)

(*b*)
```
t=linspace(0,5*pi,200);
x=t; y=t*cos(t);
z=exp(t/5)-2;
```

```
stem3(x,y,z,'filled');
xlabel('t'),ylabel('tcos(t)'),zlabel('e^t/5-1')
```

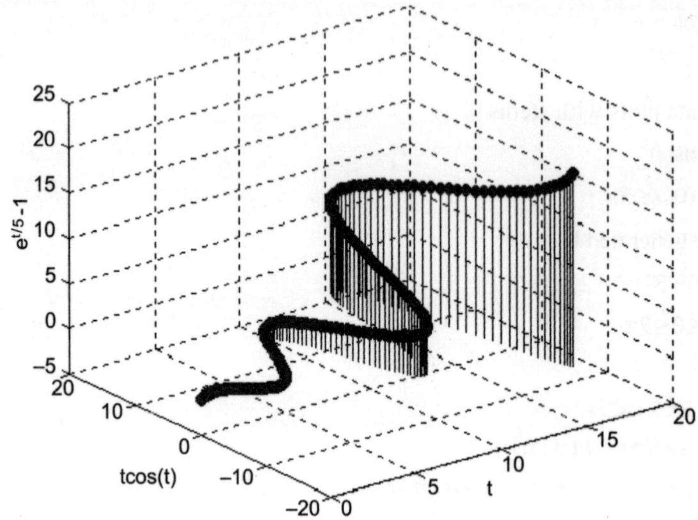

Fig. E1.11(b)

(c)
```
z=[0:0.2:1]';
r=sin(5*pi*z)+3;
cylinder(r)
```

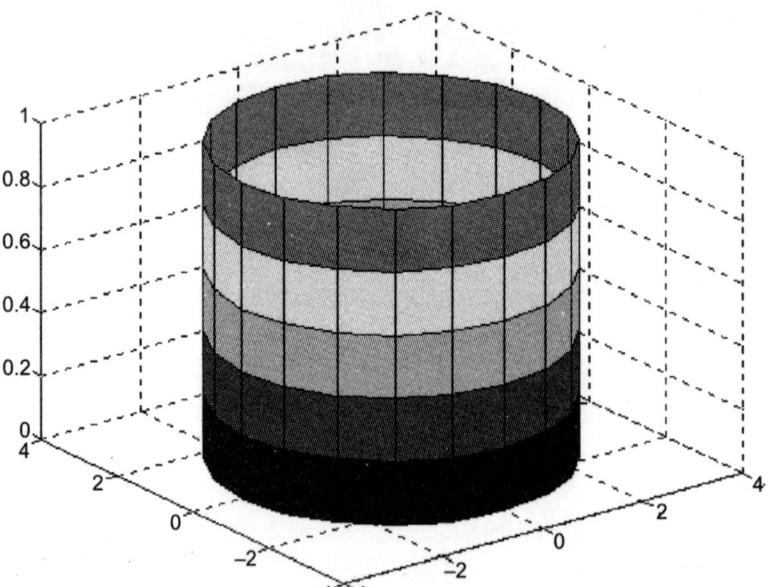

Fig. E1.11(c)

Example E1.12: Obtain the plot of the points for $0 \le t \le 6\pi$ when the coordinates x, y, z are given as a function of the parameter t as follows:

$$x = \sqrt{t}\sin(3t)$$
$$y = \sqrt{t}\cos(3t)$$
$$z = 0.8t$$

Solution:

```
% Line plots
>> t=[0:0.1:6*pi];
>> x=sqrt(t)*sin(3*t);
>> y=sqrt(t)*cos(3*t);
>> z=0.8*t;
>> plot3(x,y,z,'k','linewidth',1)
>> grid on
>> xlabel('x'); ylabel('y'); zlabel('z')
```

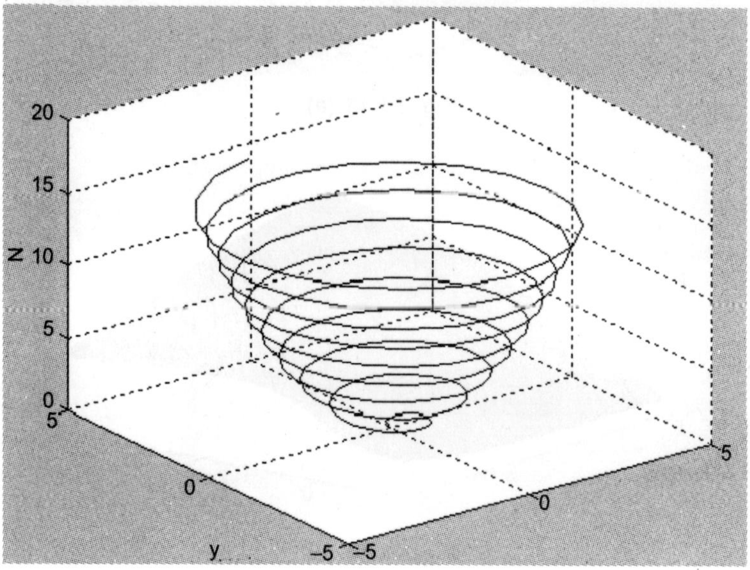

Fig. E1.12

Example E1.13: Obtain the mesh and surface plots for the function $z = \dfrac{2xy^2}{x^2 + y^2}$ over the domain $-2 \le x \le 6$ and $2 \le y \le 8$.

Solution:

```
% Mesh and surface plots
    x=-2:0·1:6;
```

```
>> y=2:0.1:8;
>> [x,y]=meshgrid(x,y);
>> z=2*x*y^2./(x^2+y^2);
>> mesh(x,y,z)
>> xlabel('x'); ylabel('y'); zlabel('z')
>> surf(x,y,z)
>> xlabel('x'); ylabel('y'); zlabel('z')
```

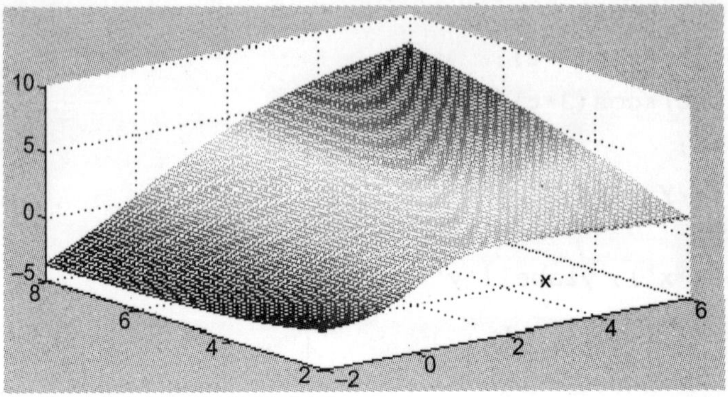

Fig. E1.13 (a)

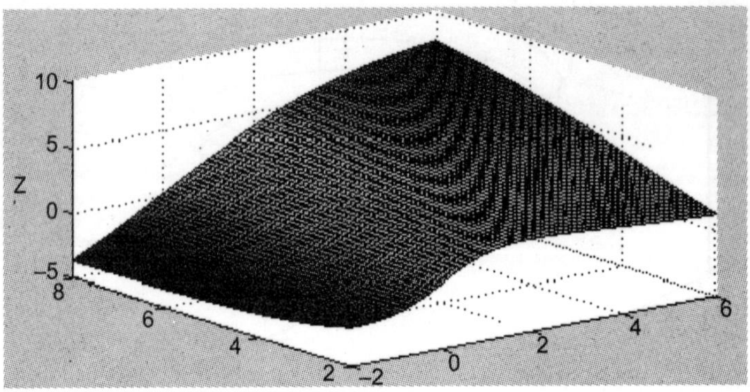

Fig. E1.13 (b)

Example E1.14: Plot the function $z = 2^{-1.5\sqrt{x^2+y^2}} \sin(x)\cos(0.5y)$ over the domain $-4 \le x \le 4$ and $-4 \le y \le 4$ using Table 1.30.

(*a*) Mesh plot
(*b*) Surface plot
(*c*) Mesh curtain plot
(*d*) Mesh and contour plot
(*e*) Surface and contour plot

Solution:

(*a*) % Mesh Plot

```
>> x=-4:0.25:4;
>> y=-4:0.25:4;
>> [x,y]=meshgrid(x,y);
>> z=2^(-1.5*sqrt(x^2 + y^2))*cos(0.5*y)*sin(x);
>> mesh(x,y,z)
>> xlabel('x');ylabel('y')
>> zlabel('z')
```

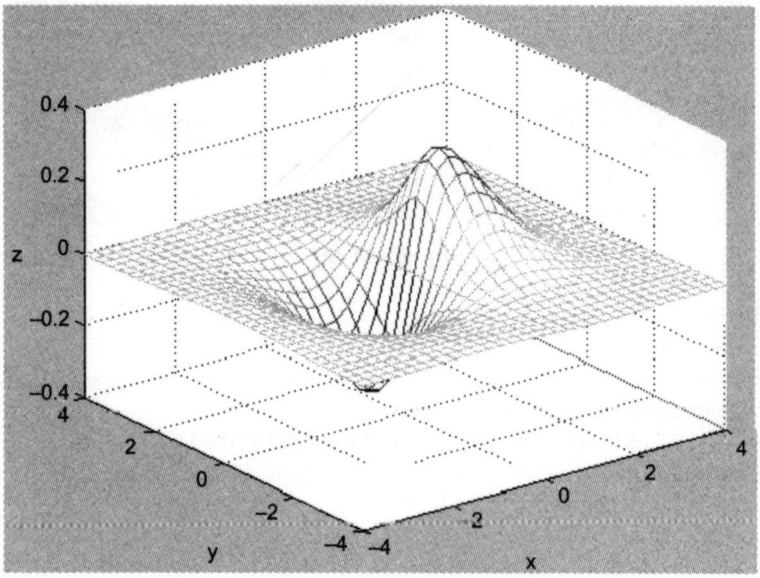

Fig. E1.14 (a)

(*b*) % Surface Plot

```
>> x=-4:0.25:4;
>> y=-4:0.25:4;
>> [x,y]=meshgrid(x,y);
>> z=2.0^(-1.5*sqrt(x^2+y^2))*cos(0.5*y)*sin(x);
>> surf(x,y,z)
>> xlabel('x'); ylabel('y')
>> zlabel('z')
```

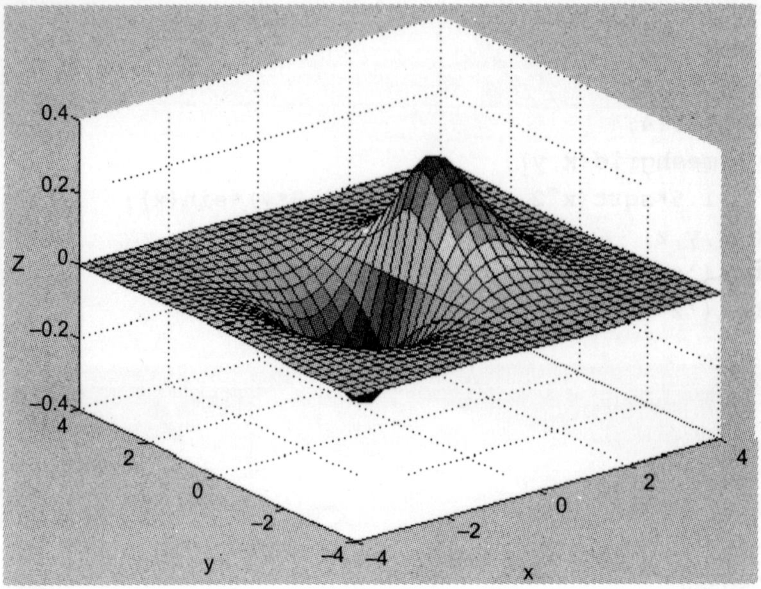

Fig. E1.14 (b)

(*c*) % Mesh Curtain Plot

```
>> x=-4.0:0.25:4;
>> y=-4.0:0.25:4;
>> [x,y]=meshgrid(x,y);
>> z=2.0^(-1.5*sqrt(x^2+y^2))*cos(05*y)*sin(x);
>> meshz(x,y,z)
>> xlabel('x');ylabel('y')
>> zlabel('z')
```

(*d*) % Mesh and Contour Plot

```
>> x=-4.0:0.25:4;
>> y=-4.0:0.25:4;
>> [x,y]=meshgrid(x,y);
>> z=2.0^(-1.5*sqrt(x^2+y^2))*cos(0.5*y)*sin(x);
>> meshc(x,y,z)
>> xlabel('x');ylabel('y')
>> zlabel('z')
```

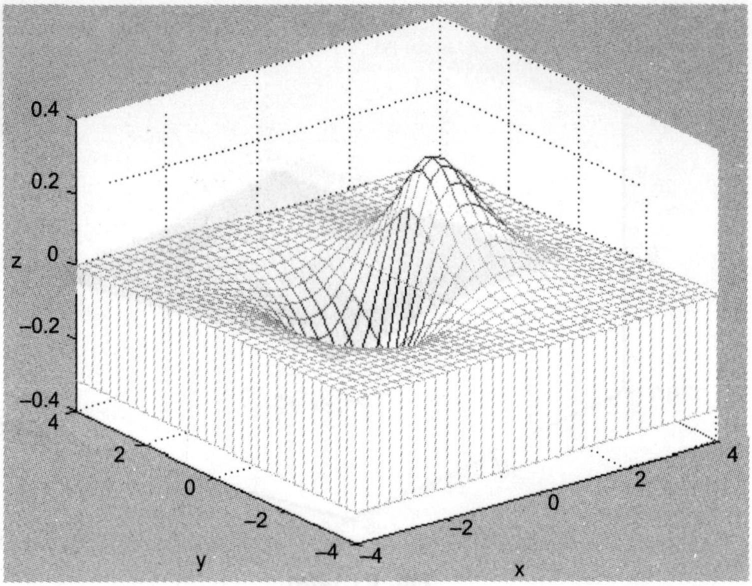

Fig. E1.14 (c)

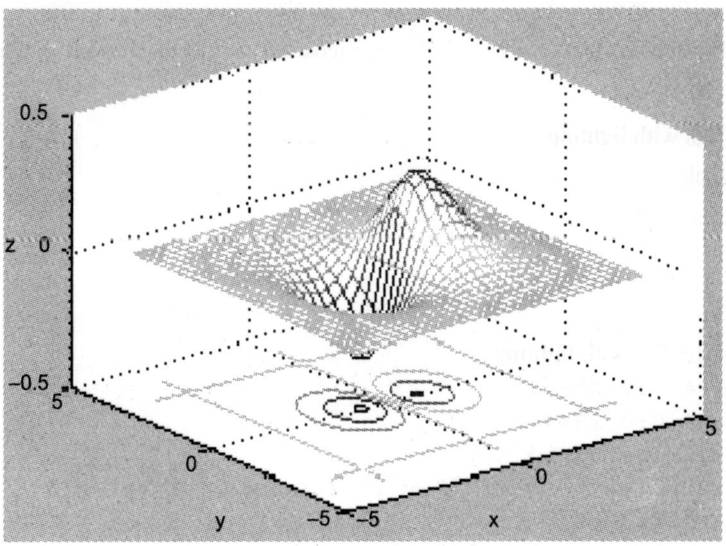

Fig. E1.14 (d)

(*e*) % Surface and Contour Plot

```
>> x=-4.0:0.25:4;
>> y=-4.0:0.25:4;
>> [x, y] =meshgrid(x, y);
>> z=2.0^(-1.5*sqrt(x^2+y^2))*cos(0.5*y)*sin(x);
>> surfc(x, y, z)
>> xlabel('x');ylabel('y')
>> zlabel('z')
```

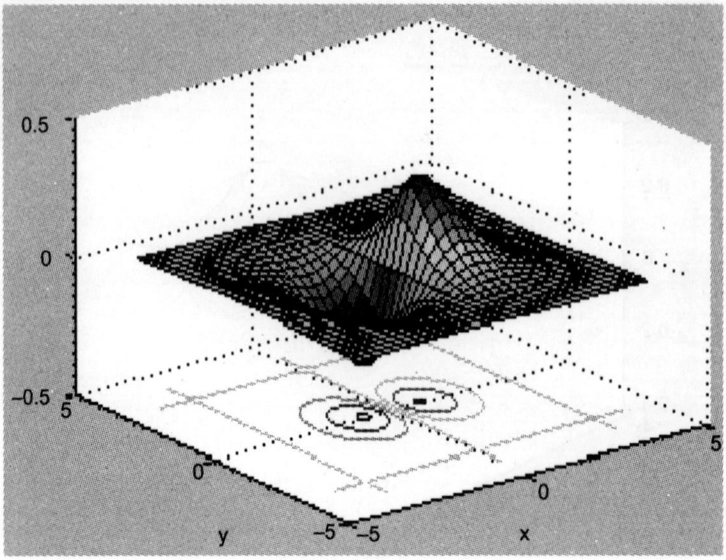

Fig. E1.14(e)

Example E1.15: Plot the function $z = 2^{-1.5\sqrt{x^2+y^2}}\sin(x)\cos(0.5y)$ over the domain $-4 \le x \le 4$ and $-4 \le y \le 4$ and using Table 1.30.

(*a*) Surface plot with lighting

(*b*) Waterfall plot

(*c*) 3-D contour plot

(*d*) 2-D contour plot

Solution:

(*a*) % Surface Plot with lighting

```
>> x=-4.0:0.25:4;
>> y=-4.0:0.25:4;
>> [x,y]=meshgrid(x,y);
>> z=2.0^(-1.5*sqrt(x^2+y^2))*cos(0.5*y)*sin(x);
>> surfl(x,y,z)
>> xlabel('x');ylabel('y')
>> zlabel('z')
```

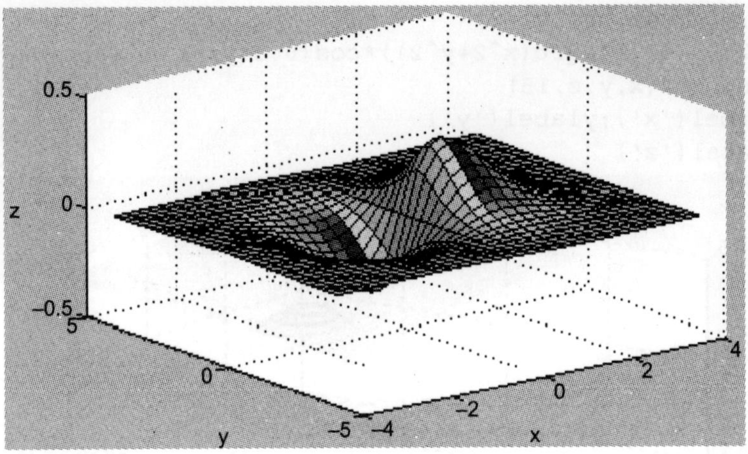

Fig. E1.15 (a)

(*b*) % Waterfall Plot

```
>> x=-4.0:0.25:4;
>> y=-4.0:0.25:4;
>> x,y]=meshgrid(x,y);
>> z=2.0^(-1.5*sqrt(x^2+y^2))*cos(0.5*y)*sin(x);
>> waterfall(x,y,z)
>> xlabel('x');ylabel('y')
>> zlabel('z')
```

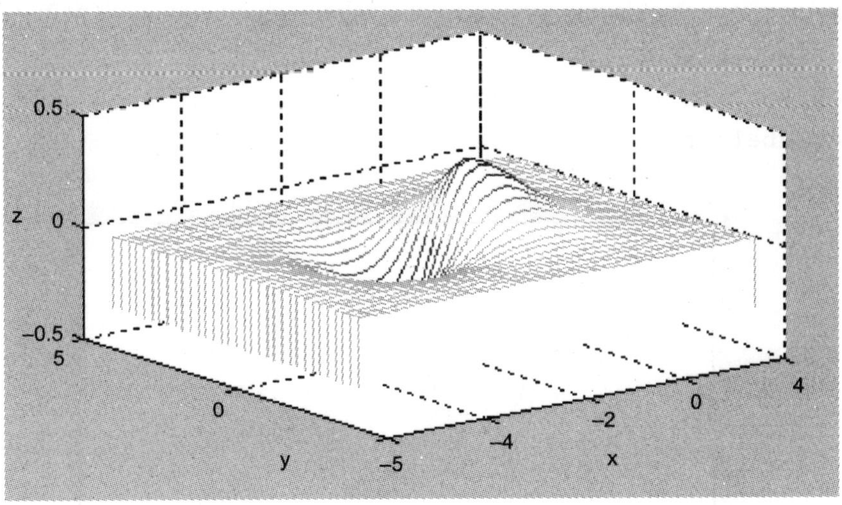

Fig. E1.15 (b)

(*c*) % 3-D Contour Plot

```
>> x=-4.0:0.25:4;
>> y=-4.0:0.25:4;
```

```
>> [x,y]=meshgrid(x,y);
>> z=2.0^(-1.5*sqrt(x^2+y^2))*cos(0.5*y)*sin(x);
>> contour3(x,y,z,15)
>> xlabel('x');ylabel('y')
>> zlabel('z')
```

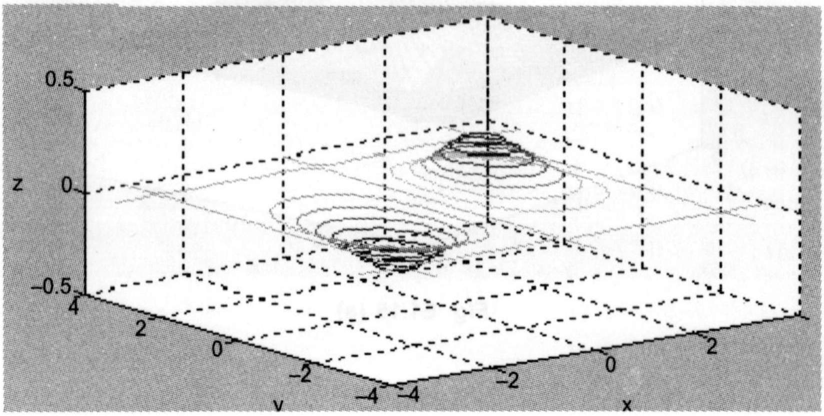

Fig. E1.15 (c)

(*d*) % 2-D Contour Plot

```
>> x=-4.0:0.25:4;
>> y=-4.0:0.25:4;
>> [x,y]=meshgrid(x,y);
>> z=2.0^(-1.5*sqrt(x^2+y^2))*cos(0.5*y)*sin(x);
>> contour(x,y,z,15)
>> xlabel('x');ylabel('y')
>> zlabel('z')
```

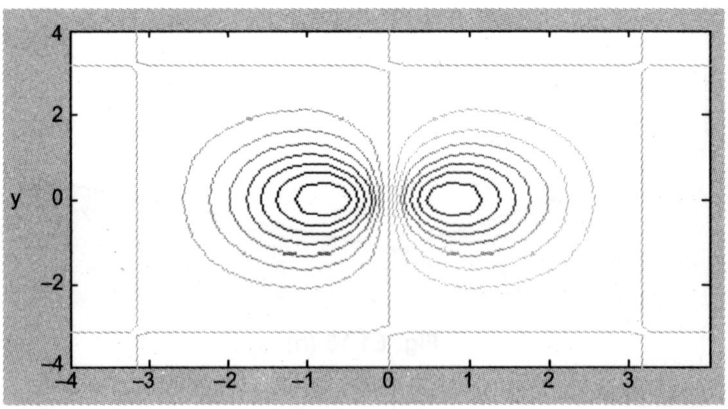

Fig. E1.15 (d)

Example E1.16: Using the functions given in Table 1.29 for plotting *x-y* data, plot the following functions:

(*a*) $f(t) = t\cos t$; $0 \le t \le 10\pi$

(*b*) $x = e^{-2t}, y = t$; $0 \le t \le 2\pi$

(*c*) $x = t, y = e^{2t}$; $0 \le t \le 2\pi$

(*d*) $x = e^t, y = 50 + e^t$; $0 \le t \le 2\pi$

(*e*) $\begin{matrix} r^2 = 3\sin 7t \\ y = r\sin t \end{matrix}$; $0 \le t \le 2\pi$

(*f*) $\begin{matrix} r^2 = 3\sin 4t \\ y = r\sin t \end{matrix}$; $0 \le t \le 2\pi$

(*g*) $y = t\sin t$; $0 \le t \le 5\pi$

Solution:

(*a*) % Use of plot command

```
>> fplot('x*cos(x)', [0,10*pi])
```

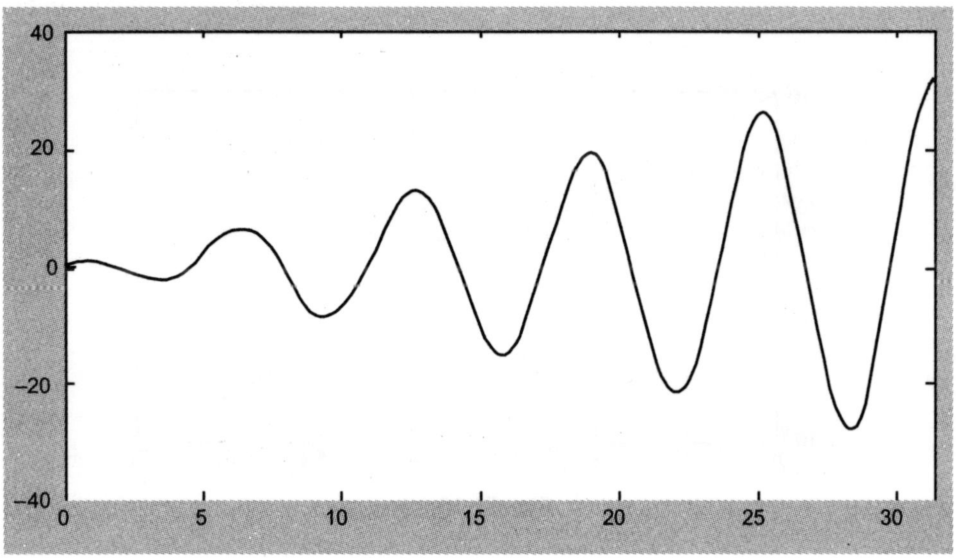

Fig. E1.16 (a)

(*b*) % Semilog x command

```
>> t=linspace(0,2*pi,200);
>> x=exp(-2*t); y=t;
>> semilog x(x,y),grid
```

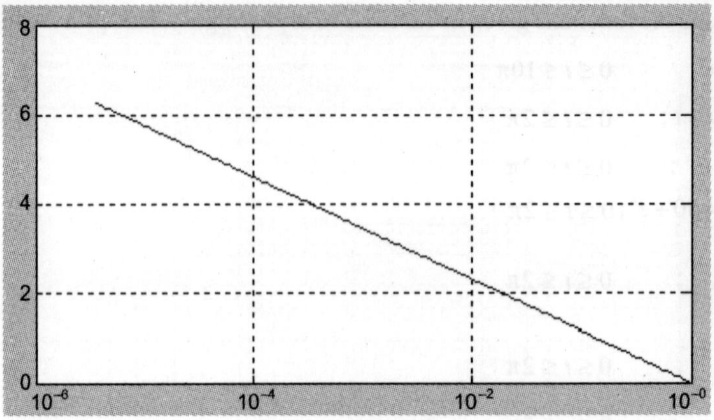

Fig. E1.16 (b)

(*c*) % Semilog y command

```
t=linspace(0,2*pi,200);
>> semilog y(t, exp(-2*t)),grid
```

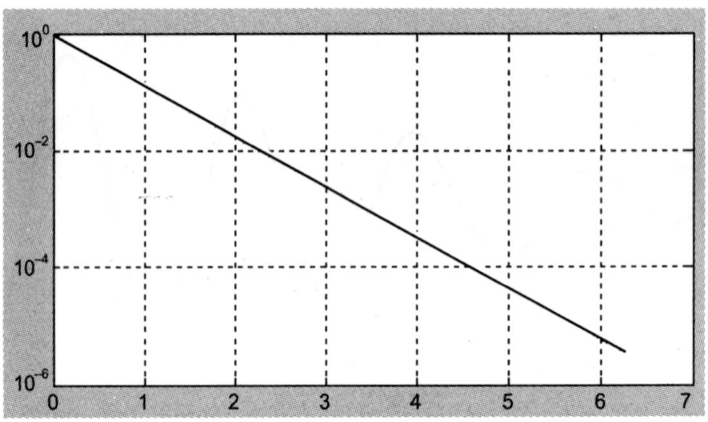

Fig. E1.16 (c)

(*d*) % Use of loglog command

```
>> t=linspace(0,2*pi,200);
>> x=exp(t);
>> y=50+exp(t);
>> loglog(x,y), grid
```

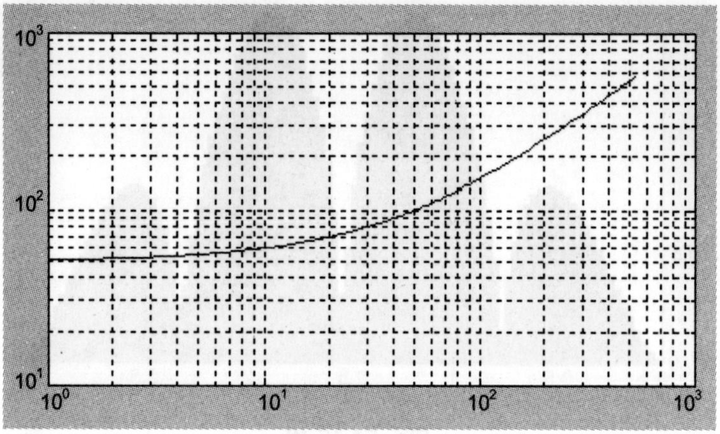

Fig. E1.16 (d)

(*e*) %Use of stairs command

```
>> t=linspace(0,2*pi,200);
>> r=sqrt(abs(3*sin(7*t)));
>> y=r*sin(t);
>> stairs(t, y)
>> axis([0 pi 0 inf]);
```

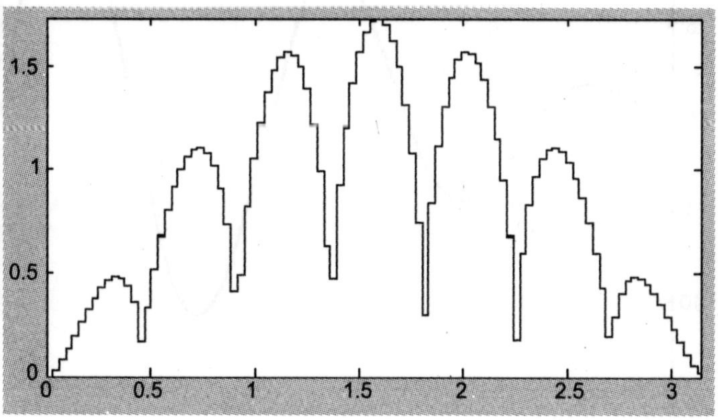

Fig. E1.16 (e)

(*f*) % Use of bar command4

```
>> t=linspace(0,2*pi,200);
>> r=sqrt(abs(3*sin(4*t)));
>> y=r*sin(t);
>> bar(t,y)
>> axis([0 pi 0 inf]);
```

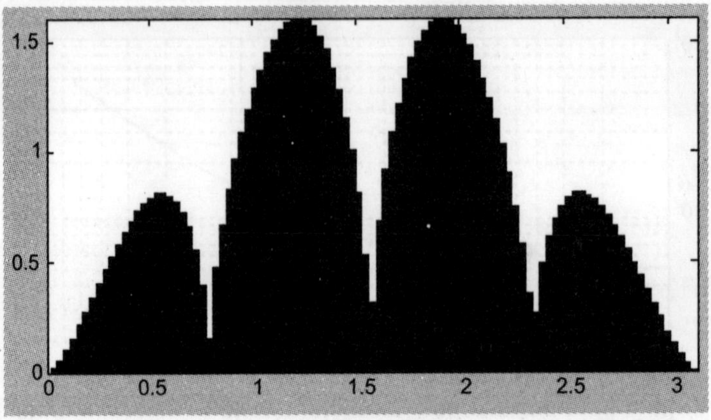

Fig. E1.16 (f)

(g) % use of comet command

```
>> q=linspace(0,5*pi,200);
>> y=q*sin(q);
>> comet(q,y)
```

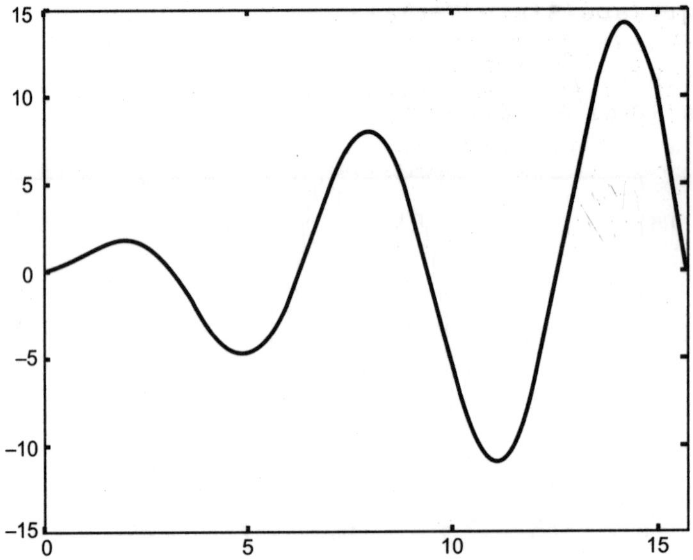

Fig. E1.16 (g)

Example E1.17: Consider the two matrices

$$A=\begin{bmatrix} 3 & 2\pi \\ 5j & 10+\sqrt{2}j \end{bmatrix} \quad \text{and} \quad B=\begin{bmatrix} 7j & -15j \\ 2\pi & 18 \end{bmatrix}$$

Using MATLAB, determine the following:

(a) $A+B$

(b) AB

(c) A^2
(d) A^T
(e) B^{-1}
(f) B^TA^T
(g) $A^2 + B^2 - AB$

Solution:

```
>> A = [3 2*pi;5j 10 + sqrt(2)*j];
>> B = [7j -15j;2*pi 18];
```

(a)
```
A + B
ans =
     3.0000 + 7.0000i     6.2832 -15.0000i
     6.2832 + 5.0000i    28.0000 + 1.4142i
```

(b)
```
>> A * B
ans =
     1.0e+002 *
     0.3948 + 0.2100i    1.1310 - 0.4500i
     0.2783 + 0.0889i    2.5500 + 0.2546i
```

(c)
```
>> A^2
ans =
       9.0000 + 31.4159i   81.6814 + 8.8858i
     -7.0711 + 65.0000i    98.0000 + 59.7002i
```

(d)
```
>> inv(A)
ans =
     0.1597 + 0.1917i    -0.1150 - 0.1042i
     0.0829 - 0.0916i     0.0549 + 0.0498i
```

(e)
```
>> B^-1
ans =
       0 -0.0817i    0.0681
       0 + 0.0285i    0.0318
```

(f)
```
>> inv(B) * inv(A)
ans =
       0.0213 - 0.0193i   - 0.0048 + 0.0128i
     - 0.0028 + 0.0016i     0.0047 - 0.0017i
```

(g)
```
>> (A^2 + B^2) - (A * B)
ans =
       1.0e + 002 *
     -0.7948 - 0.8383i      0.7358 - 2.1611i
      0.7819 + 1.0010i     1.6700 - 0.6000i
```

Example E1.18: Find the inverse of the following matrices using MATLAB:

$$(a)\begin{bmatrix}3 & 2 & 0\\ 2 & -1 & 7\\ 5 & 4 & 9\end{bmatrix} \qquad (b)\begin{bmatrix}-4 & 2 & 5\\ 7 & -1 & 6\\ 2 & 3 & 7\end{bmatrix} \qquad (c)\begin{bmatrix}-1 & 2 & -5\\ 4 & 3 & 7\\ 7 & -6 & 1\end{bmatrix}$$

Solution:

```
>> clear % Clears the workspace
>> A = [3 2 0; 2 -1 7; 5 4 9]; % Spaces separate matrix columns - semicolons separate matrix rows
>> B = [-4 2 5; 7 -1 6; 2 3 7]; % Spaces separate matrix columns - semicolons separate matrix rows
>> C = [-1 2 -5; 4 3 7; 7 -6 1]; % Spaces separate matrix columns - semicolons separate matrix rows
>> inv(A); % Finds the inverse of the selected matrix
>> inv(B); % Finds the inverse of the selected matrix
>> inv(C) % Finds the inverse of the selected matrix
% Inverse of A
ans =
   0.4805  0.2338 -0.1818
  -0.2208 -0.3506  0.2727
   0.1688  0.0260  0.0909
% Inverse of B
ans =
  -0.1773  0.0071  0.1206
  -0.2624 -0.2695  0.4184
   0.1631  0.1135  0.0709
% Inverse of C
ans =
   0.1667  0.1037  0.1074
   0.1667  0.1259 -0.0481
  -0.1667  0.0296 -0.0407
```

Example E1.19: Determine the eigenvalues and eigenvectors of matrix **A** using MATLAB

$$(a) \qquad A=\begin{bmatrix}4 & -1 & 5\\ 2 & 1 & 3\\ 6 & -7 & 9\end{bmatrix} \qquad (b)\ A=\begin{bmatrix}3 & 5 & 7\\ 2 & 4 & 8\\ 5 & 6 & 10\end{bmatrix}$$

Solution:

(*a*)
```
A = [4 -1 5; 2 1 3; 6 -7 9]
A =
    4   -1   5
    2    1   3
    6   -7   9
%The eigenvalues of A
format short e
eig(A)
ans =
    1.0000e + 001
    5.8579e - 001
    3.4142e + 000
%The eigenvectors of A
[Q,d]=eig(A)
Q =
   -5.5709e - 001    - 8.2886e - 001    - 7.3925e - 001
   -3.7139e - 001    - 3.9659e - 002    - 6.7174e - 001
   -7.4278e - 001      5.5805e - 001    - 4.7739e - 002
d =
   1.0000e + 001  0  0
   0 5.8579e-001 0
   0            0  3.4142e + 000
```

(*b*)
```
A =
   3   5   7
   2   4   8
   5   6  10
%The eigenvalues of A
format short e
eig(A)
ans =
     1.7686e + 001
    -3.4295e - 001   +1.0066e + 000i
    -3.4295e - 001   -1.0066e + 000i
%The eigenvectors of A
[Q,d]=eig(A)
Q =
   Column 1
          5.0537e - 001
          4.8932e - 001
          7.1075e - 001
```

```
    Column 2
            -2.0715e - 001 - 5.2772e - 001i
              7.1769e - 001
            -3.3783e - 001 +2.2223e - 001i

    Column 3
            - 2.0715e - 001 + 5.2772e - 001i
              7.1769e - 001
            - 3.3783e - 001- 2.2223e - 001i

d =
    Column 1
            1.7686e + 001
            0
            0

    Column 2
            0
            -3.4295e - 001 +1.0066e + 000i
            0

    Column 3
            0
            0
            -3.4295e - 001 -1.0066e + 000i
```

Example E1.20: Determine the eigenvalues and eigenvectors of **AB** using MATLAB.

$$\mathbf{A} = \begin{bmatrix} 3 & 0 & 2 & 1 \\ 1 & 2 & 5 & 4 \\ 7 & -1 & 2 & 6 \\ 1 & -2 & 3 & 4 \end{bmatrix}; \quad \mathbf{B} = \begin{bmatrix} 1 & 3 & 5 & 7 \\ 2 & -1 & -2 & 4 \\ 3 & 2 & 1 & 1 \\ 4 & 1 & 0 & 6 \end{bmatrix}$$

Solution:

% MATLAB Program

```
% The matrix "a" = A*B
>> A = [ 3 0 2 1; 1 2 5 4; 7 -1 2 6; 1 -2 3 4 ];
>> B = [ 1 3 5 7; 2 -1 -2 4; 3 2 1 1; 4 1 0 6 ];
>> a = A*B
  a =
    13  14  17  29
    36  15   6  44
    35  32  39  83
    22  15  12  26
  >> eig (a)
```

```
ans =
  98.5461
   2.2964
  -1.3095
  -6.5329
```

The eigenvectors are:

```
>> [Q, d] = eig (a)
Q =
   - 0.3263   - 0.2845    0.3908    0.3413
   - 0.3619     0.7387  - 0.7816  - 0.9215
   - 0.8168   - 0.6026    0.4769    0.0962
   - 0.3089     0.1016  - 0.0950    0.1586

d =
    98.5461  0          0          0
    0        2.2964     0          0
    0        0        - 1.3095     0
    0        0          0        - 6.5329
```

Example E1.21: Solve the following set of equations using MATLAB:

(*a*) $x_1 + 2x_2 + 3x_3 + 5x_4 = 21$

$-2x_1 + 5x_2 + 7x_3 - 9x_4 = 18$

$5x_1 + 7x_2 + 2x_3 - 5x_4 = 25$

$-x_1 + 3x_2 - 7x_3 + 7x_4 = 30$

(*b*) $x_1 + 2x_2 + 3x_3 + 4x_4 = 8$

$2x_1 - 2x_2 - x_3 - x_4 = -3$

$x_1 - 3x_2 + 4x_3 - 4x_4 = 8$

$2x_1 + 2x_2 - 3x_3 + 4x_4 = -2$

Solution:

(*a*)

```
>> A = [1 2 3 5;-2 5 7 -9; 5 7 2 -5; -1 -3 -7 7];
>> B = [21; 18; 25; 30];
>> S = A\B
S =
   - 8.9896
    14.1285
   - 5.4438
     3.6128
% Therefore x1= - 8.9896, x2=14.1285, x3= - 5.4438, x4=3.6128.
```

(*b*)

```
>> A = [1 2 3 4; 2 -2 -1 1; 1 -3 4 -4; 2 2 -3 4];
>> B = [8;-3; 8;-2];
>> S =A\B
```

```
S =
      2.0000
      2.0000
      2.0000
     -1.0000
```

% Therefore $x_1 = 2.0000$, $x_2 = 2.0000$, $x_3 = 2.0000$, $x_4 = -1.0000$.

Example E1.22: Use *diff* command for symbolic differentiation of the following functions:

(*a*) $S_1 = e^{x^8}$

(*b*) $S_2 = 3\,x^3\,e^{x^5}$

(*c*) $S_3 = 5x^3 - 7x^2 + 3x + 6$

Solution:

(*a*)
```
>> syms x
>> S1= exp (x^8);
>> diff (S1)
ans =
      8*x^7*exp(x^8)
```

(*b*)
```
>> S2=3*x^3*exp(x^5);
>> diff (S2)
ans =
      9*x^2*exp(x^5) +15*x^7*exp(x^5)
```

(*c*)
```
>> S3=5*x^3-7*x^2+3*x+6;
>> diff (S3)
ans =
      15*x^2-14*x + 3
```

Example E1.23: Use MATLAB's symbolic commands to find the values of the following integrals:

(*a*) $\int_{0.2}^{0.7} |x|\,dx$ (*b*) $\int_0^{\pi} (\cos y + 7y^2)dy$

(*c*) $\sqrt{x}$ (*d*) $7x^5 - 6x^4 + 11x^3 + 4x^2 + 8x + 9$

(*e*) $\cos a$

Solution:

(*a*)
```
>>syms x, y, a, b
>> S1= abs (x)
>> int (S1, 0.2, 0.7)
ans =
      9/40
```

(*b*)
```
>> S2=cos (y) +7*y^2
>> int (S2, 0, pi)
ans =
      7/3*pi^3
```

(*c*)
```
>> S3=sqrt (x)
>> int (S3)
ans =
    2/3*x^ (3/2)
    >> int (S3,'a', 'b')
ans =
    2/3*b^ (3/2)-2/3*a^ (3/2)
    >> int (S3, 0.4, 0.7)
ans =
    7/150*70^ (1/2)-4/75*10^ (1/2)
```

(*d*)
```
>> S4 = 7*x^5-6*x^4+11*x^3+4*x^2+8*x-9
>> int (S4)
ans =
    7/6*x^6-6/5*x^5+11/4*x^4+4/3*x^3+4*x^2-9*x
```

(*e*)
```
>> S5=cos (a)
>> int (S5)
ans =
    sin (a)
```

Example E1.24: Obtain the general solution of the following first order differential equations:

(*a*) $\frac{dy}{dt} = 5t - 6y$ (*b*) $\frac{d^2y}{dt^2} + 3\frac{dy}{dt} + y = 0$

(*c*) $\frac{ds}{dt} = Ax^3$ (*d*) $\frac{ds}{dA} = Ax^3$

Solution:

(*a*)
```
>> solve ('Dy=5*t-6*y')
ans =
    5/6*t-5/36+exp (-6*t)*C1
```

(*b*)
```
>> dsolve ('D2y +3*Dy + y = 0')
ans =
    C1*exp (1/2*(5^ (1/2)-3)*t) + C2*exp (-1/2*(5^ (1/2) +3)*t)
```

(*c*)
```
>> dsolve ('Ds =A*x^3','x')
ans =
    1/4*A*x^4 + C1
```

(*d*)
```
>> dsolve ('Ds=A*x^3', 'A')
ans =
    1/2*A^2*x^3 + C1
```

Example E1.25: Determine the solution of the following differential equations that satisfies the given initial conditions.

(*a*) $\frac{dy}{dx} = -7x^2$; $y(1) = 0.7$

(*b*) $\frac{dy}{dx} = 5x\cos^2 y$; $y(0) = \pi/4$

(*c*) $\frac{dy}{dx} = -y + e^{3x}$; $y(0) = 2$

(*d*) $\frac{dy}{dt} + 5y = 35$; $y(0) = 4$

Solution:

(*a*)
```
>> dsolve ('Dy = -7*x^2','y (1) =0.7')
ans =
     -7*x^2*t + 7*x^2 + 7/10
```

(*b*)
```
>> dsolve ('Dy=5*x*cos (y) ^2','y (0) =pi/4')
ans =
     atan (5*t*x + 1)
```

(*c*)
```
>> dsolve ('Dy = -y + exp (3*x)', 'y (0) =2')
ans =
      exp (3*x) + exp (- t)*(-exp (3*x) +2)
```

(*d*)
```
>> dsolve ('Dy + 5*y =35', 'y (0) =4')
ans =
     7 - 3*exp (-5*t)
```

Example E1.26: Given the differential equation

$$\frac{d^2x}{dt^2} + 7\frac{dx}{dt} + 5x = 8u(t)\ ;\ t \geq 0$$

Using MATLAB program, find

(*a*) $x(t)$ when all the initial conditions are zero.

(*b*) $x(t)$ when $x(0) = 1$ and $\dot{x} = 2$.

Solution:

(*a*) x (t) when all the initial conditions are zero
```
>> x = dsolve ('D2x = -7*Dx - 5*x +8', 'x (0) = 0')
x =
   8/5+ (-8/5-C2)*exp (1/2*(-7+29^ (1/2))*t) + C2*exp (-1/2*(7+29^
     (1/2))*t)
```

(*b*) x (t) when x (0) = 1 and $\dot{x}$ = 2
```
>> x = dsolve ('D2x = -7*Dx - 5*x +8', 'x (0) = 1', 'Dx (0) = 2')
```

```
x =
    8/5+ (-3/10-1/290*29^ (1/2))*exp (1/2*(-7+29^ (1/2))*t)-1/290*
        (-1+3*29^ (1/2))*29^ (1/2)*exp(-1/2*(7+29^ (1/2))*t)
```

Example E1.27: Given the differential equation

$$\frac{d^2x}{dt^2}+12\frac{dx}{dt}+15x=35\,; \qquad t\geq 0$$

Using MATLAB program, find

(*a*) $x(t)$ when all the initial conditions are zero.

(*b*) $x(t)$ when $x(0)=0$ and $\dot{x}(0)=1$.

Solution:

(*a*) x (t) when all the initial conditions are zero

```
>> x = dsolve ('D2x = -12*Dx - 15*x +35', 'x (0) = 0')
x =
    7/3+ (-7/3-C2)*exp ((-6+21^ (1/2))*t) +C2*exp (-(6+21^ (1/2))*t)
```

(*b*) x (t) when x (0) = 0 and $\dot{x}$ (0) = 1.

```
>> x = dsolve ('D2x = -12*Dx - 15*x + 35', 'x (0) = 0', 'Dx (0) = 1')
x =
    7/3+ (-7/6-13/42*21^ (1/2))*exp ((-6+21^ (1/2))*t)-1/126*(39+7*21^
        (1/2))*21^ (1/2)*exp (-(6+21^ (1/2))*t)
```

Example E1.28: Find the inverse of the following matrix using MATLAB.

$$A=\begin{bmatrix} s & 2 & 0 \\ 2 & s & -3 \\ 3 & 0 & 1 \end{bmatrix}$$

Solution:

```
>> A = [s 2 0; 2 s -3; 3 0 1];
>> inv (A)
ans =
    [s/(s^2-22),        -2/(s^2-22),     -6/(s^2-22)]
    [-11/(s^2-22),      s/(s^2-22),      3*s/(s^2-22)]
    [-3*s/(s^2-22),     6/(s^2-22),      (s^2-4)/(s^2-22)]
```

Example E1.29: Expand the following function $F(s)$ into partial fractions using MATLAB. Determine the inverse Laplace transform of $F(s)=\dfrac{1}{s^4+5s^3+7s^2}$.

Solution:

The MATLAB program for determining the partial fraction expansion is given below:

```
>> b = [0 0 0 0 1];
>> a = [1 5 7 0 0];
>> [r, p, k] = residue (b, a)
r =
      0.0510 -0.0648i
      0.0510 +0.0648i
     -0.1020
      0.1429
p =
     -2.5000 + 0.8660i
     -2.5000 - 0.8660i
      0
      0
k = [ ]
```

% From the above MATLAB output, we have the following expression:

$$F(s) = \frac{r_1}{s-p_1} + \frac{r_2}{s-p_2} + \frac{r_3}{s-p_3} + \frac{r_4}{s-p_4}$$

$$F(s) = \frac{0.0510 - 0.0648i}{s-(-2.5000+0.8660i)} + \frac{0.0510+0.0648i}{s-(-2.5000-0.8660i)} + \frac{-0.1020}{s-0} + \frac{0.1429}{s-0}$$

% Note that the row vector k is zero implies that there is no constant term in this example problem.
% The MATLAB program for determining the inverse Laplace transform of $F(s)$ is given below:

```
>> syms s
>> f = 1/(s^4 + 5*s^3 + 7*s^2);
>> ilaplace ( f )
ans =
  1/7*t-5/49+5/49*exp (-)*cos (1/2*3^ (1/2)*t) +11/147*exp (-5/2*t)*3^
  (1/2)*sin(1/2*3^(1/2)*t)
```

Example E1.30: Expand the following function $F(s)$ into partial fractions using MATLAB. Determine the inverse Laplace transform of $F(s)$.

$$F(s) = \frac{5s^2 + 3s + 6}{s^4 + 3s^3 + 7s^2 + 9s + 12}$$

Solution:

The MATLAB program for determining the partial fraction expansion is given below:

```
>> b = [0 0 5 3 6];
>> a = [1 3 7 9 12];
>> [r, p, k] = residue(b, a)
```

```
r =
      -0.5357 - 1.0394i
      -0.5357 + 1.0394i
       0.5357 - 0.1856i
       0.5357 + 0.1856i
p =
      -1.5000 + 1.3229i
      -1.5000 - 1.3229i
      -0.0000 + 1.7321i
      -0.0000 - 1.7321i
k = [ ]
```

% From the above MATLAB output, we have the following expression:

$$F(s)=\frac{r_1}{s-p_1}+\frac{r_2}{s-p_2}+\frac{r_3}{s-p_3}+\frac{r_4}{s-p_4}$$

$$F(s)=\frac{-0.5357-1.0394i}{s-(-1.500+1.3229i)}+\frac{(-0.5357+1.0394i)}{s-(-1.5000-1.3229i)}$$

$$+\frac{0.5357-0.1856i}{s-(-0+1.7321i)}+\frac{-0.5357+0.1856i}{s-(-0-1.7321i)}$$

% Note that the row vector *k* is zero implies that there is no constant term in this example problem.
% The MATLAB program for determining the inverse Laplace transform of *F*(*s*) is given below:

```
>> syms s
>> f = (5*s^2 + 3*s +6)/(s^4 + 3*s^3 + 7*s^2 + 9*s +12);
>> ilaplace(f )
ans =
      11/14*exp(-3/2*t)*7^(1/2)*sin(1/2*7^(1/2)*t)-15/14*exp(-3/
      2*t)*cos(1/2*7^(1/2)*t)+3/14*3^ (1/2)*sin(3^(1/2)*t)+15/
      14*cos(3^(1/2)*t)
```

Example E1.31: For the following function *F*(*s*):

$$F(s)=\frac{s^4+3s^3+5s^2+7s+25}{s^4+5s^3+20s^2+40s+45}$$

Using MATLAB, find the partial fraction expansion of *F*(*s*). Also, find the inverse Laplace transformation of *F*(*s*).

Solution:

$$F(s)=\frac{s^4+3s^3+5s^2+7s+25}{s^4+5s^3+20s^2+40s+45}$$

The partial fraction expansion of *F*(*s*) using MATLAB program is given as follows:

```
num = [1 3 5 7 25];
den = [1 5 20 40 45];
[r, p, k] = residue(num, den)
```

```
r =
   -1.3849 + 1.2313i
   -1.3849 - 1.2313i
    0.3849 - 0.4702i
    0.3849 + 0.4702i

p =
   -0.8554 + 3.0054i
   -0.8554 - 3.0054i
   -1.6446 +1.3799i
   -1.6446 - 1.3799i

k =
    1
```

From the MATLAB output, the partial fraction expansion of $F(s)$ can be written as follows:

$$F(s) = \frac{r_1}{(s-p_1)} + \frac{r_2}{(s-p_2)} + \frac{r_3}{(s-p_3)} + \frac{r_4}{(s-p_4)} + k$$

$$F(s) = \frac{(-1.3849 + j1.2313)}{(s + 0.8554 - j3.005} + \frac{(-1.3849 - j1.2313)}{(s + 0.8554 + j3.005)}$$

$$+ \frac{(0.3849 - j0.4702)}{(s + 1.6446 - j1.3799} + \frac{(0.3849 + j0.4702)}{(s + 1.6446 + j1.3779)} + 1$$

Example E1.32: Obtain the partial fraction expansion of the following function using MATLAB:

$$F(s) = \frac{8(s+1)(s+3)}{(s+2)(s+4)(s+6)^2}$$

Solution:

$$F(s) = \frac{8(s+1)(s+3)}{(s+2)(s+4)(s+6)^2} = \frac{(8s+8)(s+3)}{(s^2+6s+8)(s^2+12s+36)}$$

The partial fraction expansion of $F(s)$ using MATLAB program is given as follows:

```
EDU>> num=conv([8 8], [1 3]);
EDU>> den=conv([1 6 8], [1 12 36]);
EDU>> [r, p, k]= residue(num, den)
r =
     3.2500
    15.0000
    -3.0000
    -0.2500

p =
    -6.0000
    -6.0000
    -4.0000
    -2.0000

k = [ ]
```

From the above MATLAB result, we have the following expansion:

$$F(s)=\frac{r_1}{(s-p_1)}+\frac{r_2}{(s-p_2)}+\frac{r_3}{(s-p_3)}+\frac{r_4}{(s-p_4)}+k$$

$$F(s)=\frac{3.25}{(s+6)}+\frac{15}{(s-15)}+\frac{-3}{(s+3)}+\frac{-0.25}{(s+0.25)}+0$$

It should be noted here that the row vector k is zero, because the degree of the numerator is lower than that of the denominator.

$$F(s)=3.25e^{-6t}+15e^{15t}-3e^{-3t}-0.25e^{-0.25t}$$

Example E1.33: Find the Laplace transform of the following function using MATLAB.

(*a*) $f(t)=7t^3\cos(5t+60°)$
(*b*) $f(t)=-7t\,e^{-5t}$
(*c*) $f(t)=-3\cos 5t$
(*d*) $f(t)=t\sin 7t$
(*e*) $f(t)=5\,e^{-2t}\cos 5t$
(*f*) $f(t)=3\sin(5t+45°)$
(*g*) $f(t)=5\,e^{-3t}\cos(t-45°)$

Solution:

% MATLAB Program

(*a*)

```
>> syms t % tell MATLAB that "t" is a symbol.
>> f = 7 * t^3*cos(5*t + (pi/3)); % define the function.
>> laplace( f )

ans =
    -84/(s^2+25)^3*s^2+21/(s^2+25)^2+336*(1/2*s-5/2*3^(1/2))/
      (s^2+25)^4*s^3-168*(1/2*s-5/2*3^(1/2))/(s^2+25)^3*s

>> pretty(laplace(f )) % the pretty function prints symbolic output
% in a format that resembles typeset mathematics.
```

$$\frac{-84s^2}{(s^2+25)^3}+\frac{21}{(s^2+25)^2}+\frac{336\left(\frac{1}{2}s-\frac{5}{2}(3)^{1/2}\right)s\hat{}3}{(s^2+25)^4}-\frac{168\left(\frac{1}{2}s-\frac{5}{2}(3)^{1/2}\right)s}{(s^2+25)^3}$$

(*b*)

```
>> syms t x
>> f = -7*t*exp(-5*t);
>> laplace(f, x)
ans =
    -7/(x + 5)^2
```

(*c*)

```
>> syms t x
>> f = -3*cos(5*t);
>> laplace(f,x)
ans =
    -3*x/(x^2 + 25)
```

(*d*)
```
>>syms t x
>>f = t*sin(7*t);
>> laplace( f, x)
ans =
      1/(x^2+49)*sin(2*atan(7/x))
```

(*e*)
```
>>syms t x
>>f = 5*exp(-2*t)*cos(5*t);
>> laplace(f, x)
ans =
      5*(x+2)/((x+2)^2+25)
```

(*f*)
```
>>syms t x
>>f = 3*sin(5*t+(pi/4));
>> laplace( f, x)
ans =
      3*(1/2*x*2^(1/2)+5/2*2^(1/2))/(x^2 + 25)
```

(*g*)
```
>>syms t x
>>f = 5*exp(-3*t)*cos(t-(pi/4));
>> laplace( f, x)
ans =
      5*(1/2*(x + 3)*2^(1/2)+1/2*2^(1/2))/((x + 3)^2 + 1)
```

Example E1.34: Generate partial-fraction expansion of the following function:

$$F(s)=\frac{10^5(s+7)(s+13)}{s(s+25)(s+55)(s^2+7s+75)(s^2+7s+45)}$$

Solution:

Generate the partial fraction expansion of the following function:

```
numg=poly[-7 -13];
numg=poly([-7 -13]);
deng=poly([0 -25 -55 roots([1 7 75])' roots([1 7 45])']);
[numg,deng]=zp2tf (numg',deng',1e5);
Gtf=(numg,deng);
Gtf=tf(numg,deng);
G=zpk(Gtf);
[r,p,k]=residue(numg,deng)
r =
    1.0e - 017*
    0.0000
   -0.0014
    0.0254
   -0.1871
    0.1621
   -0.0001
    0.0000
    0.0011
```

```
p =
   1.0e + 006*
   4.6406
   1.4250
   0.3029
   0.0336
   0.0027
   0.0001
   0.0000
     0
k = [ ]
```

Example E1.35: Determine the inverse Laplace transform of the following functions using MATLAB.

(*a*) $F(s) = \dfrac{s}{s(s+2)(s+6)}$ (*b*) $F(s) = \dfrac{1}{s^2(s+5)}$

(*c*) $F(s) = \dfrac{3s+1}{(s^2+2s+9)}$ (*d*) $F(s) = \dfrac{s-25}{s(s^2+3s+20)}$

Solution:

(*a*)
```
>> syms s
>> f = s/(s*((s + 2)*(s + 6)));
>> ilaplace( f )
ans =
     1/2*exp(-4*t)*sinh(2*t)
```

(*b*)
```
>> syms s
>> f = 1/((s^2)*(s + 5));
>> ilaplace(f )
ans =
     1/3*t - 2/9*exp(-3/2*t)*sinh(3/2*t)
```

(*c*)
```
>>syms s
>> f = (3*s + 1)/(s^2 + 2*s + 9);
>> ilaplace( f )
ans =
     3*exp(-t)*cos(2*2^(1/2)*t)-1/2*2^(1/2)*exp(-t)*sin(2*2^(1/2)*t)
```

(*d*)
```
>>syms s
>> f = (s -25)/(s*(s^2 + 3*s +25));
>> ilaplace( f )
ans =
     5/4*exp(-3/2*t)*cos(1/2*71^(1/2)*t)+23/284*71^(1/2)*exp
     (-3/2*t)*sin(1/2*71^(1/2)*t)-5/4
```

Example E1.36: Find the inverse Laplace transform of the following function using MATLAB.

$$G(s) = \frac{(s^2+9s+7)(s+7)}{(s+2)(s+3)(s^2+12s+150)}$$

Solution:

% MATLAB Program

```
>> syms s    % tell MATLAB that "s" is a symbol.
>>G = (s^2 + 9*s +7)*(s + 7)/[(s + 2)*(s + 3)*(s^2 + 12*s + 150)]; % define
the function.
>>pretty(G) % the pretty function prints symbolic output
% in a format that resembles typeset mathematics.
```

$$\frac{(s+9s+7)(s+7)}{(s+2)(s+3)(s+12s+150)}$$

```
>> g = ilaplace(G); % inverse Laplace transform
>>pretty(g)
```

$$-7/26\exp(-2t)+\frac{44}{123}\exp(-3t)+\frac{2915}{3198}\exp(-6t)\cos(114^{½}t)$$

$$+\frac{889}{20254}\exp(-6t)114^{1/2}\ \sin(114^{1/2}t)$$

Example E1.37: Generate the transfer function using MATLAB.

$$G(s)=\frac{3(s+9)(s+21)(s+57)}{s(s+30)(s^2+5s+35)(s^2+28s+42)}$$

using

(*a*) the ratio of factors

(*b*) the ratio of polynomials

Solution:

% MATLAB Program

```
'a. The ratio of factors'
>>Gzpk = zpk([-9  -21  -57] , [0 -30 roots([1 5 35]) 'roots([1 28 42])'],3)
% zpk is used to create zero-pole-gain models or to convert TF or
% SS models to zero-pole-gain form.
'b. The ratio of polynomials'
>> Gp = tf(Gzpk)  % generate the transfer function
% Computer response:
```

ans =

(*a*) The ratio of factors

Zero/pole/gain:

$$\frac{3\ (s+9)\ (s+21)\ (s+57)}{s(s+30)\ (s+26.41)\ (s+1.59)\ (s\text{^}2 + 5s + 35)}$$

ans =

(*b*) The ratio of polynomials

Transfer function:

$$\frac{3\ s\text{^}3 + 261\ s\text{^}2 + 5697\ s + 32319}{s\text{^}6 + 63\ s\text{^}5 + 1207\ s\text{^}4 + 7700\ s\text{^}3 + 37170\ s\text{^}2 + 44100\ s}$$

Example E1.38: Generate the transfer function using MATLAB.

$$G(s) = \frac{s^4 + 20s^3 + 27s^2 + 17s + 35}{s^5 + 8s^4 + 9s^3 + 20s^2 + 29s + 32}$$

using

(*a*) the ratio of factors

(*b*) the ratio of polynomials

Solution:

% MATLAB Program

% a. the ratio of factors

```
>>Gtf = tf([1 20 27 17 35] , [1 8 9 20 29 32]) % generate the
% transfer function
% Computer response:
Transfer function:
```

$$\frac{s\text{^}4 + 20\, s\text{^}3 + 27\, s\text{^}2 + 17\, s + 35}{s\text{^}4 + 8\, s\text{^}3 + 9\, s\text{^}2 + 20\, s + 29}$$

% b. the ratio of polynomials

```
>> Gzpk = zpk(Gtf)  % zpk is used to create zero-pole-gain models
% or to convert TF or SS models to zero-pole-gain form.
% Computer response:
 Zero/pole/gain:
```

$$\frac{(s{+}18.59)\,(s{+}1.623)\,(s\text{^}2 - 0.214s + 1.16)}{(s{+}7.042)\,(s{+}1.417)\,(s\text{^}2 - 0.4593s + 2.906)}$$

1.22 SUMMARY

In this chapter, the MATLAB environment which is an interactive environment for numeric computation, data analysis and graphics was presented. Arithmetic operations, display formats, elementary built-in functions, arrays, scalars, vectors or matrices, operations with arrays including dot product, array multiplication, array division, inverse and transpose of a matrix, determinants, element by element operations, eigenvalues and eigenvectors, random number generating functions, polynomials, system of linear equation, script files, programming in MATLAB, the commands used for printing information and generating 2-D and 3-D plots, input/output in MATLAB was presented with illustrative examples. MATLAB's functions for symbolic mathematics were introduced. These functions are useful in performing symbolic operations and developing closed-form expressions for solutions to linear algebraic equations, ordinary differential equations and systems of equations. Symbolic mathematics for determining analytical expressions for the derivative and integral of an expression was also presented.

REFERENCES

Chapman, S.J., *MATLAB Programming for Engineers,* 2nd ed., Brooks/Cole, Thomson Learning, Pacific Grove, CA, 2002.

Dukkipati, R.V., *Analysis and Design of Control Systems using MATLAB*, New Age International Publishers, New Delhi, India, 2006.

Dukkipati, R.V. and Shivakumar, M. R., *MATLAB for Electrical Engineers*, New Age International Publishers, New Delhi, India, 2007.

Dukkipati, R.V. and Srinivas, J., *Solving Engineering Mechanics Problems with MATLAB*, New Age International Publishers, New Delhi, India, 2007.

Dukkipati, R.V., *MATLAB for Engineers*, New Age International Publishers, New Delhi, India, 2006.

Dukkipati, R.V., *Solving Engineering System Dynamics Problems with MATLAB*, New Age International Publishers, New Delhi, India, 2006.

Dukkipati, R.V., *Solving Vibration Analysis Problems with MATLAB*, New Age International Publishers, New Delhi, India, 2006.

Etter, D.M., *Engineering Problem Solving with MATLAB,* Prentice-Hall, Englewood Cliffs, NJ, 1993.

Gilat, Amos., *MATLAB–An Introduction with Applications*, 2nd ed., Wiley, New York, 2005.

Hanselman, D. and Littlefield, B.R., *Mastering MATLAB 6*, Prentice-Hall, Upper Saddle River, New Jersey, NJ, 2001.

Herniter, M.E., *Programming in MATLAB*, Brooks/Cole, Pacific Grove, CA, 2001.

Magrab, E.B., *An Engineers Guide to MATLAB*, Prentice-Hall, Upper Saddle River, New Jersey, NJ, 2001.

Marchand, P. and Holland, O.T., *Graphics and GUIs with MATLAB*, 3rd ed., CRC Press, Boca Raton, FL, 2003.

Moler, C., *The Student Edition of MATLAB for MS-DOS Personal Computers with 3-1/2" Disks,* MATLAB Curriculum Series, The MathWorks, Inc., 2002.

Palm, W.J. III., *Introduction to MATLAB 7 for Engineers*, McGraw-Hill, New York, NY, 2005.

Pratap, Rudra, *Getting Started with MATLAB—A Quick Introduction for Scientists and Engineers,* Oxford University Press, New York, NY, 2002.

Sigman, K. and Davis, T.A., *MATLAB Primer*, 6th ed., Chapman & Hall/CRC Press, Boca Raton, FL, 2002.

The MathWorks, Inc., *MATLAB: Application Program Interface Reference Version 6*, The MathWorks, Inc., Natick, 2000.

The MathWorks, Inc., *MATLAB: Creating Graphical User Interfaces, Version* 1, The MathWorks, Inc., Natick, 2000.

The MathWorks, Inc., *MATLAB: Function Reference,* The MathWorks, Inc., Natick, 2000.

The MathWorks, Inc., *MATLAB: Release Notes for Release 12*, The MathWorks, Inc., Natick, 2000.

The MathWorks, Inc., *MATLAB: Symbolic Math Toolbox User's Guide, Version 2*, The MathWorks, Inc., Natick, 1993–1997.

The MathWorks, Inc., MATLAB: *Using MATLAB Graphics, Version 6*, The MathWorks, Inc., Natick, 2000.

PROBLEMS

P1.1: Compute the following quantity using MATLAB in the Command Window:

$$\frac{17\left[\sqrt{5}-1\right]}{\left[15^2-13^2\right]}+\frac{5^7\log_{10}(e^3)}{\pi\sqrt{121}}+\ln(e^4)+\sqrt{11}$$

P1.2: Compute the following quantity using MATLAB in the Command Window:

$$B=\frac{\tan x+\sin 2x}{\cos x}+\log\left|x^5-x^2\right|+\cosh x-2\tanh x\,;\quad \text{for } x=5\pi/6.$$

P1.3: Compute the following quantity using MATLAB in the Command Window:

$$x=a+\frac{ab\,(a+b)}{c\,\sqrt{|ab|}}+c^a+\frac{\sqrt{14\,b}}{e^{3c}}+\ln(2)+\frac{\log_{10}c}{\log_{10}(a+b+c)}+2\sinh a-3\tanh b$$

for $a=1, b=2$ and $c=1.8$.

P1.4: Use MATLAB to create

(*a*) a row and column vectors that has the elements: 11, –3, $e^{7.8}$, ln(59), tan(p/3), 5 $\log_{10}(26)$.

(*b*) a row vector with 20 equally spaced elements in which the first element is 5.

(*c*) a column vector with 15 equally spaced elements in which the first element is –1.

P1.5: Enter the following matrix A in MATLAB and create:

$$A=\begin{bmatrix}1&2&3&4&5&6&7&8\\9&10&11&12&13&14&15&16\\17&18&19&20&21&22&23&24\\25&26&27&28&29&30&31&32\\33&34&35&36&37&38&39&40\end{bmatrix}$$

(*a*) a 4 × 5 matrix B from the 1st, 3rd and the 5th rows, and the 1st, 2nd, 4th and 8th columns of the matrix A.

(*b*) a 16 element-row vector C from the elements of the 5th row, and the 4th and 6th columns of the matrix A.

P1.6: Given the function $y=\left(x^{\sqrt{2}+0.02}+e^x\right)^{1.8}\ln x$. Determine the value of y for the following values of x: 2, 3, 8, 10, –1, –3, –5, –6.2. Solve the problem using MATLAB by first creating a vector **x**, and creating a vector **y**, using element-by-element calculations.

P1.7: Define a and b as scalars, a = 0.75, and b = 11.3, and x, y and z as the vectors, x = 2, 5, 1, 9, y = 0.2, 1.1, 1.8, 2 and z = –3, 2, 5, 4. Use these variables to calculate A given below using element-by-element computations for the vectors with MATLAB.

$$A = \frac{x^{1.1}y^{-2}z^{5}}{(a+b)^{b/3}} + a\frac{\left(\frac{z}{x}+\frac{y}{2}\right)}{z^{a}}$$

P1.8: Enter the following three matrices in MATLAB

$$A = \begin{bmatrix} 1 & 2 & 3 \\ -8 & 5 & 7 \\ -8 & 4 & 6 \end{bmatrix}, \quad B = \begin{bmatrix} 12 & -5 & 4 \\ 7 & 11 & 6 \\ 1 & 8 & 13 \end{bmatrix}, \quad C = \begin{bmatrix} 7 & 13 & 4 \\ -2 & 8 & -5 \\ 9 & -6 & 11 \end{bmatrix}$$

and show that

(*a*) $A+B=B+A$

(*b*) $A+(B+C)=(A+B)+C$

(*c*) $7(A+C)=7(A)+7(C)$

(*d*) $A*(B+C)=A*B+A*C$

P1.9: Consider the polynomials

$$p_1(s) = s^3 + 5s^2 + 3s + 10$$
$$p_2(s) = s^4 + 7s^3 + 5s^2 + 8s + 15$$
$$p_3(s) = s^5 + 15s^4 + 10s^3 + 6s^2 + 3s + 9$$

Determine $p_1(2), p_2(2)$ and $p_3(3)$.

P1.10: The following polynomials are given:

$$p_1(x) = x^5 + 2x^4 - 3x^3 + 7x^2 - 8x + 7$$
$$p_2(x) = x^4 + 3x^3 - 5x^2 + 9x + 11$$
$$p_3(x) = x^3 - 2x^2 - 3x + 9$$
$$p_4(x) = x^2 - 5x + 13$$
$$p_5(x) = x + 5$$

Use MATLAB functions with polynomial coefficient vectors to evaluate the expressions at $x = 2$.

P1.11: Determine the roots of the following polynomials:

(*a*) $p_1(x) = x^7 + 8x^6 + 5x^5 + 4x^4 + 3x^3 + 2x^2 + x + 1$

(*b*) $p_2(x) = x^6 - 7x^6 + 7x^5 + 15x^4 - 10x^3 - 8x^2 + 7x + 15$

(*c*) $p_3(x) = x^5 - 13x^4 + 10x^3 + 12x^2 + 8x - 15$

(*d*) $p_4(x) = x^4 + 7x^3 + 12x^2 - 25x + 8$

(*e*) $p_5(x) = x^3 + 15x^2 - 23x + 105$

(*f*) $p_6(x) = x^2 - 18x + 23$

(*g*) $p_7(x) = x + 7$

P1.12: An aluminium thin-walled sphere is used as a marker buoy. The sphere has a radius of 65 cm and a wall thickness of 10 mm. The density of aluminium is 2700 kg/m^3. The buoy is placed in the ocean where the density of the water is 1050 kg/m^3. Determine the height H between the top of the buoy and the surface of the water.

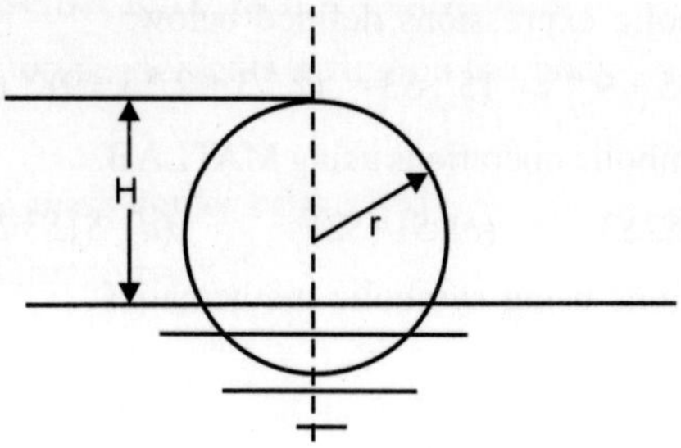

Fig. P1.12

P1.13: Determine the values of x, y and z for the following set of linear algebraic equations:

$$x_2 - 3x_3 = -7$$
$$2x_1 + 3x_2 - x_3 = 9$$
$$4x_1 + 5x_2 - 2x_3 = 15$$

P1.14: Write a simple script file to find (*a*) dot product, (*b*) cross-product of 2 vectors:

$a = \hat{j} - \hat{k}$ and $b = 3\hat{i} - \hat{j}$

P1.15: Write a function to find gradient of $f(x, y) = x^2 + y^2 - 2xy + 4$ at (*a*) (1,1), (*b*) (1,– 2) and (*c*) (0,– 3). Use the function name from command prompt.

P1.16: Write MATLAB functions $f = x^2 - 3x + 1$ and $g = e^x - 4x + 6$ and find the result $f(127)/g(5)$ from a script file.

P1.17: Plot the function $y = |x| \cos(x)$ for $-200 \le x \le 200$.

P1.18: Plot the following functions on the same plot for $0 \le x \le 2\pi$ using the plot function:

(*a*) $\sin^2(x)$

(*b*) $\cos^2 x$

(*c*) $\cos(x)$

P1.19: Plot a graph of the function $y = 45 \sin(0.4t)$ for $t \in [0, 3]$.

P1.20: Consider the function $z = 0.56 \cos(xy)$. Draw a surface plot showing variation of z with x and y. Given $x \in [0, 10]$ and $y \in [0,100]$.

P1.21: Figure P1.21 shows two boats: boat *A* travels south at a speed of 10 mph, and boat B travels east at a speed of 19 mph. The ships are positioned at 8 a.m. are also shown in figure. Write a MATLAB program to plot the distance between the ships as a function of time for the next 5 hours.

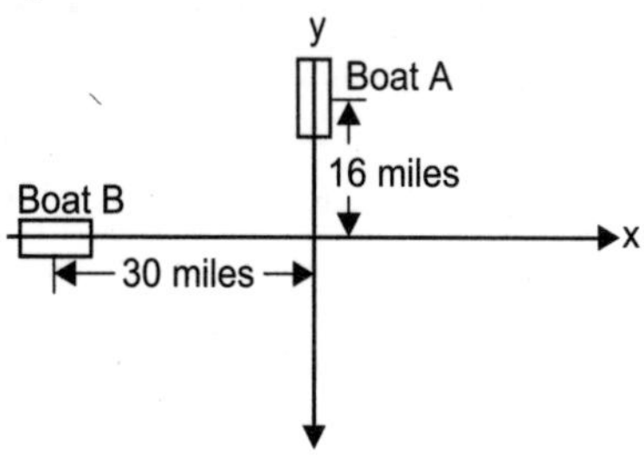

Fig. P1.21

P1.22: Consider the given symbolic expressions defined below:

$S1 =$ '2/(x – 5)'; $S2 =$ 'x ^ 5 + 9 * x – 15'; $S3 =$ '(x ^ 3 + 2 * x +9) * (x * x – 5)';

Perform the following symbolic operations using MATLAB.

(*a*) $S1S2/S3$ (*b*) $S1/S2S3$ (*c*) $S1/(S2)^2$ (*d*) $S1S3/S2$ (*e*) $(S2)^2/(S1S3)$

P1.23: Solve the following equations using symbolic mathematics:

(*a*) $x^2 + 9 = 0$

(*b*) $x^2 + 5x - 8 = 0$

(*c*) $x^3 + 11x^2 - 7x + 8 = 0$

(*d*) $x^4 + 11x^3 + 7x^2 - 19x + 28 = 0$

(*e*) $x^7 - 8x^5 + 7x^4 + 5x^3 - 8x + 9 = 0$

P1.24: Determine the values of *x*, *y* and *z* for the following set of linear algebraic equations:

$$2x + y - 3z = 11$$
$$4x - 2y + 3z = 8$$
$$-2x + 2y - z = -6$$

P1.25: Figure P1.25 shows a scale with two springs.

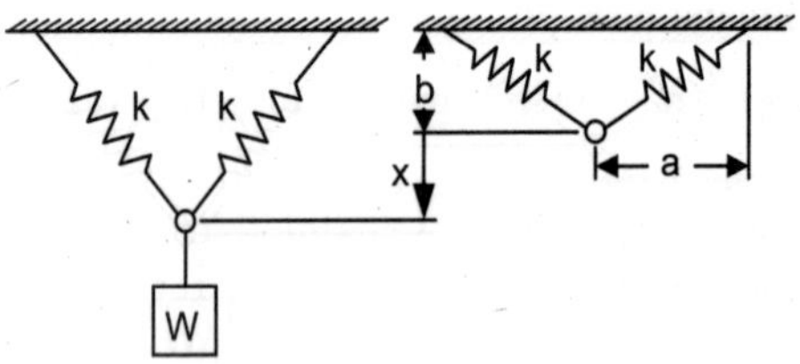

Fig. P1.25

The two springs are unstretched initially and will stretch when a mass is attached to the ring and the ring will displace downwards a distance of *x*. The weight *W* of the object is given by

$$W = \frac{2k}{\ell}(\ell - \ell_0)(b + x)$$

where ℓ_0 = initial length of a spring = $\sqrt{a^2 + b^2}$

and ℓ = the stretched length of the spring = $\sqrt{a^2 + (b + x)^2}$.

If k = spring constant,

Write a MATLAB program to determine the distance *x* when $W = 350$ N. Given $a = 0.16$ m, $b = 0.045$ m, and the spring constant $k = 3000$ N/m.

P1.26: Determine the solutions of the following first-order ordinary differential equations using MATLAB's symbolic mathematics.

(*a*) $y' = 8x^2 + 5$ with initial condition $y(2) - 0.5$.

(*b*) $y' = 5x\sin^2(y)$ with initial condition $y(0) = \pi/5$.
(*c*) $y' = 7x\cos^2(y)$ with initial condition $y(0) = 2$.
(*d*) $y' = -5x + y$ with initial condition $y(0) = 3$.
(*e*) $y' = 3y + e^{-5x}$ with initial condition $y(0) = 2$.

P1.27: For the following differential equations, use MATLAB to find $x(t)$ when (*a*) all the initial conditions are zero, (*b*) $x(t)$ when $x(0) = 1$ and $\dot{x}(0) = -1$.

(*a*) $\frac{d^2x}{dt^2} + 10\frac{dx}{dt} + 5x = 11$ (*b*) $\frac{d^2x}{dt^2} - 7\frac{dx}{dt} - 3x = 5$

(*c*) $\frac{d^2x}{dt^2} + 3\frac{dx}{dt} + 7x = -15$ (*d*) $\frac{d^2x}{dt^2} + \frac{dx}{dt} + 7x = 26$

P1.28: Figure P1.28 shows a water tank (shaped as an inverted frustum cone with a circular hole at the bottom on the side).

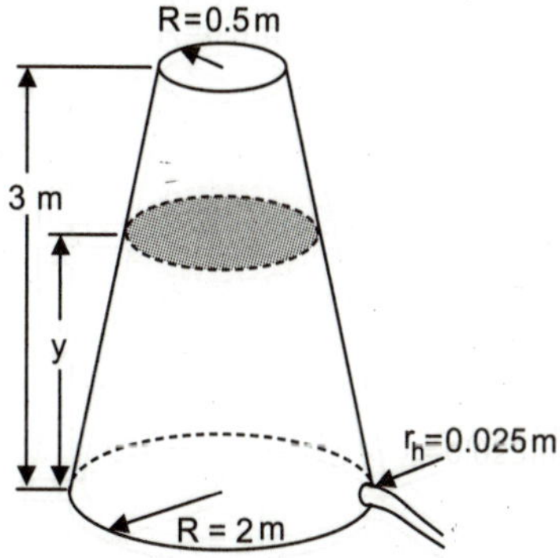

Fig. P1.28 Water tank

The velocity of water discharged through the hole is given by $v = \sqrt{2gy}$ where h = height of the water and g = acceleration due to gravity (9.81 m/s^2). The rate of discharge of water in the tank as the water drains out through the hole is given by: $\frac{dy}{dt} = -\frac{\sqrt{2gy}r_h^2}{(2-0.5y)^2}$ where y = height of water and r_h = radius of the hole. Write a MATLAB program to solve and plot the differential equation. Assume, that the initial height of the water is 2.5 m.

P1.29: An airplane uses a parachute (see Fig. P1.29) and other means of braking as it slow down on the runway after landing. The acceleration of the airplane is given by $a = -0.005\,v^2 - 4$ m/s^2

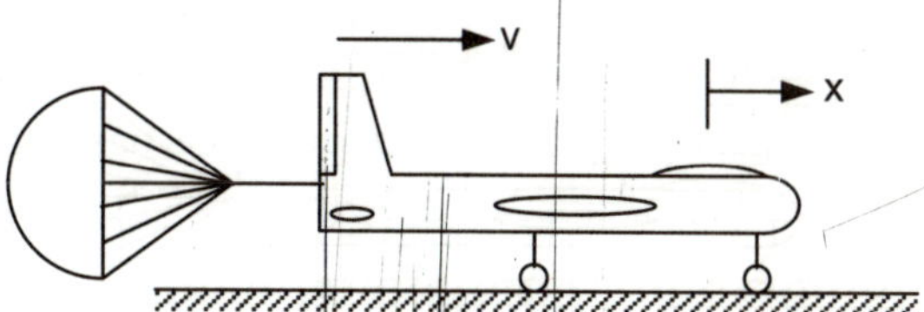

Fig. P1.29

Considering the airplane with a velocity of 500 km/h opens its parachute and starts decelerating at $t = 0$ second, write a MATLAB program to solve the differential equation and plot the velocity from $t = 0$ second until the airplane stops.

P1.30: Obtain the first and second derivatives of the following functions using MATLAB's symbolic mathematics.

(a) $F(x) = x^5 - 8x^4 + 5x^3 - 7x^2 + 11x - 9$

(b) $F(x) = (x^3 + 3x - 8)(x^2 + 21)$

(c) $F(x) = (3x^3 - 8x^2 + 5x + 9)/(x + 2)$

(d) $F(x) = (x^5 - 3x^4 + 5x^3 + 8x^2 - 13)^2$

(e) $F(x) = (x^2 + 8x - 11)/(x^7 - 7x^6 + 5x^3 + 9x - 17)$

P1.31: Determine the values of the following integrals using MATLAB's symbolic functions.

(a) $\int \left(5x^7 - x^5 + 3x^3 - 8x^2 + 7\right) dx$

(b) $\int \sqrt{x} \cos x$

(c) $\int x^{2/3} \sin^2 2x$

(d) $\int_{0.2}^{1.8} x^2 \sin x \, dx$

(e) $\int_{-1}^{-0.2} |x| \, dx$

P1.32: Use MATLAB to calculate the following integral: $\int_0^5 \frac{1}{0.8x^2 + 0.5x + 2} dx$

P1.33: Use MATLAB to calculate the following integral: $\int_0^{10} \cos^2(0.5x) \sin^4(0.5x) dx$

P1.34: The variation of gravitational acceleration g with altitude y is given by:

$$g = \frac{R^2}{(R + y)^2} g_o,$$

where $R = 6371$ km is radius of the earth and $g_o = 9.81$ m/s^2 is gravitational acceleration at sea level.
The change in the gravitational potential energy ΔU of an object that is raised up from the earth is given by:

$$\Delta U = \int_0^y mg dy$$

Determine the change in the potential energy of a satellite with a mass of 500 kg that is raised from the surface of the earth to a height of 800 km.

P1.35: Find the Laplace transform of the following function using MATLAB:

$$f(t) = 7t^3\cos(5t + 60°)$$

P1.36: Use MATLAB program to find the transforms of the following functions.

(*a*) $f(t) = -7t\,e^{-5t}$

(*b*) $f(t) = -3\cos 5t$

(*c*) $f(t) = t\sin 7t$

(*d*) $f(t) = 5\,e^{-2t}\cos 5t$

(*e*) $f(t) = 3\sin(5t + 45°)$

(*f*) $f(t) = 5\,e^{-3t}\cos(t - 45°)$

P1.37: Consider the two matrices

$$A = \begin{bmatrix} 1 & 0 & 2 \\ 2 & 5 & 4 \\ -1 & 8 & 7 \end{bmatrix} \text{ and } B = \begin{bmatrix} 7 & 8 & 2 \\ 3 & 5 & 9 \\ -1 & 3 & 1 \end{bmatrix}$$

Using MATLAB, determine the following:

(*a*) $A + B$

(*b*) AB

(*c*) A^2

(*d*) A^T

(*e*) B^{-1}

(*f*) $B^T A^T$

(*g*) $A^2 + B^2 \quad AB$

(*h*) determinant of A, determinant of B and determinant of AB.

P1.38: Use MATLAB to define the following matrices:

$$A = \begin{bmatrix} 2 & 1 \\ 0 & 5 \\ 7 & 4 \end{bmatrix}, \quad B = \begin{bmatrix} 5 & 3 \\ -2 & -4 \end{bmatrix}, \quad C = \begin{bmatrix} 2 & 3 \\ -5 & -2 \\ 0 & 3 \end{bmatrix}, \quad D = [1\ 2]$$

Compute matrices and determinants if they exist.

(*a*) $(AC^T)^{-1}$

(*b*) $|B|$

(*c*) $|AC^T|$

(*d*) $(C^TA)^{-1}$

P1.39: Consider the two matrices

$$A = \begin{bmatrix} 1 & 0 & 1 \\ 2 & 3 & 4 \\ -1 & 6 & 7 \end{bmatrix} \text{ and } B = \begin{bmatrix} 7 & 4 & 2 \\ 3 & 5 & 6 \\ -1 & 2 & 1 \end{bmatrix}$$

Using MATLAB, determine the following:

(a) $A+B$
(b) AB
(c) A^2
(d) A^T
(e) B^{-1}
(f) B^TA^T
(g) A^2+B^2-AB
(h) det A, det B and det AB.

P1.40: Find the inverse of the following Matrices:

(a) $$A=\begin{bmatrix} 3 & 2 & 1 \\ -1 & 5 & 4 \\ 5 & 7 & -9 \end{bmatrix}$$

(b) $$B=\begin{bmatrix} 1 & 6 & 3 \\ -4 & -5 & 7 \\ 8 & 4 & 2 \end{bmatrix}$$

(c) $$C=\begin{bmatrix} -1 & -2 & 5 \\ -4 & 7 & 2 \\ 7 & -8 & -1 \end{bmatrix}$$

P1.41: Determine the eigenvalues and eigenvectors of the following matrices using MATLAB.

$$A=\begin{bmatrix} 1 & -2 \\ 1 & 5 \end{bmatrix}, \quad B=\begin{bmatrix} 1 & 5 \\ -2 & 7 \end{bmatrix}$$

P1.42: If $A=\begin{bmatrix} 4 & 6 & 2 \\ 5 & 6 & 7 \\ 10 & 5 & 8 \end{bmatrix}$

Use MATLAB to determine the following:

(a) the three eigenvalues of A
(b) the eigenvectors of A
(c) Show that $AQ = Qd$ where Q is the matrix containing the eigenvectors as columns and d is the matrix containing the corresponding eigenvalues on the main diagonal and zeros elsewhere.

P1.43: Determine eigenvalues and eigenvector of **A** using MATLAB.

(a) $$A=\begin{bmatrix} 0.5 & -0.8 \\ 0.75 & 1.0 \end{bmatrix}$$

(b) $$A=\begin{bmatrix} 8 & 3 \\ -3 & 4 \end{bmatrix}$$

P1.44: Determine the eigenvalues and eigenvectors of the following matrices using MATLAB.

(*a*) $A = \begin{bmatrix} 1 & -2 \\ 1 & 3 \end{bmatrix}$

(*b*) $A = \begin{bmatrix} 1 & 5 \\ -2 & 4 \end{bmatrix}$

P1.45: Determine the eigenvalues and eigenvectors of $A * B$ using MATLAB.

$$A = \begin{bmatrix} 3 & -1 & 2 & 1 \\ 1 & 2 & 7 & 4 \\ 7 & -1 & 8 & 6 \\ 1 & -2 & 3 & 4 \end{bmatrix}, \quad B = \begin{bmatrix} 1 & 2 & 5 & 7 \\ 2 & -1 & -2 & 4 \\ 3 & 2 & 5 & 1 \\ 4 & 1 & -3 & 6 \end{bmatrix}$$

P1.46: Determine the eigenvalues and eigenvectors of A and B using MATLAB.

$$A = \begin{bmatrix} 4 & 5 & -3 \\ -1 & 2 & 3 \\ 2 & 5 & 7 \end{bmatrix}, \quad B = \begin{bmatrix} 1 & 2 & 3 \\ 8 & 9 & 6 \\ 5 & 3 & -1 \end{bmatrix}$$

P1.47: Determine the eigenvalues and eigenvectors of $A = a * b$ using MATLAB.

$$a = \begin{bmatrix} 6 & -3 & 4 & 1 \\ 0 & 4 & 2 & 6 \\ 1 & 3 & 8 & 5 \\ 2 & 2 & 1 & 4 \end{bmatrix}$$

$$b = \begin{bmatrix} 0 & 1 & 2 & 3 \\ 4 & 5 & 6 & -1 \\ 1 & 5 & 4 & 2 \\ 2 & -3 & 6 & 7 \end{bmatrix}$$

P1.48: Determine the values of x, y and z for the following set of linear algebraic equations:

$$\begin{aligned} x_2 - 3x_3 &= -7 \\ 2x_1 + 3x_2 - x_3 &= 9 \\ 4x_1 + 5x_2 - 2x_3 &= 15 \end{aligned}$$

P1.49: Determine the values of x, y and z for the following set of linear algebraic equations:

$$\begin{aligned} 2x - y &= 10 \\ -x + 2y - z &= 0 \\ -y + z &= -50 \end{aligned}$$

P1.50: Solve the following set of equations using MATLAB.

(*a*)
$$\begin{aligned} 2x_1 + x_2 + x_3 - x_4 &= 12 \\ x_1 + 5x_2 - 5x_3 + 6x_4 &= 35 \\ -7x_1 + 3x_2 - 7x_3 - 5x_4 &= 7 \\ x_1 - 5x_2 + 2x_3 + 7x_4 &= 21 \end{aligned}$$

(*b*)
$$x_1 - x_2 + 3x_3 + 5x_4 = 7$$
$$2x_1 + x_2 - x_3 + x_4 = 6$$
$$-x_1 - x_2 - 2x_3 + 2x_4 = 5$$
$$x_1 + x_2 - x_3 + 5x_4 = 4$$

P1.51: Solve the following set of equations using MATLAB.

(*a*)
$$2x_1 + x_2 + x_3 - x_4 = 10$$
$$x_1 + 5x_2 - 5x_3 + 6x_4 = 25$$
$$-7x_1 + 3x_2 - 7x_3 - 5x_4 = 5$$
$$x_1 - 5x_2 + 2x_3 + 7x_4 = 11$$

(*b*)
$$x_1 - x_2 + 3x_3 + 5x_4 = 5$$
$$2x_1 + x_2 - x_3 + x_4 = 4$$
$$-x_1 - x_2 + 2x_3 + 2x_4 = 3$$
$$x_1 + x_2 - x_3 + 5x_4 = 1$$

P1.52: Solve the following set of equations using MATLAB.

(*a*)
$$x_1 + 2x_2 + 3x_3 + 5x_4 = 21$$
$$-2x_1 + 5x_2 + 7x_3 - 9x_4 = 17$$
$$5x_1 + 7x_2 + 2x_3 - 5x_4 = 23$$
$$-x_1 - 3x_2 - 7x_3 + 7x_4 = 26$$

(*b*)
$$x_1 + 2x_2 + 3x_3 + 4x_4 = 9$$
$$2x_1 - 2x_2 - x_3 + x_4 = -5$$
$$x_1 - 3x_2 + 4x_3 - 4x_4 = 7$$
$$2x_1 + 2x_2 - 3x_3 + 4x_4 = -6$$

P1.53: Determine the inverse of the following matrix using MATLAB.

$$A = \begin{bmatrix} 3s & 2 & 0 \\ 7s & -s & -5 \\ 3 & 0 & -3s \end{bmatrix}$$

P1.54: Expand the following function $F(s)$ into partial fractions with MATLAB:

$$F(s) = \frac{5s^3 + 7s^2 + 8s + 30}{s^4 + 15s^3 + 62s^2 + 85s + 25}$$

P1.55: Determine the Laplace transform of the following time functions using MATLAB.

(*a*) $f(t) = u(t+9)$
(*b*) $f(t) = e^{5t}$
(*c*) $f(t) = (5t+7)$
(*d*) $f(t) = 5u(t) + 8e^{7t} - 12e^{-8t}$
(*e*) $f(t) = e^{-t} + 9t^3 - 7t^{-2} + 8$
(*f*) $f(t) = 7t^4 + 5t^2 - e^{-7t}$
(*g*) $f(t) = 9\,u\,t + 5e^{-3t}$

P1.56: Determine the inverse Laplace transform of the following rotational function using MATLAB:

$$F(s) = \frac{7}{s^2 + 5s + 6} = \frac{7}{(s+2)\,(s+3)}$$

P1.57: Determine the inverse transform of the following function having complex poles

$$F(s) = \frac{15}{(s^3 + 5s^2 + 11s + 10)}$$

P1.58: Determine the inverse Laplace transform of the following functions using MATLAB:

(*a*) $F(s) = \dfrac{s}{s(s+2)(s+3)(s+5)}$

(*b*) $F(s) = \dfrac{1}{s^2(s+7)}$

(*c*) $F(s) = \dfrac{5s+9}{(s^3 + 8s + 5)}$

(*d*) $F(s) = \dfrac{s-28}{s(s^2 + 9s + 33)}$.

❍ ❍ ❍

CHAPTER 2

ELECTRICAL CIRCUITS

2.1 INTRODUCTION

In this chapter, we briefly review the three types of basic passive electrical elements: resistor, inductor and capacitor.

Resistance Elements: *Ohm's Law:* The voltage drop V_R across a linear resistor is proportional to the current i_R flowing through the resistor, where the constant of proportionality is the resistance R as shown in Fig. 2.1.

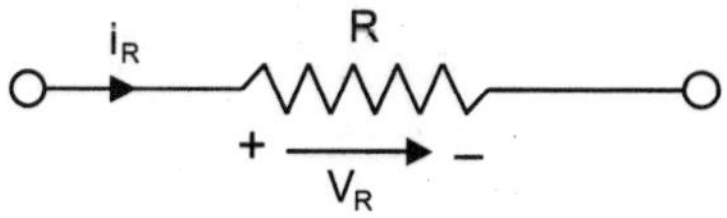

Fig. 2.1

$$V_R = R\, i_R$$

Resistors do not store electrical energy in any form but dissipate it as heat. The rate of energy dissipated (power consumed) by a resistor is given by

$$P = i_R^2 R = \frac{V_R^2}{R} \quad \text{(W or J/s)}$$

Resistors in Series: The current i passes through each element as shown in Fig. 2.2(a). The total voltage drop is given by the sum of the voltage drops across each element, or

$$V = V_1 + V_2$$

Applying Ohm's law, we obtain

$$iR_{eq} = iR_1 + iR_2$$

or $$R_{eq} = R_1 + R_2$$

The voltage drop across each resistor is then given by

$$V_1 = \left(\frac{R_1}{R_1 + R_2}\right) V$$

and $$V_2 = \left(\frac{R_2}{R_1 + R_2}\right)V$$

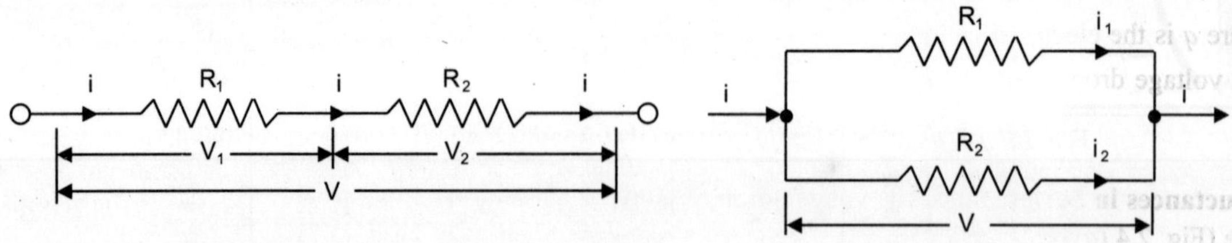

(a) Resistors in series **(b) Resistors in parallel**

Fig. 2.2

Resistors in Parallel: All the elements in the case have the same voltage applied across them as shown in Fig. 2.2 (*b*).

$$i = i_1 + i_2$$

Applying Ohm's law, we get

$$\frac{V}{R_{eq}} = \frac{V}{R_1} + \frac{V}{R_2}$$

or $$R_{eq} = \frac{R_1 R_2}{R_1 + R_2} \quad \text{...(2.1)}$$

If there are *n* resistors, we can write

$$\frac{1}{R_{eq}} = \frac{1}{R_1} + \frac{1}{R_1} + \cdots + \frac{1}{R_n}$$

Solving eq. (2.1) for the currents i_1 and i_2, we obtain

$$i_1 = \left(\frac{R_2}{R_1 + R_2}\right)i$$

$$i_2 = \left(\frac{R_1}{R_1 + R_2}\right)i$$

Inductance Elements: The voltage V_L across the inductor L is given by (see Fig. 2.3)

$$V_L = L\frac{di_L}{dt}$$

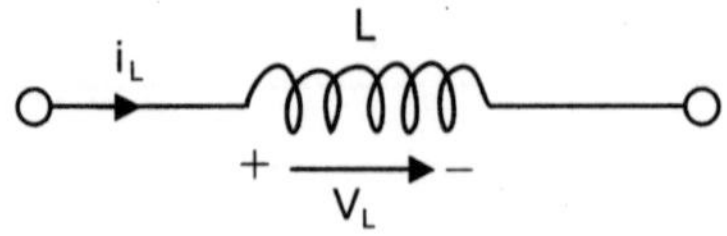

Fig. 2.3

where i_L is the current through the inductor.

The energy stored in an inductance is

$$E = \frac{1}{2}Li^2 = \frac{1}{2}L(\dot{q})^2$$

where q is the electrical charge.

The voltage drop in an inductance is

$$V_i = L\dot{i} = L\dot{q}$$

Inductances in Series: Since the voltage drop through an inductor is proportional to the inductance L, we have (Fig. 2.4 (*a*))

$$L_{eq} = L_1 + L_2$$

(a) Inductances in series

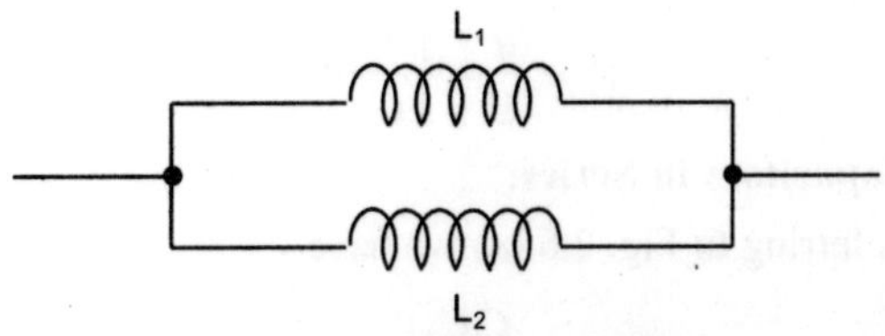

(b) Inductances in parallel

Fig. 2.4 Inductances

Inductances in Parallel: Referring to Fig. 2.4 (*b*), we have

$$L_{eq} = \frac{L_1 L_2}{L_1 + L_2}$$

Similarly, for n inductors

$$\frac{1}{L_{eq}} = \frac{1}{L_1} + \frac{1}{L_2} + \cdots + \frac{1}{L_n}$$

Capacitance Elements: Capacitance C is a measure of the quantity of charge that can be stored for a given voltage across the plates. The capacitance C of a capacitor is given by

$$C = \frac{q}{V_c}$$

where q is the quantity of charge stored and V_c is the voltage across the capacitor.

Since $i = \frac{dq}{dt}$ and $V_c = q/C$, we have

$$i = C\frac{dV_c}{dt}$$

or $$dV_c = \frac{1}{C} i\, dt$$

Hence $$V_c = \frac{1}{C}\int i_c\, dt$$

This is shown in Fig. 2.5.

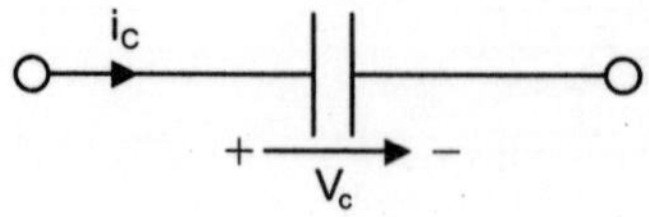

Fig. 2.5 Capacitor

The energy stored in a capacitor is given by

$$E = \frac{1}{2}CV^2$$

The voltage drop across capacitor is given by

$$V_c = \frac{q}{C} = \int \frac{i}{C}\,dt$$

Capacitors in Series:

Referring to Fig. 2.6 (*a*) we have

$$C_{eq} = \frac{C_1C_2}{C_1 + C_2}$$

For *n* capacitors

$$\frac{1}{C_{eq}} = \frac{1}{C_1} + \frac{1}{C_2} + \cdots + \frac{1}{C_n}$$

Capacitors in Parallel:

For capacitors in parallel (see Fig. 2.6 (*b*))

$$C_{eq} = C_1 + C_2$$

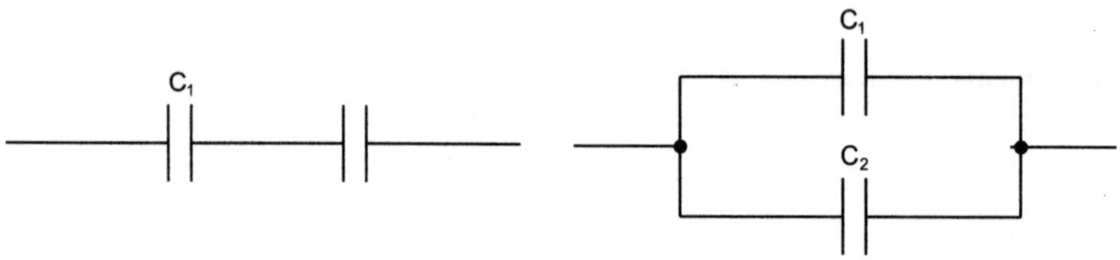

(a) Capacitors in series **(b) Capacitors in parallel**

Fig. 2.6 Capacitor

2.2 ELECTRICAL CIRCUITS

In this section, we apply Ohm's law to series and parallel circuits to determine the combined resistance of the given circuit.

Series Circuits: The combined resistance of series-connected resistors of a simple series circuit is given by the sum of the individual resistances. The voltage between points *A* and *B* of the simple series circuit shown in Fig. 2.7 is given by

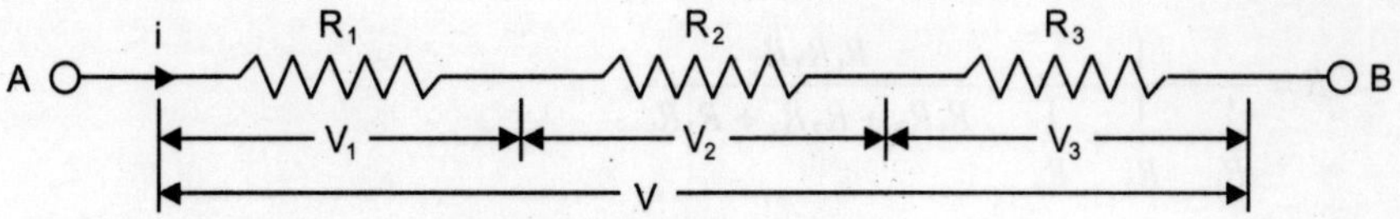

Fig. 2.7 Series circuit

$$V = V_1 + V_2 + V_3$$

where $V_1 = iR_1$

$V_2 = iR_2$

and $V_3 = iR_3$

Hence $$\frac{V}{i} = R_1 + R_2 + R_3$$

Therefore, the combined resistance R of the series circuit is given by

$$R = R_1 + R_2 + R_3$$

Parallel Circuits: For the parallel electrical circuit shown in Fig. 2.8, we can write

$$i_1 = \frac{V}{R_1}$$

$$i_2 = \frac{V}{R_2}$$

and $$i_3 = \frac{V}{R_3}$$

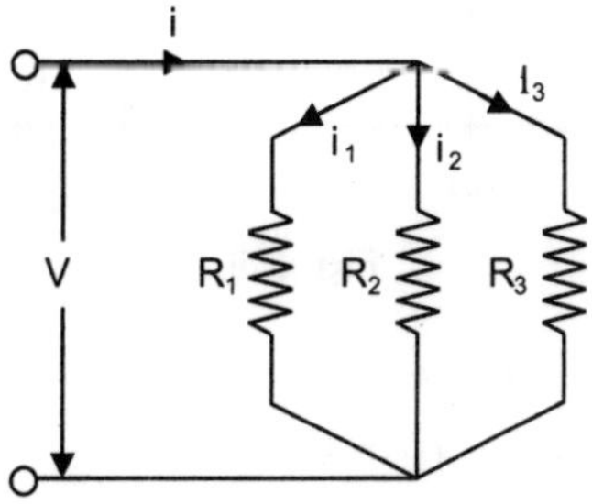

Fig. 2.8 Parallel circuit

Now $i = i_1 + i_2 + i_3$

Therefore,

$$i = \frac{V}{R_1} + \frac{V}{R_2} + \frac{V}{R_3} = \frac{V}{R}$$

where R is the combined resistance. Hence

$$\frac{1}{R} = \frac{1}{R_1} + \frac{1}{R_2} + \frac{1}{R_3}$$

Therefore, $R = \dfrac{1}{\dfrac{1}{R_1} + \dfrac{1}{R_2} + \dfrac{1}{R_3}} = \dfrac{R_1 R_2 R_3}{R_1 R_2 + R_2 R_3 + R_3 R_1}.$

2.3 KIRCHHOFF S LAWS

Kirchhoff's laws are the two most useful physical laws for modeling electrical systems. It is necessary to apply Kirchhoff's laws in solving electric circuit problems as they involve many electromotive forces such as resistance, capacitance and inductance.

The Kirchhoff's laws are stated as follows:

1. *Kirchhoff's current law (node law)*: The algebraic sum of all the currents flowing into a junction (or node) is zero (node analysis).

In other words, the sum of currents entering a node is equal to the sum of the currents leaving the same node. A *node* is an electrical circuit is a point where three or more wires are joined together. Currents going toward a node are considered positive while currents leaving a node are treated as negative.

The algebraic sum of all currents (in) a circuit node is zero. That is,

$$\sum_n (i_n)_{\text{in}} = 0$$

Referring to Fig. 2.9, Kirchhoff's current law states that

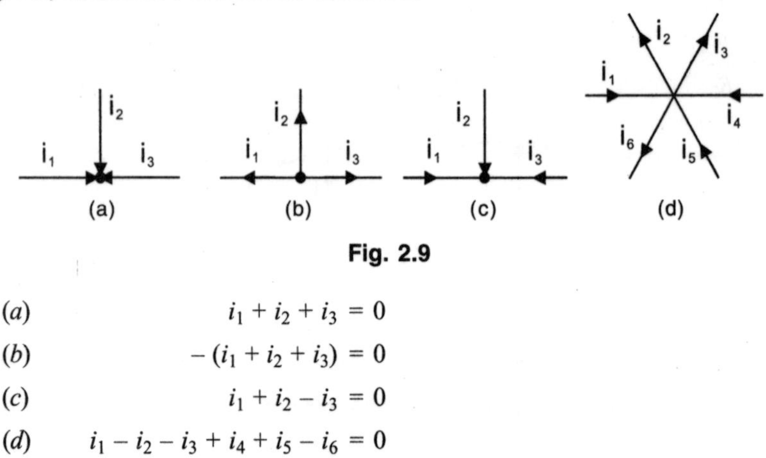

Fig. 2.9

Fig. 2.9 (*a*)	$i_1 + i_2 + i_3 = 0$
Fig. 2.9 (*b*)	$-(i_1 + i_2 + i_3) = 0$
Fig. 2.9 (*c*)	$i_1 + i_2 - i_3 = 0$
Fig. 2.9 (*d*)	$i_1 - i_2 - i_3 + i_4 + i_5 - i_6 = 0$

2. *Kirchhoff's voltage law (loop law)*: The algebraic sum of all the potential drops around a closed loop (or closed circuit) is zero (loop analysis).

In other words, the sum of the voltage drops is equal to the sum of the voltage rises around a loop. That is, the sum of all voltage drops around a circuit loop is zero. Hence

$$\Sigma V_{\text{drop}} = 0$$

or

$$\Sigma V_{\text{gain}} = 0$$

The voltage drops or voltage gains should be appropriately indicated for loop analysis. Figure 2.10 shows examples with useful sign convention.

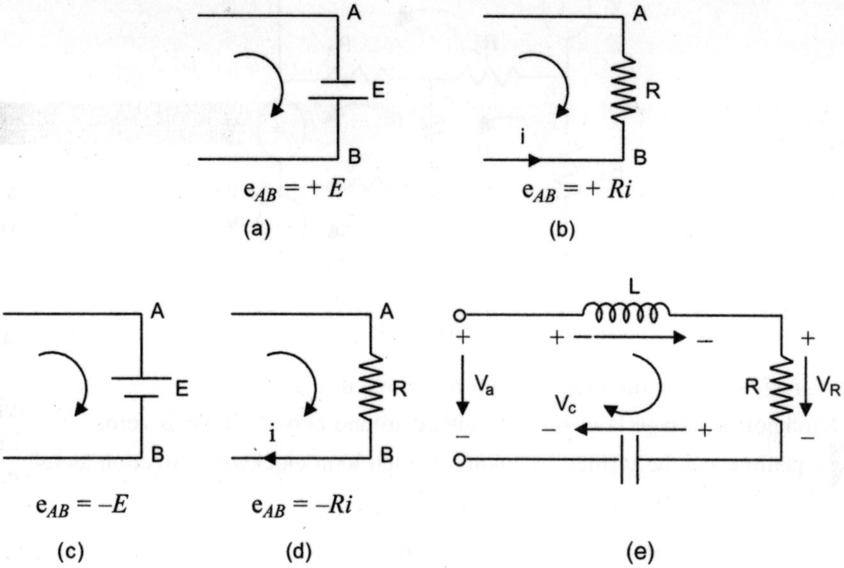

Fig. 2.10

The application of MATLAB to the analysis and design of control systems, engineering mechanics (statics and dynamics), mechanical vibration analysis, electrical circuits and numerical methods is presented in this chapter with a number of illustrative examples. The MATLAB computational approach to the transient response analysis, steps response, impulse response, ramp response and response to the simple inputs are presented. Plotting root loci, Bode diagrams, polar plots, Nyquist plot, Nichols plot and state space method are obtained using MATLAB. Extensive worked examples are included with a significant number of exercise problems to guide the student to understand and as an aid for learning about the analysis and design of control systems, engineering mechanics, vibration analysis of mechanical systems, electrical circuits, and numerical methods using MATLAB.

2.4 EXAMPLE PROBLEMS AND SOLUTIONS

Example E2.1: Figure E2.1 shows an electrical circuit with resistors and voltage sources. Write a MATLAB program to determine the current in each resistor using the mesh current method based on Kirchhoff's voltage law.

Given: $V_1 = 22$ V, $V_2 = 12$ V, $V_3 = 44$ V, $R_1 = 20\Omega$, $R_2 = 12\Omega$, $R_3 = 15\ \Omega$, $R_4 = 7\ \Omega$, $R_5 = 16\ \Omega$, $R_6 = 10\ \Omega$, $R_7 = 10\ \Omega$, $R_8 = 15\ \Omega$

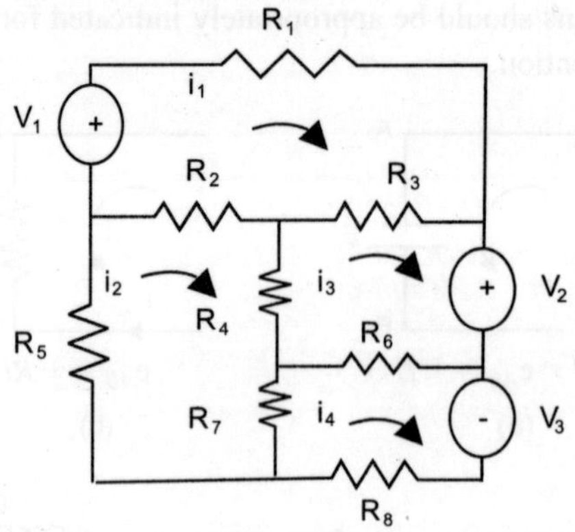

Fig. E2.1

Solution: Let i_1, i_2, i_3 and i_4 be the loop currents as shown in Fig. E2.1.

According to Kirchhoff's voltage law: sum of voltage around closed circuit is zero.

Thus, the loop equations can be written by taking in each loop clockwise direction as reference.

$$V_1 - R_1 i_1 - R_3(i_1 - i_3) - R_2(i_1 - i_2) = 0$$

$$-R_2(i_2 - i_1) - R_4(i_2 - i_3) - R_7(i_2 - i_4) - R_5 i_2 = 0$$

$$-R_3(i_3 - i_1) - V_2 - R_6(i_3 - i_4) - R_4(i_3 - i_2) = 0$$

$$V_3 - R_8 i_4 - R_7(i_4 - i_2) - R_6(i_4 - i_3) = 0$$

The equations can be written in matrix form as follows:

$$\begin{bmatrix} -(R_1+R_2+R_3) & R_2 & R_3 & 0 \\ R_2 & -(R_2+R_4+R_5+R_7) & R_4 & R_7 \\ R_3 & R_4 & -(R_3+R_4+R_6) & R_6 \\ 0 & R_7 & R_6 & -(R_6+R_7+R_8) \end{bmatrix} \begin{Bmatrix} i_1 \\ i_2 \\ i_3 \\ i_4 \end{Bmatrix} = \begin{Bmatrix} -V_1 \\ 0 \\ V_2 \\ -V_3 \end{Bmatrix}$$

MATLAB solution of this system of equations is given below:

MATLAB Program

```
%INITIALIZING THE VARIABLES
V1=22;
V2=12;
V3=44;
V=[-V1;0;V2;-V3] %CREATE THE VOLTAGE VECTOR
R1=20;
R2=12;
R3=15;
R4=7;
```

```
R5=16;
R6=10;
R7=10;
R8=15;
% CREATE THE RESISTANCE MATRIX
R=[-(R1+R2+R3) R2 R3 0;
R2 -(R2+R4+R5+R7) R4 R7;
R3 R4 -(R3+R4+R6)R6;
0 R7 R6 -(R6+R7+R8)];
% GET THE CURRENT VECTOR AS SOLUTION
I=inv(R)*V;
% ALLOT VALUES TO FOUR CURRENTS
i1=I(1)
i2=I(2)
i3=I(3)
i4=I(4)
```

The output obtained is as follows:

$V =$

–22
0
12
–44

$i_1 =$

0.8785

$i_2 =$

0.7154

$i_3 =$

0.7138

$i_4 =$

1.6655

The current in resistor $R_2 = i_1 - i_2 =$ 0.1631 A

The current in resistor $R_3 = i_1 - i_3 =$ 0.1647 A

The current in resistor $R_4 = i_2 - i_3 =$ 0.0016 A

The current in resistor $R_6 = i_4 - i_3 =$ 0.9517 A

The current in resistor $R_7 = i_4 - i_2 =$ 0.9501 A

Example E2.2: Write a MATLAB program that computes the voltage across each resistor and the power dissipated in each resistor for the circuit shown in Figure E2.2 that has resistors connected in series.

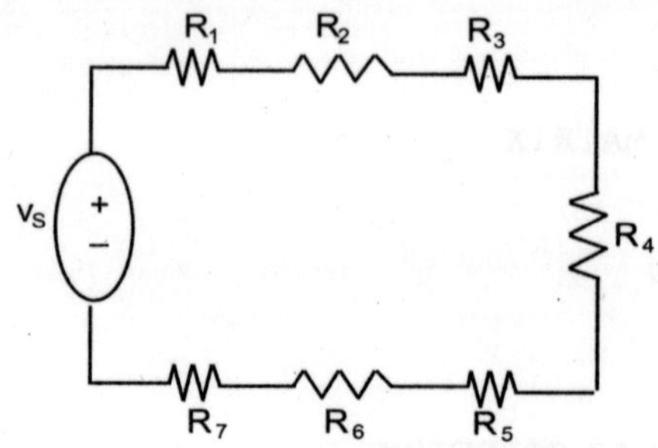

Fig. E2.2

The voltage across each of the several resistors connected in series is given by the voltage divider rule

$$v_s\ v_s\ v_s\ \ v_n\ v_n = \frac{R_n}{R_{eq}} v_s$$

where

v_n, R_n = the voltage across resistor n and its resistance,

$R_{eq} = \Sigma R_n$ = the equivalent resistance,

v_s = the source voltage.

The power dissipated in each resistor is given by $P_n = \dfrac{R_n}{R_{eq}} v_s^2$

Solution:

MATLAB program is given for the following data:

$V_s = 12\ V$, $R_1 = 10\ \Omega$, $R_2 = 7\ \Omega$, $R_3 = 6\ \Omega$, $R_4 = 9\ \Omega$, $R_5 = 4\ \Omega$, $R_6 = 7.5\ \Omega$, $R_7 = 10\ \Omega$

```
% THIS PROGRAM CALCULATES THE VOLTAGE ACROSS EACH RESISTOR
% IN A CIRCUIT THAT HAS RESISTORS CONNECTED IN SERIES
vs=input('Enter the source voltage');
rn=input('Enter values of resistors as elements in a row vector\n');
req=sum(rn);         % CALCULATING EQUIVALENT RESISTANCE
vn=rn*vs/req;        % APPLY VOLTAGE DIVIDE RULE
pn=rn*vs^2/req/2; % CALCULATING POWER IN EACH CIRCUIT
i=vs/req;  % CALCULATE CURRENT IN THE CIRCUIT
ptotal=vs*i;         % CALCULATE POWER IN THE CIRCUIT
table=[rn',vn',pn'];% CREATE TABLE
disp(' Resistance  Voltage  Power') %DISPLAY HEADINGS FOR COLUMNS
disp('(ohms)   (volts)  (watts)')
disp(table)          % DISPLAY THE VARIABLE 'TABLE'
```

```
fprintf('The curent in the circuit is %f amp',i)
fprintf('\nThe total power dissipated in the circuit is %f watts\n',ptotal)
```

MATLAB Output:

Enter the source voltage

Enter values of resistors as elements in a row vector

[10 7 6 9 4 7.5 5]

Resistance (ohm)	Voltage (volt)	Power (watt)
10.0000	2.4742	14.8454
7.0000	1.7320	10.3918
6.0000	1.4845	8.9072
9.0000	2.2268	13.3608
4.0000	0.9897	5.9381
7.5000	1.8557	11.1340
5.0000	1.2371	7.4227

The current in the circuit is 0.247423 amp.

The total power dissipated in the circuit is 2.969072 watt.

Example E2.3: Figure E2.3 shows a semiconductor diode and the current flowing through the diode is given by:

$$i_D = i_0[\exp\left(\frac{q\,v_d}{kT}\right) - 1]$$

where v_d = the voltage across the diode (volt)

i_0 = the leakeage current of the diode (amp)

k = Boltzmann's constant (1.38×10^{-23} joule/K)

q = the charge of an electorn (1.6×10^{-19} coulombs)

T = temperature (in K)

i_D = the current flow through the diode (amp)

(*a*) Write a MATLAB program to calculate the current flowing through this diode for all voltages from – 0.2 V to + 0.25 V in 0.01 V steps.

(*b*) Repeat the procedure in (a) for 70°F, 200°F and 400°F.

(*c*) Plot the current as a function of applied voltage.

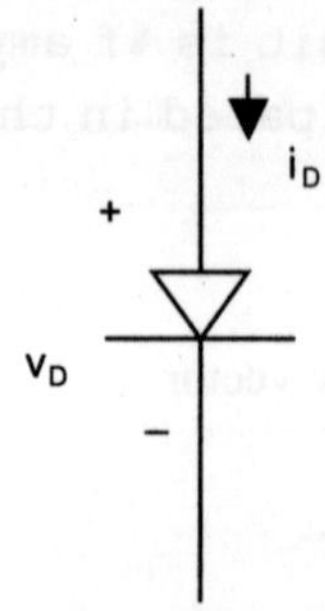

Fig. E2.3

Solution:

MATLAB program for calculation of current flow in diode is given below:

```
% INITIAL VALUES
i0=2e-4;              % leakage current in amp
k=1.38e-23;           % Boltzmann constant (J/K)
q=1.602e-19;          % charge of electron in C
vd=-0.2:0.01:0.25;% diode voltage (V)
t_f=[75 200 400];  % temperature in F
for ii=1:length(t_f)
  t_k=(5/9)*(t_f(ii)-32)+273.15;      %convert temperature to kelvin
  id=i0.*(exp((q*vd)/(k*t_k))-1);   %calculate diode current
  if ii ==1
  plot(vd,id,'-o'); % plot lines in various ways
  hold on;
  elseif ii ==2
     plot(vd,id,'--');
  elseif ii==3
     plot(vd,id,':o');
     hold off;
  end
end
legend('75 deg F','200 deg F', '400 deg F')
grid on;
title('\bf plot of diode voltage Vs diode current');
xlabel('v_{D}');
ylabel('i_{D}');
```

The output is shown in Fig. E2.3(a)

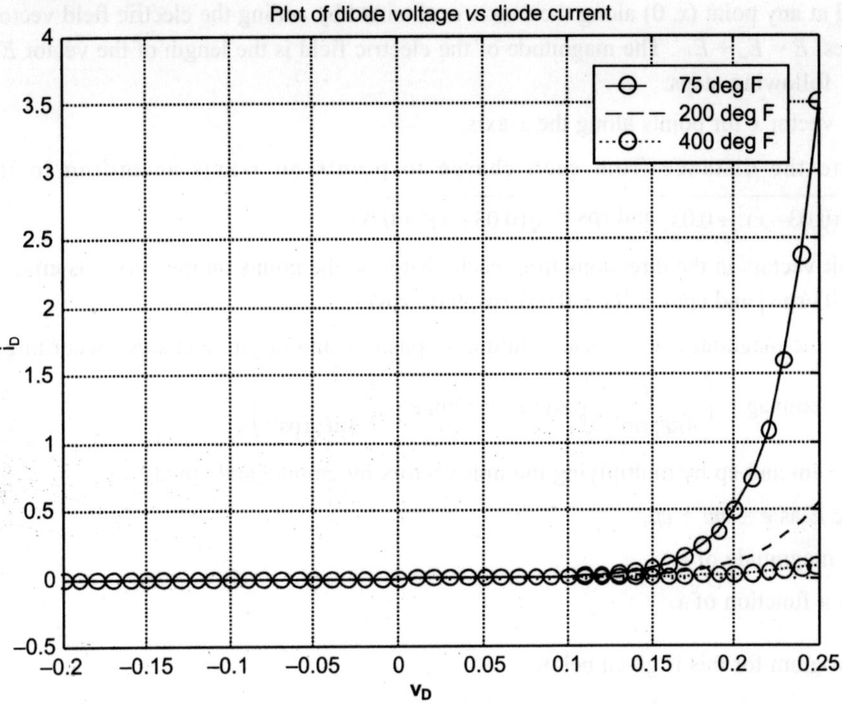

Fig. E2.3(a) MATLAB output

Example E2.4: Figure E2.4(*a*) shows the electric field at a point due to a charge which is a vector *E*. The magnitude of *E* is given by Coulomb's law $E = \left(\frac{q}{4\pi\varepsilon_0 r^2}\right)$, where *q* is magnitude of the charge, *r* is the distance between the charge and the point, and ε_0 is the permittivity constant (8.8542×10^{-12} C^2/Nm^2). The electric field *E* at any point is obtained by superposition of the electric field of each charge. An electric dipole with $q = 12 \times 10^{-19}$ C is created as shown in Fig. E2.4 (*b*).

Write a MATLAB program to determine and plot the magnitude of the electric field along the *x*-axis from $x = -8$ cm to $x = 8$ cm.

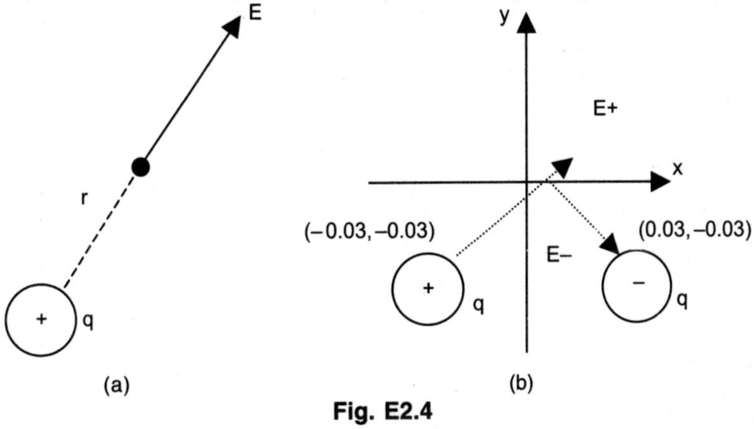

Fig. E2.4

Solution:

Electric field at any point $(x, 0)$ along the x-axis is obtained by adding the electric field vectors due to each of the charges. $E = E_- + E_+$. The magnitude of the electric field is the length of the vector E. The problem is solved by following steps:

1. Create a vector x for points along the x-axis.
2. Calculate the distance from each charge to points on x-axis according to the equations rms $= \sqrt{(0.03-x)^2+0.03^2}$ and rps $= \sqrt{(0.03+x)^2+0.03^2}$
3. Write unit vectors in the directions from each charge to the points on the x-axis as emuv = [(0.03 – x)/rms, – 0.03/rms] and epuv = [(x + 0.03)/rps, 0.02/rps]
4. Calculate the magnitude of electric field due to positive and negative charges according to Coulomb's law: E= emmag = $\left(\dfrac{q}{4\pi\varepsilon_0 \text{rms}^2}\right)$ and E_+= epmag = $\left(\dfrac{q}{4\pi\varepsilon_0 \text{rps}^2}\right)$
5. Calculate em and ep by multiplying the unit vectors by emmag and epmag.
6. Calculate E as $e = em + ep$,
7. Find the magnitude of e.
8. Plot e as a function of x.

MATLAB program for this is given below:

```
q = 12e-9;
ep = 8.8542e-12;
x =[-0.08:0.001:0.08];                    %COLUMN VECTOR OF x
rms =(0.03-x)^2+0.03^2;rm = sqrt(rms);
rps =(0.03+x)^2+0.03^2;rp = sqrt(rps);
emuv =[((0.03-x)./rm),(-0.03./rm)]; % Unit vector of em
epuv =[((0.03+x)./rp),(0.03./rp)];  % Unit vector of ep
emmag =(q/(4*pi*ep))./rms;
epmag =(q/(4*pi*ep))./rps;
em =[emmag*emuv(:,1),emmag*emuv(:,2)]; % Multiplication of magnitude and uv
ep =[epmag*epuv(:,1),epmag*epuv(:,2)];
e = em+ep;
emag = sqrt(e(:,1)^2+e(:,2)^2);
plot(x,emag,'k');
xlabel('Position along the x-axis(m)')
ylabel('Magnitude of electric field (N/C)')
title('Electric field due to an electric dipole')
```

The output of the program is shown in Fig. E2.4(*c*).

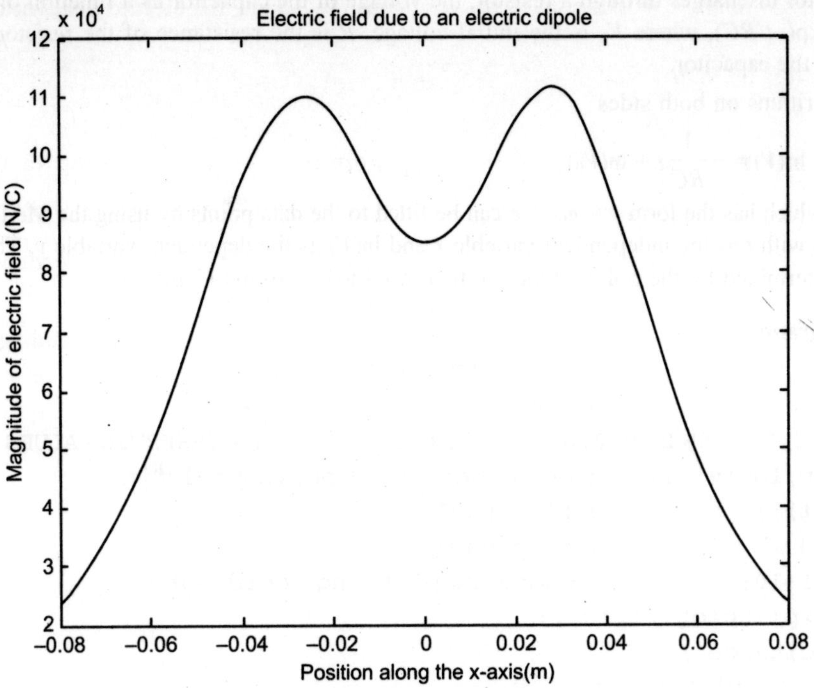

Fig. E2.4(c) MATLAB output

Example E2.5: Figure E2.5 shows a circuit to determine the electrical capacitance of an electrical capacitor.

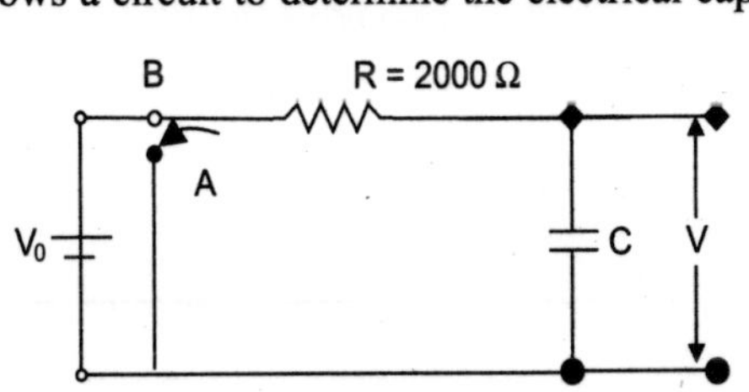

Fig. E2.5

The process involves the following steps: first the switch is connected to *B* and the capacitor is charged, then the switch is switched to *A* and the capacitor discharges through the resistor. The voltage across the capacitor is measured as the capacitor discharges. The measurements obtained are given below in a table: (*a*) Write a MATLAB program to plot the voltage as a function of time, (*b*) determine the capacitance of the capacitor by fitting an experimental curve to the data points.

Table E2.5

t(s)	1	2	3	4	5	6	7	8	9	10
V(volt)	9.5	7.35	5.25	3.65	2.85	2.05	1.25	0.95	0.75	0.61

Solution:

When a capacitor discharges through a resistor, the voltage of the capacitor as a function of time is given by: $V = V_0 \exp(-t/RC)$, where V_0 is the initial voltage, R is the resistance of the resistor and C is the capacitance of the capacitor.

By taking logarithms on both sides

$$\ln(V) = -\frac{1}{RC}t + \ln(V_0)$$

This equation which has the form $y = mx + c$ can be fitted to the data points by using the MATLAB function polyfit (x, y, 1) with t as the independent variable x and $\ln(V)$ as the dependent variable y. The coefficients m and c are determined by the polyfit function then used to determine C and V_0.

MATLAB Program:

```
r=2000;                      % RESISTANCE VALUE
t=1:10;                      % time in seconds
v=[9.5 7.35 5.25 3.65 2.85 2.05 1.25 0.95 0.75 0.61]; % OBSERVED VALUES of voltage
p=polyfit(t,log(v),1);       % one dimensional polynomial fit
c=-1/(r*p(1));               % finding C
v0=exp(p(2));                % finding V0
tplot=0:0.1:10;              % choosing plotting coordinates
vplot=v0*exp(-tplot./(r*c));
disp('Capacitance');c
plot(t,v, 'o',tplot,vplot)
xlabel('t(s)')
ylabel('voltage');
```

MATLAB Output:

```
Capacitance
c =
   0.0016
```

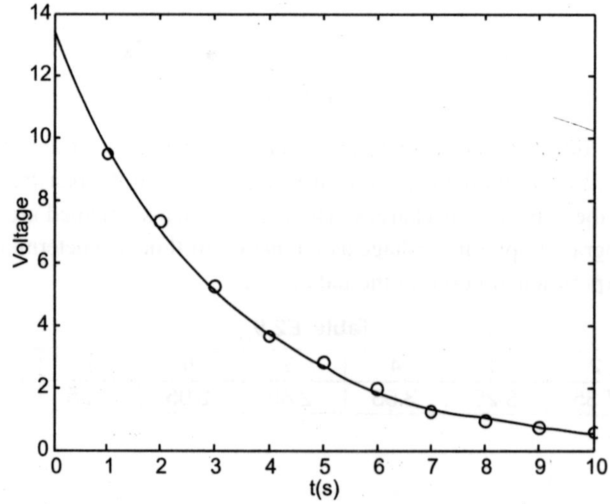

Fig. E2.5(a) MATLAB output

Example E2.6: A series RLC circuit driven by a sinusoidal AC voltage source (120 ∠0° volts) is shown in Fig. E2.6. The impedance of the inductor is given by $ZL = j2\pi fL$, where $j = \sqrt{-1}$, f is frequency of the voltage source (Hz) and L is the inductance (Henries). The impedance of the capacitor is given by $\frac{-j}{2\pi fC}$, where C is the capacitance (farads). The current I flowing is given by Kirchhoff's voltage law that is $i = \frac{120\angle 0^\circ}{R + j2\pi fL - j/(2\pi fC)}$. Write a MATLAB program to calculate and plot (*a*) the magnitude of the current as function of frequency for the range 100 kHz to 10 MHz. (*b*) the phase angle as a function of frequency for the range 100 kHz to 10 MHz. (*c*) the magnitude and phase angle of the current as a function of frequency on two subplots of a single figure.

Given $R = 120\,\Omega$, $L = 0.15$ mH and C = 0.26 nF

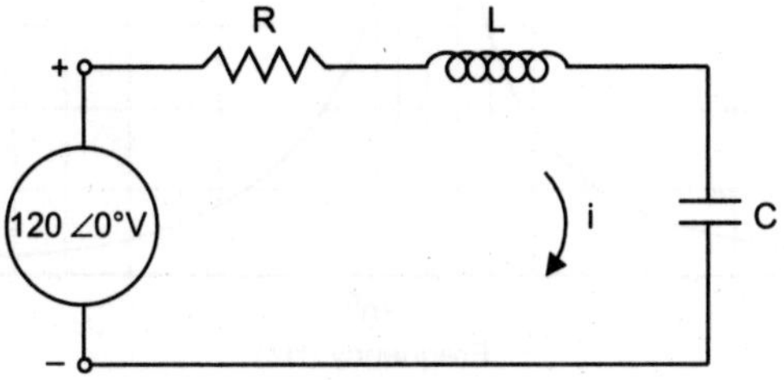

Fig. E2.6

Solution:

This can be attempted as a complex number option in MATLAB.

(a) Magnitude of current:

```
f=100000:50000:10000000;
        %INITIALIZE RANGE OF FREQUENCY
vs=120;
c=0.265e-9;
L=0.15e-3;
r=120;
i0=vs./(r+j*2*pi*f*L-j./(2*pi*f*c)); %CALCULATE OUTPUT CURRENT
semilogx(f,abs(i0));
        %PLOT ON LOG-LINEAR SCALE
title('\bfPlot of magnitude of current flow vs frequency');
xlabel('\bfFrequency (Hz)');
ylabel('\bfCurrent (A)');
grid on;
```

The output obtained is shown in Fig. E2.6 (*a*).

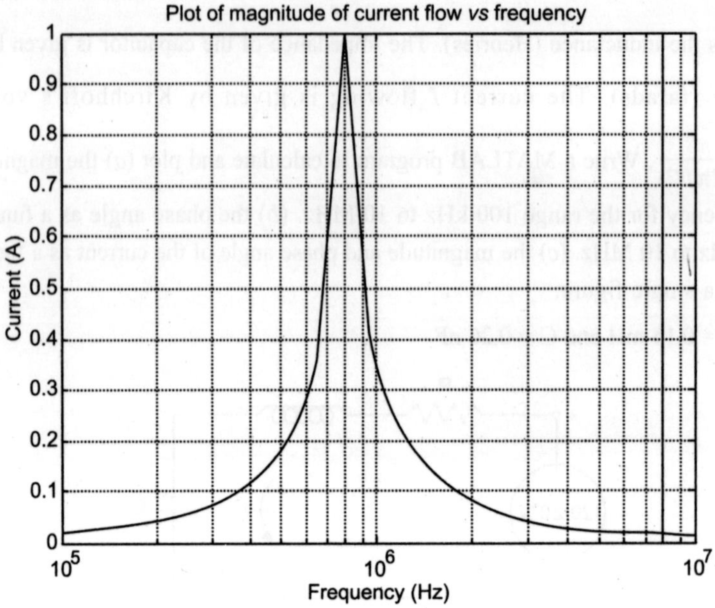

Fig. E2.6(a) MATLAB output

(b) Phase angle

```
f=100000:50000:10000000;
      %INITIALIZE RANGE OF FREQUENCY
vs = 120;
c=0.265e-9;
L=0.15e-3;
r=120;
i0=vs./(r+j*2*pi*f*L-j./(2*pi*f*c)); %CALCULATE OUTPUT CURRENT
phase = angle(i0)*180/pi;
figure(1);
semilogx(f,phase,'LineWidth',2);
      %PLOT ON LOG-LINEAR SCALE
title('\bfPlot of phase of current flow Vs frequency');
xlabel('\bfFrequency (Hz)');
ylabel('\bfCurrent (A)');
grid on;
```

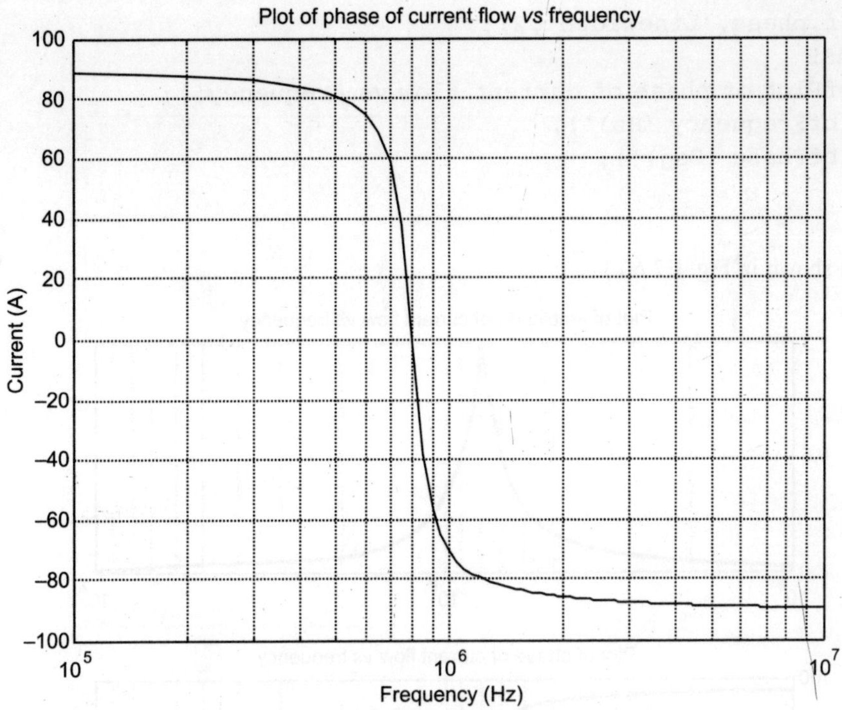

Fig. E2.6(b) MATLAB output

(c) Both phase angle and magnitude on single plot

```
f=100000:50000:10000000;
      %INITIALIZE RANGE OF FREQUENCY
vs=120;
c=0.265e-9;
L=0.15e-3;
r=120;
w=2*pi*f; %CALCULATE W
i0=vs./(r+j*2*pi*f*L-j./(2*pi*f*c)); %CALCULATE OUTPUT CURRENT
phase=angle(i0)*180/pi;
      %PHASE ANGLE IN DEGREES
figure(1);
subplot(2,1,1);
      %SUB-PLOT-1
semilogx(f,abs(i0),'Linewidth',2);
      %MAGNITUDE
title('\bfPlot of amplitude of current flow Vs frequency');
ylabel('\bfAmplitude (A)');
grid on;
subplot(2,1,2);    % SUB-PLOT-2
```

```
semilogx(f,phase,'Linewidth',2);
    %PHASE
title('\bfPlot of phase of current flow vs frequency');
xlabel('\bfFrequency (Hz)');
ylabel('\bfPhase (Deg)');
grid on;
```

The output is shown in Fig. E2.6(*c*)

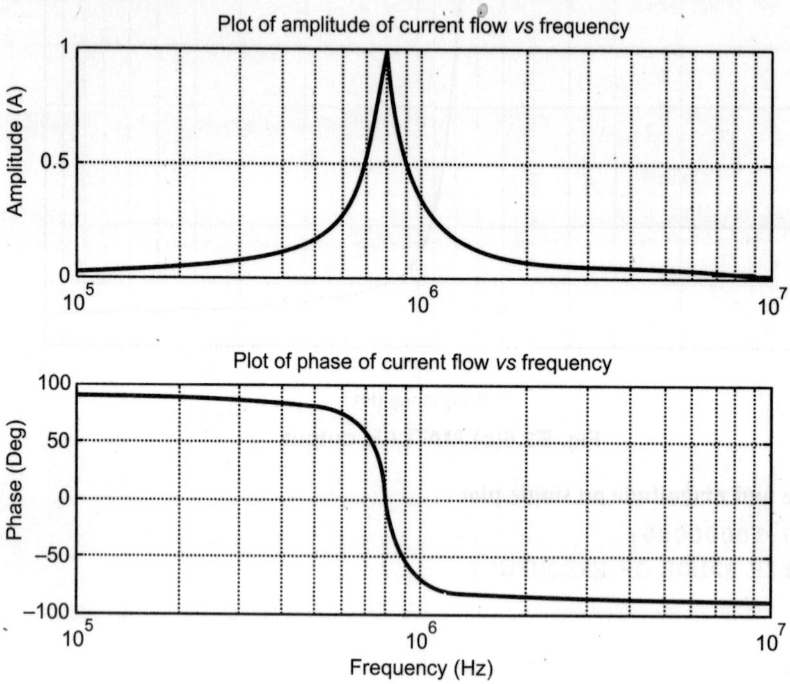

Fig. E2.6(c) MATLAB output

Example E2.7: The Table below gives the viscosity μ of an oil at different temperatures. Write a MATLAB program to determine an equation that can be fitted to the data.

T(°C)	−20	0	20	40	60	80	100	120
10^{-5} (N-S/m^2)	4.2	0.4	0.092	0.034	0.016	0.0077	0.0046	0.0033

Solution:

Usually viscosity varies with absolute temperature exponentially. To have a best fit of the given points, a curved exponential figure is suitable, whose equations can be written as:

$$\mu = \exp(aT^2 + bT + c)$$

Taking logarithms and simplifying

$$\log\mu = aT^2 + bT + c.$$

here the constants can be obtained from the polyfit function polyfit(T, logμ, 2), then finally μ is obtained from the exponential relation and ploted as a function of temperature in Kelvin.

MATLAB program for this application is shown below:

```
TC=-20:20:120;
%TEMPERATURE RANGE IN DEGREE CENTRIGRADE
mu=[4.2 0.4 0.092 0.034 0.016 0.0077 0.0046 0.0033]; %GIVEN VISCOSITIES
TK=TC + 273; % TEMPERATURE IN KELVIN
p=polyfit(TK,log(mu),2) % POLYNOMIAL FITTING WITH LOG(MU) AND TK, SECOND ORDER
Tplot=273+[-20:120];% DEFINING TK AS AN ARRAY
muplot=exp(p(1)*Tplot^2+p(2)*Tplot+p(3));%CORRESPONDING MU ARRAY
semilogy(TK,mu,'o',Tplot,muplot,'-')%PLOTTING ON SEMI-LOG SCALE
xlabel('\bfTemperature K');
ylabel('\bfViscosity in N-S/meter square');
```

Figure E2.7 (a) shows the MATLAB output.

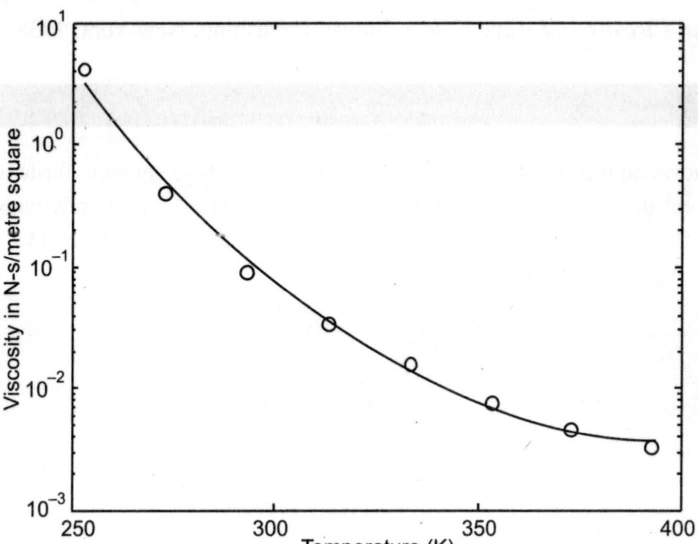

Fig. E2.7 (a) MATLAB output

REFERENCES

Cogdell, J.R., *Foundations of Electrical Circuits,* Prentice-Hall, Englewood Cliffs, NJ, 1999.

Dorf, R.C., and Svoboda, J.A., *Introduction to Electric Circuits,* Wiley, New York, NY, 2006.

Fogiel, M., and Ogden, J.R., *The Electric Circuits Problem Solver: A Complete Solution Guide to Any Textbook,* Research & Education Association, 1998.

Hayt, W.H., and Kemmerly, J.E., *Engineering Circuit Analysis,* 5th ed., McGraw-Hill, New York, NY, 1993.

Johnson, D.E., Johnson, J.R. Hilburn, J.L., and Scott, P.D., *Electric Circuit Analysis,* 3rd ed., Wiley, New York, 1997.

Johnson, D.E., *Basic Electric Circuit Analysis,* 5th ed., Wiley, New York, 2006.

Johnson, D.E., Hilburn, J.L., Johnson, J.R., and Scott, P.D., *Electric Circuit Analysis,* 3rd ed., Prentice-Hall, Englewood Cliffs, NJ, 1990.

Nahvi, M., *Schaums Outline of Electrical Circuits,* 4th ed., McGraw-Hill, New York, NY, 2002.

Nilsson, J.W., *Electrical Circuits,* 7th ed., Prentice-Hall, Englewood Cliffs, NJ, 2004.

Paul, C.R., *Fundamentals of Electric Circuit Analysis,* Wiley, New York, 2000.

Singh Guru, B., and Warrier, R., *Electric Circuits—Analysis and Design,* Oxford University Press, Oxford, 2005.

Smith, R.J., and Dorf, R.C., *Circuits, Systems, and Devices,* 5th ed., Wiley, New York, 1992.

Starr, A.T., *Electrical Circuits and Wave Filters,* Pitman Publishing, New York, 1938.

PROBLEMS

P2.1: Figure P2.1 shows an electrical circuit with resistors and voltage sources. Write a MATLAB program to determine the current in each resistor, using the mesh current method based on Kirchhoff's second voltage law. Given $V_1 = 37$ V, $V_2 = 19$ V, $V_3 = 25$ V, $R_1 = 16\ \Omega$, $R_2 = 19\ \Omega$, $R_3 = 11\ \Omega$, $R_4 = 10\ \Omega$, $R_5 = 6\ \Omega$, $R_6 = 15\ \Omega$, $R_7 = 9\ \Omega$, $R_8 = 14\ \Omega$, $R_9 = 6\ \Omega$ and $R_{10} = 3\ \Omega$.

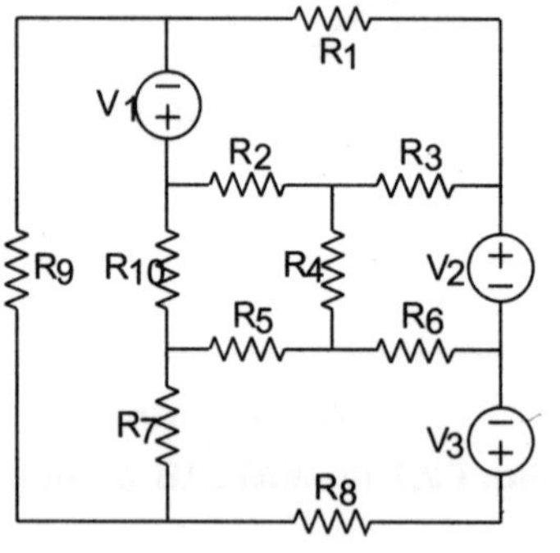

Fig. P2.1

P2.2: Write a MATLAB program in a script file that computes the current through each resistor and the power dissipated in each in a circuit that has resistors connected in parallel as shown in Fig. P2.2. Use the script file for the circuit shown in Fig. P2.2.

Note that when several resistors are connected in a circuit in parallel, the current through each of them is given by

$$i_n = \frac{v_s}{R_n}$$

where i_n and R_n are the current through resistors n and its resistance, respectively, and v_s is the source voltage. The equivalent resistance, R_{eq}, is given by

$$\frac{1}{R_{eq}} = \frac{1}{R_1} + \frac{1}{R_2} + \dots + \frac{1}{R_n}$$

The source current is given by: $i_s = v_s / R_{eq}$, and the power P_n, dissipated in each resistor is given by: $P_n = v_s i_n$.

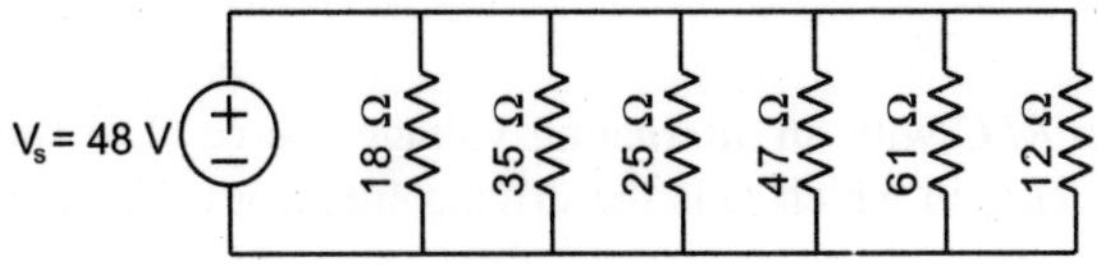

Fig. P2.2

P2.3: Figure P2.3 shows an electrical circuit with a voltage source, v_s with an internal resistance, r_s and a load resistance, R_L. The power P dissipated in the load is given by

$$P = \frac{v_s^2 R_L}{(R_L + r_s)^2}$$

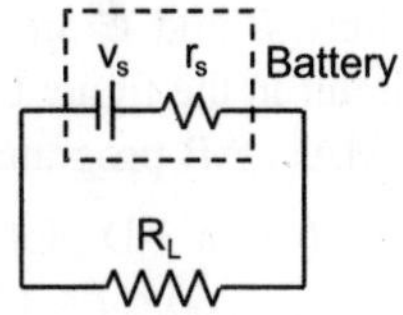

Fig. P2.3

Write a MATLAB program to plot the power P as a function of R_L for $1 \le R_L \le 12\ \Omega$ given that $v_s = 12$ V, and $r_s = 3\ \Omega$.

P2.4: Figure P2.4(a) shows a resistor of $R = 5\ \Omega$ and an inductor $L - 1.4$ H connected in a circuit to a voltage source (RL circuit). When the voltage source applies a rectangular voltage pulse with an amplitude of $V = 12$V and a duration of 0.5s as shown in Fig.P2.4(b), the current $i(t)$ in the circuit as a function of time is given by

$$i(t) = \frac{V}{R}(1 - e^{(-Rt)/L}) \quad \text{for } 0 \le t \le 0.5s$$

$$i(t) = e^{-(Rt)/L} \frac{V}{R}(e^{(0.5R)/L}/1) \quad \text{for } 0.5 \le t$$

Write a MATLAB program to plot the current as a function of time for $0 \le t \le 3s$.

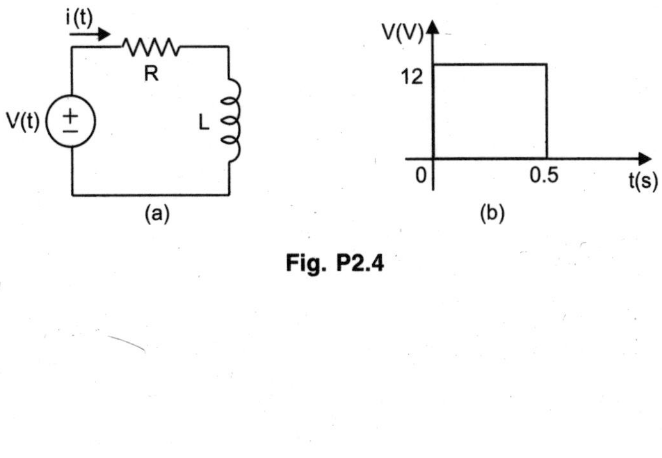

Fig. P2.4

P2.5: The ratio of the magnitude of the voltage in a low-pass *RC* filter shown in Fig. P2.5 is given by

$$RV = \left|\frac{V_0}{V_i}\right| = \frac{1}{\sqrt{1+(\omega RC)^2}}$$

where ω is the frequency of the input signal.

Write a user-defined MATLAB function that calculates the magnitude ratio. Write a program in script file that uses the lowpass function to generate a plot of *RV* as a function of ω for $10^{-2} \le \omega \le 10^6$ rad/s. Run the script file with $R = 1300\ \Omega$, and $C = 9\ \mu F$.

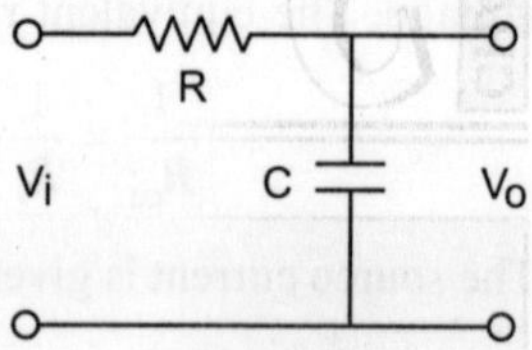

Fig. P2.5

P2.6: Figure P2.6 shows an *RLC* with an alternating voltage source. The source voltage v_s is given by $v_s = v_m \sin(\omega_d t)$ where $\omega_d = 2\pi f_d$ in which f_d is the driving frequency. The amplitude of the current, *I*, is given by

$$I = \frac{v_m}{\sqrt{R^2 + (\omega_d L - 1/(\omega_d C))^2}}$$

where *R* and *C* are the resistance of the resistor and capacitance of the capacitor, respectively. For the circuit in the figure $C = 16 \times 10^{-6}$ F, $L = 250 \times 10^{-3}$ H, $v_m = 25$ V. Write a MATLAB program to make

(*a*) a 3-D plot of *I* (*z* axis) as a function of ω_d (*x* axis) for $60 \le f \le 110$ Hz, and a function of *R* (*y* axis) for $10 \le R \le 40\ \Omega$

(*b*) a plot that is a projection on the *x*-*z* plane. Estimate from this plot the natural frequency of the circuit. Compare the estimate with the calculated value of $1/(2\pi(\sqrt{LC}))$.

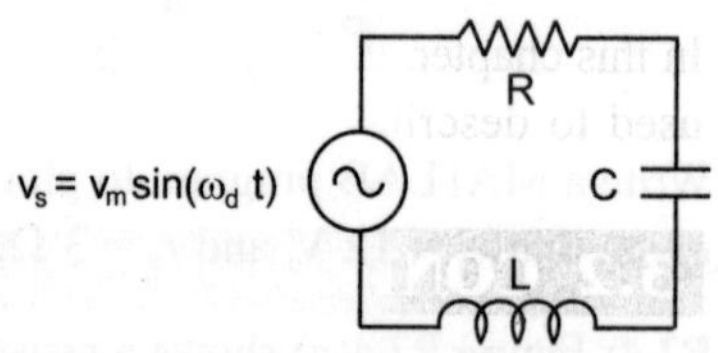

Fig. P2.6

P2.7: Figure P2.7 shows an *RC* circuit includes a voltage source v_s, a resistor $R = 50\ \Omega$ and a capacitor $C = 0.001$ F. The differential equation that describes the response of the circuit given by

$$\frac{dv_c}{dt} + \frac{1}{RC}v_c = \frac{1}{RC}v_s$$

where v_c is the voltage of the capacitor. Initially, $v_s = 0$, and then at $t = 0$ the voltage source is changed. Find the response of the circuit for the following three cases:

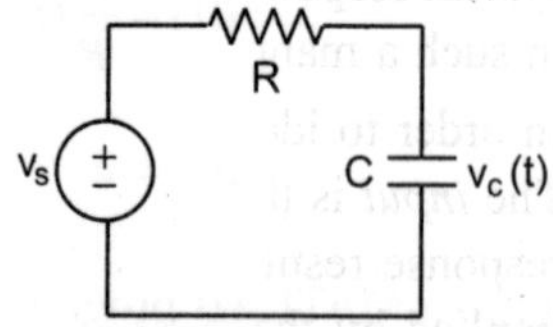

Fig. P2.7

(*a*) $v_s = 12$ V for $t \ge 0$.

(*b*) $v_s = 12 \sin(2.60\pi t)$ V for $t \ge 0$.

(*c*) $v_s = 12$ V for $0 \le t \le 0.01$s, and then $v_s = 0$ for $t \ge 0.01$s.

Solve each case for $0 \le t \le 0.2$ s. For each case plot v_s and v_c *vs.* time using a MATLAB program.

❍❍❍

CHAPTER 3

CONTROL SYSTEMS

3.1 INTRODUCTION

In this chapter, we present a brief introduction and overview of control systems. Some of the terms commonly used to describe the operation, analysis and design of control systems are presented.

3.2 CONTROL SYSTEMS

Control systems in an interdisciplinary field covering many areas of engineering and sciences. Control systems exist in many systems of engineering, sciences and in human body. *Control* means to regulate, direct, command or govern. A *system* is a collection, set, or arrangement of elements (subsystems). A *control system* is an interconnection of components forming a system configuration that will provide a desired system response. Hence, a control system is an arrangement of physical components connected or related in such a manner as to command, regulate, direct or govern itself or another system.

In order to identify, delineate or define a control system, we introduce two terms: *input* and *output* here. The *input* is the stimulus, excitation or command applied to a control system, and the *output* is the actual response resulting from a control system. The *output* may or may not be equal to the specified response implied by the input. Inputs could be physical variables or abstract ones such as *reference*, *set point* or *desired* values for the output of the control system. Control systems can have more than one input or output. The input and the output represent the desired response and the actual response respectively. A control system provides an output or response for a given input or stimulus, as shown in Fig. 3.1.

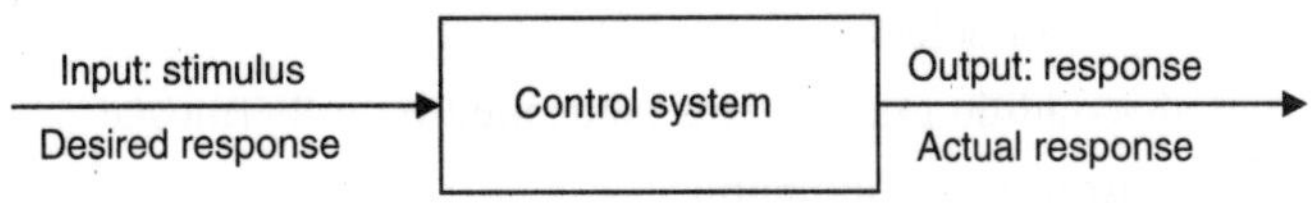

Fig. 3.1 Description of a control system

The output may not be equal to the specified response implied by the input. If the output and input are given, it is possible to identify or define the nature of the system's components. Broadly speaking, there are three basic types of control systems:

(*a*) Man-made control systems

(*b*) Natural, including biological-control systems

(*c*) Control systems whose components are both man-made and natural.

An electric switch is a man-made control system controlling the electricity-flow. The simple act of pointing at an object with a finger requires a biological control system consisting chiefly of eyes, the arm, hand and finger and the brain of a person, where the input is precise-direction of the object with respect to some reference and the output is the actual pointed direction with respect to the same reference. The control system consisting of a person driving an automobile has components, which are clearly both man-made and biological. The driver wants to keep the automobile in the appropriate lane of the roadway. The driver accomplishes this by constantly watching the direction of the automobile with respect to the direction of road. Figure 3.2 is an alternate way of showing the basic entities in a general control system.

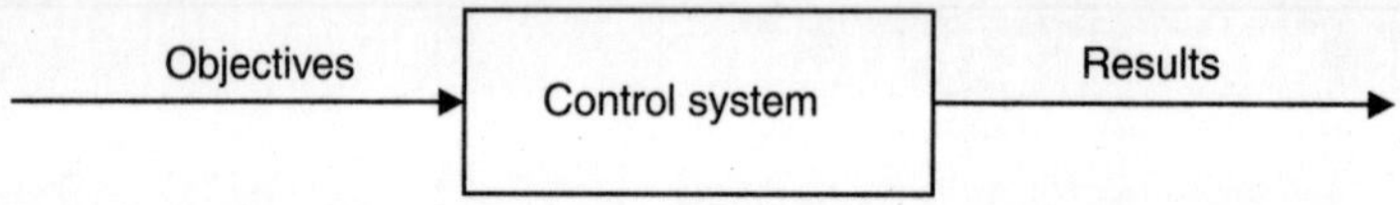

Fig. 3.2 Components of a control system

In the steering control of an automobile for example, the direction of two front wheels can be regarded as the result or controlled output variable and the direction of the steering wheel as the actuating signal or objective. The control-system in this case is composed of the steering mechanism and the dynamics of the entire automobile. As another example, consider the idle-speed control of an automobile engine, where it is necessary to maintain the engine idle speed at a relatively low-value (for fuel economy) regardless of the applied engine loads (like airconditioning, power steering, etc.). Without the idle-speed control, any sudden engine-load application would cause a drop in engine speed that might cause the engine to stall. In this case, throttle angle and load-torque are the inputs (objectives) and the engine-speed is the output. The engine is the controlled process of the system. A few more applications of control-systems can be found in the print wheel control of an electronic type writer, the thermostatically controlled heater or furnace which automatically regulates the temperature of a room or enclosure, and the sun tracking control of solar collector dish.

Control system applications are found in robotics, space-vehicle systems, aircraft autopilots and controls, ship and marine control systems, intercontinental missile guidance systems, automatic control systems for hydrofoils, surface-effect ships, and high-speed rail systems including the magnetic levitation systems.

3.3 EXAMPLES OF CONTROL SYSTEMS

Control systems find numerous and widespread applications from everyday to extraordinary in science, industry and home. Here are a few examples:

(*a*) Home heating and air-conditioning systems controlled by a thermostat

(*b*) The cruise (speed) control of an automobile

(*c*) Manual control:

(*i*) Opening or closing of a window for regulating air temperature or air quality

(*ii*) Activation of a light switch to regulate the illumination in a room

(*iii*) Human controlling the speed of an automobile by regulating the gas supply to the engine

(*d*) Automatic traffic control (signal) system at roadway intersections
(*e*) Control system which automatically turns on a room lamp at dusk, and turns it off in daylight
(*f*) Automatic hot water heater
(*g*) Environmental test-chamber temperature control system
(*h*) An automatic positioning system for a missile launcher
(*i*) An automatic speed control for a field-controlled DC motor
(*j*) The attitude control system of a typical space vehicle
(*k*) Automatic position-control system of a high speed automated train system
(*l*) Human heart using a pacemaker
(*m*) An elevator-position control system used in high-rise multilevel buildings.

3.4 CONTROL SYSTEM CONFIGURATIONS

There are two control system configurations: open-loop control system and closed-loop control system.

(*a*) ***Block:*** A block is a set of elements that can be grouped together, with overall characteristics described by an input/output relationship as shown in Fig. 3.3. A block diagram is a simplified pictorial representation of the cause and effect relationship between the input(s) and output(s) of a physical system.

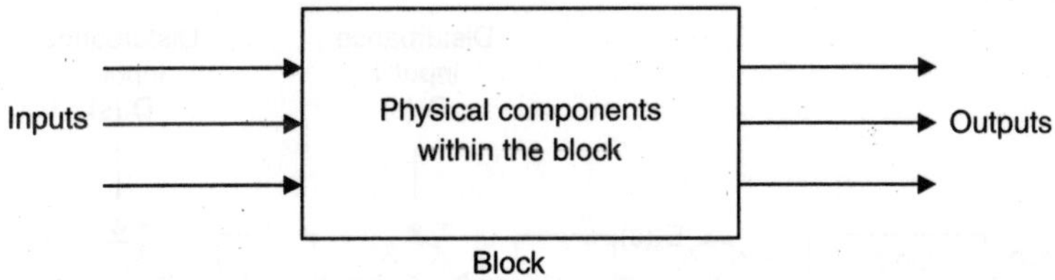

Fig. 3.3 Block diagram

The simplest form of the block diagram is the single block as shown in Fig. 3.3. The input and output characteristics of entire groups of elements within the block can be described by an appropriate mathematical expressions as shown in Fig. 3.4.

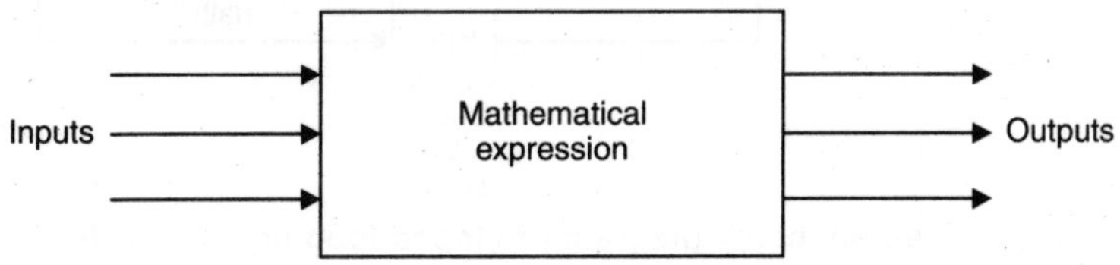

Fig. 3.4 Block representation

(*b*) ***Transfer function:*** The transfer function of a system (or a block) is defined as the ratio of output to input as shown in Fig. 3.5.

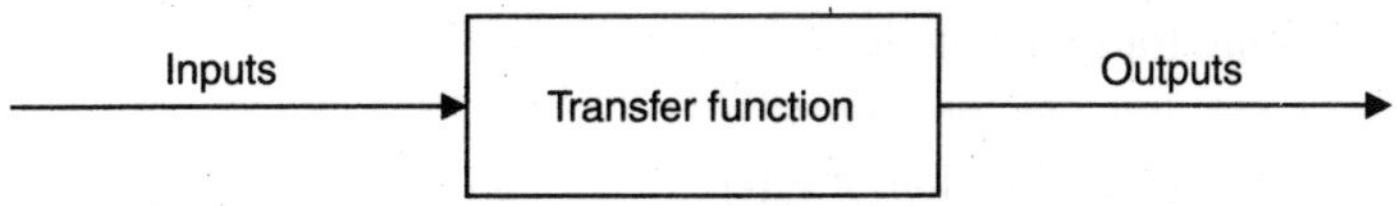

Fig. 3.5 Transfer function

$$\text{Transfer function} = \frac{Output}{Input}$$

Transfer functions are generally used to represent a mathematical model of each block in the block diagram representation. All the signals are transfer functions on the block diagrams. For instance, the time function reference input is $r(t)$, and its transfer function is $R(s)$ where t is time and s is the Laplace transform variable or complex frequency.

(c) ***Open-loop control system:*** A general block diagram of open-loop system is shown in Fig. 3.6.

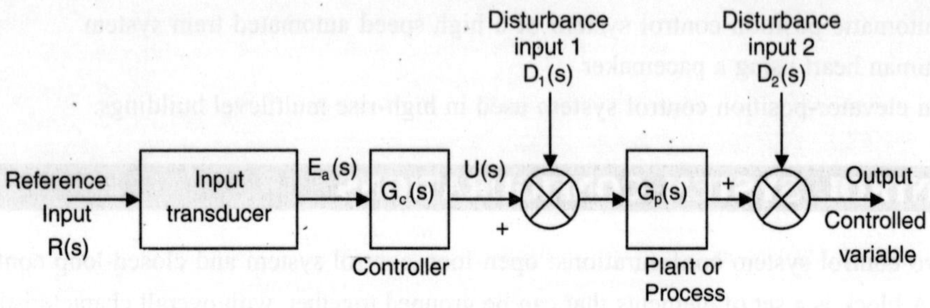

Fig. 3.6 General block diagram of open-loop control system

(d) ***Closed-loop (feedback control) System:*** The general architecture of a closed-loop control system is shown in Fig. 3.7.

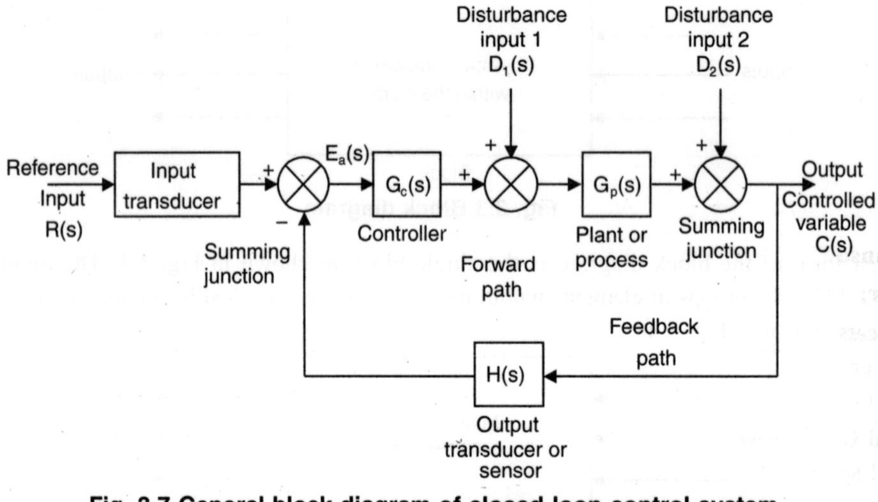

Fig. 3.7 General block diagram of closed-loop control system

3.5 CONTROL SYSTEM TERMINOLOGY

The variables in Figs. 3.6 and 3.7 are defined as follows:

$C(s)$ controlled output, transfer function of $c(t)$

$D(s)$ disturbance input, transfer function of $d(t)$

$E_a(s)$ actuating error, transfer function of $e_a(t)$

$G_a(s)$ transfer function of the actuator

$G_c(s)$ transfer function of the controller

$G_p(s)$ transfer function of the plant or process

$H(s)$ transfer function of the sensor or output transducer = $G_s(s)$

$R(s)$ reference input, transfer function of $r(t)$.

Summing Point: As shown in Fig. 3.8, the block is a small circle called a summing point with the appropriate plus or minus sign associated with the arrows entering the circle. The output is the algebraic sum of the inputs. There is no limit on the number of inputs entering a summing point.

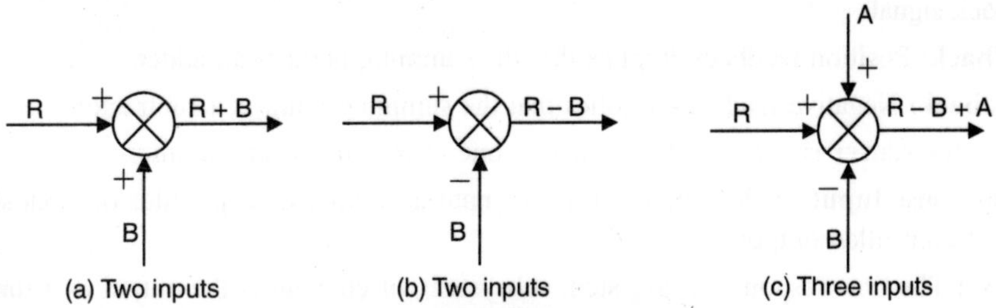

Fig. 3.8 Summing point

Take-off Point: A take-off point allows the same signal or variable as input to more than one block or summing point, thus permitting the signal to proceed unaltered along several different paths to several destinations as shown in Fig. 3.9.

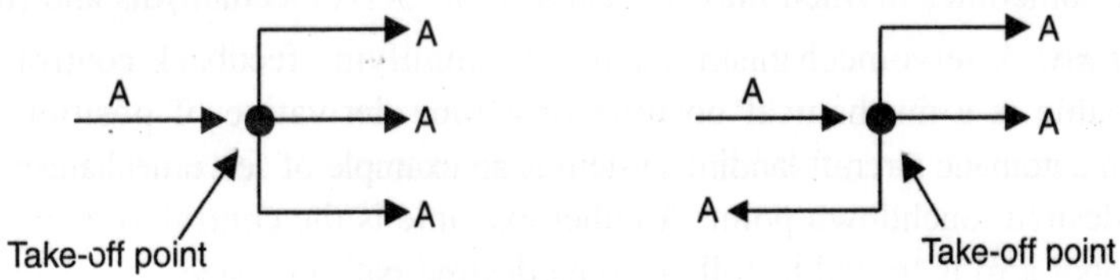

Fig. 3.9 Take-off point

Input Transducer: Input transducer converts the form of input to that used by the controller.

Controller: The controller drives a process or plant.

Plant, Process or Controlled System $G_p(s)$: The plant, process or controlled system is the system, subsystem, process or object controlled by the feedback control system. For example, the plant can be a furnace system where the output variable is temperature.

Controlled Output C(s): The controlled output $C(s)$ is the output variable of the plant under the control of the control system.

Forward Path: The forward path is the transmission path from the summing point to the controlled output.

Feedback Path: The feedback path is the transmission path from the controlled output back to the summing point.

Feed Forward (Control) Elements: The feed forward (control) elements are the components of the forward path that generate the control signal applied to the plant or process. The feed forward (control) elements include controller(s), compensator(s) or equalization elements and amplifiers.

Feedback Elements: The feedback elements establish the fundamental relationship between the controlled output $C(s)$ and the primary feedback signal $B(s)$. They include sensors of the controlled output, compensators and controller elements.

Reference Input R(s): The reference input is an external signal applied to the control system generally at the first summing input, so as to command a specified action of the process or plant. It typically represents ideal or desired process or plant output response.

Primary Feedback Signal: The primary feedback signal is a function of the controlled output summed algebraically with the reference input to establish the actuating or error signal. An open-loop system has no primary feedback signal.

Actuating or Error Signal: The actuating or error signal is the reference input signal plus or minus the primary feedback signal.

Positive Feedback: Position feedback implies that the summing point is an adder.

Negative Feedback: Negative feedback implies that the summing point is a subtractor.

Transducer: A transducer is a device that converts one energy form into another.

Disturbance or Noise Input: A disturbance or noise input is an undesired stimulus or input signal affecting the value of the controlled output.

Time Response: The time response of a system subsystem, or element is the output as a function of time, generally following the application of a prescribed input under specified operating conditions.

3.6 CONTROL SYSTEM CLASSES

Control systems are sometimes divided into two classes: (a) Servomechanisms and (b) Regulators.

(a) ***Servomechanisms:*** A servomechanism is a power-amplifying feedback control system in which the controlled variable is a mechanical position or a time derivative of position such as velocity or acceleration. An automatic aircraft landing system is an example of servomechanism. The aircraft follows a ramp to the desired touchdown point. Another example is the control system of an industrial robot in which the robot arm is forced to follow some desired path in space.

(b) ***Regulators:*** A regulator or regulating system is a feedback control system in which the reference input or command is constant for long periods of time, generally for the entire time interval during which the system is operational. Such an input is known as *set point*. An example of a regulator control system is the human biological system that maintains the body temperature at approximately 98.6°F in an environment that usually has a different temperature.

3.6.1 Supplementary Terminology

(*a*) *Linear System*: A linear system is a system where input/output relationships may be represented by a linear differential equation. The plant is linear if it can be accurately described using a set of linear differential equations. This attribute indicates that system parameters do not vary as a function of signal level.

Similarly, the plant is a lumped-parameter (rather than distributed parameter) system if it can be described using ordinary (rather than partial) differential equations. This condition is generally accomplished if the physical size of the system is very small in comparison to the wavelength of the highest frequency of interest.

(*b*) *Time-Variant System:* A time-variant is a system if the parameters vary as a function of time. Thus, a time-variant system is a system described by a differential equation with variable coefficients. A linear time variant system is described by linear differential equations with variable coefficients. A rocket-burning fuel system is an example of time variant system since the rocket mass varies during the flight as the fuel is burned.

(c) *Time-Invariant System:* A time-invariant system is a system described by a differential equation with constant coefficients. Thus, the plant is time invariant if the parameters do not change as a function of time. A linear time invariant system is described by linear differential equations with constant coefficients. A single degree of freedom spring mass viscous damper system is an example of a time-invariant system provided the characteristics of all the three components do not vary with time.

(d) *Multivariable Feedback System:* The block diagram representing a multivariable feedback system where the interrelationships of many controlled variables are considered is shown in Fig. 3.10.

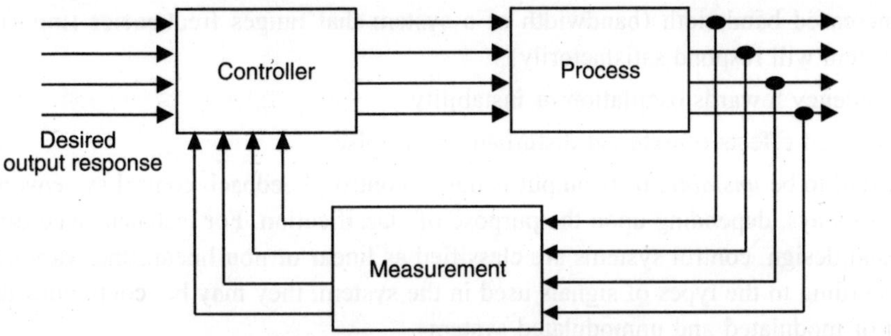

Fig. 3.10 Multivariable control system

3.7 FEEDBACK SYSTEMS

Feedback is the property of a closed-loop system, which allows the output to be compared with the input to the system such that the appropriate control action may be formed as some function of the input and output.

For more accurate and more adaptive control, a link or feedback must be provided from output to the input of an open-loop control system. So, the controlled signal should be fed back and compared with the reference input, and an actuating signal proportional to the difference of input and output must be sent through the system to correct the error. In general, feedback is said to exist in a system when a closed sequence of cause and effect relations exists between system variables. A closed-loop idle-speed control system is shown in Fig. 3.11. The reference input N_r sets the desired idle-speed. The engine idle speed *N* should agree with the reference value N_r and any difference such as the load-torque T is sensed by the speed-transducer and the error detector. The controller will operate on the difference and provide a signal to adjust the throttle angle to correct the error.

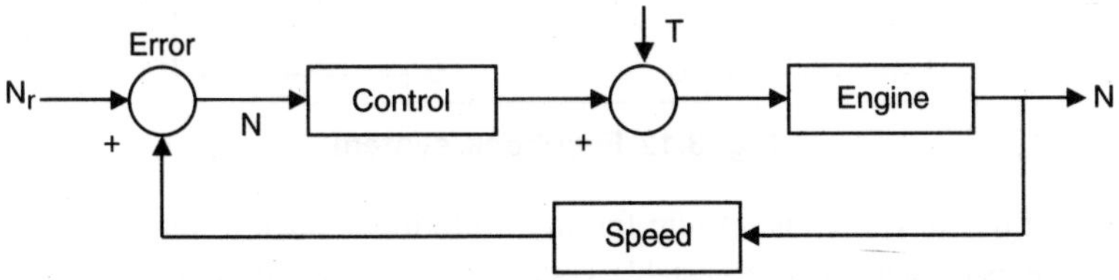

Fig. 3.11 Closed-loop idle-speed control system

3.8 ANALYSIS OF FEEDBACK

The most important features, the presence of feedback impacts to a system are the following:

(*a*) Increased accuracy: its ability to reproduce the input accurately

(*b*) Reduced sensitivity of the ratio of output to input for variations in system characteristics and other parameters

(*c*) Reduced effects of non-linearities and distortion

(*d*) Increased bandwidth (bandwidth of a system that ranges frequencies (input) over which the system will respond satisfactorily)

(*e*) Tendency towards oscillation or instability

(*f*) Reduced effects of external disturbances or noise.

A system is said to be *unstable*, if its output is out of control. Feedback control systems may be classified in a number of ways, depending upon the purpose of classification. For instance, according to the method of analysis and design, control systems are classified as linear or non-linear, time-varying or time-variant systems. According to the types of signals used in the system, they may be: continuous data and discrete-data system or modulated and unmodulated systems.

Consider the simple feedback configuration shown in Fig. 3.12, where *R* is the input signal, *C* is the output signal, *E* is error and *B* is feedback signal.

The parameters *G* and *H* are constant-gains. By simple algebraic manipulations, it can be shown that the input-output relation of the system is given by

$$M = \frac{C}{R} = \frac{G}{1+GH}$$

The general effect of feedback is that it may increase or decrease the gain *G*. In practical control systems, *G* and *H* are functions of frequency, so the magnitude of $(1 + GH)$ is greater than 1 in one frequency range, but less than 1 in another. Thus, feedback affects the gain *G* of a non-feedback system by a factor $(1 + GH)$.

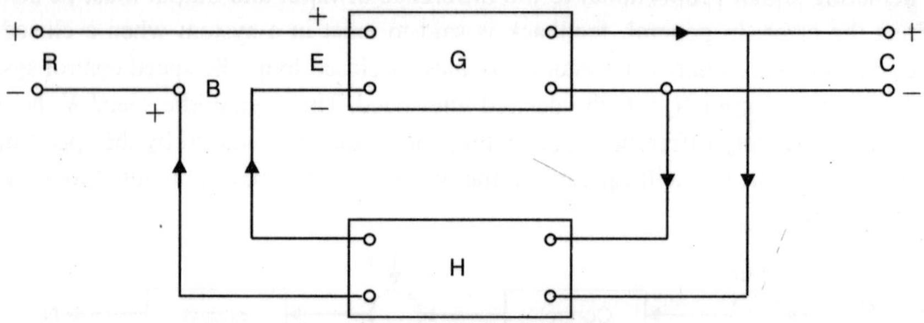

Fig. 3.12 Feedback system

If $GH = -1$, the output of the system is infinite for any finite input, such a state is called unstable system-state. Alternatively, feedback stabilizes an unstable system and the sensitivity of a gain of the overall system *M* to the variation in *G* is defined as:

$$S_G^M = \frac{\partial M / M}{\partial G / G} = \frac{\text{Percentage change in } M}{\text{Percentage change in } G}$$

where ∂M denotes incremental change in M due to incremental change in G (∂G). One can write sensitivity-function as:

$$S_G^M = \frac{\partial M / M}{\partial G / G} = \frac{1}{1 + GH}$$

By increasing GH, the magnitude of the sensitivity-function is made arbitrarily small.

3.9 CONTROL SYSTEM ANALYSIS AND DESIGN OBJECTIVES

Control systems engineering consists of *analysis* and *design* of control systems configurations. Control systems are *dynamic*, in that they respond to an input by first undergoing a transient response before attaining a steady-state response which corresponds to the input. There are three main objectives of control systems analysis and design. They are:

1. Producing the response to a transient disturbance which is acceptable
2. *Minimizing the steady-state errors*: Here, the concern is about the accuracy of the steady-state response
3. *Achieving stability:* Control systems must be designed to be stable. Their natural response should decay to a zero values as time approaches infinity, or oscillate.

Analysis is investigation of the properties and performance of an existing control system. Design is the selection and arrangement of the control system components to perform a prescribed task. The design of control systems is accomplished in two ways: *design by analysis* in which the characteristics of an existing or standard system configuration are modified, and *design by synthesis* in which the form of the control system is obtained directly from its specifications.

3.10 MATLAB APPLICATION

The application of MATLAB to the analysis and design of control systems, engineering mechanics (statics and dynamics), mechanical vibration analysis, electrical circuits and numerical methods is presented in this chapter with a number of illustrative examples. The MATLAB computational approach to the transient response analysis, steps response, impulse response, ramp response and response to the simple inputs are presented. Plotting root loci, Bode diagrams, polar plots, Nyquist plot, Nichols plot and state space method are obtained using MATLAB. Extensive worked examples are included with a significant number of exercise problems to guide the student to understand and as an aid for learning about the analysis a nd design of control systems, engineering mechanics, vibration analysis of mechanical systems, electrical circuits and numerical methods using MATLAB.

3.10.1 Transient Response Analysis

When the numerator and denominator of a closed-loop transfer function are known, the commands **step (num, den), step (num, den, t)** in MATLAB can be used to generate plots of unit-step responses. Here, t is the user specified time.

3.10.2 Response to Initial Condition

Case 1: *State Space Approach*

Consider a system defined in state space given by

$$\dot{\mathbf{x}} = \mathbf{Ax} \qquad ...(3.1)$$

$$\mathbf{x}\,(0) = \mathbf{x_0}$$

Assuming that there is no external input acting on the system, the response **x(t)** knowing the initial condition $x(0)$ and that **x** is an n-vector, is obtained as follows:

Taking Laplace transform of both sides of Eq. (3.1), we obtain

$$s\,\mathbf{x}(s) - \mathbf{x}(0) = \mathbf{AX}(s) \qquad ...(3.2)$$

Equation (3.2) can be rearranged as

$$s\,\mathbf{x}(s) = \mathbf{AX}(s) + \mathbf{x}(0) \qquad ...(3.3)$$

Taking inverse Laplace transform of Eq. (3.3), we get

$$\dot{\mathbf{x}} = A\mathbf{x} + \mathbf{x}(0)\,\ddot{a}(t) \qquad ...(3.4)$$

Defining $\dot{\mathbf{z}} = \mathbf{x}$, Eq. (3.4) can be written as

$$\ddot{\mathbf{z}} = \mathbf{A}\,\dot{\mathbf{z}} + \mathbf{x}(0)\,\ddot{a}(t) \qquad ...(3.5)$$

Integrating Eq. (3.5), we obtain

$$\dot{\mathbf{z}} = A\,\mathbf{z} + \mathbf{x}(0)\,1(t) = \mathbf{Az} + \mathbf{B}\,u \qquad ...(3.6)$$

where $\mathbf{B} = \mathbf{x}(0)$ and $u = 1(t)$

Noting that $\dot{\mathbf{z}} = \mathbf{x}$ and $x(t) = \dot{\mathbf{z}}(t)$, we have

$$\mathbf{x} = \dot{\mathbf{z}} = A\,\mathbf{z} + \mathbf{B}\,u \qquad ...(3.7)$$

The response to initial condition is obtained by solving Eqs. (3.6) and (3.7).

The corresponding MATLAB command used to obtain the response curves are given as follows:

```
[x, z, t] = step (A, B, A, B);
  x1 = [1 0 0 ...0] * x';
  x2 = [1 0 0 ...0] * x';
  .   .
  .   .
  .   .
  xn = [0 0 0 ...1] * x';
 plot (t, x1, x2,..., t, xn
```

Case 2: *State Space Approach*

Consider the system defined in state space is by

$$\dot{\mathbf{x}} = \mathbf{Ax} \quad \mathbf{x}(0) = \mathbf{x_0} \qquad ...(3.8)$$

$$\mathbf{y} = \mathbf{Cx} \qquad ...(3.9)$$

where **x** is an n vector and **y** is an m vector.

By defining $\dot{\mathbf{z}} = \mathbf{x}$ ...(3.10)

we obtain

$$\dot{\mathbf{z}} = \mathbf{Az} + \mathbf{x}(0)\ 1(t) = \mathbf{Az} + \mathbf{B}\ u \qquad ...(3.11)$$

where

$$\mathbf{B} = \mathbf{x}(0) \text{ and } u = 1(t) \qquad ...(3.12)$$

Since $\mathbf{x} = \dot{\mathbf{z}}$, Eq. (3.9) becomes

$$\dot{\mathbf{y}} = \mathbf{C}\dot{\mathbf{z}} \qquad ...(3.13)$$

From Eqs. (3.11) and (3.13), we obtain

$$\mathbf{y} = \mathbf{C}\,(\mathbf{Az} + \mathbf{B}u) = \mathbf{CAz} + \mathbf{CB}u \qquad ...(3.14)$$

The response of the system is obtained from the Eqs. (3.11) and (3.14) to a given initial condition

The following MATLAB commands may be used to obtain the response curves:

```
[y, z, t ] = step (A, B, C*A, C*B);
y1 = [1 0 0 ...0] * y' ;
y2 = [0 1 0 ...0] * y' ;                ...(3.15)
.      .
.      .
ym = [0 0 0 ...1] * y' ;
plot (t, y1, t, y2, ........, t, ym).
```

3.11 SECOND-ORDER SYSTEMS

The standard form of a second-order system is defined by

$$G(s) = \frac{\omega_n^{\ 2}}{s^2 + 2\xi\omega_n s + \omega_n^2} \qquad ...(3.16)$$

where

ξ is the damping ratio of the system and ω_n is the undamped natural frequency of the system.

The dynamic behaviour of the second order system is then described in terms of two parameters ξ and ù$_n$.

If $0 < \xi < 1$, the closed loop poles are complex conjugates and lie in the left-half plane. The system is called underdamped, and the transient response is oscillatory. If $\xi = 0$, the transient response does not die out. If $\xi = 1$, the system is called critically damped. Overdamped system corresponds to $\xi = 1$.

Given ω_n and ξ, then the MATLAB command

```
printsys (num, den)
```

or

```
printsys(num, den, s)
```

prints the num/den as a ratio of polynomials in s.

The unit-step response of the transfer-function system using MATLAB is obtained with the use of step-response commands with left-hand arguments.

```
c = step ( num, den, t )
```

or

```
[y, x, t] = step (num, den, t).
```

3.12 ROOT LOCUS PLOTS

Consider the system equation

$$1+\frac{K(s+z_1)(s+z_2)\cdots(s+z_n)}{(s+p_1)(s+p_2)\cdots(s+p_n)}=0 \qquad ...(3.17)$$

Equation (3.17) can be written as

$$1+K\frac{num}{den}=0 \qquad ...(3.18)$$

where *num* is the numerator of the polynomial and *den* is the denominator polynomial, and *K* is the gain ($K > 0$). The vector *K* contains all the gain values for which the closed loop poles are to be computed. The root loci is plotted by using the MATLAB command

rlocus (num, den)

The gain vector *K* is supplied by the user.

The matrix *r* and gain vector *K* are obtained by the following MATLAB commands:

```
[r, k] = rlocus (num, den)
[r, k] = rlocus (num, den, k)
[r, k] = rlocus (A, B, C, D)
[r, k] = rlocus (A, B, C, D, K)                    ...(3.19)
[r, k] = rlocus (sys)
```

In Eqs. (3.19), *r* has length *K* rows and length [den – 1] columns containing the complex root locations. For plotting the root loci, the MATLAB command plot (*r*, ' ') is used.

The following MATLAB command are used for plotting the root loci with mark '0' or 'x':

```
r = rlocus (num, den)
plot (r, '0') or plot (r, 'x')
```

MATLAB provides its own set of gain values used to compute a root locus plot. It also uses the automatic axis scaling features of the plot command.

3.13 BODE DIAGRAMS

Bode diagrams are rectangular plots. Bode diagram are also known as logarithmic plot and consist of two graphs: the first one is a plot of the logarithmic of the magnitude of a sinusoidal transfer function, the second one is a plot of the phase angle. Both these graphs are plotted against the frequency on a logarithmic scale.

The MATLAB command "bode" obtains the magnitudes and phase angles of the frequency response of continuous time, linear, time invariant systems.

The MATLAB bode commands commonly used are:

```
Bode(num, den)
bode(num, den, w)
bode(A, B, C, D)                                   ...(3.20)
bode(A, B, C, D, w)
bode(sys)
```

where w is the frequency vector.

MATLAB bode commands with left hand arguments commonly used are:

```
[mag, phase, w] = bode (num, den)
[mag, phase, w] = bode (num, den, w)
[mag, phase, w] = bode (A, B, C, D)
[mag, phase, w] = bode (A, B, C, D, w)                ...(3.21)
[mag, phase, w] = bode (A, B, C, D, iu, w)
[mag, phase, w] = bode (sys)
```

The MATLAB commands given in Eq. (3.21) returns the frequency response of the system in matrices mag, phase and w. The plot is not drawn on the screen. The matrices mag, phase provide the magnitudes and phase angles of frequency response of the system, computed at the specified frequency points.

The magnitude may be converted into decibels using the MATLAB statement

magdB = 20 * log 10 (mag) ...(3.22)

In MATLAB, the following command

```
logspace (d1, d2)                                     ...(3.23)
```

or

```
logspace(d1, d2, n). logspace(d1, d2)                 ...(3.24)
```

are used to specify the frequency range that will generate a vector of 50 points logarithmically equally speed between decades 10^{d1} and 10^{d2}.

The MATLAB command

```
w = logspace (-1, 2)                                  ...(3.25)
```

may be used to generate 50 points between 0.1 and 100 rad/sec.

Similarly, the MATLAB command

```
logspace (d1, d2, n)                                  ...(3.26)
```

generates n points logarthimatically equally spaced between 10^{d1} and 10^{d2} where by the n points include both the endpoints.

3.14 NYQUIST PLOTS

Nyquist plots are also used in the frequency-response representation of linear, time invariant, continuous time feedback control systems. Nyquist plots are polar plots.

The MATLAB command

```
nyquist (num, den)                                    ...(3.27)
```

Draw the Nyquist plot of the transfer function

$$G(s) = \frac{num(s)}{den(s)} \qquad ...(3.28)$$

where num and den contain the polynomial coefficients in descending powers of s. The other MATLAB command uses for drawing Nyquist plots are:

```
nyquist (num, den, w)
nyquist (A, B, C, D)
nyquist (A, B, C, D, w)
nyquist (A, B, C, D, iu, w)                    ...(3.29)
nyquist (sys)
```

where w is the frequency vector.

The MATLAB command involving the user-specified vector w in Eq. (3.29) computes the frequency response at the specified frequency points.

The following MATLAB commands

```
[re, im,w ] = nyquist (num, den)
[re, im,w ] = nyquist (num, den, w)
[re, im,w ] = nyquist (A, B, C, D)
[re, im,w ] = nyquist (A, B, C, D, w)          ...(3.30)
[re, im,w ] = nyquist (A, B, C, D, iu, w)
[re, im,w ] = nyquist (sys)
```

are used to obtain the frequency response of the system in the matrices *re*, *im* and *w*. The plot is not drawn on the screen. The matrices *re* and *im* contain the real and imaginary parts of the frequency response of the system, computed at the frequency points specificated in the vector *w*.

3.15 NICHOLS CHART

The chart consisting of the *M* and *N* loci in the log magnitude versus phase diagram is called the Nichols chart. The *G(jw)* locus drawn on the Nichols chart gives both the gain characteristics and phase characteristics of the closed loop transfer function at the same time. The Nichols chart contains curves of constant closed loop magnitude and phase angle. The Nichols chart is symmetric about the 180° axis. The *M* loci are centered about the critical point (0 dB, –180). The Nichols chart is useful in determining the frequency response of the closed loop from that of the open loop. The Nichols chart is produced by using the MATLAB command nichols(num, den). The command *n* grid creates the dotted lines that allow reading closed-loop gain and phase from the Nichols chart. In order to customize the axes of the Nichols chart, the MATLAB command **axis** is used.

3.16 GAIN MARGIN, PHASE MARGIN, PHASE CROSSOVER FREQUENCY AND GAIN CROSSOVER FREQUENCY

The MATLAB command

```
[Gm, pm, wcp, wcg] = margin (sys)              ...(3.31)
```

can be used to obtain the gain margin, phase margin, phase crossover frequency and gain crossover frequency.

In Equation (3.31), Gm is the gain margin, pm is the phase margin, wcp is the phase crossover frequency, and wcg is the gain crossover frequency.

The following MATLAB command is commonly used for obtaining the resonant peak and resonant frequency:

```
[mag, phase, w] = bode (num, den, w)
```

or

```
[mag, phase, w] = bode (sys, w)
[Mp, k] = max (mag)                                    ...(3.32)
resonant peak = 20 * log 10 (Mp)
resonant frequency = w (k)
```

The following lines are used in MATLAB program to obtain bandwidth:

```
n = 1
while 20 * log 10 (mag (n)) > -3
    n = n + 1
    end                                                ...(3.33)
    bandwidth = w (n)
```

3.17 TRANSFORMATION OF SYSTEM MODELS

In this section, we consider two cases of transformation of system models:

1. Transformation of system model from transfer function to state space
2. Transformation of system model from state space to transfer function

3.17.1 Transformation of System Model from Transfer Function to State Space

The closed-loops transfer function can be written as

$$\frac{Y(s)}{U(s)} = \frac{numerator\ of\ polynomial\ in\ s}{denominator\ of\ polynomial\ in\ s} = \frac{num}{den} \qquad ...(3.34)$$

The state space representation is obtained by the MATLAB command

```
[A, B, C, D] = tf 2ss (num, den)                       ...(3.35)
```

3.17.2 Transformation of System Model from State Space to Transfer Function

The transfer function from state space equations is obtained by using the MATLAB command:

```
[num, den] = ss2tf (A, B, C, D, iu)                    (3.36)
```

where *iu* corresponds to the system with more than one input. iu is either 1, 2 or 3, where 1 implies input u_1, 2 implies input u_2 and 3 implies input u_3.

For system with only one input, the MATLAB command

```
[num, den ] = ss2tf (A, B, C, D)                       ...(3.37)
```

or

```
[num, den ] = ss2tf (A, B, C, D, 1)                    ...(3.38)
```

may be used

3.18 BODE DIAGRAMS OF SYSTEMS DEFINED IN STATE SPACE

Let the control system defined in state space be

$$\dot{\mathbf{x}} = \mathbf{Ax} + \mathbf{Bu}$$

$$\mathbf{y} = \mathbf{Cx} + \mathbf{Du} \quad ...(3.39)$$

where

A = state matrix (*nxn* matrix)

B = control matrix (*nxr* matrix)

C = output matrix (*mxn* matrix)

D = output matrix (*mxn* matrix)

u = control vector (*r* – vector)

x = state vector (*n* – vector)

y = output vector (*m* – vector)

The MATLAB command **bode[A, B, C, D]** may be used to obtain the Bode diagram of this system. In fact, the command **bode[A, B, C, D]** gives a series of Bode plots, one for each input of the system, with the frequency range automatically determined.

If we use the scalar *iu* as an index into the inputs of the control system that specifies which input is to be used for the Bode plot, then the MATLAB command **Bode[A, B, C, D iu]** produces the Bode plots from the input *iu* to all the outputs ($y_1, y_2, \ldots, y_m$) of the system with the frequency range automatically determined.

If the system has three inputs, then $\mathbf{u} = \begin{bmatrix} u_1 \\ u_2 \\ u_3 \end{bmatrix}$

For a system with only one input *u*, then the MATLAB command

Bode[A, B, C, D] ...(3.40)

or

Bode [A, B, C, D, 1] can be used. ...(3.41)

3.19 NYQUIST PLOTS OF A SYSTEM DEFINED IN STATE SPACE

Consider the system defined in state space given by Equation (3.39). Nyquist plots of the system defined in Eq. (3.39) may be obtained by using the MATLAB command

nyquist (A, B, C, D) ...(3.42)

The MATLAB command given by Eq. (3.42) produces a series of Nyquist plots one corresponding to each input and output combination of the system, with the frequency range automatically determined.

If we used the scalar *iu* as an index to the inputs of the control system that specifies which input is to be used for the Nyquist plot, then the MATLAB command nyquist `(A,B,C,D,iu,w)` produces Nyquist plots from the input to all the outputs ($y_1, y_2, \ldots, y_m$) of the system with the frequency range automatically determined.

The MATLAB command

```
nyquist (A, B, C, D, iu, w)                                          ...(3.43)
```

considers the user-supplied frequency vector *w*. The vector *w* specifies the frequency at which the frequency response should be determined.

3.20 TRANSIENT-RESPONSE ANALYSIS IN STATE SPACE

In this section, we present the transient-response analysis of systems in state space using MATLAB. Specifically, we present the step response, impulse, ramp response and responses to other forms of simple inputs.

3.20.1 Unit Step Response

For a control system defined in a state space form as in Eq. (3.39), the MATLAB command

```
step (A, B, C, D)                                                    ...(3.44)
```

will generate plots of unit step responses, with the time vector automatically determined provided *t* is not explicitly provided in the step commands.

The MATLAB command step (sys) may also be used to obtain the unit-step response of a system.

The command

```
step (sys)                                                           ...(3.45)
```

can be used where the system is defined by

```
sys = tf (num, den)                                                  ...(3.46)
```

or

```
sys = ss (A, B, C, D)                                                ...(3.47)
```

The following MATLAB step commands with left hand arguments are used then no plot is shown on the screen:

```
[y, x, t] = step [num, den, t]
[y, x, t] = step (A, B, C, D, iu)                                    ...(3.48)
[y, x, t] = step (A, B, C, D, iu, t )
```

Hence, in order to obtain the response curves, plot commands should be used. The matrices *x* and *y* contain the state response of the system and the output respectively, computed at the time points *t*. In Eq. (3.48), *iu* is a scalar index of the inputs of the system, which specifies the input to be used for the response, and *t* is the user specified time. The step command in Eq. (3.48) can be used to obtain a series of step response plots, one for each input and output combination of

$$\dot{\mathbf{x}} = \mathbf{Ax} + \mathbf{Bu}$$

$$\mathbf{y} = \mathbf{Cx} + \mathbf{Du} \qquad ...(3.49)$$

when the system involves multiple inputs and multiple outputs.

3.20.2 Impulse Response

The following MATLAB commands may be used to obtain the unit impulse response of a control system:

```
impulse (num, den)                                                   ...(3.50)
impulse(A, B, C, D)                                                  ...(3.51)
```

```
[y, x, t] = impulse (num, den)                    ...(3.52)
[y, x, t] = impulse (num, den, t)                 ...(3.53)
[y, x, t] = impulse (A, B, C, D)                  ...(3.54)
[y, x, t] = impulse (A, B, C, D, iu)              ...(3.55)
[y, x, t] = impulse (A, B, C, D, iu, t)           ...(3.56)
```

The command in Eq. (3.50) impulse (num, den) shows the plots of the unit impulse response on the monitor (screen). The command in Eq. (3.51), impulse (*A*, *B*, *C*, *D*) produces a series of unit impulse-response plots one for each input and output combination of the system defined in Eq. (3.39) with the time vector automatically obtained. The vector *t* in Eqs. (3.53) and (3.56) is the user supplied time vector, which specifies the times at which the impulse response is to be obtained. The scalar *iu* in Eqs. (3.55) and (3.56) is an index into the inputs of the system and specifies which input is to be used for the impulse response. The matrices *x* and *y* in Eqs. (3.52) to (3.56) contain the state responses of the system and the output respectively, evaluated at the time points *t*.

3.20.3 Unit Ramp Response

Consider the system described in state space as

$$\dot{\mathbf{x}} = \mathbf{Ax} + \mathbf{Bu}$$

$$\mathbf{y} = \mathbf{Cx} + \mathbf{Du} \qquad ...(3.57)$$

where u is the unit ramp function.

When all the initial conditions are zeros, the unit ramp response is the integral of the unit step response. Therefore, the unit ramp response is given by

$$z = \int_0^t y dt \qquad ...(3.58)$$

or

$$\dot{\mathbf{z}} = \mathbf{y} = \mathbf{x}_1 \qquad ...(3.59)$$

Defining

$$\mathbf{z} = \mathbf{x}_3 \qquad ...(3.60)$$

Equation (3.59) can be written as

$$\dot{\mathbf{x}}_3 = \mathbf{x}_1 \qquad ...(3.61)$$

Combining Eqs. (3.57) and (3.61), we can write

$$\dot{\mathbf{x}} = \mathbf{AAx} + \mathbf{BBu}$$

$$\mathbf{z} = \mathbf{CCx} + \mathbf{DDu} \qquad ...(3.62)$$

The MATLAB command

```
[z, x, t] = step (AA, BB, CC, DD)                 ...(3.63)
```

can be used to obtain the unit-ramp response curve z (t).

3.20.4 Response to Arbitrary Input

The response to an arbitrary input can be obtained by using the following MATLAB commands:

```
lsim (num, den, t)                                ...(3.64)
lsim (A, B, C, D, u, t)                           ...(3.65)
```

```
y = lsim (num, den, r, t)                                    ...(3.66)
y = lsim (A, B, C, D, u, t)                                  ...(3.67)
```

The MATLAB commands in Eqs. (3.64) to (3.67) will generate the response to input time function *r* or *u*

3.21 RESPONSE TO INITIAL CONDITION IN STATE SPACE

Consider the system defined in state space by

$$\dot{\mathbf{x}} = \mathbf{Ax} + \mathbf{Bu}, \mathbf{x}(0) = \mathbf{x}_0 \quad ...(3.68)$$

$$\mathbf{y} = \mathbf{Cx} + \mathbf{Du} \quad ...(3.69)$$

The MATLAB command

```
initial (A, B, C, D, [initial condition], t)                 ...(3.70)
```

may be used to provide the response to the initial condition.

3.22 EXAMPLE PROBLEMS AND SOLUTIONS

Example E3.1: Reduce the system shown in Fig. E3.1 to a single transfer function, $T(s) = C(s)/R(s)$ using MATLAB. The transfer functions are given as

$$G_1(s) = \frac{1}{(s+7)}$$

$$G_2(s) = \frac{1}{(s^2+6s+5)}$$

$$G_3(s) = \frac{1}{(s+8)}$$

$$G_4(s) = \frac{1}{s}$$

$$G_5(s) = \frac{7}{(s+3)}$$

$$G_6(s) = \frac{1}{(s^2+7s+5)}$$

$$G_7(s) = \frac{5}{(s+5)}$$

$$G_8(s) = \frac{1}{(s+9)}$$

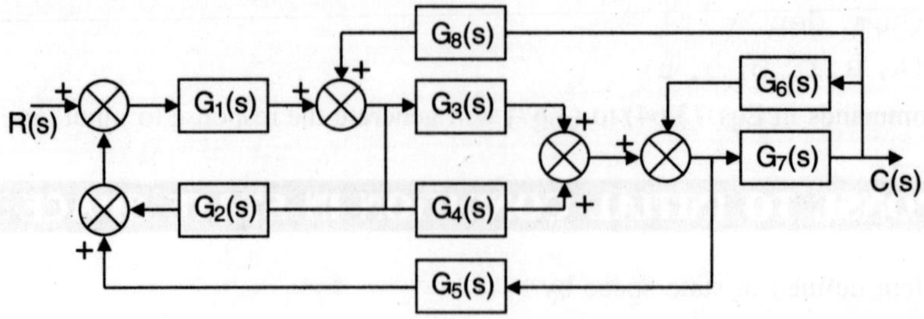

Fig. E3.1

The transfer functions are given as:

G1 $(s) = 1/(s + 7)$

G2 $(s) = 1/(s^2 + 6s + 5)$

G3 $(s) = 1/(s + 8)$

G4 $(s) = 1/s$

G5 $(s) = 7/(s + 3)$

G6 $(s) = 1/(s^2 + 7s + 5)$

G7 $(s) = 5/(s + 5)$

G8 $(s) = 1/(s + 9)$

Solution:

% MATLAB Program

```
G1 = tf ([0 0 1], [0 1 7]);
G2 = tf ([0 0 1], [1 6 5]);
G3 = tf ([0 0 1], [0 1 8]);
G4 = tf ([0 0 1], [0 1 0]);
G5 = tf ([0 0 7], [0 1 3]);
G6 = tf ([0 0 1], [1 7 5]);
G7 = tf ([0 0 5], [0 1 5]);
G8 = tf ([0 0 1], [0 1 9]);
G9 = tf ([0 0 1], [0 0 1]);
T1 = append (G1, G2, G3, G4, G5, G6, G7, G8, G9);
Q = [ 1 -2 -5 9 ]
     2 1 8 0
     3 1 8 0
     4 1 8 0
     5 3 4 -6
     6 7 0 0
     7 3 4 -6
     8 7 0 0];
```

```
Inputs = 9;
Outputs = 7;
Ts = connect (T1, Q, Inputs, Outputs);
T = Tf (Ts) computer response
Transfer function:
10 s^7 + 290 s^6 + 3350 s^5 + 1.98e004 s^4 + 6.369e004 s^3 + 1.089e005 s^2
+ 8.895e004 s + 2.7e004 s^10 + 45 s^9 + 866 s^8 + 9305 s^7 + 6.116e004 s^6 +
2.533e005 s^5 + 6.57e005 s^4 + 1.027e006 s^3 + 8.909e005 s^2 + 3.626e005 s
+ 4.2e004
```

Example E3.2: For each of the second order systems below, find ξ, ω_n, *Ts*, *Tp*, *Tr*, % overshoot and plot the step response using MATLAB.

$$(a)\quad T(s) = \frac{130}{s^2 + 15s + 130}$$

$$(b)\quad T(s) = \frac{0.045}{s^2 + 0.025s + 0.045}$$

$$(c)\quad T(s) = \frac{10^8}{s^2 + 1.325 \times 10^3 s + 10^8}$$

Solution:

(*a*)

```
>> clf
>> numa=130;
>> dena=[1 15 130];
>> Ta=tf(numa, dena)
Transfer function:
        130
  ----------------
  s^2 + 15s + 130
>> omegana=sqrt (dena(3))
  omegana = 11.4018
>> zetaa=dena(2)/(2*omegana)
  zetaa = 0.6578
>> Tsa=4/ (zetaa*omegana)
  Tsa = 0.5333
>> Tpa=pi/ (omegana*sqrt(1-zetaa^2))
  Tpa = 0.3658
>> Tra=(1.76*zetaa^3-.417*zetaa^2 + 1.039*zetaa + 1)/ omegana
  Tra =  0.1758
>> percenta=exp(-zetaa*pi/ sqrt(1-zetaa^2))*100
  percenta = 6.4335
>> subplot(221)
```

```
>> step(Ta)
>> title('(a)')
>> '(b)'
   ans =
```

(*b*)

```
>> numb=.045;
>> denb=[1 .025 .045];
>> Tb=tf(numb,denb)
Transfer function:
            0.045
   ----------------------
   s^2 + 0.025s + 0.045
>> omeganb=sqrt(denb(3))
   omeganb=0.2121
>> zetab=denb(2)/(2*omeganb)
   zetab=0.0589

>> Tsb=4/ (zetab*omeganb)
   Tsb = 320
>> Tpb=pi/ (omeganb*sqrt(1-zetab^2))
   Tpb = 14.8354
>> Trb=(1.76*zetab^3 -.417*zetab^2 + 1.039*zetab + 1)/ omeganb
   Trb = 4.9975
>> percentb=exp(-zetab*pi/ sqrt(1-zetab^2))*100
   percentb = 83.0737
>> subplot(222)
>> step(Tb)
>> title('(b)')
>> '(c)'
   ans =
```

(*c*)

```
>> numc=10E8;
>> denc=[1 1.325*10E3 10E8];
>> Tc=tf(numc, denc)
Transfer function:
              1e009
      ----------------------
      s^2 + 13250s + 1e009
```

```
>> omeganc=sqrt(denc(3))
   omeganc = 3.1623e+004
>> zetac=denc (2)/(2*omeganc)
   zetac = 0.2095
>> Tsc = 4/ (zetac*omeganc)
   Tsc = 6.0377e-004
>> Tpc =pi/ (omeganc*sqrt (1-zetac^2))
   Tpc = 1.0160e-004
>> Trc = (1.76*zetac^3 -.417*zetac^2 + 1.039*zetac + 1)/ omeganc
   Trc = 3.8439e-005
>> percentc =exp (-zetac*pi/ sqrt (1-zetac^2))*100
   percentc = 51.0123
>> subplot (223)
>> step (Tc)
>> title ('(c)')
```

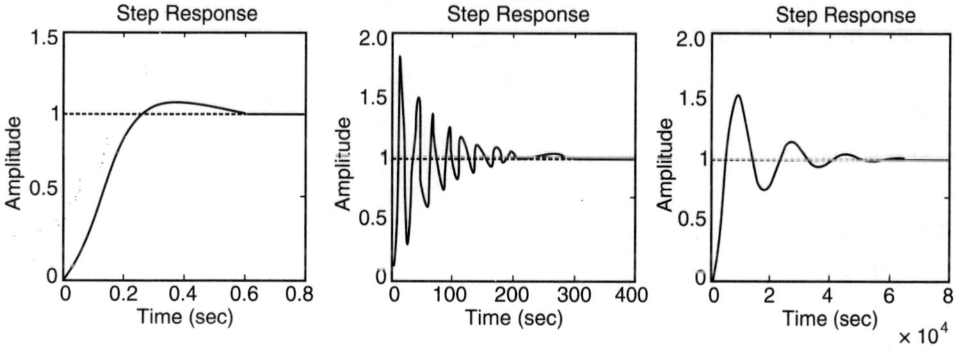

Fig. E3.2

Example E3.3: Determine the pole locations for the system shown below using MATLAB.

$$\frac{C(s)}{R(s)} = \frac{s^3 - 6s^2 + 7s + 15}{s^5 + s^4 - 5s^3 - 9s^2 + 11s - 12}$$

Solution:

```
>> %MATLAB Program
>> den= [1 1 -5 -9 11 -12];
>> A=roots (den)
A =
     -2.1586 + 1.2396i
     -2.1586 - 1.2396i
      2.3339
      0.4917 + 0.7669i
      0.4917 - 0.7669i
```

Example E3.4: Determine the pole locations for the unity feedback system shown below using MATLAB.

$$G(s) = \frac{150}{(s+5)(s+7)(s+9)(s+11)}$$

Solution:

```
>> %MATLAB Program
>> numg =150
numg = 150
>> deng =poly ([-5 -7 -9 -11]);
>> 'G(s)'
ans =
G(s)
>> G=tf (numg, deng)
Transfer function:
                        150
     ---------------------------------------------
     s^4 + 32  s^3 + 374  s^2 + 1888 s + 3465
>> 'Poles of G(s)'
ans =
Poles of G(s)
>> pole (G)
ans =
   -11.0000
    -9.0000
    -7.0000
    -5.0000
>> 'T(s)'
ans =
T(s)
>> T=feedback (G, 1)
Transfer function:
                        150
     ---------------------------------------------
     s^4 + 32  s^3 + 374  s^2 + 1888 s + 3615
>> pole (T)
ans =
     -10.9673+1.9506i
     -10.9673-1.9506i
      -5.0327+1.9506i
      -5.0327-1.9506i
```

Example E3.5: A plant to be controlled is described by a transfer function

$$G(s) = \frac{s+7}{s^2+9s+30}$$

Obtain the root locus plot using MATLAB.

Solution:

```
>> %MATLAB Program
>> clf
>> num = [1 7];
>> den = [1 9 30];
>> rlocus (num, den);
```

Computer response is shown in Fig. E3.5.

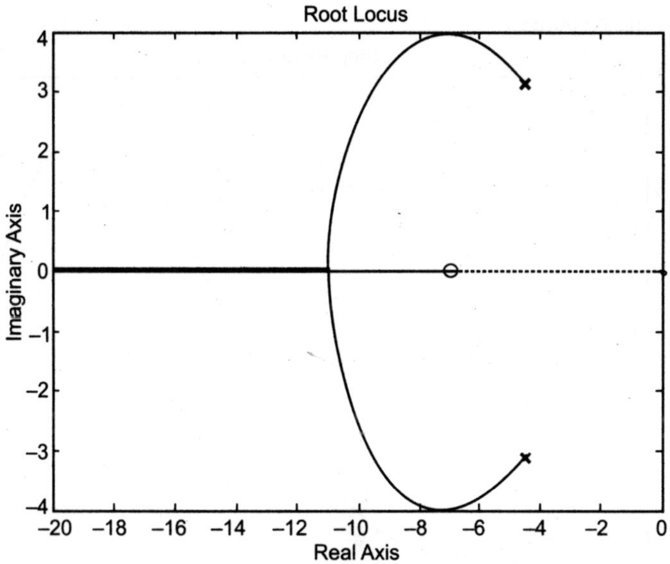

Fig. E3.5

Example E3.6: For the unity feedback system shown in Fig. E3.6, *G*(*s*) is given as

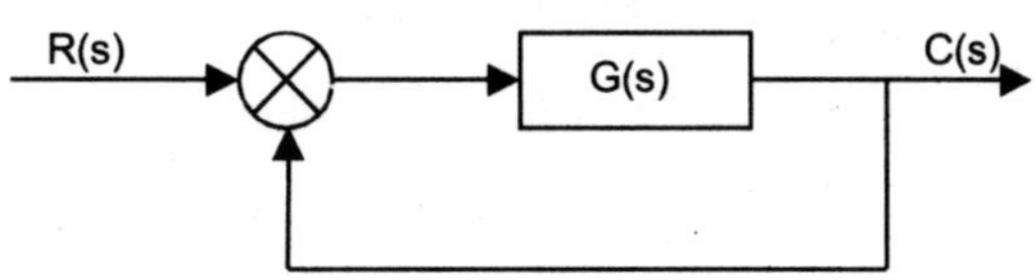

Fig. E3.6

$$G(s) = \frac{30(s^2-5s+3)}{(s+1)\,(s+2)\,(s+4)\,(s+5)}$$

Determine the closed-loop step response using MATLAB.

Solution:

```
>>%MATLAB Program
>>numg=40*[1 -5 7];
>> deng =poly ([-1 -2 -4 -5]);
>> G=tf (numg, deng);
>> T=feedback (G, 1)
```

Transfer function:

```
        40s^2 - 200s + 280
-----------------------------------
s^4 + 12s^3 + 89s^2 - 122s + 320
```

```
>> step (T)
```

Computer response:

Figure E3.6 (a) shows the response.

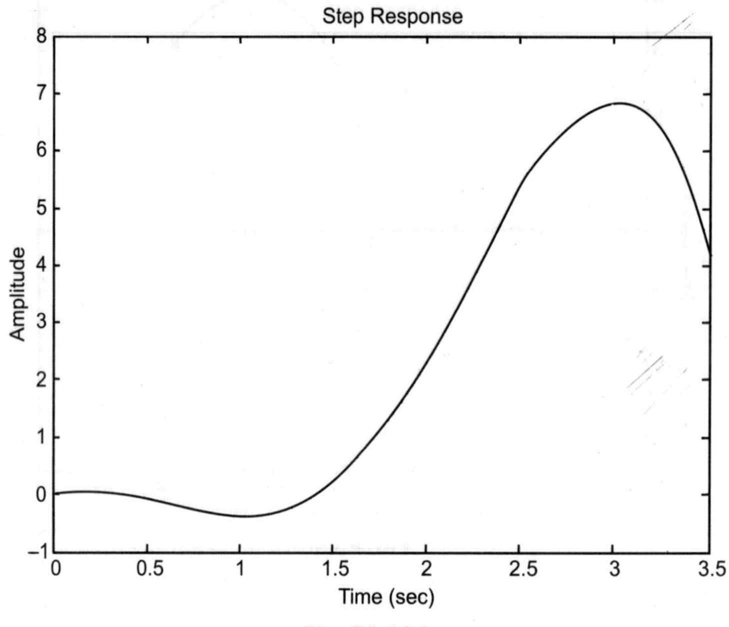

Fig. E3.6(a)

Simulation shows over 30% overshoot and non minimum-phase behaviour. Hence, the second-order approximation is not valid.

Example E3.7: Determine the accuracy of the second-order approximation using MATLAB to simulate the unity feedback system shown in Fig. E3.7 where

$$G(s) = \frac{12(s^2 + 3s + 9)}{(s^2 + 3s + 9)(s + 1)(s + 5)}$$

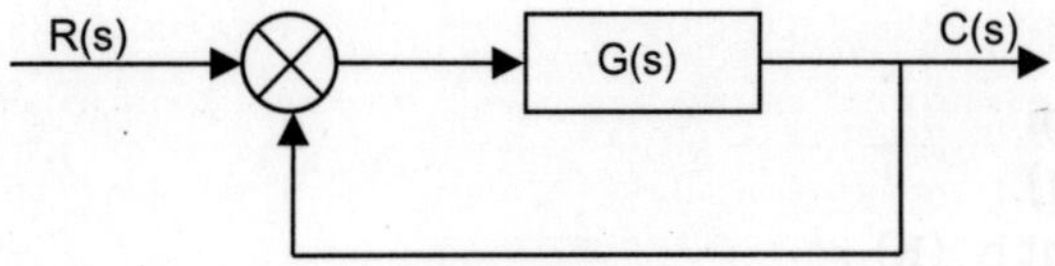

Fig. E3.7

Solution:

```
>>%MATLAB Program
>> numg=12*[1 3 9];
>> deng =conv ([1 3 9], poly ([-1 -5]));
>> G=tf (numg, deng);
>> T=feedback (G, 1);
>> step (T)
```

Computer response [see Fig. E3.7 (a)].

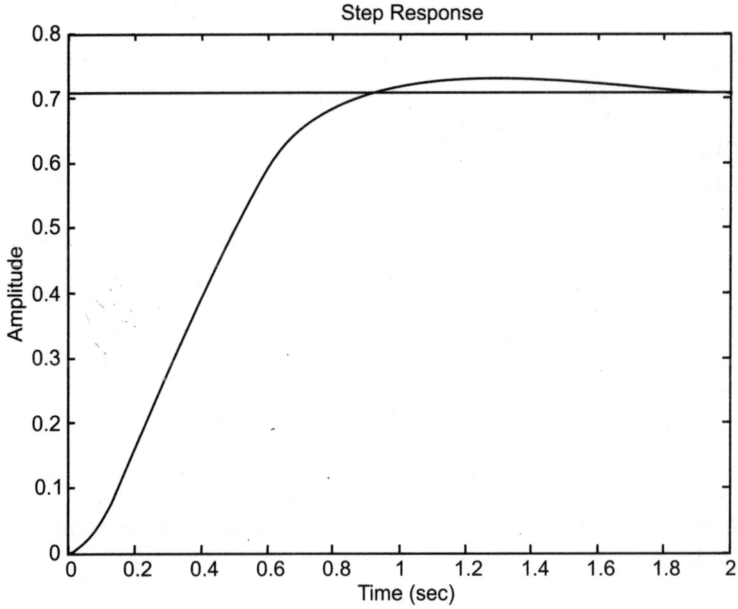

Fig. E3.7 (a)

Example E3.8: For the unity feedback system shown in Fig. E3.8 with

$$G(s) = \frac{K(s+1)}{s(s+1)(s+5)(s+6)},$$

determine the range of K for stability using MATLAB.

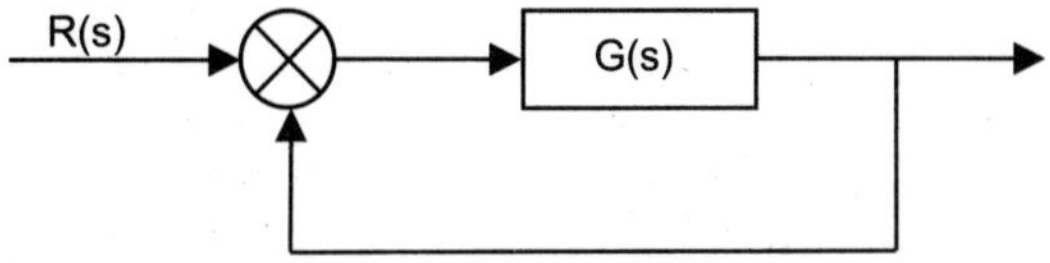

Fig. E3.8

Solution:

```
>>%MATLAB Program
>> K= [0:0.2:200];
>> for i =1: length (K);
>> deng=poly ([0 -1 -5 -6]);
>> dent=deng+ [0 0 0 K (i) K (i)];
>> R=roots (dent);
>> A=real(R);
>> B=max (A);
>> if B>0
>> R
>> K=K (i)
>> break
>> end
>> end
```

Computer response:

R =

–10.0000
–0.5000 + 4.4441*i*
–0.5000 – 4.4441*i*
–1.0000

A =

–10.0000
–0.5000
–0.5000
–1.0000

B =

–0.5000

Example E3.9: Write a program in MATLAB to obtain the Nyquist and Nichols plots for the following transfer function for k=30.

$$G(s) = \frac{k(s+1)(s+3+7i)(s+3-7i)}{(s+1)(s+3)(s+5)(s+3+7i)(s+3-7i)}$$

Solution:

```
>>%MATLAB Program
>>%Simple Nyquist and Nichols plots
>> clf
>> z= [-1 -3+7*i -3-7*i];
>> p= [-1 -3 -5 -3+7*i -3-7*i];
>> k=30;
>> [num, den] =zp2tf (z', p', k);
```

```
>> subplot (211), nyquist (num, den)
>> subplot (212), Nichols (num, den)
>> ngrid
>> axis ([50 360 -40 30])
```

Computer response:

The Nyquist and Nichols plots are shown in Fig. E3.9.

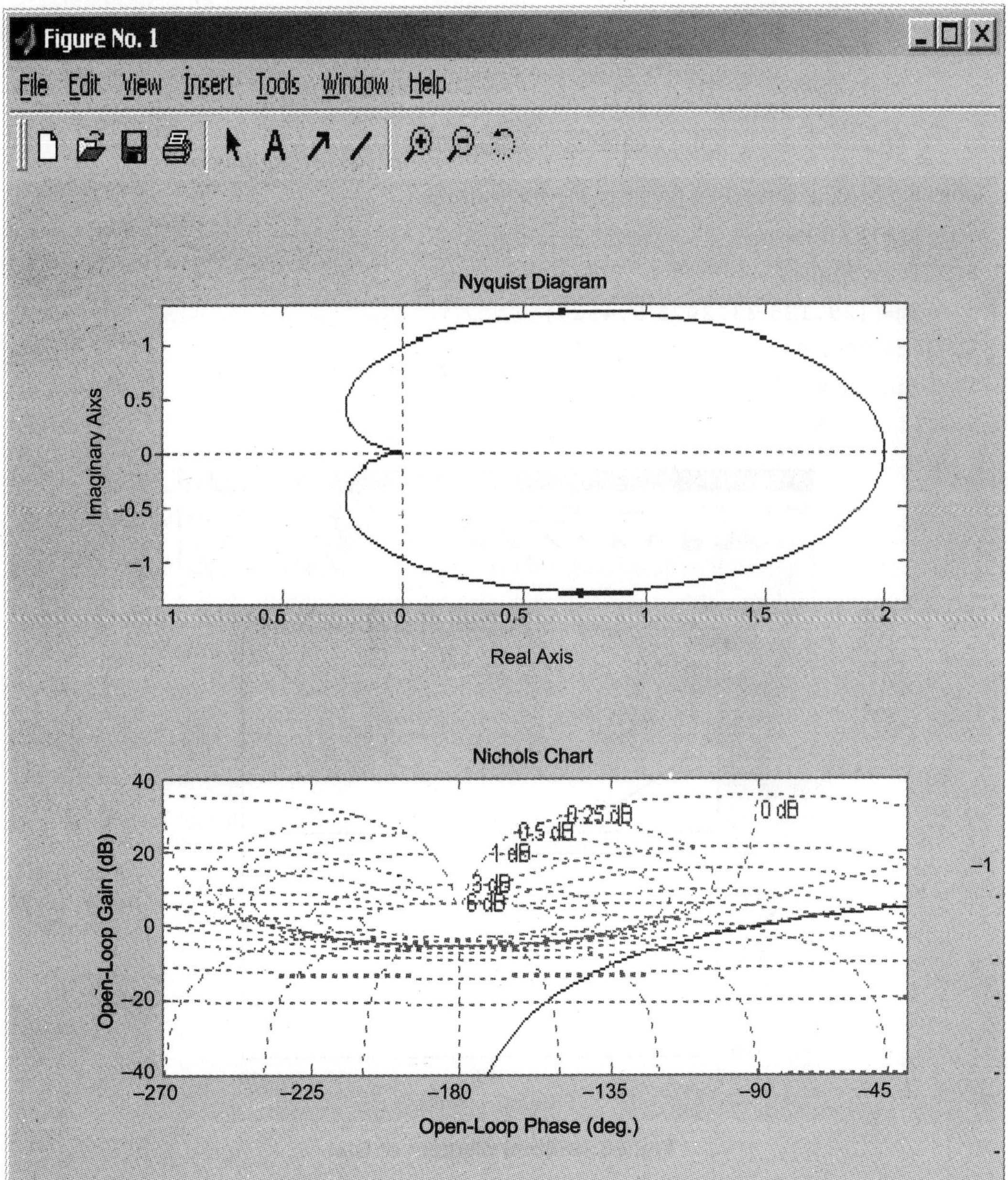

Fig. E3.9

Example E3.10: A PID controller is given by

$$G_c(s) = 29.125\frac{(s+0.57)^2}{s}$$

Draw a Bode diagram of the controller using MATLAB.

Solution:

$$G_c(s) = \frac{29.125(s^2+1.14s+0.3249)}{s}$$

$$= \frac{29.125s^2+33.2025s+9.4627}{s}$$

The following MATLAB program produces the Bode diagram

```
>> % MATLAB Program
>> % Bode diagram
>> num= [29.125 33.2025 9.4627];
>> den= [0 1 0];
>> bode (num, den)
>> title ('Bode diagram of G(s)')
```

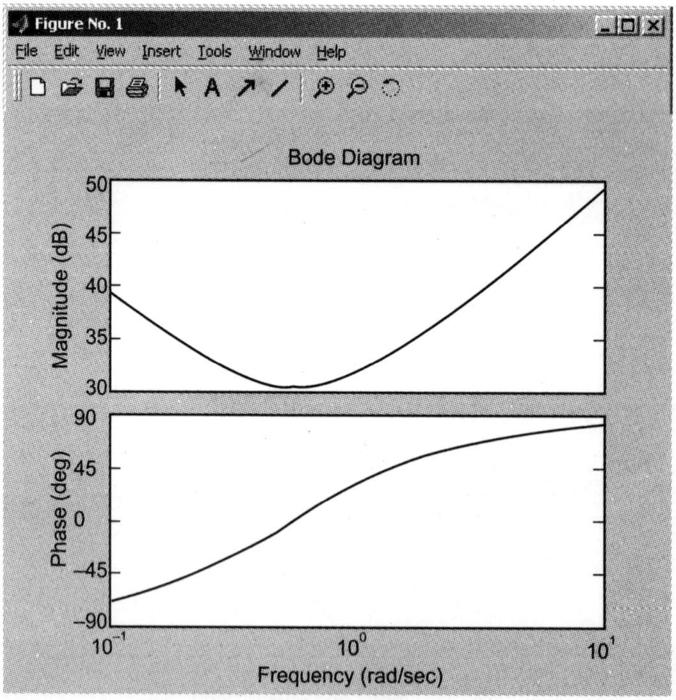

Fig. E3.10 Bode diagram of G(s)

Example E3.11: For the closed-loop system defined by

$$\frac{C(s)}{R(s)} = \frac{1}{s^2 + 2\zeta s + 1}$$

(*a*) plot the unit-step response curves *c*(*t*) for æ =0, 0.1, 0.2, 0.4, 0.5, 0.6, 0.8, and 1.0. ù$_n$ is normalized to 1.

(*b*) plot a three-dimensional plot of (a).

Solution:

```
>> % Two-dimensional plot and three-dimensional plot of unit-step
>> %response curves for the standard second-order system with wn =1
>> %and zeta = 0, 0.1, 0.2, 0.4, 0.5, 0.6, 0.8, and 1.0
>> t=0:0.2:10;
>> zeta= [0 0.1 0.2 0.4 0.5 0.6 0.8 1.0];
>> for n=1:8;
>> num= [0 0 1];
>> den= [1 2*zeta (n) 1];
>> [y (1:51, n), x, t] = step (num, den, t);
>> end
>> %Two-dimensional diagram with the command plot (t, y)
>> plot (t, y)
>> grid
>> title ('Plot of unit-step response curves')
>> xlabel ('t Sec')
>> ylabel ('Response')
>> text (4.1, 1.86, '\zeta=0')
>> text (3.0, 1.7,'0.1')
>> text (3.0, 1.5,'0.2')
>> text (3.0, 1.22,'0.4')
>> text (2.9, 1.1,'0.5')
>> text (4.0, 1.08,'0.6')
>> text (3.0, 0.9, '0.8')
>> text (4.0, 0.9,'1.0')
>> %For three-dimensional plot, we use the command mesh (t, eta, y')
>> mesh (t, eta, y')
>> title ('Three-dimensional plot of unit-step response curves')
>> xlabel ('t Sec')
>> ylabel ('\zeta')
>> zlabel ('Response')
```

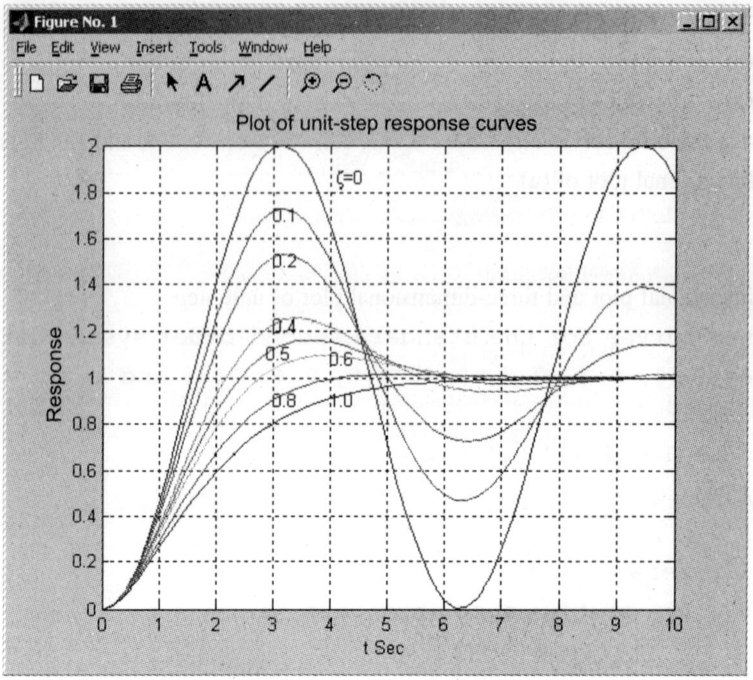

Fig. E3.11 (a) Plot of unit-step response curves

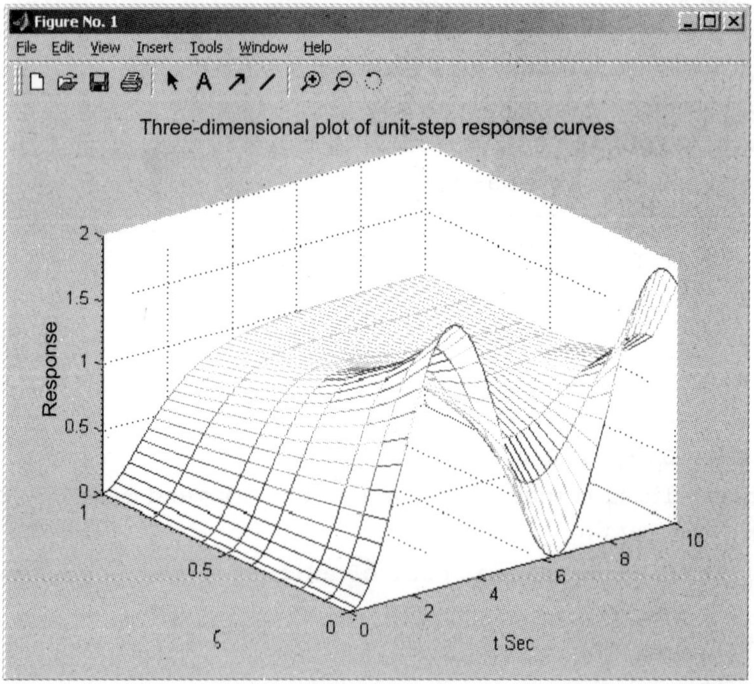

Fig. E3.11 (b) Three-dimensional plot of unit-step response curves

Example E3.12: A closed-loop control system is defined by

$$\frac{C(s)}{R(s)} = \frac{2\zeta s}{s^2 + 2\zeta s + 1}$$

where æ is the damping ratio. For æ = 0.1, 0.2, 0.3, 0.4, 0.5, 0.6, 0.7, 0.8, 0.9, and 1.0 using MATLAB. Plot.

(*a*) a two-dimensional diagram of unit-impulse response curves

(*b*) a three-dimensional plot of the response curves.

Solution: A MATLAB program that produces a two-dimensional diagram of unit-impulse response curves and a three-dimensional plot of the response curves is given below:

```
>> % To plot a two-dimensional diagram
>> t = 0:0.2:10;
>> zeta = [0.1 0.2 0.3 0.4 0.5 0.6 0.7 0.8 0.9 1.0];
>> for n=1:10;
>> num = [0 2*zeta (n) 1];
>> den = [1 2*zeta (n) 1];
>> [y (1:51, n), x, t]=impulse (num,den,t);
>> end
>> plot (t, y)
>> grid
>> title ('Plot of unit-impulse response curves')
>> xlabel ('t Sec')
>> ylabel ('Response')
>> text (2.0,0.85,'0.1')
>> text (1.5,0.75,'0.2')
>> text (1.5,0.6,'0.3')
>> text (1.5,0.5,'0.4')
>> text (1.5,0.38,'0.5')
>> text (1.5,0.25,'0.6')
>> text (1.7,0.12,'0.7')
>> text (2.0,-0.1, '0.8')
>> text (1.5, 0.0, '0.9')
>> text (.5, 1.5,'1.0')
>> % Three–dimensional plot
>> mesh (t, eta, 'y')
>> title ('Three-dimensional plot')
>> xlabel ('t Sec')
>> ylabel ('\zeta')
>> zlabel ('Response')
```

The two-dimensional diagram and three-dimensional diagram produced by this MATLAB program are shown in Figs. E3.12 (a) and (b) respectively.

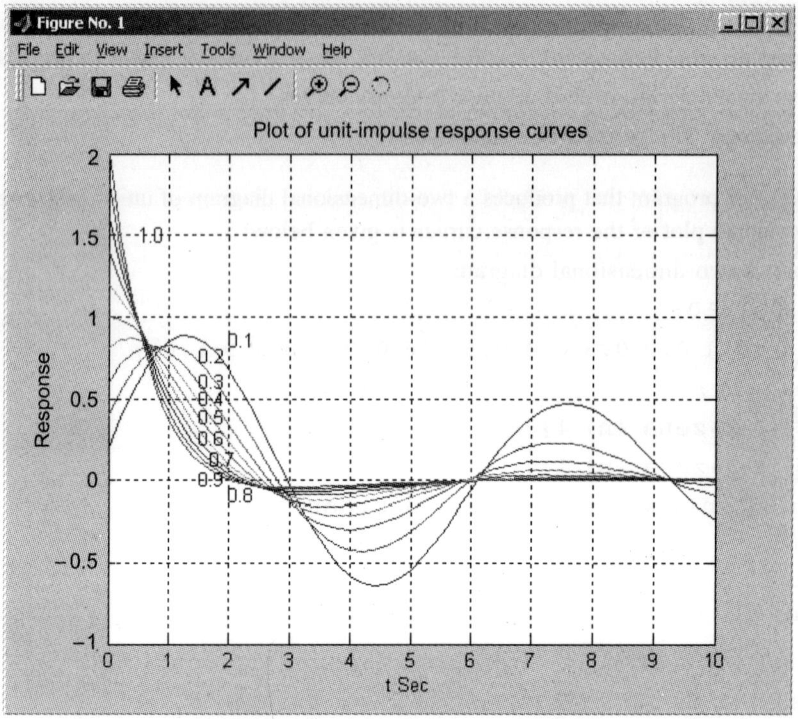

Fig. E3.12 (a) Two-dimensional plot

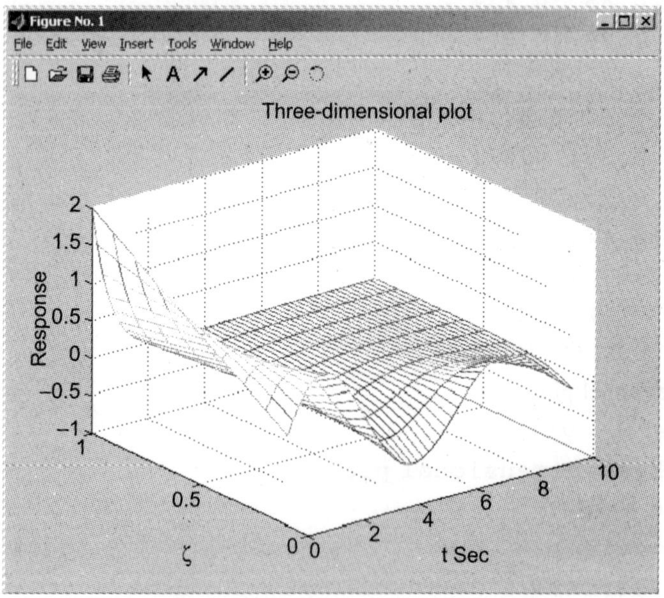

Fig. E3.12 (b) Three-dimensional plot

Example E3.13: For the system shown in Fig. E3.13, write a program in MATLAB that will use an open-loop transfer function *G*(*s*):

$$G(s) = \frac{50(s+1)}{s(s+3)(s+5)}$$

$$G(s) = \frac{25(s+1)(s+7)}{s(s+2)(s+4)(s+8)}$$

(*a*) Obtain a Bode plot

(*b*) Estimate the percent overshoot, settling time and peak time

(*c*) Obtain the closed-loop step response.

Solution:

(*a*) >> %MATLAB Program

```
>> G=zpk ([-1], [0 -3 -5], 50)
>> G=tf (G)
>> bode (G)
>> title ('System 1')
>> %title ('System 1')
>> pause
>> %Find phase margin
>> [Gm, Pm, Wcg, Wcp] =margin (G);
>> w-1:.01:20;
>> [M, P, w] =bode (G, w);
>> % Find bandwidth
>> for k=1:1: length (M);
>> if 20*log10 (M (k)) +7<=0;
>> 'Mag'
>> 20*log10 (M (k))
>> 'BW'
>> wBW =w (k)
>> break
>> end
>> end
>> %Find damping ratio, percent overshoot, settling time and peak time
>> for z=0:.01:10
>> Pt=atan (2*z/ (sqrt (-2*z^2+sqrt (1+4*z^4))))*(180/pi);
>> if (Pm-Pt) <=0
>> z;
>> Po=exp (-z*pi/sqrt (1-z^2));
>> Ts= (4/ (wBW*z))*sqrt ((1-2*z^2) +sqrt (4*z^4-4*z^2+2));
>> Tp = (pi/ (wBW*sqrt (1-z^2)))*sqrt ((1-2*z^2) +sqrt (4*z^4-4*z^2+2));
>> fprintf('Bandwidth=%g', wBW)
>> fprintf('Phase margin=%g', Pm)
```

```
>> fprintf(', Damping ratio=%g', z)
>> fprintf(', Percent overshoot=%g', Po*100)
>> fprintf(', Settling time=%g', Ts)
>> fprintf(', Peak time=%g', Tp)
>> break
>> end
>> end
>> T=feedback (G, 1);
>> step (T)
>> title ('Step response system 1')
>> %title ('Step response system 1')
```

Computer response:

Zero/pole/gain:

$$\frac{50\,(s+1)}{s(s+3)(s+5)}$$

Transfer function:

$$\frac{50\,s+50}{s\char`^3+8s\char`^2+15s}$$

The Bode plot is shown in Fig. E3.13 (a)

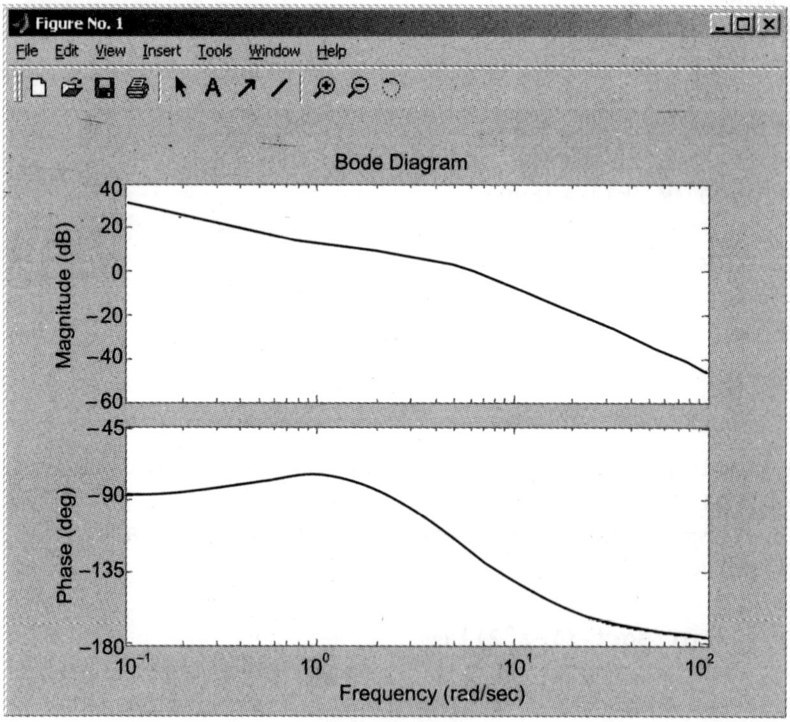

Fig. E3.13 (a)

ans =

Mag

ans =

    –3.0032

ans =

BW

wBW =

    9.7900

Bandwidth = 9.79, Phase margin = 53.892, Damping ratio = 0.59, Percent overshoot = 10.0693, Settling time = 0.804303, Peak time = 0.461606

The step response is shown in Fig. E3.13(b)

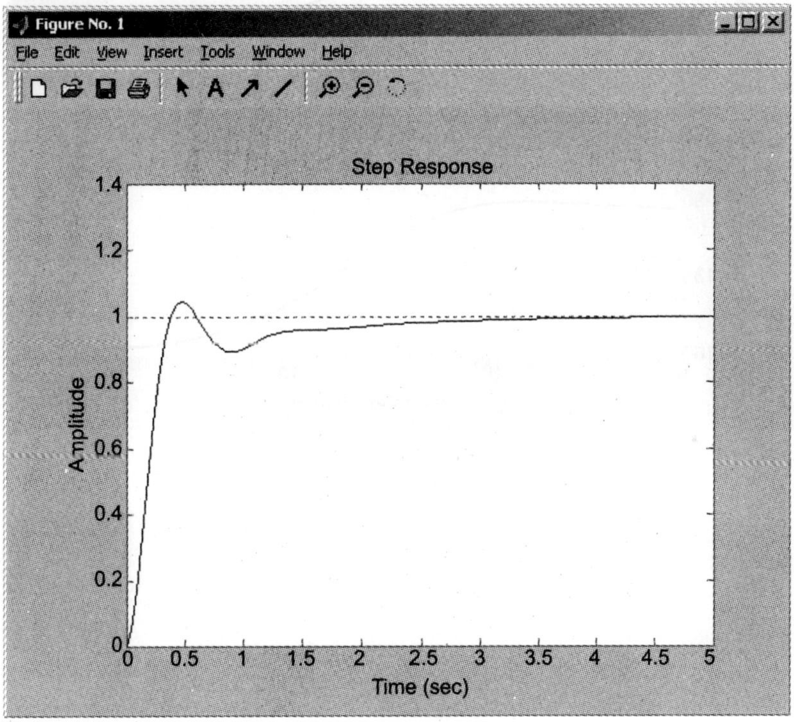

Fig. E3.13 (b)

(*b*) Likewise, for this problem

    >> G = zpk ([–1 –7], [0 –2 –4 –8], 25)

    >> G = tf (G)

The following Bode plot and step response are obtained [see Figs. E3.13(c) and (d)].

Zero/pole/gain:

$$\frac{25(s+1)(s+7)}{s(s+2)(s+4)(s+8)}$$

Transfer function:

$$\frac{25s\text{^}2+200s+175}{s\text{^}4+14s\text{^}3+56s\text{^}2+64s}$$

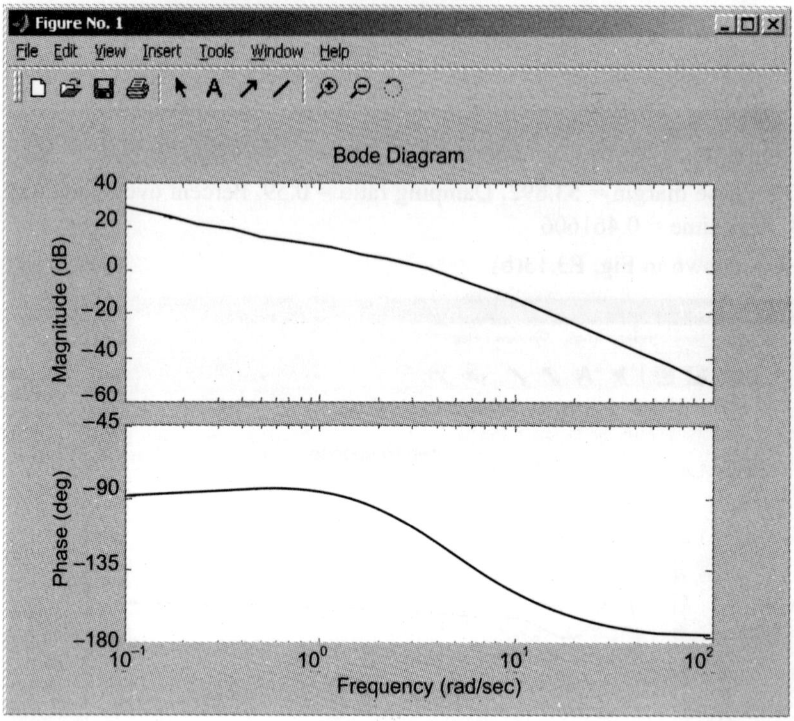

Fig. E3.13(c)

ans =

Mag

ans =

  −7.0110

ans =

BW

wBW =

  6.5500

Bandwidth = 6.55, Phase margin = 63.1105, Damping ratio = 0.67, Per cent overshoot = 5.86969, Settling time = 0.959175, Peak time = 0.679904

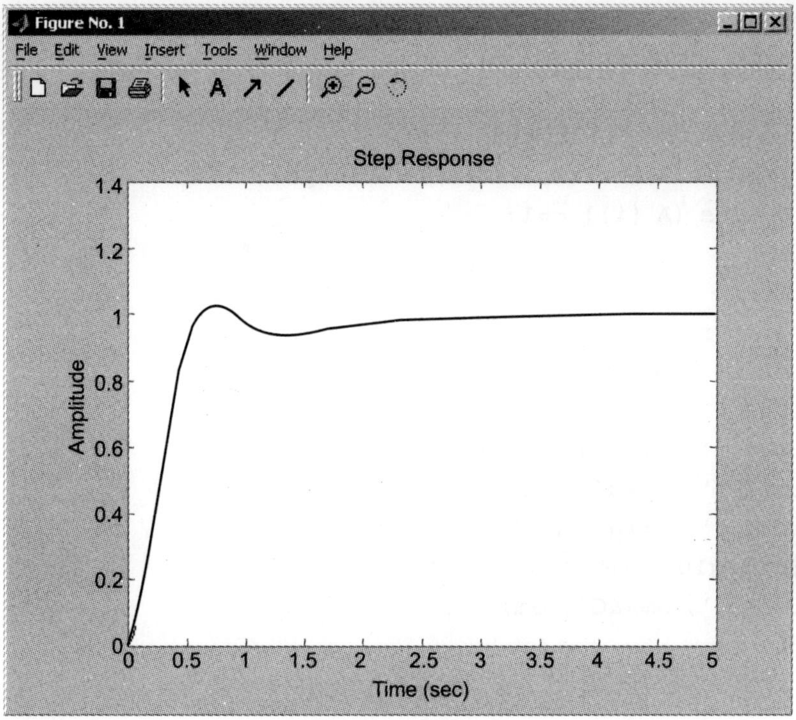

Fig. E3.13 (d)

Example E3.14: Write a program in MATLAB for a unity-feedback system with

$$G(s) = \frac{K(s+7)}{(s^2+3s+52)(s^2+2s+35)}$$

(*a*) plot the Nyquist diagram

(*b*) display the real-axis crossing value and frequency.

Solution:

```
>> %MATLAB Program
>> numg= [1 7]
>> deng=conv ([1 3 52], [1 2 35]);
>> G=tf (numg, deng)
>> 'G(s)'
>> Gap=zpk (G)
>> inquest (G)
>> axis ([-3e-3, 4e-3,-5e-3, 5e-3])
```

```
>> w=0:0.1:100;
>> [re, im] =nyquis t (G, w);
>> for i=1:1: length (w)
>> M (i) =abs (re (i) +j*im (i));
>> A (i) =atan2 (im (i), re (i))*(180/pi);
>> if 180-abs (A (i)) <=1;
>> re (i);
>> im (i);
>> K=1/abs (re (i));
>> fprintf ('\nw =%g', w (i))
>> fprintf (', Re=%g', re (i))
>> fprintf (', Im =%g', im (i))
>> fprintf (', M=%g', M (i))
>> fprintf (', K=%g', K)
>> Gm=20*log10 (1/M (i));
>> fprintf (', Gm=&G', Gm)
>> break
>> end
>> end
```

Computer response:

numg =

    1   7

Transfer function:

$$\frac{s+7}{s^4+5s^3+93s^2+209s+1820}$$

ans =

G(s)

Zero/pole/gain:

$$\frac{(s+7)}{(s^2+2s+35)(s^2+3s+52)}$$

The Nyquist plot is shown in Fig. E3.14.

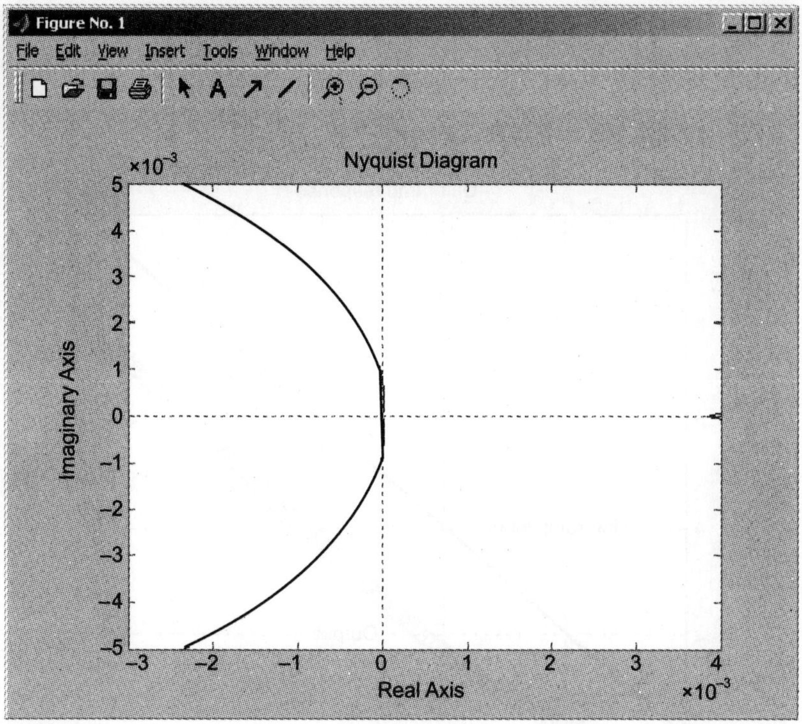

Fig. E3.14

Example E3.15: Determine the unit-ramp response of the following system using MATLAB and lsim command.

$$\frac{C(s)}{R(s)} = \frac{1}{3s^2 + 2s + 1}$$

Solution:

```
>> % MATLAB Program
>> % Unit-ramp response
>> num = [0 0 1];
>> den = [3 2 1];
>> t=0:0.1:10;
>> r=t;
>> y =lsim(num,den,r,t);
>> plot(t, r,'-', t,y, 'o')
>> grid
>> title('Unit-ramp response')
>> xlabel('t Sec')
>> ylabel('Unit-ramp input and output')
>> text(1.0, 4.0, 'Unit-ramp input')
>> text(5.0,2.0, 'Output')
```

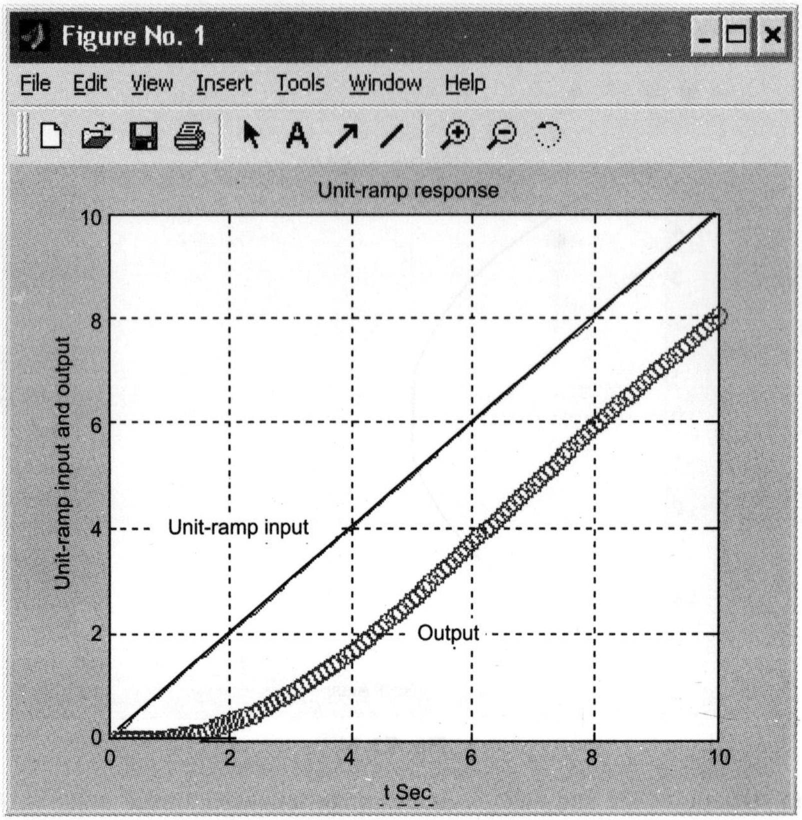

Fig. E3.15 Unit-ramp response

Example E3.16: A higher-order system is defined by

$$\frac{C(s)}{R(s)} = \frac{7s^2 + 16s + 10}{s^4 + 5s^3 + 11s^2 + 16s + 10}$$

(*a*) plot the unit-step response curve of the system using MATLAB

(*b*) obtain the rise time, peak time, maximum overshoot and settling time using MATLAB.

Solution:

```
>> %Unit-step response curve
>> num=[0 0 7 16 10];
>> den=[1 5 11 16 10];
>> t=0:0.02:20;
>> [y,x,t]=step(num,den,t);
>> plot(t, y)
>> grid
```

```
>> title('Unit-step response')
>> xlabel('t Sec')
>> ylabel('Output y(t)')
```

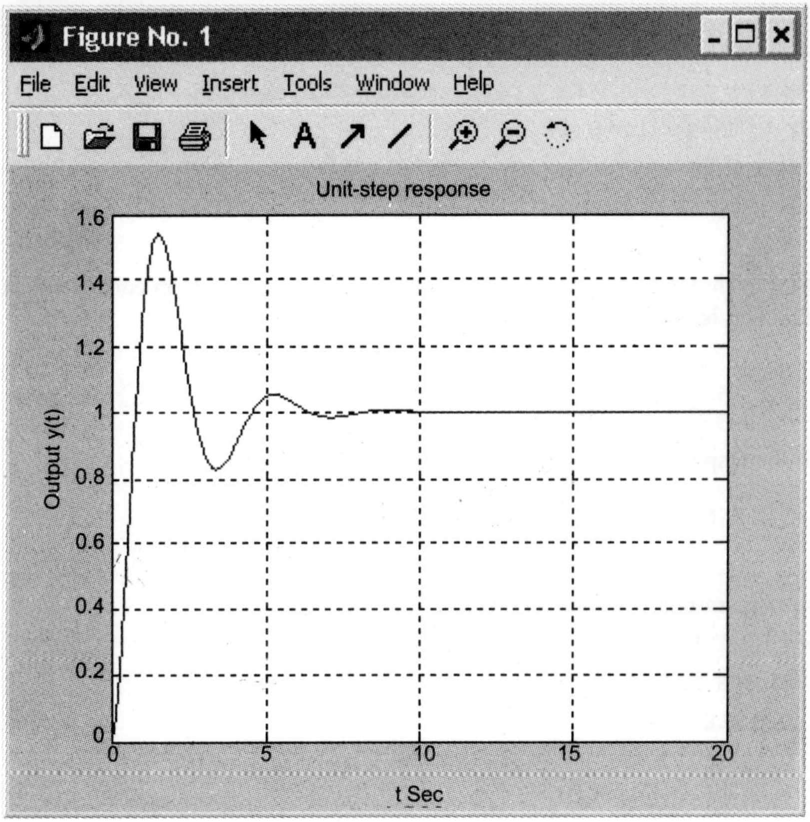

Fig. E3.16 Unit-step response

```
>> %Response to rise from 10% to 90% of its final value
>> r1=1;while y(r1)<0.1,r1=r1+1;end
>> r2=1;while y(r2)<0.9,r2=r2+1;end
>> rise_time=(r2-r1)*0.02

rise_time =
        0.5400
>> [ymax,tp]=max(y);
>> peak_time=(tp-1)*0.02
```

```
peak_time =
          1.5200
>> max_overshoot = ymax-1
max_overshoot =
          0.5397
>> s=1001;while y(s)>0.98 & y(s)<1.02;s=s-1;end
>> settling_time=(s-1)*0.02
settling_time =
          6.0200
```

Example E3.17: Obtain the unit-ramp response of the following closed-loop control system whose closed-loop transfer function is given by

$$\frac{C(s)}{R(s)} = \frac{s+12}{s^3+5s^2+8s+12}$$

Determine also the response of the system when the input is given by

$$r = e^{-0.7t}$$

Solution:

```
>> % Unit-ramp response – lsim command
>> num= [0 0 1 12];
>> den= [1 5 8 12];
>> t=0:0.1:10;
>> r=t;
>> y=lsim(num,den,r,t);
>> plot (t,r, '-', t,y, 'o')
>> grid
>> title('Unit-ramp response')
>> xlabel('t Sec')
>> ylabel('Output')
>> text(3.0,6.5, 'Unit-ramp input')
>> text(6.2,4.5, 'Output')
```

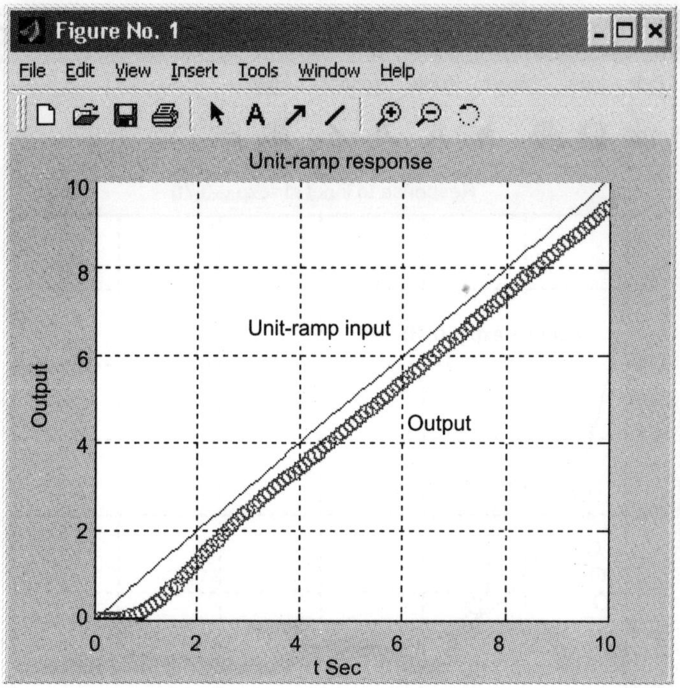

Fig. E3.17(a) Unit-ramp response curve

```
>> %Input r1=exp(-0.7t)
>> num=[0 0 1 12];
>> den=[1 5 8 12];
>> t=0:0.1:12;
>> r1=exp(-0.7*t);
>> y1=lsim(num,den,r1,t);
>> plot(t,r1, '-', t,y1, 'o')
>> grid
>> title('Response to input r1=exp(-0.7t)')
>> xlabel('t Sec')
>> ylabel('Input and output')
>> text(0.5,0.9, 'Input r1=exp(-0.7t)')
>> text(6.3,0.1, 'Output')
```

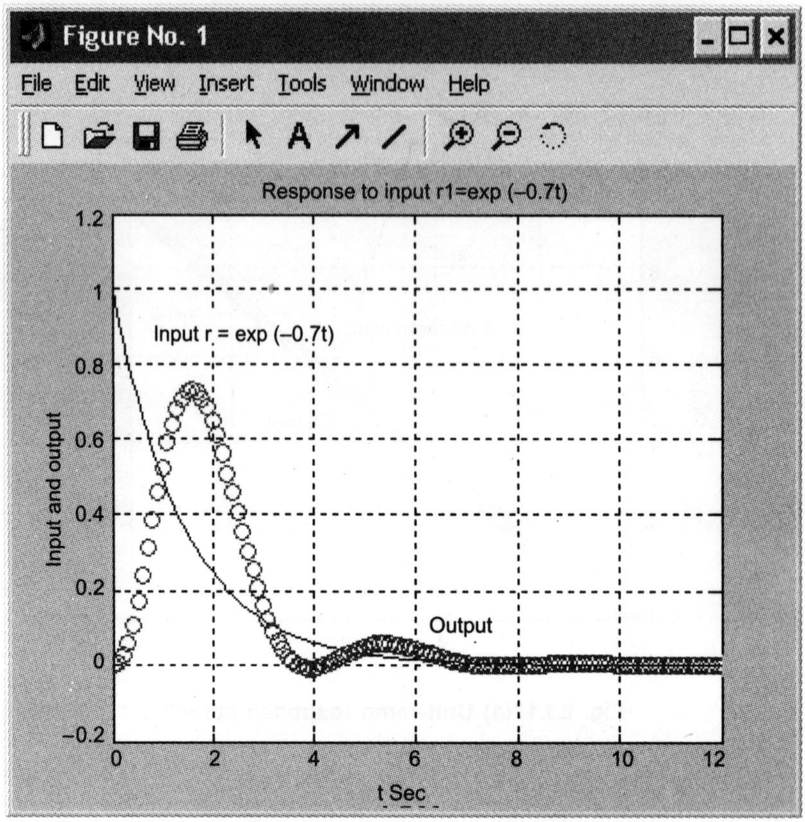

Fig. E3.17(b) Response curve for input r= $e^{-0.7t}$

Example E3.18: A unity-feedback control system is defined by the following feedforward transfer function

$$G(s) = \frac{K}{s(s^2+7s+9)}$$

(*a*) determine the location of the closed-loop poles, if the value of gain is equal to 3

(*b*) plot the root loci for the system using MATLAB.

Solution:

```
>> % MATLAB Program to find the closed-loop poles
>> p=[1 7 9 3];
>> roots(p)
ans =
      -5.4495
      -1.0000
      -0.5505
```

```
>> % MATLAB Program to plot the root-loci
>> num=[0 0 0 1];
>> den=[1 5 9 0];
>> rlocus(num,den);
>> axis('square')
>> grid
>> title('Root-locus plot of G(s)')
```

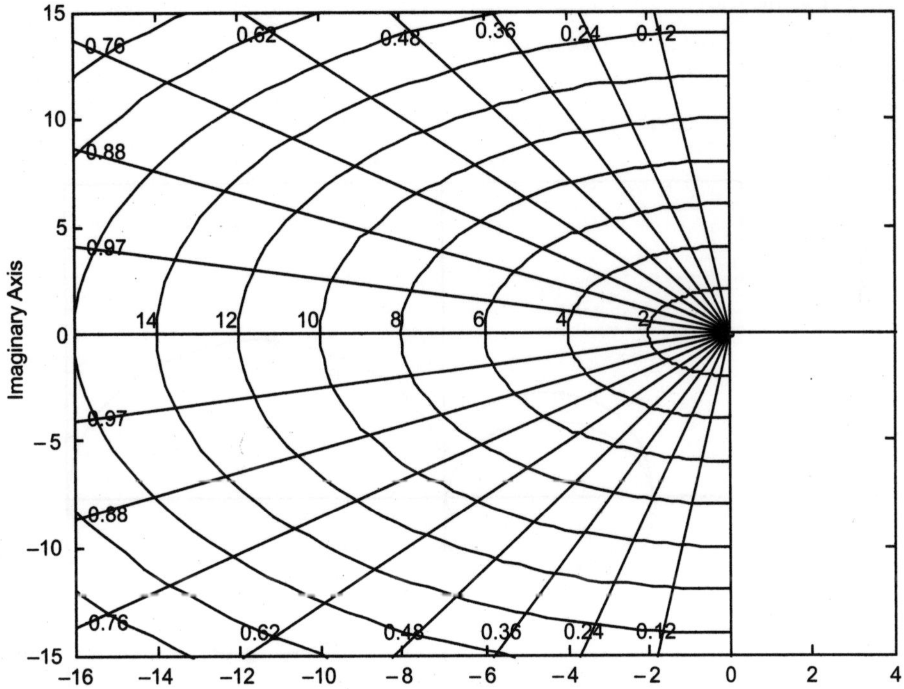

Fig. E3.18 Root-locus plot of G(s)

Example E3.19: The open-loop transfer function of a unity-feedback control system is given by

$$G(s) = \frac{1}{s^3 + 0.4s^2 + 7s + 1}$$

(*a*) draw a Nyquist plot of G(s) using MATLAB

(*b*) determine the stability of the system.

Solution:

```
>> % Open-loop poles
>> p =[1 0.4 7 1];
>> roots(p)
```

```
ans =
      -0.1282 + 2.6357i
      -0.1282 - 2.6357i
      -0.1436
>> % Nyquist plot
>> num = [0 0 0 1];
>> den = [1 0.4 7 1];
>> nyquist(num,den)
>> v=[-3 3 -2 2];axis(v);axis('square')
>> grid
>> title('Nyquist plot of G(s)')
```

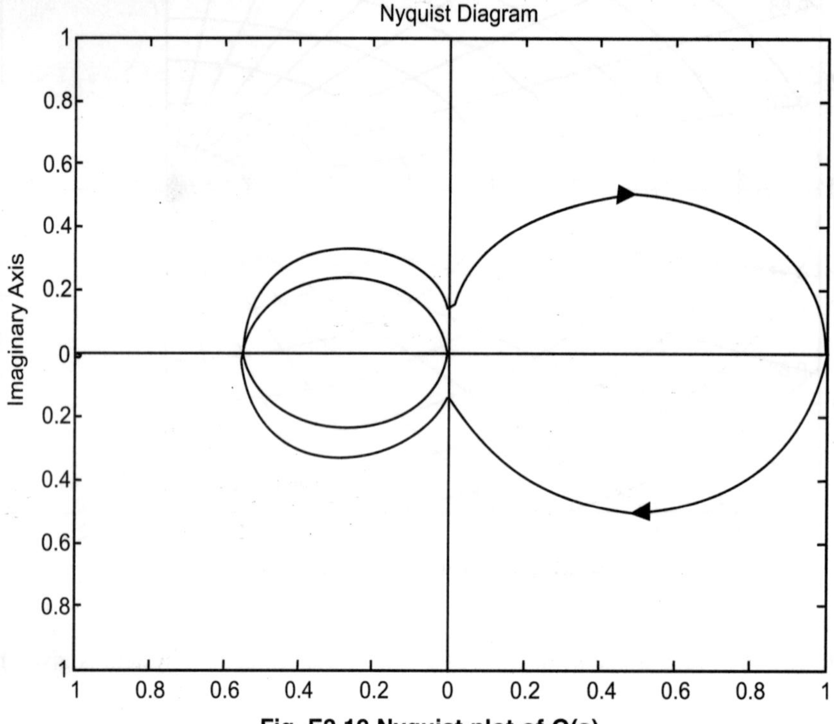

Fig. E3.19 Nyquist plot of G(s)

There are two open-loop poles in the right half *s* plane and no encirclement of the critical point, the closed-loop system is unstable.

Example E3.20: For the closed-loop control system shown in Fig. E3.20, obtain the range of gain *K* for stability and plot a root-locus diagram for the system.

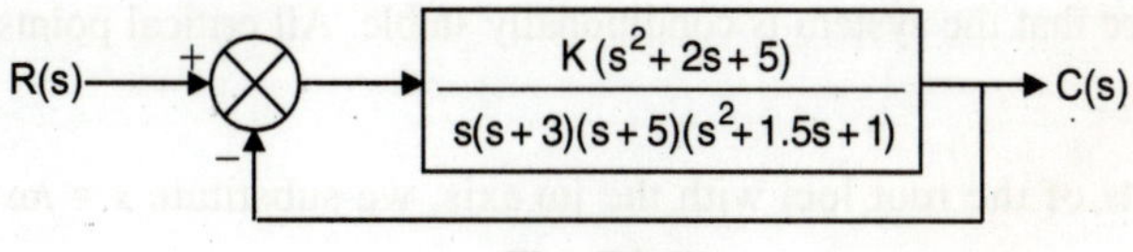

Fig. E3.20

Solution:

The range of gain K for stability is obtained by first plotting the root loci and then finding critical points (for stability) on the root loci. The open-loop transfer function $G(s)$ is

$$G(s) = \frac{K(s^2+2s+5)}{s(s+3)(s+5)(s^2+1.5s+1)}$$

$$= \frac{K(s^2+2s+5)}{s^5+9.5s^4+28s^3+20s^2+15s}$$

A MATLAB program to generate a plot of the root loci for the system is given below. The resulting root-locus plot is shown in Fig. E3.20(a).

% MATLAB Program

```
num = [0  0    0 1 2 5];
den = [1  9.5  28 20 15 0];
rlocus(num,den)
v = [-8  2    -5 5]; axis(v); axis('square')
grid
title('Root-Locus Plot')
```

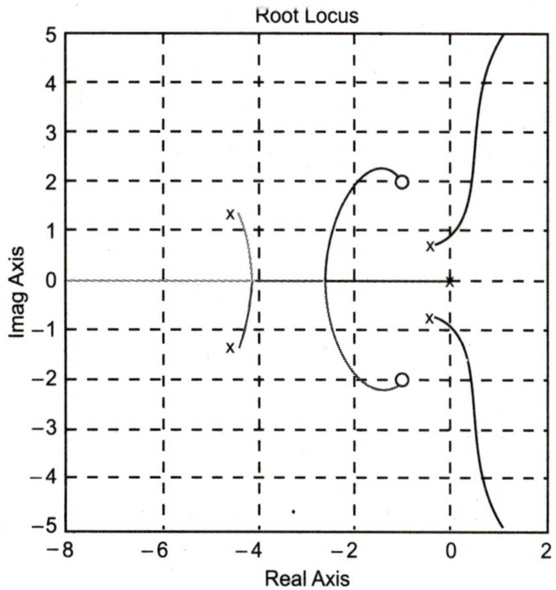

Fig. E3.20 (a)

From Fig. E3.20(a), we notice that the system is conditionally stable. All critical points for stability lie on the $j\omega$ axis.

To obtain the crossing points of the root loci with the jω axis, we substitute $s = j\omega$ into the characteristic equation

$$s^5 + 9.5s^4 + 28s^3 + 20s^2 + 15s + K(s^2 + 2s + 5) = 0$$

or $(j\omega)^5 + 9.5(j\omega)^4 + 28(j\omega)^3 + (20 + K)(j\omega)^2 + (15 + 2K)(j\omega) + 5K = 0$

or

$$[9.5\omega^4 - (20 + K)\omega^2 + 5K] + j[\omega^5 - 28\omega^3 + (15 + 2K)\omega] = 0$$

Equating the real part and imaginary part equal to zero, respectively, we get

$$9.5\omega^4 - (20 + K)\omega^2 + 5K = 0 \quad ...(1)$$

$$\omega^5 - 28\omega^3 + (15 + 2K)\omega = 0 \quad ...(2)$$

Equation (2) can be written as

$$\omega = 0$$

or $$\omega^4 - 28\omega^2 + 15 + 2K = 0 \quad ...(3)$$

$$K = \frac{-\omega^4 + 28\omega^2 - 15}{2} \quad ...(4)$$

Substituting Eq.(4) into Eq.(1), we obtain

$$9.5\omega^4 - [20 + \tfrac{1}{2}(-\omega^4 + 28\omega^2 - 15)]\,\omega^2 - 2.5\omega^4 + 70\omega^2 - 37.5 = 0$$

or

$$0.5\omega^6 - 2\omega^4 + 57.5\omega^2 - 37.5 = 0$$

The roots of the above equation can be obtained by MATLAB program given below.

% MATLAB Program

```
a = [0.5 0 - 2  0  57.5  0  -37.5];
roots(a)
```

MATLAB Output:

```
ans =
    -2.4786 + 2.1157i
    -2.4786 - 2.1157i
     2.4786 + 2.1157i
     2.4786 - 2.1157i
     0.8155
    -0.8155
```

The root-locus branch in the upper half plane that goes to infinity crosses the jω axis at ω = 0.8155. The gain values at these crossing points are given by

$$K = \frac{-0.8155^4 + 28\times 0.8155^2 - 15}{2} = 1.5894 \quad \text{for} \quad \omega = 0.8155$$

For this K value, we obtain the range of gain K for stability as

$$1.5894 > K > 0$$

Example E3.21: For the control system shown in Fig. E3.21:

(*a*) plot the root loci for the system
(*b*) find the value of K such that the damping ratio ζ of the dominant closed-loop poles is 0.6
(*c*) obtain all closed-loop poles
(*d*) plot the unit-step respond curve using MATLAB.

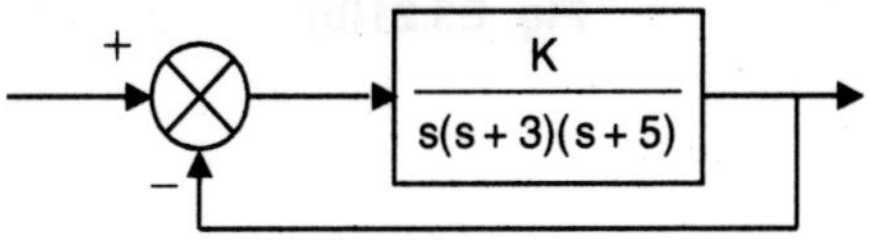

Fig. E3.21

Solution:

(*a*) The MATLAB program given below generates a root-locus plot for the given system. The resulting plot is shown in Fig. E3.21(a).

```
% MATLAB Program
num = [0    0   0  1];
den = [1    8  15  0];
rlocus(num,den)
v = [-6   4  -5   5]; axis(v); axis('square')
grid
title('Root-Locus Plot')
```

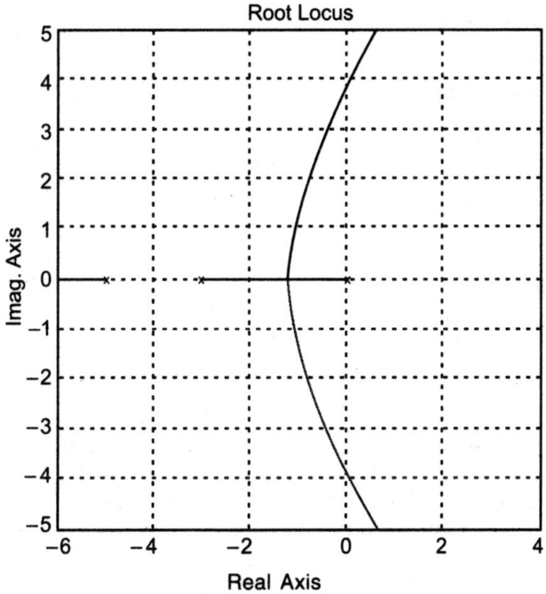

Fig. E3.21(a)

(*b*) We note that the constant ζ points $(0 < \zeta < 1)$ lie on a straight line having angle θ from the $j\omega$ axis as shown in Fig. E3.21(b).

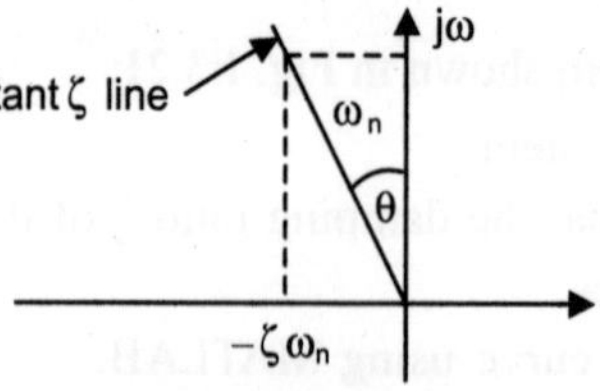

Fig. E3.21(b)

From Fig. E3.21(b), we obtain

$$\sin\theta = \frac{\zeta\omega_n}{\omega_n} = \zeta$$

Also that $\zeta = 0.6$ line can be defined by

$$s = -0.75a + ja$$

where a is a variable $(0 < a < \infty)$. To obtain the value of K such that the damping ratio ζ of the dominant closed-loop poles is 0.6, we determine the intersection of the line $s = -0.75a + ja$ and the root locus. The intersection point can be obtained by solving the following simultaneous equations for a.

$$s = -0.75a + ja \qquad \text{...(1)}$$

$$s(s+3)(s+5) + K = 0 \qquad \text{...(2)}$$

From Eqs. (1) and (2), we obtain

$$(-0.75a + ja)(-0.75a + ja + 3)(-0.75a + ja + 5) + K = 0$$

or

$$(1.8281a^3 - 2.1875a^2 - 3a + K) + j(0.6875a^3 - 7.5a^2 + 15a) = 0$$

Equating the real part and imaginary part of the above equation to zero, respectively, we obtain

$$1.8281a^3 - 2.1875a^2 - 3a + K = 0 \qquad \text{...(3)}$$

$$0.6875a^3 - 7.5a^2 + 4a = 0 \qquad \text{...(4)}$$

Equation (4) can be rewritten as

$$a = 0$$

or

$$0.6875a^2 - 7.5a + 4 = 0$$

or

$$a^2 - 10.90991a + 5.8182 = 0$$

or

$$(a - 0.5623)(a - 10.3468) = 0$$

Therefore, $a = 0.5323$ or $a = 10.3468$

From Eq.(3), we obtain

$$K = -1.8281a^3 + 2.1875a^2 + 3a = 2.0535 \quad \text{for } a = 0.5626$$

$$K = -1.8281a^3 + 2.1875a^2 + 3a = -1759.74 \text{ for } a = 10.3468$$

Since the K value is positive for $a = 0.5623$ and negative for $a = -10.3468$, we select $a = 0.5623$. The required gain K is 2.0535.

The characteristic equation with $K = 2.0535$ is then

$$s(s + 3)(s + 5) + 2.0535 = 0$$

or

$$s^3 + 8s^2 + 15s + 2.0535 = 0$$

(*c*) The closed-loop poles can be obtained by the following MATLAB program.

```
% MATLAB Program
p = [1 8  15  2.0535];
roots(p)
ans =
      -5.1817
      -2.6699
      -0.1484
Hence, the closed-loop poles are located at
      s = -5.1817, s=-2.6699, s = -4.1565.
```

(*d*) The unit-step response of the system for K = 2.0535 can be obtained from the following MATLAB program. The resulting unit-step response curve is shown in Fig. E3.21(c).

```
% MATLAB Program
num = [0    0     0    2.0535];
den = [1    8    15    2.0535];
step(num,den)
grid
title('Unit-Step Response')
xlabel('t Sec')
ylabel('Output').
```

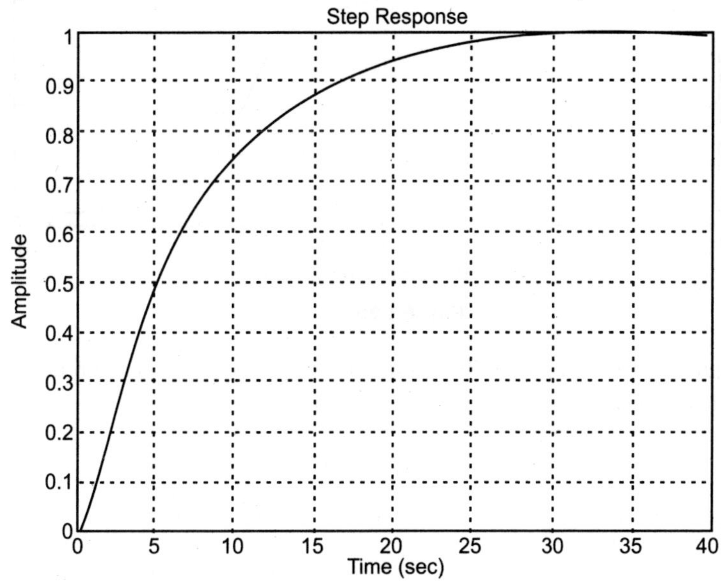

Fig. E3.21 (c)

Example E3.22: The open-loop transfer function of a unity-feedback control system is given by

$$G(s) = \frac{K}{s(s^2 + s + 5)}$$

(*a*) determine the value of gain *K* such that the phase margin is 50°

(*b*) find the gain margin for the gain *K* obtained in (*a*).

Solution:

$$G(s) = \frac{K}{s(s^2 + s + 5)}$$

The undamped natural frequency is $\sqrt{5}$ rad/s and the damping ratio of $0.1.\sqrt{5}$ from the denominator. Let the frequency corresponding to the angle of –130° (Phase Margin of 50°) be ω_1 and therefore

$$\angle G(j\omega_1) = -130^\circ$$

The Bode diagram is shown in Fig. E3.22 from MATLAB program.

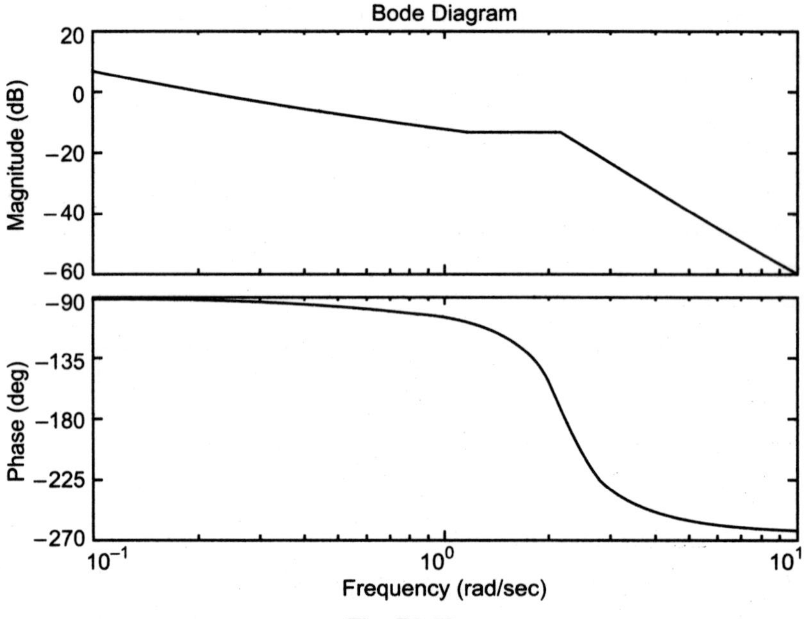

Fig. E3.22

From Fig. E3.22, the required phase margin of 50° and occurs at the frequency ω =1.06 rad/s. The magnitude of $G(j\omega)$ at this frequency is then –7 dB. The gain *K* must then satisfy

$$20\log K = 7 \text{ dB}$$

or $$K = 2.23$$

Example E3.23: Obtain the state-space representation of the following system using MATLAB.

$$\frac{C(s)}{R(s)} = \frac{35s + 7}{s^3 + 5s^2 + 36s + 7}.$$

Solution:

A MATLAB program to obtain a state-space representation of this system is given below.

% MATLAB Program

```
>> num=[0 0 35 7];
>> den=[1 5 36 7];
>> g=tf(num,den)

Transfer function:
```

$$\frac{35s+7}{s\hat{}3+5s\hat{}2+36s+7}$$

```
>> [A,B,C,D]=tf2ss(num,den)
A =
    -5 -36  -7
     1   0   0
     0   1   0
B =
     1
     0
     0
C =
     0  35   7
D =
     0
```

From the MATLAB output, we obtain the following state space equations:

$$\begin{bmatrix} \dot{x}_1 \\ \dot{x}_2 \\ \dot{x}_3 \end{bmatrix} = \begin{bmatrix} -5 & -36 & -7 \\ 1 & 0 & 0 \\ 0 & 1 & 0 \end{bmatrix} \begin{bmatrix} x_1 \\ x_2 \\ x_3 \end{bmatrix} + \begin{bmatrix} 1 \\ 0 \\ 0 \end{bmatrix} u$$

$$y = [0 \ \ 7] \begin{bmatrix} x_1 \\ x_2 \\ x_3 \end{bmatrix} + [0]u$$

Example E3.24: Find the transfer function for the following system using MATLAB.

$$\begin{bmatrix} \dot{x}_1 \\ \dot{x}_2 \\ \dot{x}_3 \end{bmatrix} = \begin{bmatrix} 0 & 1 & 0 \\ -5 & -2 & 0 \\ 0 & 2 & -6 \end{bmatrix} \begin{bmatrix} x_1 \\ x_2 \\ x_3 \end{bmatrix} + \begin{bmatrix} 0 & 0 \\ 3 & -1 \\ 5 & 0 \end{bmatrix} u$$

$$y = \begin{bmatrix} 1 & 0 & 0 \\ 0 & 0 & 1 \end{bmatrix} \begin{bmatrix} x_1 \\ x_2 \\ x_3 \end{bmatrix}$$

Solution:

The transfer function matrix is given by

$$G(s) = C[sI - A]^{-1} B$$

where
$$A = \begin{bmatrix} 0 & 1 & 0 \\ -5 & -2 & 0 \\ 0 & 2 & -6 \end{bmatrix} \quad B = \begin{bmatrix} 0 & 0 \\ 3 & -1 \\ 5 & 0 \end{bmatrix} \quad C = \begin{bmatrix} 1 & 0 & 0 \\ 0 & 0 & 1 \end{bmatrix}$$

Hence
$$G(s) = \begin{bmatrix} 1 & 0 & 0 \\ 0 & 0 & 1 \end{bmatrix} \begin{bmatrix} s & -1 & 0 \\ 5 & s+2 & 0 \\ 0 & -2 & s+6 \end{bmatrix} \begin{bmatrix} 0 & 0 \\ 3 & -1 \\ 5 & 0 \end{bmatrix}$$

```
>> % MATLAB Program
>> syms s
>> C=[1 0 0;0 0 1];
>> M=[s -1 0;5 s +2 0; 0 -2 s+6];
>> B=[0 0;3 -1;5 0];
>> C*inv(M)*B

ans =
     [3/(s^2+2*s+5), -1/(s^2+2*s+5)]
     [6*s/(s^3+8*s^2+17*s+30)+5/(s+6),  -2*s/(s^3+8*s^2+17*s+30)]
```

Example E3.25: Determine the transfer function $G(s) = Y(s)/R(s)$, for the following system representation in state space form.

$$\dot{x} = \begin{bmatrix} 0 & 3 & 7 & 0 \\ 0 & 0 & 1 & 0 \\ 0 & 0 & 0 & 1 \\ -5 & -6 & 9 & 5 \end{bmatrix} x + \begin{bmatrix} 0 \\ 5 \\ 7 \\ 2 \end{bmatrix} r$$

$$y = [1\ 3\ 6\ 5]\, x$$

Solution:

```
    A=[0 3 5 0;0 0 1 0;0 0 0 1;-5 -6 8 5];
    B=[0;5;7;2];
    C=[1 3 7 5];
    D=0;
    statespace=ss(A,B,C,D)
a =
         x1  x2  x3   x4
    x1   0    3   5    0
    x2   0    0   1    0
    x3   0    0   0    1
    x4  -5   -6   8    5
b =
         u1
    x1   0
    x2   5
    x3   7
    x4   2
c =
         x1  x2  x3   x4
    y1   1    3   7    5
d =
         u1
    y1   0

Continuous-time model.

[A,B,C,D]=tf 2ss(num,den);
G=tf(num,den)
```

Transfer function:

$$\frac{s^4+3s^3+10s^2+5s+6}{s^5+7s^4+8s^3+6s^2}.$$

Example E3.26: Determine the transfer function and poles of the system represented in state space as follows using MATLAB.

$$\dot{x}=\begin{bmatrix} 9 & -3 & -1 \\ -3 & 2 & 0 \\ 6 & 8 & -2 \end{bmatrix}+\begin{bmatrix} 1 \\ 2 \\ 3 \end{bmatrix}u(t)$$

$$y = [2 \quad 9 \quad -12]\,x\,;\; x(0) = \begin{bmatrix} 0 \\ 0 \\ 0 \end{bmatrix}$$

Solution:

% MATLAB Program

```
>> A = [8 -3 4;-7 1 0;3 4 -7]
A =
      8  -3    4
     -7   1    0
      3   4   -7
>> B=[1;3;8]
B =
      1
      3
      8
>> C=[1  7  -2]
C =
      1   7  -2
>> D=0
D =
      0
>> [numg,deng]=ss2tf(A,B,C,D,1)
numg =
     1.0e + 003 *
     0           0.0060      0.0730   -2.8770
deng =
     1.0000   -2.0000    -88.0000    33.0000
>> G=tf(numg,deng)
```

Transfer function:

```
        6s^2 + 73s - 2877
      ---------------------
      s^3 - 2s^2 - 88s + 33
```

```
>> poles=roots(deng)
poles  =
         10.2620
         -8.6344
          0.3724
```

Example E3.27: A control system is defined by

$$\begin{bmatrix} \dot{x}_1 \\ \dot{x}_2 \end{bmatrix} = \begin{bmatrix} 0 & 1 \\ -25 & -9 \end{bmatrix} \begin{bmatrix} x_1 \\ x_2 \end{bmatrix} + \begin{bmatrix} 1 & 1 \\ 0 & 1 \end{bmatrix} \begin{bmatrix} u_1 \\ u_2 \end{bmatrix}$$

$$\begin{bmatrix} y_1 \\ y_2 \end{bmatrix} = \begin{bmatrix} 1 & 0 \\ 0 & 1 \end{bmatrix} \begin{bmatrix} x_1 \\ x_2 \end{bmatrix}$$

Plot the four sets of Bode diagrams f or the system [two for input1, and two for input 2] using MATLAB.

Solution: There are 4 sets of Bode diagrams (2 for input1 and 2 for input 2)

```
>> % Bode Diagrams
>> A=[0 1;-25 -9];
>> B=[1 1;0 1];
>> C=[1 0;0 1];
>> D=[0 0;0 0];
>> bode(A,B,C,D)
```

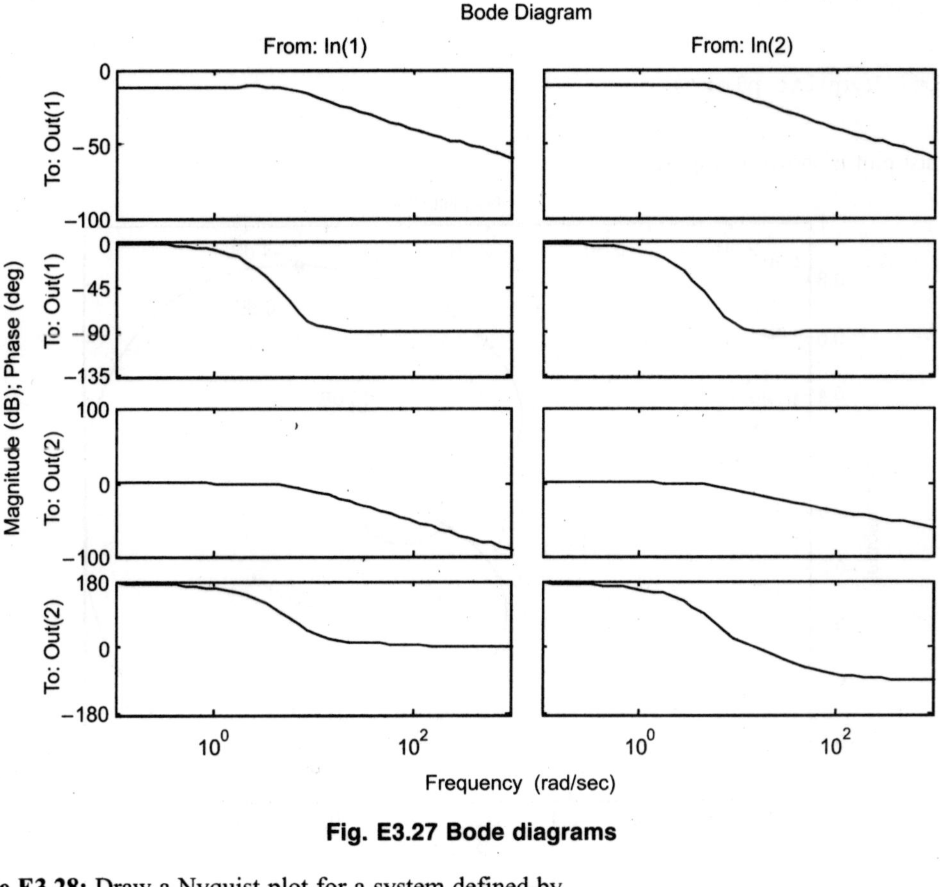

Fig. E3.27 Bode diagrams

Example E3.28: Draw a Nyquist plot for a system defined by

$$\begin{bmatrix} \dot{x}_1 \\ \dot{x}_2 \end{bmatrix} = \begin{bmatrix} 0 & 1 \\ -25 & 5 \end{bmatrix} \begin{bmatrix} x_1 \\ x_2 \end{bmatrix} + \begin{bmatrix} 0 \\ 20 \end{bmatrix} u$$

$$y = [1 \quad 0]\begin{bmatrix} x_1 \\ x_2 \end{bmatrix} + [0]u$$

using MATLAB.

Solution: Since the system has a single input *u* and a single output *y*, a Nyquist plot can be obtained by using the command nyquist (*A*, *B*, *C*, *D*) or nyquist (*A*, *B*, *C*, *D*, 1).

```
>> % MATLAB Program
>> A=[0 1;-25 5];
>> B=[0;20];
>> C=[1 0];
>> D=[0];
>> nyquist(A,B,C,D)
>> grid
>> title('Nyquist plot')
```

The Nyquist plot is shown in Figure E3.28.

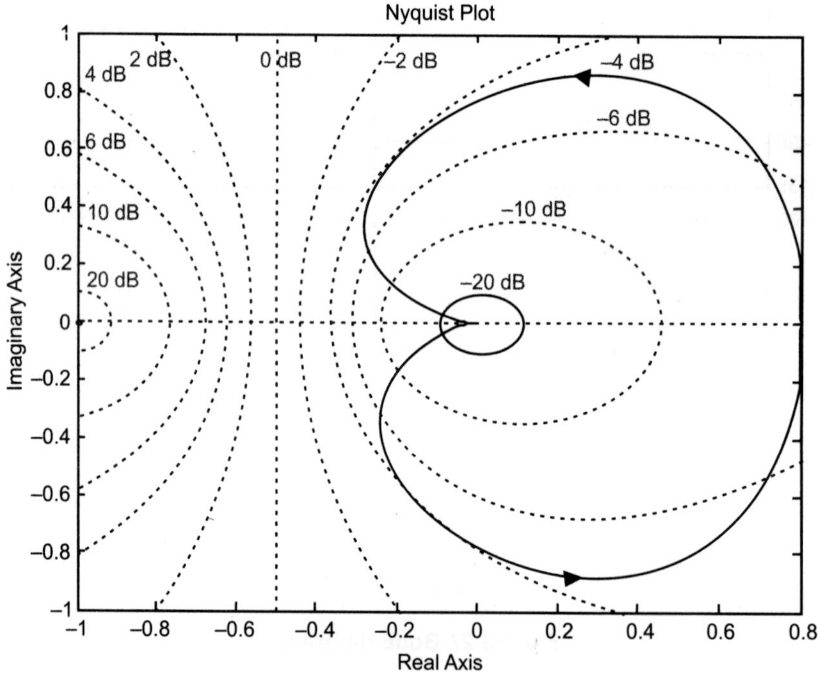

Fig. E3.28 Nyquist plot

Example E3.29: Obtain the unit-step response, unit-ramp response, and unit-impulse response of the following system using MATLAB.

$$\begin{bmatrix} \dot{x}_1 \\ \dot{x}_2 \end{bmatrix} = \begin{bmatrix} -1 & -1.5 \\ 2 & 0 \end{bmatrix} \begin{bmatrix} x_1 \\ x_2 \end{bmatrix} + \begin{bmatrix} 1.5 \\ 0 \end{bmatrix} u$$

$$y = \begin{bmatrix} 1 & 0 \end{bmatrix} \begin{bmatrix} x_1 \\ x_2 \end{bmatrix}$$

where u is the input and y is the output.

Solution:

```
>> % Unit-step response
>> A=[-1 -1.5;2 0];
>> B=[1.5;0];
>> C=[1 0];
>> D=[0];
>> y,x,t]=step(A,B,C,D);
>> plot(t,y)
>> grid
>> title('Unit-step response')
>> xlabel('t Sec')
>> ylabel('Output')
```

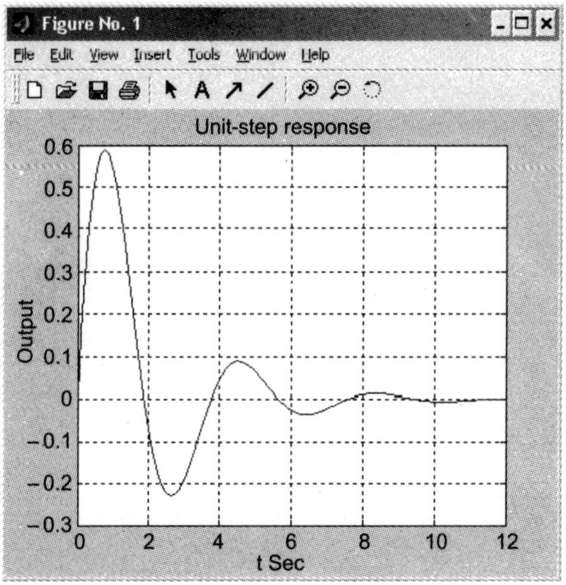

Fig. E3.29 (a) Unit-step response

```
>> % Unit-ramp response
>> A=[-1 -1.5; 2 0];
>> B=[1.5; 0];
```

```
>> C=[1 0];
>> D=[0];
>> % New enlarged state and output equations
>> AA=[A zeros (2, 1); C 0];
>> BB=[B; 0];
>> CC=[0 1];
>> DD=[0];
>> [z, x, t] =step (AA, BB, CC, DD);
>> x3= [0 0 1]*x'; plot (t, x3, t, t,'-')
>> grid
>> title ('Unit-ramp response')
>> xlabel ('t Sec')
>> ylabel ('Output and unit-ramp input')
>> text (12, 1.2,'Output')
```

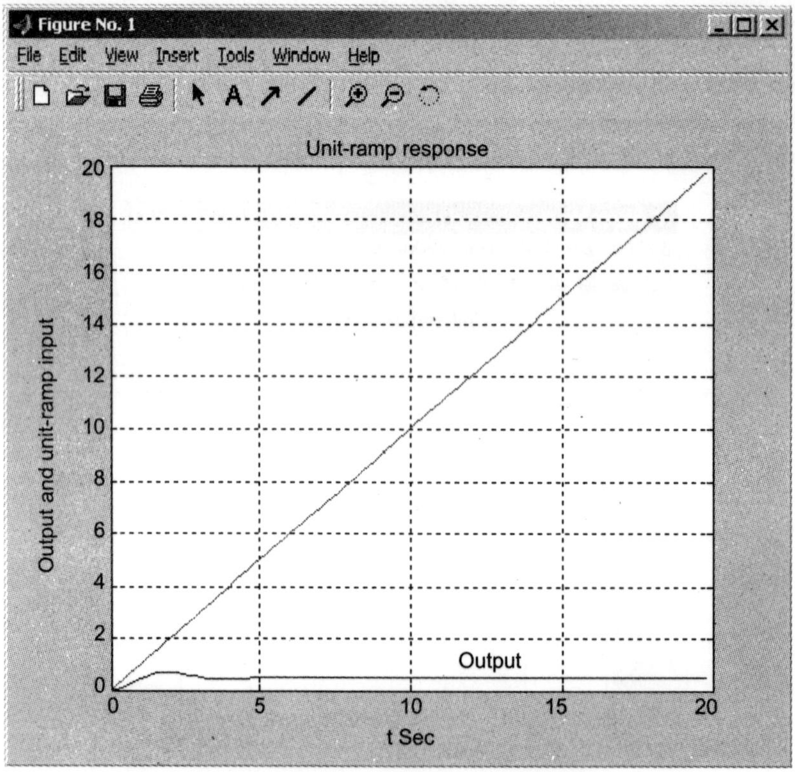

Fig. E3.29 (b) Unit-ramp response

```
>> % Unit-impulse response
>> A= [-1 -1.5; 2 0];
>> B= [1.5; 0];
```

```
>> C= [1 0];
>> D= [0];
>> impulse (A, B, C, D)
```

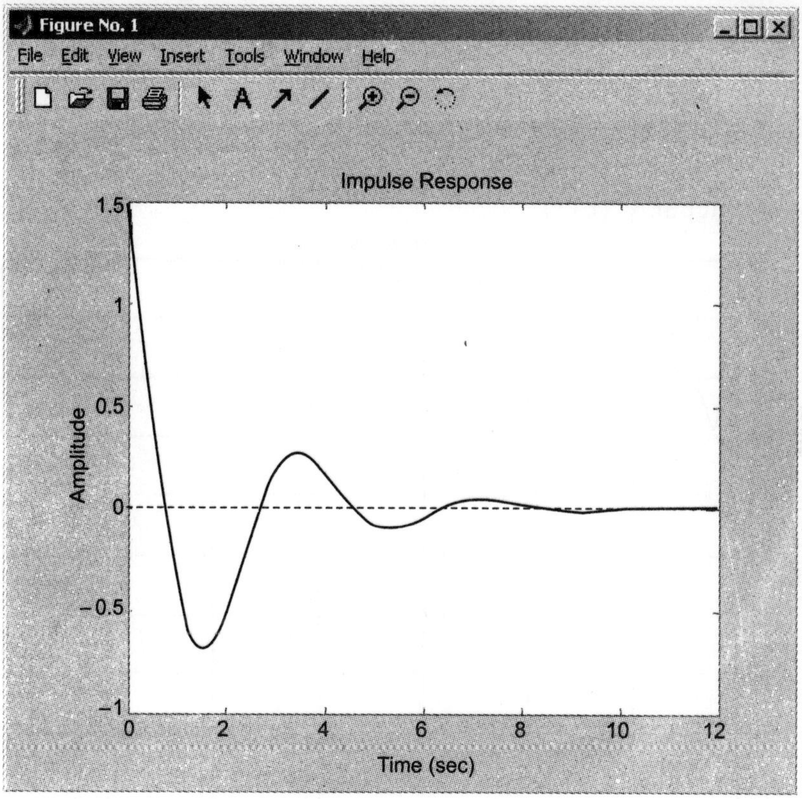

Fig. E3.29(c) Unit-impulse response

Example E3.30: Obtain the unit-step response and unit-ramp response of the following system using MATLAB.

$$\begin{bmatrix} \dot{x}_1 \\ \dot{x}_2 \\ \dot{x}_3 \end{bmatrix} = \begin{bmatrix} -5 & -30 & -5 \\ 1 & 0 & 0 \\ 0 & 1 & 0 \end{bmatrix} \begin{bmatrix} x_1 \\ x_2 \\ x_3 \end{bmatrix} + \begin{bmatrix} 1 \\ 0 \\ 0 \end{bmatrix} u$$

$$y = \begin{bmatrix} 0 & 20 & 5 \end{bmatrix} \begin{bmatrix} x_1 \\ x_2 \\ x_3 \end{bmatrix} + [0]u$$

Solution:

```
>> % MATLAB Program
>> A=[-5 -30 -5; 1 0 0; 0 1 0];
```

```
>> B=[1; 0; 0];
>> C=[0 20 5];
>> D=[0];
>> [y, x, t]=step (A, B, C, D);
>> plot(t, y)
>> grid
>> title('Unit-response')
>> xlabel('t Sec')
>> ylabel('Output y (t)')
```

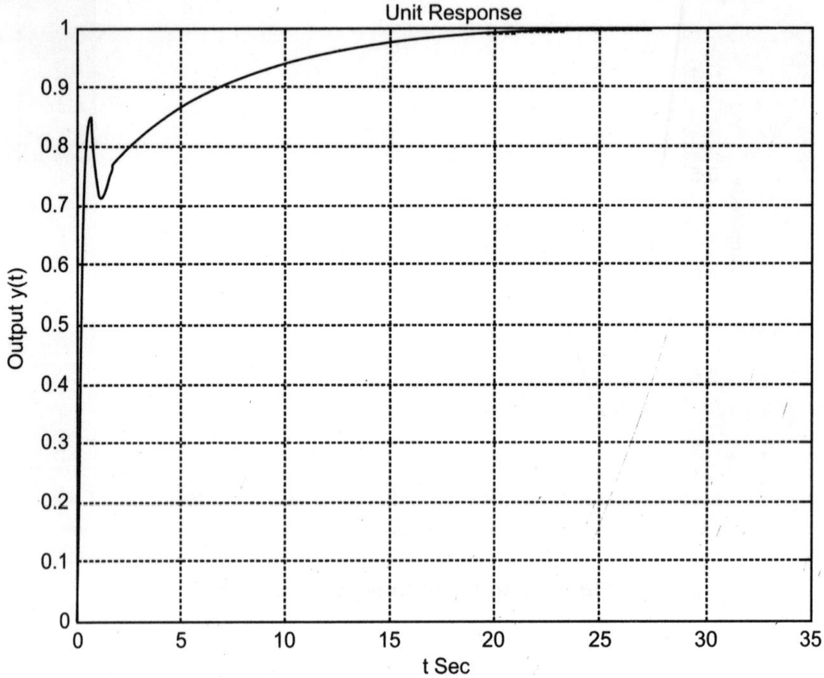

Fig. E3.30(a) Unit-step response

Unit-ramp response:

$$AA = \begin{bmatrix} -5 & -30 & -5 & 0 \\ 1 & 0 & 0 & 0 \\ 0 & 1 & 0 & 0 \\ 0 & 25 & 5 & 0 \end{bmatrix} = \begin{bmatrix} & & & 0 \\ & A & & 0 \\ & & & 0 \\ 0 & 25 & 5 & 0 \end{bmatrix} = A \text{ [zeros (2, 1); C 0]}$$

$$BB = \begin{bmatrix} 1 \\ 0 \\ 0 \\ 0 \end{bmatrix} = \begin{bmatrix} B \\ \\ 0 \end{bmatrix}$$

$$CC = \begin{bmatrix} 0 & 25 & 5 & 0 \end{bmatrix} = \begin{bmatrix} C & 0 \end{bmatrix}$$

```
>> % MATLAB Program
>> A =[-5 -30 -5; 1 0 0; 0 1 0];
>> B =[1; 0; 0];
>> C =[0 25 5];
>> D =[0];
>> AA =[A zeros (3, 1); C 0];
>> BB =[B; 0];
>> CC =[C 0];
>> DD =[0];
>> t=0:0.01:5;
>> [z, x, t] =step (AA, BB, CC, DD, 1, t);
>> P =[0 0 0 1]*x';
>> plot (t, P, t, t)
>> grid
>> title ('Unit-ramp response')
>> xlabel ('t Sec')
>> ylabel ('Input and output')
```

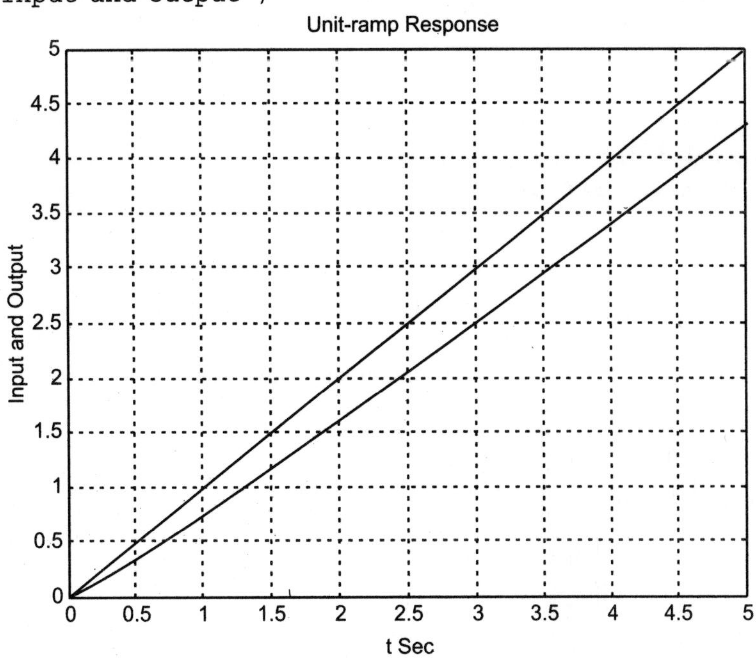

Fig. E3.30 (b) Unit-ramp response

Example E3.31: Consider the system

$$\begin{bmatrix} \dot{x}_1 \\ \dot{x}_2 \\ \dot{x}_3 \end{bmatrix} = \begin{bmatrix} 3 & 0 & 0 \\ 0 & 1 & 0 \\ 0 & 3 & 2 \end{bmatrix} \begin{bmatrix} x_1 \\ x_2 \\ x_3 \end{bmatrix}$$

The output is given by

$$y = \begin{bmatrix} 1 & 1 & 1 \end{bmatrix} \begin{bmatrix} x_1 \\ x_2 \\ x_3 \end{bmatrix}$$

(*a*) determine the observability of the system using MATLAB

(*b*) show that the system is completely observable if the output is given by

$$\begin{bmatrix} y_1 \\ y_2 \end{bmatrix} = \begin{bmatrix} 1 & 1 & 1 \\ 1 & 3 & 2 \end{bmatrix} \begin{bmatrix} x_1 \\ x_2 \\ x_3 \end{bmatrix}$$

using MATLAB.

Solution:

```
>> % MATLAB Program
>> A = [3 0 0; 0 1 0; 0 3 2];
>> C = [1 1 1];
>> rank ([C' A'*C' A'^2*C'])
ans =
    3
>> A= [3 0 0; 0 1 0; 0 3 2];
>> C= [1 1 1; 1 3 2];
>> rank ([C' A'*C' A'^2*C'])
ans =
    3
```

From the above, we observe that the system is observable and controllable.

Example E3.32: Consider the following state equation and output equation

$$\begin{bmatrix} \dot{x}_1 \\ \dot{x}_2 \\ \dot{x}_3 \end{bmatrix} = \begin{bmatrix} -1 & -3 & -2 \\ 0 & -2 & 1 \\ 1 & 0 & -1 \end{bmatrix} \begin{bmatrix} x_1 \\ x_2 \\ x_3 \end{bmatrix} + \begin{bmatrix} 3 \\ 0 \\ 1 \end{bmatrix} u$$

$$y = \begin{bmatrix} 1 & 1 & 0 \end{bmatrix} \begin{bmatrix} x_1 \\ x_2 \\ x_3 \end{bmatrix}$$

Determine if the system is completely state controllable and completely observable using MATLAB.

Solution:

The controllability and observability of the system can be obtained by examining the rank condition of

$$[B\ AB\ A^2B] \text{ and } [C'\ A'C'\ (A')^2\ C']$$

```
>> % MATLAB Program
>> A = [-1 -3 -2; 0 -2 1; 1 0 -1];
>> B = [3; 0; 1];
>> C = [1 1 0];
>> D = [0];
>> rank ([B A*B A^2*B])

ans=
    3
    >> rank ([C' A'*C' A'^2*C'])
ans=
    3
```

We observe the rank of [B AB A^2B] is 3 and the rank of **[C′ A′*C′ (A′) ^{2}*C′]** is 3, the system is completely statc controllable and observable.

Example E3.33: Determine the eigenvalues of the following system using MATLAB.

$$\dot{x} = \begin{bmatrix} 0 & 2 & 0 \\ 0 & 2 & -9 \\ -2 & 2 & 5 \end{bmatrix} x + \begin{bmatrix} 0 \\ 0 \\ 2 \end{bmatrix} r$$

$$y = [0 \quad 0 \quad 1]\, x$$

Solution:

```
>> A = [0 2 0; 0 2 -7; -2 2 5]; %Define the matrix above
>> eig (A) %Calculate the eigenvalues of matrix A.
ans =
    2.0000
    2.5000 + 3.4278i
    2.5000 - 3.4278i
```

REFERENCES

Anand, D.K., *Introduction to Control Systems,* 2nd ed., Pergamon Press, New York, NY, 1984.

Atkinson, P., *Feedback Control Theory for Engineers,* 2nd ed., Heinemann, 1977.

Bateson, R.N., *Introduction to Control System Technology*, Prentice-Hall, Upper Saddle River, NJ, 2002.

Bayliss, L.E., *Living Control Systems*, English Universities Press Limited, London, UK, 1966.

Beards, C.F., *Vibrations and Control System,* Ellis Horwood, 1988.

Benaroya, H., *Mechanical Vibration—Analysis, Uncertainties, and Control*, Prentice-Hall, Upper Saddle River, NJ, 1998.

Bode, H.W., *Network Analysis and Feedback Design*, Van Nostrand Reinhold, New York, NY, 1945.

Bolton, W., *Control Engineering*, 2nd ed., Addison Wesley Longman Ltd., Reading, MA, 1998.

Brogan, W.L., *Modern Control Theory*, Prentice-Hall, Upper Saddle River, NJ, 1985.

Buckley, R.V., *Control Engineering,* Macmillan, New York, NY, 1976.

Burghes, D., and Graham, A., *Introduction to Control Theory Including Optimal Control,* Ellis Horwood, 1980.

Cannon, R.H., *Dynamics of Physical Systems*, McGraw-Hill, New York, NY, 1967.

Chesmond, C.J., *Basic Control System Technology,* Edward Arnold, 1990.

Clark, R.N., *Introduction to Automatic Control Systems*, Wiley, New York, NY, 1962.

D'Azzo, J.J. and Houpis, C.H., *Linear Control System Analysis and Design: Conventional and Modern*, 4th ed., McGraw-Hill, New York, NY, 1995.

Dorf, R.C. and Bishop, R.H., *Modern Control Systems*, 9th ed., Prentice-Hall, Upper Saddle River, NJ, 2001.

Dorsey, John, *Continuous and Discrete Control Systems*, McGraw-Hill, New York, NY, 2002.

Douglas, J., *Process Dynamics and Control,* Volumes I and II, Prentice-Hall, Englewood Cliffs, NJ, 1972.

Doyle, J.C., Francis, B.A. and Tannenbaum, A., *Feedback Control Theory,* Macmillan, New York, NY, 1992.

Dransfield, P., and Habner, D.F., *Introducing Root Locus*, Cambridge University Press, Cambridge, 1973.

Dukkipati, R.V., *Control Systems,* Narosa Publishing House, New Delhi, India, 2005.

Dukkipati, R.V., *Engineering System Dynamics,* Narosa Publishing House, New Delhi, India, 2004.

Dukkipati, R.V., *Vibration Analysis,* Narosa Publishing House, New Delhi, India, 2004.

Evans, W.R., *Control System Dynamics*, McGraw-Hill, New York, NY, 1954.

Eveleigh, V.W., *Control System Design,* McGraw-Hill, New York, NY, 1972.

Franklin, G.F., David Powell, J. and Abbas Emami-Naeini, *Feedback Control of Dynamic Systems*, 3rd ed., Addison Wesley, Reading, MA, 1994.

Friedland, B., *Control System Design*, McGraw-Hill, New York, NY, 1986.

Godwin, Graham E., Graebe, Stefan F. and Salgado, Maria E., *Control System Design*, Prentice-Hall, Upper Saddle River, NJ, 2001.

Grimble, Michael J., *Industrial Control Systems Design*, Wiley, New York, NY, 2001.

Gupta, S., *Elements of Control Systems*, Prentice-Hall, Upper Saddle River, NJ, 2002.

Guy, J.J., *Solution of Problems in Automatic Control*, Pitman, 1966.

Healey, M., *Principles of Automatic Control*, Hodder and Stoughton, 1975.

Jacobs, O.L.R., *Introduction to Control Theory*, Oxford University Press, 1974.

Johnson, C. and Malki, H., *Control Systems Technology*, Prentice-Hall, Upper Saddle River, NJ, 2002.

Kailath, T., *Linear Systems*, Prentice-Hall, Upper Saddle River, NJ, 1980.

Kuo, B.C., *Automatic Control Systems*, 6th ed., Prentice-Hall, Englewood Cliffs, NJ, 1991.

Leff, P.E.E., *Introduction to Feedback Control Systems*, McGraw-Hill, New York, NY, 1979.

Levin, W.S., *Control System Fundamentals*, CRC Press, Boca Raton, FL, 2000.

Levin, W.S., *The Control Handbook*, CRC Press, Boca Raton, FL, 1996.

Lewis, P. and Yang, C., *Basic Control Systems Engineering*, Prentice-Hall, Upper Saddle River, NJ, 1997.

Marshall, S.A., *Introduction to Control Theory*, Macmillan, 1978.

Mayr, O., *The Origins of Feedback Control*, MIT Press, Cambridge, MA, 1970.

Mees, A.J., *Dynamics of Feedback Systems,* Wiley, New York, NY, 1981.

Nise, Norman, S., *Control Systems Engineering*, 3rd ed., Wiley, New York, NY, 2000.

Ogata, K., *Modern Control Engineering*, 3rd ed., Prentice-Hall, Englewood Cliffs, NJ, 1997.

Ogata, K., *State Space Analysis of Control Systems*, Prentice-Hall, Upper Saddle River, NJ, 1967.

Ogata, K., *System Dynamics*, 3rd ed., Prentice-Hall, Upper Saddle River, NJ, 1998.

Palm III, W.J., *Control Systems Engineering*, Wiley, New York, NY, 1986.

Paraskevopoulos, P.N., *Modern Control Engineering*, Marcel Dekker, Inc., New York, NY, 2003.

Phillips, C.L. and Harbour, R.D., *Feedback Control Systems,* 4th ed., Prentice-Hall, Upper Saddle River, NJ, 2000.

Power, H.M. and Simpson, R.J., *Introduction to Dynamics and Control*, McGraw-Hill, New York, NY, 1978.

Raven, F.H., *Automatic Control Engineering*, 4th ed., McGraw-Hill, New York, NY, 1987.

Richards, R.J., *An Introduction to Dynamics and Control*, Longman, 1979.

Richards, R.J., *Solving Problems in Control*, Longman Scientific & Technical, Wiley, New York, NY, 1993.

Rohrs, C.E., Melsa, J.L. and Schultz, D.G., *Linear Control Systems*, McGraw-Hill, New York, NJ, 1993.

Rowell, G. and Wormley, D., *System Dynamics*, Prentice-Hall, Upper Saddle River, NJ, 1999.

Schwarzenbach, J. and Jill, K.F., *System Modeling and Control*, 2nd ed., Arnold, 1984.

Shearer, J.L., Kulakowski, B.T. and Gardner, J.F., *Dynamic Modeling and Control of Engineering Systems*, 2nd ed., Prentice-Hall, Upper Saddle River, NJ, 1997.

Shinners, S. M., *Modern Control System Theory and Design*, 2nd ed., Wiley Interscience, New York, NY, 1998.

Sinha, N.K., *Control Systems,* Holt Rinehart and Winston, New York, NY, 1986.

Smith, O.J.M., *Feedback Control Systems*, McGraw-Hill, New York, NY, 1958.

Stefano,D.III., Stubberud, A.R. and Williams, I.J., *Schaum's Outline Series Theory and Problems of Feedback and Control Systems,* McGraw-Hill, New York, NY, 1967.

Thompson, S., *Control Systems: Engineering and Design*, Longman, 1989.

Truxal, J.G., *Control System Synthesis*, McGraw-Hill, New York, NY, 1955.

Umez-Eronini, E., *System Dynamics and Control*, Brooks/Cole Publishing Company, Pacific Grove, CA, 1999.

Vu, H.V., *Control Systems*, McGraw-Hill Primis Custom Publishing, New York, NY, 2002.

Vukic, Z., Kuljaca, L., Donlagic, D. and Tesnjak, S., *Nonlinear Control Systems*, Marcel Dekker, Inc., New York, NY, 2003.

Welbourn, D.B., *Essentials of Control Theory*, Edward Arnold, 1963.

Weyrick, R.C., *Fundamentals of Automatic Control*, McGraw-Hill, New York, NY, 1975.

PROBLEMS

P3.1: [Reduction of multiple subsystems]: Reduce the system shown in Fig. P3.1 to a single transfer function, $T(s) = C(s)/R(s)$ using MATLAB.

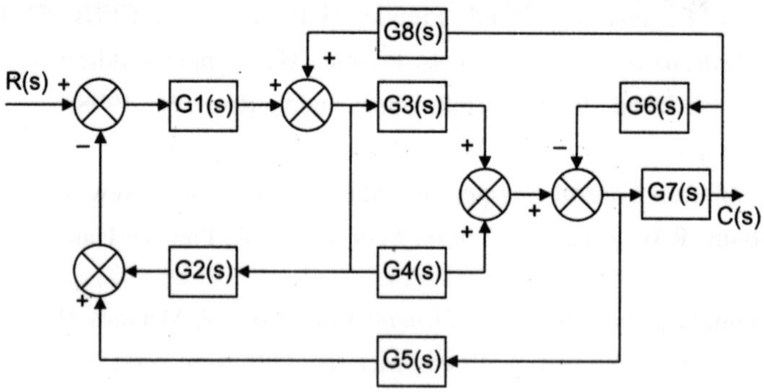

Fig. P3.1

The transfer functions are given as

$G_1(s) = 1/(s + 3)$

$G_2(s) = 1/(s^2 + 3s + 5)$

$G_3(s) = 1/(s + 7)$

$G_4(s) = 1/s$

$G_5(s) = 7/(s + 5)$

$G_6(s) = 1/(s^2 + 3s + 5)$

$G_7(s) = 5/(s + 6)$

$G_8(s) = 1/(s + 8)$

P3.2: Obtain the unit-step response plot for the unity-feedback control system whose open loop transfer function is

$$G(s) = \frac{8}{s(s+1)(s+3)}$$

using MATLAB. Determine also the rise time, peak time, maximum overshoot and settling time in the unit-step response plot.

P3.3: Obtain the unit-acceleration response curve of the unity-feedback control system whose open loop transfer function is given by

$$G(s) = \frac{8(s+1)}{s^2(s+3)}$$

using MATLAB. The unit-acceleration input is defined by

$$r(t) = \frac{1}{2}t^2 (t \geq 0)$$

P3.4: The feed forward transfer function $G(s)$ of a unity-feedback system is given by

$$G(s) = \frac{k(s+3)^2}{(s^2+5)(s+4)^2}$$

Plot the root loci for the system using MATLAB.

P3.5: For the unity feedback shown in Fig. P3.5, where

$$G(s) = \frac{K}{s(s+3)(s+4)(s+5)}$$

Obtain the following:

(*a*) display a root locus and pause

(*b*) draw a close-up of the root locus where the axes go from –2 to 0 on the real axis and –2 to 2 on the imaginary axis

(*c*) overlay the 15% overshoot line on the close-up root locus

(*d*) allow you to select interactively the point where the root locus crosses the 15% overshoot line, and respond with the gain at that point as well as all of the closed-loop poles at that gain

(*e*) find the step response at the gain for 15% overshoot.

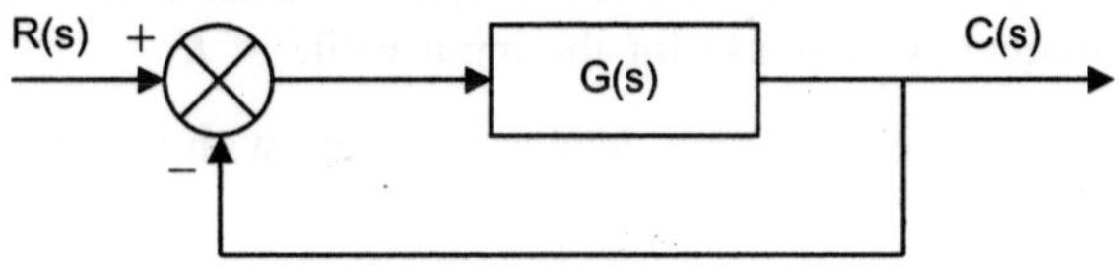

Fig. P3.5

P3.6: For the system shown in Fig. P3.6, determine the following using MATLAB

(*a*) display a root locus and phase

(*b*) display a close-up of the root locus where the axes go from –2 to 2 on the real axis and –2 to 2 on the imaginary axis

(*c*) overlay the 0.707 damping ratio line on the close-up root locus

(*d*) obtain the step response at the gain for 0.707 damping ratio.

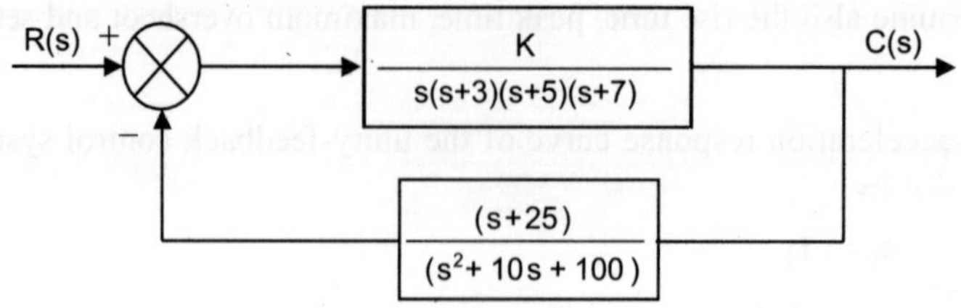

Fig. P3.6

P3.7: Write a program in MATLAB to obtain a Bode plot for the transfer function

$$G(s) = \frac{(5s^3 + 51s^2 + 20s + 400)}{(s^4 + 12s^3 + 60s^2 + 300s + 250)}$$

P3.8: Write a program in MATLAB for the unity feedback system with $G(s) = K/[s(s + 7)\ (s + 15)]$ so that the value of gain K can be input. Display the Bode plots of t, a system for the input value of K. Determine and display the gain and phase margin for the input value of K.

P3.9: Write a program in MATLAB for the system shown in Fig. P3.9 so that the value of K can be input ($K = 40$).

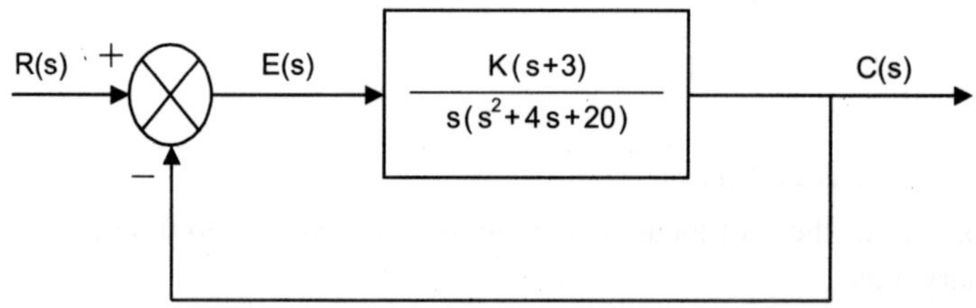

Fig. P3.9

(*a*) Display the closed-loop magnitude and phase frequency response for unity feedback system with an open-loop transfer function, $KG(s)$.

(*b*) Determine and display the peak magnitude, frequency of the peak magnitude and bandwidth for the closed-loop frequency response for the input value of K.

P3.10: Write a program in MATLAB for a unity feedback system with the forward-path transfer function given by

$$G(s) = \frac{7(s+3)}{s(s^2 + 4s + 12)}$$

(*a*) Draw a Nichols plot of an open-loop transfer function

(*b*) The user can read the Nichols plot display and enter the value of M_p

(*c*) Obtain the closed-loop magnitude and phase plots.

(*d*) Display the expected values of percent overshoot, settling time and peak time

(*e*) Plot the closed-loop step response.

P3.11: For the system shown in Fig. P3.11, write a program in MATLAB that will use an open-loop transfer function $G(s)$.

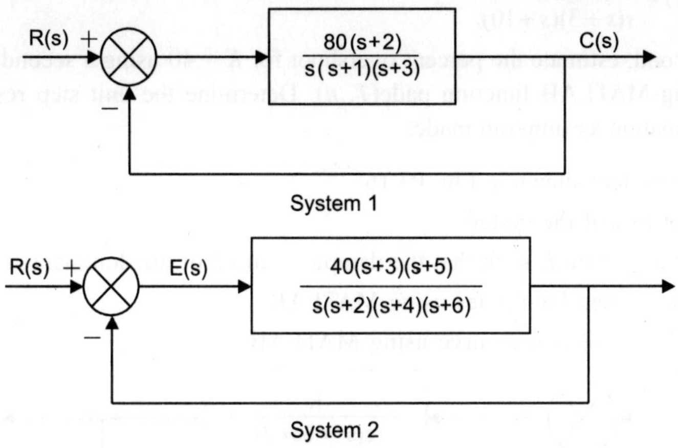

Fig. P3.11

(*a*) Obtain a Bode plot

(*b*) Estimate the percent overshoot, settling time and peak time

(*c*) Obtain the closed-loop step response.

P3.12: Write a program in MATLAB for a unity-feedback system with

$$G(s) = \frac{K(s+3)}{(s^2+5s+80)(s^2+4s+20)}$$

(*a*) Plot the Nyquist diagram

(*b*) Display the real-axis crossing value and frequency.

P3.13: Write a program in MATLAB to obtain the Nyquist and Nichols plots for the following transfer function for $k = 30$.

$$G(s) = \frac{k(s+1)(s+2+5i)(s+2-5i)}{(s+2)(s+5)(s+7)(s+2+7i)(s+2-7i)}$$

P3.14: Write a program in MATLAB for a unity feedback system with the forward-path transfer function given by

$$G(s) = \frac{7(s+3)}{s(s^2+4s+12)}$$

(*a*) Draw a Nichols plot of an open-loop transfer function

(*b*) The user can read the Nichols plot display and enter the value of M_p

(*c*) Obtain the closed-loop magnitude and phase plots.

(*d*) Display the expected values of percent overshoot, settling time and peak time.

(*e*) Plot the closed-loop step response.

P3.15: For a unit feedback system with the forward-path transfer function

$$G(s) = \frac{K}{s(s+3)(s+10)}$$

and a delay of 0.5 second, estimate the percent overshoot for $K = 40$ using a second-order approximation. Model the delay using MATLAB function pade(T, n). Determine the unit step response and check the second-order approximation assumption made.

P3.16: For the control system shown in Fig. P3.16:

(*a*) plot the root loci of the system

(*b*) find the value of gain K such that the damping ratio ξ of the dominant closed-loop poles is 0.5

(*c*) obtain all the closed-loop poles using MATLAB

(*d*) plot the unit-step response curve using MATLAB.

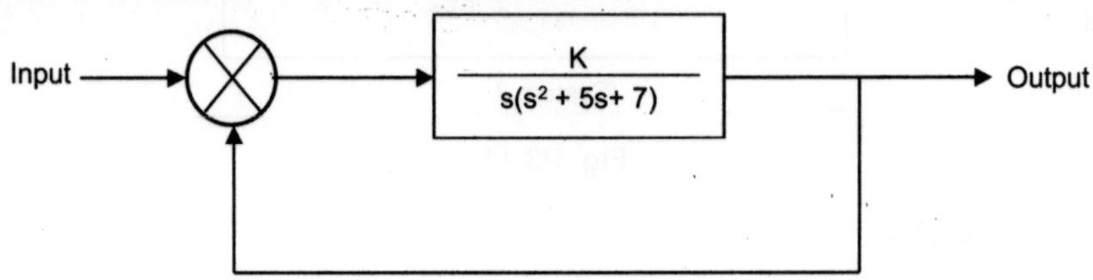

Fig. P3.16

P3.17: Figure P3.17 shows a position control system with velocity feedback. What is the response $c(t)$ to the unit step input?

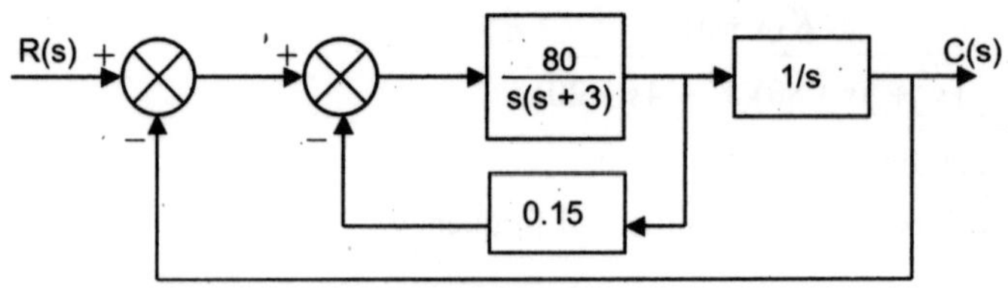

Fig. P3.17

P3.18: The open-loop transfer function $G(s)H(s)$ of a control system is

$$G(s)H(s) = \frac{K}{s(s+0.5)(s^2+0.5s+8)} = \frac{K}{s^4+s^3+8.25s^2+4s}$$

Plot the root loci for the system using MATLAB.

P3.19: Design a compensator for the system shown in Fig. P3.19 such that the dominant closed-loop poles are located at $s = -1 \pm j\sqrt{3}$.

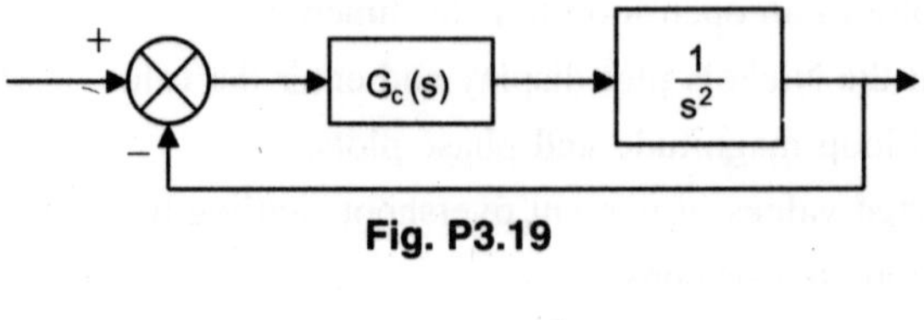

Fig. P3.19

P3.20: For the control system shown in Fig. P3.20:

(*a*) design a PID control $G_c(s)$ such that the dominant closed-loop poles located at $s = -1 \pm j1$.

(*b*) select $a = 0.6$ for the PID controller and find the values of K and b.

(*c*) root-locus plot using MATLAB.

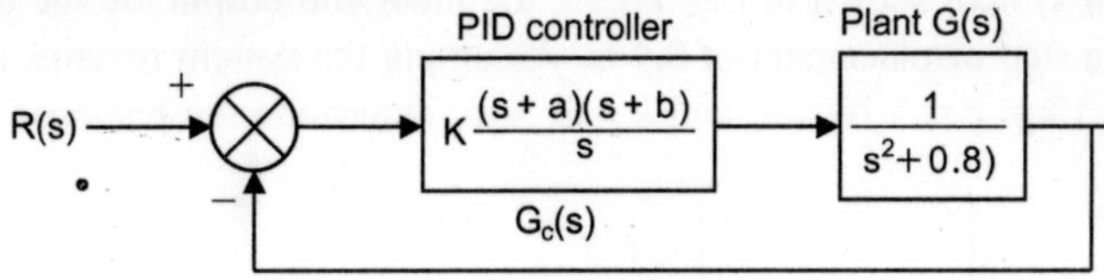

Fig. P3.20

P3.21: Draw a Bode diagram of the open-loop transfer function $G(s)$ of the closed-loop system shown in Fig. P3.21 and obtain the phase margin and gain margin.

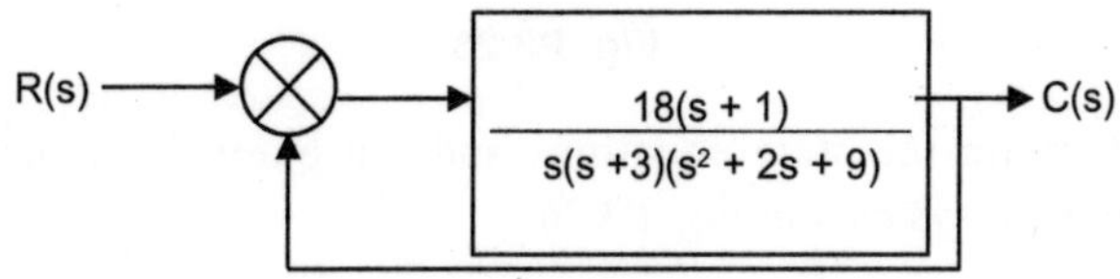

Fig. P3.21

P3.22: A block diagram of a process control system is shown in Fig. P3.22. Find the range of gain for stability.

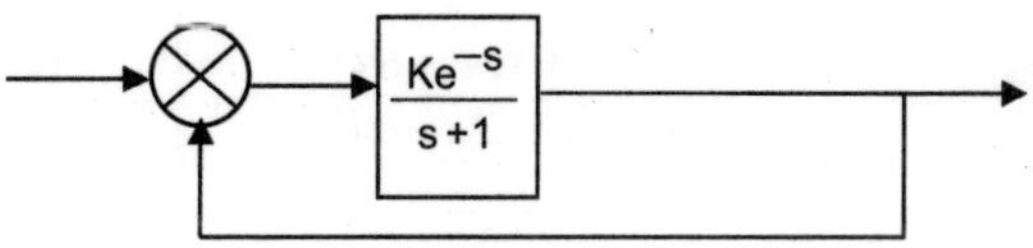

Fig. P3.22

P3.23: For the control system shown in Fig. P3.23:

(*a*) draw a Bode diagram of the open-loop transfer function

(*b*) find the value of the gain K such that the phase margin is 50°

(*c*) find the gain margin of the system with the gain obtained in (b).

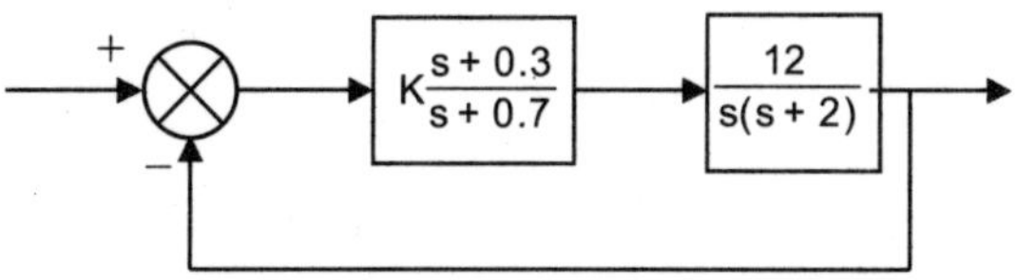

Fig. P3.23

P3.24: Obtain the unit-step response and unit-ramp response of the following system using MATLAB.

$$\begin{bmatrix} \dot{x}_1 \\ \dot{x}_2 \\ \dot{x}_3 \end{bmatrix} = \begin{bmatrix} -5 & -25 & -5 \\ 1 & 0 & 0 \\ 0 & 1 & 0 \end{bmatrix} \begin{bmatrix} x_1 \\ x_2 \\ x_3 \end{bmatrix} + \begin{bmatrix} 1 \\ 0 \\ 0 \end{bmatrix} u$$

$$y = [0 \quad 25 \quad 5]\begin{bmatrix} x_1 \\ x_2 \\ x_3 \end{bmatrix} + [0]u$$

P3.25: For the mechanical system shown in Fig. P3.25, the input and output are the displacement x and y respectively. The input is a step displacement of 0.4 m. Assuming the system remains linear throughout the transient period and m = 3 kg, c = 3 N-s/m, and k = 1 N/m, determine the response of the system using MATLAB.

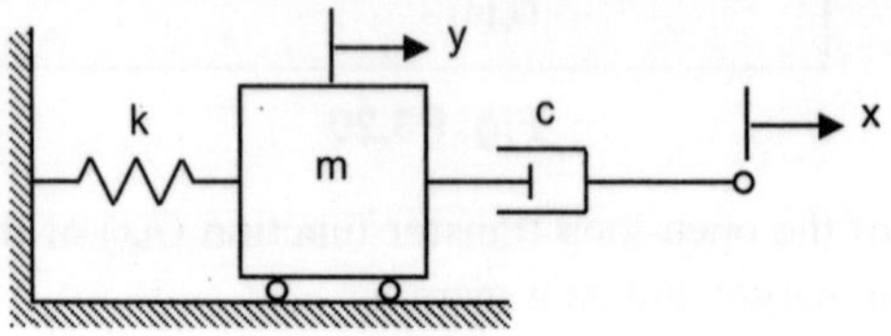

Fig. P3.25

P3.26: Using MATLAB, write the state equations and the output equation for the phase-variable representation for the following systems in Fig. P3.26.

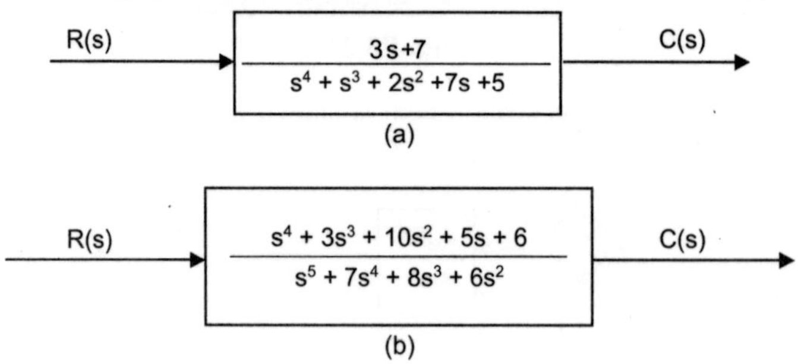

Fig. P3.26

P3.27: Determine the transfer function and poles of the system represented in state space as following using MATLAB.

$$\dot{x} = \begin{bmatrix} 9 & -5 & 2 \\ -4 & 1 & 0 \\ 3 & 5 & -7 \end{bmatrix} x + \begin{bmatrix} 2 \\ 5 \\ 7 \end{bmatrix} u(t)$$

$$y = [1 \quad 7 \quad -2]\,x; \; x(0) = \begin{bmatrix} 0 \\ 0 \\ 0 \end{bmatrix}$$

P3.28: Obtain the root locus diagram of a system defined in state space using MATLAB. The system equations are

$$\dot{x} = Ax + Bu \text{ and } y = Cx + Du \text{ and } u = r - y$$

where r is the input and y is the output.

The matrices **A, B, C,** and **D** are:

$$A=\begin{bmatrix}0 & 1 & 0\\ 0 & 0 & 1\\ -150 & -50 & -15\end{bmatrix} \quad B=\begin{bmatrix}0\\ 1\\ -15\end{bmatrix}$$

$$C=\begin{bmatrix}1 & 0 & 0\end{bmatrix}$$

$$D=\begin{bmatrix}0\end{bmatrix}$$

P3.29: Obtain the Bode diagram of the following system using MATLAB.

$$\begin{bmatrix}\dot{x}_1\\ \dot{x}_2\end{bmatrix}=\begin{bmatrix}0 & 1\\ -30 & 7\end{bmatrix}\begin{bmatrix}x_1\\ x_2\end{bmatrix}+\begin{bmatrix}0\\ 30\end{bmatrix}u$$

$$y=[1 \quad 0]\begin{bmatrix}x_1\\ x_2\end{bmatrix}$$

The input of the system is u and the output is y.

P3.30: A control system is defined by

$$\begin{bmatrix}\dot{x}_1\\ \dot{x}_2\end{bmatrix}=\begin{bmatrix}-1 & -2\\ 7.5 & 0\end{bmatrix}\begin{bmatrix}x_1\\ x_2\end{bmatrix}+\begin{bmatrix}1 & 1\\ 1 & 0\end{bmatrix}\begin{bmatrix}u_1\\ u_2\end{bmatrix}$$

$$\begin{bmatrix}y_1\\ y_2\end{bmatrix}=\begin{bmatrix}1 & 0\\ 0 & 1\end{bmatrix}\begin{bmatrix}x_1\\ x_2\end{bmatrix}+\begin{bmatrix}0 & 0\\ 0 & 0\end{bmatrix}\begin{bmatrix}u_1\\ u_2\end{bmatrix}$$

Write a MATLAB program to obtain the following plots:

(*a*) two Nyquist plots for the input u_1 in one diagram

(*b*) two Nyquist plots for the input u_2 in one diagram.

P3.31: Obtain the unit-ramp response of the system defined by

$$\begin{bmatrix}\dot{x}_1\\ \dot{x}_2\end{bmatrix}=\begin{bmatrix}0 & 2\\ -3 & -1\end{bmatrix}\begin{bmatrix}x_1\\ x_2\end{bmatrix}+\begin{bmatrix}0\\ 2\end{bmatrix}u$$

$$y=[1 \quad 0]\begin{bmatrix}x_1\\ x_2\end{bmatrix}$$

where u is the unit-ramp input. Use lsim command to obtain the response.

P3.32: Obtain the response curves $y(t)$ using MATLAB for the following system.

$$\begin{bmatrix}\dot{x}_1\\ \dot{x}_2\end{bmatrix}=\begin{bmatrix}-1 & 1\\ -1 & 0\end{bmatrix}\begin{bmatrix}x_1\\ x_2\end{bmatrix}+\begin{bmatrix}0\\ 2\end{bmatrix}u$$

$$y=[1 \quad 0]\begin{bmatrix}x_1\\ x_2\end{bmatrix}$$

The input u is given by:

(*a*) u = unit-step input

(*b*) $u = e^{-t}$

The initial state $x(0) = 0$.

P3.33: Plot the step response using MATLAB for the following system represented in state space, where u(t) is the unit step.

$$\dot{x} = \begin{bmatrix} -3 & 2 & 0 \\ 0 & -7 & 1 \\ 0 & 0 & -4 \end{bmatrix} x + \begin{bmatrix} 0 \\ 1 \\ 1 \end{bmatrix} u(t)$$

$$y = \begin{bmatrix} 0 & 1 & 1 \end{bmatrix} x;$$

$$x(0) = \begin{bmatrix} 0 \\ 0 \\ 0 \end{bmatrix}$$

P3.34: Diagonalize the following system using MATLAB.

$$\dot{x} = \begin{bmatrix} -10 & -5 & 7 \\ 15 & 4 & -12 \\ -8 & -3 & 6 \end{bmatrix} x + \begin{bmatrix} 1 \\ 2 \\ 3 \end{bmatrix} r$$

$$y = \begin{bmatrix} 1 & -2 & 3 \end{bmatrix} x$$

P3.35: Determine to unit-ramp response of the system defined by

$$\begin{bmatrix} \dot{x}_1 \\ \dot{x}_2 \end{bmatrix} = \begin{bmatrix} 0 & 2 \\ -3 & -3 \end{bmatrix} \begin{bmatrix} x_1 \\ x_2 \end{bmatrix} + \begin{bmatrix} 0 \\ 2 \end{bmatrix} u$$

$$y = \begin{bmatrix} 1 & 0 \end{bmatrix} \begin{bmatrix} x_1 \\ x_2 \end{bmatrix}$$

using MATLAB where u is the unit-ramp input. Use lsim command in MATLAB.

P3.36: Obtain the unit-impulse response of the following system using MATLAB

$$\begin{bmatrix} \dot{x}_1 \\ \dot{x}_2 \end{bmatrix} = \begin{bmatrix} 0 & 1 \\ -1 & -2 \end{bmatrix} \begin{bmatrix} x_1 \\ x_2 \end{bmatrix} + \begin{bmatrix} 0 \\ 1 \end{bmatrix} u$$

$$y = \begin{bmatrix} 1 & 1 \end{bmatrix} \begin{bmatrix} x_1 \\ x_2 \end{bmatrix} + [0]u.$$

P3.37: A control system is defined by

$$\begin{bmatrix} \dot{x}_1 \\ \dot{x}_2 \\ \dot{x}_3 \end{bmatrix} = \begin{bmatrix} -1 & -3 & -3 \\ 0 & -2 & 1 \\ 2 & 0 & -1 \end{bmatrix} \begin{bmatrix} x_1 \\ x_2 \\ x_3 \end{bmatrix} + \begin{bmatrix} 3 \\ 0 \\ 1 \end{bmatrix} u$$

$$y = \begin{bmatrix} 1 & 2 & 0 \end{bmatrix} \begin{bmatrix} x_1 \\ x_2 \\ x_3 \end{bmatrix}$$

Determine the controllability and observability of the system using MATLAB.

P3.38: Determine the eigenvalues of the following system using MATLAB.

$$\dot{x} = \begin{bmatrix} 0 & 1 & 0 \\ 0 & 1 & -5 \\ -2 & 1 & 3 \end{bmatrix} x + \begin{bmatrix} 0 \\ 0 \\ 1 \end{bmatrix} u$$

$$y = \begin{bmatrix} 0 & 0 & 1 \end{bmatrix} x$$

P3.39: For the following path of a unity feedback system in state space representation, determine if the closed-loop system is stable using the Routh-Hurwitz criterion and MATLAB.

$$\dot{x} = \begin{bmatrix} 0 & 1 & 0 \\ 0 & 1 & 5 \\ -3 & -4 & -5 \end{bmatrix} x + \begin{bmatrix} 0 \\ 0 \\ 1 \end{bmatrix} u$$

$$y = \begin{bmatrix} 0 & 1 & 1 \end{bmatrix} x$$

P3.40: Consider the differential equation system given by

$$\ddot{y} + 4\dot{y} + 3y = 0, \quad y(0) = 0.2 \text{ and } \dot{y}(0) = 0.1$$

Find the state space equation for the system. Also, obtain the response $y(t)$ of the system subject to the given initial conditions using MATLAB.

❍ ❍ ❍

CHAPTER 4

NUMERICAL METHODS

4.1 INTRODUCTION

In this chapter, we introduce the solution of system of linear algebraic equations using such methods as the Gauss elimination method, LU decomposition method, Choleski's decomposition, Gauss-Seidel method, Gauss-Jordan method and Jacobi method. A procedure based on Jacobi rotations, the Householder factorization, symmetric matrix eigenvalue problems, Jacobi method, Householder reduction to tridiagonal form, Sturn sequence and QR method are presented for the treatment of algebraic eigenvalue problems. Numerical examples using MATLAB are provided to illustrate the procedures.

4.2 SYSTEM OF LINEAR ALGEBRAIC EQUATIONS

Here, we consider the solution of n linear, algebraic equations in n unknowns. A system of algebraic equations has the form

$$\begin{bmatrix} A_{11} & A_{12} & \cdots & A_{1n} \\ A_{21} & A_{22} & \cdots & A_{2n} \\ \vdots & \vdots & \vdots & \vdots \\ A_{n1} & A_{n2} & \cdots & A_{nn} \end{bmatrix} \begin{bmatrix} x_1 \\ x_2 \\ \vdots \\ x_n \end{bmatrix} = \begin{bmatrix} b_1 \\ b_2 \\ \vdots \\ b_n \end{bmatrix} \quad \text{...(4.1)}$$

where the coefficients A_{ij} and the constants b_j are known, and x_i represents the unknowns.

Equation (4.1) is simply written as

$$Ax = b$$

4.3 GAUSS ELIMINATION METHOD

Consider the equations at some instant during the elimination phase.

$$\left[\begin{array}{ccccccccc|c} A_{11} & A_{12} & A_{13} & \cdots & A_{1k} & \cdots & A_{1j} & \cdots & A_{1n} & b_1 \\ 0 & A_{22} & A_{23} & \cdots & A_{2k} & \cdots & A_{2j} & \cdots & A_{2n} & b_2 \\ 0 & 0 & A_{33} & \cdots & A_{3k} & \cdots & A_{3j} & \cdots & A_{3n} & b_3 \\ \vdots & \vdots & \vdots & \vdots & \vdots & \vdots & \vdots & \vdots & \vdots & \vdots \\ 0 & 0 & 0 & \cdots & A_{kk} & \cdots & A_{kj} & \cdots & A_{kn} & b_k \\ \hline \vdots & \vdots & \vdots & \vdots & \vdots & \vdots & \vdots & \vdots & \vdots & \vdots \\ 0 & 0 & 0 & \cdots & A_{ik} & \cdots & A_{ij} & \cdots & A_{in} & b_i \\ \vdots & \vdots & \vdots & \vdots & \vdots & \vdots & \vdots & \vdots & \vdots & \vdots \\ 0 & 0 & 0 & \cdots & A_{nk} & \cdots & A_{nj} & \cdots & A_{nn} & b_n \end{array}\right] \begin{array}{l} \\ \\ \\ \\ \leftarrow \text{pivot row} \\ \\ \leftarrow \text{row being transformed} \\ \\ \\ \end{array} \quad ...(4.2)$$

In the above Eq.(4.2), the first k rows of A have already been transformed to upper triangular form. Hence, the current pivot equation is the kth equation and all the equations below it are still to be transformed. Let the ith row be a typical row below the pivot equation that is to be transformed. We obtain this by multiplying the pivot row by $\lambda = A_{ik}/A_{kk}$ and subtracting it from the i-th row. Then

$$A_{ij} \leftarrow A_{ij} - \lambda A_{kj} \qquad j = k, k+1, \ldots, n \qquad ...(4.3)$$

$$b_i \leftarrow b_i - \lambda b_k$$

In order to transform the entire coefficient matrix to upper triangular form, k and i in Eqs. (4.3) and (4.4) should have the ranges $k = 1, 2, \ldots, n-1$ (choose the pivot row), $i = k + 1, k + 2, \ldots, n$ (selects the row to be transformed).

The augmented coefficient matrix after Gauss elimination has the form

$$[A/b] = \left[\begin{array}{ccccc|c} A_{11} & A_{12} & A_{13} & \cdots & A_{1n} & b_1 \\ 0 & A_{22} & A_{23} & \cdots & A_{2n} & b_2 \\ 0 & 0 & A_{33} & \cdots & A_{3n} & b_3 \\ \vdots & \vdots & \vdots & \vdots & \vdots & \vdots \\ 0 & 0 & 0 & \cdots & A_{nn} & b_n \end{array}\right]$$

The last equation, $A_{nn}\, x_n = b_n$, is solved first, giving

$$x_n = b_n / A_{nn}$$

Now conducting the back substitution, we have the solution as

$$x_k = \left(b_k - \sum_{j=k+1}^{n} A_{kj}\, x_j \right) \frac{1}{A_{kk}} \qquad k = n-1, n-2, \ldots \qquad ...(4.4)$$

4.4 LU DECOMPOSITION METHODS

Any square matrix A can be written as a product of a lower triangular matrix L and an upper triangular matrix U.

$$A = LU$$

The process of computing L and U for a given A is known as *LU decomposition* or *LU factorization*.

The given equations can be rewritten as $LUx = b$ and using the notation $Ux = y$, then

$$Ly = b$$

which can be solved for y by forward substitution.

Hence, $Ux = y$ which gives x by the back substitution process.

4.5 CHOLESKI S DECOMPOSITION

Choleski's decomposition $A = LL^T$ requires that A to be symmetric. The decomposition process involves taking square roots of certain combinations of the elements of A.

A typical element in the lower triangular portion of LL^T is of the form,

$$\left(LL^T\right)_{ij} = L_{i1}L_{j1} + L_{i2}L_{j2} + \cdots + L_{ij}L_{jj} = \sum_{k=1}^{j} L_{ik}L_{jk} \qquad i \geq j$$

Equating this term to the corresponding element of A gives

$$A_{ij} = \sum_{k=1}^{j} L_{ik}L_{jk} \qquad i = j,\ j+1,\ \ldots,\ n \qquad j = 1, 2, \ldots, n \qquad \text{...(4.5)}$$

Taking the term containing L_{ij} outside the summation in Eq.(4.5), we obtain

$$A_{ij} = \sum_{k=1}^{j-1} L_{ik}L_{jk} + L_{ij}L_{jj}$$

If $i = j$, then the solution is

$$L_{ij} = \sqrt{A_{ij} - \sum_{k-1}^{j-1} L_{jk}^2} \qquad j = 2, 3, \ldots, n$$

or a non-diagonal term, we get

$$L_{ij} = \left(A_{ij} - \sum_{k=1}^{j-1} L_{ik}L_{jk}\right) \Big/ L_{jj} \qquad j = 2, 3, \ldots, n-1 \qquad i = j+1, j+2, \ldots, n$$

4.6 GAUSS-SEIDEL METHOD

The equations $Ax = b$ can be written in scalar form as

$$\sum_{j=1}^{n} A_{ij}x_j = b_i \qquad i = 1, 2, \ldots, n$$

Extracting the term containing x_i from the summation sign gives

$$A_{ii}x_i + \sum_{\substack{j=1 \\ j \neq i}}^{n} A_{ij}x_j = b_i \qquad i = 1, 2, \ldots, n$$

Solving for x_i, we obtain

$$x_i = \frac{1}{A_{ii}}\left(b_i - \sum_{\substack{j=1 \\ j\neq i}}^{n} A_{ij}x_j\right) \quad i = 1, 2, \ldots, n$$

Hence, the iterative scheme is

$$x_i \leftarrow \frac{1}{A_{ii}}\left(b_i - \sum_{\substack{j=1 \\ j\neq i}}^{n} A_{ij}x_j\right) \quad i = 1, 2, \ldots, n$$

We start by choosing the starting vector x. The procedure for Gauss-Seidel algorithm is summarized here with relaxation:

(*a*) conducting k iterations with $\omega = 1$ (or $k = 10$). After the kth iteration record $\Delta x^{(k)}$.

(*b*) carryout additional p iterations ($p \geq 1$) and record $\Delta x^{(k+p)}$ after the last iteration.

(*c*) perform all subsequent iterations with $\omega = \omega_{opt}$, where

$$\omega_{opt} = \frac{2}{1+\sqrt{1-\left(\Delta x^{(k+p)} / \Delta x^{(k)}\right)^{1/p}}}$$

4.7 GAUSS-JORDAN METHOD

Let us consider a system of linear algebraic equations, in the matrix form

$$[A]\{x\} = \{b\}$$

where, for simplification, $[A]$ is of order 3×3. The augmented matrix is

$$\begin{bmatrix} a_{11} & a_{12} & a_{13} & b_1 \\ a_{21} & a_{22} & a_{23} & b_2 \\ a_{31} & a_{32} & a_{33} & b_3 \end{bmatrix} \quad \ldots(4.6)$$

The solution of equation (4.6) is

$$[I]\{x\} = [A]^{-1}\{b\}$$

where $[I]$ is the identity matrix. The augmented matrix is

$$\begin{bmatrix} 1 & 0 & 0 & \alpha_1 \\ 0 & 1 & 0 & \alpha_2 \\ 0 & 0 & 1 & \alpha_3 \end{bmatrix} \quad \ldots(4.7)$$

In the Gauss-Jordan method the augmented matrix (4.6) is converted to the augmented matrix (4.7) by a series of operations similar to the Gaussian elimination method. In the Gaussian elimination method an upper triangular matrix is derived while in the Gauss-Jordan method an identity matrix is derived.

4.8 JACOBI METHOD

This is an iterative technique solving with an assumed solution vector and successive refinement by iteration. The system of equations for consideration is

$$a_{11}x_1 + a_{12}x_2 + a_{13}x_3 \ldots + a_{1n}x_n = b_1$$
$$a_{21}x_1 + a_{22}x_2 + a_{23}x_3 \ldots + a_{2n}x_n = b_2$$
$$\ldots \quad \ldots \quad \ldots \quad \ldots$$
$$\ldots \quad \ldots \quad \ldots \quad \ldots$$
$$a_{i1}x_1 + a_{i2}x_2 + a_{i3}x_3 \ldots + a_{in}x_n = b_i$$
$$\ldots \quad \ldots \quad \ldots \quad \ldots$$
$$a_{n1}x_1 + a_{n2}x_2 + a_{n3}x_3 \ldots + a_{nn}x_n = b_n \qquad \ldots(4.8)$$

Rewriting the above equations

$$x_1 = (b_1 - a_{12}x_2 - a_{13}x_3 - \ldots - a_{1n}x_n)/a_{11}$$
$$x_2 = (b_2 - a_{21}x_1 - a_{23}x_3 - \ldots - a_{2n}x_n)/a_{22}$$
$$\ldots \quad \ldots \quad \ldots \quad \ldots$$
$$x_i = (b_i - a_{i1}x_i - a_{i2}x_2 \ldots a_{ii-1}n_{i-1} - a_{ii+1}x_{i+1} \ldots a_{in}x_n)/a_{ii}$$
$$\ldots \quad \ldots \quad \ldots \quad \ldots$$
$$x_n = (b_n - a_{n1}x_1 - a_{n2}x_2 \ldots a_{nn-1}x_{n-1})/a_{nn} \qquad \ldots(4.9)$$

This procedure is valid only if all the diagonal elements are non zero. The equations are to be rearranged suitably to avoid the non zero elements in the main diagonal.

Substituting the values of x_i^r any stage in the iterative process on the right hand side of equations (4.9) gives the values to the next stage, *i.e.*, x_i^{r+1}. In other words, the scheme is given by the system of equations (4.10) with a superscript r on the right side and a superscript $r + 1$ on the left hand side. Rewriting the equations,

$$x_1^{r+1} = (b_1 - a_{12}x_2^r - a_{13}x_3^r - \cdots - a_{1n}x_n^r)/a_{11}$$
$$x_2^{r+1} = (b_2 - a_{21}x_1^r - a_{23}x_3^r - \cdots - a_{2n}x_n^r)/a_{22}$$
$$\ldots \quad \ldots \quad \ldots \quad \ldots$$
$$x_i^{r+1} = (b_i - a_{i1}x_i^r - a_{i2}x_2^r \cdots - a_{ii-1}x_{i-1}^r - a_{ii+1}n_{i+1}^r \ldots a_{in}x_n^r)/a_{ii}$$
$$\ldots \quad \ldots \quad \ldots \quad \ldots$$
$$\ldots \quad \ldots \quad \ldots \quad \ldots$$
$$x_n^{r+1} = (b_n - a_{n1}x_1^r - a_{n2}x_2^r - \cdots a_{n,n-1}x_{n-1}^r)/a_{nn} \qquad \ldots(4.10)$$

The sequence $x^0, x^1, x^2, \ldots$ generated by the equations of (4.10) gives a sequence which converges to the solutions vector x which satisfies the set of equations given in Eq.(4.8), *i.e.*, $[A]\{x\} = \{b\}$.

Equation (4.10) in the matrix form is as follows

$$x^{r+1} = \{V\} + [B]\{x\}^r \qquad \ldots(4.11)$$

$$\text{where } \{V\} = \begin{Bmatrix} \dfrac{b_1}{a_{11}} \\ \dfrac{b_2}{a_{22}} \\ \cdots \\ \dfrac{b_i}{a_{ii}} \\ \cdots \\ \dfrac{b_n}{a_{nn}} \end{Bmatrix}$$

$$\text{and} \qquad [B] = \begin{bmatrix} 0 & a_{12}/a_{11} & a_{13}/a_{11} & \cdots & \cdots & \cdots & a_{1n}/a_{11} \\ a_{21}/a_{22} & 0 & a_{23}/a_{22} & \cdots & \cdots & \cdots & a_{2n}/a_{22} \\ \cdots & \cdots & \cdots & \cdots & \cdots & \cdots & \cdots \\ a_{i1}/a_{ii} & a_{i2}/a_{ii} & \cdots & 0 & a_{ii+1}/a_{ii} & \cdots & a_{ii}/a_{nn} \\ \cdots & \cdots & \cdots & \cdots & \cdots & \cdots & \cdots \\ a_{n1}/a_{nn} & \cdots & \cdots & \cdots & a_{n,n-1}/a_{nn} & \cdots & 0 \end{bmatrix}$$

The system of equations given in Eq. (4.8) can be written in the form

$$\{x\} = \{v\} + [B]\{x\} \qquad \text{...(4.12)}$$

Now we can construct expressions for $x^{(1)}$... $x^{(2)}$... in terms of $x^{(0)}$

$$\begin{aligned} \{x\}^1 &= \{v\} + [B]x^0 \\ \{x\}^2 &= \{v\} + [B]x^1 \\ &= \{v\} + [B](\{v\} + [B]x^{(0)}) \\ &= \{v\} + [B](\{v\} + [B]^2x^0) \\ \{x\}^3 &= \{v\} + [B]\{x\}^{(2)} \\ &= \{v\} + [B](\{v\} + [B]\{v\} + [B]^2x^{(0)}) \\ &= \{v\} + [B]\{v\} + [B]^2\{v\} + [B]^3x^0 \end{aligned}$$

Generalizing

$$x^{(r)} = \{v\} + [B]\{v\} + [B]^2\{v\} + \cdots + [B]^{r-1}\{v\} + [B]^r x^{(0)}$$

Finally

$$x^{(r)} = ([I] + [B] + [B]^2 + [B]^3 \cdots + [B]^{r-1})\{v\} + [B]^{(r)}x^{(0)} \qquad \text{...(4.13)}$$

Here, we notice that $([I] + [B] + [B]^2 + [B]^3 \ldots [B]^{r-1})$ is a matrix geometric progression. It is possible to obtain the sum of r terms of the above expressions. Let us denote

$$\begin{aligned} s_r &= [I] + [B] + [B]^2 + [B]^3 \cdots + [B]^{r-1} \\ &= ([I] - [B]^r)([I] - [B])^{-1} \end{aligned}$$

provided $([I] - [B])$ is non-singular. Here we see that as $r \to \infty$ the limit of the sum exists if $[B]^r \to 0$, in this case $s_r \to s = ([I] - [B])^{-1}$.

Hence in Eq.(4.13) x^r will converge to the vector $\{x\}$ provided $[B]^r \to 0$ as $r \to \infty$. Then the vector $\{x\}$ can be written as

$$\{x\} = ([I] - [B]^{-1}\{v\})$$

This means that $([I] - [B])\ \{x\} = (v)$ and hence $\{x\} = [B]\{x\} + \{v\}$. This is just the equation (4.12).

4.9 THE HOUSEHOLDER FACTORIZATION

This method transforms the matrix into an upper triangular form by making use of reflection matrices; we have

$$[P_H]^T[A]$$

where

$$[P_H]^T = [P_{n-1}]^T \ldots [P_2]^T[P_1]^T$$

The $[S_H]$ is an upper triangular matrix. The matrices $[P_i]^T$, $i = 1, \ldots, n-1$ are reflection matrices computed in such a way that $[P_i]^T$ reduce the subdiagonal elements in column i of the coefficient matrix.

Then we have

$$[P_i]T = \begin{bmatrix} [I_{i-1}] & 0 \\ 0 & [P_i] \end{bmatrix}$$

here $[I_{i-1}]$ is the identity matrix of size $i-1$

and $$[\tilde{P}_i] = 1 - \theta\{w\}\ \{w\}^T;$$

where $$\theta = \frac{2}{\{w_i\}^T\{w_i\}}$$

Here $[\tilde{P}_i]$ is a symmetric matrix and $\{w_i\}$ is a vector of size $n - i + 1$. The vector $\{w_i\}$ will be chosen as explained later.

Because $[\tilde{P}_i]$ is symmetric, $[P_i]^T = [P_i]$.

Now solution of the equation $[A]\{x\} = \{b\}$ can be obtained by the following equation

$$[A] = [P_H][S_H]$$

where $\{v\} = [S_H]\ \{x\}$.

The vector $\{v\}$ is obtained as $\{v\} = [P_H]^T\{b\}$.

To explain the transformation, as a first step let us compute the $[P_1]$,

i.e., $$[\tilde{A}] = [P_1][A] \qquad ...(4.14)$$

and $$[A] = [a_1\ ;\ A_1]$$

where a_1 is the first column of $[A]$. Then, we have

$$[P_1] = I - \theta\{w_1\}\{w_1\}^T$$

Here we have the first element of the vector $[P_1][a_1]$ to be non zero since the sub-diagonal elements of the column 1 of matrix $[\tilde{A}]$ is required to be zero.

Now choose the vector $\{w_1\}$ such that it must fulfill the condition

$$(I - \theta\{w_1\}\{w_1\}^T)[a_1] = \pm \|a_1\|_2\, e_1 \qquad \text{...(4.15)}$$

where e_1 is a non-dimensional unit vector from Eq. (4.15).

$$[a_1] - \theta\{w_1\} = \pm\, \|a_1\|_2\, e_1$$

where θ is a constant and equal to $e\{w_1\}^T\{w_1\}$.

Let us set $\theta = 1.0$, then we obtain

$$\{w_1\} = [a_1] + \text{sign}\,(a_{11})\, \|a_1\|_2\, e_1$$

From equation (4.14) we can get

$$\{v_1\}^T = \{w_1\}^T[A]$$

hence, $$[\tilde{A}] = [A] - \theta(\{w_1\}\{v_1\}^T)$$

The factorization is explained in the example.

4.10 SYMMETRIC MATRIX EIGENVALUE PROBLEMS

The standard matrix eigenvalue problem is

$$Ax = \lambda x \qquad \text{...(4.16)}$$

where A is a given $n \times n$ matrix. The objective here is to find the scalar λ and the vector x.

Equation (4.16) can be rewritten as

$$(A - \lambda I)x = 0$$

A non-trivial solution exists only if

$$|A - \lambda I| = 0 \qquad \text{...(4.17)}$$

Expansion of Eq.(4.17) gives the polynomial equation called the *characteristic equation*.

$$a_1\lambda^n + a_2\lambda^{n-1} + \cdots + a_n\lambda + a_{n+1} = 0$$

which has the roots λ_i, $i = 1, 2, \ldots, n$, called the *eigenvalues* of the matrix A. The solutions of x_i of $(A - \lambda_i I)$ $x = 0$ are known as *eigenvectors*.

4.11 JACOBI METHOD

Applying the transformation $x = Px^*$ in Eq.(4.16) where P is a non-singular matrix, we can write

$$P^{-1}APx^* = \lambda P^{-1}Px^*$$

or $$A^*x^* = \lambda x^* \qquad \text{...(4.18)}$$

where $A^* = P^{-1}AP$.

Matrices that have the same eigenvalues are deemed to be *similar* and the transformation between them is called a *similarity transformation*. Diagonalizing A^*, Eq.(4.18) can be written as

$$\begin{bmatrix} A_{11}^* - \lambda & 0 & \cdots & 0 \\ 0 & A_{22}^* - \lambda & \cdots & 0 \\ \vdots & \vdots & \vdots & \vdots \\ 0 & 0 & \cdots & A_{nn}^* - \lambda \end{bmatrix} \begin{bmatrix} x_1^* \\ x_2^* \\ \vdots \\ x_n^* \end{bmatrix} = \begin{bmatrix} 0 \\ 0 \\ \vdots \\ 0 \end{bmatrix}, \qquad ...(4.19)$$

Solving Eq.(4.19), we obtain

$$\lambda_1 = A_{11}^*,\ \lambda_2 = A_{22}^*,\ ...\lambda_n = A_{nn}^*$$

$$x_1^* = \begin{bmatrix} 1 \\ 0 \\ \vdots \\ 0 \end{bmatrix} \quad x_2^* = \begin{bmatrix} 0 \\ 1 \\ \vdots \\ 0 \end{bmatrix} \quad \cdots \quad x_n^* = \begin{bmatrix} 0 \\ 0 \\ \vdots \\ 1 \end{bmatrix}$$

or $$x^* = \begin{bmatrix} x_1^* & x_2^* & \cdots & x_n^* \end{bmatrix} = I$$

Therefore, the eigenvector matrix of A is

$$X = Px^* = PI = P$$

The transformation matrix P is the eigenvector matrix of A and the eigenvalues of A are the diagonal terms of A^*.

Jacobi Rotation Matrix:

Consider the special transformation in the plane rotation

$$x = Rx^*$$

where
$$R = \begin{bmatrix} & & k & & & \ell & & \\ 1 & 0 & 0 & 0 & 0 & 0 & 0 & 0 \\ 0 & 1 & 0 & 0 & 0 & 0 & 0 & 0 \\ 0 & 0 & c & 0 & 0 & s & 0 & 0 \\ 0 & 0 & 0 & 1 & 0 & 0 & 0 & 0 \\ 0 & 0 & 0 & 0 & 1 & 0 & 0 & 0 \\ 0 & 0 & -s & 0 & 0 & c & 0 & 0 \\ 0 & 0 & 0 & 0 & 0 & 0 & 1 & 0 \\ 0 & 0 & 0 & 0 & 0 & 0 & 0 & 1 \end{bmatrix} \begin{matrix} \\ \\ k \\ \\ \\ \\ \ell \\ \\ \\ \end{matrix}$$

R is called the *Jacobi rotation matrix* and $R^{-1} = R^T$.

Also $$A^* = R^{-1}AR = R^T AR$$

The matrix A^* has the same eigenvalues as the original matrix A and it is also symmetric.

Jacobi Diagonalization:

The Jacobi diagonalization procedure uses only the upper half of the matrix and is summarized below:

(*a*) Obtain the largest absolute value off-diagonal element $A_{k\ell}$ in the upper half of A.

(*b*) Compute ϕ, t, c and s

$$\phi = \frac{A_{kk} - A_{\ell\ell}}{2A_{k\ell}}$$

$$t = \frac{1}{2\phi}$$

$$c = \frac{1}{\sqrt{1+t^2}}$$

$$s = tc$$

(*c*) Compute τ from $\tau = \dfrac{s}{1+c}$

(*d*) Modify the elements in the upper half of A:

$$A^*_{kk} = A_{kk} - t\,A_{k\ell}$$

$$A^*_{\ell\ell} = A_{\ell\ell} - t\,A_{k\ell}$$

$$A^*_{k\ell} = A^*_{\ell k} = 0$$

$$A^*_{ki} = A^*_{ik} = A_{ki} - s\left(A_{\ell i} + \tau A_{ki}\right), \quad i \neq k, i \neq \ell$$

$$A^*_{\ell i} = A^*_{i\ell} = A_{\ell i} + s\left(A_{ki} - \tau A_{\ell i}\right), \quad i \neq k, i \neq \ell$$

where $\tau = \dfrac{s}{1+c}$

(*e*) Update the matrix P

$$P^*_{ik} = P_{ik} - s\left(P_{i\ell} + \tau P_{ik}\right)$$

$$P^*_{i\ell} = P_{i\ell} + s\left(P_{ik} - \tau P_{i\ell}\right)$$

Repeat the procedure until the $A_{k\ell} < \in$, where $\in$ is the error tolerance.

4.12 HOUSEHOLDER REDUCTION TO TRIDIAGONAL FORM

The computational procedure is carried out with $i = 1, 2, \ldots, n-2$ as described below:

(*a*) Define A' as the $(n-i) \times (n-i)$ lower-right hand portion of A

(*b*) Let $x = [A_{i+1,\,i}\;\; A_{i+2,\,i} \ldots A_{n,\,i}]^T$

(*c*) Compute $|x|$. Let $k = |x|$ if $x_1 > 0$ and $k = -|x|$ if $x_1 < 0$

(*d*) Let $u = [k + x_1\; x_2 x_3 \ldots x_{n-i}]^T$

(*e*) Compute $H = |u|^2/2$

(*f*) Compute $V = A'u/H$

(*g*) Compute $g = u^T v/2H$

(*h*) Compute $w = V - gu$

(*i*) Compute the transformation $A \leftarrow A' - w^T u - u^T w$

(*j*) Set $A_{i,i+1} = A_{i+1,\,i} = -k$

4.13 STURN SEQUENCE

Consider a symmetric tridiagonal matrix. Its characteristic polynomial can be computed with 3(*n* – 1) multiplications as described below:

$$P_n(\lambda) = |A - \lambda I| = \begin{bmatrix} d_1 - \lambda & c_1 & 0 & 0 & \cdots & 0 \\ c_1 & d_2 - \lambda & c_2 & 0 & \cdots & 0 \\ 0 & c_2 & d_3 - \lambda & c_3 & \cdots & 0 \\ 0 & 0 & c_3 & d_4 - \lambda & \cdots & 0 \\ \vdots & \vdots & \vdots & \vdots & \vdots & \vdots \\ 0 & 0 & \cdots & 0 & c_{n-1} & d_n - \lambda \end{bmatrix}$$

$$P_0(\lambda) = 1$$

$$P_1(\lambda) = d_1 - \lambda$$

$$P_i(\lambda) = (d_i - \lambda)P_{i-1}(\lambda) - c_{i-1}^2 P_{i-2}(\lambda), \qquad i = 2, 3, \ldots, n$$

The polynomials $P_0(\lambda)$, $P_1(\lambda)$, …, $P_n(\lambda)$ form a *sturn sequence*. The number of sign changes in the sequence $P_0(a)$, $P_1(a)$, …, $P_n(a)$ is equal to the number of roots of $P_n(\lambda)$ that are smaller than *a*. If a member $P_i(a)$ of the sequence is zero, its sign is to be taken opposite to that of $P_{i-1}(a)$.

4.14 QR METHOD

In the preceding section, we have described the Jacob's method which is a reliable method but it requires a large computation time and is valid only for real symmetric matrices. The QR method on the other hand is numerically extremely stable and is applicable to a general matrix. This method also provides a basis for developing a general purpose procedure for determining the eigenvalues and eigenvectors.

The method utilizes the fundamental property that a real matrix can be written as

$$[A] = [Q][U]$$

where [*Q*] is orthogonal and [*U*] is upper triangular. This is contrary to the decomposition in the form [*L*][*U*] where [*L*] is the unit lower matrix and [*U*] is the upper triangular matrix. The property can be proved as follows.

As in Jacobi's method we introduce here the rotations matrix and denote it by [R·(p, q, θ)] to indicate the rows that contain the non-zero, off-diagonal elements. Note that [*R*] is orthogonal.

$$[R(p,q,\theta)] = \begin{bmatrix} 1 & & & & & & & \\ & 1 & & & & & & \\ & & \cos\theta & & & \sin\theta & & \\ & & & 1 & & & & \\ & & & & 1 & & & \\ & & -\sin\theta & & & \cos\theta & & \\ & & & & & & 1 & \\ & & p & & & q & & 1 \end{bmatrix} \begin{matrix} \\ \\ p \\ \\ \\ q \\ \\ \\ \end{matrix}$$

If any vector $\{x\}$ is multiplied by $[R.(p, q, \theta)]$ such that $y = [R]\{x\}$, then

$$y_p = r_{pp}x_p + r_{pq}x_q = \cos\theta\, x_p + \sin\theta\, x_q$$

and
$$Y_q = r_{qp}x_p + r_{qq}x_q = -\sin\theta\, x_p + \cos\theta\, x_q$$

i.e., $y_i = x_i$ if $i \neq p$ or q. Therefore it is necessary to select θ such that y_p or y_q is equal to zero. It should also be noted that if $x_p = x_q = 0$ then $y_p = y_q = 0$. If we write

$$[A] = \left(x^{(1)}x^{(2)}...x^{(n)}\right)$$

then
$$[R(p,q,\theta)][A] = \left(y^{(1)}y^{(2)}...y^{(n)}\right)$$

An element in either pth row or qth row is reduced by a proper choice of θ. Thus, all the elements in the first column except the first element can be made zero by suitable values of θ, and they remain zero even after multiplying with $[R]$. Similarly for all other columns elements are made zero for the elements below the diagonal elements by proper choice of θ values. Thus, we obtain an upper triangular matrix by forming the product

$$[u] = R\left(n, n-1, \theta_{n,n-1}\right)R\left(n, n-2, \theta_{n,n-2}\right)...R\left(3,1,\theta_{3,1}\right)R\left(2,1,\theta_{2,1}\right)[A]$$

$$= \left(\prod_{j=1}^{n-1}\prod_{i=j+1}^{n} R\left(i, j, \theta_{ij}\right)\right)[A]$$

Since $[R]$ is an orthogonal matrix, the products of $[R]$ are also orthogonal. Hence, we have $[U] = [S][A]$ where $[S]$ is orthogonal an $d[U]$ is upper triangular. Since $[S]$ is orthogonal, we have $[A] = [S]^{-1}[U] = [S]^T[\mathrm{U}]$. If $[Q] = [S]^T$, then $[A] = [Q][U]$.

We can construct a sequence of matrices $[A_0]$, $[A_1][A_2]$... where

$$[A_0] = [A] = [Q_0][A_0],\ [Q_k][A_k] = [Q_{k-1}][A_{k-1}]$$

for all values of $k \geq 1$. That is, we start with $[A_0] = [A]$ and put it in the form $[Q_0][U_0]$ to obtain $[Q_0]$ and $[U_0]$ and then obtain $[A_1]$ which is equal to the product of $[U_0][Q_0]$ in reverse order. Repeating this procedure, we can obtain any number of sequence.

$[A]$	$= [A_0] = [Q_0][U_0]$	determines $[Q_0]$ and $[U_0]$
$[A_1]$	$= [U_0][Q_0]$	determines $[A_1]$
	$= [Q_1][U_1]$	determines $[Q_1]$ and $[U_1]$
$[A_2]$	$= [U_1][Q_1]$	determines $[A_2]$
	$= [Q_2][U_2]$	determines $[Q_2]$ and $[U_2]$
$[A_k]$	$= [U_{k-1}][Q_{k-1}]$	determines $[A_k]$
	$= [Q_k][U_k]$	determines $[Q_k]$ and $[U_k]$

From the above sequence, we can show that the product $Q_0Q_1Q_2...Q_k$ converges as $k \to \infty$. Then $[A_k]$ converges to an upper triangular matrix with the eigenvalues of $[A]$ as its diagonal elements. This can be proved as follows. We have

$$[A_k] = [Q_k][U_k] = [U_{k-1}][Q_{k-1}] \quad ...(4.20)$$

$$[A_{k-1}] = [Q_{k-1}][U_{k-1}] \quad ...(4.21)$$

From which

$$[U_{k-1}] = [Q_{k-1}]^{-1}[A_{k-1}] \quad ...(4.22)$$

Substituting Eq. (4.22) in Eq.(4.20), we get

$$[A_k] = [Q_{k-1}]^{-1}[A_{k-1}][Q_{k-1}]$$

Hence $[A_k]$ is similar to $[A_{k-1}]$. This implies that $[A_k]$ is similar to $[A_0] = [A]$. Therefore, it has the same eigenvalues as $[A]$. Also

$$[A_{k-1}] = [Q_{k-2}]^{-1}[A_{k-2}][Q_{k-2}]$$

Thus $$[A_{k+1}] = [Q_k]^{-1}[Q_{k-1}]^{-1}[Q_0]^{-1}[A][Q_0][Q_1]...[Q_k] = [P_k]^{-1}[A][P_k]$$

where $$[P_k] = [Q_0][Q_1]...[Q_k]$$

If $k \to \infty [P_k]$ exists and we denote it by $[P]$.

Then $$\lim_{k\to\infty} Q_k = \lim_{k\to\infty}\left([P_{k-1}]^{-1}[P_k]\right) = \left(\lim_{k\to\infty}[P_{k-1}]^{-1}\right)\left(\lim_{k\to\infty}[P_k]\right) = [P]^{-1}[P] = [I]$$

Here, we have two limiting conditions

1. $$[A_k] = [P_{k-1}]^{-1}[A][P_{k-1}]$$

which means

$$\lim_{k\to\infty}[A_k] = \left(\lim_{k\to\infty}[P_{k-1}]^{-1}\right)[A]\left(\lim_{k\to\infty}[P_{k-1}]\right) = [P]^{-1}[A][P]$$

Therefore, the limit $[A_k]$ is similar to $[A]$ and hence has the same eigenvalues as $[A]$.

2. $$[A_k] = [Q_k][U_k]$$

that is $$\lim_{k\to\infty}[A_k] = \left(\lim_{k\to\infty}[Q_k]\right)\left(\lim_{k\to\infty}[U_k]\right)$$

here we have

$$\lim_{k\to\infty}[Q_k] = [I]$$

which results in

$$\lim_{k\to\infty}[A_k] = \lim_{k\to\infty}[U_k]$$

Since every $[U_k]$ is an upper triangular matrix, the limit of $[A_k]$ is also an upper triangular matrix.

The accuracy of this method mainly depends on the effectiveness of the algorithm used for decompositions of $[A_k]$ into $[Q_k][U_k]$. The limit $k \to \infty$ can exist for large size problems.

4.15 EXAMPLE PROBLEMS AND SOLUTIONS

Example E4.1: Use Gaussian elimination scheme to solve the set of equations.

$$2x_1 + x_2 - 3x_3 = 11$$
$$4x_1 - 2x_2 + 3x_3 = 8$$
$$-2x_1 + 2x_2 - x_3 = -6$$

Solution:

```
>> A = [2 1 -3;4 -2 3; -2 2 -1];
>> b = [11;8; -6];
>> format long
>> [x,det] = gauss(A,b)
x =
     3
    -1
    -2
det = -22
function [x, det] = gauss(A, b)
% Solves A*x = b by Gauss elimination and finds det(A)
% USAGE: [x, det] = gauss(A,b)
if size(b, 2) > 1; b = b'; end  % b column vector
n = length(b);
for k = 1:n - 1 % Elimination
for i = k + 1:n
if A (i, k) ~ = 0
lambda = A(i, k)/A(k, k);
A(i, k +1:n) = A(i, k +1:n) - lambda * A(k, k + 1:n);
b(i) = b(i) - lambda*b(k);
end
end
end
if nargout == 2; det = prod(diag(A)); end
for k = n: - 1:1 % Back substitution
b(k) = (b(k) - A(k, k + 1:n)*b(k + 1:n))/A(k, k);
end
x = b;
```

MATLAB Solution [Using built-in function]:

```
>> A = [2 1 -3; 4 -2 3; -2 2 -1];
>> B = [11; 8; -6];
>> x = inv(A)*B
>> x = A\B
x =
    3
   -1
   -2
>> x = inv(A)*B
x =
  3.0000
 -1.0000
 -2.0000
```

Example E4.2: Using Gaussian elimination method, solve the system of linear equations:

$$
\begin{aligned}
2x_1 + x_2 + x_3 - x_4 &= 10 \\
x_1 + 5x_2 - 5x_3 + 6x_4 &= 25 \\
-7x_1 + 3x_2 - 7x_3 - 5x_4 &= 5 \\
x_1 - 5x_2 + 2x_3 + 7x_4 &= 11
\end{aligned}
$$

Solution:

```
EDU >> Run_pr_E4.2
A =
    2   1   1  -1
    1   5  -5   6
   -7   3  -7  -5
    1  -5   2   7
B =
   10
   25
    5
   11
x =
    25.3587
   -19.6143
   -28.9058
    -7.8027
det =
 -223.0000
x =
    25.3587
   -19.6143
   -28.9058
    -7.8027
```

Run_pr_E4.2.m

```
A = [2 1 1 -1;1 5 -5 6; -7 3 -7 -5; 1 -5 2 7];
b = [10;25;5;11];
[x, det] = gauss(A,b)
x = A\b
```

gauss.m

function [x,det] = gauss(A,b)

```
% Solves A*x = b
if size(b,2) > 1; b = b'; end
n = length(b);
for k = 1:n-1
for i= k+1:n
if A(i,k) ~ = 0
lambda = A(i,k)/A(k,k);
A(i,k+1:n) = A(i,k+1:n) - lambda*A(k,k+1:n);
b(i)= b(i) - lambda*b(k);
end
end
end
if nargout == 2; det = prod(diag(A)); end
for k = n:-1:1
b(k) = (b(k) - A(k,k+1:n)*b(k+1:n))/A(k,k);
end
x = b;
```

MATLAB Solution [Using built-in function]:

```
>> A = [2 1 1 -1;1 5 -5 6;-7 3 -7 -5;1 -5 2 7];
>> B = [10;25;5;11];
>> x = A\B
x =
   25.3587
  -19.6143
  -28.9058
   -7.8027
>> x = inv(A)*B
x =
   25.3587
```

```
-19.6143
-28.9058
 -7.8027
```

Example E4.3: Tridiagonalize the given matrix $[A] = \begin{bmatrix} 4 & 3 & 2 & 1 \\ 3 & 8 & 6 & 12 \\ 2 & 6 & 8 & 3 \\ 1 & 2 & 3 & 4 \end{bmatrix}$ by Householder's method.

Solution:

The following program is used

```
%Input - A is an nxn symmetric matrix
A = [4 3 2 1; 3 8 6 12;2 6 8 3; 1 2 3 4];

%Output - T is a tridiagonal matrix

[n,n] = size(A);
for k = 1:n - 2
  s = norm(A(k +1:n, k));
  if (A(k + 1, k)<0)
    s = -s;
  end
  r = sqrt(2*s*(A(k +1, k) + s));
  W(1:k) = zeros(1,k);
  W(k + 1) = (A(k + 1,k) + s)/r;
  W(k + 2:n) = A(k + 2:n, k)'/r;
  V(1:k) = zeros(1, k);
  V(k+1:n) = A(k + 1:n, k + 1:n)*W(k + 1:n)';
  c = W(k + 1:n)*V(k + 1:n)';
  Q(1:k) = zeros(1, k);
  Q(k + 1:n) = V(k+1:n) - c*W(k + 1:n);
  A (k + 2: n, k) = zeros(n - k - 1,1);
  A (k, k + 2: n) = zeros (1, n - k - 1);
  A(k +1, k) = -s;
  A(k, k + 1) = -s;
   A(k + 1:n, k + 1:n) =A(k + 1:n, k + 1:n) - 2*W(k + 1:n)'*Q(k + 1:n) -2*Q(k +
1:n)'*W(k+1:n);
end
T=A;
fprintf ('Matrix in tridiagonal form is\n');
disp(T)
```

Matrix in tridiagonal form is

```
 4.0000  -3.7417    0         0
-3.7417  14.5714    2.6245    0
 0        2.6245    2.6878   -0.7622
 0        0        -0.7622    2.7407
```

Example E4.4: Use the QR factorization method with Householder transformation to calculate the eigenvalues and the corresponding eigenvectors of the matrix [*K*], where

$$[K] = \begin{bmatrix} 5 & -4 & 1 & 0 \\ -4 & 6 & -4 & 1 \\ 1 & -4 & 6 & -4 \\ 0 & 1 & -4 & 5 \end{bmatrix}$$

Solution:

MATLAB Solution [Using built-in function]:

```
>> A = [5 - 4 1 0; - 4 6  - 4 1; 1- 4 6 - 4; 0 1 -4 5];
>> kmax = 200;
>> [eigs,A] = eig_QR(A, kmax)
eigs =
   13.0902
    6.8541
    1.9098
    0.1459
A =
   13.0902     0.0000     0.0000    -0.0000
   -0.0000     6.8541     0.0000     0.0000
    0.0000    -0.0000     1.9098     0.0000
    0          0         -0.0000     0.1459
>> A = [5 - 4 1 0; - 4 6 - 4 1;1 - 4 6 - 4;0 1 - 4 5];
>> [Q,d] = eig(A)
Q =
  - 0.3717   - 0.6015     0.6015   - 0.3717
  - 0.6015   - 0.3717   - 0.3717     0.6015
  - 0.6015     0.3717   - 0.3717   - 0.6015
  - 0.3717     0.6015     0.6015     0.3717
d =
    0.1459     0          0          0
    0          1.9098     0          0
    0          0          6.8541     0
    0          0          0         13.0902
```

```
function [eigs,A] = eig_QR(A,kmax)
%Find eigenvalues by using QR factorization
if nargin<2, kmax = 200; end
for k = 1:kmax
[Q,R] = qr(A); %A = Q*R; R=Q'*A=Q^-1*A
A = R*Q; %A = Q^-1*A*Q
end
eigs = diag(A);

function [Q,R] = qr_my(A)
%QR factorization
N = size(A,1); R=A; Q = eye(N);
for k =1:N - 1
H = Householder(R(:,k), k);
R = H*R;
Q = Q*H;
end

function H = Householder(x,k)
%Householder transform to zero out tail part starting from k+1
H = eye(N) - 2*w*w'; %Householder matrix
N = length(x);
w = zeros(N,1);
w(k) = (x(k) + g)/c; w(k + 1:N) = x(k + 1:N)/c;
tmp = sum(x (k+1: N). ^2);
c =sqrt((x(k) + g)^2 + tmp);
g = sqrt(x(k)^2 + tmp);
```

Example E4.5: Using Choleski's method of solution, solve the following linear equations.

$$x_1 + x_2 + x_3 = 7$$
$$3x_1 + 3x_2 + 4x_3 = 23$$
$$2x_1 + x_2 + x_3 = 10$$

Solution:

MATLAB Solution [Using built-in function]:

Choleski's method:

```
>> A = [1 1 1;3 3 4;2 1 1];
>> B = [7;23;10];
>> [L,U] = lu(A)
```

```
L =
        0.3333   -0.0000   1.0000
        1.0000    0         0
        0.6667    1.0000    0

U =
        3.0000    3.0000   4.0000
        0        -1.0000  -1.6667
        0         0       -0.3333
>> L*U
ans =
        1.0000    1.0000   1.0000
        3.0000    3.0000   4.0000
        2.0000    1.0000   1.0000
>> d = L\B
d =
       23.0000
       - 5.3333
       - 0.6667
>> x = U\d
x =
        3.0000
        2.0000
        2.0000
```

Check with MATLAB [Using built-in function]:

```
>> A = [1 1 1;3 3 4;2 1 1];
>> B = [7;23;10];
>> x = A\B
x =
      3.0000
      2.0000
      2.0000
>> x = inv(A)*B
x =
      3.0000
      2.0000
      2.0000
```

Example E4.6: Solve the system of equations by Choleski's factorization method.

$$12x_1 - 6x_2 - 6x_3 - 1.5x_4 = 1$$
$$-6x_1 + 4x_2 + 3x_3 + 0.5x_4 = 2$$
$$-6x_1 + 3x_2 + 6x_3 + 1.5x_4 = 3$$
$$-1.5x_1 + 0.5x_2 + 1.5x_3 + x_4 = 4$$

Solution:

MATLAB Solution [Using built-in function]:

Choleski's method:

```
>> A = [12 - 6 - 6 - 1.5; - 6 4 3 0.5; - 6 3 6 1.5; - 1.5 0.5 1.5 1];
>> B = [1; 2; 3; 4];
>> [L,U] = lu(A)
L =
     1.0000        0         0         0
    -0.5000   1.0000         0         0
    -0.5000        0    1.0000         0
    -0.1250  -0.2500   -0.2500    1.0000
U =
    12.0000  -6.0000   -6.0000   -1.5000
          0   1.0000         0   -0.2500
          0        0    3.0000    0.7500
          0        0         0    0.5625
>> L*U
ans =
    12.0000  -6.0000   -6.0000   -1.5000
    -6.0000   4.0000    3.0000    0.5000
    -6.0000   3.0000    6.0000    1.5000
    -1.5000   0.5000    1.5000    1.0000
>> d = L\B
d =
     1.0000
     2.5000
     3.5000
     3.8750
>> x=U\d
x =
     2.7778
     4.2222
    -0.5556
     6.8889
```

MATLAB Solution [Using built-in function]:

```
>> A = [12 -6 -6 -1.5; -6 4 3 0.5; -6 3 6 1.5; -1.5 0.5 1.5 1];
>> B = [1;2;3;4];
>> x = A\B
x =
       2.7778
       4.2222
      -0.5556
       6.8889
>> x = inv(A)*B
x =
       2.7778
       4.2222
      -0.5556
       6.8889
```

Example E4.7: Solve the set of equations given in Example E4.3. Use Jacobi method.

Solution:

```
>> A = [3 1 -1; 4 -10 1; 2 1 5]; >> b = [-2 3 4]';
>> [x,k] = jacobi(A,b,[0 0 0]',1.e-10)
Jacobi iteration has converged in 38 iterations.
x =
      -0.2462
      -0.3026
       0.9590
k =
      38
```

```
function [x, k, diff] = jacobi(A,b,x0,tol,kmax)
% Jacobi iteration on the system Ax = b.
if nargin<3, x0 = zeros(size(b));, end
if nargin<4, tol = 1e-10;, end
if nargin<5, kmax = 100;, end
if min(abs(diag(A)))<eps
error('Coefficient matrix has zero diagonal entries, iteration cannot be performed.\r')
end
[n m] = size(A);
xold = x0;
```

```
k = 1;, diff = [];
while k< = kmax
  xnew = b;
  for i = 1:n
    for j = 1:n
      if j~ = i
        xnew(i) = xnew(i) - A(i,j)*xold(j);
      end
    end
    xnew(i) = xnew(i)/A(i,i);
  end
  diff(k) = norm(xnew-xold,2);
  if diff(k)<tol
      fprintf('Jacobi iteration has converged in %d iterations.\r', k)
      x = xnew;
      return
  end
  k = k+1;, xold = xnew;
end
fprintf('Jacobi iteration failed to converge.\r')
x = xnew;
```

Example E4.8: Find the solution to the equations using Jacobi method with initial values [0 0 0 0].

$$\begin{bmatrix} 4 & 2 & 0 & 0 \\ 2 & 8 & 2 & 0 \\ 0 & 2 & 8 & 2 \\ 0 & 0 & 2 & 4 \end{bmatrix} \begin{Bmatrix} x_1 \\ x_2 \\ x_3 \\ x_4 \end{Bmatrix} = \begin{Bmatrix} 4 \\ 0 \\ 0 \\ 0 \end{Bmatrix}$$

Solution:

```
>> A = [4 2 0 0;2 8 2 0;0 2 8 2;0 0 2 4];
>> b = [4;0;0;0];
>> x0 = [0 0 0 0]';
>> [x,k] = jacobi(A,b,x0,1.e - 10)
Jacobi iteration has converged in 34 iterations.
x =
     1.1556
    -0.3111
     0.0889
    -0.0444
```

```
k =
    34
```

```
function [x, k, diff] = jacobi(A,b,x0,tol,kmax)
% Jacobi iteration on the system Ax = b.
if nargin<3, x0 = zeros(size(b));, end
if nargin<4, tol = 1e - 10;, end
if nargin<5, kmax = 100;, end
if min(abs(diag(A)))<eps
error('Coefficient matrix has zero diagonal entries, iteration cannot be
performed.\r')
end
[n m] = size(A);
xold = x0;
k = 1;, diff = [];
while k< = kmax
  xnew = b;
  for i = 1:n
    for j = 1:n
      if j~ = i
        xnew(i) = xnew(i) - A(i,j)*xold(j);
      end
    end
    xnew(i) = xnew(i)/A(i,i);
  end
  diff(k) = norm(xnew - xold,2);
  if diff(k)<tol
      fprintf('Jacobi iteration has converged in %d iterations.\r', k)
      x = xnew;
      return
  end
  k = k+1;, xold = xnew;
end
fprintf('Jacobi iteration failed to converge.\r')
x = xnew;
```

Example E4.9: Find the solution to the equations using Gauss-Seidel method.

$$\begin{bmatrix} 4 & 2 & 0 & 0 \\ 2 & 8 & 2 & 0 \\ 0 & 2 & 8 & 2 \\ 0 & 0 & 2 & 4 \end{bmatrix} \begin{Bmatrix} x_1 \\ x_2 \\ x_3 \\ x_4 \end{Bmatrix} = \begin{Bmatrix} 4 \\ 0 \\ 0 \\ 0 \end{Bmatrix}$$

Solution:

MATLAB Solution Using built-in function]:

```
>> A = [4 2 0 0;2 8 2 0;0 2 8 2;0 0 2 4];
>> B = [4;0;0;0];
>> x = A\B
x =
     1.1556
    -0.3111
     0.0889
    -0.0444
>> x=inv(A)*B
x =
     1.1556
    -0.3111
     0.0889
    -0.0444
>> A = [4 2 0 0;2 8 2 0;0 2 8 2;0 0 2 4];
>> b = [4;0;0;0];
>> tol = 1.0e - 9;
>> format long;
>> xguess = [1- 0.5 0.1 - 0.2];
>> [x,iter] = GAUSSD(A,b,xguess,tol)
x =
  1.15555555568491 -0.31111111117579  0.08888888892123 -0.04444444446061
iter =
    16
```

```
function [Y,iter] = GAUSSD(A,r,yguess,tol)
% GAUSSD will iteratively solve Ay = r
n = length(r); Y = yguess; dy = ones(n,1); iter = 0;
while norm(dy)/norm(Y) > tol
for i = 1:n
if abs(A(i,i))<100*eps;error('zero pivot found');end
dy(i) = r(i)/A(i,i);
```

```
for j = 1:n
dy(i) = dy(i) - A(i,j)*Y(j)/A(i,i);
end
Y(i) = Y(i) + dy(i);
end
iter = iter + 1;
if iter>1000; error('not converging in 1000 steps');end
end
```

Example E4.10: Solve the system of equations given by $[A]\{x\} = \{b\}$ using Gauss-Seidel method. The matrices $[A]$ and $\{b\}$ are given below.

$$[A] = \begin{bmatrix} 4 & 2 & 0 & 0 \\ 2 & 8 & 2 & 0 \\ 0 & 2 & 8 & 2 \\ 0 & 0 & 2 & 4 \end{bmatrix}, \ \{b\} = \begin{Bmatrix} 4 \\ 0 \\ 0 \\ 14 \end{Bmatrix}$$

Solution:

MATLAB Solution [Using built-in function]:

```
>> A = [4 2 0 0;2 8 2 0;0 2 8 2;0 0 2 4];
>> b = [4;0;0;14];
>> x = A\b
x =
     1.0000
     0
    -1.0000
     4.0000
>> x = inv(A)*b
x =
     1.0000
    -0.0000
    -1.0000
     4.0000
>> A= [4 2 0 0;2 8 2 0;0 2 8 2;0 0 2 4];
>> b = [4;0;0;14];
>> xguess = [1 -0.5 0.1 -0.2];
>> tol = 1.0e-9;
>> format long;
>> [x,iter] = GAUSSD(A,b,xguess,tol)
x =
   1.00000000075670 -0.00000000037835 -0.99999999981083 3.99999999990541
iter =
   17
```

```
function [Y,iter] = GAUSSD(A,r,yguess,tol)
% GAUSSD will iteratively solve Ay = r
n = length(r); Y = yguess; dy = ones(n,1); iter = 0;
while norm(dy)/norm(Y) > tol
for i = 1:n
if abs(A(i,i))<100*eps;error('zero pivot found');end
dy(i) = r(i)/A(i,i);
for j = 1:n
dy(i) = dy(i) - A(i,j)*Y(j)/A(i,i);
end
Y(i) = Y(i) + dy(i);
end
iter = iter + 1;
if iter>1000; error('not converging in 1000 steps');end
end
```

Example E4.11: Solve the system of equations given below by Householder's factorization method:

$$\begin{bmatrix} 4 & -1 & 0 & 0 \\ -1 & 4 & -1 & 0 \\ 0 & -1 & 4 & -1 \\ 0 & 0 & -1 & 4 \end{bmatrix} \begin{Bmatrix} x_1 \\ x_2 \\ x_3 \\ x_4 \end{Bmatrix} = \begin{Bmatrix} 1 \\ 0 \\ 0 \\ 0 \end{Bmatrix}$$

Solution:

```
>> A = [4 -1 0 0;-1 4 -1 0;0 -1 4 -1;0 0 -1 4];
>> b = [1;0;0;0];
>> householder(A)
ans =
     4     1     0     0
    -2     4    -1     0
     0     2     4     1
     0     0     1     4
>> [L,U] = lu(A)
L =
     1.0000    0          0          0
    -0.2500    1.0000     0          0
     0        -0.2667     1.0000     0
     0         0         -0.2679     1.0000
U =
     4.0000   -1.0000     0          0
     0         3.7500    -1.0000     0
     0         0          3.7333    -1.0000
     0         0          0          3.7321
```

```
>> L*U

ans =
     4    -1     0     0
    -1     4    -1     0
     0    -1     4    -1
     0     0    -1     4
>> A = [4 -1 0 0;-1 4 -1 0;0 -1 4 -1;0 0 -1 4];
>> d = L\b
d =
      1.0000
      0.2500
      0.0667
      0.0179
>> x = U\d
x =
      0.2679
      0.0718
      0.0191
      0.0048
```

MATLAB Solution [Using built-in function]:

```
>> A = [4 -1 0 0;-1 4 -1 0;0 -1 4 -1;0 0 -1 4];
>> B = [1;0;0;0];
>> x = A\B
x =
      0.2679
      0.0718
      0.0191
      0.0048
>> x = inv(A)*B
x =
      0.2679
      0.0718
      0.0191
      0.0048
```

```
function A = householder(A)
% Householder reduction of A to tridiagonal form A = [c\d\c]
%Extract c and d by d = diag(A), c = diag(A,1)
%Usage: A = householder(A)
```

```
n = size(A,1);
for k = 1:n-2
u = A(k+1:n,k);
uMag = sqrt(dot(u,u));
if u(1)<0;uMag = -uMag; end
u(1) = u(1)+uMag;
A(k+1:n,k) = u;
H = dot(u,u)/2;
v = A(k+1:n,k+1:n)*u/H;
g = dot(u,v)/(2*H);
v = v-g*u;
A(k+1:n,k+1:n) = A(k+1:n,k+1:n)-v*u'-u*v';
A(k,k+1) = -uMag;
d = diag(A);
c = diag(A,1);
end
```

Example E4.12: Solve the system of equations given below by Householder's factorization method:

$$\begin{bmatrix} 4 & 2 & 1 & 1 \\ 2 & 10 & 2 & 1 \\ 1 & 2 & 4 & 2 \\ 1 & 2 & 4 & 8 \end{bmatrix} \begin{Bmatrix} x_1 \\ x_2 \\ x_3 \\ x_4 \end{Bmatrix} = \begin{Bmatrix} 10 \\ 20 \\ 30 \\ 40 \end{Bmatrix}$$

Solution:

```
>> A = [4 2 1 1;2 10 2 1;1 2 4 2;1 2 4 8];
% Householder reduction of A to tridiagonal form A = [c\d\c]
% Extract c and by d = diag(A) andc = diag(A,1)
>> householder(A)
ans =
      4.0000   -2.4495    1.0000    1.0000
      4.4495   12.4082   -1.8257   -2.6330
      1.0000    2.6422    2.4400    0.3427
      1.0000   -1.6330    2.3427    7.1517
>> b = [10;20;30;40];
>> A = [4 2 1 1;2 10 2 1;1 2 4 2;1 2 4 8];
>> [L,U] = lu(A)
L =
      1.0000    0         0         0
      0.5000    1.0000    0         0
      0.2500    0.1667    1.0000    0
      0.2500    0.1667    1.0000    1.0000
```

```
U =
      4.0000    2.0000     1.0000     1.0000
      0         9.0000     1.5000     0.5000
      0         0          3.5000     1.6667
      0         0          0          6.0000
>> L*U
ans =
      4     2     1     1
      2    10     2     1
      1     2     4     2
      1     2     4     8
>> d = L\b
d =
     10
     15
     25
     10
>> x = U\d
x =
      0.2381
      0.5159
      6.3492
      1.6667
```

```
function A = householder(A)
% Householder reduction of A to tridiagonal form A = [c\d\c]
% Extract c and d by d = diag(A), c = diag(A,1)
% Usage: A = householder(A)
n = size(A,1);
for k = 1:n - 2
u = A(k+1:n,k);
uMag = sqrt(dot(u,u));
if u(1)<0;uMag = -uMag; end
u(1) = u(1)+uMag;
A(k+1:n,k) = u;
H = dot(u,u)/2;
v = A(k+1:n,k+1:n)*u/H;
g = dot(u,v)/(2*H);
v = v-g*u;
A(k+1:n,k+1:n) = A(k+1:n,k+1:n)-v*u'-u*v';
A(k,k+1) = -uMag;
d = diag(A);
```

```
c = diag(A,1);
end
```

MATLAB Solution [Using built-in function]:

```
>> A = [4 2 1 1;2 10 2 1;1 2 4 2;1 2 4 8];
>> B = [10;20;30;40];
>> x = A\B
x =
      0.2381
      0.5159
      6.3492
      1.6667
>> x = inv(A)*B
x =
      0.2381
      0.5159
      6.3492
      1.6667
```

Example E4.13: Use the method of Gaussian elimination to solve the following system of linear equations:

$$x_1 + x_2 + x_3 - x_4 = 2$$
$$4x_1 + 3x_2 + x_3 + x_4 = 11$$
$$x_1 - x_2 - x_3 + 2x_4 = 0$$
$$2x_1 + x_2 + 2x_3 - 2x_4 = 2$$

Solution:

Gaussian elimination method eliminates (makes zero) all coefficients below the main diagonal of the two-dimensional array. It does so by adding multiples of some equations to others in a symmetric way. Elimination makes the array of new coefficients have an upper triangular form since the lower triangular coefficients are all zero. Upper triangular equations can be solved by back substitution. Back substitution first solves last equation which has only one unknown $x(N) = b(N)/A(N, N)$.

Thus, it is a two phase procedure.

(1) Forward elimination (Upper triangularization): First reduce the coefficients of first column of A below main diagonal to zero using first row. Then do same for the second column using second row.

(2) Back substitution: In this step, starting from the last equation, each of the unknowns is found.

Pitfalls of the method:

There are two pitfalls of Gauss elimination method:

Division by zero: It is possible that division by zero may occur during forward elimination steps.

Round-off error: Gauss Elimination Method is prone to round-off errors.

The following MATLAB code is written for this problem

```
% This will perform Gaussian elmination
% on the matrix that you pass to it.
% i.e., given A and b it can be used to find x,
%     Ax = b
%
% A - matrix for the left hand side.
% b - vector for the right hand side
% This performs Gaussian elminiation to find x.
% MATRIX DEFINITION
A = [1 1 1 -1;4 3 1 1;1 -1 -1 2;2 1 2 -2];
b = [2;11;0;2];
% Perform Gaussian Elimination
 for j = 2:N,
   for i = j:N,
     m = A(i,j-1)/A(j-1, j-1);
     A(i,:) = A(i,:) - A(j-1,:)*m;
     b(i) = b(i) - m*b(j-1);
   end
 end
disp('Upper triangular form of given matrix is=')
disp(A)
disp('b=')
disp(b)

% BACK-SUBSTITUTION
% Perform back substitution
 x = zeros(N,1);
 x(N) = b(N)/A(N,N);
  for j = N-1:-1:1,
   x(j) = (b(j)-A(j,j+1:N)*x(j+1:N))/A(j,j);
 end
disp('final solution is');
disp(x);
```

Output appears like this:

```
N
    = 4
```

```
Upper triangular form of given matrix is =
    1.0000    1.0000    1.0000   -1.0000
    0        -1.0000   -3.0000    5.0000
    0         0         4.0000   -7.0000
    0         0         0          0.2500
b =
    2
    3
   -8
    1
final solution is
   -1
    2
    5
    4
```

Check with MATLAB built-in function:

```
>> A = [1 1 1 -1;4 3 1 1;1 -1 -1 2;2 1 2 -2];
>> b = [2;11;0;2];
>> x = A\b
x =
   -1.0000
    2.0000
    5.0000
    4.0000
```

Example E4.14: Solve the following system of equations using Choleski's factorization.

$$x_1 + x_2 + x_3 - x_4 = 2$$
$$x_1 - x_2 - x_3 + 2x_4 = 0$$
$$4x_1 + 4x_2 + x_3 + x_4 = 11$$
$$2x_1 + x_2 + 2x_3 - 2x_4 = 2$$

Solution:

Choleski's factorization is basically applicable to only symmetric positive definite matrices.

Here original matrix $[A]$ is decomposed as follows:

1. Form $[A] = L{\cdot}L^T$ where L is lower triangular matrix
2. Forward substitution to solve $Ly = b$ for y
3. Back substitution to solve $L^Tx = y$ for x

For non-symmetric matrix a LU decomposition scheme can be employed using MATLAB function '*lu*(*A*)'.

Complete MATLAB program is given below to solve the problem.

```
A = [1 1 1 -1;1 -1 -1 2;4 4 1 1;2 1 2 -2];
b = [2;0;11;2];
```

```
[L,U] = lu(A);
% solution of y
y = L\b;
%final solution x
x = U\y;
fprintf('Solution of the equations is\n');
disp(x)
Output is as follows:
Solution of the equations is
        1.0000
        2.0000
       -1.0000
        0.0000
```

Check with MATLAB built-in function:

```
>> A= [1 1 1 -1;1 -1 -1 2;4 4 1 1;2 1 2 -2];
b = [2;0;11;2];
>> x = A\b
x =

        1.0000
        2.0000
       -1.0000
        0.0000
```

Example E4.15: Using the Gauss-Seidel method, solve the system of equations given below:

$$x + 2y + z = 0$$
$$3x + y - z = 0$$
$$x - y + 4z = 3$$

Solution:

The Gauss-Seidel method is a technique used to solve a linear system of equations. In solving equations $AX = b$, first the matrix A is written as: $A = D + L + U$ where the matrices D, L, and U represent the diagonal, negative strictly lower triangular, and negative strictly upper triangular parts of the coefficient matrix A. Then the solution is given for every iteration counter k as:

$$X^{(k+1)} = (D + L)^{-1}(-U\, X^{(k)} + b) \qquad \text{Gauss-Seidel Method}$$
$$X^{(k+1)} = D^{-1}(-(L + U)\, X^{(k)} + b) \qquad \text{Jacobi Method}$$

Disadvantages:

1. The matrix $(D + L)$ is not always invertible. One must check that the values on the diagonal are non-zero before starting the iteration because it can lead to unpredictable results.

2. The spectral radius of the matrix $(D + L)^{-1} * U$ must have a modulus < 1 for the iteration to work correctly. Think of the spectral radius (the largest value of the set of eigenvalue modules) as being the greatest scalar factor that can be applied to a vector. If it is greater than 1, iteration on the corresponding eigenvector will result in an infinite limit.

Complete MATLAB program for solving given system of equations is given below:

```
% The display consists of a table of x-values with iterates of x1, x2, ..., xn
% in each column.
A = [1 2 1;3 1 -1;1 -1 4];b = [0;0;3];
X0 = zeros(size(b)); % starting vector
tole = 1e-6;kstop = 30;% error tolerance and max. iterations
[n,n] = size(A);
P = tril(A);% lower triangular form
k = 0;r = b-A*X0;
r0 = norm(r);er = norm(r);
X = X0;
[L,U] = lu(P);
fprintf('iter#\tX(1)\t\tX(2)\n');
while er>tole & k<kstop
  fprintf('%d\t%f\t%f\n',k,X(1),X(2));
  k = k+1;
  dx = L\r;
  dx = U\dx;
  X = X+dx;
  r = b-A*X;
  er = norm(r)/r0;
  erp(k) = norm(r)/r0;
end
X
plot(erp, '-p');
grid on;
xlabel('Iteration #');
ylabel('normalized error');
```

Output of the program is as follows:

Final solution is $X =$

```
   1.0e + 024 *
  -1.7510
   5.5007
   1.8129
```

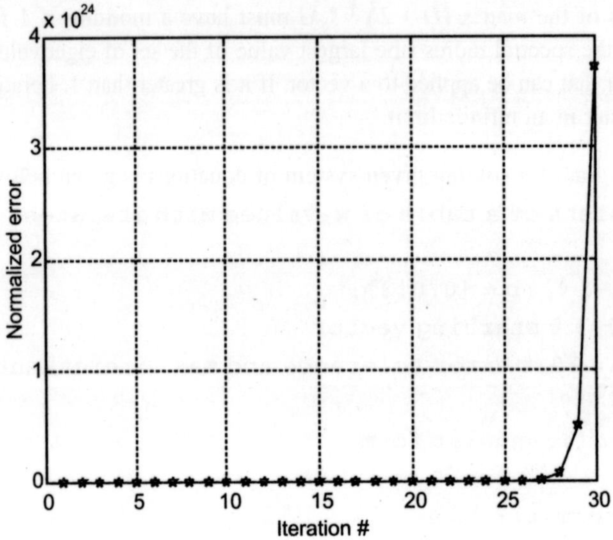

Fig. E4.15

Here the method fails due to reason (2) given above.

Check with MATLAB built-in function:

```
>> A = [1 2 1;3 1 -1;1 -1 4];b = [0;0;3];
>> x = A\b
x =
      0.3333
     -0.4444
      0.5556
```

Example E4.16: Using the Gauss-Seidel method, solve the system of equations given below:

$$4x - y + z = 10$$
$$-x + 4y - 2z = -2$$
$$x - 2y + 4z = 5$$

Solution:

MATLAB program for this problem is given below.

```
A = [4 -1 1;-1 4 -2;1 -2 4];
b = [10;-2;5];
X0 = zeros(size(b)); % starting vector
tole = 1e-6;kstop = 30;% error tolerance and max. iterations
[n,n] = size(A);
P = tril(A);% lower triangular form
k = 0;r = b-A*X0;
r0 = norm(r);er = norm(r);
```

```
X = X0;
[L,U] = lu(P);
fprintf('iter#\tX(1)\t\tX(2)\n');
while er>tole & k<kstop
  fprintf('%d\t%f\t%f\n',k,X(1),X(2));
  k = k+1;
  dx = L\r;
  dx = U\dx;
  X = X+dx;
  r = b-A*X;
  er = norm(r)/r0;
  erp(k) = norm(r)/r0;
end
X
plot(erp, '-p');
grid on;
xlabel('Iteration #');
ylabel('normalized error');
```

Output of the program is as follows:

iter#	X(1)	X(2)
0	0.000000	0.000000
1	2.500000	0.125000
2	2.359375	0.433594
3	2.389160	0.535767
4	2.403793	0.561245
5	2.407893	0.566810
6	2.408845	0.567927
7	2.409044	0.568137
8	2.409082	0.568174

The final solution is

$X =$

2.4091

0.5682

0.9318

The variation of error in each cycle is shown in Fig. E4.16.

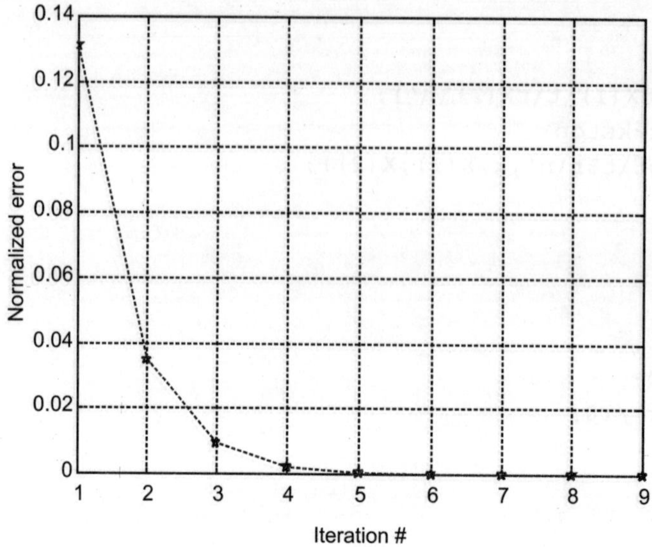

Fig. E4.16 MATLAB output

Check with MATLAB built-in function:

```
>> A = [4 -1 1;-1 4 -2;1 -2 4];b= [10; -2;5];
>> x = A\b
x =
        2.4091
        0.5682
        0.9318
```

Example E4.17: Use the Jacobi method to determine the eigenvalues and eigenvectors of the following matrix

$$A = \begin{bmatrix} 11 & 2 & 8 \\ 2 & 2 & -10 \\ 9 & -10 & 5 \end{bmatrix}$$

Solution:

A solution is guaranteed for all real symmetric matrices when Jacobi's method is used. This limitation is not severe since many practical problems of applied mathematics and engineering involve symmetric matrices. From a theoretical viewpoint, the method embodies techniques that are found in more sophisticated algorithms. For instructive purposes, it is worthwhile to investigate the details of Jacobi's method.

Start with the real symmetric matrix A. Then construct the sequence of orthogonal matrices $R_1, R_2, R_3, \ldots, R_n$ as follows:

$$D_0 = A$$

and $D_j = R_j^T D_j R_j$ for $j = 1,2,\ldots$.

It is possible to construct the sequence $\{R_j\}$ so that

$$\lim_{j \to D_j} = D = \text{diag}(\lambda_1, \lambda_2, \ldots\ldots, \lambda_n)$$

In practice, we will stop when the off-diagonal elements are close to zero. Then we will have $D_m \approx D$.

The complete program is shown below:

```
A = [11 2 8;2 2 -10;9 -10 5];
%Output - V is the nxn matrix of eigenvectors
%      - D is the diagonal nxn matrix of eigenvalues
D = A;
[n,n] = size(A);
V = eye(n);
%Calculate row p and column q of the off-diagonal element
%of greatest magnitude in A
[m1 p] = max(abs(D-diag(diag(D))));
[m2 q] = max(m1);
p = p(q);
i = 1;
while(i<10)
  % Zero out Dpq and Dqp
  t = D(p,q)/(D(q,q)-D(p,p));
  c = 1/sqrt(t^2+1);
  s = c*t;
  R = [c s;-s c];
  D([p q],:) = R'*D([p q],:);
  D(:,[p q]) = D(:,[p q])*R;
  V(:,[p q]) = V(:,[p q])*R;
  [m1 p] = max(abs(D-diag(diag(D))));
  [m2 q] = max(m1);
  p = p(q);
  i = i+1;
end
D = diag(diag(D))
fprintf('final eigenvalues are %f\t%f\t%f\n',D(1,1),D(2,2),D(3,3));
```

The output of the program is as follows:

```
D =

   18.4278         0         0
         0   -9.2213         0
         0         0    8.7934

final eigenvalues are    18.427839    -9.221279    8.793440
```

Check with MATLAB built-in function:

```
>> A = [11 2 8;2 2 -10;9 -10 5];
>> [Q,D] = eig(A)
Q =
     0.3319    -0.6460    -0.6277
    -0.6599     0.3380    -0.6966
    -0.6741    -0.6845     0.3475
D =
    -9.2213     0          0
     0         18.4308     0
     0          0          8.7905
```

Example E4.18: Transform the matrix $A = \begin{bmatrix} 4 & 3 & 2 & 1 \\ 3 & 4 & 1 & 2 \\ 2 & 1 & 4 & 3 \\ 1 & 2 & 3 & 4 \end{bmatrix}$ into tridiagonal form using Householder reduction. Also determine the transformation matrix.

Solution:

Suppose that A is a symmetric $n \times n$ matrix.

Start with $A_0 = A$

Construct the sequence $P_1, P_2, ..., P_{n-1}$ of Householder matrices, so that $A_k = P_k A_{k-1} P_k$ for $k = 1, 2, ..., n-2$, where A_k has zeros below the subdiagonal in columns 1, 2, …, k. Then A_{n-2} is a symmetric tridiagonal matrix that is similar to A. This process is called Householder's method.

```
%Input - A is an nxn symmetric matrix
A=[4 3 2 1;3 4 1 2;2 1 4 3;1 2 3 4];
%Output - T is a tridiagonal matrix
[n,n] = size(A);
for k = 1:n-2
  s = norm(A(k+1:n,k));
  if (A(k+1,k)<0)
    s = -s;
  end
  r = sqrt(2*s*(A(k+1,k)+s));
  W(1:k) = zeros(1,k);
  W(k+1) = (A(k+1,k)+s)/r;
  W(k+2:n) = A(k+2:n,k)'/r;
  V(1:k) = zeros(1,k);
  V(k+1:n) = A(k+1:n,k+1:n)*W(k+1:n)';
  c = W(k+1:n)*V(k+1:n)';
```

```
    Q(1:k) = zeros(1,k);
    Q(k+1:n) = V(k+1:n)-c*W(k+1:n);
    A(k+2:n,k) = zeros(n-k-1,1);
    A(k,k+2:n) = zeros(1,n-k-1);
    A(k+1,k) = -s;
    A(k,k+1) = -s;
    A(k+1:n,k+1:n) = A(k+1:n,k+1:n) ...
      -2*W(k+1:n)'*Q(k+1:n)-2*Q(k+1:n)'*W(k+1:n);
end
T = A;
fprintf('Matrix in tridiagonal form is\n');
disp(T);
```

The output of the program is given below:

Matrix in tridiagonal form is

```
 4.0000   -3.7417    0        0
-3.7417    6.5714    2.7180   0
 0         2.7180    3.0529   1.2403
 0         0         1.2403   2.3757
```

Example E4.19: Use the Sturn sequence property to find the interval of the smallest eigenvalue of

$$A = \begin{bmatrix} 2 & -1 & 0 & 0 \\ -1 & 2 & -2 & 0 \\ 0 & -2 & 2 & -1 \\ 0 & 0 & -1 & 2 \end{bmatrix}$$

Solution: The sequence $\{f_k(a)\}$ and $\{f_k(b)$ can be used to determine the number of roots of $f_n(\lambda)$, which are contained in $[a, b]$.

The sequence $\{f_0, f_1, ..., fn\}$ forms a Sturn sequence of polynomials; and such sequences have special properties. Given a point b, calculate

$$\{f_0(b), f_1(b), ..., f_n(b)\}$$

and observe the signs of these quantities. If some $f_j(\lambda) = 0$, then choose the sign of $f_j(\lambda)$ to be opposite to that of $f_{j-1}(\lambda)$. It can be shown that

$$f_j(\lambda) = 0 \Rightarrow f_{j-1}(\lambda) \neq 0$$

Having obtain a sequence of signs from flet $s(\lambda)$ denote the number of agreements of sign between consecutive members of the sign sequence.

The MATLAB program for this presented below:

```
%Given the diagonals c and d of A = [c\d\c] and the value of l, this function returns
the sturn sequence P0(l), P1(l), P2(l), ........ Pn(l). Note that Pn(l) = |A-λl|
A = [2 -1 0 0;-1 2 -2 0;0 -2 2 -1;0 0 -1 2];
d = diag(A)';
c = [-1 -2 -1];
lam = input('Enter guess value lambda\n');
n = length(d)+1;
p = ones(n,1);
p(2) = d(1)-lam;
for i = 2:n-1
  p(i+1) = (d(i)-lam)*p(i)-(c(i-1)^2)*p1(i-1);
end
fprintf('sturn sequence p(%f) is\n',lam);
disp(p);
%%% number of sign changes in the sturn sequence p is
%%% number eigenvalues of matrix A that are smaller than
%%% lam_min
n = length(p);
oldsign = 1;
num_eval = 0;
for i = 2:n
  psign = sign(p(i));
  if psign = 0 psign = -oldsign;
  end
  if psign*oldsign <0
    num_eval = num_eval+1;
  end
  oldsign = psign;
end
fprintf('Number of eigenvalues less than lamda = %f are %d\n', lam, num_eval);
Output of the program is as follows (in two runs)
>>Enter guess value lambda
0
sturn sequence p(0.000000) is
     1
     2
     4
     0
    -4
```

Number of eigenvalues less than lamda = 0.000000 are 1

» sturn

Enter guess value lambda

−1

sturn sequence p(−1.000000) is

1

3

9

19

53

Number of eigenvalues less than lamda = − 1.000000 are 0

Hence, lowest eigen value lies between 0 and −1.

Example E4.20: Use Gaussian elimination scheme to solve the set of equations:

$$2x_1 + x_2 - 3x_3 = 11$$
$$4x_1 - 2x_2 + 3x_3 = 8$$
$$-2x_1 + 2x_2 - x_3 = -6$$

Solution:

Writing the equation in the form of $[A]X = B$ and applying forward elimination and back-substitution, we obtain

$$U = \begin{bmatrix} 2 & 1 & -3 \\ 0 & -4 & 9 \\ 0 & 0 & 2.75 \end{bmatrix} \quad \text{and right hand side} = \begin{bmatrix} 11 \\ -14 \\ -5 \end{bmatrix}$$

Finally, the solution from back substitution becomes $X = \begin{bmatrix} 3 \\ -1 \\ -2 \end{bmatrix}$

The complete MATLAB program is given below:

```
% Ax = b
% A - matrix for the left hand side.
% b - vector for the right hand side
% This performs Gaussian elminiation to find x.
% MATRIX DEFINITION
A = [2 1 -3;4 -2 3;-2 2 -1];
b = [11;8;-6];
N = max(size(A));
% Perform Gaussian (FORWARD) elimination
 for j = 2:N,
   for i = j:N,
     m = A(i,j-1)/A(j-1,j-1);
     A(i,:) = A(i,:) -A(j-1,:)*m;
```

```
      b(i) = b(i) - m*b(j-1);
    end
  end
disp('Upper triangular form of given matrix is =')
disp(A);
disp('b = ');
disp(b);
% BACK-SUBSTITUTION
% Perform back substitution
 x = zeros(N,1);
 x(N) = b(N)/A(N,N);
 for j = N-1:-1:1,
  x(j) = (b(j)-A(j,j+1:N)*x(j+1:N))/A(j,j);
 end
disp('final solution is');disp(x);
```

Output is as follows:

The final solution is

```
     3
    -1
    -2
```

Check with MATLAB built-in function:

```
>> A = [2 1 -3;4 -2 3;-2 2 -1];
b = [11;8;-6];
>> x = A\b
x =
      3
     -1
     -2
```

Example E4.21: Solve the system of linear equations by Gaussian elimination method:

$$6x_1 + 3x_2 + 6x_3 = 30$$
$$2x_1 + 3x_2 + 3x_3 = 17$$
$$x_1 + 2x_2 + 2x_3 = 11$$

Solution:

Writing the equation in the form of $[A]X=B$ and apply forward elimination and back-substitution

The complete MATLAB program and output are given below:

```
%  A - matrix for the left hand side.
%  b - vector for the right hand side.
% This performs Gaussian elminiation to find x.
% MATRIX DEFINITION
```

```
A = [6 3 6;2 3 3;1 2 2];
b = [30;17;11];
N = max(size(A))

% Perform Gaussian Elimination
 for j = 2:N,
   for i = j:N,
     m = A(i, j-1)/A(j-1, j-1);
     A(i,:) = A(i,:) - A(j-1,:)*m;
     b(i) = b(i) -m*b(j-1);
   end
 end
disp('Upper triangular form of given matrix is =')
disp(A)
disp('b =')
disp(b)

% BACK-SUBSTITUTION
% Perform back substitution
 x = zeros(N,1);
 x(N) = b(N)/A(N,N);
 for j = N-1:-1:1,
  x(j) = (b(j)-A(j,j+1:N)*x(j+1:N))/A(j,j);
 end
disp('final solution is');
disp(x);
disp('matlab solution is');
x = inv(A)*b
```

OUTPUT is given below:

N=

3

Upper triangular form of given matrix is =

6.0000	3.0000	6.0000
0	2.0000	1.0000
0	0	0.2500

b =

30.0000
7.0000
0.7500

The final solution is

```
1
2
3
```

MATLAB solution is

```
x =
     1
     2
     3
```

Check with MATLAB built-in function:

```
>> A = [6 3 6;2 3 3;1 2 2];
b = [30;17;11];
>>
>> x=A\b

x =
    1
    2
    3
```

Example E4.22: Using Choleski's method, solve the following linear equations:

$$x_1 + x_2 + x_3 = 7$$
$$3x_1 + 3x_2 + 4x_3 = 23$$
$$2x_1 + x_2 + x_3 = 10$$

Solution: The complete program and output are given below:

```
A = [1 1 1;3 3 4;2 1 1];
b = [7;23;10];
[L,U] = lu(A);
% solution of y
y = L\b;
%final solution x
x = U\y;
fprintf('Solution of the equations is\n');
disp(x)
Solution of the equations is
      3.0000
      2.0000
      2.0000
```

Check with MATLAB built-in function:

```
>> A = [1 1 1;3 3 4;2 1 1];
b = [7;23;10];
>> x = A\b
x =
        3.0000
        2.0000
        2.0000
```

Example E4.23: Solve the system of equations by Choleski's factorization method:

$$12x_1 - 6x_2 - 6x_3 - 1.5x_4 = 1$$
$$-6x_1 + 4x_2 + 3x_3 + 0.5x_4 = 2$$
$$-6x_1 + 3x_2 + 6x_3 + 1.5x_4 = 3$$
$$-1.5x_1 + 0.5x_2 + 1.5x_3 + x_4 = 4$$

Solution:

Here the matrix [*A*] is symmetric.

Program and the output are given below:

```
A = [12 -6 -6 -1.5;-6 4 3 0.5;-6 3 6 1.5; -1.5 0.5 1.5 1];
b = [1;2;3;4];
[L,U] = lu(A);
% solution of y
y = L\b;
%final solution x
x = U\y;
fprintf('Solution of the equations is\n');
disp(x)
```

The solution of the equations is

```
        2.7778
        4.2222
       -0.5556
        6.8889
```

Check with MATLAB built-in function:

```
>> A = [12 -6 -6 -1.5; -6 4 3 0.5; -6 3 6 1.5; -1.5 0.5 1.5 1];
b = [1;2;3;4];
>> x = A\b
x =
        2.7778
        4.2222
       -0.5556
        6.8889
```

Example E4.24: Find the solution to the equations using Gauss-Seidel method

$$\begin{bmatrix} 4 & 2 & 0 & 0 \\ 2 & 8 & 2 & 0 \\ 0 & 2 & 8 & 2 \\ 0 & 0 & 2 & 4 \end{bmatrix} \begin{Bmatrix} x_1 \\ x_2 \\ x_3 \\ x_4 \end{Bmatrix} = \begin{Bmatrix} 4 \\ 0 \\ 0 \\ 0 \end{Bmatrix}$$

Solution:

The complete MATLAB program is given below with outputs of the program

```
A = [4 2 0 0; 2 8 2 0; 0 2 8 2; 0 0 2 4];b = [4;0;0;0];
X0 = zeros(size(b)); % starting vector
tole = 1e-6;kstop = 30;% error tolerance and max. iterations
[n,n] = size(A);
P = tril(A);% lower triangular form
k = 0;r = b-A*X0;
r0 = norm(r);er = norm(r);
X = X0;
[L,U] = lu(P);
fprintf('iter#\tX(1)\t\tX(2)\t\tX(3)\t\tX(4)\n');
while er>tole & k<kstop
  fprintf('%d\t%f\t%f\t%f\t%f\n',k,X(1),X(2),X(3),X(4));
  k = k+1;
  dx = L\r;
  dx = U\dx;
  X = X+dx;
  r = b - A*X;
  er = norm(r)/r0;
  erp(k) = norm(r)/r0;
end
X
```

The output is as follows:

```
X =
        1.1556
      - 0.3111
        0.0889
      - 0.0444
```

Check with MATLAB built-in function:

```
>> A = [4 2 0 0;2 8 2 0;0 2 8 2;0 0 2 4];b = [4;0;0;0];
>> x = A\b
```

```
x =
      1.1556
     -0.3111
      0.0889
     -0.0444
```

Example E4.25: Solve the system of equations given by $[A]\{X\}=\{b\}$ using Gauss-Seidel method. The matrices $[A]$ and $\{b\}$ are given below:

$$[A]=\begin{bmatrix}4 & 2 & 0 & 0\\ 2 & 8 & 2 & 0\\ 0 & 2 & 8 & 2\\ 0 & 0 & 2 & 4\end{bmatrix} \text{ and } \{b\}=\begin{Bmatrix}4\\ 0\\ 0\\ 14\end{Bmatrix}$$

Solution:

The following program and output are presented:

```
A = [4 2 0 0; 2 8 2 0; 0 2 8 2; 0 0 2 4];b = [4;0;0;14];
X0 = zeros(size(b)); % starting vector
tole = 1e-6;kstop = 30;% error tolerance and max.iterations
[n,n] = size(A);
P = tril(A);% lower triangular form
k = 0;r = b-A*X0;
r0 = norm(r);er = norm(r);
X = X0;
[L,U] = lu(P);
fprintf('iter#\tX(1)\t\tX(2)\t\tX(3)\t\tX(4)\n');
while er>tole & k<kstop
  fprintf('%d\t%f\t%f\t%f\t%f\n',k,X(1),X(2),X(3),X(4));
  k = k+1;
  dx = L\r;
  dx = U\dx;
  X = X+dx;
  r = b-A*X;
  er = norm(r)/r0;
  erp(k) = norm(r)/r0;
end
X
```

The output is as follows:

```
X =
      1.0000
    – 0.0000
    – 1.0000
      4.0000
```

Check with MATLAB built-in function:

```
>> A = [4 2 0 0; 2 8 2 0; 0 2 8 2; 0 0 2 4]; b = [4;0;0;14];
>> x = A\b
x =
      1.0000
      0
     -1.0000
      4.0000
```

Example E4.26: Use the Jacobi's method to determine the eigenvalues and eigenvectors of matrix

$$[A] = \begin{bmatrix} 4 & -1 & -2 \\ -1 & 3 & 3 \\ -2 & 3 & 1 \end{bmatrix}$$

Solution:

The complete computer program is given below:

```
A = [4 -1 -2;-1 3 3;-2 3 1];
%Output - V is the nxn matrix of eigenvectors
% - D is the diagonal nxn matrix of eigenvalues
D = A;
[n,n] = size(A);
V = eye(n);
%Calculate row p and column q of the off-diagonal element
%of greatest magnitude in A
[m1 p] = max(abs(D-diag(diag(D))));
[m2 q] = max(m1);
p = p(q);
i = 1;
while(i<20)
  %Zero out Dpq and Dqp
    t = D(p,q)/(D(q,q)-D(p,p));
    c = 1/sqrt(t^2+1);
    s = c*t;
    R = [c s;-s c];
  D([p q],:) = R'*D([p q],:);
  D(:,[p q]) = D(:,[p q])*R;
  V(:,[p q]) = V(:,[p q])*R;
  [m1 p] = max(abs(D-diag(diag(D))));
  [m2 q] = max(m1);
  p = p(q);
  i = i+1;
end
D = diag(diag(D))
fprintf('Final eigenvalues are %f\t%f\t%f\n',D(1,1),D(2,2),D(3,3));
```

The output is as follows:

D =

2.6916	0	0
0	6.6956	0
0	0	–1.3872

The final eigenvalues are 2.691611, 6.695589 and –1.387200

Check with MATLAB built-in function:

```
>> A = [4 -1 -2;-1 3 3;-2 3 1];
>> [Q,D] = eig(A)
Q =
      0.2114     0.7636    -0.6102
     -0.5184     0.6168     0.5923
      0.8286     0.1911     0.5262
D =
     -1.3872     0          0
      0          2.6916     0
      0          0          6.6956
```

Example E4.27: Find the eigenvalues and eigenvectors of $[A] = \begin{bmatrix} 6 & -2 & 1 & -1 \\ -2 & 4 & -2 & 1 \\ 1 & -2 & 4 & -2 \\ -1 & 1 & -2 & 4 \end{bmatrix}$ with the Jacobi's method.

Solution:

The following MALTAB program is used for this:

```
A = [6 -2 1 -1;-2 4 -2 1;1 -2 4 -2;-1 1 -2 4];
%Output - V is the nxn matrix of eigenvectors
% - D is the diagonal nxn matrix of eigenvalues
D = A;
[n,n] = size(A);
V = eye(n);
%Calculate row p and column q of the off-diagonal element
%of greatest magnitude in A
[m1 p] = max(abs(D-diag(diag(D))));
[m2 q] = max(m1);
p = p(q);
i = 1;
while(i<100)
  %Zero out Dpq and Dqp
  t = D(p,q)/(D(q,q) -D(p,p));
```

```
  c = 1/sqrt(t^2+1);
  s = c*t;
  R = [c s;- s c];
  D([p q],:) = R'*D([p q],:);
  D(:,[p q]) = D(:,[p q])*R;
  V(:,[p q]) = V(:,[p q])*R;
  [m1 p] = max(abs(D-diag(diag(D))));
  [m2 q] = max(m1);
  p = p(q);
  i = i+1;
end
D = diag(diag(D))
fprintf('Eigenvectors are\n')
disp(V)
```

The output is as follows:

D =

9.1025	0	0	0
0	1.5186	0	0
0	0	4.5880	0
0	0	0	2.7910

The eigenvectors are

V =

0.6043	0.1788	– 0.7250	– 0.2778
– 0.5006	0.5421	– 0.0252	– 0.6744
0.4721	0.7046	0.4915	0.1976
– 0.4016	0.4215	– 0.4818	0.6550

Check with MATLAB built-in function:

```
>> A = [6 -2 1 -1;-2 4 -2 1;1 -2 4 -2;-1 1 -2 4];
>> [Q,D] = eig(A)
Q =
    -0.1788    -0.2778     0.7250    -0.6043
    -0.5421    -0.6744     0.0252     0.5006
    -0.7046     0.1976    -0.4915    -0.4721
    -0.4215     0.6550     0.4818     0.4016
D =
     1.5186    0          0          0
     0         2.7910     0          0
     0         0          4.5880     0
     0         0          0          9.1025
```

Example E4.28: Transform the matrix $[A]=\begin{bmatrix} 7 & 2 & 3 & -1 \\ 2 & 8 & 5 & 1 \\ 3 & 5 & 12 & 9 \\ -1 & 1 & 9 & 7 \end{bmatrix}$ into tridiagonal form using Householder reduction.

Solution:

The following program is used.

```
%Input - A is an nxn symmetric matrix
A = [7 2 3 -1;2 8 5 1;3 5 12 9;-1 1 9 7];

%Output - T is a tridiagonal matrix
[n,n] = size(A);
for k = 1:n-2
  s = norm(A(k+1:n,k));
  if (A(k+1,k)<0)
    s = -s;
  end
  r = sqrt(2*s*(A(k+1,k)+s));
  W(1:k) = zeros(1,k);
  W(k+1) = (A(k+1,k)+s)/r;
  W(k+2:n) = A(k+2:n,k)'/r;
  V(1:k) = zeros(1,k);
  V(k+1:n) = A(k+1:n,k+1:n)*W(k+1:n)';
  c = W(k+1:n)*V(k+1:n)';
  Q(1:k) = zeros(1,k);
  Q(k+1:n) = V(k+1:n)-c*W(k+1:n);
  A(k+2:n,k) = zeros(n-k-1,1);
  A(k,k+2:n) = zeros(1,n-k-1);
  A(k+1,k) = -s;
  A(k,k+1) = -s;
 A(k+1:n,k+1:n) = A(k+1:n,k+1:n)-2*W(k+1:n)'*Q(k+1:n)-2*Q(k+1:n)'*W(k+1:n);
end
T = A;
fprintf ('Matrix in tridiagonal form is\n');
disp(T)
```

The output is as follows:

The matrix in tridiagonal form is

```
 7.0000   -3.7417    0         0
-3.7417   10.6429    9.1309    0
 0         9.1309   10.5942    4.7716
 0         0         4.7716    5.7629
```

REFERENCES

Abramowitz, M. and Stegun, I., *Handbook of Mathematical Functions,* Dover Press, New York, 1964.

Akai, T.J., *Applied Numerical Methods for Engineers*, Wiley, New York, NY, 1993.

Al-Khafaji, A.W. and Tooley, J.R., *Numerical Methods in Engineering Practice*, Holt, Rinehart and Winston, New York, 1986.

Allen, M. and Issaaccson, E., *Numerical Analysis for Applied Science*, Wiley, New York, 1998.

Ames, W.F., *Numerical Methods for Partial Differential Equations*, 3rd ed., Academic Press, New York, 1992.

Ascher,U., Mattheij, R. and Russell, R., *Numerical Solution of Boundary Value Problems for Ordinary Differential Equations,* Prentice-Hall, Englewood Cliffs, NJ, 1988.

Atkinson, K. and Han, W., *Elementary Numerical Analysis*, 3rd ed, Wiley, New York, 2004.

Atkinson, K.E., *An Introduction to Numerical Analysis*, 2nd ed., Wiley, New York, NY, 1993.

Atkinson, L.V. and Harley, P.J., *Introduction to Numerical Methods with PASCAL*, Addison-Wesley, Reading, MA, 1984.

Atkinson, L.V., Harley, P.J. and Hudson, J.D., *Numerical Methods with FORTRAN 77*, Addison-Wesley, Reading, MA, 1989.

Axelsson, K., *Iterative Solution Methods,* Cambridge University Press, Cambridge, UK, 1994.

Ayyub, B.M. and McCuen, R.H., *Numerical Methods for Engineers*, Prentice-Hall, Upper Saddle River, New Jersey, NJ, 1996.

Baker, A.J., *Finite Element Computational Fluid Mechanics*, McGraw-Hill, New York, 1983.

Balagurusamy, E., *Numerical Methods*, Tata McGraw-Hill, New Delhi, India, 2002.

Bathe, K.J. and Wilson, E.L., *Numerical Methods in Finite Element Analysis*, Prentice-Hall, Englewood Cliffs, NJ, 1976.

Bhat, R.B. and Chakraverty, S., *Numerical Analysis in Engineering*, Narosa Publishing House, New Delhi, India, 2004.

Bhat, R.B. and Gouw, G .J., *Numerical Methods in Engineering*, Simon and Schuster Custom Publishing, Needham Heights, MA, 1996.

Bjorck, A., *Numerical Methods for Least Squares Problems*, Society for Industrial and Applied Mathematics (SIAM), Philadelphia, PA, 1996.

Booth, A.D., *Numerical Methods*, Academic Press, New York, 1958.

Brice, C., Luther, H.A., and Wilkes, J.O., *Applied Numerical Methods*, New York, NY, 1969.

Buchanan, J.L. and Turner, P.R., *Numerical Methods and Analysis,* McGraw-Hill, New York, 1992.

Burden, R.L. and Faires, J.D., *Numerical Analysis,* 6th ed., Brooks/Cole, Pacific Grove, 1997.

Carnahan, B., Luther, A. and Wilkes, J.O., *Applied Numerical Methods,* Wiley, New York, 1969.

Chapra, S.C. and Canale, R.P., *Introduction to Computing for Engineers*, 2nd ed., McGraw-Hill, New York, 1994.

Chapra, S.C., and Canale, R.P., *Numerical Methods for Engineers with Personal Computers*, McGraw-Hill, New York, 1985.

Chapra, S.C., *Applied Numerical Methods with MATLAB for Engineers and Scientists*, McGraw-Hill, New York, 2005.

Chapra, S.C., *Numerical Methods for Engineers with Software and Programming Applications*, 4th ed., McGraw-Hill, New York, NY, 2002.

Cheney, W. and Kincaid, D., *Numerical Mathematics and Computing*, 2nd ed., Brooks/Cole, Monterey, CA, 1994.

Chui, C., *An Introduction to Wavelets*, Academic Press, Burlington, MA, 1992.

Consatantinides, A., *Applied Numerical Methods with Personal Computers*, McGraw-Hill, New York, 1987.

Conte, S.D. and DeBoor, C.W., *Elementary Numerical Analysis: An Algorithm Approach*, 2nd ed., McGraw-Hill, New York, NY, 1972.

Dahlquist, G. and Bjorck, A., *Numerical Methods*, Prentice-Hall, Englewood Cliffs, NJ, 1974.

Davis, P. and Rabinowitz, P., *Methods of Numerical Integration,* Academic Press, 2nd ed., New York, 1998.

Demmel, J.W., *Applied Numerical Linear Algebra*, Society for Industrial and Applied Mathematics (SIAM), Philadelphia, PA, 1997.

Dennis, J.E. and Schnabel, R.B., *Numerical Methods for Unconstrained Optimization and Non-linear Equations,* Society for Industrial and Applied Mathematics (SIAM), Philadelphia, PA, 1996.

Epperson, J.F., *An Introduction to Numerical Methods and Analysis*, Wiley, New York, NY, 2001.

Fadeev, D.K., and Fadeeva, V.N., *Computational Methods of Linear Algebra*, Freeman, San Francisco, 1963.

Fadeeva, V.N., (Trans. Curtis D. Benster), *Computational Methods of Linear Algebra,* Dover, New York, 1959.

Fatunla, S.O., *Numerical Methods for Initial Value Problems in Ordinary Differential Equations*, Academic Press, San Diego, 1988.

Ferziger, J.H., *Numerical Methods for Engineering Applications*, 2nd ed., Wiley, New York, NY, 1998.

Forbear, C.E., *Introduction to Numerical Analysis*, Addison-Wesley, Reading, MA, 1969.

Forsythe, G.E. and Wasow, W.R., *Finite-Difference Methods for Partial Differential Equations*, Wiley, New York, 1960.

Forsythe, G.E. Malcolm, M.A. and Moler, C.B., *Computer Methods for Mathematical Computation,* Prentice-Hall, Englewood Cliffs, NJ, 1977.

Froberg, C.E., *Introduction to Numerical Analysis*, Addison-Wesley, Reading, MA, 1965.

Gautschi, W., *Numerical Analysis: An Introduction*, Birkhauser, Boston, MA, 1997.

Gear, C.W., *Numerical Initial Value Problems in Ordinary Differential Equations,* Prentice-Hall, Englewood Cliffs, NJ, 1971.

Gerald, C.F. and Wheatley, P.O., *Applied Numerical Analysis*, 5th ed., Addison-Wesley, Reading, MA, 1994.

Gladwell, J. and Wait, R., *A Survey of Numerical Methods of Partial Differential Equations,* Oxford University Press, New York, 1979.

Goldberg, D.E., *Genetic Algorithms in Search, Optimization and Machine Learning,* Addison-Wesley, Reading, MA, 1989.

Golub, G.H. and Van Loan, C.F., *Matrix Computations*, 3rd ed., Johns Hopkins University Press, Baltimore, MD, 1996.

Greenbaum, A., *Iterative Methods for Solving Linear Systems*, Society for Industrial and Applied Mathematics (SIAM), Philadelphia, PA, 1997.

Griffiths, D.V. and Smith, I.M., *Numerical Methods for Engineers,* Oxford University Press, 1991.

Guest, P.G., *Numerical Methods of Curve Fitting*, Cambridge University Press, New York, 1961.

Hager, W.W., *Applied Numerical Algebra*, Prentice-Hall, Upper Saddle River, NJ, 1998.

Hamming, R.W., *Numerical Methods for Scientists and Engineers*, 2nd ed., McGraw-Hill, New York, 1973.

Henrici, P.H., *Elements of Numerical Analysis,* Wiley, New York, 1964.

Higham, N.J., *Accuracy and Stability of Numerical Algorithms*, Society for Industrial and Applied Mathematics (SIAM), Philadelphia, PA, 1996.

Hildebrand, F.B., *Introduction to Numerical Analysis*, 2nd ed., McGraw-Hill, New York, NY, 1974.

Hoffman, J., *Numerical Methods for Engineers and Scientists*, McGraw-Hill, New York, 1992.

Hornbeck, R.W., *Numerical Methods*, Quantum, New York, 1975.

Householder, A.S., *Principles of Numerical Analysis*, McGraw-Hill, New York, 1953.

Householder, A.S., *The Theory of Matrices in Numerical Analysis*, Blaisdell, New York, 1964.

Iserles, A., *A First Course in the Numerical Analysis of Differential Equations,* Cambridge University Press, New York, 1996.

Issaccson, E. and Keller, H.B. and Bishop, H., Analysis *of Numerical Methods*, Wiley, New York, 1966.

Jacobs, D. (ed.), *The State of the Art in Numerical Analysis*, Academic Press, London, 1977.

Jacques, I. and Colin, J., *Numerical Analysis*, Chapman and Hall, New York, 1987.

Jain, M.K., *Numerical Analysis for Scientists and Engineers*, S.B.W. Publishers, New Delhi, India, 1971.

James, M.L., Smith, G.M. and Wolford, J.C., *Applied Numerical Methods for Digital Computations with FORTRAN and CSMP*, 3rd ed., Harper & Row, New York, 1985.

Johnson, L.W., Riess, R.D., *Numerical Analysis*, 2nd ed., Addison-Wesley, Reading, MA, 1982.

Johnston, R.L., *Numerical Methods: A Software Approach*, Wiley, New York, 1982.

Kahaneer, D., Moher, C. and Nash, S., *Numerical Methods and Software*, Prentice-Hall, Englewood Cliffs, NJ, 1989.

Keller, H.B., *Numerical Methods for Two-Point Boundary Value Problems*, Wiley, New York, 1968.

Kelley, C.T., *Iterative Methods of Optimization*, Society for Industrial and Applied Mathematics (SIAM), Philadelphia, PA, 1999.

Kharab, A. and Guenther, R.B., *An Introduction to Numerical Methods—A MATLAB Approach*, CRC Press, Boca Raton, FL, 2001.

Kincaid, D. and Cheney, W., *Numerical Analysis: Mathematics of Scientific Computing,* Brooks/Cole, Pacific Grove, CA, 1996.

Kress, R., *Numerical Analysis*, Springer-Verlag, New York, 1998.

Krishnamurthy, E.V. and Sen, S.K., *Numerical Algorithms*, East-West Publishers, New Delhi, India, 1986.

Krommer, A. R. and Ueberhuber, C.W., *Computational Integration*, Society for Industrial and Applied Mathematics (SIAM), Philadelphia, PA, 1998.

Lambert, J.D., *Numerical Methods for Ordinary Differential Equations—The Initial Value Problems,* Wiley, New York, NY, 1991.

Lapidus, L. and Pinder, G.F., *Numerical Solution of Ordinary Differential Equations in Science and Engineering*, Wiley, New York, 1981.

Lapidus, L., and Seinfield, J.H., *Numerical Solution of Partial Differential Equations*, Academic Press, New York, 1971.

Lastman, G.J. and Sinha, N.K., *Microcomputer Based Numerical Methods for Science and Engineering,* Saunders College Publishing, New York, NY, 1989.

Levy, H. and Baggott, E.A., *Numerical Solutions of Differential Equations,* Dover, New York, 1950.

Maron, M.J., *Numerical Analysis, A Practical Approach*, Macmillan, New York, 1982.

Mathews, J.H., *Numerical Methods for Mathematics, Science and Engineering*, 2nd ed., Prentice-Hall of India, New Delhi, India, 1994.

Milne, W.E., *Numerical Solution of Differential Equations*, Wiley, New York, 1953.

Moin, P., *Fundamentals of Engineering Numerical Analysis*, Cambridge University Press, New York, 2001.

Morton, K.W. and Mayers, D.F., *Numerical Solution of Partial differential Equations: An Introduction*, Cambridge University Press, Cambridge, UK, 1994.

Myron, A. and Issacson, E.L., *Numerical Analysis for Applied Science*, Wiley, Hoboken, NJ, 1998.

Na, T.Y., *Computational Methods in Engineering Boundary Value Problems*, Academic Press, New York, 1979.

Nakamura, S., *Computational Methods in Engineering and Science,* Wiley, New York, NY, 1977.

Nielson, K.L., *Methods in Numerical Analysis,* Macmillan Company, New York, 1964.

Noble, B., *Numerical Methods,* Vol. 2, Oliver and Boyd, Edinburgh, 1964.

Nocedal, J. and Wright, S.J., Numerical Optimization, Springer-Verlag, New York, 1999.

Ortega, J.M., *Numerical Analysis—A Second Course*, Academic Press, New York, NY, 1972.

Powell, M., *Approximation Theory and Methods*, Cambridge University Press, Cambridge, UK, 1981.

Press, W.H., Teukolsky, S.A., Vetterling, W.T. and Flannery, B.P., *Numerical Recipes: The Art of Scientific Computing*, 2nd ed., Cambridge University Press, New York, 1992.

Quarteroni, A., Sacco, R. and Saleri, F., *Numerical Mathematics,* Springer-Verlag, New York, 2000.

Ralston, A., and Rabinowitz, P., *A First Course in Numerical Analysis*, 2nd ed., McGraw-Hill, New York, 1978.

Ralston, A. and Wilf, H.S., eds., *Mathematical Methods for Digital Computers,* Vol. 1 and 2, Wiley, New York, 1967.

Rao, K.S., *Numerical Methods for Scientists and Engineers*, Prentice-Hall, New Delhi, India, 2001.

Rao, S.S., *Applied Numerical Methods for Engineers and Scientists*, Prentice-Hall, Upper Saddle River, New Jersey, NJ, 2002.

Ratschek, H. and Rokne, J., *Computer Methods for the Range of Functions*, Ellis Horwood, Chichester, 1984.

Rice, J.R., *Numerical Methods, Software and Analysis*, McGraw-Hill, New York, 1983.

Sastry, S.S., *Introductory Methods of Numerical Analysis*, Prentice-Hall of India, New Delhi, India, 2001.

Scarborough, J.B., *Numerical Mathematical Analysis*, 6th ed., John Hopkins Press, Baltimore, MD, 1966.

Scheid, F., *Schaum's Outline of Theory and Problems in Numerical Analysis*, 2nd ed., Schaum's Outline Series, McGraw-Hill, New York, 1988.

Schiesser, W.E., *Computational Mathematics in Engineering and Applied Science*, CRC Press, Boca Raton, FL, 1994.

Shampine, L.F., *Numerical Solution of Ordinary Differential Equations*, Chapman and Hall, New York, 1994.

Sharma, J.N., *Numerical Methods for Engineers and Scientists,* Narosa Publishing House, New Delhi, India, 2004.

Smith, G.D., *Numerical Solution of Partial Differential Equations: Finite Difference Methods*, 3rd ed., Oxford University Press, Oxford, 1985.

Smith, W.A., *Elementary Numerical Analysis*, Prentice-Hall, Englewood Cliffs, NJ, 1986.

Snyder, M.A., *Chebyshev Methods in Numerical Approximation*, Prentice-Hall, Englewood Cliffs, NJ, 1966.

Stanton, R.G., *Numerical Methods for Science and Engineering*, Prentice-Hall of India, New Delhi, India, 1967.

Stark, P.A., *Introduction to Numerical Methods*, Macmillan, New York, 1970.

Stewart, G.W., *Matrix Algorithms,* Vol. 1, *Basic Decompositions,* Society for Industrial and Applied Mathematics (SIAM), Philadelphia, PA, 1998.

Stoer, J. and Bulirsch, R., *Introduction to Numerical Analysis*, Springer-Verlag, New York, 1980.

Stroud, A., and Secrets, D., *Gaussian Quadrature Formulas*, Prentice-Hall, Englewood Cliffs, 1966.

Stroud, A.H., *Numerical Quadrature and Solution of Ordinary Differential Equations*, Springer-Verlag, New York, 1974.

Taylor, J.R., *An Introduction to Error Analysis*, University Science Books, Mill Valley, CA, 1982.

Traub, J.F., *Iterative Methods for the Solution of Equations*, Prentice-Hall, Englewood Cliffs, NJ, 1964.

Trefethen, L.N. and Bau, D., *Numerical Linear Algebra*, Society for Industrial and Applied Mathematics (SIAM), Philadelphia, PA, 1997.

Tyrtyshnikov, E.E., *A Brief Introduction to Numerical Analysis*, Birkhauser, Boston, 1997.

Ueberhuber, C.W., *Numerical Computation 1: Methods, Software, and Analysis*, Springer-Verlag, New York, 1997.

Ueberhuber, C.W., *Numerical Computation 2: Methods, Software, and Analysis*, Springer-Verlag, New York, 1997.

Vemuri, V. and Karplus, W.J., *Digital Computer Treatment of Partial Differential Equations,* Prentice-Hall, Englewood Cliffs, NJ, 1981.

Vichnevetsky, R., *Computer Methods for Partial Differential Equations, Vol. 1: Elliptic Equations and the Finite Element Method*, Prentice-Hall, Englewood Cliffs, NJ, 1981.

Vichnevetsky, R., *Computer Methods for Partial Differential Equations, Vol. 2: Initial Value Problems,* Prentice-Hall, Englewood Cliffs, NJ, 1982.

Wendroff, B., *Theoretical Numerical Analysis*, Academic Press, New York, 1966.

Wilkinson, J.H., *Rounding Errors in Algebraic Processes*, Dover, New York, 1994.

Yokowitz, S. and Szidarovsky, F., *An Introduction to Numerical Computation*, Macmillan, New York, 1986.

Yong, D.M. and Gregory, R.T., *A Survey of Numerical Mathematics,* Vol. 1 and 2, Addison-Wesley, Reading, MA, 1972.

Young, D., *Iterative Solution for Large Linear Systems,* Academic Press, New York, 1971.

PROBLEMS

P4.1: Use the method of Gaussian elimination to solve the following system of linear equations:

$$x_1 + x_2 + x_3 - x_4 = 2$$
$$4x_1 + 4x_2 + x_3 - x_4 = 11$$
$$x_1 - x_2 - x_3 + 2x_4 = 0$$
$$2x_1 + x_2 + 2x_3 - 2x_4 = 2$$

P4.2: Use Gaussian elimination method to solve the system of equations $[A]\{x\} = \{b\}$ where

$$A = \begin{bmatrix} 1 & 1 & 1 & 1 \\ 2 & -1 & 3 & 0 \\ 0 & 2 & 0 & 3 \\ -1 & 0 & 2 & 1 \end{bmatrix}, \qquad b = \begin{Bmatrix} 3 \\ 3 \\ 1 \\ 0 \end{Bmatrix}$$

P4.3: Solve the following set of equations by Gauss-Jordan method.

$$2x_1 + x_2 - 3x_3 = 11$$
$$4x_1 - 2x_2 + 3x_3 = 8$$
$$-2x_1 + 2x_2 - x_3 = -6$$

P4.4: Use Gauss-Jordan method to solve the following set of equations.

$$\begin{bmatrix} 5 & -4 & 1 & 0 & 0 \\ -4 & 6 & -4 & 1 & 0 \\ 1 & -4 & 6 & -4 & 1 \\ 0 & 1 & -4 & 6 & -4 \\ 0 & 0 & 1 & -4 & 5 \end{bmatrix} \begin{Bmatrix} x_1 \\ x_2 \\ x_3 \\ x_4 \end{Bmatrix} = \begin{Bmatrix} 1 \\ 2 \\ 3 \\ 2 \\ 1 \end{Bmatrix}$$

P4.5: Solve the following system of equations using Choleski's factorizations.

$$x_1 + x_2 + x_3 - x_4 = 2$$
$$x_1 - x_2 - x_3 + 2x_4 = 0$$
$$4x_1 + 4x_2 + x_3 + x_4 = 11$$
$$2x_1 + x_2 + 2x_3 - 2x_4 = 2$$

P4.6: Use Choleski's method of solution for Problem P4.2.

P4.7: Use Jacobi iterative scheme to obtain the solutions of the following system of equations.

$$x + 2y + z = 0$$
$$3x + y - z = 0$$
$$x - y + 4z = 3$$

P4.8: Use Jacobi iterative scheme to obtain the solution for Problem P4.1.

P4.9: Use Gauss-Seidel method to solve the following system of equations in Problem P4.7.

P4.10: Solve the system of equations in Problem P4.2 using Gauss-Seidel method.

P4.11: Solve the following set of equations in Problem P4.5 using Householder's factorization method.

P4.12: Use the Householder reduction to transfer the following matrix A into tridiagonal form and solve the set of equations $Ax = b$, where

$$A = \begin{bmatrix} 7 & 2 & 3 & -1 \\ 2 & 8 & 5 & 1 \\ 3 & 5 & 12 & 9 \\ -1 & 1 & 9 & 7 \end{bmatrix} \quad b = \begin{bmatrix} 2 \\ -3 \\ 5 \\ 7 \end{bmatrix}$$

P4.13: Determine the eigenvalues and eigenvectors of the following matrix using Jacobi method.

$$[A] = \begin{bmatrix} 11 & 2 & 8 \\ 2 & 2 & -10 \\ 9 & -10 & 5 \end{bmatrix}$$

P4.14: Use Jacobi method to compute the eigenvalues and the corresponding eigenvectors of the following matrix A:

$$[A] = \begin{bmatrix} 4 & 3 & 2 & 1 \\ 3 & 4 & 1 & 2 \\ 2 & 1 & 4 & 3 \\ 1 & 2 & 3 & 4 \end{bmatrix}$$

❍❍❍

CHAPTER 5

OPTIMIZATION

5.1 INTRODUCTION

Optimization is minimizing or maximizing a function. The function $F(x)$ is called the *merit function* or *objective function*. The components of x are known as the design variables.

The minimum point must be bracketed before a minimization algorithm can be used. The bracketing procedure consists of starting with an initial value of x_0 and moving downhill computing the functions at $x_1, x_2, x_3, \ldots$ until the point x_n is reached where $f(x)$ increases for the first time. The minimum point is now bracketed in the interval (x_{n-2}, x_n). The increasing in step size follows as $h_{i+1} = c\, h_i$ where $c > 1$.

Suppose the minimum of $f(x)$ has been bracketed in the interval (a, b) of length h. To telescope the interval, the function at $x_1 = b - Rh$ and $x_2 = a + Rh$ is evaluated. If $f_1 > f_2$, then the minimum lies in (x_1, b); otherwise it is located in (a, x_2).

Next, we evaluate the function at $x_2 = a + Rh'$ and repeat the process. We noted that $x_2 - x_1 = 2\,Rh - h$ and $x_1 - a = h' - Rh'$ or $2Rh - h = h' - Rh'$ and substituting $h' = Rh$, we obtain $R = 0.618033989$. The number of telescopings required to reduce h from $|b - a|$ to an error tolerance $\in$ is given by

$$n = \frac{\ln(\in / |b-a|)}{\ln R} = -2.078087 \ln \frac{\in}{|b-a|}.$$

5.2 CONJUGATE GRADIENT METHODS

The objective here is to minimize $F(x)$, where the components of x are the n independent design variables. Consider the quadratic function

$$F(x) = c - \sum_i b_i x_i + \frac{1}{2}\sum_i \sum_j A_{ij} x_i x_j$$

$$= c - b^T x + \frac{1}{2} x^T A x \qquad \text{...(5.1)}$$

Differentiating Eq.(5.1) w.r.t. x_i gives

$$\frac{\partial F}{\partial x_i} = -b_i + \sum_j A_{ij} x_j$$

or in vector notation

$$\nabla F = -b + Ax \qquad \text{...(5.2)}$$

where ∇F is the *gradient* of F.

The gradient along u when the motion takes place along the line $x = x_0 + su$, where s is the distance moved is given by

$$\nabla F\big|_{x_0+su} = -b + A(x_0 + su) = \nabla F\big|_{x_0} + s\,Au$$

If the change in the gradient sAu is perpendicular to a vector V, then

$$V^T Au = 0 \qquad \text{...(5.2A)}$$

The directions of u and V are said to be mutually *conjugate.*

5.3 NEWTON S METHOD

Newton's method is a gradient method and can be conveniently used to optimize functions with several parameters. Let the function to be optimized be $U(\overline{x})$, where $\overline{x}$ is the vector of parameters $x_1, x_2, \ldots, x_n$. The function $U(\overline{x})$ can be expanded in the Taylor's series about a point $\overline{x}^*$ as

$$U(\overline{x}) = U(\overline{x}^*) + \sum_{i=1}^{n} \frac{\partial U(\overline{x}^*)}{\partial X_i}(x_i - x_i^*)$$

Newton's method uses only two terms in the series. Expressing in concise form, the above series can be written as

$$U(\overline{x}) = U(\overline{x}^*) + g^{-T}(\overline{x}^*)(\overline{x} - \overline{x}^*) \qquad \text{...(5.3)}$$

where $\overline{g}(\overline{x}^*)$ is the vector of first derivatives given by

$$\overline{g}(\overline{x}^*) = \left[\frac{\partial U(\overline{x}^*)}{\partial x_1}, \frac{\partial U(\overline{x}^*)}{\partial x_2}, \ldots\right]^T$$

The minimum $U(\overline{x}^*)$ obtained by setting

$$\frac{\partial U}{\partial x_i} = 0$$

In Eq.(5.3) which yields the set of equations

$$\overline{g}(\overline{x}^*) + \overline{J}(\overline{x}^*)(\overline{x} - \overline{x}^*) = 0 \qquad \text{...(5.4)}$$

where $\bar{J}(\bar{x}^*)$ is the Jacobian matrix of second derivatives given by

$$\bar{J}(\bar{x}^*) = \begin{vmatrix} \frac{\partial^2 U(\bar{x}^*)}{\partial x_1^2} & \frac{\partial^2 U(\bar{x}^*)}{\partial x_1 \partial x_2} & \cdots\cdots & \frac{\partial^2 U(\bar{x}^*)}{\partial x_1 \partial x_n} \\ \frac{\partial^2 U(\bar{x}^*)}{\partial x_n \partial x_1} & & \cdots\cdots & \frac{\partial^2 U(\bar{x}^*)}{\partial x_n^2} \end{vmatrix}$$

A set of linear algebraic equations in the unknown x_i's are given by Eq.(5.4). If $\bar{x}^*$ is taken as $\bar{x}_k$, the kth point in the step by step search for the minimum, then solution of Eq. (5.4) given $(k + 1)$st approximation. Writing Eq.(5.4) in the form

$$\bar{g}(\bar{x}_k) = \bar{J}(\bar{x}_k)(\bar{x}_{k+1} - \bar{x}_k) = 0 \qquad \text{...(5.5)}$$

It is possible to obtain an iterative form for the solution as

$$\bar{x}_{k+1} = \bar{x}_k - [\bar{J}(\bar{x}_k)]^{-1}\bar{g}(\bar{x}_k)$$

It is not actually necessary to obtain the inverse of the matrix $\bar{J}[\bar{x}_k]$ to solve for the new approximation $\bar{x}_k$. It is possible to write Eq.(5.5) in the form

$$\bar{J}(\bar{x}_k)\bar{\delta}_k = -\bar{g}(\bar{x}_k)$$

where $\bar{\delta}_k = \bar{x}_{k+1} - \bar{x}_k$.

5.4 THE CONCEPT OF QUADRATIC CONVERGENCE

Conjugate Directions for a Quadratic Function

The gradient method is expressed as

$$\bar{x}_{k+1} = \bar{x}_k - \lambda_k \bar{g}(\bar{x}_k) \qquad \text{...(5.6)}$$

or in the form

$$\bar{\delta}_k = -\lambda_k \bar{g}(\bar{x}_k)$$

During each iteration λ_k is selected to minimize $U(\bar{x}_{k+1})$ in the gradient direction. A gradient search tends to zig-zig quite badly a particularly for quadratic functions. If it is possible to establish the best direction to take for a quadratic function, it would likely also be better for most other non-linear functions. This is called quadratic convergence and the approach is rather surprisingly successful. Equation (5.6) has the general form, in this case, given by

$$\bar{x}_{k+1} = \bar{x}_k + \lambda_k \bar{C}(\bar{x}_k) \qquad \text{...(5.7)}$$

where $\bar{C}(\bar{x}_k)$ defines the conjugate direction vector at each step. The general quadratic form is

$$U(\bar{x}) = \frac{1}{2}\bar{x}^T\bar{A}\bar{x} + \bar{B}^T\bar{x} + d \qquad \text{...(5.8)}$$

where $\bar{A}$ is a matrix and $\bar{B}$ is a vector.

It is required to determine a means of establishing conjugate directions for an optimization function of this form and show that they give convergence to the minimum. For this we require $\bar{A}$ to be a positive-define matrix, which means it must be such that all quadratic terms of Eq.(5.8) are positive. This is equivalent to requiring Eq.(5.8) to be convex so that it has a minimum. $\bar{A}$ will also be symmetric since

$$\frac{\partial^2 U}{\partial x_i \partial x_j} = A_{ij} = \frac{\partial^2 U}{\partial x_j \partial x_i} = A_{ji}$$

and consequently $\bar{A}^{-1}$ is also symmetric. For convenience, let

$$\bar{g}(\bar{x}_k) = \bar{g}_k;\ \bar{g}(\bar{x}) = \bar{g};\ \bar{C}(\bar{x}_k) = \bar{C}_k$$

Note that the gradient vector of the quadratic (5.8) is

$$\bar{g} = \bar{A}\bar{x} + \bar{B} \qquad \text{...(5.9)}$$

Equation (5.7) is iterated for successive steps from i to $(n - 1)$, to obtain

$$\bar{x}_n = \bar{x}_i + \sum_{k=1}^{n-1} \lambda_k \bar{C}_k$$

Premultiplying both sides by $\bar{A}$ and adding $\bar{B}$, we get

$$\bar{A}\bar{x}_n = \bar{B} = \bar{A}\bar{x}_i + B + \sum_{k=i}^{n-1} \lambda_k \bar{A}\bar{C}_k \qquad \text{...(5.10)}$$

Using Eq.(5.9) this becomes

$$\bar{g}_n = \bar{g}_i + \sum_{k=i}^{n-1} \lambda_k \bar{A}\bar{C}_k$$

Finally, premultiplying by $\bar{C}_{i-1}^T$,

$$\bar{C}_{i-1}^T \bar{g}_n = \bar{C}_{i-1}^T \bar{g}_1 + \sum_{k=1}^{n-1} \lambda_k \bar{C}_{i-1}^T \bar{A}\bar{C}_k \qquad \text{...(5.11)}$$

It can be demonstrated intuitively that $\bar{C}_{i-1}^T \bar{g}_i$ is zero by the following reasoning. In the $i - 1$ step, $\bar{C}_{i-1}$ is followed to a minimum for U, with takes us to $\bar{x}_1$ and therefore the gradient $\bar{g}_i$ is normal to $\bar{C}_{i-1}$. Consequently,

$$\bar{C}_{i-1}^T \bar{g}_i = 0$$

This can be demonstrated more rigorously as follows. Consider λ_{i-1} as a variable that is being adjusted to minimize U and bring the search to $\bar{x}_i$. Consequently,

$$\frac{dU}{d\lambda_{j-1}} = \frac{\partial U}{\partial x_1}\frac{dx_1}{d\lambda_{i-1}} + \frac{\partial U}{\partial x_2}\frac{dx_2}{d\lambda_{i-1}} + \cdots + \frac{\partial U}{\partial x_n}\frac{dx_n}{d\lambda_{i-1}} \qquad \text{...(5.12)}$$

Referring to Fig. 5.1, the search vector $\bar{C}_{i-1}$ at the origin has components $C_{1,\,i-1}, \ldots, C_{n,\,i-1}$, and the search moves along vector $\lambda_{i-1}C_{i-1}$ from x_{i-1} to x_1. In general, then, for any value of λ_{i-1},

$$\bar{x} = \bar{x}_{i-1} + \lambda_{i-1}\bar{C}_{i-1}$$

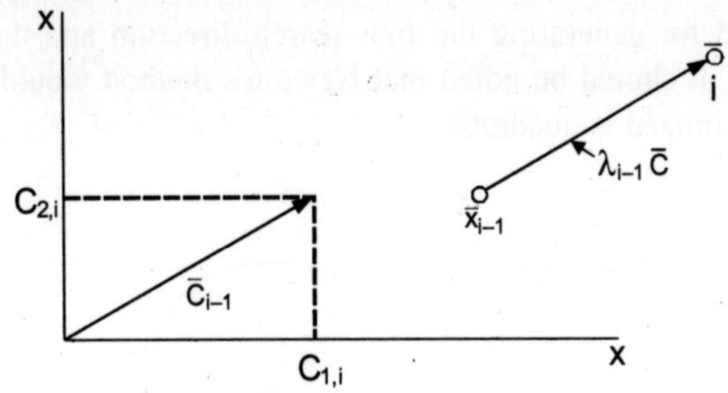

Fig. 5.1 The (i – 1)th search step

Taking the derivative with respect to λ_{i-1}, results in

$$\frac{d\bar{x}}{d\lambda_{i-1}} = \frac{d\bar{x}_{i-1}}{d\lambda_{i-1}} + \bar{C}_{i-1}$$

Since $\bar{x}_{i-1}$ is constant at this state in the search, we have

$$\bar{C}_{i-1} = \frac{d\bar{x}}{d\lambda_{i-1}}$$

Thus, Eq.(5.12) can be written for any value of λ_{i-1} as

$$\frac{dU}{d\lambda_{i-1}} = \bar{C}_{i-1}^T \bar{g}$$

Now at $\bar{x}_1$, $dU/d\lambda_{i-1}$ must be zero for a minimum U. Thus, we have

$$\bar{C}_{i-1}^T \bar{g} = 0$$

Consequently, Eq.(5.11) reduces to

$$\bar{C}_{i-1}^T \bar{g}_n = \sum_{k=i}^{n-1} \lambda_k \bar{C}_{i-1}^T \bar{A} \bar{C}_k \qquad ...(5.13)$$

The conjugate vectors are defined as those satisfying

$$\bar{C}_i^T \bar{A} \bar{C}_j = 0 \qquad ...(5.14)$$

For $i \neq j$. Since $\bar{A}$ must be a positive-define matrix as defined above, the summation term of Eq.(5.13) is zero so that

$$\bar{C}_{i-1}^T \bar{g}_n = 0 \qquad ...(5.15)$$

The theory of n-dimensional vectors states that if we construct a set of n-vectors all orthogonal or conjugate to each other, then any other vector can be written as a linear combination of these vectors. Therefore, no other vector can be orthogonal to all of the original n-vectors other than the zero vector. Since Eq.(5.15) is an expression of orthogonally of the nth gradient vector with all n conjugate vectors, then $\bar{g}_n$ must be zero, which is the condition for the minimum of the quadratic. Thus, the minimum of the quadratic can be found in the n steps if the search directions are conjugate.

The conjugate directions in two dimensions are shown in Fig. 5.2. The first search direction is the gradient vector, which is chosen arbitrarily. The second direction is conjugate to the first one. Several methods have been proposed for generating the first search direction and these methods are applied to non-quadratic functions also. It should be noted that Newton's method would go to the minimum in one step if the function to be minimized is quadratic.

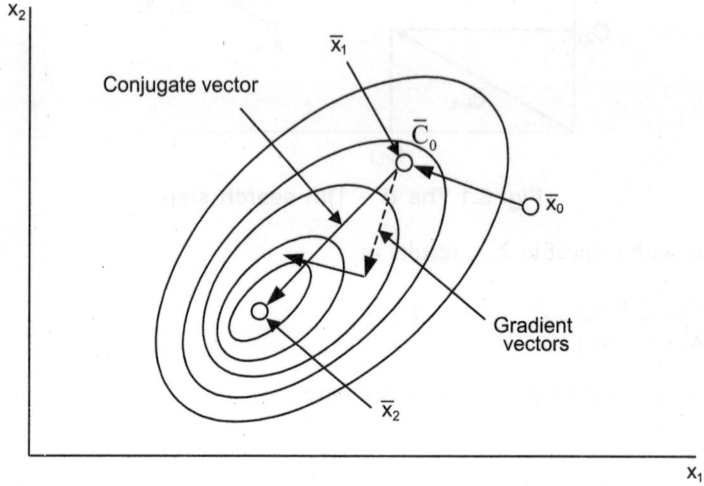

Fig. 5.2 Conjugate directions

5.5 POWELL'S METHOD

For an optimization problem involving n design variables, the basic algorithm is described below:

(*a*) select a point x_0 in the design space

(*b*) select the starting vectors V_i, $i = 1, 2, \ldots, n$

(*c*) do with $i = 1, 2, \ldots, n$

minimize $F(x)$ along the line thro x_{i-1} in the direction of V_i.

assume the minimum point as x_i

end do

(*d*) $V_{n+1} \leftarrow x_0 - x_n$

minimize $F(x)$ along the line thro x_0 in the direction of V_{n+1}

assume the minimum point as x_{n+1}

if $|x_{n+1} - x_0| < \in$ exit loop

do with $i = 1, 2, \ldots, n$

$V_i \leftarrow V_{i+1}$

end do

end cycle

The minimum point of a quadratic surface is reached in n cycles.

5.6 FLETCHER-REEVES METHOD

The algorithm is described below:

(*a*) select a starting point x_0

(*b*) $g_0 \leftarrow -\nabla F(x_0)$

(*c*) $V_0 \leftarrow g_0$

(*d*) loop with $i = 0, 1, 2, \ldots$

minimize $F(x)$ along V_i; x_{i+1} is the minimum point assumed

$g_{i+1} \leftarrow -\nabla F(x_{i+1})$

if $|g_{i+1}| < \epsilon$ or $|F(x_{i+1}) - F(x_i)| < \epsilon$ exit loop

$r \leftarrow (g_{i+1} \cdot g_{i+1})/(g_i \cdot g_i)$

$V_{i+1} \leftarrow g_{i+1} + rV_i$

end loop

The method will find the minimum of a quadratic function in n iterations. Also, V_i and V_{i+1} are mutually conjugate. In other words,

$$V_i^T A V_{i+1} = 0 \text{ and } g_i \cdot g_{i+1} = 0.$$

5.7 HOOKE AND JEEVES METHOD

Hooke and Jeeves method is a sequential technique each step of which consists of two kinds of moves, the exploratory move and the pattern move.

General procedure:

1. Start with an arbitrarily chosen point $X_1 = \begin{Bmatrix} x_1 \\ x_2 \\ \vdots \\ x_n \end{Bmatrix}$, called the starting base point and prescribed step lengths Δx_i in each of the coordinate directions u_i, $i = 1, 2, \ldots, n$. Set $k = 1$.
2. Compute $f_k = f(\mathbf{X}_k)$. Set $i = 1$, $\mathbf{Y}_{k0} = \mathbf{X}_k$, and start the exploratory move as stated in step 3.
3. The variable x_i is perturbed about the current temporary base point $\mathbf{Y}_{k,\,i-1}$ to obtain the new temporary base point as

$$\mathbf{Y}_{k,i} = \begin{cases} \mathbf{Y}_{k,i-1} + \Delta x_i \mathbf{u}_i & \text{if } f^+ = f(\mathbf{Y}_{k,i-1} + \Delta x_i \mathbf{u}_i) \\ & \quad < f = f(\mathbf{Y}_{k,i-1}) \\ \mathbf{Y}_{k,i-1} - \Delta x_i \mathbf{u}_i & \text{if } f^- = f(\mathbf{Y}_{k,i-1} - \Delta x_i \mathbf{u}_i) \\ & \quad < f = f(\mathbf{Y}_{k,i-1}) \\ & \quad < f^+ = f(\mathbf{Y}_{k,i-1} + \Delta x_i \mathbf{u}_i) \\ \mathbf{Y}_{k,i-1} & \text{if } f = f(\mathbf{Y}_{k,i-1}) < \min(f^+, f^-) \end{cases}$$

This process is continued for $i = 1, 2, \ldots,$ until x_n is perturbed to find $\mathbf{Y}_{k,n}$.

4. If the point $\mathbf{Y}_{k,n}$ remains same as $\mathbf{X}_k$, reduce the step lengths Δx_i (say, by a factor of 2), set $i = 1$ and go to step 3. If $\mathbf{Y}_{k,n}$ is different from $\mathbf{X}_k$, obtain the new base point as

$$\mathbf{X}_{k+1} = \mathbf{Y}_{k,n}$$

and go to step 5.

5. With the help of the base points $\mathbf{X}_k$ and $\mathbf{X}_{k+1}$, establish a pattern direction $\mathbf{S}$ as

$$\mathbf{S} = \mathbf{X}_{k+1} - \mathbf{X}_k$$

and find a point $\mathbf{Y}_{k+1,0}$ as

$$\mathbf{Y}_{k+1,0} = \mathbf{X}_{k+1} + \lambda\mathbf{S} \quad \text{...(5.16)}$$

where λ is the step-length, which can be taken as 1 for simplicity. Alternatively, we can solve a one-dimensional minimization problem in the direction $\mathbf{S}$ and use the optimum step length λ^* in place of λ in Eq.(5.16).

6. Set $k = k + 1$, $f_k = f(\mathbf{Y}_{k0})$, $i = 1$, and repeat step 3. If at the end of step 3, $f(\mathbf{Y}_{k,n}) < f(\mathbf{X}_k)$, we take the new base point as $\mathbf{X}_{k+1} = \mathbf{Y}_{k,n}$ and go to step 5. On the other hand, if $f(\mathbf{Y}_{k,n}) \geq f(\mathbf{X}_k)$, set $\mathbf{X}_{k+1} \equiv \mathbf{Y}_k$, reduce the step lengths Δx_i, set $k = k + 1$, and go to step 2.

7. The process is assumed to have converged whenever the step lengths fall below a small quantity ε. Thus, the process is terminated if

$$\max(\Delta x_i) < \varepsilon.$$

5.8 INTERIOR PENALTY FUNCTION METHOD

In the interior penalty function methods, a new function (ϕ function) is constructed by augmenting a penalty term to the objective function. The penalty term is chosen such that its value will be small at points away from the constraint boundaries and will tend to infinity as the constraint boundaries are approached. Thus, once the unconstrained minimization of $\phi(\mathbf{X}, r_k)$ is started from any feasible point $\mathbf{X}_1$, the subsequent points generated will always lie within the feasible domain since the constraint boundaries act as barriers during the minimization process. The ϕ function defined as

$$\phi(\mathbf{X}, r_k) = f(\mathbf{X}) - r_k \sum_{j=1}^{m} \frac{1}{g_j(\mathbf{X})}$$

Since the above equation does not allow any constraint to be violated, it requires a feasible starting point for the search toward the optimum point. The iteration procedure of this method can be summarized as follows:

Iterative process:

1. Start with an initial feasible point $\mathbf{X}_1$ satisfying all the constraints with strict inequality sign, that is, $g_j(\mathbf{X}_1) < 0$ for $j = 1, 2, \ldots, m$ and an initial value for $r_1 > 0$. Set $k = 1$.
2. Minimize $\phi(\mathbf{X}, r_k)$ by using any of the unconstrained minimization methods and obtain the solution $\mathbf{X}^*_k$.
3. Test whether $\mathbf{X}^*_k$ is the optimum solution of the original problem. If $\mathbf{X}^*_k$ is found to be optimum, terminate the process or else, go to the next step.

4. Find the value of the next penalty parameter, r_{k+1}, as

$$r_{k+1} = cr_k$$

where $c < 1$.

5. Set the new value of $k = k + 1$, take the new starting point as $\mathbf{X}_1 = \mathbf{X}^*_k$, and go to step 2.

All these aspects are discussed in the following paragraphs.

Starting Feasible Point $\mathbf{X}_1$:

1. Select an arbitrary point $\mathbf{X}_1$ and evaluate the constraints $g_j(\mathbf{X})$ at the point $\mathbf{X}_1$. Since the point $\mathbf{X}_1$ is arbitrary, it may not satisfy all the constraints with strict inequality sign. If r out of a total of m constraints are violated, renumber the constraints such that the last r constraints will become the violated ones, that is,

$$g_j(\mathbf{X}_1) < 0,\ j = 1, 2, \ldots, m - r$$
$$g_j(\mathbf{X}_1) \geq 0,\ j = m - r + 1, m - r + 2, \ldots, m$$

2. Identify the constraint that is violated most at the point $\mathbf{X}_1$, that is, obtain the integer k such that $g_k(\mathbf{X}_1) = \max[g_j(\mathbf{X}_1)]$ for $j = m - r + 1, m - r + 2, \ldots, m$

3. Formulate a new optimization problem as:

Find $\mathbf{X}$ which minimizes $g_k(\mathbf{X})$
subject to

$$g_j(\mathbf{X}) \leq 0, \qquad j = 1, 2, \ldots, m - r$$
$$g_j(\mathbf{X}) - g_k(\mathbf{X}_1) \leq 0, \qquad j = m - r + 1, m - r + 2, \ldots, k - 1, k + 1, \ldots, m$$

4. Solve the optimization problem formulated in step 3 by taking the point $\mathbf{X}_1$ as a feasible starting point using the interior penalty function method. Note that this optimization method can be terminated whenever the value of the objective function $g_k(\mathbf{X})$ drops below zero. The solution obtained $\mathbf{X}_M$ will satisfy at least one more constraint than did the original point $\mathbf{X}_1$.

5. If all the constraints are not satisfied at the point $\mathbf{X}_M$, set the new starting point as $\mathbf{X}_1 = \mathbf{X}_M$, and renumber the constraints such that the last r constraints will be the unsatisfied ones (this value of r will be different from the previous value), and go to step 2.

This procedure is repeated until all the constraints are satisfied and a point $\mathbf{X}_1 = \mathbf{X}_M$ is obtained for which $g_j(\mathbf{X}_1) < 0, j = 1, 2, \ldots, m$.

Initial Value of the Penalty Parameter (r_1):

Since the unconstrained minimization of $\phi(\mathbf{X}, r_k)$ is to be carried out for a decreasing sequence of r_k, it might appear that by choosing a very small value of r_1, we can avoid an excessive number of minimizations of the function ϕ. But from a computational point of view, it will be easier to minimize the unconstrained function $\phi(\mathbf{X}, r_k)$ if r_k is large. A moderate value has to be choosen for the initial penalty parameter (r_1). In practice, a value of r_1 that gives the value of $\phi(\mathbf{X}_1, r_1)$ approximately equal to 1.1 to 2.0 times the value of $f(\mathbf{X}_1)$ has been found to be quite satisfactory in achieving quick convergence of the process. Hence, for any initial feasible starting point $\mathbf{X}_1$, the value of r_1 can be taken as

$$r_1 \simeq 0.1 \text{ to } 1.0 \frac{f(\mathbf{X}_1)}{-\Sigma_{j=1}^{m} 1/g_j(\mathbf{X}_1)} \qquad \text{...(5.17)}$$

Subsequent Values of the Penalty Parameter:

Once the initial value of r_k is chosen, the subsequent values of r_k is selected so that

$$r_{k+1} < r_k \tag{5.18}$$

The values of r_k are chosen such that

$$r_{k+1} < cr_k \tag{5.19}$$

where $c < 1$. The value of c can be taken as 0.1, 0.2 or 0.5.

Convergence Criteria:

The process will be terminated whenever the following conditions are satisfied.

The relative difference between the values of the objective function obtained at the end of any two consecutive unconstrained minimizations falls below a small number ε_1, that is,

$$\left|\frac{f(\mathbf{X}_k^*) - f(\mathbf{X}_{k-1}^*)}{f(\mathbf{X}_k^*)}\right| \le \varepsilon_1$$

The difference between the optimum points $\mathbf{X}_k^*$ and $\mathbf{X}_{k-1}^*$ becomes very small. This can be judged in several ways. Some of them are given below:

$$|(\Delta\mathbf{X})_i| \le \varepsilon_2$$

where $\Delta\mathbf{X} = \mathbf{X}_k^* - \mathbf{X}_{k-1}^*$, and $(\Delta\mathbf{X})_i$ is the ith component of the vector $\Delta\mathbf{X}$.

$$\max|(\Delta\mathbf{X})_i| \le \varepsilon_3$$

$$|\Delta\mathbf{X}| = [(\Delta\mathbf{X})_1^2 + (\Delta\mathbf{X})_2^2 + \cdots + (\Delta\mathbf{X})_n^2]^{1/2} \le \varepsilon_4$$

It is advisable to normalize the constraints so that they vary between –1 and 0 as far as possible.

If the constraints are not normalized, the problem can still be solved effectively by defining different penalty parameters for different constraints as

$$\phi(\mathbf{X}, r_k) = f(\mathbf{X}) - r_k \sum_{j=1}^{m} \frac{R_j}{g_j(\mathbf{X})}$$

where $R_1, R_2, \ldots, R_m$ are selected such that the contributions of different $g_j(\mathbf{X})$ to the ϕ function will be approximately the same at the initial point $\mathbf{X}_1$.

5.9 EXAMPLE PROBLEMS AND SOLUTIONS

Example E5.1: Minimize the following function using Newton's method.

$$f(x, y) = x_1^2 - x_1x_2 - 5x_1 + x_2^2 - x_2$$

Use initial guesses, $x = 0$ and $y = 0$.

Solution:

```
>> fn=inline('x(1)^2-x(1)*x(2)-5*x(1)+x(2)^2-x(2)','x');
>> gn=inline('[2*x(1)-x(2)-5  -x(1)+2*x(2)-1]','x');
```

```
>> x0=[0 0];TolX=1e-4;TolFun=1e-6;MaxIter=100;
>> [x0,g0, xx]=newtons(gn,x0,TolX,MaxIter)
x0 =
      3.6667  2.3333
g0 =
      1.0e-015 *
      0        -0.4441
xx =
      3.6667   2.3333
      3.6667   2.3333
```

function g= jacob(f,x,h,varargin)

```
%Jacobian of f(x)
if nargin<3,  h=.0001; end
N= length(x); h2= 2*h; %h12=12*h;
x=x(:).'; I= eye(N);
for n=1:N
f1=feval(f,x+I(n,:)*h,varargin{:});
f2=feval(f,x-I(n,:)*h,varargin{:});
f3=feval(f,x+I(n,:)*h2,varargin{:});
f4=feval(f,x-I(n,:)*h2,varargin{:});
f12=(f1-f2)/h2;
f12=(8*(f1-f2)-f3+f4)/h12;
g(:,n)=f12(:);
end
if sum(sum(isnan(g)))==0&rank(g)<N
format short e
fprintf('At x=%12.6e, Jacobian singular with J=',x);
disp(g); format short;
end
```

function [x,fx,xx]=newtons(f,x0,TolX,MaxIter,varargin)

```
% newtons.m  to solve a set of nonlinear eqs
% input:f=a 1st-order vector ftn equivalent to a set of equations
% x0=the initial guess of the solution
% TolX=the upper limit of |x(k)-x(k-1)|
% MaxIter=the maximum # of iteration
% Output: x=the point which the algorithm has reached
% fx=f(x(last))
% xx=the history of x
```

```
h=1e-5; TolFun=eps; EPS=1e-6;
fx=feval(f,x0,varargin{:});
Nf=length(fx); Nx=length(x0);
if Nf~=Nx, error('Incompatible dimensions of f and x0!'); end
if nargin<4, MaxIter=100; end
if nargin<3, TolX=EPS; end
xx(1,:)=x0(:).';
%fx0= norm(fx);
for k=1: MaxIter
J=jacob(f,xx(k,:),h,varargin{:});
if rank(J)<Nx
k=k-1; fprintf('Warning: Jacobian singular! with det(J)=%12.6e\n',det(J));
break;
else
dx= -J\fx(:); %-[dfdx]^-1*fx;
end
xx(k+1,:)= xx(k,:)+dx.';
fx= feval(f,xx(k+1,:),varargin{:}); fxn=norm(fx);
% if fxn<fx0, break; end
%end
if fxn<TolFun|norm(dx)<TolX, break; end
%fx0= fxn;
end
x= xx(k+1,:);
if k==MaxIter
fprintf('Do not depend on this, though the best in %d iterations\n',MaxIter)
end
```

Example E5.2: Minimize the two-variable objective function

$$f(x_1, x_2) = x_1^2 - 2x_1x_2 - 4x_1 + x_2^2 - x_2$$

Use initial values: (0,0).

Solution:

```
>> fn=inline('10*x(1)^2-10*x(1)*x(2)+3*x(2)^2+2*x(1)','x');
>> gn=inline('[20*x(1)-10*x(2)+2  -10*x(1)+6*x(2)]','x');
>> x0=[0 0];TolX=1e-4;TolFun=1e-6;MaxIter=50;
>> [x0,g0,xx]=newtons(gn,x0,TolX,MaxIter)
x0=
      -0.6000  -1.0000
g0=
       0          0
```

```
xx =
       0         0
      -0.6000   -1.0000
      -0.6000   -1.0000
```

function g= jacob(f,x,h,varargin)

```
%Jacobian of f(x)
if nargin<3,  h=.0001; end
N= length(x); h2= 2*h; %h12=12*h;
x=x(:).'; I= eye(N);
for n=1:N
f1=feval(f,x+I(n,:)*h,varargin{:});
f2=feval(f,x-I(n,:)*h,varargin{:});
f3=feval(f,x+I(n,:)*h2,varargin{:});
f4=feval(f,x-I(n,:)*h2,varargin{:});
f12=(f1-f2)/h2;
f12=(8*(f1-f2)-f3+f4)/h12;
g(:,n)=f12(:);
end
if sum(sum(isnan(g)))==0&rank(g)<N
format short e
fprintf('At x=%12.6e, Jacobian singular with J=',x);
disp(g); format short;
end
```

function [x,fx,xx]= newtons(f,x0,TolX,MaxIter,varargin)

```
% newtons.m to solve a set of nonlinear eqs
% input: f = a 1st-order vector ftn equivalent to a set of equations
% x0 = the initial guess of the solution
% TolX = the upper limit of |x(k)-x(k-1)|
% MaxIter= the maximum # of iteration
% Output: x=the point which the algorithm has reached
% fx=f(x(last))
% xx=the history of x
h=1e-5; TolFun=eps; EPS=1e-6;
fx=feval(f,x0,varargin{:});
Nf=length(fx); Nx=length(x0);
if Nf~=Nx, error('Incompatible dimensions of f and x0!'); end
if nargin<4, MaxIter=100; end
if nargin<3, TolX=EPS; end
xx(1,:)=x0(:).';
```

```
%fx0= norm(fx);
for k=1: MaxIter
J=jacob(f,xx(k,:),h,varargin{:});
if rank(J)<Nx
k=k-1; fprintf('Warning: Jacobian singular! with det(J)=%12.6e\n',det(J));
break;
else
dx= -J\fx(:); %-[dfdx]^-1*fx;
end
xx(k+1,:)= xx(k,:)+dx.';
fx= feval(f,xx(k+1,:),varargin{:}); fxn=norm(fx);
% if fxn<fx0, break; end
%end
if fxn<TolFun|norm(dx)<TolX, break; end
%fx0= fxn;
end
x= xx(k+1,:);
if k==MaxIter
fprintf('Do not depend on this, though the best in %d iterations\n',MaxIter)
end
```

Example E5.3: Fit a polynomial by quadratic approximation and determine the values of X at which $F(X)$ is minimum.

X	$F(X)$
1	8
2	3
3	17

Solution:

X	$F(X)$
1	8
2	3
3	17

Let $F(X) = a_0 + a_1X + a_2X^2$. From the given data, we have

$$a_0 + a_1 + a_2 = 8$$
$$a_0 + 2a_1 + 4a_2 = 3$$
$$a_0 + 3a_1 + 9a_2 = 17$$

solving above equations using MATLAB give

```
>> A=[1 1 1;1 2 4;1 3 9];
>> b=[8;3;17];
```

```
>> x=A\b
x =
       32.0000
      -33.5000
        9.5000
>> x=inv(A)*b
x =
       32.0000
      -33.5000
        9.5000
      a0 = 32
      a1 = -33.5
      a2 = 9.5
>> x=[1 2 3];y=[8 3 17]; a2a1a0=polyfit(x,y,2)
a2a1a0 =
      9.50000000000001    -33.50000000000002    32.00000000000003
```

and the function is

$$F(X) = 32 - 33.5X + 9.5X^2$$

For finding minimum of the function, we find the first derivative of the function

$\dfrac{dF(X)}{dX} = -33.5 + 19X = 0$; for a minima or maxima

Thus, $X = 1.763$

To check for minima or maxima, we find second derivative of the function $\dfrac{d^2F(X)}{dX^2} = 19 > 0$; thus it's a minimum.

The minimum value of $F(X)$ at X is

$F(X = 1.763) = 2.462$

Example E5.4: Fit a polynomial by quadratic approximation and determine the values of X at which $F(X)$ is minimum.

X	$F(X)$
1	–7
2	5
3	14

Solution:

X	$F(X)$
1	–7
2	5
3	14

Let $F(X) = a_0 + a_1X + a_2X^2$. From the given data, we have

$$a_0 + a_1 + a_2 = -7$$
$$a_0 + 2a_1 + 4a_2 = 5$$
$$a_0 + 3a_1 + 9a_2 = 14$$

Solving above equations give

$$a_0 = -22$$
$$a_1 = 16.5$$
$$a_2 = -1.5$$

```
>> x=[1 2 3];y=[-7 5 14];a2a1a0=polyfit(x,y,2)
a2a1a0 =
        -1.50000000000000    16.50000000000002    -22.00000000000003
```

and the function is

$$F(X) = -22 + 16.5X - 1.5X^2$$

For finding minimum of the function, we find the first derivative of the function $\frac{dF(X)}{dX} = 16.5 - 3X = 0$; for a minimum or maximum

thus, $X = 5.5$

To check for minima or maxima, we find second derivative of the function $\frac{d^2F(X)}{dX^2} = -3 < 0$; thus it's a maximum.

Thus, for the given function there is no absolute minimum. The function attains its minimum values at $\pm\infty$.

MATLAB Solution:

```
% Problem 3.2
clc
clear
disp('Fit a Polynomial by Quadratic Aproximation')
x1=1;
x2=2;
x3=3;
f1=-7;
f2=5;
f3=14;
fx1=[1 x1 (x1)];
fx2=[1 x2 2*x2];
fx3=[1 x3 3*x3];
a=[fx1;fx2;fx3]
b=[f1 ;f2; f3]
poly_values=inv(a)*b
```

```
%solve for min
disp('(derivative) d(f(x))/dx= -3*x+16.5')
disp('Thus minimum is x=-16.5/3 ~ 5.5')
disp('Second derivative d2(f(x))/d2x=-3<0')
disp('Thus no absolute minimum')
```

Example E5.5: Use Powell's method to find the minimum of the function

$$f = 120(y - x^2)^2 + (1 - x)^2$$

Start with (–1, 1).

Solution:

```
function y = fex3_17(X)
y = 120*(X(2)-X(1)^2)^2+(1-X(1))^2;
>> global X FUNC
>> FUNC = @fex3_17;
>> X=[-1.0,1.0];
>> [xMin,fMin,numCycles]=powell
xMin =
      1.0000
      1.0000
fMin =
      4.8369e-021
numCycles =
      12
```

function [xMin,fMin,nCyc] = powell(h,tol)

```
% Powell's method
% h=initial search increment=0.1
% tol=error tolerance=1.0e-6
% X=starting point
% FUNC=function that returns f
% xMin=minimum point
% fMin=miminum value of f
% nCyc=number of cycles to convergence
global X FUNC V
if nargin <2; tol=1.0e-6; end
if nargin <1; h=0.1; end
if size(X,2)>1; X=X'; end
n = length(X);
df = zeros(n,1);
```

```
u = eye(n);
for j = 1:40        % 40 cycles
xOld = X;
fOld = feval(FUNC,xOld);
for i = 1:n
V = u(1:n,i);
[a,b] = goldBracket(@fLine,0.0,h);
[s,fMin] = goldSearch(@fLine,a,b);
df(i) = fOld - fMin;
fOld = fMin;
X = X + s*V;
end
V = X - xOld;
[a,b] = goldBracket(@fLine,0.0,h);
[s,fMin] = goldSearch(@fLine,a,b);
X = X + s*V;
% convergence criterion
if sqrt(dot(X-xOld,X-xOld)/n) < tol
xMin = X; nCyc = j; return
end
iMax = 1; dfMax = df(1);
for i = 2:n
if df(i) > dfMax
iMax = i; dfMax = df(i);
end
end
for i = iMax:n-1
u(1:n,i) = u(1:n,i+1);
end
u(1:n,n) = V;
end
error('No converge')

function z = fLine(s)
global X FUNC V
z = feval(FUNC,X+s*V);
```

Example E5.6: Use Powell's method to find the minimum of the function

$$f(x) = 9x_1^2 + 4x_2^2 - 8x_1x_2 + 3x_1$$

Start with $x_0 = [0 \quad 0]^T$.

Solution:

```
function y = fex3_18(X)
y = 9*X(1)^2+4*X(2)^2-8*X(1)*X(2)+3*X(1);
>> global X FUNC
>> FUNC = @fex3_18;
>> X=[-1.0,1.0];
>> [xMin,fMin,numCycles]=powell

xMin =
      -0.3000
      -0.3000
fMin =
      -0.4500
numCycles =
      2
```

function [xMin,fMin,nCyc]=powell(h,tol)

```
% Powell's method
% h   = initial search increment  = 0.1
% tol = error tolerance  = 1.0e-6
% X = starting point
% FUNC = function that returns f
% xMin = minimum point
% fMin = miminum value of f
% nCyc = number of cycles to convergence
global X FUNC V
if nargin < 2; tol = 1.0e-6; end
if nargin < 1; h = 0.1; end
if size(X,2) > 1; X = X'; end
n = length(X);
df = zeros(n,1);
u = eye(n);
for j = 1:40     % 40 cycles
xOld = X;
fOld = feval(FUNC,xOld);
for i = 1:n
V = u(1:n,i);
[a,b] = goldBracket(@fLine,0.0,h);
[s,fMin] = goldSearch(@fLine,a,b);
df(i) = fOld - fMin;
fOld = fMin;
X = X + s*V;
```

```
end
V = X - xOld;
[a,b] = goldBracket(@fLine,0.0,h);
[s,fMin] = goldSearch(@fLine,a,b);
X = X + s*V;
% convergence criterion
if sqrt(dot(X-xOld,X-xOld)/n) < tol
xMin = X; nCyc = j; return
end
iMax = 1; dfMax = df(1);
for i = 2:n
if df(i) > dfMax
iMax = i; dfMax = df(i);
end
end
for i = iMax:n-1
u(1:n,i) = u(1:n,i+1);
end
u(1:n,n) = V;
end
error('No converge')

function z = fLine(s)
global X FUNC V
z = feval(FUNC,X+s*V);
```

Example E5.7: Use Fletcher-Reeves method to locate the minimum of function

$$F(x) = 10x_1^2 + 3_2^2 - 10x_1, x_2 + 2x_1.$$

Start with $[0 \quad 0.05]^T$.

Solution:

```
Global X FUNC DFUNC V
>> FUNC=@fex3_19;DFUNC=@dfex3_19;X=[0,0.5];
>> [xMin,fMin,nCyc]=fletcherReeves
xMin =
      -0.6000
      -1.0000
fMin =
      -0.6000
nCyc =
      3
```

function [xMin,fMin,nCyc] = FletcherReeves(h,tol)

```
% Fletcher-Reeves method
% h = initial search increment = 0.1
% tol = error tolerance = 1.0e-6
% X = starting point
% FUNC = handle of function that returns f
% DFUNC = handle of function that returns grad(f)
% xMin = minimum point
% fMin = miminum value of f
% nCyc = # of cycles to convergence
global X FUNC DFUNC V
if nargin < 2; tol = 1.0e-6; end
if nargin < 1; h = 0.1; end
if size(X,2) > 1; X = X'; end
n = length(X);
g0 = -feval(DFUNC,X);
V = g0;
for i = 1:50
[a,b] = goldBracket(@fLine,0.0,h);
[s,fMin] = goldSearch(@fLine,a,b);
X = X + s*V;
g1 = -feval(DFUNC,X);
if sqrt(dot(g1,g1)) <= tol
xMin = X; nCyc = i; return
end
gamma = dot((g1 - g0),g1)/dot(g0,g0);
V = g1 + gamma*V;
g0 = g1;
end
error('Method did not converge')
function z = fLine(s)
global X FUNC V
z = feval(FUNC,X+s*V);
```

function [a,b] = goldBracket(func,x1,h)

```
% Brackets the minimum point of f(x)
% func = returns f(x)
% x1= starting value of x
% h = initial step size
% a, b = limits on x
c = 1.618033989;
f1 = feval(func,x1);
```

```
x2 = x1 + h; f2 = feval(func,x2);
if f2 > f1
h = -h;
x2 = x1 + h; f2 = feval(func,x2);
if f2 > f1
a = x2; b = x1 - h; return
end
end
% Search loop
for i = 1:100
h = c*h;
x3 = x2 + h; f3 = feval(func,x3);
if f3 > f2
a = x1; b = x3; return
end
x1 = x2; f1 = f2; x2 = x3; f2 = f3;
end
error('Failed to find minimum')
```

function [xMin,fMin] = goldSearch(func,a,b,tol)

```
% Golden section search method
% func = function that returns f(x)
% a, b = limits of the interval for the minimum
% tol = error tol = 1.0e-6
% fMin = min of f(x)
% xMin = x at min point
if nargin < 4; tol = 1.0e-6; end
nIter = ceil(-2.078087*log(tol/abs(b-a)));
R = 0.618033989;
C = 1.0 - R;
x1 = R*a + C*b;
x2 = C*a + R*b;
f1 = feval(func,x1);
f2 = feval(func,x2);
for i =1:nIter
if f1 > f2
a = x1; x1 = x2; f1 = f2;
x2 = C*a + R*b;
f2 = feval(func,x2);
else
b = x2; x2 = x1; f2 = f1;
x1 = R*a + C*b;
```

```
f1 = feval(func,x1);
end
end
if f1 < f2; fMin = f1; xMin = x1;
else; fMin = f2; xMin = x2;
end
```

Example E5.8: Use Fletcher-Reeves method to find the minimum of function in Problem EN3.18. Start with $[0 \quad 0.05]^T$.

Solution:

```
Global X FUNC DFUNC V
X=[0,0];
>> FUNC=@fex3_20;DFUNC=@dfex3_20;X=[0,0];
>> [xMin,fMin,nCyc]=FletcherReeves

xMin =
      -0.3000
      -0.3000
fMin =
      -0.4500
nCyc =
      3
```

function [xMin,fMin,nCyc] = FletcherReeves(h,tol)

```
% Fletcher-Reeves method
% h = initial search increment = 0.1
% tol= error tolerance = 1.0e-6
% X = starting point
% FUNC = handle of function that returns f
% DFUNC = handle of function that returns grad(f)
% xMin = minimum point
% fMin = miminum value of f
% nCyc = # of cycles to convergence
global X FUNC DFUNC V
if nargin < 2; tol = 1.0e-6; end
if nargin < 1; h = 0.1; end
if size(X,2) > 1; X = X'; end
n = length(X);
g0 = -feval(DFUNC,X);
V = g0;
for i = 1:50
```

```
[a,b] = goldBracket(@fLine,0.0,h);
[s,fMin] = goldSearch(@fLine,a,b);
X = X + s*V;
g1 = -feval(DFUNC,X);
if sqrt(dot(g1,g1)) <= tol
xMin = X; nCyc = i; return
end
gamma = dot((g1 - g0),g1)/dot(g0,g0);
V = g1 + gamma*V;
g0 = g1;
end
error('Method did not converge')
function z = fLine(s)
global X FUNC V
z = feval(FUNC,X+s*V);
```

function [a,b] = goldBracket(func,x1,h)

```
% Brackets the minimum point of f(x)
% func =  returns f(x)
% x1= starting value of x
% h = initial step size
% a, b = limits on x
c = 1.618033989;
f1 = feval(func,x1);
x2 = x1 + h; f2 = feval(func,x2);
if f2 > f1
h = -h;
x2 = x1 + h; f2 = feval(func,x2);
if f2 > f1
a = x2; b = x1 - h; return
end
end
% Search loop
for i = 1:100
h = c*h;
x3 = x2 + h; f3 = feval(func,x3);
if f3 > f2
a = x1; b = x3; return
end
x1 = x2; f1 = f2; x2 = x3; f2 = f3;
end
error('Failed to find minimum')
```

function [xMin,fMin] = goldSearch(func,a,b,tol)

```
% Golden section search method
% func = function that returns f(x)
% a, b = limits of the interval for the minimum
% tol = error tol = 1.0e-6
% fMin = min of f(x)
% xMin = x at min point
if nargin < 4; tol = 1.0e-6; end
nIter = ceil(-2.078087*log(tol/abs(b-a)));
R = 0.618033989;
C = 1.0 - R;
x1 = R*a + C*b;
x2 = C*a + R*b;
f1 = feval(func,x1);
f2 = feval(func,x2);
for i =1:nIter
if f1 > f2
a = x1; x1 = x2; f1 = f2;
x2 = C*a + R*b;
f2 = feval(func,x2);
else
b = x2; x2 = x1; f2 = f1;
x1 = R*a + C*b;
f1 = feval(func,x1);
end
end
if f1 < f2; fMin = f1; xMin = x1;
else; fMin = f2; xMin = x2;
end
```

Example E5.9: Minimize the following function $f(x)$ by the penalty function method:

$$f(x) = [(x_1 + 2)^2 + 5(x_2 - 2)^2]\,[(x_1 - 1.5)^2 + 0.5(x_2 - 0.5)^2]$$

subject to
$$\begin{bmatrix} -x_1 \\ -x_2 \\ 3x_1 - x_1x_2 + 4x_2 - 6 \\ 2x_1 + x_2 - 5 \\ 3x_1 - 4x_2^2 - 4x_2 \end{bmatrix} \le \begin{bmatrix} 0 \\ 0 \\ 0 \\ 0 \\ 0 \end{bmatrix}.$$

Solution:

```
>> % Penalty function method
>> clear,clf
>> f='f321p';
>> x0=[0.4 0.5];
>> TolX=1e-5;TolFun=1e-9;alpha0=1;
>> TolX=1e-5;
>> MaxIter=100;
>> [x0_Nelder,f0_Nelder]=opt_Nelder(f,x0,TolX,TolFun,MaxIter) % Nelder
method
x0_Nelder =
      1.4423    0.6540
f0_Nelder =
      0.3176
>> [fc_Nelder,f0_Nelder,c0_Nelder]=f321p(x0_Nelder) % Its results
fc_Nelder =
      0.3176
f0_Nelder =
      0.3176
c0_Nelder =
     -1.4423
     -0.6540
     -0.0002
     -1.4613
     -0.0002

>> [x0_s,f0_s]=fminsearch(f,x0) %MATLAB built-in fminsearch()
x0_s =
      1.4421    0.6540
f0_s =
      0.3178
>> [fc_s,f0_s,c0_s]=f321p(x0_s) % its results
fc_s =
      0.3178
f0_s =
      0.3178
c0_s =
     -1.4421
     -0.6540
     -0.0009
     -1.4618
     -0.0001
```

```
>> [x0_u,f0_u]=fminunc(f,x0) % MATLAB built-in fminunc
Warning: Gradient must be provided for trust-region method;
  using line-search method instead.
> In fminunc at 243
Maximum number of function evaluations exceeded;
 increase options.MaxFunEvals
x0_u =
      1.4311    0.6599
f0_u =
      0.3637
>> [fc_u,f0_u,c0_u]=f321p(x0_u) % its results
fc_u =
      0.3637
f0_u =
      0.3637
c0_u =
      -1.4311
      -0.6599
      -0.0114
      -1.4778
      -0.0880
```

function [fc,f,c]=f321p(x)

```
f=((x(1)+2)^2+5*(x(2)-2)^2)*((x(1)-1.5)^2+0.5*(x(2)-0.5)^2);
c=[-x(1); -x(2); 3*x(1)-x(1)*x(2)+4*x(2)-6;2*x(1)+x(2)-5;
   3*x(1)-4*x(2)^2-4*x(2)]; % Constraint vector
v=[1 1 1 1 1];e=[1 1 1 1 1]';% Weighting coefficient vector
fc=f+v*((c>0).*exp(e.*c)); % New objective function
```

function [xo,fo]=opt_Nelder(f,x0,TolX,TolFun,MaxIter)

```
N=length(x0);
if N==1 %for 1-dimensional case
[xo,fo]=opt_quad(f,x0,TolX,TolFun); return
end
S= eye(N);
for i=1:N %repeat the procedure for each subplane
i1=i+1; if i1>N, i1=1; end
abc=[x0; x0+S(i,:); x0+S(i1,:)]; %each directional subplane
fabc=[feval(f,abc(1,:)); feval(f,abc(2,:)); feval(f,abc(3,:))];
[x0,fo]=Nelder0(f,abc,fabc,TolX,TolFun,MaxIter);
if N<3, break; end %No repetition needed for a 2-dimensional case
end
xo=x0;
```

function [xo,fo]=opt_quad(f,x0,TolX,TolFun,MaxIter)

```
%search for the minimum of f(x) by quadratic approximation method
if length(x0)>2, x012=x0(1:3);
else
if length(x0)==2, a=x0(1); b=x0(2);
else a=x0-10; b=x0+10;
end
x012= [a (a+b)/2 b];
end
f012= f(x012);
[xo,fo]=opt_quad0(f,x012,f012,TolX,TolFun,MaxIter);
```

function [xo,fo]=opt_quad0(f,x012,f012,TolX,TolFun,k)

```
x0= x012(1); x1= x012(2); x2= x012(3);
f0= f012(1); f1= f012(2); f2= f012(3);
nd= [f0-f2 f1-f0 f2-f1]*[x1*x1 x2*x2 x0*x0; x1 x2 x0]';
x3= nd(1)/2/nd(2); f3=feval(f,x3); %Eq.(7.1-4)
if k<=0|abs(x3-x1)<TolX|abs(f3-f1)<TolFun
xo=x3;  fo=f3;
if k==0, fprintf('Just the best in given # of iterations'), end
else
if x3<x1
if f3<f1, x012=[x0 x3 x1]; f012= [f0 f3 f1];
else  x012=[x3 x1 x2]; f012= [f3 f1 f2];
end
else
if f3<=f1, x012=[x1 x3 x2]; f012= [f1 f3 f2];
else  x012=[x0 x1 x3]; f012= [f0 f1 f3];
end
end
[xo,fo]=opt_quad0(f,x012,f012,TolX,TolFun,k-1);
end
```

Example E5.10: Minimize $f(x) = x_1^2 + x_2^2 - 6x_1 - 8x_2 + 10$

subject to $4x_1^2 + x_2^2 \le 0$

$3x_1 + 5x_2 \le 0$

Using penalty function method.

Solution:

```
% Penalty function method
clear,clf
```

```
f='f322p';
x0=[0.4 0.5];
TolX=1e-5;TolFun=1e-9;alpha0=1;
TolX=1e-5; MaxIter=100;
[x0_Nelder,f0_Nelder]=opt_Nelder(f,x0,TolX,TolFun,MaxIter) % Nelder method
[fc_Nelder,f0_Nelder,c0_Nelder]=f322p(x0_Nelder) % Its results
[x0_s,f0_s]=fminsearch(f,x0) %MATLAB built-in fminsearch()
[fc_s,f0_s,c0_s]=f322p(x0_s) % its results
[x0_u,f0_u]=fminunc(f,x0) % MATLAB built-in fminunc
[fc_u,f0_u,c0_u]=f322p(x0_u) % its results

>> [x0_Nelder,f0_Nelder]=opt_Nelder(f,x0,TolX,TolFun,MaxIter) % Nelder
method
x0_Nelder =
      0.4412  -0.2647
f0_Nelder =
      9.7353
>> [fc_Nelder,f0_Nelder,c0_Nelder]=f322p(x0_Nelder) % Its results
fc_Nelder =
      9.7353
f0_Nelder =
      9.7353
c0_Nelder =
     -0.7085
     -0.0000

>> [x0_s,f0_s]=fminsearch(f,x0) %MATLAB built-in fminsearch()
x0_s =
      0.4412  -0.2647
f0_s =
      9.7353
>> [fc_s,f0_s,c0_s]=f322p(x0_s) % its results
fc_s =
      9.7353
f0_s =
      9.7353

c0_s =
     -0.7085
     -0.0000
```

```
>> [x0_u,f0_u]=fminunc(f,x0) % MATLAB built-in fminunc
Warning: Gradient must be provided for trust-region method;
 using line-search method instead.
> In fminunc at 243
Optimization terminated: relative infinity-norm of gradient less than
options.TolFun.
x0_u =
      0.4867   -0.1888
f0_u =
      10.5382
>> [fc_u,f0_u,c0_u]=f322p(x0_u) % its results
fc_u =
      10.5382
f0_u =
      8.8627
c0_u =
      -0.9119
      0.5161
```

function [fc,f,c]=f322p(x)

```
f=(x(1)^2+x(2)^2-6*x(1)-8*x(2)+10);
c=[-4*x(1)^2+x(2)^2; 3*x(1)+5*x(2)]; % Constraint vector
v=[1 1];e=[1 1 ]';% Weighting coefficient vector
fc=f+v*((c>0).*exp(e.*c)); % New objective function
```

function [xo,fo]=opt_quad(f,x0,TolX,TolFun,MaxIter)

```
%search for the minimum of f(x) by quadratic approximation method
if length(x0)>2, x012=x0(1:3);
else
if length(x0)==2, a=x0(1); b=x0(2);
else a=x0-10; b=x0+10;
end
x012= [a (a+b)/2 b];
end
f012= f(x012);
[xo,fo]=opt_quad0(f,x012,f012,TolX,TolFun,MaxIter);
```

function [xo,fo]=opt_quad0(f,x012,f012,TolX,TolFun,k)

```
x0= x012(1); x1= x012(2); x2= x012(3);
f0= f012(1); f1= f012(2); f2= f012(3);
nd= [f0-f2 f1-f0 f2-f1]*[x1*x1 x2*x2 x0*x0; x1 x2 x0]';
x3= nd(1)/2/nd(2); f3=feval(f,x3); 78ikol
```

```
if k<=0|abs(x3-x1)<TolX|abs(f3-f1)<TolFun
xo=x3;  fo=f3;
if k==0, fprintf('Just the best in given # of iterations'), end
else
if x3<x1
if f3<f1, x012=[x0 x3 x1]; f012= [f0 f3 f1];
else  x012=[x3 x1 x2]; f012= [f3 f1 f2];
end
else
if f3<=f1, x012=[x1 x3 x2]; f012= [f1 f3 f2];
else  x012=[x0 x1 x3]; f012= [f0 f1 f3];
end
end
[xo,fo]=opt_quad0(f,x012,f012,TolX,TolFun,k-1);
end
```

Example E5.11: Find the minimum point of the following objective function $f(x)$ using quadratic approximation method.

$$f(x) = \frac{(x_2^2 - 5)}{8} - 1$$

Solution:

```
>> clear,clf
>> f323=inline('(x.*x-5).^2/8-1', 'x');
>> a=0;b=3;TolX=1e-6;TolFun=1e-9;MaxIter=100;
>> [x0q,f0q]-opt_quad(f323,[a,b],TolX,TolFun,MaxIter)
x0q =
      2.2361
f0q =
     -1.0000
>> % x0q= minimum point and f0q = its function value in above
>> [x0q,f0q]=fminbnd(f323,a,b) % MATLAB built-in function
x0q =
      2.2361
f0q =
     -1.0000
```

function [xo,fo]=opt_quad(f,x0,TolX,TolFun,MaxIter)

```
%search for the minimum of f(x) by quadratic approximation method
if length(x0)>2, x012=x0(1:3);
else
if length(x0)==2, a=x0(1); b=x0(2);
```

```
else a=x0-10; b=x0+10;
end
x012= [a (a+b)/2 b];
end
f012= f(x012);
[xo,fo]=opt_quad0(f,x012,f012,TolX,TolFun,MaxIter);
```

function [xo,fo]=opt_quad0(f,x012,f012,TolX,TolFun,k)

```
x0= x012(1); x1= x012(2); x2= x012(3);
f0= f012(1); f1= f012(2); f2= f012(3);
nd= [f0-f2 f1-f0 f2-f1]*[x1*x1 x2*x2 x0*x0; x1 x2 x0]';
x3= nd(1)/2/nd(2); f3=feval(f,x3); %Eq.(7.1-4)
if k<=0|abs(x3-x1)<TolX|abs(f3-f1)<TolFun
xo=x3; fo=f3;
if k==0, fprintf('Just the best in given # of iterations'), end
else
if x3<x1
if f3<f1, x012=[x0 x3 x1]; f012= [f0 f3 f1];
else  x012=[x3 x1 x2]; f012= [f3 f1 f2];
end
else
if f3<=f1, x012=[x1 x3 x2]; f012= [f1 f3 f2];
else  x012=[x0 x1 x3]; f012= [f0 f1 f3];
end
end
[xo,fo]=opt_quad0(f,x012,f012,TolX,TolFun,k-1);
end
```

Example E5.12: Find the minimum point of the following objective function $f(x)$ using quadratic approximation method.

Solution:

```
>> clear,clf
>> f324=inline('(x.*x+3).^2/10+exp(x)-7','x');
>> a=0;b=3;TolX=1e-6;TolFun=1e-9;MaxIter=100;
>> [x0q,f0q]=opt_quad(f324,[a,b],TolX,TolFun,MaxIter)
x0q =
      -0.4793
f0q =
      -5.3377
>> % x0q= minimum point and f0q = its function value
>> [x0q,f0q]=fminbnd(f324,a,b) % MATLAB built-in function
```

```
x0q =
     5.6302e-005
f0q =
    -5.0999
```

function [xo,fo]=opt_quad(f,x0,TolX,TolFun,MaxIter)

```
%search for the minimum of f(x) by quadratic approximation method
if length(x0)>2, x012=x0(1:3);
else
if length(x0)==2, a=x0(1); b=x0(2);
else a=x0-10; b=x0+10;
end
x012= [a (a+b)/2 b];
end
f012= f(x012);
[xo,fo]=opt_quad0(f,x012,f012,TolX,TolFun,MaxIter);
```

function [xo,fo]=opt_quad0(f,x012,f012,TolX,TolFun,k)

```
x0= x012(1); x1= x012(2); x2= x012(3);
f0= f012(1); f1= f012(2); f2= f012(3);
nd= [f0-f2 f1-f0 f2-f1]*[x1*x1 x2*x2 x0*x0; x1 x2 x0]';
x3= nd(1)/2/nd(2); f3=feval(f,x3); %Eq.(7.1-4)
if k<=0|abs(x3-x1)<TolX|abs(f3-f1)<TolFun
xo=x3;  fo=f3;
if k==0, fprintf('Just the best in given # of iterations'), end
else
if x3<x1
if f3<f1, x012=[x0 x3 x1]; f012= [f0 f3 f1];
else x012=[x3 x1 x2]; f012= [f3 f1 f2];
end
else
if f3<=f1, x012=[x1 x3 x2]; f012= [f1 f3 f2];
else  x012=[x0 x1 x3]; f012= [f0 f1 f3];
end
end
[xo,fo]=opt_quad0(f,x012,f012,TolX,TolFun,k-1);
end
```

Example E5.13: Use the MATLAB *fminbnd* function to find the maximum of $f(x) = 8 \sin x - \frac{x^2}{14}$ with the interval $x_\ell = 0$ and $x_u = 7$.

Solution:

First we create an .m file to hold the function

```
function f=fx(x)
f=-(8*sin(x)-x^2/14)
```

The negative sign is for minimization.

```
>> x=fminbnd('fx', 0,7)
```

The result from MATLAB program is

```
f =
      -7.8268
x =
       1.5432
```

Example E5.14: Use the MATLAB *fminsearch* function to find the maximum of $f(x, y) = 3xy + 8x - x^2 - 9y^2$, using initial guesses, $x = -1$ and $y = 1$.

Solution:

Create an m file to hold the function

```
function f=fxy(x)
f=-(3*x(1)*x(2)+8*x(1)-x(1)^2-9*x(2)^2)
```

Invoke the fminsearch function with

```
>> x=fminsearch('fxy',[-1,1])
f =
     -21.3333
x =
        5.3334    0.8889
```

Examples E5.15 to E5.20 are based on Tutorials and Demos from MATLAB (The Mathworks, Inc.)

Example E5.15: This is an unconstrained minimization example. Find the set of values $[x_1, x_2]$ that solve

$$\min_x f(x) = e^{x_1}(4x_1^2 + 2x_2^2 + 4x_1x_2 + 2x_2 + 0.9)$$

Starting guess: $x^0 = [-1, 1]$.

Solution:

MATLAB Solution [Using built-in function]:

```
Write an m-file objfun.m
function f=objfun(x)
f=exp(x(1))*(4*x(1)^2+2*x(2)^2+4*x(1)*x(2)+2*x(2)+0.9);

Write one of the unconstrained optimization routines:
>> x0=[-1,1]; % Starting guess at the solution
>> options=optimset('LargeScale', 'off');
>> [x,fval,exitflag,output]=fminunc(@objfun,x0,options)
```

```
Optimization terminated: relative infinity-norm of gradient less than
options.TolFun.

x =
      0.5000   -1.0000
fval =
      3.6609e-016
exitflag =
    1
output =
      iterations: 8
       funcCount: 66
        stepsize: 1
      firstorderopt: 7.3704e-008
       algorithm: 'medium-scale: Quasi-Newton line search'
       message: 'Optimization terminated: relative infinity-norm of gradient
less than options.TolFun.'
```

Example E5.16: This is a non-linear inequality constrained example. Find x that solves

$$\min_{x} f(x) = e^{x_1}(4x_1^2 + 2x_2^2 + 4x_1x_2 + 2x_2 + 0.9)$$

subject to the constraints

$$x_1x_2 - x_1 - x_2 \leq -2.0$$
$$x_1x_2 \geq -10$$

Starting guess: $x^0 = [-1, 1]$.

Solution: The constraints are written in the form $c(x) \leq 0$.

$$x_1x_2 - x_1 - x_2 + 2 \leq 0$$
$$-x_1x_2 - 10 \leq 0$$

MATLAB Solution [Using built-in function]:

```
Write an m-file objfun.m
function f=objfun(x)
f=exp(x(1))*(4*x(1)^2+2*x(2)^2+4*x(1)*x(2)+2*x(2)+0.9);

Write an m-file confun.m for the constraints:
function [c,ceq]=confun(x)
%Nonlinear inequality constraints
c=[2+x(1)*x(2)-x(1)-x(2);-x(1)*x(2)-10];
%Nonlinear inequality constraints
ceq=[];
```

Invoke constrained optimization routine:

```
>> x0=[-1,1]; % Initial guess at the solution
>> options=optimset('LargeScale', 'off');
>> [x,fval]=fmincon(@objfun,x0,[],[],[],[],[],[],@confun,options)
Optimization terminated: first-order optimality measure less
 than options.TolFun and maximum constraint violation is less
 than options.TolCon.
Active inequalities (to within options.TolCon = 1e-006):
  lower     upper    ineqlin   ineqnonlin
                        1
                        2
x =
      -9.5474   1.0474
fval =
       0.0236
>> [c,ceq]=confun(x)
c =
       1.0e-007 *
      -0.9035
       0.9035
ceq =
      []
```

Example E5.17: This is a constrained optimization example: inequalities and bounds.

Minimize $f(x) = e^{x_1}(4x_1^2 + 2x_2^2 + 4x_1x_2 + 2x_2 + 0.9)$

subject to $2 + x_1x_2 - x_1 - x_2 \le 0$

$-x_1x_2 \le 0$

$x_1 \ge 0$

$x_2 \ge 0$

Initial values: $x^0 = [-1, 1]$.

Solution:

MATLAB Solution [Using built-in function]:

function f=objfun(x)

```
f=exp(x(1))*(4*x(1)^2+2*x(2)^2+4*x(1)*x(2)+2*x(2)+0.9);
```

function [c,ceq]=confun(x)

```
%Nonlinear inequality constraints
c=[2+x(1)*x(2)-x(1)-x(2);-x(1)*x(2)-10];
%Nonlinear inequality constraints
ceq=[];
```

```
>> x0=[-1,1]; % Initial guess at the solution
>> lb=[0,0];   % Lower bounds
>> ub=[];   % Upper bounds
>> options=optimset('LargeScale', 'off');
>> [x,fval]=fmincon(@objfun,x0,[],[],[],[],lb,ub,@confun,options)
Optimization terminated: first-order optimality measure less
than options.TolFun and maximum constraint violation is less
than options.TolCon.
Active inequalities (to within options.TolCon = 1e-006):
  lower     upper    ineqlin   ineqnonlin
    1          1
x =
      0          1.5000
fval =
      8.5000
>> [c,ceq]=confun(x)
c =
      0
      -10
ceq =
      []
```

Example E5.18: This is a constrained example with gradients.

Minimize $f(x) = e^{x_1}(4x_1^2 + 2x_2^2 + 4x_1x_2 + 2x_2 + 0.9)$

subject to $2 + x_1x_2 - x_1 - x_2 \le 0$

$-x_1x_2 \le 0$

Initial values: $x^0 = [-1, 1]$.

Solution:

MATLAB Solution [Using built-in function]:

Write an m-file for the objective function and gradient:

The objective function and its gradient are defined in the *m*-file *objgrad.m* as follows:

```
function [f,G]=objfungrad(x)
f=exp (x(1))*(4*x(1)^2+2*x(2)^2+4*x(1)*x(2)+2*x(2)+0.9);
t=exp(x(1))*(4*x(1)^2+2*x(2)^2+4*x(1)*x(2)+2*x(2)+0.9);
G=[t+exp(x(1))*(8*x(1)+4*x(2)),
   exp(x(1))*(4*x(1)+4*x(2)+2)];
```

Write an m-file for the nonlinear constraints and the gradients of the nonlinear constraints:

The constraints and their partial derivatives are contained in the *m*-file *confungrad.m:*

function[c,ceq,dc,dceq]=confungrad(x)

```
c=[2+x(1)*x(2)-x(1)-x(2);
   -x(1)*x(2)-10];
dc=[x(2)-1,-x(2);
   x(1)-1,-x(1)];
ceq=[];
dceq=[];
```

7

Invoke constrained optimization routine:

Define a guess at the solution:

```
>> x0=[-1,1];
>> options=optimset('LargeScale', 'off');
>> options=optimset(options, 'GradObj', 'on','GradConstr', 'on');
>> lb=[],ub=[], % no lower or upper bounds
>> [x,fval]=fmincon(@objfungrad,x0,[],[],[],[],lb,ub,@confungrad,options)
Optimization terminated: first-order optimality measure less
 than options.TolFun and maximum constraint violation is less
 than options.TolCon.
Active inequalities (to within options.TolCon = 1e-006):
  lower      upper     ineqlin   ineqnonlin
                          1
                          2
x =
      -9.5474    1.0474
fval =
       0.0236
>> [c,ceq]=confungrad(x)  % check the constraint values at x
c =
       1.0e-007 *
      -0.9032
       0.9032
ceq =
      []
```

Example E5.19:

Minimize $\quad f(x) = e^{x_1}(4x_1^2 + 2x_2^2 + 4x_1x_2 + 2x_2 + 0.9)$

subject to $\quad x_1^2 + x_2^2 = 1$

$\quad -x_1x_2 \geq -10$

Initial values: $\quad x^0 = [-1, 1]$.

Solution:

MATLAB Solution [Using built-in function]:

The objective function nd its gradient re-defined in the *m-file objfun.m* as follows:

function f=objfun(x)

```
f=exp(x(1))*(4*x(1)^2+2*x(2)^2+4*x(1)*x(2)+2*x(2)+0.9);
```

The m-file confuneq.m contains the equality and inequality constraints:

```
function [c,ceq]=confuneq(x)
c=-x(1)*x(2)-10;
ceq=x(1)^2+x(2)-1;
```

Define a guess at the solution:

```
>> x0=[-1,1];
```

We will use the option as below:

```
>> options=optimset('LargeScale', 'off');
```

Call the optimization algorithm:

```
>> [x,fval,exitflag,output]=fmincon(@objfun,x0,[],[],[],[],[],[],@confuneq,
options);
Optimization terminated: first-order optimality measure less than options.
TolFun
 and maximum constraint violation is less than options.TolCon.
No active inequalities.
>> x
x =
      -0.7488   0.4393
```

The function value at the solution is

```
>> fval
fval =
        1.4621
```

The constraint values at the solution are

```
>> [c,ceq]=confuneq(x)


c =
      -9.6710
ceq =
        6.4376e-009
```

The total number of function evaluations was

```
>> output.funcCount
ans =
       21
```

Changing the default termination tolerances

```
Consider the original unconstrained problem solved first
Minimize f(x)= exp(x(1))*(4*x(1)^2+2*x(2)^2+4*x(1)*x(2)+2*x(2)+0.9
This time we will solve it more accurately by overriding the default
termination criteria (options.TolX and options.TolFun).
Create an anonymous function of the objective to be minimized:
>> fun=@(x) exp(x(1))*(4*x(1)^2+2*x(2)^2+4*x(1)*x(2)+2*x(2)+0.9);
>> fun
fun =
   @(x) exp(x(1))*(4*x(1)^2+2*x(2)^2+4*x(1)*x(2)+2*x(2)+0.9)
Make a guess at the solution as
>> x0=[-1,1];
Set the optimization options: turn off the large-scale algorithms (the
default):
>> options=optimset('LargeScale', 'off');
Override the default termination criteria:
% Termination tolerances on X and f.
>> options=optimset(options, 'TolX',1e-3, 'TolFun',1e-3);
Call the optimization algorithm:
>> [x,fval,exitflag,output]=fminunc(fun,x0,options);

Optimization terminated: relative infinity-norm of gradient less than
options.TolFun.
The optimizer has found a solution at
>> x
x =
      0.5246   -1.0248
The function value at the solution is
>> fval
fval =
     -0.1669
The total number of function evaluations was
>> output.funcCount
ans =
      48
Set optimization options: turn off the large scale algorithms (the default):
>> options=optimset(options,'Display','iter');
>> [x,fval,exitflag,output]=fminunc(fun,x0,options);
```

Iteration	Func-count	f(x)	Step-size	First-order optimality
0	3	1.80261	0.736	
1	9	1.68824	0.377066	0.295
2	30	–0.124807	21.3836	0.964
3	36	–0.160866	0.239618	0.158
4	45	–0.166915	0.0531349	0.0219
5	48	–0.166933	1	0.00114

Optimization terminated: relative infinity-norm of gradient less than options.TolFun.

Example E5.20: Optimal Fit of a Non-linear Function

This is a demonstration of the optimal fitting of a non-linear function to a set of data. It uses FMINSEARCH, an implementation of the Nelder-Mead simplex (direct search) algorithm, to minimize a non-linear function of several variables.

Solution:

MATLAB Solution [Using built-in function]:

First, create some sample data and plot it.

```
>> t = (0:.1:2)';
y = [6 4 3 2 1.8990 1.5 1.2 1.1 1.03      0.8 0.68 0.61 0.59 0.39 0.39 0.54 0.34
0.13   0.2 0.17 0.26]';
plot(t,y,'ro'); hold on; h = plot(t,y,'b'); hold off;
title('Input data'); ylim([0 6])
```

The goal is to fit the following function with two linear parameters and two non-linear parameters to the data:

```
y = C(1)*exp(-lambda(1)*t) + C(2)*exp(-lambda(2)*t)
```

To fit this function, we've create a function FITFUN. Given the non-linear parameter (lambda) and the data (t and y), FITFUN calculates the error in the fit for this equation and updates the line (h).

type fitfun

```
function err = fitfun(lambda,t,y)
% FITFUN Used by FITDEMO.
% FITFUN(lambda,t,y) returns the error between the data and the values
% computed by the current function of lambda.
% FITFUN assumes a function of the form
% y =  c(1)*exp(-lambda(1)*t) + ... + c(n)*exp(-lambda(n)*t)
% with n linear parameters and n non-linear parameters.
A = zeros(length(t),length(lambda));
for j = 1:length(lambda)
   A(:,j) = exp(-lambda(j)*t);
end
c = A\y;
z = A*c;
err = norm(z-y);
```

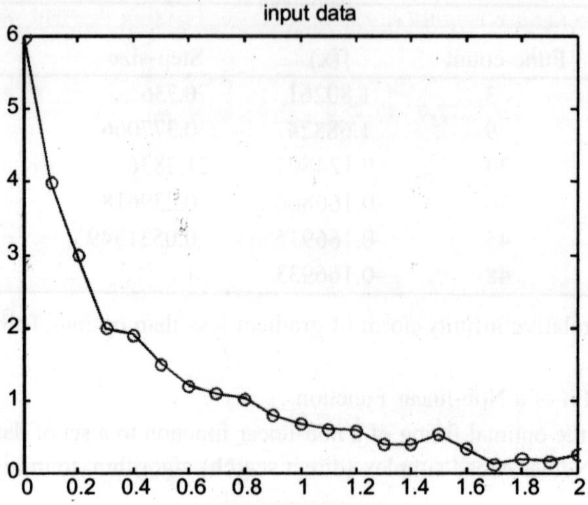

Fig. E5.20 (a)

Make a guess for initial estimate of lambda (start) and invoke FMINSEARCH. It minimizes the error returned from FITFUN by adjusting lambda. It returns the final value of lambda. Use an output function to plot intermediate fits.

```
start = [1;0];
% We use an anonymous function to pass additional parameters t, y, h to the
% output function.
>> start = [1;0];
>> outputFcn = @(x,optimvalues,state)
   fitoutputfun(x,optimvalues,state,t,y,h);
options = optimset('OutputFcn',outputFcn,'TolX',0.1);
estimated_lambda = fminsearch(@(x)fitfun(x,t,y),start,options)
estimated_lambda =
      7.0269
      1.3427
```

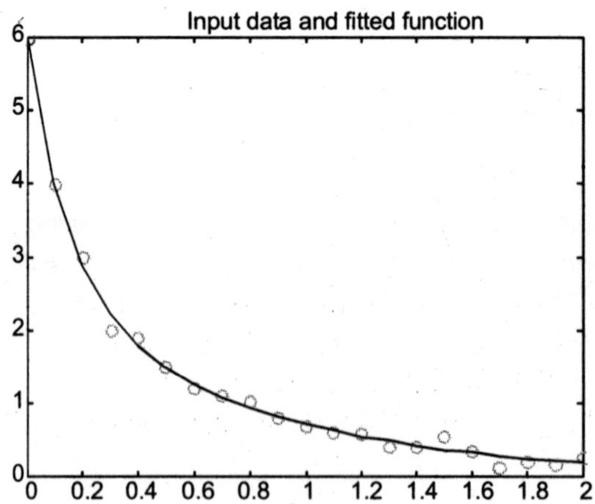

Fig. E5.20(b)

Example E5.21: Minimize $f(x_1, x_2) = 90\,(x_2 - x_1^2)^2 + (1 - x_1)^2$ using the starting point

$x_1 = -1.1, x_2 = 1.0$

Solution:

```
The minimum = 0 at x = 1, y = 1
EDU>> Run_EN_5_21
x =
        1.0000     1.0000
fval =
        7.2476e-010
```

```
Run_EN_5_21
y=@(x)90*(x(2)-x(1)^2)^2+(1-x(1))^2;
x,fval]=fminsearch(y,[-1.1,1.0])
```

Example E5.22: Minimize $f = 0.60 - 0.70/(1. + x^2) - 0.5*\tan^{-1}(1/x)$

Solution:

The minimum value of the function is $f = -0.8286$ at $x = 0.1001$

```
EDU>> Run_EN_5_22
f =
   @(x)0.60-0.70/(1. + x.^2)-0.5*atan(1/x)
x =
      0.1001
f =z
    -0.8286
Run_EN_5_22
f = @(x)0.60 - 0.70/(1. + x.^2)- 0.5*atan(1/x)
x = fminbnd(f, .1,1.0)
f = 0.60 - 0.70/(1. + x.^2) - 0.5*atan(1/x)
```

Example E5.23: Use the MATLAB fminbnd function to find the maximum of

$$y = (3*(\sin(x)) - (x^2/12)$$

Solution:

The graph of this function is given below. By inspection, the maximum value of the function is close to 2.8 and occurs at approximately $x = 1.5$.

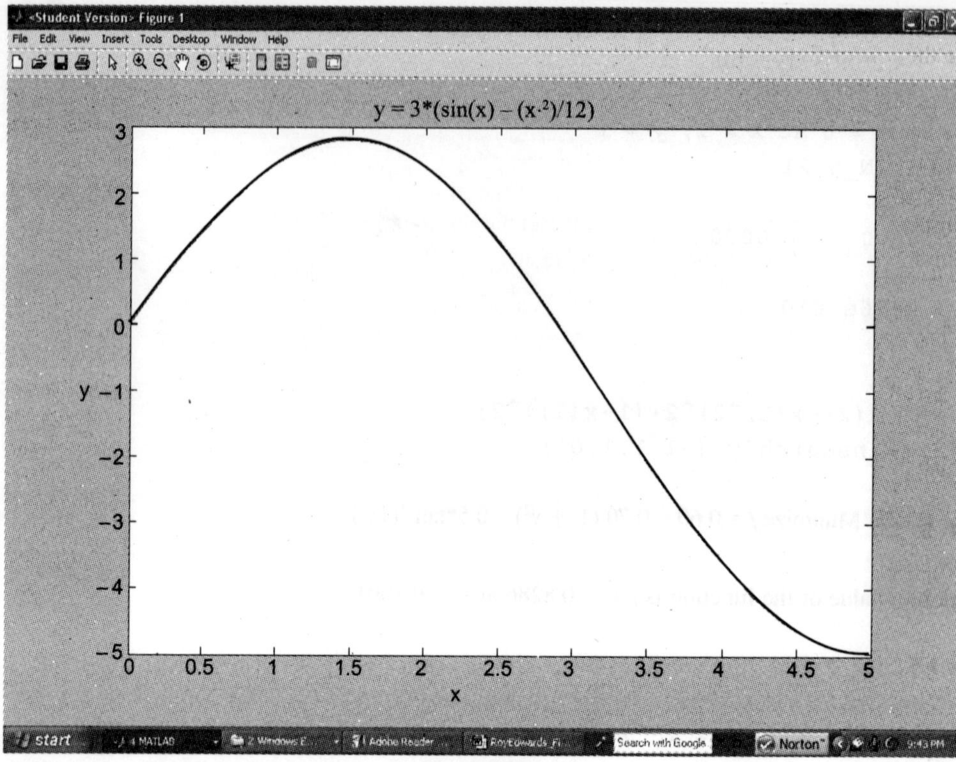

Fig. E5.23

To compute the exact value of the *maximum* of the function, calculate the negative of the function (y). Use fminbnd on this new function (fun) to calculate the minimum value. The maximum of the original function occurs at the same x as the minimum of the new function. The maximum value of the original function is the negative of the new function.

```
EDU>> Run_EN_5_23
fun =
    @(x)(-1.0)* (3*(sin(x))-(x.^2)/12)
x =
        1.4880
fun =
       -2.8052
```

Therefore, the maximum of the original function, f, is

$y = 2.8052$ at

$x = 1.4880$

```
Run_EN_5_23
fun = @(x)(-1.0)* (3*(sin(x)) - (x.^2)/12)
x = fminbnd(fun, 0,5.0)
fun = -1.0 * (3*(sin(x)) - (x.^2)/12)
```

Example E5.24: Using the MATLAB function fminsearch,
Maximize the function

$f(x_1, x_2) = 3*x_1*x_2 + 5*x_1 - x_1^2 - 3*x_2^2$ with initial guess
$x_1 = -1.0, x_2 = 1.0$

Solution:
The minimum of $-f$ occurs at $x = 10.0$ $y = 5.0$ and the minimum has a value of -25.0.
The maximum of the original function, f, occurs at $x = 10.0$ $y = 5.0$ and has a value of 25.0.

```
EDU>> Run_EN_5_24
x =
      10.0000   5.0000
fval =
     -25.0000
```

```
Run_EN_5_24
y=@(x)-1.0 * (3.*x(1).*x(2)+5.*x(1) -x(1).^2 - 3.*(x(2).^2));
[x,fval] = fminsearch(y,[-1.0,1.0])
```

Example E5.25: Use Powell's method to find the *minimum* of the function:

$f = 120(y - x^2)^2 + (1 - x)^2$ starting with (–1, 1)

Solution:

```
The minimum = 0 at x = 1, y = 1
EDU>> Run_EN_5_25
y =
      4.8369e-021
xMin =
      1.0000
      1.0000
fMin =
      4.8369e-021 (which is 0)
nCyc =
      12
```

```
Run_EN_5_25
global X FUNC
FUNC = @fpr3_15;
X=[-1.0;1.0];
[xMin,fMin,nCyc]=Powell
```

```
fpr5_25
function y = fpr3_15(X)
y=120*(X(2)-X(1)^2)^2 + (1.-X(1))^2
```

Example E5.26: Find the minimum of the function $f = 90(y - x^2)^2 + (1 - x)^2$ with Powell's method starting at the point (–1, 1).

Solution:

Let $\overline{X}_0$ be an initial guess at the location of the minimum of the function $z = f(\overline{X}) = f(x_1, x_2, ..., x_n)$. Assume that the partial derivatives of the function are not available. An intuitively appealing approach to approximating a minimum of the function f is to generate the next approximation $\overline{X}_1$ by proceeding successively to a minimum of f along each of the n standard base vectors. This process can be called the taxi-cab method and generates the sequence of points

$$\overline{X}_0 = \overline{P}_0, \overline{P}_1, \overline{P}_2 ..., \overline{P}_n = \overline{X}_1$$

Along each standard base vector $\overline{E}_k = (0,...0,1_k,0,...,0)$ the function f is a function of one variable, and the minimization of f might be accomplished by the application of either the golden ratio or Fibonacci searches if f is unimodal in this search direction. The iteration is then repeated to generate a sequence of points $\{\overline{X}_k\}_{k=0}$. Unfortunately, the method is, in general, inefficient due to the geometry of multivariable functions.

Choose N =2 and select two direction vectors $U_1 = \begin{bmatrix} 1 \\ 0 \end{bmatrix}$ and $U_2 = \begin{bmatrix} 0 \\ 1 \end{bmatrix}$.

Start with point $P_0 = X = \begin{bmatrix} -1 \\ 1 \end{bmatrix}$ and construct $P_1 = P_0 + \lambda_1 U_1 = \begin{bmatrix} -1+\lambda_1 \\ 1 \end{bmatrix}$ by moving in the directions U_1 by optimal length λ_1. Substituting P_1 in f, a one-dimensional objective function is formed in λ_1, which is solved for minimum. Then λ_1 is substituted in P_1 and new point P_2 is evaluated as $P_2 = P_1 + \lambda_2 U_2$ by moving in the directions U_2 by optimal length λ_2 in the similar manner.

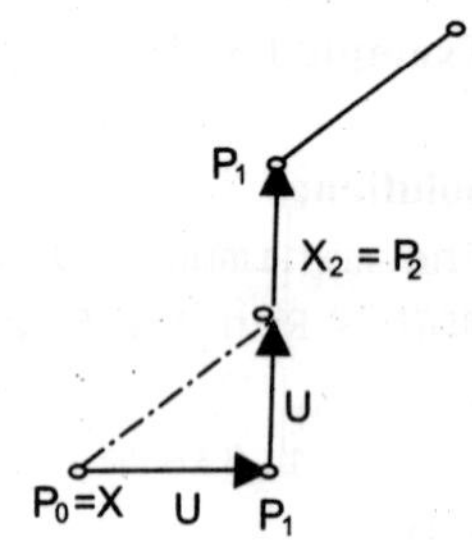

Fig. E5.26 (a)

Then change the new search directions as $U_1 = \begin{bmatrix} 0 \\ 1 \end{bmatrix}$ and $U_2 = P_2 - P_0$. The process is repeated for several iterations to get the best unconstrained optimum point X_n. For obtaining the optimum lengths λ_i an unconstrained one-dimensional problem is to be solved. The method is illustrated in Fig. E5.26(a).

The solution by other method (Nedler and Meed' Simplex) is as follows with MATLAB readymade function:

Outputs with the function 'obj.m' given below is as follows:

```
function f =obj(x)
f=90*(x(2)-x(1)^2)^2+(1-x(1))^2;
>> [x fval]=fminsearch('obj',[-1,1]);
>> x
x=1.0000        1.0000
>> fval
fval=0.000
```

The complete flow chart of the method is shown in Fig. E5.26(b).

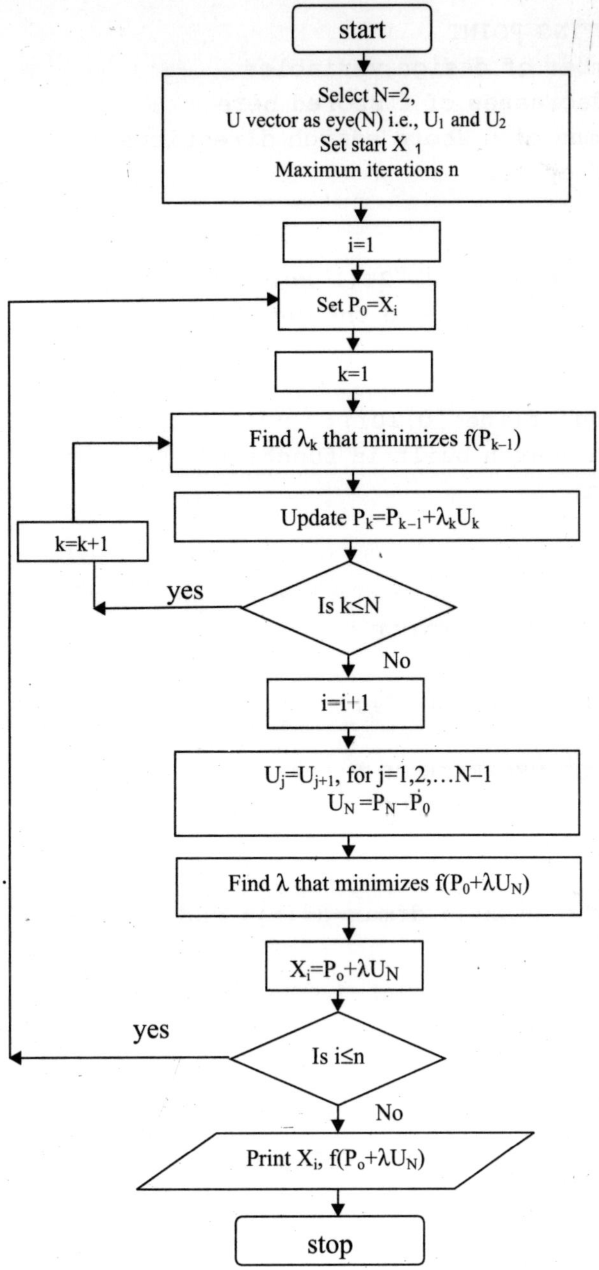

Fig. E5.26 (b)

The program is as follows:

```
global X V
X=[-1;1];   %STARTING POINT
N=length(X);% number of design variables
df=zeros(N,1);% decreases of f stored here
u=eye(N);  % columns of u store search directions V
n=30;  % Number of cycles
for j=1:n
  xold=X;
  fold=90*(xold(2)-xold(1)^2)^2+(1-xold(1))^2;
  % FIRST N line searches record the decrease of f
  for i=1:N
   V=u(1:N,i);
   [s fmin]=fminbnd('fline',0,10);
   %Golden section search built in function
   df(i)=fold-fmin;
   fold=fmin;
   X=X+s*V;
  end
  % LAST LINE SEARCH IN THE CYCLE
  V=X-xold;
  [s fmin]=fminbnd('fline',0,10);
  X=X+s*V;
  % IDENTIFY BIGGEST DECREASE OF F
  % AND UPDATE SEARCH DIRECTIONS
  imax=1; dfmax=df(1);
  for i=2:N
    if df(i)>dfmax   imax=i; dfmax=df(i); end
  end
  for i=imax:N-1
    u(1:N,i)=u(1:N,i+1);
  end
  u(1:N,N)=V;
end
fprintf('Optimum point after %d cycles is\n',n);
fprintf('%f\n%f\n',X(1),X(2));
```

The function with file name 'fline.m' used is as follows:

```
function z=fline(s)
global X V
b1=V(1);
b2=V(2);
a1=X(1);a2=X(2);
```

```
p1=a1+s*b1;p2=a2+s*b2;
z=90*(p2-p1^2)^2+(1-p1)^2;
```

The output is as follows:
Optimum point after 30 cycles is
1.003135
1.000263

Example E5.27: Use the Fletcher-Reeves method to locate the minimum of $f(x) = 9x_1^2 + 3x_2^2 - 8x_1x_2 + 2x_1$. Start with $X_o=[0\ 0]^T$.

Solution:

This method is also called conjugate gradient method. It is modification of Cauchy's method of gradient decent algorithm. The complete algorithm is given below:
Given x^0 perform the following steps:

1. Compute $\nabla f(x^0)$ and set $u^1 = -\nabla f(x^0)$.
2. For $i = 1, 2, ..., n$ do:

   2.1 Set $x^i = x^{i-1} + \lambda_i u^i$ where λ_i such that

   $$f(x^{i-1} + \lambda_i u^i) = \min_{\lambda} f(x^{i-1} + \lambda u^i) \text{ (line search)}$$

   2.2 Compute $\nabla f(x^i)$,

   2.3 If convergence criteria satisfied, then STOP and $x^* \cong x^i$, else go to Step 2.4

   2.4 If $1 \le i \le n-1, u^{i+1} = -\nabla f(x^i) + \beta_i u^i$
3. Set $x^0 = x^n$ and go to Step 2 (restart).

Here $\beta_i = \dfrac{|\nabla f_i|^2}{|\nabla f_{i-1}|^2}$.

In this problem $\nabla f = \begin{bmatrix} 18x_1 - 8x_2 + 2 \\ 6x_2 - 8x_1 \end{bmatrix}$ and $X^0 = \begin{bmatrix} 0 \\ 0 \end{bmatrix}$

Iteration 1:

Thus $U^1 = -\nabla f(X^0) = \begin{bmatrix} 2 \\ 0 \end{bmatrix}$.

For $i = 1$, find $X^1 = X^0 + \lambda_1 U^1 = \begin{bmatrix} 2\lambda_1 \\ 0 \end{bmatrix}$ and substituting in function f and find the minimum value of f and corresponding λ_1 and X^1.

Compute $\nabla f(X^1)$

Iteration 2:

$$U^2 = -\nabla f_1 + \frac{|\nabla f_1|^2}{|\nabla f_0|^2}\, U^1$$

$X^2 = X^1 + \lambda_2 U^2$ and perform line search to find the minimum of $f(X^2) = f(\lambda_2)$

Again compute $\nabla f\,(X^2)$. Stop if it is equal to zero otherwise continue.

Complete program is given below:

```
% CONJUGATE GRADIENT METHOD
global X V
X=[0;0];
N=length(X);
g0=-feval('df',X);
V=g0;
n=50;
for i=1:n
  [s fmin]=fminbnd('fline',-10,10);
  X=X+s*V
  g1=-feval('df',X);
  gamma=(norm(g1)/norm(g0))^2;
  V=g1+gamma*V;
  g0=g1;
end
fprintf('Minimum point for this function is \n');
fprintf('%f\n%f\n',X(1),X(2));
This requires the following function files
%LINEAR FUNCTION OF s
function z=fline(s)
global V X
p1=X(1)+s*V(1);
p2=X(2)+s*V(2);
z=9*p1^2+3*p2^2-8*p1*p2+2*p1;
%GRADIENT FUNCTION
function y=df(X)
y=[18*X(1)-8*X(2)+2;6*X(2)-8*X(1)];
```

The output is as follows:

Minimum point for this function is

–0.272727

–0.363636

Exact output obtained from the function fminsearch('fxy',[–1,1]) is

–0.2727

–0.3637

Example E5.28: Find the minimum of the function $f(X) = 4x_1^2 + 3x_2^2 - 5x_1x_2 - 8x_1$ starting from (0, 0) using Powell's method

Solution: The process is shown in Fig. E5.28.

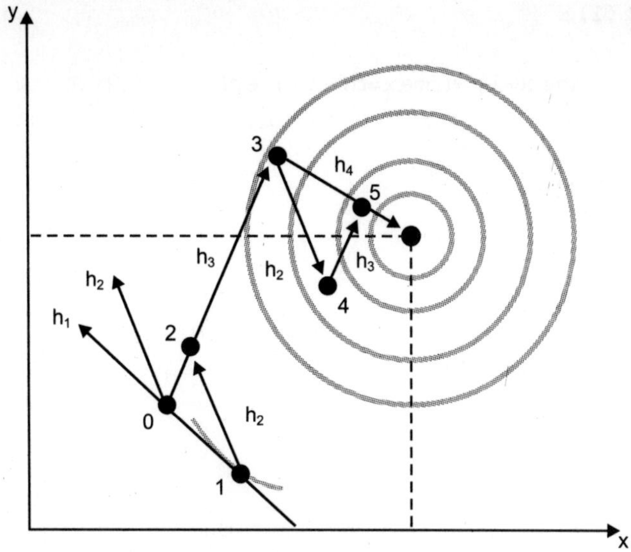

Fig. E5.28

Complete Program is as follows:

```
global  X V
X=[-1;1];  %STARTING POINT
N=length(X);% number of design variables
df=zeros(N,1);% decreases of f stored here
u=eye(N); % columns of u store search directions V
n=30;  % Number of cycles
for j=1:n
  xold=X;
  fold=4*xold(1)^2+3*xold(2)^2-5*xold(1)*xold(2)-8*xold(1);
  % FIRST N line searches record the decrease of f
  for i=1:N
   V=u(1:N,i);
   [s fmin]=fminbnd('fline',0,10);
   %Golden section search built in function
   df(i)=fold-fmin;
   fold=fmin;
   X=X+s*V;
  end
  % LAST LINE SEARCH IN THE CYCLE
  V=X-xold;
  [s fmin]=fminbnd('fline',0,10);
```

```
  X=X+s*V;
  % IDENTIFY BIGGEST DECREASE OF F
  % AND UPDATE SEARCH DIRECTIONS
  imax=1; dfmax=df(1);
  for i=2:N
    if df(i)>dfmax   imax=i; dfmax=df(i); end
  end
  for i=imax:N-1
    u(1:N,i)=u(1:N,i+1);
  end
  u(1:N,N)=V;
end
fprintf('Optimum point after %d cycles is\n',n);
fprintf('%f\n%f\n',X(1),X(2));

Function is
function z=fline(s)
global X V
b1=V(1);
b2=V(2);
a1=X(1);a2=X(2);
p1=a1+s*b1;p2=a2+s*b2;
z=4*p1^2+3*p2^2-5*p1*p2-8*p1;
Optimum point after 30 cycles is
2.091345
1.739733
Actual output from MATLAB function fminsearch('fxy', [0 0]) is
2.0870
1.7392
```

Example E5.29: Find the minimum value of the function $f(X) = 7x_1^2 + 5x_2^2 - 8x_1x_2 - 5x_1$ starting from (0, 0) using Powell's method.

Solution: The following program is used

```
global  X V
X=[0;0];    %STARTING POINT
N=length(X);% number of design variables
df=zeros(N,1);% decreases of f stored here
u=eye(N);  % columns of u store search directions V
n=30;  % Number of cycles
for j=1:n
  xold=X;
```

```
 fold=7*xold(1)^2+5*xold(2)^2-8*xold(1)*xold(2)-5*xold(1);
 % FIRST N line searches record the decrease of f
 for i=1:N
  V=u(1:N,i);
  [s fmin]=fminbnd('fline',0,10);
  %Golden section search built in function
  df(i)=fold-fmin;
  fold=fmin;
  X=X+s*V;
 end
 % LAST LINE SEARCH IN THE CYCLE
 V=X-xold;
 [s fmin]=fminbnd('fline',0,10);
 X=X+s*V;
 % IDENTIFY BIGGEST DECREASE OF F
 % AND UPDATE SEARCH DIRECTIONS
 imax=1; dfmax=df(1);
 for i=2:N
   if df(i)>dfmax   imax=i; dfmax=df(i); end
 end
 for i=imax:N-1
   u(1:N,i)=u(1:N,i+1);
 end
 u(1:N,N)=V;
end
fprintf('Optimum point after %d cycles is\n',n);
fprintf('%f\n%f\n',X(1),X(2));
Function used is as follows:
function z=fline(s)
global X V
a1=X(1);a2=X(2);
b1=V(1);
b2=V(2);
p1=a1+s*b1;p2=a2+s*b2;
z=7*p1^2+5*p2^2-8*p1*p2-5*p1;
Optimum point after 30 cycles is
0.657916
0.528062
```

The actual output from MATLAB fminsearch function is

0.6579

0.5263

Example E5.30: Repeat problem E5.30 using Fletcher-Reeves method.

Solution:

Given $f(x_1, x_2) = 4x_1^2 + 3x_2^2 - 5x_1x_2 - 8x_1$

Here gradient $df = [8x_1 - 5x_2 - 8;\ 6x_2 - 5x_1]^T$

Complete program is given below:

```
% CONJUGATE GRADIENT METHOD
global X V
X=[0;0];
N=length(X);
g0=-feval('df',X);
V=g0;
n=50;
for i=1:n
  [s fmin]=fminbnd('fline',-10,10);
  X=X+s*V
  g1=-feval('df',X);
  gamma=(norm(g1)/norm(g0))^2;
  V=g1+gamma*V;
  g0=g1;
end
fprintf('Minimum point for this function is \n');
fprintf('%f\n%f\n',X(1),X(2));
```

This requires the following function files

```
%LINEAR FUNCTION OF s
function z=fline(s)
global V X
p1=X(1)+s*V(1);
p2=X(2)+s*V(2);
z=4*p1^2+3*p2^2-5*p1*p2-8*p1;
%GRADIENT FUNCTION
function y=df(X)
y=[8*X(1)-5*X(2)-8;6*X(2)-5*X(1)];
```

The output is as follows:

Minimum point for this function is

2.086957

1.739130

The actual output is $[2.087 \quad 1.7392]^T$

Example E5.31: Repeat problem E5.31 using Fletcher-Reeves method.

Solution:

Given $f(x_1, x_2) = 7x_1^2 + 5x_2^2 - 8x_1x_2 - 5x_1$

Here gradient df = $[14x_1 - 8x_2 - 5;\ 10x_2 - 8x_1]^T$

Complete program is as follows:

```
global X V
X=[0;0];
N=length(X);
g0=-feval('df',X);
V=g0;
n=50;
for i=1:n
  [s fmin]=fminbnd('fline',-10,10);
  X=X+s*V
  g1=-feval('df',X);
  gamma=(norm(g1)/norm(g0))^2;
  V=g1+gamma*V;
  g0=g1;
end
fprintf('Minimum point for this function is \n');
fprintf('%f\n%f\n',X(1),X(2));

Functions are
function z=fline(s)
global V X
p1=X(1)+s*V(1);
p2=X(2)+s*V(2);
z=7*p1^2+5*p2^2-8*p1*p2-5*p1;
%GRADIENT FUNCTION
function y=df(X)
y=[14*X(1)-8*X(2)-5; 10*X(2)-8*X(1)];
```

The output is as follows:

Minimum point for this function is

0.657895

0.526316

The actual output from MATLAB function is $[0.6579\ \ 0.5263]^T$.

REFERENCES

1. **Arora, J.S.,** *Introduction to Optimum Design*, McGraw-Hill, New York, 1989.
2. **Papalambros, P.Y. and Wilde, D.J.,** *Principles of Optimal Design*, Cambridge University Press, Cambridge, 1988.
3. **Siddall, J.N.,** *Optimal Engineering Design: Principles and Applications,* Marcel Dekker, New York, 1982.
4. **Rao, S.S.,** *Optimization: Theory and Applications,* 2nd ed., Wiley, New York, 1984.
5. **Vanderplatts, G.N.,** *Numerical Optimization Techniques for Engineering Design with Applications,* McGraw-Hill, New York, 1984.
6. **Fox, R.L.,** *Optimization Methods for Engineering Design*, Addison-Wesley, Reading, MA, 1972.
7. **Recklaitis, G.V., Ravindran, A. and Ragsdell, K.M.,** *Engineering Optimization: Methods and Applications*, Wiley, New York, 1983.
8. **Shoup, T.E. and Mistree, F.,** *Optimization Methods with Applications for Personal Computers*, Prentice-Hall, Englewood Cliffs, NJ, 1987.

PROBLEMS

P5.1: Minimize $f(x_1, x_2) = x_1 - 0.5x_2 + 2x_1^2 + 2x_1x_2 + x_2^2$ using Newton's method. Starting point: (0, 0).

P5.2: Use Newton's method to find the maximum of $f(x) = 5 \sin x - \frac{8}{19}x^2$ with the initial guess of $x_0 = 1, 8$.

P5.3: Fit a polynomial by quadratic approximation and find the value of x at which $F(x)$ is minimum.

x	$F(x)$
1	12
2	7
3	20

P5.4: Fit a polynomial by quadratic approximation and find the value of x at which $F(x)$ is minimum.

x	$F(x)$
1	20
2	–17
3	15

P5.5: Find the minimum of the following function using Powell's method:

$$F(x) = 4x_1^2 + 3x_2^2 - 5x_1x_2 - 8x_1$$

Starting from (0, 0).

P5.6: Find the minimum of the following function using Powell's method:

$$F(x) = 7x_1^2 + 5x_2^2 - 8x_1x_2 - 5x_1$$

Starting from (0, 0).

P5.7: Repeat Problem P5.5 using Fletcher-Reeves method.

P5.8: Repeat Problem P5.6 using Fletcher-Reeves method.

P5.9: Minimize $f(x_1, x_2) = x_1 - x_2 + 2x_1^2 + 2x_1x_2 + x_2^2$ starting from the point (0, 0) using Hook and Jeeves method.

P5.10: Repeat Problem P5.1 using Hooke and Jeeves method.

P5.11: Minimize $f(x_1, x_2) = (x_1 - 1)^2 + (x_2 - 1)^2$

subject to
$$g_1(x_1, x_2) = -x_1 \le 0$$
$$g_2(x_1, x_2) = -x_2 \le 0$$
$$g_3(x_1, x_2) = x_1^2 + x_2^2 - 1 \le 0$$

P5.12: Minimize $f(x_1, x_2) = (x_1 - 1)^2 + x_2^2$

subject to
$$g_2(x_1, x_2) = -x_2 \le 0$$
$$g_3(x_1, x_2) = x_2 - (1 - x_1)^2 \le 0$$

P5.13: Use the MATLAB *fminbnd* function to find the minimum of the function in Problem P5.9.

P5.14: Minimize $f(x_1, x_2) = 90(x_2 - x_1)^2 + (1 - x_1)^2$ using the starting point ($x_1 = -1.1, x_2 = 1.0$). Use MATLAB built-in function *fminsearch*.

P5.15:

(a) Minimize $(x_1 - x_2)^2 + (x_2 - x_3)^4$.
Initial guess: (–2.5, 2, 2)

(b) Minimize $x_1x_4(x_1 + x_2 + x_3) + x_3$
Initial guess: (1, 4, 5, 1).

P5.16:

Minimize $x_1 + 2x_2 + 3x_3 + \exp(x_1x_4)$
Initial guess: (1, 2, 1, 2).

P5.17:

Minimize $f(x) = x_1 + 54x_2 + 3x_3$

subject to
$$x_1 + 5x_2 - x_3 \ge 4$$
$$-x_1 + x_2 + 2x_3 \ge 1$$
$$-x_1 + 3x_2 + 3x_3 \ge 5$$
$$-3x_1 + 8x_2 - 5x_3 \ge 3$$

Initial guess: $x^0 = (0, 1, 1)$.

P5.18:

Minimize $f(x) = x_1 + 5x_2$

subject to $x_1 + x_2 \le 3$

$-x_1 + x_2 \le 1.5$

Initial guess: $x^0 = (-1, 1)$.

P5.19: Solve Problem P5.17 with $x_1, x_2, x_3 \ge 0$.

P5.20: Solve Problem P5.18 with $x_1, x_2 \ge 0$.

P5.21:

Minimize $f(x) = 100(x_2 - x_1^2)^2 + (1 - x_1)^2$

subject to $x_1 + 1 \ge 0$

$1 - x_2 \ge 0$

$5x_2 - x_1 - 1 \ge 0$

$2 - x_1 - 2x_2 \ge 0$

Initial guess: [–1, 1].

P5.22:

Minimize $f(x) = x_1^2 + x_2^2 + x_3^2$

subject to $1 - x_2x_3 \ge 0$

$x_1 - x_3 \ge 0$

$x_1 - x_2^2 + x_2x_3 - 5 = 0$

$0 \le x_1 \le 5$

$0 \le x_2 \le 3$

$0 \le x_3 \le 4$

Initial guess: [–1, 1].

P5.23:

Minimize $f(x) = 2x_1 - 3(x_2 - 4)^2$

subject to $x_1^2 + x_2^2 - 10 \le 0$

$x_1^2 + (x_2 - 4)^4 \le 0$

Initial guess: [–1, 1].

P5.24:

Minimize $f(x) = (x_1 - x_2)^2 + x_2$

subject to $1 - x_1 + x_2 \le 1$

$x_1 + 2x_2 \le 4$

$x_1 \ge 0$

$x_2 \ge 0$

Initial guess: [2, 0].

❍ ❍ ❍

CHAPTER 6

Direct Numerical Integration Methods

6.1 INTRODUCTION

The behaviour of many dynamic systems undergoing time-dependant changes (transients) can be described by ordinary differential equations. When the solution to the differential equation(s) of motion of a dynamic system cannot be obtained in closed form, a numerical procedure is warranted. Many numerical integration methods are available for the approximate solution of such equation(s) of motion. All the numerical integration methods have two basic characteristics. First, they do not satisfy the differential equation(s) at all time t, but only at discrete time intervals, say Δt apart. Secondly, within each time interval Δt, a specific type of variation of the displacement X, velocity $\dot{X}$, and acceleration $\ddot{X}$ is assumed. Thus, several numerical integration schemes are available depending on the type of variation assumed for X, $\dot{X}$ and $\ddot{X}$ within each time interval Δt.

In this chapter, we discuss several widely used step-by-step numerical integration schemes for solutions of both single and multi degree of freedom systems. A brief description of these methods is presented for linear dynamic response analysis and their application is illustrated by several examples.

6.2 SINGLE-DEGREE OF FREEDOM SYSTEM

The general equation of a viscously damped single degree of freedom dynamical system, which is linear, can be expressed in the following general form:

$$M\ddot{X} + C\dot{X} + KX = F(t) \qquad ...(6.1)$$

where M, C and K are the mass, damping and stiffness of the system; $F(t)$ is the applied force; and X, $\dot{X}$ and $\ddot{X}$ are the displacement, velocity and acceleration of the system.

6.2.1 Finite Difference Method

If the equilibrium relation (6.1) is regarded as an ordinary differential equation with constant coefficients, it follows that any convenient *finite difference* expressions to approximate the velocities and accelerations in terms of displacements can be used. The central idea in the *finite difference* method is to use approximations to derivatives. Hence, the general differential equation such as (6.1) and the associated boundary conditions, if any, are replaced by the corresponding finite difference equations. The continuous variable t is replaced by the discrete variable t_i and the differential equation is solved progressively in time increments $h = \Delta t$ starting from known initial conditions. The solution obtained is approximate but by suitably selecting the time increment the accuracy of the solution can be improved.

In this method, we replace the solution domain with a finite number of points, known as mesh or grid points, and obtain the solution at these points. The mesh or grid points are generally equally spaced along the independent coordinate as shown in Fig. 6.1. Central difference method is based on the Taylor's series expansion of X_{i+1} and X_{i-1} about the grid point i.

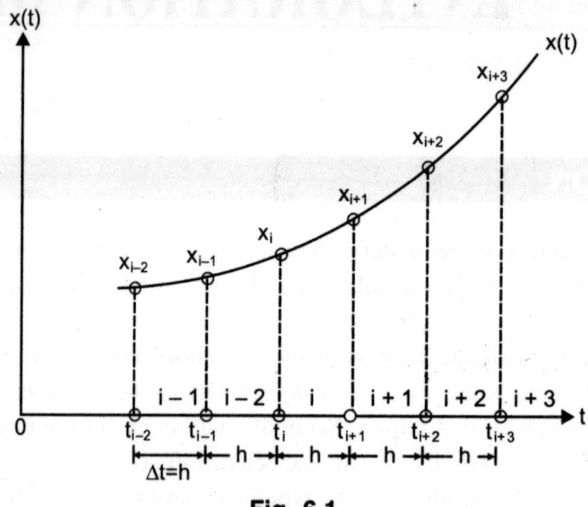

Fig. 6.1

$$X_{i+1} = X_i + h\dot{X}_i + \frac{h^2}{2}\ddot{X}_i + \frac{h^3}{6}\dddot{X}_i + \cdots \qquad \text{...(6.2)}$$

$$X_{i-1} = X_i - h\dot{X}_i + \frac{h^2}{2}\ddot{X}_i - \frac{h^3}{6}\dddot{X}_i + \cdots \qquad \text{... (6.3)}$$

where $X_i = X(t = t_i)$ and the interval $h = t_{i+1} - t_i = \Delta t$. By taking the first two terms only and subtracting Eq. (6.3) from (6.2), we obtain

$$\dot{X}_i = \frac{1}{2h}(X_{i+1} - X_{i-1}) \qquad \text{...(6.4)}$$

Adding Eqs. (6.3) and (6.2), we get

$$\ddot{X}_i = \frac{1}{h^2}(X_{i-1} - 2X_i + X_{i+1}) \qquad \text{...(6.5)}$$

Although there exist a number of finite difference schemes, here we consider only two methods selected for their simplicity. They are the Central Difference Method and the Runge-Kutta method.

6.2.2 Central Difference Method

Let the duration over which the numerical solution of Eq. (6.1) is required be divided into n equal parts of interval $h = \Delta t$ each. The initial conditions are assumed to be given by $X(t = 0) = X_0$ and $\dot{X}(t = 0) = \dot{X}_0$. The accuracy of the solution always depends on the size of the time step. The critical time step is given by $\Delta t_{cri} = \tau_n/\pi$, where τ_n is the natural period of the system. If Δt is selected to be larger than Δt_{cri}, the method becomes unstable, that is the truncation of higher order terms or rounding-off in the computer causes errors to grow and makes the dynamic response calculations meaningless. Numerical methods, which require the use of time, step Δt smaller than the critical time step Δt_{cri} are said to be conditionally stable. A safe rule to use is to choose $h \le \tau_n/10$. Substituting Eqs. (6.5) and (6.4) for $\ddot{X}_i$ and $\dot{X}_i$ respectively in Eq. (6.1) at mesh or grid point i give

$$M\left\{\frac{X_{i+1} - 2X_i + X_{i-1}}{(\Delta t)^2}\right\} + C\left\{\frac{X_{i+1} - X_{i-1}}{2\Delta t}\right\} + KX_i = F_i \qquad \text{...(6.6)}$$

where $X_i = X(t_i)$ and $F_i = F(t_i)$. Solving Eq. (6.6) for X_{i+1} gives

$$X_{i+1} = \left\{\frac{1}{\frac{M}{(\Delta t)^2} + \frac{C}{2\Delta t}}\right\}\left[\left\{\frac{2M}{(\Delta t)^2} - K\right\}\{X_i\} + \left\{\frac{C}{2\Delta t} - \frac{M}{(\Delta t)^2}\right\}X_{i-1} + F_i\right] \qquad \text{...(6.7)}$$

which is known as the recurrence formula.

Thus, the displacement of the mass, X_{i+1}, can be calculated using Eq. (6.7) if we know the previous displacements, X_i, X_{i+1} and the present external force F_i. Repeated application of Eq. (6.7) gives us the response time history of the behaviour of the system. Since the solution of X_{i+1} given in Eq.(6.7) is based on the previous displacement X_i given in Eq. (6.6), the integration procedure is known as an explicit integration method. Note that in order to compute X_1, both X_0 and X_{-1} are required but the initial conditions provide only the values of X_0 and $\dot{X}_0$. Therefore, the central difference method is not self-starting. However, the value of X_{-1} can be obtained from Eqs. (6.4) and (6.5) as follows. First calculate the value of $\ddot{X}_0$ by substituting the given values of X_0 and $\dot{X}_0$ in Eq. (6.1) as follows,

$$\ddot{X}_0 = \frac{1}{M}\left[F(t = 0) - C\dot{X}_0 - KX_0\right] \qquad \text{...(6.8)}$$

The value of X_{-1} is then obtained by the application of Eqs. (6.4) and (6.5) at $i = 0$.

$$X_{-1} = X_0 - \Delta t\,\dot{X}_0 + \frac{(\Delta t)^2}{2}\ddot{X}_0 \qquad \text{...(6.9)}$$

6.2.3 Runge-Kutta Method

In the Runge-Kutta method, an approximation to $X_{t+\Delta t}$ is obtained from X_t in such a way that the power series expansion of the approximation coincides, up to terms of a certain order $(\Delta t)^N$ in the time interval Δt, with the actual Taylor series expansion of $(t + \Delta t)$ in powers of Δt. The method is based on the assumption that the higher derivatives exist at points required.

The Runge-Kutta method is self-starting and has the advantage that no initial values are needed beyond the prescribed values. A brief discussion of its basis is represented here. In the Runge-Kutta method, the second-order differential equation is first reduced to two first-order equations. Consider the differential equation for the single degree of freedom system given in Eq. (6.1). Equation (6.1) can be rewritten as

$$\ddot{X} = \frac{1}{M}\left[F(t) - C\dot{X} - KX\right] = f\,(X, \dot{X}, t) \qquad ...(6.10)$$

By letting $X_1 = X$ and $X_2 = \dot{X}$, Eq. (6.10) can be reduced to the following two first-order equations;

$$\dot{X}_1 = X_2$$

$$\dot{X}_2 = f(X_1, X_2, t) \qquad ...(6.11)$$

By defining

$$\bar{X}(t) = \begin{Bmatrix} X_1(t) \\ X_2(t) \end{Bmatrix}$$

and $$\bar{F}(t) = \begin{Bmatrix} x_2 \\ f(x_1, x_2, t) \end{Bmatrix}$$

the following recurrence formula is obtained to find the values of $\bar{X}(t)$ at mesh or grids points t_i according to the fourth order Runge-Kutta method. We omit the details of the derivation of the method.

$$\bar{X}_{i+1} = \bar{X}_i + \frac{1}{6}\left[\bar{K}_1 + 2\bar{K}_2 + 2\bar{K}_3 + \bar{K}_4\right]$$

where $\bar{K}_1 = h\bar{F}(\bar{X}_i, t_i)$

$$\bar{K}_2 = h\bar{F}(\bar{X}_i + \frac{1}{2}\bar{K}_1, t_i + \frac{1}{2}h)$$

$$\bar{K}_3 = h\bar{F}(\bar{X}_i + \frac{1}{2}\bar{K}_2, t_i + \frac{1}{2}h) \qquad ...(6.12)$$

and $$\bar{K}_4 = h\bar{F}(\bar{X}_i + \frac{1}{2}\bar{K}_3, t_{i+1})$$

Although the Runge-Kutta method does not require the computation of derivatives beyond the first, its higher accuracy is obtained by four evaluations of the first derivatives to obtain agreement with the Taylor series solution through terms of order h^4. Since the fourth-order Runge-Kutta method is an explicit method, the maximum time step is usually governed by stability considerations. The change in time step can be easily implemented between iterations and hence the method can be considered as an inherently stable method. The main drawback of the method is that each forward step requires several computations of the functions thus increasing the computational cost. The Runge-Kutta method is applicable and extendable to a system of differential equations.

6.3 MULTI-DEGREE OF FREEDOM SYSTEM

The general form of the equations of motion for a multi-degree of freedom system are written as

$$[M]\{\ddot{X}\} + [C]\{\dot{X}\} + [K]\{X\} = \{F(t)\} \qquad ...(6.13)$$

where $[M]$, $[C]$ and $[K]$ are the mass, damping and stiffness matrices for the system and $\{\ddot{X}\}, \{\dot{X}\}$ and $\{X\}$ refer to the acceleration, velocity and displacement vectors, respectively. $\{F(t)\}$ is the force vector. Several numerical direct integrating schemes are available to determine the approximate solution of a system of equations of motion. For a linear dynamic system, matrices $[M]$, $[C]$ and $[K]$ are independent of time and therefore remain unchanged during the integration procedure. These matrices vary with time for a non-linear dynamic system and must be modified during the integration of equations of motion. For the solution of equations of motion for a linear dynamic system, either the normal mode superposition method of dynamic analysis or direct numerical integration methods can be used. However, for the solution of non-linear equations of motion, direct numerical integration methods are generally recommended.

In a direct integration method, the system of equations of motion is integrated successively by using a step by step numerical procedure. No transformation of the equations of motion is needed prior to integration and using difference formulas that involve one or more increments of time usually approximates time derivatives. Basically there are two principal approaches used in the direct integration method: explicit and implicit schemes. In an explicit scheme, the response quantities are expressed in terms of previously determined values of displacement, velocity and acceleration. In an implicit scheme, the difference equations are combined with the equations of motion, and the displacements are calculated directly by solving the equations.

In this section, only selected numerical integration schemes widely used for linear and non-linear dynamic analyses are considered. Three explicit and four implicit direct integration schemes are examined. A brief description of these schemes is presented and their application is illustrated. The explicit schemes presented are the central difference method, two-cycle iteration with trapezoidal rule and fourth-order Runge-Kutta. The implicit schemes include the Houbolt, Wilson-Theta, Newark-Beta and Park Stiffly stable methods. The accuracy, stability and efficiency of these schemes are examined by comparing the results for sample problems.

6.4 EXPLICIT SCHEMES

As mentioned earlier, in an explicit formulation, the response quantities are expressed in terms of previously determined values of displacement, velocity and acceleration.

6.4.1 Central Difference Method

The procedure indicated for the case of a single degree of freedom system can be directly extended to this case. Consider a displacement time history curve as shown in Fig. 6.2. At the middle of the time interval Δt, the velocity is given by

$$\dot{X}_{i+\frac{1}{2}} = \frac{X_{i+1} - X_i}{\Delta t} \quad ...(6.14)$$

and

$$\dot{X}_{i-\frac{1}{2}} = \frac{X_i - X_{i-1}}{\Delta t} \quad ...(6.15)$$

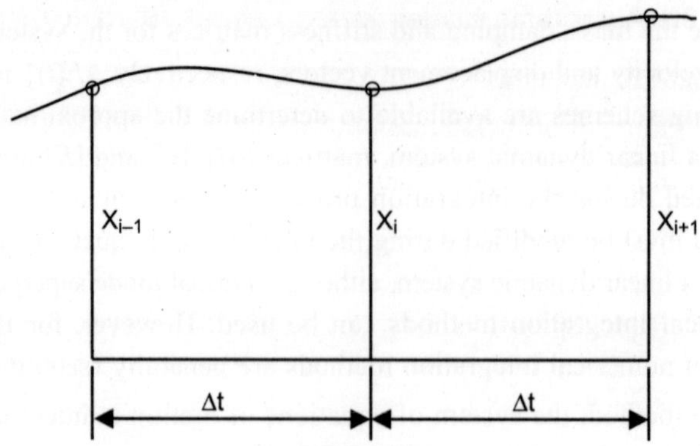

Fig. 6.2

The acceleration is

$$\ddot{X}_i = \frac{\dot{X}_{i+\frac{1}{2}} - \dot{X}_{i-\frac{1}{2}}}{\Delta t} \qquad \text{...(6.16)}$$

Substituting $\dot{X}_{i+\frac{1}{2}}$ and $\dot{X}_{i-\frac{1}{2}}$ from the Eqs. (6.14) and (6.15) into Eq. (6.16), we get

$$\ddot{X}_i = \frac{1}{\Delta t^2}(X_{i+1} - 2X_i + X_{i-1}) \qquad \text{...(6.17)}$$

The difference formulas in the central difference method for velocity and acceleration are written in terms of displacement as

$$\{\dot{X}_t\} = \frac{1}{2\Delta t}[\{X_{t+\Delta t}\} - \{X_{t-\Delta t}\}] \qquad \text{...(6.18)}$$

$$\{\ddot{X}_t\} = \frac{t}{\Delta t^2}[\{X_{t+\Delta t}\} - 2\{X_t\} + \{X_{t-\Delta t}\}] \qquad \text{...(6.19)}$$

Substituting $\{\dot{X}_t\}$ and $\{\ddot{X}_t\}$ from Eqs. (6.18) and (6.19), respectively into Eq. (6.13), we get

$$[\overline{M}]\ \{X_{t+\Delta t}\} = \{\overline{F_t}\} \qquad \text{...(6.20)}$$

where $[\overline{M}]$, the effective mass matrix, and $\{\overline{F_t}\}$, the effective force vector, is given by

$$[\overline{M}] = \frac{1}{\Delta t^2}[M]\ \frac{1}{2\Delta t}\ [C] \qquad \text{...(6.21)}$$

$$\{\overline{F_t}\} = \{F_t\} - ([K] - \frac{2}{\Delta t^2}[M])\ \{X_t\} - (\frac{1}{\Delta t^2}[M] - \frac{1}{2\Delta t}[C]\ )\ \{X_{t-\Delta t}\} \qquad \text{...(6.22)}$$

At time $t+\Delta t$, the displacements $\{X_{t+\Delta t}\}$ can be computed by solving Eq. (6.20), and the velocities and accelerations at time t are determined by substituting these values of $\{X_{t+\Delta t}\}$ into Eqs. (6.18) and (6.19). Note that the calculation of $\{X_{t+\Delta t}\}$ involves $\{X_t\}$ and $\{X_{t-\Delta t}\}$. Hence, in order to obtain the solution at time Δt, a special starting procedure is needed. Table 6.1 summarizes the time integration schedule as suitable for integration in the computer.

Table 6.1 Algorithms based on the central difference method

(*a*) Initial Computations:

1. Form stiffness [*K*], mass [*M*] and damping [*C*] matrices.
2. Initialize $\{X_0\}, \{\dot{X}_0\}$ and $\{\{\ddot{X}_0\}$.
3. Select time step Δt and calculate integration constants a_i:

$$a_0 = \frac{1}{\Delta t^2};\ a_1 = \frac{1}{2\Delta t};\ a_2 = 2a_0;\ a_3 = \frac{1}{a_2}.$$

4. Calculate $\{X_{-\Delta t}\} = \{X_0\} - \Delta t\{\dot{X}_0\} + a_3\{\ddot{X}_0\}$.
5. Form effective mass matrix $\left[\overline{M}\right] = a_0[M] + a_1[C]$.
6. Triangularize $\left[\overline{M}\right]$: $\left[\overline{M}\right] = [L]\ [D]\ [L]^T$.

(*b*) For each time step:

1. Calculate effective force vector at time *t*:

$$\left\{\overline{F}_t\right\} = \{F_t\} - ([K] - a_2[M])\ \{X_t\} - (a_0[M] - a_1[C]\ )\ \{X_{t-\Delta t}\}$$

2. Solve for displacements at time $t + \Delta t$:

$$\left[\overline{M}\right]\ \{X_{t+\Delta t}\} = \left[\overline{F}_t\right]$$

3. Calculate $\{\dot{X}\}$, and $\{\ddot{X}\}$ at time *t*:

$$\{\dot{X}_t\} = a_1(-\{X_{t-\Delta t}\} - \{X_{t+\Delta t}\}\ )$$
$$\{\ddot{X}_t\} = a_0(\ \{X_{t-\Delta t}\} - 2\{X_t\} + \{X_{t+\Delta t}\}\ )$$

The local truncation error of this method is of the order of Δt^2. An important consideration in the use of the central difference method is that the integration method requires that the time step Δt smaller than a critical value, Δt_{cr}, which is limited by the highest frequency of the discrete system ω_{max}, where

$$\Delta t \le \Delta t_{cr} \le \frac{2}{\omega_{max}} \qquad \text{...(6.23)}$$

If the time step is longer than Δt_{cr}, the integration is unstable, meaning that any errors resulting from the numerical integration of round off in the computer grow and make the dynamic response calculations questionable.

6.4.2 Two-Cycle Iteration with Trapezoidal Rule

The equations of motion at any time *t* are expressed in the incremental form as

$$[M]\{\Delta\ddot{X}_t\} = \{\Delta F_t\} - [K]\{\Delta X_t\} - [C]\{\Delta\dot{X}_t\} \qquad \text{...(6.24)}$$

The increments in the velocities and displacements are estimated by the use of the following relationships in the first iteration cycle:

For the first time step:

$$\{\Delta\dot{X}_t\} = \Delta t\{\ddot{X}_{t-\Delta t}\} \qquad \text{...(6.25)}$$

For other time steps:

$$\{\Delta\dot{X}_t\} = 2\Delta t\{\ddot{X}_{t-\Delta t}\} - \{\Delta\dot{X}_{t-\Delta t}\} \qquad \text{...(6.26)}$$

$$\{\dot{X}_t\} = \{\dot{X}_{t-\Delta t}\} + \{\Delta\dot{X}_t\} \qquad \text{...(6.27)}$$

$$\{\Delta X_t\} = \frac{1}{2}\Delta t\left[\{\dot{X}_{t-\Delta t}\} + \{\dot{X}_t\}\right] \qquad \text{...(6.28)}$$

By substituting the relations $\{\Delta\dot{X}_t\}$ and $\{\Delta X_t\}$ from Eqs. (6.26) and (6.28) into Eq. (6.24), we obtain the increments in the accelerations as

$$\{\Delta\ddot{X}_t\} = [M]^{-1}(\{\Delta F_t\} - [K]\{\Delta X_t\} - [C]\{\Delta\dot{X}_t\}) \qquad \text{...(6.29)}$$

These are then employed to obtain the estimate of the acceleration at time *t* as

$$\{\ddot{X}_t\} = \{\ddot{X}_{t-\Delta t}\} + \{\Delta\ddot{X}_t\} \qquad \text{...(6.30)}$$

In the second iteration cycle, the increments in the velocities and the accelerations are refined as

$$\{\Delta\dot{X}_t\} = \frac{1}{2}\Delta t(\{\ddot{X}_{t-\Delta t}\} + \{\ddot{X}_t\}) \qquad \text{...(6.31)}$$

$$\{\dot{X}_t\} = \{\dot{X}_{t-\Delta t}\} + \{\Delta\dot{X}_t\} \qquad \text{...(6.32)}$$

$$\{\Delta X_t\} = \frac{1}{2}\Delta t(\{\dot{X}_{t-\Delta t}\} + \{\dot{X}_t\}) \qquad \text{...(6.33)}$$

Finally, the relations for $\{\Delta\dot{X}_t\}$ and $\{\Delta X_t\}$ in Eqs. (6.31) and (6.33) are substituted into Eq. (6.29) to compute the new increments in the accelerations. These are then used in Eq. (6.30) to calculate the accelerations at time *t*. The computational algorithm based on this method is summarized in Table 6.2.

Table 6.2 Algorithm based on two-cycle iteration with trapezoidal rule

1. Form stiffness $[K]$, mass $[M]$ and damping $[C]$ matrices
2. Initialize $\{X_0\}, \{\dot{X}_0\}$ and $\{\ddot{X}_0\}$
3. Select time step Δt and calculate for the first time step in the first iteration cycle: $\{\Delta\dot{X}_t\} = \Delta t\{\ddot{X}_{t-\Delta t}\}$
4. For other time steps:

$$\{\Delta\dot{X}_t\} = 2\Delta t\{\ddot{X}_{t-\Delta t}\} - \{\Delta\dot{X}_{t-\Delta t}\}$$

$$\{\dot{X}_t\} = \{\dot{X}_{t-\Delta t}\} + \{\Delta\dot{X}_t\}$$

$$\{\Delta X_t\} = \frac{\Delta t}{2}(\{\dot{X}_{t-\Delta t}\} - \{\dot{X}_t\})$$

Contd...

5. Compute $\{\Delta\ddot{X}_t\}$ and $\{\ddot{X}_t\}$ at time t:

$$\{\Delta\ddot{X}_t\}=[M]^{-1}(\{\Delta F_t\}-[K]\{\Delta X_t\}-[C]\{\Delta\dot{X}_t\})$$
$$\{\ddot{X}_t\}=\{\ddot{X}_{t-\Delta t}\}+\{\Delta\ddot{X}_t\}$$

6. Second iteration cycle:

$$\{\Delta\dot{X}_t\}=\frac{\Delta t}{2}(\{\ddot{X}_{t-\Delta t}\}+\{\ddot{X}_t\})$$
$$\{\dot{X}_t\}=\{\dot{X}_{t-\Delta t}\}+\{\Delta\dot{X}_t\}$$
$$\{\Delta X_t\}=\frac{\Delta t}{2}(\{\dot{X}_{t-\Delta t}\}+\{\dot{X}_t\})$$

7. Compute $\{\Delta\ddot{X}_t\}$ in step 5 using $\{\Delta\dot{X}_t\}$, $\{\dot{X}_t\}$ and $\{\Delta X_t\}$ from step 6.
8. Finally, compute $\{\ddot{X}_t\}$ from step 5, using $\{\ddot{X}_t\}$ and $\{\Delta\ddot{X}_t\}$ from step 7.

6.4.3 Fourth-Order Runge-Kutta Method

In the fourth-order Runge-Kutta method, the system of second-order differential Eq. (6.13) is converted into state variable form. That is, both the displacements and velocities are treated as unknowns $\{y\}$ defined by

$$\{y\}=\begin{Bmatrix}\{X\}\\ \hline \{\dot{X}\}\end{Bmatrix} \qquad \text{...(6.34)}$$

Using Eq. (6.34), Eq.(6.13) can be rewritten as

$$\{\ddot{X}\}=-[M]^{-1}[K]\{X\}-[M]^{-1}[C]\{\dot{X}\}+[m]^{-1}\{F(t)\} \qquad \text{...(6.35)}$$

Using the identity

$$\{\dot{y}\}=\{\dot{y}\} \qquad \text{...(6.36)}$$

we obtain from Eqs. (6.35) and (6.36)

$$\{\dot{y}\}=\begin{Bmatrix}\{\dot{X}\}\\ \hline \{\ddot{X}\}\end{Bmatrix}=\left[\begin{array}{c|c}[0] & [I]\\ \hline -[M]^{-1}[K] & -[M]^{-1}[C]\end{array}\right]\begin{Bmatrix}\{X\}\\ \hline \{\dot{X}\}\end{Bmatrix}+\begin{Bmatrix}0\\ \hline [M]^{-1}\{F(t)\}\end{Bmatrix} \qquad \text{...(6.37)}$$

or
$$\{\dot{y}\}=[E]\{y\}+\{F^*(t)\} \qquad \text{...(6.38)}$$

That is
$$\{\dot{y}\}=\{f(t,y)\} \qquad \text{...(6.39)}$$

In the Runge-Kutta method, an approximation to $\{y_{t+\Delta t}\}$ is obtained from $\{y_t\}$ in such a way that the power series expansion of the approximation coincides, up to the terms of a certain order $(\Delta t)^N$ in the time interval Δt, with the actual Taylor series expansion of $(t+\Delta t)$ in powers of Δt. This method has the advantage that no initial values are required beyond the prescribed ones. The general fourth-order algorithms are based on formulas of the form

$$\{y_{t+\Delta t}\} = \{y_t\} + \Delta t(aK_1 + bK_2 + cK_3 + dK_4) \quad ...(6.40)$$

where a, b, c and d are constants and K_1, K_2, K_3 and K_4 are the approximate derivative values computed in the interval $t_K < t < t_{K+\Delta t}$. Several fourth order algorithms have been proposed. The following is due to Runge-Kutta and we omit presenting the details of its derivation.

$$\{y_{t+\Delta t}\} = \{y_t\} + \frac{\Delta t}{6}[K_1 + 2K_2 + 2K_3 + K_4] \quad ...(6.41)$$

in which

$$K_1 = f(t, y_t)$$

$$K_2 = f\left(t + \frac{\Delta t}{2}, y_t + K_1\frac{\Delta t}{2}\right)$$

$$K_3 = f\left(t + \frac{\Delta t}{2}, y_t + K_2\frac{\Delta t}{2}\right) \quad ...(6.42)$$

$$K_4 = f(t + \Delta t, y_t + K_3\Delta t)$$

The Runge-Kutta algorithm does not require the calculation of higher derivatives. This method is completely self-starting and the step size can be changed easily between iterations and hence the method can be considered inherently stable. The truncation error e_t for the fourth-order Runge-Kutta scheme is of the form

$$e_t = c(\Delta t)^5 \quad ...(6.43)$$

where c is constant, which depends on $f(t, y)$ and its higher-order partial derivatives. Runge-Kutta method generates an artificial damping that unduly suppresses the amplitude of the response of a dynamic system to some extent.

6.5 IMPLICIT SCHEMES

In an implicit scheme, the difference equations are combined with the equations of motion, and the displacements are calculated directly by solving the equations.

6.5.1 Houbolt Method

The Houbolt method is based on third-order interpolation of displacements X_t, and the multi-step implicit formulas for $\dot{X}_t$ are $\ddot{X}_t$ obtained in terms of X_t by using backward differences.

The difference formulas are summarized in the following with reference to Fig. 6.3. By considering a cubic curve that passes through the four successive ordinates, the following equations can be obtained:

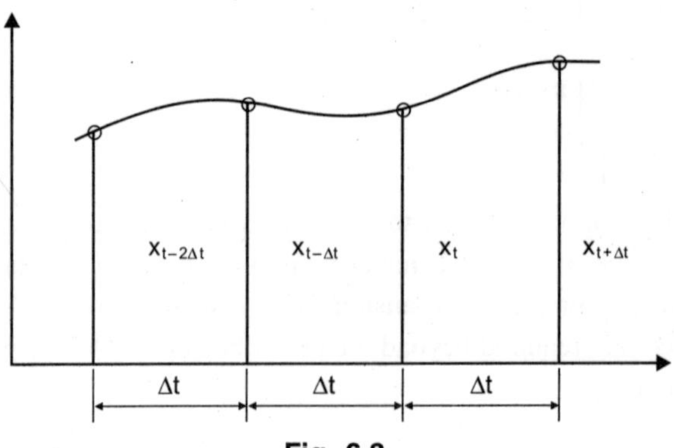

Fig. 6.3

$$X_t = X_{t+\Delta t} - \Delta t \dot{X}_{t+\Delta t} + \frac{\Delta t^2}{2}\ddot{X}_{t+\Delta t} - \frac{\Delta t^3}{6}\dddot{X}_{t+\Delta t} \qquad ...(6.44)$$

$$X_{t-\Delta t} = X_{t+\Delta t} - (2\Delta t)\dot{X}_{t+\Delta t} + \frac{(2\Delta t)^2}{2}\ddot{X}_{t+\Delta t} - \frac{(2\Delta t)^3}{6}\dddot{X}_{t+\Delta t} \qquad ...(6.45)$$

$$X_{t-2\Delta t} = X_{t+\Delta t} - (3\Delta t)\dot{X}_{t+\Delta t} + \frac{(3\Delta t)^2}{2}\ddot{X}_{t+\Delta t} - \frac{(3\Delta t)^3}{6}\dddot{X}_{t+\Delta t} \qquad ...(6.46)$$

Solving Eqs. (6.44) to (6.46) for $\ddot{X}_{t+\Delta t}$ and $\dot{X}_{t+\Delta t}$, we get

$$\ddot{X}_{t+\Delta t} = \frac{1}{\Delta t^2}(2X_{t+\Delta t} - 5X_t + 4X_{t-\Delta t} - X_{t-2\Delta t}) \qquad ...(6.47)$$

$$\dot{X}_{t+\Delta t} = \frac{1}{6\Delta t}(11X_{t+\Delta t} - 18X_t + 9X_{t-\Delta t} - 2X_{t-2\Delta t}) \qquad ...(6.48)$$

The difference formulas in the Houbolt algorithm are, therefore, given by

$$\{\ddot{X}_{t+\Delta t}\} = \frac{1}{\Delta t^2}\left[2\{X_{t+\Delta t}\} - 5\{X_t\} + 4\{X_{t-\Delta t}\} - \{X_{t-2\Delta t}\}\right] \qquad ...(6.49)$$

$$\{\dot{X}_{t+\Delta t}\} = \frac{1}{6\Delta t}\left[11\{X_{t+\Delta t}\} - 18\{X_t\} + 9\{X_{t-\Delta t}\} - 2\{X_{t-2\Delta t}\}\right] \qquad ...(6.50)$$

By substituting the expressions for $\{\ddot{X}_{t+\Delta t}\}$ and $\{\dot{X}_{t+\Delta t}\}$ from (6.49) and (6.50), respectively, into (6.13), we get

$$\left[\overline{M}\right]\{X_{t+\Delta t}\} = \left\{\overline{F_{t+\Delta t}}\right\} \qquad ...(6.51)$$

where $\left[\overline{M}\right]$ is the effective mass matrix and $\left\{\overline{F_{t+\Delta t}}\right\}$ is the effective force vector.

$$\left[\overline{M}\right] = \frac{2}{\Delta t^2}[M] + \frac{11}{6\Delta t}[C] + [K] \qquad ...(6.52)$$

$$\begin{aligned}\left\{\overline{F_{t+\Delta t}}\right\} = \{F_{t+\Delta t}\} &+ \left(\frac{5}{\Delta t^2}[M] + \frac{3}{\Delta t}[C]\right)\{X_t\} \\ &- \left(\frac{4}{\Delta t^2}[M] + \frac{3}{2\Delta t}[C]\right)\{X_{t-\Delta t}\} + \left(\frac{1}{\Delta t^2}[M] + \frac{1}{3\Delta t}[C]\right)\{X_{t-2\Delta t}\}\end{aligned} \qquad ...(6.53)$$

Note that the equilibrium equation at time $t+\Delta t$, Eq. (6.51) is used in finding the solution for $\{X_{t+\Delta t}\}$. For this reason, this method is called an implicit integration method. It can be seen that the velocities and accelerations at time $t+\Delta t$ are obtained by substituting for $\{X_{t+\Delta t}\}$ in (6.50) and (6.49) respectively. Also that a knowledge of X_t, $X_{t-\Delta t}$ and $X_{t-2\Delta t}$ is needed to find solution for $\{X_{t+\Delta t}\}$. Since there is no direct method available to find $\{X_{t-\Delta t}\}$ and $\{X_{t-2\Delta t}\}$, initially we use the central difference method to find solution at time Δt and $2\Delta t$. This makes the method non-self starting. The method also requires large computer storage to store displacements for the previous time steps. The step by step procedure to be used in the Houbolt method is summarized in Table 6.3. A basic difference between the Houbolt method in Table 6.3 and the central difference method in Table 6.2 is the appearance of the stiffness matrix K as a factor to the required displacements $X_{t+\Delta t}$. The term $KX_{t+\Delta t}$ appears because the equilibrium is considered at time $t+\Delta t$ and not at time t as in the central difference method. There is no critical time-step limit, and Δt can in general be selected much larger than that given for the central difference method.

Table 6.3 Algorithm based on Houbolt method

(*a*)	Initial Computations: 1. Form stiffness [*K*], mass [*M*] and damping [*C*] matrices 2. Initialize $\{X_0\},\{\dot{X}_0\}$ and $\{\ddot{X}_0\}$. 3. Select time step Δt and calculate integration constants: $a_0=\frac{2}{\Delta t^2};\ a_1=\frac{11}{6\Delta t};\ a_2=\frac{5}{\Delta t^2};\ a_3=\frac{3}{\Delta t};\ a_4=-2a_0;\ a_5=\frac{-a_3}{2};$ $a_6=\frac{a_0}{2};\ a_7=\frac{a_3}{9}.$ 4. Use special starting procedure, such as central-difference method to calculate. $\{X_{\Delta t}\}$ and $\{X_{2\Delta t}\}$. 5. Calculate effective stiffness matrix: $[\overline{K}]=[K]+a_0[M]+a_1[C]$ 6. Triangularize $[\overline{K}]:[\overline{K}]=[L]\ [D]\ [L]^T$
(*b*)	For each time step: 1. Calculate effective force vector at time $t+\Delta t$: $\{\overline{F}_{t+\Delta t}\}=\{F_{t+\Delta t}\}+[M]\ (a_2\{X_t\}+a_4\{X_{t-\Delta t}\}+a_6\{X_{t-2\Delta t}\})$ $+[C]\ (a_3\{X_t\}+a_5\{X_{t-\Delta t}\}+a_7\{X_{t-2\Delta t}\})$ 2. Solve for displacements at time $t+\Delta t$ $[\overline{K}]\ \{X_{t+\Delta t}\}=\{\overline{F_{t+\Delta t}}\}$ 3. Calculate $\{\dot{X}\}$ and $\{\ddot{X}\}$ at time $t+\Delta t$: $\{\dot{X}_{t+\Delta t}\}=a_1\{X_{t+\Delta t}\}-a_3\{X_t\}-a_5\{X_{t-\Delta t}\}-a_7\{X_{t-2\Delta t}\}$ $\{\ddot{X}_{t+\Delta t}\}=a_0\{X_{t+\Delta t}\}-a_2\{X_t\}-a_4\{X_{t-\Delta t}\}-a_6\{X_{t-2\Delta t}\}$

6.5.2 Wilson Theta Method

The Wilson Theta Method assumes that the acceleration of the system varies linearly between two instants of time. Referring to Fig. 6.4, the acceleration is assumed to be linear from time *t* between , $t_i = i\Delta t$ to time $t_{i+\theta} = t_i + \theta\Delta t$, where $\theta \geq 1.0$. Because of this reason, the method is known as the Wilson Theta method. If τ is the increase in time *t* between *t* and $t+\theta\Delta t$ ($0 \leq \tau \leq \theta\Delta t$), then for time interval *t* to $t+\theta\Delta t$, it can be assumed that

$$\ddot{X}_{t+\tau} = \ddot{X}_t + \frac{\tau}{\theta\Delta t}(\ddot{X}_{t+\theta\Delta t} - \ddot{X}_t) \qquad ...(6.54)$$

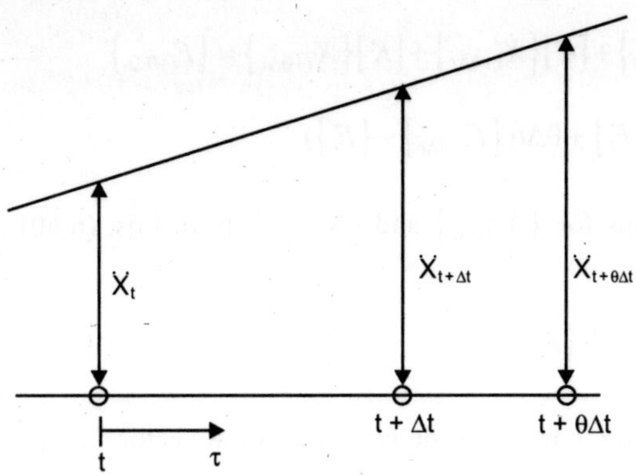

Fig. 6.4

Successive integration for Eq. (6.54) gives the following expressions for $\dot{X}_{t+\tau}$ and $X_{t+\tau}$:

$$\dot{X}_{t+\tau} = \dot{X}_t + \ddot{X}_t\tau + \frac{\tau^2}{2\theta\Delta t}(\ddot{X}_{t+\theta\Delta t} - \ddot{X}_t) \qquad ...(6.55)$$

$$X_{t+\tau} = X_t + \dot{X}_t\tau + \frac{1}{2}\ddot{X}_t\tau^2 + \frac{\tau^3}{6\theta\Delta t}(\ddot{X}_{t+\theta\Delta t} - \ddot{X}_t) \qquad ...(6.56)$$

Substituting $\tau = \theta\Delta t$ into thc above Eqs. (6.55) and (6.56), we obtain the following expressions for $\dot{X}$ and X at time $t+\theta\Delta t$:

$$\dot{X}_{t+\theta\Delta t} = \dot{X}_t + \frac{\theta\Delta t}{2}(\ddot{X}_t + \ddot{X}_{t+\theta\Delta t}) \qquad ...(6.57)$$

$$X_{t+\theta\Delta t} = X_t + \theta\Delta t\,\dot{X}_t + \frac{\theta^2\Delta t^2}{6}(\ddot{X}_{t+\theta\Delta t} + 2\ddot{X}_t) \qquad ...(6.58)$$

Solving Eqs. (6.57) and (6.58) for $\ddot{X}_{t+\theta\Delta t}$ and $\dot{X}_{t+\theta\Delta t}$ in terms of $\ddot{X}_{t+\theta\Delta t}$, we get

$$\ddot{X}_{t+\theta\Delta t} = \frac{6}{\theta^2\Delta t^2}(X_{t+\theta\Delta t} - X_t) - \frac{6}{\theta\Delta t}(\dot{X}_t) - 2\ddot{X}_t$$

$$\dot{X}_{t+\theta\Delta t} = \frac{3}{\theta\Delta t}(X_{t+\theta\Delta t} - X_t) - 2\dot{X}_t - \frac{\theta\Delta t}{2}\ddot{X}_t \qquad ...(6.59)$$

The difference formulas in the Wilson Theta algorithm are then given by

$$\{\ddot{X}_{t+\theta\Delta t}\} = \frac{6}{\theta^2\Delta t^2}(\{X_{t+\theta\Delta t}\} - \{X_t\}) - \frac{6}{\theta\Delta t}\{\dot{X}_t\} - 2\{\ddot{X}_t\} \qquad ...(6.60)$$

$$\{\ddot{X}_{t+\theta\Delta t}\} = \frac{3}{\theta\Delta t}(\{X_{t+\theta\Delta t}\} - \{X_t\}) - 2\{\dot{X}_t\} - \frac{\theta\Delta t}{2}\{\ddot{X}_t\} \qquad ...(6.61)$$

We employ Eq. (6.13) at time $t+\Delta t$ to obtain a solution for displacement, velocity and acceleration at time $t+\Delta t$. Since accelerations vary linearly, a linear projected force vector is used such that

$$[M]\{\ddot{X}_{t+\theta\Delta t}\}+[C]\{\dot{X}_{t+\theta\Delta t}\}+[K]\{X_{t+\theta\Delta t}\}=\{F_{t+\theta\Delta t}\} \quad ...(6.62)$$

where $\{F_{t+\theta\Delta t}\}=\{F_t\}+\theta\Delta t(\{F_{t+\theta\Delta t}\}-\{F_t\})$.

By substituting the expressions for $\{\ddot{X}_{t+\theta\Delta t}\}$ and $\{\dot{X}_{t+\theta\Delta t}\}$ from Eqs. (6.60) and (6.61), respectively, into Eq.(6.62), we get

$$[\overline{M}]\{X_{t+\theta\Delta t}\}=\{\overline{F}_{t+\Delta t}\} \quad ...(6.63)$$

where the effective mass matrix $[\overline{M}]$ and the effective force vector $\{\overline{F}_{t+\Delta t}\}$ are given by

$$[\overline{M}]=\frac{6}{\theta^2\Delta t^2}[M]+\frac{3}{\theta\Delta t}[C]+[K] \quad (6.64)$$

$$\begin{aligned}\{\overline{F}_{t+\theta\Delta t}\}&=\{F_{t+\theta\Delta t}\}+(\frac{6}{\theta^2\Delta t^2}[M]+\frac{3}{\theta\Delta t}[C])\{X_t\}\\&+(\frac{6}{\theta\Delta t}[M]+2[C])\{\dot{X}_t\}+(2[M]+\frac{\theta\Delta t}{2}[C])\ \{\ddot{X}_t\}\end{aligned} \quad (6.65)$$

The solution of Eq. (6.63) gives $\{X_{t+\theta\Delta t}\}$ which is then substituted into the following relationships to obtain the displacements, velocities and accelerations at time $t+\Delta t$.

$$\{\ddot{X}_{t+\Delta t}\}=\frac{6}{\theta^2\Delta t^2}(\{X_{t+\theta\Delta t}\}-\{X_t\})-\frac{6}{\theta^2\Delta t}\{\dot{X}_t\}+\left(1-\frac{3}{\theta}\right)\{\ddot{X}_t\} \quad ...(6.66)$$

$$\{\dot{X}_{t+\Delta t}\}=\{\dot{X}_t\}+\frac{\Delta t}{2}(\{\ddot{X}_{t+\Delta t}\}-\{\ddot{X}_t\}) \quad ...(6.67)$$

$$\{X_{t+\Delta t}\}=\{X_t\}+\Delta t\{\dot{X}_t\}+\frac{\Delta t^2}{6}(\{\ddot{X}_{t+\Delta t}\}-2\{\ddot{X}_t\}) \quad ...(6.68)$$

When $\theta = 1.0$, the method reduces to the linear acceleration scheme. The method is unconditionally stable for linear dynamic systems when $\theta \geq 1.37$, and a value of $\theta = 1.4$ is often used for non-linear dynamic systems. It may also be noted that no special starting procedures are needed, since $X, \dot{X}$ and $\ddot{X}$ are expressed at time $t+\Delta t$ in terms of the same quantities at time t only. The complete algorithm used in the Wilson Theta method is given in Table 6.4.

Table 6.4 Algorithm based on Wilson Theta method

(*a*) Initial Computations:

1. Form stiffness [*K*], mass [*M*] and damping [*C*] matrices
2. Initialize $\{X_0\},\{\dot{X}_0\}$ and $\{\ddot{X}_0\}$.
3. Select time step Δt and calculate integration constants, $\theta = 1.4$(say):

$$a_0 = \frac{6}{(\theta\Delta t)^2};\; a_1 = \frac{3}{\theta\Delta t};\; a_2 = 2a_1;\; a_3 = \frac{\theta\Delta t}{2};\; a_4 = \frac{a_0}{\theta};\; a_5 = \frac{-a_2}{\theta};$$

$$a_6 = 1 - \frac{3}{\theta};\; a_7 = \frac{\Delta t}{2};\; a_8 = \frac{\Delta t^2}{6}.$$

4. Form effective stiffness matrix:

$$\left[\overline{K}\right] = [K] + a_0[M] + a_1[C]$$

5. Triangularize $\left[\overline{K}\right] : \left[\overline{K}\right] = [L][D][L]^{\mathrm{T}}$

(*b*) For each time step:

1. Calculate effective force vector at time $t + \Delta t$:

$$\left\{\overline{F_{t+\theta\Delta t}}\right\} = \{F_t\} + \theta\,(\{F_{t+\Delta t}\} - \{F_t\}) + [M]\,(a_0\{X_t\} + a_2\{\dot{X}_t\} + 2\{\ddot{X}_t\})$$
$$+ [C]\,(a_1\{X_1\} + 2\{\dot{X}_t\} + a_3\{\ddot{X}_t\})$$

2. Solve for displacements at time $t + \theta\Delta t$:

$$\left[\overline{K}\right]\{X_{t+\theta\Delta t}\} = \left\{\overline{F_{t+\theta\Delta t}}\right\}$$

3. Calculate $\{X\},\{\dot{X}\}$ and $\{\ddot{X}\}$ at time $t + \Delta t$:

$$\{\ddot{X}_{t+\Delta t}\} = a_4(\{X_{t+\theta\Delta t}\} - \{X_t\}) + a_5\{\dot{X}_t\} + a_6\{\ddot{X}_t\}$$
$$\{\dot{X}_{t+\Delta t}\} = \{\dot{X}_t\} + a_7(\{\ddot{X}_{t+\Delta t}\} + \{\ddot{X}_t\})$$
$$\{X_{t+\Delta t}\} = \{X_t\} + \Delta t\{\dot{X}_t\} + a_8(\{\ddot{X}_{t+\Delta t}\} + 2\{\ddot{X}_t\})$$

6.5.3 Newmark Beta Method

The Newmark Beta integration method is also based on the assumption that the acceleration varies linearly between two instants of time. Two parameters α and β are used in this method, which can be changed to suit the requirements of a particular problem. The expressions for velocity and displacements are given by

$$\dot{X}_{t+\Delta t} = \dot{X}_t + \left[(1-\alpha)\ddot{X}_t + \alpha\ddot{X}_{t+\Delta t}\right]\Delta t \quad ...(6.69)$$

$$X_{t+\Delta t} = X_t + \dot{X}_t\Delta t + \left[\left(\frac{1}{2} - \beta\right)\ddot{X}_t + \beta\ddot{X}_{t+\Delta t}\right]\Delta t^2 \quad ...(6.70)$$

The parameters α and β indicate how much the acceleration enters into the velocity and displacement equations at the end of the interval Δt. Therefore, α and β are chosen to obtain the desired integration accuracy and stability. When α =1/6 and β =1/2, Eqs. (6.69) and (6.70) correspond to the linear acceleration method (which can also be obtained using θ =1 in Wilson method). When α =1/2 and β = 0, the acceleration is constant and equal to $\ddot{X}_t$ during each time interval Δt. If α = 1/2 and β = 1/8, the acceleration is constant from the beginning as $\ddot{X}_t$ and then changes to $\ddot{X}_{t+\Delta t}$ in the middle of the time interval Δt. When α = 1/2 and β = 1/4, this corresponds to the assumption that the acceleration remains constant at an average value of $(\ddot{X}_t + \ddot{X}_{t+\Delta t})/2$. The finite difference formulas for the Newmark Beta scheme are

$$\{\ddot{X}_{t+\Delta t}\} = \frac{1}{\beta \Delta t^2}(\{X_{t+\Delta t}\} - \{X_t\}) - \frac{1}{\beta \Delta t}\{\dot{X}_t\} - \left(\frac{1}{2\beta} - 1\right)\{\ddot{X}_t\} \quad \text{...(6.71)}$$

$$\{\dot{X}_{t+\Delta t}\} = \frac{\alpha}{\beta \Delta t}(\{X_{t+\Delta t}\} - \{X_t\}) - \left(\frac{\alpha}{\beta} - 1\right)\{\dot{X}_t\} - \Delta t\left(\frac{\alpha}{2\beta} - 1\right)\{\ddot{X}_t\} \quad \text{...(6.72)}$$

Equation (6.13) can be employed to obtain a solution for displacements, velocity and accelerations at time $t + \Delta t$. Therefore, by substituting the expressions for $\{\ddot{X}_{t+\Delta t}\}$ and $\{\dot{X}_{t+\Delta t}\}$ from Eqs. (6.71) and (6.72), respectively, into Eq. (6.13), we get

$$[\overline{M}]\{X_{t+\Delta t}\} = \{\overline{F_{t+\Delta t}}\} \quad \text{...(6.73)}$$

where the effective mass matrix $[\overline{M}]$ and the effective force vector $\{\overline{F_{t+\Delta t}}\}$ are given by

$$[\overline{M}] = \frac{1}{\beta \Delta t^2}[M] + \frac{\alpha}{\beta \Delta t}[C] + [K] \quad \text{...(6.74)}$$

$$\begin{aligned}\{\overline{F}_{t+\Delta t}\} = \{F_{t+\Delta t}\} &+ \left[\left(\frac{1}{2\beta} - 1\right)[M] + \Delta t\left(\frac{\alpha}{2\beta} - 1\right)[C]\right]\{\ddot{X}_t\} \\ &+ \left[\frac{1}{\beta \Delta t}[M] + \left(\frac{\alpha}{\beta} - 1\right)[C]\right]\{\dot{X}_t\} \\ &+ \left[\frac{1}{\beta \Delta t^2}[M] + \frac{\alpha}{\beta \Delta t}[C]\right]\{X_t\}\end{aligned} \quad \text{...(6.75)}$$

Solution of Eq. (6.73) gives $\{X_{t+\Delta t}\}$, which is then substituted into Eqs. (6.71) and (6.72) in order to obtain the accelerations and velocities at time $t + \Delta t$. One of the features of Newmark Beta method is that for linear systems the amplitude is conserved and the response is unconditionally stable, provided that $\alpha \geq \frac{1}{2}$ and $\beta \geq \frac{1}{4}\left(\alpha + \frac{1}{2}\right)^2$. For values of $\alpha = \frac{1}{2}$ and $\beta = \frac{1}{4}$, the largest truncation errors occur in the frequency of the response as opposed to other β values. It is also important to note that unless $\beta = \frac{1}{2}$, there is a spurious damping introduced, proportional to $\beta - \frac{1}{2}$. If β = 0, a negative damping results; this involves a self-excited vibration arising solely from the numerical procedure. In a likewise manner, if β is greater than $\frac{1}{2}$, a positive damping is introduced which reduces the magnitude of the response even without real damping in the problem. For a multi-degree of freedom system in which a number of modes constitute the total response, the peak amplitude may not be correct. The complete algorithm using the Newmark Beta integration method is given in Table 6.5.

Table 6.5 Algorithm based on Newmark Beta method

(*a*) Initial Computations:

1. Form stiffness [*K*], mass [*M*] and damping [*C*] matrices
2. Initialize $\{X_0\}, \{\dot{X}_0\}$ and $\{\ddot{X}_0\}$.
3. Select time step Δt, parameters α and β, and calculate integration constants,

$$\beta \geq 0.5;\ \alpha \geq 0.25\,(0.5+\beta)^2$$

$$a_0 = \frac{1}{\beta(\Delta t)^2};\ a_1 = \frac{\alpha}{\beta\Delta t};\ a_2 = \frac{1}{\beta\Delta t};\ a_3 = \frac{1}{2\beta} - 1;\ a_4 = \frac{\alpha}{\beta} - 1;$$

$$a_5 = \frac{\Delta t}{2}\left(\frac{\alpha}{\beta} - 2\right);\ a_6 = \Delta t(1-\beta);\ a_7 = \beta\Delta t$$

4. Form effective stiffness matrix:

$$\left[\overline{K}\right] = [K] + a_0[M] + a_1[C]$$

5. Triangularize $\left[\overline{K}\right] : \left[\overline{K}\right] = [L]\ [D]\ [L]^T$

(*b*) For each time step:

1. Calculate effective force vector at time $t + \Delta t$:

$$\left\{\overline{F}_{t+\Delta t}\right\} = \{F_{t+\Delta t}\} + [M]\ (a_0\{X_t\} + a_2\{\dot{X}_t\} + a_3\{\ddot{X}_t\})$$
$$+ [C]\ (a_1\{X_t\} + a_4\{\dot{X}_t\} + a_5\{\ddot{X}_t\})$$

2. Solve for displacements at time $t + \Delta t$

$$\left[\overline{K}\right]\ \{X_{t+\Delta t}\} = \left\{\overline{F}_{t+\Delta t}\right\}$$

3. Calculate $\{\dot{X}\}$ and $\{\ddot{X}\}$ at time $t + \Delta t$:

$$\{\ddot{X}_{t+\Delta t}\} = a_0(\{X_{t+\Delta t}\} - \{X_t\}) - a_2\{\dot{X}_t\} - a_3\{\ddot{X}_t\}$$
$$\{\dot{X}_{t+\Delta t}\} = a_1(\{X_{t+\Delta t}\} - \{X_t\}) - a_4\{\dot{X}_t\} - a_5\{\ddot{X}_t\}$$

6.5.4 Park Stiffly Stable Method

The Park Stiffly Stable method is an accurate method for low frequency ranges and stable for all higher-frequency components. Using a linear combination of the following two difference formulas derives the velocity in the Park Stiffly Stable method:

$$\dot{X}_{t+\Delta t} = \frac{1}{6\Delta t}[11X_{t+\Delta t} - 18X_t + 9X_{t-\Delta t} - 2X_{t-2\Delta t}] \quad \text{...(6.76)}$$

$$\dot{X}_{t+\Delta t} = \frac{1}{2\Delta t}(2X_{t+\Delta t} - 4X_t + X_{t-\Delta t}) \quad \text{...(6.77)}$$

The linear combination of (6.76) and (6.77) gives

$$\dot{X}_{t+\Delta t} = \frac{1}{4\Delta t}(3X_{t+\Delta t} - 4X_t + X_{t-\Delta t}) + \frac{1}{12\Delta t}(11X_{t+\Delta t} - 18X_t + 9X_{t-\Delta t} - 2X_{t-2\Delta t}) \quad \text{...(6.78)}$$

or

$$\dot{X}_{t+\Delta t} = \frac{1}{6\Delta t}(10X_{t+\Delta t} - 15X_t + 6X_{t-\Delta t} - X_{t-2\Delta t}) \quad \text{...(6.79)}$$

Similarly, for the acceleration, we obtain

$$\ddot{X}_{t+\Delta t} = \frac{1}{6\Delta t}(10\dot{X}_{t+\Delta t} - 15\dot{X}_t + 6\dot{X}_{t-\Delta t} - \dot{X}_{t-2\Delta t}) \quad \text{...(6.80)}$$

The difference formulas in the Park Stiffly method are given by

$$\{\ddot{X}_{t+\Delta t}\} = \frac{1}{6\Delta t}\left[10\{\dot{X}_{t+\Delta t}\} - 15\{\dot{X}_t\} + 6\{\dot{X}_{t-\Delta t}\} - \{\dot{X}_{t-2\Delta t}\}\right] \quad \text{...(6.81)}$$

$$\{\dot{X}_{t+\Delta t}\} = \frac{1}{6\Delta t}\left[10\{X_{t+\Delta t}\} - 15\{X_t\} + 6\{X_{t-\Delta t}\} - \{X_{t-2\Delta t}\}\right] \quad \text{...(6.82)}$$

We consider Eq. (6.13) to obtain solution for the displacements, velocities and accelerations at time $t + \Delta t$. By substituting the expressions for $\{\ddot{X}_{t+\Delta t}\}$ and $\{\dot{X}_{t+\Delta t}\}$ from (6.81) and (6.82), respectively, into (6.13), we get

$$|\bar{M}|\{X_{t+\Delta t}\} = \{\bar{F}_{t+\Delta t}\} \quad \text{...(6.83)}$$

where the effective mass matrix $[\bar{M}]$ and the effective force vector $\{\bar{F}_{t+\Delta t}\}$ are given by

$$[\bar{M}] = \frac{100}{36\Delta t^2}[M] - \frac{10}{6\Delta t}[C] + [K] \quad \text{...(6.84)}$$

$$\{\bar{F}_{t+\Delta t}\} = \frac{15}{6\Delta t}[M]\{\dot{X}_t\} - \frac{1}{\Delta t}[M]\{\dot{X}_{t-\Delta t}\} + \frac{1}{6\Delta t}[M]\{\dot{X}_{t-2\Delta t}\} + \left(\frac{150}{36\Delta t^2}[M] + \frac{15}{6\Delta t}[C]\right)\{X_t\} - \left(\frac{10}{6\Delta t^2}[M] + \frac{1}{\Delta t}[C]\right)\{X_{t-\Delta t}\} + \left(\frac{1}{36\Delta t^2}[M] + \frac{1}{6\Delta t}[C]\right)\{X_{t-2\Delta t}\} \quad \text{...(6.85)}$$

The solution of Eq.(6.83) gives $\{X_{t+\Delta t}\}$, which is then substituted in Eq.(6.82) to obtain velocities. The values of $\{X_{t+\Delta t}\}$ are then obtained by the use of Eq.(6.81). Note that in the Park Stiffly stable method, the calculation of $\{X_{t+\Delta t}\}$ requires the displacements and velocities at t, $t-\Delta t$ and $t-2\,\Delta t$. Therefore, in order to obtain the solution at time Δt and $2\Delta t$, a special starting procedure is needed, which makes the method non-self starting. The complete algorithm based on Park Stiffly stable method used in the integration is given in Table 6.6. The method requires a large computer memory in order to store the displacements and velocities for the two previous time steps.

Table 6.6 Algorithm based on Park Stiffly stable method

(*a*) Initial Computations:

1. Form stiffness [*K*], mass [*M*] and damping [*C*] matrices
2. Initialize $\{X_0\},\{\dot{X}_0\}$ and $\{\ddot{X}_0\}$.
3. Select time step Δt and calculate integration constants:

$$a_0=\frac{10}{6\Delta t};\; a_1=\frac{-15}{6\Delta t};\; a_2=\frac{1}{\Delta t};\; a_3=\frac{-1}{6\Delta t};$$

4. Form effective stiffness matrix:

$$\left[\bar{K}\right]=a_0^2\left[M\right]-a_0\left[C\right]+\left[K\right]$$

5. Triangularize $\left[\bar{K}\right]:\left[\bar{K}\right]=\left[L\right]\left[D\right]\left[L\right]^T$

(*b*) For each time step:

1. Calculate effective force vector at time $t+\Delta t$:

$$\left\{\bar{F}_{t+\Delta t}\right\}=(-a_1\left\{\dot{X}_t\right\}-a_2\left\{\dot{X}_{t-\Delta t}\right\}-a_3\left\{\dot{X}_{t-2\Delta t}\right\}-a_0a_1\left\{X_t\right\}-a_0a_2\left\{X_{t-\Delta t}\right\}$$
$$+a_3^2\left\{X_{t-2\Delta t}\right\})\left[M\right]-(a_1\left\{X_t\right\}+a_2\left\{X_{t-\Delta t}\right\}+a_3\left\{X_{t-2\Delta t}\right\})\left[C\right]$$

2. Solve for displacements at time $t+\Delta t$

$$|\bar{M}|\left\{X_{t+\Delta t}\right\}=\left\{\bar{F}_{t+\Delta t}\right\}$$

3. Calculate $\left\{\dot{X}\right\}$ and $\left\{\ddot{X}\right\}$ at time $t+\Delta t$:

$$\left\{\dot{X}_{t+\Delta t}\right\}=a_0\left\{X_{t+\Delta t}\right\}+a_1\left\{X_t\right\}+a_2\left\{X_{t-\Delta t}\right\}+a_3\left\{X_{t-2\Delta t}\right\}$$
$$\left\{\ddot{X}_{t+\Delta t}\right\}=a_0\left\{\dot{X}_{t+\Delta t}\right\}+a_1\left\{\dot{X}_t\right\}+a_2\left\{\dot{X}_{t-\Delta t}\right\}+a_3\left\{\dot{X}_{t-2\Delta t}\right\}$$

6.6 EXAMPLE PROBLEMS AND SOLUTIONS

Example E6.1: Find the response of a viscously damped single degree of freedom system subjected to a force

$$F(t)=F_0\left(1-\sin\frac{\pi t}{2t_0}\right)$$

with the following data: $F_0 = 2$ N, $t_0 = \pi$ seconds, $m = 2$ kg, $c = 0.3$ Ns/m and $k = 1$ N/m. The values of the displacement and velocity of the mass at $t = 0$ are zero. Use the central difference method. Choose $\Delta t = 1$, 0.1 and 0.5 seconds and compare the results.

Solution: This is a single-degree of freedom system problem with all initial conditions zero. The following MATLAB program is executed to obtain the results.

```
% INITIAL VALUES
m=2;k=1;c=0.3;dt=0.1;
x0=0;x0d=0;
F0=2;
T=5;
x0dd=inv(m)*(F0-c*x0d-k*x0);
xprev=x0-(dt*x0d)+((dt^2)*x0dd/2);
a0=1/dt^2;a1=1/(2*dt);a2=2*a0;
mbar=a0*m+a1*c;
  t=0;
  v(1)=x0d;a(1)=x0dd;
  i=1;
  for t=0:dt:T+dt
  X(i)=x0;
  f=F0*(1-sin(0.5*t));
fbar=f+(a2*m-k)*x0+(a1*c-a0*m)*xprev;
  x=inv(mbar)*fbar;
  xprev=x0;
  x0=x;
  i=i+1;
  p=i;
  end
  for i=2:p-1
    if i<p-1
    v(i)=(X(i+1)-X(i-1))/(2*dt);
    a(i)=(X(i+1)-2*X(i)+X(i-1))/dt^2;
    end
  end
  fprintf('\ntime\t\tdisplacement\tvelocity\tacceleration\n');
  i=1;
  for t=0:dt:T
    fprintf('%f\t%f\t%f\t%f\n',t,X(i),v(i),a(i));
    i=i+1;
  end
  t=[0:dt:T+dt];
  plot(t,X,'-p');
xlabel('time(s)');
```

The output of the program is shown below for various values of Δt.
when Δt =1 sec, the following results are obtained

time	displacement	velocity	acceleration
0.000000	0.000000	0.000000	1.000000
1.000000	0.500000	0.590965	0.181930
2.000000	1.181930	0.433220	–0.497419
3.000000	1.366441	–0.144974	–0.658969
4.000000	0.891982	–0.606607	–0.264297
5.000000	0.153226	–0.536092	0.405328

When Δt = 0.5 sec, the following results are obtained

time	displacement	velocity	acceleration
0.000000	0.000000	0.000000	1.000000
0.500000	0.125000	0.407252	0.629008
1.000000	0.407252	0.620473	0.223877
1.500000	0.745473	0.638891	–0.150209
2.000000	1.046143	0.491762	–0.438307
2.500000	1.237235	0.231599	–0.602342
3.000000	1.277742	–0.075255	–0.625078
3.500000	1.161980	–0.359295	–0.511081
4.000000	0.918447	–0.558261	–0.284782
4.500000	0.603719	–0.625966	0.013962
5.000000	0.292481	–0.538461	0.336057

When Δt = 0.1 sec, the following results are obtained

time	displacement	velocity	acceleration
0.000000	0.000000	0.000000	1.000000
0.100000	0.005000	0.096651	0.933023
0.200000	0.019330	0.186429	0.862537
0.300000	0.042286	0.269009	0.789068
0.400000	0.073132	0.344120	0.713147
0.500000	0.111110	0.411543	0.635310
0.600000	0.155441	0.471113	0.556092
0.700000	0.205332	0.522719	0.476028
0.800000	0.259985	0.566303	0.395644
0.900000	0.318593	0.601858	0.315459
1.000000	0.380356	0.629430	0.235982
1.100000	0.444479	0.649114	0.157706
1.200000	0.510179	0.661055	0.081110
1.300000	0.576690	0.665443	0.006652
1.400000	0.643268	0.662514	–0.065229
1.500000	0.709193	0.652547	–0.134117
1.600000	0.773777	0.635860	–0.199624
1.700000	0.836365	0.612810	–0.261384
1.800000	0.896339	0.583787	–0.319064
1.900000	0.953122	0.549216	–0.372359

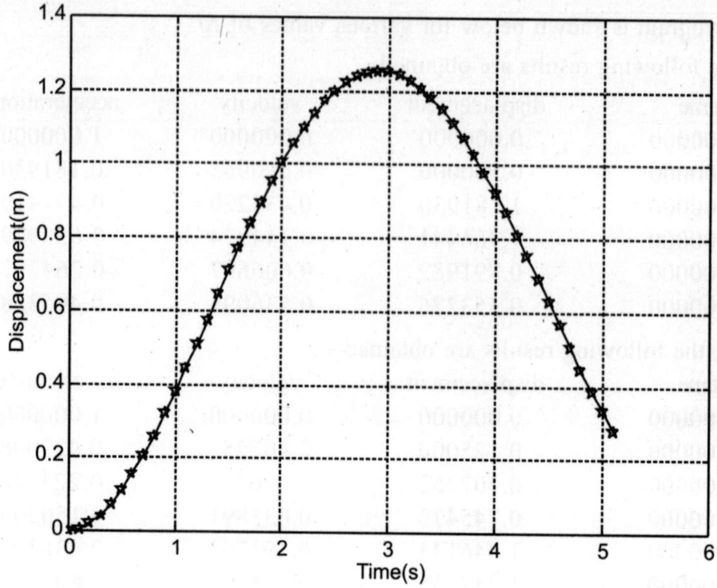

Fig. E6.1 Displacement response plot for Δt = 0.1 sec.

Example E6.2: Find the solution of the equation $5\ddot{X} + 2.5\dot{X} + 4000X = F(t)$, where $F(t)$ is as shown in Fig. E6.2 for the duration $0 \le t \le 1$. Assume that $X_0 = \dot{X}_0 = 0$ and $\Delta t = 0.05$. Use the central difference method.

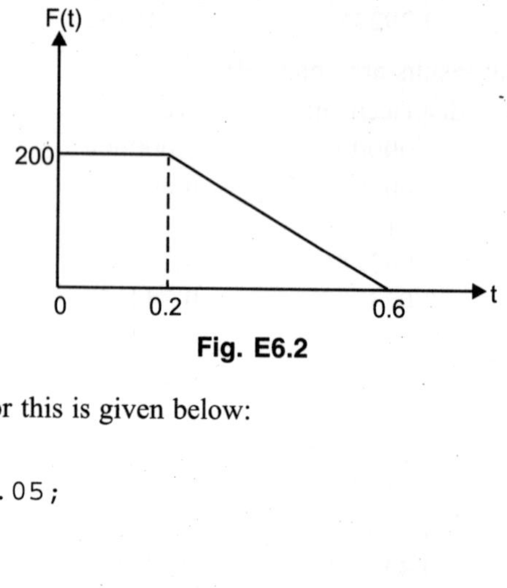

Fig. E6.2

Solution: MATLAB program for this is given below:

```
% INITIAL VALUES
m=5;k=4000;c=2.5;dt=0.05;
x0=0;x0d=0;
F0=200;
T=1;
x0dd=inv(m)*(F0-c*x0d-k*x0);
xprev=x0-(dt*x0d)+((dt^2)*x0dd/2);
a0=1/dt^2;a1=1/(2*dt);a2=2*a0;
mbar=a0*m+a1*c;
  t=0;
```

```
v(1)=x0d;a(1)=x0dd;
i=1;
for t=0:dt:T+dt
X(i)=x0;
if t<=0.2 f=F0;
else if (t>0.2 & t<=0.6) f=-(F0/0.4)*(t-0.6);
 else if t>0.6 f=0;
   end
  end
end
     fbar=f+(a2*m-k)*x0+(a1*c-a0*m)*xprev;
x=inv(mbar)*fbar;
xprev=x0;
x0=x;
i=i+1;
p=i;
end
for i=2:p-1
 if i<p-1
 v(i)=(X(i+1)-X(i-1))/(2*dt);
 a(i)=(X(i+1)-2*X(i)+X(i-1))/dt^2;
  end
end
fprintf('\ntime\t\tdisplacement\tvelocity\tacceleration\n');
i=1;
for t=0:dt:T
 fprintf('%f\t%f\t%f\t%f\n',t,X(i),v(i),a(i));
  i=i+1;
end
t=[0:dt:T+dt];
plot(t,X,'-p');
     xlabel('time(s)');
     ylabel('displacement(m)');
     grid on;
```

The output is as follows:

time	displacement	velocity	acceleration
0.000000	0.000000	0.000000	40.000000
0.050000	0.050000	0.987654	–0.493827
0.100000	0.098765	–0.000000	–39.012346
0.150000	0.050000	–0.963268	0.481634
0.200000	0.002439	0.000000	38.049078

0.250000	0.050000	0.816027	–5.408013
0.300000	0.084041	–0.246914	–37.109594
0.350000	0.025309	–1.042791	5.274482
0.400000	–0.020238	–0.006097	36.193308
0.450000	0.024699	0.770130	–5.144248
0.500000	0.056775	–0.240967	–35.299646
0.550000	0.000602	–0.998028	5.017230
0.600000	–0.043028	–0.011896	34.428050
0.650000	–0.000587	0.849928	0.044924
0.700000	0.041965	0.011602	–33.577975
0.750000	0.000573	–0.828943	–0.043815
0.800000	–0.040929	–0.011316	32.748889
0.850000	–0.000559	0.808475	0.042733
0.900000	0.039918	0.011036	–31.940274
0.950000	0.000545	–0.788513	–0.041678
1.000000	–0.038933	–0.010764	31.151626

Figure E6.2(a) shows the response history.

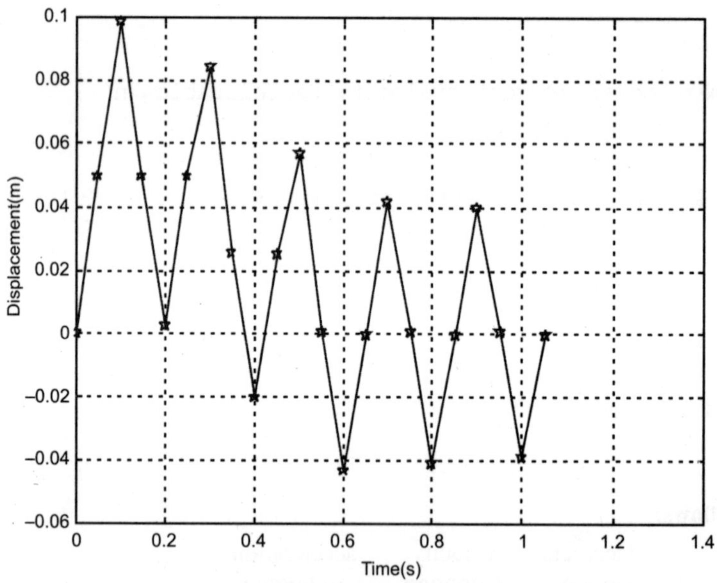

Fig. E6.2 (a) MATLAB output for Δt = 0.05s

Example E6.3: Solve numerically the differential equation $4\ddot{X} + 2000X = F(t)$ with the initial conditions $X_0 = \dot{X}_0 = 0$ and forcing function $F(t)$ as shown in Fig. E6.3. Use central difference method with $\Delta t = 0.02$ sec.

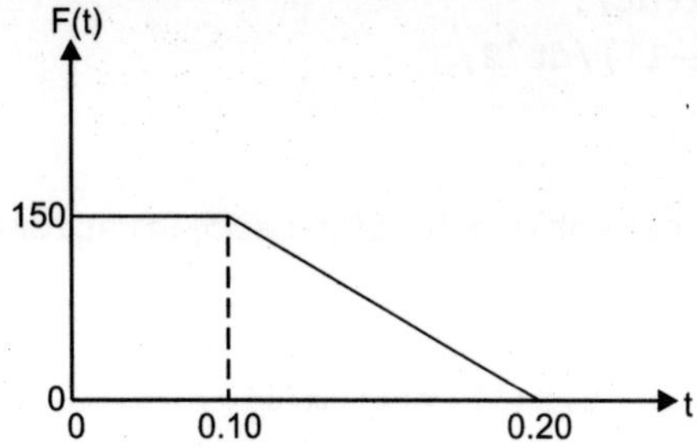

Fig. E6.3

Solution: Here the complete MATLAB program is shown below:

```
% INITIAL VALUES
     m=4;k=2000;c=0;dt=0.02;
     x0=0;x0d=0;
     F0=150;
     T=1;
     x0dd=inv(m)*(F0-c*x0d-k*x0);
     xprev=x0-(dt*x0d)+((dt^2)*x0dd/2);
     a0=1/dt^2;a1=1/(2*dt);a2=2*a0;
     mbar=a0*m+a1*c;
  t=0;
  v(1)=x0d;a(1)=x0dd;
  i=1;
  for t=0:dt:T+dt
  X(i)=x0;
  if t<=0.1 f=F0;
  else if (t>0.1 & t<=0.2) f=-(F0/0.1)*(t-0.2);
    else if t>0.2 f=0;
      end
    end
  end
     fbar=f+(a2*m-k)*x0+(a1*c-a0*m)*xprev;
  x=inv(mbar)*fbar;
  xprev=x0;
  x0=x;
  i=i+1;
  p=i;
```

```
 end
 for i=2:p-1
  if i<p-1
 v(i)=(X(i+1)-X(i-1))/(2*dt);
 a(i)=(X(i+1)-2*X(i)+X(i-1))/dt^2;
  end
 end
fprintf('\ntime\t\tdisplacement\tvelocity\tacceleration\n');
i=1;
for t=0:dt:T
 fprintf('%f\t%f\t%f\t%f\n',t,X(i),v(i),a(i));
  i=i+1;
end
t=[0:dt:T+dt];
plot(t,X,'-p');
     xlabel('time(s)');
     ylabel('displacement(m)');
     grid on;
```

The output is given below:

time	displacement	velocity	acceleration
0.000000	0.000000	0.000000	37.500000
0.020000	0.007500	0.712500	33.750000
0.040000	0.028500	1.282500	23.250000
0.060000	0.058800	1.596000	8.100000
0.080000	0.092340	1.590300	–8.670000
0.100000	0.122412	1.266540	–23.706000
0.120000	0.143002	0.614472	–41.500800
0.140000	0.146991	–0.310490	–50.995440
0.160000	0.130582	–1.323355	–50.290992
0.180000	0.094057	–2.221548	–39.528346
0.200000	0.041720	–2.825432	–20.860030
0.220000	–0.018961	–2.939229	9.480291
0.240000	–0.075849	–2.465181	37.924555
0.260000	–0.117568	–1.498096	58.783907
0.280000	–0.135773	–0.231392	67.886478
0.300000	–0.126824	1.081590	63.411753
0.320000	–0.092509	2.178254	46.254678
0.340000	–0.039693	2.839268	19.846667

0.360000	0.021061	2.932428	–10.530677
0.380000	0.077604	2.439102	–38.801886
0.400000	0.118625	1.457956	–59.312718
0.420000	0.135922	0.185219	–67.961006
0.440000	0.126034	–1.124562	–63.017093
0.460000	0.090940	–2.209431	–45.469761
0.480000	0.037657	–2.852413	–18.828477
0.500000	–0.023157	–2.924913	11.578502
0.520000	–0.079340	–2.412430	39.669781
0.540000	–0.119654	–1.417461	59.827104
0.560000	–0.136038	–0.139000	68.019006
0.580000	–0.125214	1.167261	62.607106
0.600000	–0.089348	2.240070	44.673786
0.620000	–0.035611	2.864865	17.805708
0.640000	0.025247	2.916687	–12.623511
0.660000	0.081056	2.385171	–40.528028
0.680000	0.120654	1.376622	–60.326940
0.700000	0.136121	0.092748	–68.060463
0.720000	0.124364	–1.209676	–62.181894
0.740000	0.087734	–2.270164	–43.866946
0.760000	0.033557	–2.876620	–16.778609
0.780000	–0.027331	–2.907751	13.665450
0.800000	–0.082753	–2.357333	41.376419
0.820000	–0.121624	–1.335447	60.812104
0.840000	–0.136171	–0.046473	68.085368
0.860000	–0.123483	1.251797	61.741559
0.880000	–0.086099	2.299706	43.049438
0.900000	–0.031495	2.887675	15.747429
0.920000	0.029408	2.898109	–14.704065
0.940000	0.084429	2.328921	–42.214747
0.960000	0.122565	1.293948	–61.282479
0.980000	0.136187	0.000186	–68.093715
1.000000	0.122572	–1.293613	–61.286209

Figure E6.3(a) shows the response history.

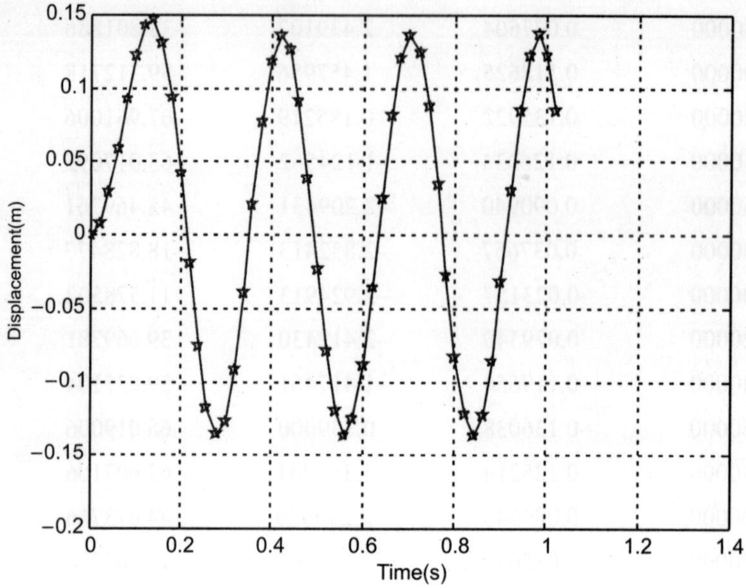

Fig. E6.3(a) Response history

Example E6.4: Solve numerically the solution to the problem of a spring mass system excited by a triangular impulse. The differential equation of motion and the initial conditions are given as

$$0.5\ddot{X} + 8\pi^2 X = F(t)$$

with $\qquad X_1 = \dot{X}_1 = 0$

The triangular force is defined in Fig. E6.4. Use central difference method with $\Delta t = 0.05$ sec.

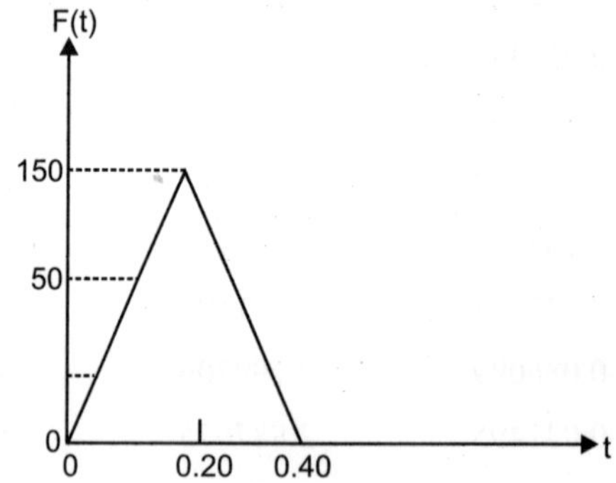

Fig. E6.4

Solution: The following MATLAB program is developed:

```
% INITIAL VALUES
m=0.5;k=8*pi^2;c=0;dt=0.05;
x0=0;x0d=0;
```

```
F0=0;F=150;
T=1;
x0dd=inv(m)*(F0-c*x0d-k*x0);
xprev=x0-(dt*x0d)+((dt^2)*x0dd/2);
a0=1/dt^2;a1=1/(2*dt);a2=2*a0;
mbar=a0*m+a1*c;
t=0;
v(1)=x0d;a(1)=x0dd;
i=1;
for t=0:dt:T+dt
X(i)=x0;
if t<=0.2 f=(F*t/0.2);
else if (t>0.2 & t<=0.4) f=-(F/0.2).*(t-0.4);
   else if t>0.4 f=0;
    end
  end
 end
      fbar=f+(a2*m-k)*x0+(a1*c-a0*m)*xprev;
 x=inv(mbar)*fbar;
 xprev=x0;
 x0=x;
 i=i+1;
 p=i;
 end
 for i=2:p-1
  if i<p-1
 v(i)=(X(i+1)-X(i-1))/(2*dt);
 a(i)=(X(i+1)-2*X(i)+X(i-1))/dt^2;
  end
 end
 fprintf('\ntime\t\tdisplacement\tvelocity\tacceleration\n');
 i=1;
 for t=0:dt:T
  fprintf('%f\t%f\t%f\t%f\n',t,X(i),v(i),a(i));
  i=i+1;
 end
 t=[0:dt:T+dt];
 plot(t,X,'-p');
     xlabel('time(s)');
     ylabel('displacement(m)');
     grid on;
```

The output is given below:

time	displacement	velocity	acceleration
0.000000	0.000000	0.000000	0.000000
0.050000	0.000000	1.875000	75.000000
0.100000	0.187500	6.759780	120.391187
0.150000	0.675978	12.725905	118.253838
0.200000	1.460091	17.418045	69.431745
0.250000	2.417782	15.233816	–156.800902
0.300000	2.983472	3.285518	–321.131034
0.350000	2.746334	–13.709851	–358.683716
0.400000	1.612487	–29.042788	–254.633742
0.450000	–0.157945	–34.785091	24.941603
0.500000	–1.866022	–26.794791	294.670399
0.550000	–2.837424	–8.226331	448.067983
0.600000	–2.688655	13.589754	424.575418
0.650000	–1.478448	30.040819	233.467197
0.700000	0.315427	34.632244	–49.810180
0.750000	1.984776	25.551408	–313.423286
0.800000	2.870567	6.383280	–453.301838
0.850000	2.623104	–15.304866	–414.223998
0.900000	1.340081	–30.950893	–211.617078
0.950000	–0.471985	–34.377997	74.532916
1.000000	–2.097719	–24.233212	331.258494

Figure E6.4(a) shows the plot of the response versus time.

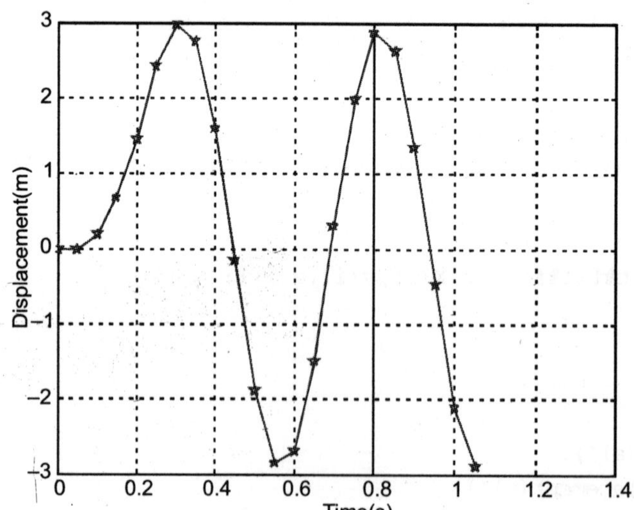

Fig. E6.4 (a) MATLAB output for Δt = 0.05s

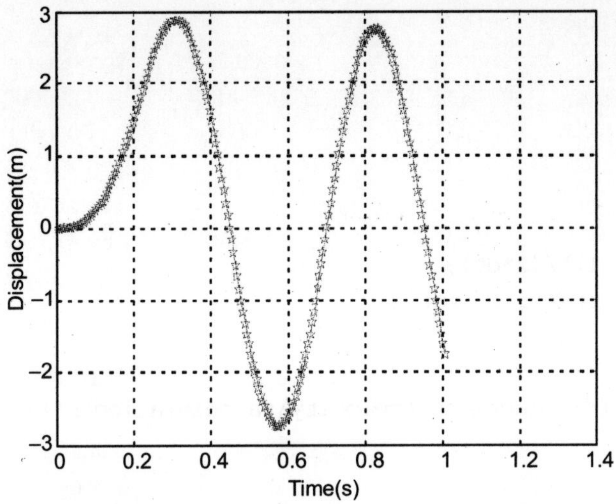

Fig. E6.4(b) MATLAB output for Δ*t* = 0.005s

Example E6.5: Solve the following nonlinear vibration problem, using the central difference method.

$$M\ddot{X} + C\dot{X} + KX + K{*}X^3 = F\cos\omega t$$

with $M = 1.0$, $C = 0.5$, $K = 1.0$, $= K^* = 0.5$, $\Delta t = 0.05$, $t_{max} = 5.0$, and the initial conditions $X_0 = \dot{X}_0 = 0$. Plot the variation of X with t. Take $\omega = 1$ and $F = 10$.

Solution: Here in X_{i+1} an additional term with $-K{*}X_i^3$ will come and other things will remain same. Assuming $F = 10$N, the following MATLAB program is developed.

```
% INITIAL VALUES
    m=1;k=1;c=0.5;ks=0.5;dt=0.05;
    x0=0;x0d=0;omega=1;
    F0=10;
    T=5;
    x0dd=inv(m)*(F0-c*x0d-k*x0);
    xprev=x0-(dt*x0d)+((dt^2)*x0dd/2);
    a0=1/dt^2;a1=1/(2*dt);a2=2*a0;
    mbar=a0*m+a1*c;
t=0;
v(1)=x0d;a(1)=x0dd;
i=1;
for t=0:dt:T+dt
X(i)=x0;
f=F0*cos(omega*t);
% NON-LINEAR TERM
fbar=f+(a2*m-k)*x0+(a1*c-a0*m)*xprev-ks*(x0^3);
x=inv(mbar)*fbar;
```

```
xprev=x0;
x0=x;
i=i+1;
p=i;
end
for i=2:p-1
  if i<p-1
 v(i)=(X(i+1)-X(i-1))/(2*dt);
 a(i)=(X(i+1)-2*X(i)+X(i-1))/dt^2;
  end
end
fprintf('\ntime\t\tdisplacement\tvelocity\tacceleration\n');
i=1;
for t=0:dt:T
 fprintf('%f\t%f\t%f\t%f\n',t,X(i),v(i),a(i));
  i=i+1;
end
t=[0:dt:T+dt];
plot(t,X,'-p');
     xlabel('time(s)');
```

The output of the program is given below:

time	displacement	velocity	acceleration
0.000000	0.000000	0.000000	10.000000
0.050000	0.012500	0.493210	9.728397
0.100000	0.049321	0.971789	9.414766
0.150000	0.109679	1.433672	9.060536
0.200000	0.192688	1.876835	8.665983
0.250000	0.297362	2.299209	8.229010
0.300000	0.422609	2.698528	7.743753
0.350000	0.567215	3.072103	7.199215
0.400000	0.729819	3.416537	6.578158
0.450000	0.908869	3.727404	5.856518
0.500000	1.102560	3.998908	5.003655
0.550000	1.308760	4.223595	3.983832
0.600000	1.524919	4.392175	2.759342
0.650000	1.747977	4.493550	1.295680
0.700000	1.974274	4.515166	–0.431058
0.750000	2.199494	4.443769	–2.424815
0.800000	2.418651	4.266666	–4.659319
0.850000	2.626160	3.973458	–7.069001

0.900000	2.815997	3.558129	–9.544163
0.950000	2.981973	3.021179	–11.933829
1.000000	3.118115	2.371360	–14.058926
1.050000	3.219109	1.626489	–15.735916
1.100000	3.280764	0.812907	–16.807359
1.150000	3.300400	–0.036584	–17.172266
1.200000	3.277105	–0.886080	–16.807592
1.250000	3.211792	–1.700621	–15.774049
1.300000	3.107043	–2.450079	–14.204274
1.350000	2.966784	–3.112116	–12.277189
1.400000	2.795832	–3.673705	–10.186361
1.450000	2.599413	–4.131135	–8.110872
1.500000	2.382718	–4.488775	–6.194716
1.550000	2.150536	–4.757067	–4.536959
1.600000	1.907011	–4.950278	–3.191475
1.650000	1.655508	–5.084393	–2.173152
1.700000	1.398572	–5.175400	–1.467123
1.750000	1.137968	–5.238034	–1.038230
1.800000	0.874769	–5.284965	–0.839002
1.850000	0.609472	–5.326325	–0.815407
1.900000	0.342136	–5.369468	–0.910322
1.950000	0.072525	–5.418854	–1.065097
2.000000	–0.199749	–5.475975	–1.219747

etc.

Figure E6.5 shows the MATLAB response.

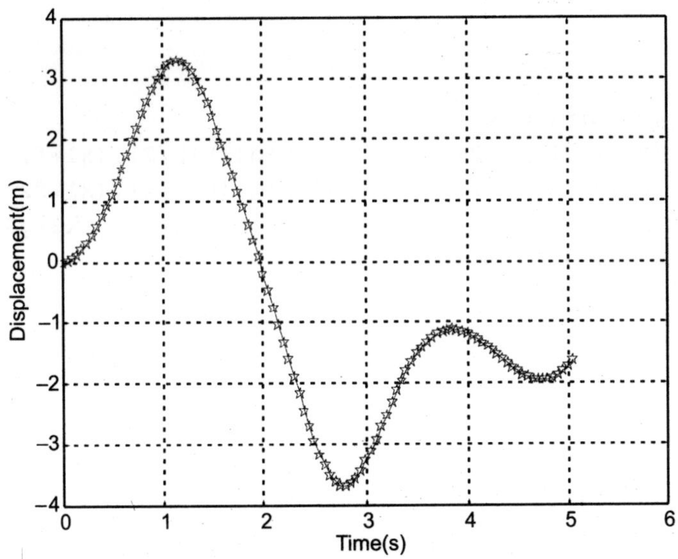

Fig. E6.5 MATLAB output for Δt = 0.05 s

Example E6.6: Solve Example 6.1 using the fourth-order Runge-Kutta method.

Solution: Here $\dot{Y} = f(x_1, x_2, t)$ is a vector of functions

For single degree of freedom system, it contains

$$\dot{Y} = \begin{Bmatrix} \dot{x} \\ \ddot{x} \end{Bmatrix} = f(x_1, x_2, t) = \begin{Bmatrix} x_2 \\ \dfrac{1}{m}(F(t) - kx_1 - cx_2) \end{Bmatrix}$$

Final solution takes the form

$$Y_{i+1} = Y_i + \frac{\Delta t}{6}[K_1 + 2K_2 + 2K_3 + K_4], \text{ where}$$

$$K_1 = f(x_1, x_2, t) = \begin{Bmatrix} p \\ q \end{Bmatrix}$$

$$K_2 = f(x_1 + p/2, x_2 + q/2, t + \Delta t/2) = \begin{Bmatrix} r \\ s \end{Bmatrix}$$

$$K_3 = f(x_1 + r/2, x_2 + q/2, t + \Delta t/2) = \begin{Bmatrix} u \\ v \end{Bmatrix}$$

$$K_4 = f(x_1 + u, x_2 + v, t + \Delta t) = \begin{Bmatrix} m \\ n \end{Bmatrix}$$

Complete MATLAB program for computing the response and its derivative in every time step is given below:

```
dt=0.5;T=10;
h=dt;
x1=0;
x2=0;
i=1;
for t=0:h:T
f1=h*f(t,x1,x2); g1=h*g(t,x1,x2);
f2=h*f((t+h/2),(x1+f1/2),(x2+g1/2));g2=h*g((t+h/2),(x1+f1/2),(x2+g1/2));
f3=h*f((t+h/2),(x1+f2/2),(x2+g2/2));g3=h*g((t+h/2),(x1+f2/2),(x2+g2/2));
f4=h*f((t+h),(x1+f3),(x2+g3)); g4=h*g((t+h),(x1+f3),(x2+g3));
x1=x1+((f1+f4)+2*(f2+f3))/6.0;
x2=x2+((g1+g4)+2*(g2+g3))/6.0;
X(i)=x1;
Y(i)=x2;
i=i+1;
end
t=[0:h:T];
plot(t,X,'-p',t,Y,'-*');
grid on;
xlabel('time(s)');
legend('displacement(m)','velocity(m/s)',2)
```

This program is executed with two other separate programs f.m and g.m given below:

```
%file f.m
function v1=f(t,x1,x2)
v1=x2;
%file g.m
function v2=g(t,x1,x2)
k=1; m=1; c=0;
F=100*(1-cos(t));
v2=(F-k*x1-c*x2)/m;
```

The output values of the data are presented below:

time	displacement	velocity
0.000000	0.000000	0.000000
0.500000	0.110437	0.411687
1.000000	0.379029	0.629789
1.500000	0.707386	0.653171
2.000000	1.004189	0.510442
2.500000	1.198540	0.253323
3.000000	1.249282	–0.052604
3.500000	1.149336	–0.338363
4.000000	0.924789	–0.541854
4.500000	0.629191	–0.616591
5.000000	0.334076	–0.537864

The output of the program is shown in Fig. E6.6.

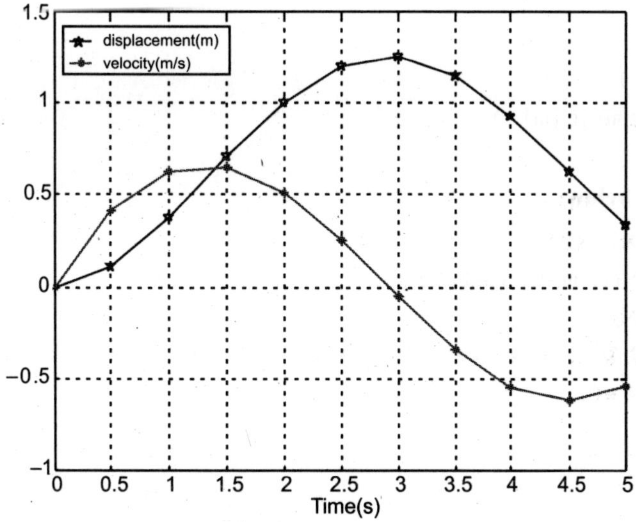

Fig. E6.6 MATLAB output

Example E6.7: Solve Example E6.2 using the fourth-order Runge-Kutta method.

Solution: MATLAB program for this problem is given below. Only change occurs in defining the function *g*. Here $dt = 0.05$s and $T = 1$s.

```
dt=0.05;T=1;
h=dt;
x1=0; % displacement
x2=0; % velocity
i=1;
fprintf('time\t\tdisplacement\tvelocity\n');
for t=0:h:T
fprintf('%f\t%f\t%f\n',t,x1,x2);
X(i)=x1;
Y(i)=x2;
f1=h*f(t,x1,x2); g1=h*g(t,x1,x2);
f2=h*f((t+h/2),(x1+f1/2),(x2+g1/2));g2=h*g((t+h/2),(x1+f1/2),(x2+g1/2));
f3=h*f((t+h/2),(x1+f2/2),(x2+g2/2));g3=h*g((t+h/2),(x1+f2/2),(x2+g2/2));
f4=h*f((t+h),(x1+f3),(x2+g3)); g4=h*g((t+h),(x1+f3),(x2+g3));
x1=x1+((f1+f4)+2*(f2+f3))/6.0;
x2=x2+((g1+g4)+2*(g2+g3))/6.0;
i=i+1;
end
time=[0:h:T];
plot(time,X,'-p');
grid on;
xlabel('time(s)');
ylabel('displacement(m)')
```

function g.m is given below:

```
function v2=g(t,x1,x2)
            k=4000; m=5; c=2.5;
   if t<=0.2 F=200;
   else if (t>0.2 & t<=0.6) F=-(200/0.4)*(t-0.6);
   else if t>0.6 F=0;
   end
   end
   end
     v2=(F-k*x1-c*x2)/m;
```

The output is as follows:

time	displacement	velocity
0.000000	0.000000	0.000000
0.050000	0.041253	1.316874
0.100000	0.091824	0.439092
0.150000	0.071773	–1.031937
0.200000	0.019836	–0.736985
0.250000	0.018390	0.574514
0.300000	0.056157	0.655850
0.350000	0.060285	–0.490566
0.400000	0.018109	–0.945601
0.450000	–0.009407	–0.071506
0.500000	0.009400	0.627115
0.550000	0.030533	0.077915
0.600000	0.010993	–0.730337
0.650000	–0.022121	–0.405278
0.700000	–0.017213	0.518375
0.750000	0.014055	0.535490
0.800000	0.020088	–0.285294
0.850000	–0.005878	–0.574286
0.900000	–0.019935	0.063796
0.950000	–0.001387	0.535146
1.000000	0.017375	0.121352

The displacement response is shown in Fig. E6.7

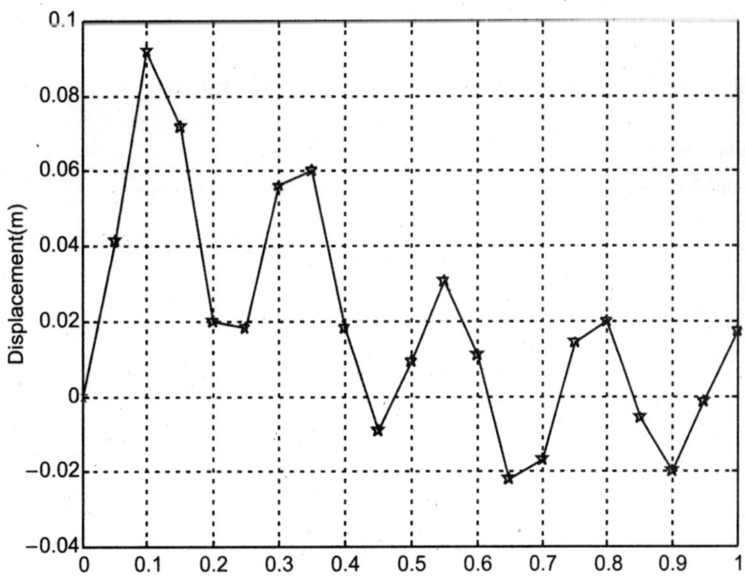

Fig. E6.7 MATLAB output

Example E6.8: Solve Example 6.3 by the Runge-Kutta method.

Solution: MATLAB program for this problem is given below. Only change occurs in defining the function *g*. Here $dt = 0.05$s and $T = 1$s.

```
t=0.02;T=1;
h=dt;
x1=0; % displacement
x2=0; % velocity
i=1;
fprintf('time\t\tdisplacement\tvelocity\n');
for t=0:h:T
fprintf('%f\t%f\t%f\n',t,x1,x2);
X(i)=x1;
Y(i)=x2;
f1=h*f(t,x1,x2); g1=h*g(t,x1,x2);
f2=h*f((t+h/2),(x1+f1/2),(x2+g1/2));g2=h*g((t+h/2),(x1+f1/2),(x2+g1/2));
f3=h*f((t+h/2),(x1+f2/2),(x2+g2/2));g3=h*g((t+h/2),(x1+f2/2),(x2+g2/2));
f4=h*f((t+h),(x1+f3),(x2+g3)); g4=h*g((t+h),(x1+f3),(x2+g3));
x1=x1+((f1+f4)+2*(f2+f3))/6.0;
x2=x2+((g1+g4)+2*(g2+g3))/6.0;
i=i+1;
end
time=[0:h:T];
plot(time,X,'-p');
grid on;
xlabel('time(s)');
ylabel('displacement(m)')
The function g.m defining the force signal is given below:

function v2=g(t,x1,x2)
      k=2000; m=4; c=0;
   if t<=0.1 F=150;
   else if (t>0.1 & t<=0.2) F=-(150/0.1)*(t-0.2);
   else if t>0.2 F=0;
   end
   end
   end
v2=(F-k*x1-c*x2)/m;
```

The output of the program is as follows:

time	displacement	velocity
0.000000	0.000000	0.000000
0.020000	0.007375	0.725000
0.040000	0.028041	1.307417
0.060000	0.057936	1.632787
0.080000	0.091181	1.637183
0.100000	0.121242	1.319778
0.120000	0.141711	0.669243
0.140000	0.146114	–0.260185
0.160000	0.130641	–1.285790
0.180000	0.095386	–2.205969
0.200000	0.044333	–2.839867
0.220000	–0.014931	–2.989164
0.240000	–0.071253	–2.550901
0.260000	–0.113564	–1.611284
0.280000	–0.133548	–0.355057
0.300000	–0.127280	0.970822
0.320000	–0.095995	2.105735
0.340000	–0.045845	2.826625
0.360000	0.013311	2.991841
0.380000	0.069845	2.568967
0.400000	0.112643	1.641187
0.420000	0.133296	0.390919
0.440000	0.127747	–0.936053
0.460000	0.097088	–2.078891
0.480000	0.047349	–2.812982
0.500000	–0.011691	–2.994079
0.520000	–0.068427	–2.586645
0.540000	–0.111707	–1.670828
0.560000	–0.133025	–0.426696
0.580000	–0.128194	0.901173
0.600000	–0.098165	2.051764
0.620000	–0.048845	2.798940
0.640000	0.010071	2.995880

0.660000	0.067001	2.603933
0.680000	0.110755	1.700204
0.700000	0.132735	0.462383
0.720000	0.128622	–0.866188
0.740000	0.099228	–2.024359
0.760000	0.050333	–2.784500
0.780000	–0.008450	–2.997242
0.800000	–0.065566	–2.620828
0.820000	–0.109788	–1.729309
0.840000	–0.132425	–0.497977
0.860000	–0.129031	0.831104
0.880000	–0.100275	1.996680
0.900000	–0.051812	2.769666
0.920000	0.006829	2.998167
0.940000	0.064122	2.637329
0.960000	0.108805	1.758141
0.980000	0.132097	0.533471
1.000000	0.129421	–0.795925

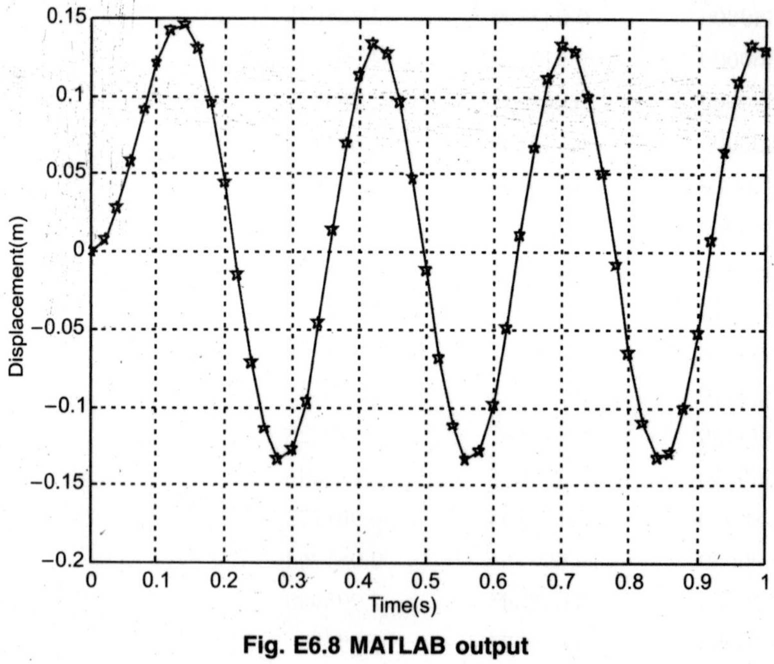

Fig. E6.8 MATLAB output

Example E6.9: Solve Example E6.4 by the Runge-Kutta method.

Solution: Triangular pulse is defined with the following MATLAB m function

```
function v2=g(t,x1,x2)
k=8*pi^2;m=0.5; c=0;
if t<=0.2 F=(150*t/0.2);
else if (t>0.2 & t<=0.4) F=-(150/0.2)*(t-0.4);
else if t>0.4 F=0;
end
end
end
v2=(F-k*x1-c*x2)/m;
```

Here *dt* = 0.05s and *T* = 1s. The output is shown below:

time	displacement	velocity
0.000000	0.000000	0.000000
0.050000	0.031250	1.813315
0.100000	0.231900	6.553226
0.150000	0.706315	12.411526
0.200000	1.454472	17.155388
0.250000	2.309559	15.351753
0.300000	2.826498	4.081899
0.350000	2.627673	–12.352850
0.400000	1.608467	–27.686924
0.450000	0.008154	–34.265866
0.500000	–1.593966	–27.784720
0.550000	–2.587509	–10.723309
0.600000	–2.594445	10.409650
0.650000	–1.612934	27.559532
0.700000	–0.017719	34.195743
0.750000	1.582951	27.798535
0.800000	2.579242	10.815730
0.850000	2.592074	–10.273897
0.900000	1.617357	–27.432202
0.950000	0.027244	–34.125340
1.000000	–1.571956	–27.811835

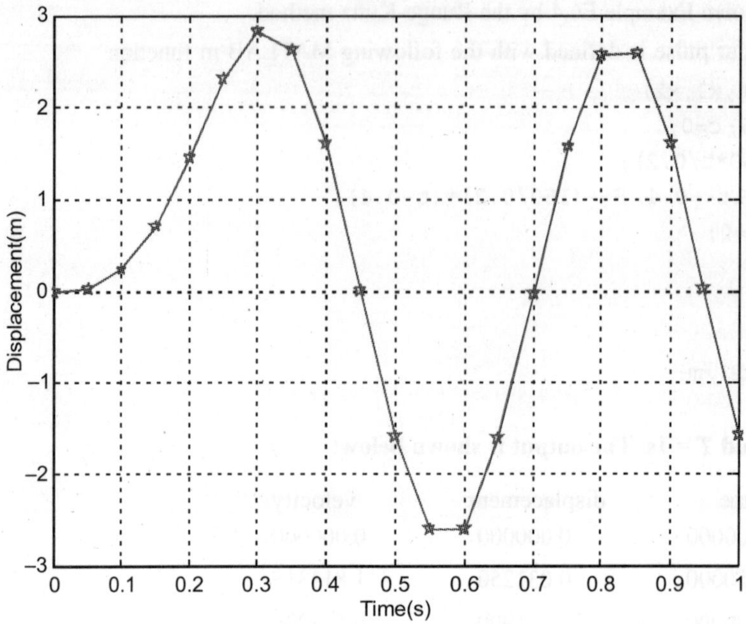

Fig. E6.9 MATLAB output

Example E6.10: Solve Example E6.5 by the Runga-Kutta method.

Solution: Here, the function defining the system g.m is given below:

```
function v2=g(t,x1,x2)
k=1;m=1; c=0.5;omega=1;
ks=0.5 % CUBIC STIFFNESS
F=10*cos(omega*t);
v2=(F-k*x1-c*x2-ks*x1^3)/m;
```

The output is given below for *dt* = 0.05s and *T* = 5s

time	displacement	velocity
0.000000	0.000000	0.000000
0.050000	0.012391	0.493389
0.100000	0.049095	0.972141
0.150000	0.109327	1.434195
0.200000	0.192202	1.877534
0.250000	0.296734	2.300105
0.300000	0.421830	2.699660
0.350000	0.566273	3.073539
0.400000	0.728700	3.418380
0.450000	0.907555	3.729795
0.500000	1.101028	4.002029
0.550000	1.306982	4.227665
0.600000	1.522864	4.397443
0.650000	1.745611	4.500284

0.700000	1.971567	4.523624
0.750000	2.196426	4.454170
0.800000	2.415222	4.279150
0.850000	2.622401	3.988046
0.900000	2.811982	3.574682
0.950000	2.977828	3.039377
1.000000	3.114021	2.390700
1.050000	3.215294	1.646314
1.100000	3.277487	0.832466
1.150000	3.297926	–0.018051
1.200000	3.275671	–0.869257
1.250000	3.211578	–1.686035
1.300000	3.108154	–2.438054
1.350000	2.969237	–3.102755
1.400000	2.799563	–3.666911
1.450000	2.604294	–4.126654
1.500000	2.388573	–4.486248
1.550000	2.157169	–4.756089
1.600000	1.914225	–4.950445
1.650000	1.663116	–5.085340
1.700000	1.406414	–5.176825
1.750000	1.145909	–5.239713
1.800000	0.882705	–5.286762
1.850000	0.617325	–5.328190
1.900000	0.349853	–5.371441

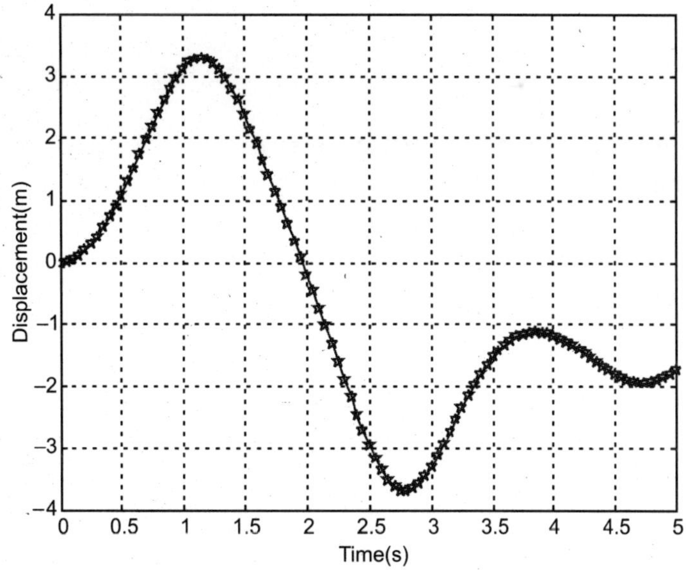

Fig. E6.10 MATLAB output

Example E6.11: Find the response of the two degree of freedom system when $F_1(t) = 0$ and $F_2(t) = 10$, using the central difference method. The mass, stiffness and damping matrices for this system are given as

$$[M]=\begin{bmatrix}1 & 0\\0 & 10\end{bmatrix},\ [K]=\begin{bmatrix}11 & -1\\-1 & 1\end{bmatrix},\ [C]=\begin{bmatrix}0.5 & -0.1\\-0.1 & 0.1\end{bmatrix}$$

All the initial conditions are given as zero. Use $\Delta t = 0.05$

Solution: The procedure is modified for matrices instead of scalars. Complete program is given below:

```
% INITIAL VALUES
M=[1 0;0 10];
K=[21 -1;-1 1];
 C=[0.5 -0.1;-0.1 0.1];
dt=0.05;
x0=[0;0];x0d=[0;0];
F0=[0;10];
T=2;
x0dd=inv(M)*(F0-C*x0d-K*x0);
xprev=x0-(dt.*x0d)+((dt^2).*(x0dd/2));
a0=1/dt^2;a1=1/(2*dt);a2=2*a0;
mbar=(a0.*M)+(a1.*C);
  t=0;
  v(:,1)=x0d;a(:,1)=x0dd;
  i=1;
  fprintf('time\t\tX(1)\t\tX(2)\n');
  for t=0:dt:T+dt
  X(:,i)=x0;
  F=F0;
  Fbar=F+(a2.*M-K)*x0+(a1.*C-a0.*M)*xprev;
  x=inv(mbar)*Fbar;
  xprev=x0;
  x0=x;
  fprintf('%f\t%f\t%f\n',t,X(1,i),X(2,i));
  i=i+1;
  p=i;
  end
  for i=2:p-1
  if i<p-1
```

```
v(:,i)=(X(:,i+1)-X(:,i-1)).*(1/(2*dt));
a(:,i)=(X(:,i+1)-2*X(:,i)+X(:,i-1)).*(1/dt^2);
 end
 end
 t=[0:dt:T+dt];
 plot(t,X(1,:),'-p',t,X(2,:),'-*');
xlabel('time(s)');
 ylabel('displacement(m)');
 legend('DOF-1','DOF-2',2);
 grid on;
```

The output of the program is as follows:

time	X(1)	X(2)
0.000000	0.000000	0.000000
0.050000	-0.000000	0.001250
0.100000	0.000015	0.004998
0.150000	0.000067	0.011243
0.200000	0.000178	0.019981
0.250000	0.000376	0.031210
0.300000	0.000688	0.044924
0.350000	0.001142	0.061120
0.400000	0.001762	0.079793
0.450000	0.002571	0.100937
0.500000	0.003586	0.124545
0.550000	0.004821	0.150611
0.600000	0.006281	0.179128
0.650000	0.007969	0.210088
0.700000	0.009880	0.243481
0.750000	0.012004	0.279301
0.800000	0.014325	0.317535
0.850000	0.016824	0.358176
0.900000	0.019481	0.401212
0.950000	0.022271	0.446631
1.000000	0.025170	0.494422

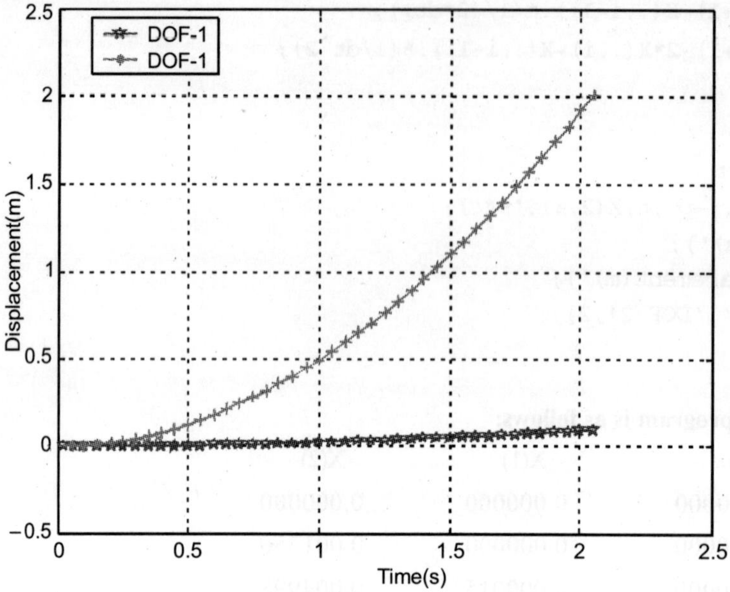

Fig. E6.11 MATLAB output response

Example E6.12: Solve Example E6.11 using the two-cycle iteration with trapezoidal rule.

Solution: For an undamped system the following equations are applicable.

We now have: $\left(\dfrac{4}{\Delta t^2}[M]+[K]\right)U_{n-1} = R_{n+1} + [M]\left(\dfrac{4}{\Delta t^2}U_n + \dfrac{4}{\Delta t}\dot{U}_n + \ddot{U}_n\right)$

The initial conditions are: $U_0 = 0, \dot{U}_0 = 0,\ \ddot{U}_0 = [M]^{-1}(R_0 - [K]U_0)$.

$$\ddot{U}_{n+1} = \frac{4}{\Delta t^2}[U_{n+1} - U_n] - \frac{4}{\Delta t}\dot{U}_n - \ddot{U}_n, \dot{U}_{n+1} = \frac{\Delta t}{2}[\ddot{U}_{n+1} + \ddot{U}_n] + \dot{U}_n = \frac{2}{\Delta t}[U_{n+1} - U_n] - \dot{U}_n$$

Complete program for damped vibrating system is given below:

% INITIAL VALUES

```
M=[1 0;0 10];
K=[21 -1;-1 1];
C=[0.5 -0.1;-0.1 0.1];
dt=0.05;
T=2;dt=0.05;
t=[0:dt:T];
i=1;
x(:,i)=[0;0];xd(:,i)=[0;0];
f(:,i)=[0;10];
xdd(:,i)=inv(M)*(f(:,i)-C*xd(:,i)-K*x(:,i));
% FIRST time step
dxd(:,2)=dt*xdd(:,1);
```

```
for i=2:length(t)
f(:,i)=[0;10];
df(:,i)=f(:,i)-f(:,i-1);
xd(:,i)=xd(:,i-1)+dxd(:,i);
dx(:,i)=(dt/2)*(xd(:,i-1)+xd(:,i));
dxdd(:,i)=inv(M)*(df(:,i)-K*dx(:,i)-C*dxd(:,i));
xdd(:,i)=xdd(:,i-1)+dxdd(:,i);
% UPDATING VALUES OF VELOCITY AND DISPLACMENT IN CURRENT CYCLE
dxd(:,i)=(dt/2)*(xdd(:,i-1)+xdd(:,i));
xd(:,i)=xd(:,i-1)+dxd(:,i);
dx(:,i)=(1/2)*(xd(:,i-1)+xd(:,i));
% REVISED DISPLACMENT IN CURRENT CYCLE
x(:,i)=x(:,i-1)+dx(:,i);
% DELTA x DOT FOR NEXT CYCLE
dxd(:,i+1)=2*dt*xdd(:,i)-dxd(:,i);
end
fprintf('time\t\tX(1)\t\tX(2)\n');
p=1
for time=0:dt:T
 fprintf('%f\t%f\t%f\n',time,x(1,p),x(2,p));
 p=p+1;
end
plot(t,x(1,:),'-p',t,x(2,:),'-*');
     xlabel('time(s)');
ylabel('displacement(m)');
legend('DOF-1','DOF-2',2);
     grid on;
```

The output is as follows:

time	X(1)	X(2)
0.000000	0.000000	0.000000
0.050000	0.000078	0.024992
0.100000	0.000492	0.099950
0.150000	0.001642	0.224830
0.200000	0.004000	0.399578
0.250000	0.008087	0.624125
0.300000	0.014442	0.898392
0.350000	0.023594	1.222290
0.400000	0.036037	1.595716
0.450000	0.052204	2.018558
0.500000	0.072446	2.490690
0.550000	0.097016	3.011977
0.600000	0.126057	3.582274
0.650000	0.159599	4.201422
0.700000	0.197561	4.869252

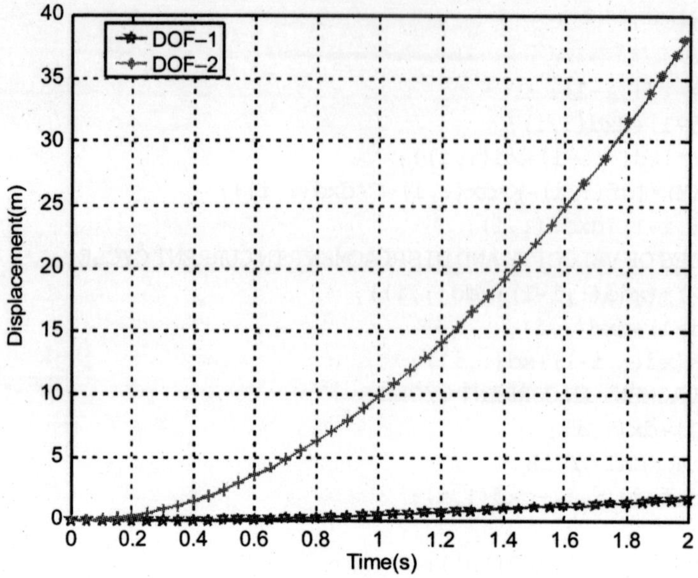

Fig. E6.12 MATLAB output

Example E6.13: Solve Example E6.11 using the fourth-order Runge-Kutta method.

Solution:

Here $\dot{Y} = f(x_1, x_2, x_3, x_4, t)$, where $Y = \begin{Bmatrix} x_1 \\ x_2 \\ x_3 \\ x_4 \end{Bmatrix}$ and $= f(x_1, x_2, x_3, x_4, t) = \begin{Bmatrix} x_3 \\ x_4 \\ \dot{x}_3 \\ \dot{x}_4 \end{Bmatrix}$

where $\begin{Bmatrix} \dot{x}_3 \\ \dot{x}_4 \end{Bmatrix} = -[M]^{-1}[K]\begin{Bmatrix} x_1 \\ x_2 \end{Bmatrix} - [M]^{-1}[C]\begin{Bmatrix} x_3 \\ x_4 \end{Bmatrix} + [M]^{-1}F(t)$

In total it can be written as $\begin{Bmatrix} \dot{x}_1 \\ \dot{x}_2 \\ \dot{x}_3 \\ \dot{x}_4 \end{Bmatrix} = \begin{bmatrix} [0] & [I] \\ -[M]^{-1}[K] & -[M]^{-1}[C] \end{bmatrix} \begin{Bmatrix} x_1 \\ x_2 \\ x_3 \\ x_4 \end{Bmatrix} + \begin{bmatrix} [0] \\ [M]^{-1}F(t) \end{bmatrix}$

or $\dot{Y} = [E]Y + F$

Thus instead of defining functions as in SDOF system, here entire thing will come in one program. The following program is developed based on the above equations.

```
dt=0.05;T=1;
h=dt;
x1=0;x2=0;  % displacements
x3=0;x4=0;  % velocity
```

```
M=[1 0;0 10];K=[2 1 -1;-1 1];C=[0.5 -0.1;-0.1 0.1];f=[0;10];
E=[zeros(size(M)) eye(size(M));-inv(M)*K-inv(M)*C];
F=[0;0;inv(M)*f];
i=1;
Y=[x1;x2;x3;x4];
fprintf('time\t\tX(1)\t\tX(2)\n');
for t=0:h:T
 X(:,i)=Y;
 fprintf('%f\t%f\t%f\n',t,Y(1),Y(2));
 K1=h*(E*Y+F);
 K2=h*(Y+(0.5*K1))+F);
 K3=h*(Y+(0.5*K2))+F)
 K4=h*(Y+K3+F)
 Y=Y+(K1+2*K2+2*K3+K4)/6;
 i=i+1;
end
time=[0:h:T];
plot(time,X(1,:),'-p',time,X(2,:),'-*');
grid on;
xlabel('time(s)');
ylabel('displacement(m)')
legend('DOF-1','DOF-2');
```

The output is shown below:

time	X(1)	X(2)
0.000000	0.000000	0.000000
0.050000	0.000002	0.001250
0.100000	0.000020	0.004998
0.150000	0.000074	0.011242
0.200000	0.000188	0.019980
0.250000	0.000388	0.031208
0.300000	0.000702	0.044922
0.350000	0.001156	0.061118
0.400000	0.001776	0.079790
0.450000	0.002584	0.100933
0.500000	0.003597	0.124541
0.550000	0.004828	0.150606
0.600000	0.006285	0.179122
0.650000	0.007969	0.210081
0.700000	0.009874	0.243474
0.750000	0.011993	0.279292
0.800000	0.014309	0.317526

0.850000	0.016805	0.358166
0.900000	0.019458	0.401200
0.950000	0.022246	0.446618
1.000000	0.025144	0.494409

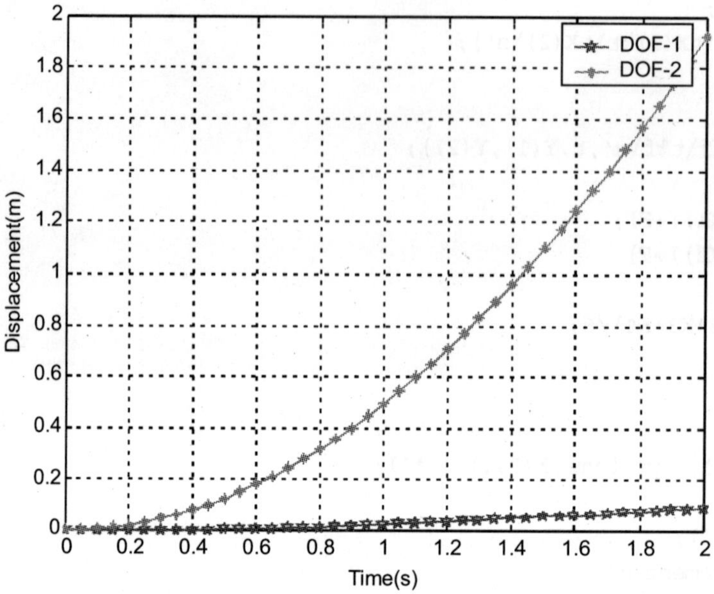

Fig. E6.13 MATLAB output

Example E6.14: Solve Example E6.11 using the Houbolt method.

Solution: In Houbolt's method for obtaining first two displacements $X\Delta t$ and $X2t$, central difference method is employed. Then three step Houbolt's algorithm is used. Velocities and accelerations are likewise defined. Complete MATLAB program is given below:

```
K=[21 -1;-1 1];
M=[1 0;0 10];
C=[0.5 -0.1;-0.1 0.1];
dt=0.05;T=2;
X0=[0;0];X0d=[0;0];F=[0;10];
t=[0:dt:T];
X(:,2)=X0;
X0dd=inv(M)*(F-C*X0d-K*X0);
% USING CENTRAL DIFFERENCE METHOD TO OBTAIN PREVIOUS 3 VALUES
Xprev=X0-(dt*X0d)+((dt^2)*(X0dd/2));
a0=1/dt^2;a1=1/(2*dt);a2=2*a0;
mbar=(a0*M)+(a1*C);
kbar=(K-a2*M);
cbar=(a0*M-a1*C);
```

```
X(:,1)=X0;
Fbar=F-kbar*X0-cbar*Xprev;
X(:,2)=inv(mbar)*Fbar;
Fbar=F-kbar*X(:,2)-cbar*X0;
X(:,3)=inv(mbar)*Fbar;

% HOUBOLT METHOD BEGINS
a0=2/(dt^2);a1=11/(6*dt);a2=5/(dt^2);a3=3/dt;a4=-2*a0;
a5=-a3/2;a6=a0/2;a7=a3/9;
Kb=K+a0*M+a1*C;
p=3;
for i=3:length(t)
  F=[0;10];% F(t+2dt)
   Fb=F+M*(a2*X(:,i)+a4*X(:,i-1)+a6*X(:,i-2))+ C*(a3*X(:,i)+a5*X(:,i-
1)+a7*X(:,i-2));
  X(:,i+1)=inv(Kb)*Fb;
  Xdd(:,i+1)=a0*X(:,i+1)-a2*X(:,i)-a4*X(:,i-1)-a6*X(:,i-2);
  Xd(:,i+1)=a1*X(:,i+1)-a3*X(:,i)-a5*X(:,i-1)-a7*X(:,i-2);
  p=p+1;
end
fprintf('\ntime\t\tX1\t\tX2\n');
for i=1:p
  time(i)=(i-1)*dt;
  fprintf('%f\t%f\t%f\n',time(i),X(1,i),X(2,i))
end
plot(time,X(1,:), '-p',time,X(2,:),'-*');
grid on;
xlabel('time(s)');
ylabel('displacement (m)');
legend('DOF-1','DOF-2');
```

The output of the program is given below:

time	X(1)	X(2)
0.000000	0.000000	0.000000
0.050000	–0.000000	0.001250
0.100000	0.000015	0.004998
0.150000	0.000069	0.011243
0.200000	0.000184	0.019980
0.250000	0.000387	0.031207
0.300000	0.000704	0.044920

0.350000	0.001161	0.061114
0.400000	0.001782	0.079784
0.450000	0.002588	0.100924
0.500000	0.003595	0.124528
0.550000	0.004817	0.150590
0.600000	0.006260	0.179102
0.650000	0.007927	0.210055
0.700000	0.009814	0.243443
0.750000	0.011912	0.279255
0.800000	0.014208	0.317483
0.850000	0.016686	0.358115
0.900000	0.019325	0.401142
0.950000	0.022104	0.446553
1.000000	0.025000	0.494334

Figure E6.14 shows the plot of histories of two degrees of freedom.

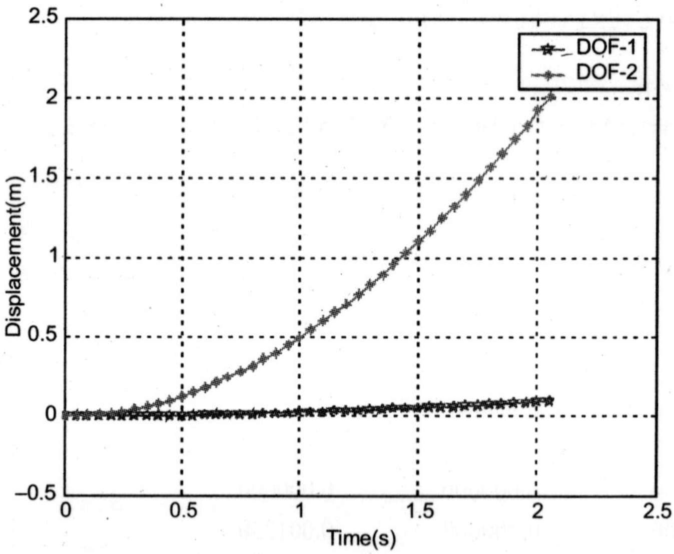

Fig. E6.14 MATLAB output (Houbolt's method)

Example E6.15: Solve Example E6.11 by the Wilson Theta method.

Solution: Here, theta is chosen as 1.4 and followed the algorithm. The complete MATLAB program is given below:

```
K=[21 -1;-1 1];
```

```
M=[1 0;0 10];
C=[0.5 -0.1;-0.1 0.1];
dt=0.05;T=2;
X0=[0;0];X0d=[0;0];F0=[0;10];
X0dd=inv(M)*(F0-C*X0d-K*X0);
theta=1.4;
a0=6/(theta*dt)^2;a1=3/(theta*dt);a2=2*a1;
a3=2;a4=(1/2*theta*dt);a5=-a2/theta;
a6=1-3/theta;
a7=dt/2;a8=dt^2/6;
Kb=K+a0*M+a1*C;
i=1;
X(:,1)=X0;Xd(:,1)=X0d;Xdd(:,1)=X0dd;t=0;
fprintf('time(s)\t\tX1\t\tX2\n');
fprintf('%f\t%f\t%f\n',t,X(1,1),X(2,1));
for t=dt:dt:T
 i=i+1;
 F=[0;10];
 Ftb=F0+M*(a0*X(:,i-1)+a2*Xd(:,i-1)+a3*Xdd(:,i-1))+C*(a1*X(:,i-1)
      +a3*Xd(:,i-1)+a4*Xdd(:,i-1))+theta*(F-F0);
 Xt(:,i)=inv(Kb)*Ftb;
 Xdd(:,i)=(a0/theta)*(Xt(:,i)-X(:,i-1))+a5*Xd(:,i-1)+a6*Xdd(:,i-1);
 Xd(:,i)=Xd(:,i-1)+a7*(Xdd(:,i)+Xdd(:,i-1));
 X(:,i)=X(:,i-1)+dt*Xd(:,i-1)+a8*(Xdd(:,i)+2*Xdd(:,i-1));
 F0=F;
 fprintf('%f\t%f\t%f\n',t,X(1,i),X(2,i));
end
t=[0:dt:T];
plot(t,X(1,:),'-p',t,X(2,:),'-*')
xlabel('time(s)');
ylabel('displacement(m)');
legend('DOF-1','DOF-2');
grid on;
```

The output is shown below:

time	X(1)	X(2)
0.000000	0.000000	0.000000
0.050000	0.000003	0.001250
0.100000	0.000022	0.004998

0.150000	0.000079	0.011242
0.200000	0.000197	0.019979
0.250000	0.000400	0.031206
0.300000	0.000717	0.044919
0.350000	0.001173	0.061113
0.400000	0.001793	0.079784
0.450000	0.002598	0.100926
0.500000	0.003607	0.124531
0.550000	0.004831	0.150595
0.600000	0.006279	0.179109
0.650000	0.007952	0.210065
0.700000	0.009847	0.243455
0.750000	0.011954	0.279271
0.800000	0.014259	0.317502
0.850000	0.016745	0.358138
0.900000	0.019392	0.401169
0.950000	0.022176	0.446584
1.000000	0.025074	0.494370
1.050000	0.028063	0.544516
1.100000	0.031122	0.597008
1.150000	0.034233	0.651833
1.200000	0.037379	0.708978
1.250000	0.040549	0.768426
1.300000	0.043738	0.830164
1.350000	0.046942	0.894174
1.400000	0.050165	0.960442
1.450000	0.053413	1.028950
1.500000	0.056697	1.099681

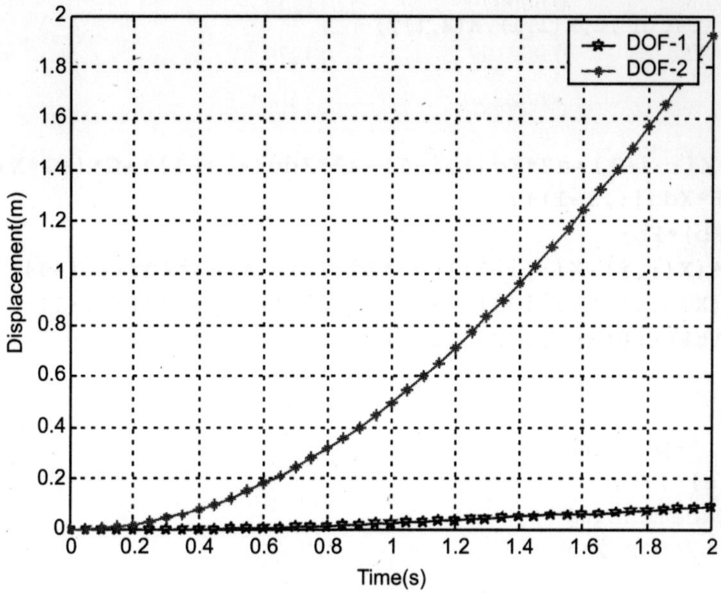

Fig. E6.15 MATLAB response (Wilson theta)

Example E6.16: Solve Example E6.11 by the Newmark Beta method.

Solution:

Table E6.11 The Newmark Scheme

• $u_{n+1} = u_n + hv_n + h^2(1/2-\beta)a_n + h^2\beta a_{n+1}$
• $v_{n+1} = v_n + h(1-\gamma)a_n + h\gamma a_{n+1}$
• $Ma_{n+1} + Cv_{n+1} + Ku_{n+1} = F_{n+1}$

Here for $\beta = 0.5$ and $\gamma = 1/6$, the following values are obtained. The MATLAB program is shown below:

```
K= [21 -1;-1 1];
M= [1 0; 0 10];
C= [0.5 -0.1;-0.1 0.1];
dt=0.05;T=2;
X0=[0;0];X0d=[0;0];F=[0;10];
X0dd=inv(M)*(F-C*X0d-K*X0);
beta=0.5;gamma=1/6;%0.25*(0.5+beta);
a0=1/(beta*dt^2);a1=gamma/(beta*dt);a2=1/(beta*dt);
a3=(1/2*beta)-1;a4=(gamma/beta-1);a5=0.5*(gamma/beta-2)*dt;
a6=dt*(1-beta);a7=beta*dt;
Kb=K+a0*M+a1*C;
i=1;
X(:,1)=X0;Xd(:,1)=X0d;Xdd(:,1)=X0dd;t=0;
fprintf('time(s)\t\tX1\t\tX2\n');
```

```
fprintf('%f\t%f\t%f\n',t,X(1,1),X(2,1));
for t=dt:dt:T
 i=i+1;
 F=[0;10];
  Fb=F+M*(a0*X(:,i-1)+a2*Xd(:,i-1)+a3*Xdd(:,i-1))+C*(a1*X(:,i-1)+a4*Xd
    (:,i-1)+a5*Xdd(:,i-1));
  X(:,i)=inv(Kb)*Fb;
  Xdd(:,i)=a0*(X(:,i)-X(:,i-1))-a2*Xd(:,i-1)-a3*Xdd(:,i-1);
  Xd(:,i)=a1*(X(:,i)-X(:,i-1))-a4*Xd(:,i-1)-a5*Xdd(:,i-1);
  fprintf('%f\t%f\t%f\n',t,X(1,i),X(2,i));
end
t=[0:dt:T];
plot(t,X(1,:),'-p',t,X(2,:),'-*')
xlabel('time(s)');
ylabel('displacement(m)');
legend('DOF-1','DOF-2');
grid on;
```

The output is as follows:

time	X(1)	X(2)
0.000000	0.000000	0.000000
0.050000	0.000005	0.000312
0.100000	0.000017	0.002654
0.150000	0.000045	0.007027
0.200000	0.000102	0.013427
0.250000	0.000205	0.021853
0.300000	0.000372	0.032303
0.350000	0.000622	0.044774
0.400000	0.000976	0.059264
0.450000	0.001454	0.075768
0.500000	0.002075	0.094284
0.550000	0.002854	0.114806
0.600000	0.003808	0.137330
0.650000	0.004947	0.161851
0.700000	0.006278	0.188365
0.750000	0.007804	0.216864
0.800000	0.009526	0.247345
0.850000	0.011437	0.279799
0.900000	0.013529	0.314220
0.950000	0.015790	0.350601
1.000000	0.018203	0.388935

Figure E6.16 shows the plot of histories of two-degree of freedom.

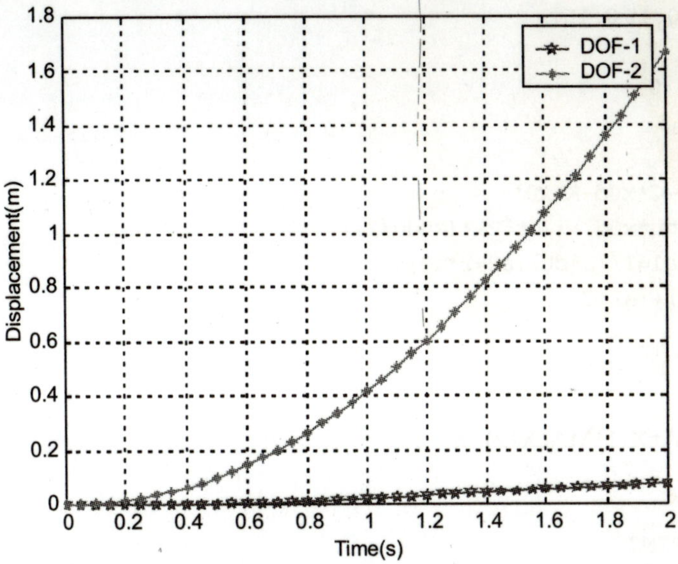

Fig. E6.16 MATLAB output Newmark method

Example E6.17: The numerical values of the mass, damping and stiffness are chosen as $M_1 = 1$, $M_2 = 10$, $C_1 = 0$, $C_2 = 0.15$, $K_1 = 19$ and $K_2 = 1$. The initial conditions are selected as zero and the forcing vector is

$$\begin{Bmatrix} F_1(t) \\ F_2(t) \end{Bmatrix} = \begin{Bmatrix} 0 \\ 5 \end{Bmatrix} \text{ for } t > 0$$

and
$$\begin{Bmatrix} F_1(t) \\ F_2(t) \end{Bmatrix} = \begin{Bmatrix} 0 \\ 0 \end{Bmatrix} \text{ for } t < 0$$

In matrix motion, these equations may be written as

$$\begin{bmatrix} M_1 & 0 \\ 0 & M_2 \end{bmatrix} \begin{bmatrix} \ddot{X}_1 \\ \ddot{X}_2 \end{bmatrix} + \begin{bmatrix} C_1 + C_2 & -C_2 \\ -C_2 & C_2 \end{bmatrix} \begin{bmatrix} \dot{X}_1 \\ \dot{X}_2 \end{bmatrix}$$

$$+ \begin{bmatrix} K_1 + K_2 & -K_2 \\ -K_2 & K_2 \end{bmatrix} \begin{Bmatrix} X_1 \\ X_2 \end{Bmatrix} + \begin{Bmatrix} -0.5K_2(X_2 - X_1)^3 \\ 0.5K_2(X_2 - X_1)^3 \end{Bmatrix} = \begin{Bmatrix} F_1 \\ F_2 \end{Bmatrix}$$

Take $\Delta t = 0.05$ sec. Use the central difference method and compute the response of the system.

Solution: Substituting the given values the following matrices is obtained:

$$M = \begin{bmatrix} 1 & 0 \\ 0 & 10 \end{bmatrix}, \; C = \begin{bmatrix} 0.15 & -0.15 \\ -0.15 & 0.15 \end{bmatrix} \; K = \begin{bmatrix} 20 & -1 \\ -1 & 1 \end{bmatrix}, F = \begin{Bmatrix} 0 \\ 5 \end{Bmatrix}$$

So, the non-linear spring force is added to the external force equation without confusion.

Complete MATLAB program is given below:

```
% INITIAL VALUES
 M=[1 0;0 10];
```

```
K=[20 -1;-1 1];
C=[0.15 -0.15;-0.15 0.15];
dt=0.05;
x0=[0;0];x0d=[0;0];
F0=[0;5];
T=2;
x0dd=inv(M)*(F0-C*x0d-K*x0);
      xprev=x0-(dt*x0d)+((dt^2)*(x0dd/2));
      a0=1/dt^2;a1=1/(2*dt);a2=2*a0;
      mbar=(a0*M)+(a1*C);
t=0;
v(:,1)=x0d;a(:,1)=x0dd;
i=1;
fprintf('time\t\tX(1)\t\tX(2)\n');
for t=0:dt:T+dt
X(:,i)=x0;
% NON-LINEAR SPRING
Fr=[-0.5*1*(X(2,i)-X(1,i))^3;0.5*1*(X(2,i)-X(1,i))^3];
F=F0+Fr;
Fbar=F+(a2*M-K)*x0+(a1*C-a0*M)*xprev;
x=inv(mbar)*Fbar;
xprev=x0;
x0=x;
fprintf('%f\t%f\t%f\n',t,X(1,i),X(2,i));
i=i+1;
p=i;
end
for i=2:p-1
if i<p-1
v(:,i)=(X(:,i+1)-X(:,i-1))*(1/(2*dt));
a(:,i)=(X(:,i+1)-2*X(:,i)+X(:,i-1))*(1/dt^2);
end
end
t=[0:dt:T+dt];
plot(t,X(1,:),'-p',t,X(2,:),'-*');
      xlabel('time(s)');
ylabel('displacement(m)');
legend('DOF-1','DOF-2',2);
grid on;
```

The output is as follows:

time	X(1)	X(2)
0.000000	0.000000	0.000000
0.050000	–0.000000	0.000625
0.100000	0.000011	0.002499
0.150000	0.000046	0.005620
0.200000	0.000121	0.009988
0.250000	0.000251	0.015599
0.300000	0.000453	0.022452
0.350000	0.000743	0.030543
0.400000	0.001134	0.039871
0.450000	0.001640	0.050433
0.500000	0.002270	0.062224

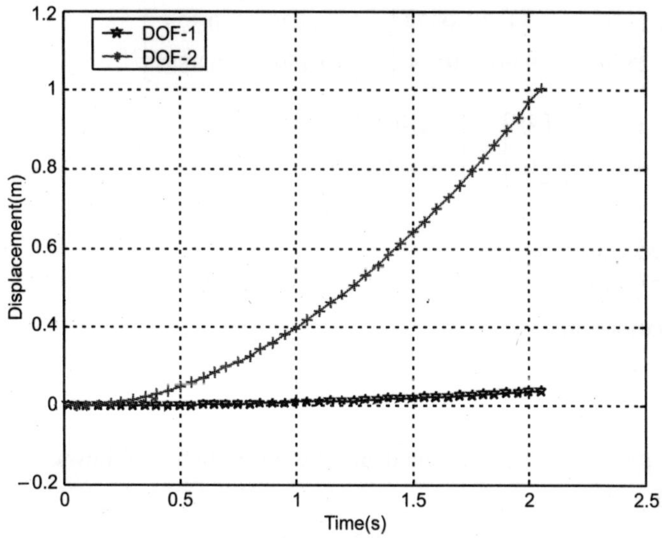

Fig. E6.17 MATLAB output

Example E6.18: Consider a simple system for which the governing equilibrium equations are

$$[M] = \begin{bmatrix} 2 & 0 \\ 0 & 1 \end{bmatrix}$$

$$[K] = \begin{bmatrix} 4 & -1 \\ -1 & 3 \end{bmatrix}$$

$$[C] = \begin{bmatrix} 0 & 0 \\ 0 & 0 \end{bmatrix}$$

and $F_1(t) = 0, F_2(t) = 10$

(*a*) calculate the transformation matrix for this system and thus establish the decoupled equations of equilibrium on the basis of mode shape vectors.

(*b*) compute the exact response by integrating each of the two decoupled equilibrium equations.

Solution:

(*a*) Transformation matrix of the system is obtained from eigenvalue problem.

Solving the undamped eigenvalue equation, we obtain eigenvector as

$$X = \begin{bmatrix} -0.8069 & 0.3437 \\ -0.5907 & -0.9391 \end{bmatrix} \text{ corresponding to eigenvalues } \lambda = \begin{bmatrix} 1.634 \\ 3.366 \end{bmatrix}$$

Find modal masses m_1= sqrt(X_1'MX_1) = 1.2850

m_2= sqrt(X_2'MX_2) = 1.0574

Now the transformation matrix is

$$\phi = \begin{bmatrix} -0.8069/1.2850 & 0.3437/1.0574 \\ -0.5907/1.2850 & -0.9391/1.0574 \end{bmatrix} = \begin{bmatrix} -0.628 & 0.325 \\ -0.4597 & -0.8881 \end{bmatrix}$$

$$\phi' F = \begin{bmatrix} -0.628 & 0.325 \\ -0.4597 & -0.8881 \end{bmatrix}' \begin{bmatrix} 0 \\ 10 \end{bmatrix} = \begin{bmatrix} -4.597 \\ -8.8808 \end{bmatrix}$$

Thus the decoupled equations are

[ϕ'$M\phi$] + [ϕ'$K\phi$] U = ϕ'F

That is modal equations are:

$\ddot{u}_1 + 1.634\, u_1 = -4.597$

$\ddot{u}_2 + 3.366\, u_2 = -8.8808$

(*b*) Each of these equations is solved independently by integration as follows:

Solution is u = C.F + P.I.,

where C.F. = complementary function = $e^{-\xi\omega_n t}$ $(A \cos \omega_d t + B \sin \omega_d t)$ and

P.I. = Particular integral = f/ω_n^2

The constants A and B are obtained with initial condition $u(0)$ and $\dot{u}(0)$

$u(t) = \xi\omega_n(A \cos \omega_d t + B \sin \omega_d t) + f/\omega_n^2$

$\dot{u} = e(B\omega_d - \xi\omega_n A) \cos \omega_d t - (A\omega_d + \xi\omega_n B)\sin \omega_d t)$

Hence $u(0) = A + f/\omega_n^2$ or $A = u(0) - f/\omega_n^2$

and $\dot{u}(0) = (B\omega_d - \xi\omega_n A)$ or $B = [\dot{u}(0) + \xi\omega_n A]/\omega_d$

If there is no damping $\xi = 0$, thus $B = \dot{u}(0)/\omega_n$

Also with zero initial conditions we can write the solutions as follows:

$u_1 = f_1/\,\omega_{n2}^2\,(1 - \cos\,\omega_{n1}t)$ and $u_2 = f_2/\,\omega_{n2}^2\,(1 - \cos\,\omega_{n2}t)$

or $u_1 = [-4.597/1.634]\ (1 - \cos\,1.2783t)$ and $u_2 = [-\,8.8808/3.366]\ (1 - \cos\,1.8347t)$

$= -\,2.8133\ (1 - \cos\,1.2783t)$ $\qquad = -\,2.6384\ (1 - \cos\,1.8347t)$

Finally the response in original coordinates is obtained as follows:

$$X = \phi U = \begin{bmatrix} -0.628 & 0.325 \\ -0.4597 & -0.8881 \end{bmatrix} \begin{bmatrix} -2.8133(1-\cos 1.2783t) \\ -2.6384(1-\cos 1.8347t) \end{bmatrix}$$

$$= \begin{bmatrix} 0.9091(1-\cos 1.2783t) \\ 3.6364(1-\cos 1.8347t) \end{bmatrix}$$

The following program is used to obtain the transformation matrix:

```
M=[2 0;0 1];
K=[4 -1;-1 3];
F=[0;10];
[u,W]=eig(K,M);
for i=1:2
 wn(i)=sqrt(W(i,i));
end
[w,I]=sort(wn);
for j=1:2
U(:,j)=u(:,I(j)); %ARRANGE MODAL VECTORS IN ASCENDING ORDER
end
%MODAL MASSES
m1=sqrt(U(:,1)'*M*U(:,1));
m2=sqrt(U(:,2)'*M*U(:,2));
phi=[U(:,1)/m1;U(:,2)/m2]; %transformation matrix

%PLOT RESPONSES
t=[0:0.1:5];
u1=-2.8133*(1-cos(1.2783*t));u2=-2.6384*(1-cos(1.8347*t));
x1=0.9091*(1-cos(1.2783*t));x2=3.6364*(1-cos(1.8347*t));
subplot(2,1,1); %SUB-PLOT-1
plot(t,u1,'-p',t,u2,'-*');
```

```
title('\bfPlot of Modal amplitudes');
xlabel('\bfTime(s)');
legend('At frequency-1=1.2783 rad/s','At frequency-2=1.8347 rad/s');
grid on;
subplot(2,1,2);       % SUB-PLOT-2
plot(t,x1,'-p',t,x2,'-*');
title('\bfPlot of Original amplitudes');
xlabel('\bfTime(s)');
legend('At DOF-1', 'At DOF-2');
grid on;
```

The output of the program is shown in Fig. E6.18.

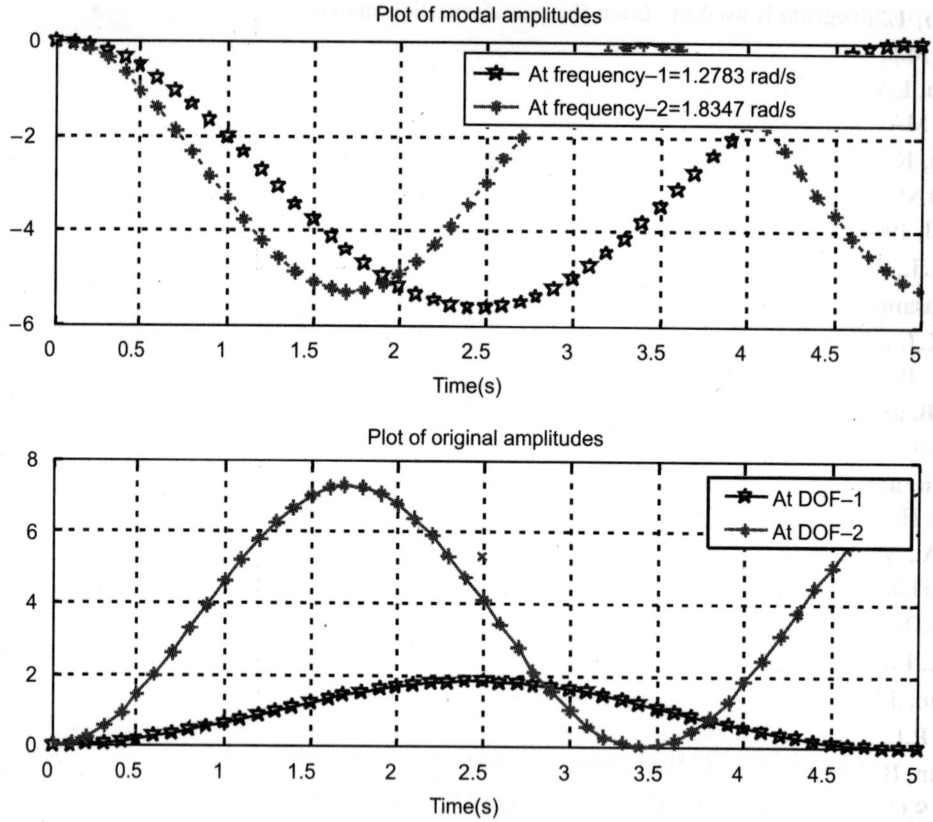

Fig. E6.18 Output of the MATLAB program

REFERENCES

Abramowitz, M. and Stegun, I., *Handbook of Mathematical Functions,* Dover Press, New York, 1964.

Akai, T.J., *Applied Numerical Methods for Engineers*, Wiley, New York, NY, 1993.

Al-Khafaji, A.W. and Tooley, J.R., *Numerical Methods in Engineering Practice*, Holt, Rinehart and Winston, New York, 1986.

Allen, M. and Iaacson, E., *Numerical Analysis for Applied Science*, Wiley, New York, 1998.

Ames, W.F., *Numerical Methods for Partial Differential Equations*, 3rd ed., Academic Press, New York, 1992.

Ascher,U., Mattheij, R. and Russell, R., *Numerical Solution of Boundary Value Problems for Ordinary Differential Equations,* Prentice-Hall, Englewood Cliffs, NJ, 1988.

Atkinson, K. and Han, W., *Elementary Numerical Analysis*, 3rd ed., Wiley, New York, 2004.

Atkinson, K.E., *An Introduction to Numerical Analysis*, 2nd ed., Wiley, New York, NY, 1993.

Atkinson, L.V. and Harley, P.J., *Introduction to Numerical Methods with PASCAL*, Addison-Wesley, Reading, MA, 1984.

Atkinson, L.V., Harley, P.J. and Hudson, J.D., *Numerical Methods with FORTRAN 77*, Addison-Wesley, Reading, MA, 1989.

Axelsson, K., *Iterative Solution Methods,* Cambridge University Press, Cambridge, UK, 1994.

Ayyub, B.M. and McCuen, R.H., *Numerical Methods for Engineers*, Prentice-Hall, Upper Saddle River, New Jersey, NJ, 1996.

Baker, A.J., *Finite Element Computational Fluid Mechanics*, McGraw-Hill, New York, 1983.

Balagurusamy, E., *Numerical Methods*, Tata McGraw-Hill, New Delhi, India, 2002.

Bathe, K.J. and Wilson, E.L., *Numerical Methods in Finite Element Analysis*, Prentice-Hall, Englewood Cliffs, NJ, 1976.

Bhat, R.B. and Chakraverty, S., *Numerical Analysis in Engineering*, Narosa Publishing House, New Delhi, India, 2004.

Bhat, R.B. and Gouw, G.J., *Numerical Methods in Engineering*, Simon and Schuster Custom Publishing, Needham Heights, MA, 1996.

Bjorck, A., *Numerical Methods for Least Squares Problems*, Society for Industrial and Applied Mathematics (SIAM), Philadelphia, PA, 1996.

Booth, A.D., *Numerical Methods*, Academic Press, New York, 1958.

Brice, C., Luther, H.A and Wilkes, J.O., *Applied Numerical Methods*, New York, NY, 1969.

Buchanan, J.L. and Turner, P.R., *Numerical Methods and Analysis,* McGraw-Hill, New York, 1992.

Burden, R.L. and Faires, J.D., *Numerical Analysis,* 6th ed., Brooks/Cole, Pacific Grove, 1997.

Carnahan, B., Luther, A. and Wilkes, J.O., *Applied Numerical Methods,* Wiley, New York, 1969.

Chapra, S.C. and Canale, R.P., *Introduction to Computing for Engineers*, 2nd ed., McGraw-Hill, New York, 1994.

Chapra, S.C., and Canale, R.P., *Numerical Methods for Engineers with Personal Computers*, McGraw-Hill, New York, 1985.

Chapra, S.C., *Applied Numerical Methods with MATLAB for Engineers and Scientists*, McGraw-Hill, New York, 2005.

Chapra, S.C., *Numerical Methods for Engineers with Software and Programming Applications*, 4th ed., McGraw-Hill, New York, NY, 2002.

Cheney, W. and Kincaid, D., *Numerical Mathematics and Computing*, 2nd ed., Brooks/Cole, Monterey, CA, 1994.

Chui, C., *An Introduction to Wavelets*, Academic Press, Burlington, MA, 1992.

Consatantinides, A., *Applied Numerical Methods with Personal Computers*, McGraw-Hill, New York, 1987.

Conte, S.D., and DeBoor, C.W., *Elementary Numerical Analysis: An Algorithm Approach*, 2nd ed., McGraw-Hill, New York, NY, 1972.

Dahlquist, G. and Bjorck, A., *Numerical Methods*, Prentice-Hall, Englewood Cliffs, NJ, 1974.

Davis, P. and Rabinowitz, P., *Methods of Numerical Integration,* Academic Press, 2nd ed., New York, 1998.

Demmel, J.W., *Applied Numerical Linear Algebra*, Society for Industrial and Applied Mathematics (SIAM), Philadelphia, PA, 1997.

Dennis, J.E. and Schnabel, R.B., *Numerical Methods for Unconstrained Optimization and Non-linear Equations,* Society for Industrial and Applied Mathematics (SIAM), Philadelphia, PA, 1996.

Epperson, J.F., *An Introduction to Numerical Methods and Analysis*, Wiley, New York, NY, 2001.

Fadeev, D.K., and Fadeeva, V.N., *Computational Methods of Linear Algebra*, Freeman, San Francisco, 1963.

Fadeeva, V.N., (Trans. Curtis D. Benster), *Computational Methods of Linear Algebra,* Dover, New York, 1959.

Fatunla, S.O., *Numerical Methods for Initial Value Problems in Ordinary Differential Equations*, Academic Press, San Diego, 1988.

Ferziger, J.H., *Numerical Methods for Engineering Applications*, 2nd ed., Wiley, New York, NY, 1998.

Forbear, C. E., *Introduction to Numerical Analysis*, Addison-Wesley, Reading, MA, 1969.

Forsythe, G.E., and Wasow, W.R., *Finite-Difference Methods for Partial Differential Equations*, Wiley, New York, 1960.

Forsythe, G.E., Malcolm, M.A. and Moler, C.B., *Computer methods for Mathematical Computation,* Prentice-Hall, Englewood Cliffs, NJ, 1977.

Froberg, C.E., *Introduction to Numerical Analysis*, Addison-Wesley, Reading, MA, 1965.

Gautschi, W., *Numerical Analysis: An Introduction*, Birkhauser, Boston, MA, 1997.

Gear, C.W., *Numerical Initial Value Problems in Ordinary Differential Equations,* Prentice-Hall, Englewood Cliffs, NJ, 1971.

Gerald, C.F. and Wheatley, P.O., *Applied Numerical Analysis*, 5th ed., Addison-Wesley, Reading, MA, 1994.

Gladwell, J. and Wait, R., *A Survey of Numerical Methods of Partial Differential Equations,* Oxford University Press, New York, 1979.

Goldberg, D.E., *Genetic Algorithms in Search, Optimization and Machine Learning,* Addison-Wesley, Reading, MA, 1989.

Golub, G.H. and Van Loan, C.F., *Matrix Computations*, 3rd ed., John Hopkins University Press, Baltimore, MD, 1996.

Greenbaum, A., *Iterative Methods for Solving Linear Systems*, Society for Industrial and Applied Mathematics (SIAM), Philadelphia, PA, 1997.

Griffiths, D.V. and Smith, I.M., *Numerical Methods for Engineers,* Oxford University Press, 1991.

Guest, P.G., *Numerical Methods of Curve Fitting*, Cambridge University Press, New York, 1961.

Hager, W.W., *Applied Numerical Algebra*, Prentice-Hall, Upper Saddle River, NJ, 1998.

Hamming, R.W., *Numerical Methods for Scientists and Engineers*, 2nd ed., McGraw-Hill, New York, 1973.

Henrici, P.H., *Elements of Numerical Analysis,* Wiley, New York, 1964.

Higham, N.J., *Accuracy and Stability of Numerical Algorithms*, Society for Industrial and Applied Mathematics (SIAM), Philadelphia, PA, 1996.

Hildebrand, F.B., *Introduction to Numerical Analysis*, 2nd ed., McGraw-Hill, New York, NY, 1974.

Hoffman, J., *Numerical Methods for Engineers and Scientists*, McGraw-Hill, New York, 1992.

Hornbeck, R.W., *Numerical Methods*, Quantum, New York, 1975.

Householder, A.S., *Principles of Numerical Analysis*, McGraw-Hill, New York, 1953.

Householder, A.S., *The Theory of Matrices in Numerical Analysis*, Blaisdell, New York, 1964.

Iserles, A., *A First Course in the Numerical Analysis of Differential Equations,* Cambridge University Press, New York, 1996.

Issaccson, E. and Keller, H.B. and Bishop, H., *Analysis of Numerical Methods*, Wiley, New York, 1966.

Jacobs, D. (ed.), *The State of the Art in Numerical Analysis*, Academic Press, London, 1977.

Jacques, I. and Colin, J., *Numerical Analysis*, Chapman and Hall, New York, 1987.

Jain, M.K., *Numerical Analysis for Scientists and Engineers*, S.B.W. Publishers, New Delhi, India, 1971.

James, M.L., Smith, G.M. and Wolford, J.C., *Applied Numerical Methods for Digital Computations with FORTRAN and CSMP*, 3rd ed., Harper & Row, New York, 1985.

Johnson, L.W., Riess, R.D., *Numerical Analysis*, 2nd ed., Addison-Wesley, Reading, MA, 1982.

Johnston, R.L., *Numerical Methods: A Software Approach*, Wiley, New York, 1982.

Kahaneer, D., Moher, C. and Nash, S., *Numerical Methods and Software*, Prentice-Hall, Englewood Cliffs, NJ, 1989.

Keller, H.B., *Numerical Methods for Two-Point Boundary Value Problems*, Wiley, New York, 1968.

Kelley, C.T., *Iterative Methods of Optimization*, Society for Industrial and Applied Mathematics (SIAM), Philadelphia, PA, 1999.

Kharab, A. and Guenther, R.B., *An Introduction to Numerical Methods—A MATLAB Approach,* CRC Press, Boca Raton, FL, 2001.

Kincaid, D. and Cheney, W., *Numerical Analysis: Mathematics of Scientific Computing,* Brooks/Cole, Pacific Grove, CA, 1996.

Kress, R., *Numerical Analysis*, Springer-Verlag, New York, 1998.

Krishnamurthy, E.V. and Sen, S.K., *Numerical Algorithms*, East-West Publishers, New Delhi, India, 1986.

Krommer, A.R. and Ueberhuber, C.W., *Computational Integration*, Society for Industrial and Applied Mathematics (SIAM), Philadelphia, PA, 1998.

Lambert, J.D., *Numerical Methods for Ordinary Differential Equations—The Initial Value Problems,* Wiley, New York, NY, 1991.

Lapidus, L. and Pinder, G.F., *Numerical Solution of Ordinary Differential Equations in Science and Engineering*, Wiley, New York, 1981.

Lapidus, L. and Seinfield, J.H., *Numerical Solution of Partial Differential Equations*, Academic Press, New York, 1971.

Lastman, G.J. and Sinha, N.K., *Microcomputer Based Numerical Methods for Science and Engineering,* Saunders College Publishing, New York, NY, 1989.

Levy, H. and Baggott, E.A., *Numerical Solutions of Differential Equations,* Dover, New York, 1950.

Maron, M.J., *Numerical Analysis, A Practical Approach,* Macmillan, New York, 1982.

Mathews, J.H., *Numerical Methods for Mathematics, Science and Engineering,* 2nd ed., Prentice-Hall of India, New Delhi, India, 1994.

Milne, W.E., *Numerical Solution of Differential Equations,* Wiley, New York, 1953.

Moin, P., *Fundamentals of Engineering Numerical Analysis,* Cambridge University Press, New York, 2001.

Morton, K.W. and Mayers, D.F., *Numerical Solution of Partial Differential Equations: An Introduction,* Cambridge University Press, Cambridge, UK, 1994.

Myron, A. and Issacson, E.L., *Numerical Analysis for Applied Science,* Wiley, Hoboken, NJ, 1998.

Na, T.Y., *Computational Methods in Engineering Boundary Value Problems,* Academic Press, New York, 1979.

Nakamura, S., *Computational Methods in Engineering and Science,* Wiley, New York, NY, 1977.

Nielson, K.L., *Methods in Numerical Analysis,* Macmillan Company, New York, 1964.

Noble, B., *Numerical Methods,* Vol. 2, Oliver and Boyd, Edinburgh, 1964.

Nocedal, J. and Wright, S.J., *Numerical Optimization,* Springer-Verlag, New York, 1999.

Ortega, J.M., *Numerical Analysis—A Second Course,* Academic Press, New York, NY, 1972.

Powell, M., *Approximation Theory and Methods,* Cambridge University Press, Cambridge, UK, 1981.

Press, W.H., Teukolsky, S.A., Vetterling, W.T. and Flannery, B.P., *Numerical Recipes: The Art of Scientific Computing,* 2nd ed., Cambridge University Press, New York, 1992.

Quarteroni, A., Sacco, R., and Saleri, F., *Numerical Mathematics,* Springer-Verlag, New York, 2000.

Ralston, A. and Rabinowitz, P., *A First Course in Numerical Analysis,* 2nd ed., McGraw-Hill, New York, 1978.

Ralston, A. and Wilf, H.S., eds., *Mathematical Methods for Digital Computers,* Vol. 1 and 2, Wiley, New York, 1967.

Rao, K.S., *Numerical Methods for Scientists and Engineers,* Prentice-Hall, New Delhi, India, 2001.

Rao, S.S., *Applied Numerical Methods for Engineers and Scientists,* Prentice-Hall, Upper Saddle River, New Jersey, NJ, 2002.

Ratschek, H., and Rokne, J., *Computer Methods for the Range of Functions,* Ellis Horwood, Chichester, 1984.

Rice, J.R., *Numerical Methods, Software and Analysis,* McGraw-Hill, New York, 1983.

Sastry, S.S., *Introductory Methods of Numerical Analysis,* Prentice-Hall of India, New Delhi, India, 2001.

Scarborough, J.B., *Numerical Mathematical Analysis,* 6th ed., John Hopkins Press, Baltimore, MD, 1966.

Scheid, F., *Schaum's Outline of Theory and Problems in Numerical Analysis,* 2nd ed., Schaum's Outline Series, McGraw-Hill, New York, 1988.

Schiesser, W.E., *Computational Mathematics in Engineering and Applied Science,* CRC Press, Boca Raton, FL, 1994.

Shampine, L.F., *Numerical Solution of Ordinary Differential Equations,* Chapman and Hall, New York, 1994.

Sharma, J.N., *Numerical Methods for Engineers and Scientists,* Narosa Publishing House, New Delhi, India, 2004.

Smith, G.D., *Numerical Solution of Partial Differential Equations: Finite Difference Methods*, 3rd ed., Oxford University Press, Oxford, 1985.

Smith, W.A., *Elementary Numerical Analysis*, Prentice-Hall, Englewood Cliffs, NJ, 1986.

Snyder, M.A., *Chebyshev Methods in Numerical Approximation*, Prentice-Hall, Englewood Cliffs, NJ, 1966.

Stanton, R.G., *Numerical Methods for Science and Engineering*, Prentice-Hall of India, New Delhi, India, 1967.

Stark, P.A., *Introduction to Numerical Methods*, Macmillan, New York, 1970.

Stewart, G.W., *Matrix Algorithms,* Vol. 1, *Basic Decompositions,* Society for Industrial and Applied Mathematics (SIAM), Philadelphia, PA, 1998.

Stoer, J., and Bulirsch, R., *Introduction to Numerical Analysis*, Springer-Verlag, New York, 1980.

Stroud, A., and Secrets, D., *Gaussian Quadrature Formulas*, Prentice-Hall, Englewood Cliffs, 1966.

Stroud, A.H., *Numerical Quadrature and Solution of Ordinary Differential Equations*, Springer-Verlag, New York, 1974.

Taylor, J.R., *An Introduction to Error Analysis*, University Science Books, Mill Valley, CA, 1982.

Traub, J.F., *Iterative Methods for the Solution of Equations*, Prentice-Hall, Englewood Cliffs, NJ, 1964.

Trefethen, L.N. and Bau, D., *Numerical Linear Algebra*, Society for Industrial and Applied Mathematics (SIAM), Philadelphia, PA, 1997.

Tyrtyshnikov, E.E., *A Brief Introduction to Numerical Analysis*, Birkhauser, Boston, 1997.

Ueberhuber, C.W., *Numerical Computation 1: Methods, Software, and Analysis*, Springer-Verlag, New York, 1997.

Ueberhuber, C.W., *Numerical Computation 2: Methods, Software, and Analysis*, Springer-Verlag, New York, 1997.

Vemuri, V. and Karplus, W.J., *Digital Computer Treatment of Partial Differential Equations,* Prentice-Hall, Englewood Cliffs, NJ, 1981.

Vichnevetsky, R., *Computer Methods for Partial Differential Equations,* Vol. 1: *Elliptic Equations and the Finite Element Method*, Prentice-Hall, Englewood Cliffs, NJ, 1981.

Vichnevetsky, R., *Computer Methods for Partial Differential Equations,* Vol. 2: *Initial Value Problems,* Prentice-Hall, Englewood Cliffs, NJ, 1982.

Wendroff, B., *Theoretical Numerical Analysis*, Academic Press, New York, 1966.

Wilkinson, J.H., *Rounding Errors in Algebraic Processes*, Dover, New York, 1994.

Yokowitz, S. and Szidarovsky, F., *An Introduction to Numerical Computation*, Macmillan, New York, 1986.

Yong, D.M., and Gregory, R.T., *A Survey of Numerical Mathematics,* Vol. 1 and 2, Addison-Wesley, Reading, MA, 1972.

Young, D., *Iterative Solution for Large Linear Systems,* Academic Press, New York, 1971.

PROBLEMS

P6.1: Determine the vibratory response of an undamped single degree of freedom system with $M = 2$, and $K = 2$. Assume the initial conditions for the velocity and displacement at $t = 0$ to be equal to 1. Use the Runge-Kutta method with a time step of 0.5 seconds.

P6.2: Determine the free vibratory response of a viscously damped single degree of freedom system with $M = C = K = 2$. Assume the initial conditions for the velocity and displacement at $t = 0$ to be equal to 1. Use the fourth-order Runge-Kutta method with time step of 0.5 seconds.

P6.3: Solve Problem P6.2 with $C = 3$ using the fourth-order Runge-Kutta method.

P6.4: Find the solution of the differential equation for an undamped single degree of freedom system with $M = 5$, $C = 2$ and $K = 300$ and the forcing function is defined as

$$F(t) = 200 \text{ for } 0 < t < 0.2$$

and $$F(t) = (1000 - 2000t)/3 \quad \text{for } 0.2 < t < 0.5$$

with the initial conditions of displacement and velocity as zero. Use the fourth-order Runge-Kutta method.

P6.5: Find the vibratory response of a single degree of freedom system with $M = 1$, $C = 0.2$, $K = 1$, and $F(t) = 5$ with the initial conditions for velocity and displacement as zero. Take time step of 0.5 seconds. Use the fourth order Runge-Kutta method.

P6.6: Find the response of the two degree of freedom system when $F_1(t) = 0$ and $F_2(t) = 10$, using the central difference method. The mass, stiffness and damping matrices for this system as shown in Fig. P6.5 are given as

$$[M] = \begin{bmatrix} 1 & 0 \\ 0 & 10 \end{bmatrix}, \ [K] = \begin{bmatrix} 21 & -1 \\ -1 & 1 \end{bmatrix}, \ [C] = \begin{bmatrix} 0.5 & -0.1 \\ -0.1 & 0.1 \end{bmatrix}$$

All the initial conditions are given as zero and use the central difference method with $\Delta t = 0.001$ seconds.

P6.7: Solve Problem P6.6 using the fourth-order Runge-Kutta method

P6.8: Solve Problem P6.6 using the Houbolt method.

P6.9: Solve Problem P6.6 by the Park Stiffly Stable method.

P6.10: Solve Problem P6.6 by the Wilson Theta method with theta = 1.5.

P6.11: Solve Problem P6.6 by the Newmark Beta method with alpha = 0.5 and beta = 1/6.

P6.12: Solve Problem P6.6 using the two-cycle iteration with trapezoidal rule.

P6.13: Find the response of the two degree of freedom system when $F_1(t) = 0$ and $F_2(t) = 10$, using the central difference method. The mass, stiffness and damping matrices for this system are given as

$$[M] = \begin{bmatrix} 1 & 0 \\ 0 & 2 \end{bmatrix}, \ [K] = \begin{bmatrix} 6 & -2 \\ -2 & 8 \end{bmatrix}, \ [C] = \begin{bmatrix} 0 & 0 \\ 0 & 0 \end{bmatrix}$$

All the initial conditions are given as zero and $\Delta t = 0.2421$ seconds.

P6.14: Find the response of the two degree of freedom system when $F_1(t) = 0$ and $F_2(t) = 0$, using the Wilson-theta method. The mass, stiffness and damping matrices for this system are given as

$$[M]=\begin{bmatrix}1 & 0\\0 & 1\end{bmatrix},\quad [K]=\begin{bmatrix}2 & 2\\2 & 5\end{bmatrix},\quad [C]=\begin{bmatrix}0 & 0\\0 & 0\end{bmatrix}$$

Assuming initial conditions to be

$$x_0=\begin{Bmatrix}1\\0\end{Bmatrix},\ \dot{x}_0=\begin{Bmatrix}0\\0\end{Bmatrix} \text{ and } \Delta t = 0.25 \text{ seconds.}$$

P6.15: Solve Problem P6.14 using Newmark's beta method, alpha = 0.25 and beta = 0.5.

P6.16: Find the response of the two degree of freedom system when $F_1(t) = \sin 2t$ and $F_2(t) = \sin 2t$, using the fourth-order Runge-Kutta method. The differential equations of this system are given as

$$\begin{bmatrix}2 & 0\\0 & 1\end{bmatrix}\begin{Bmatrix}\ddot{x}_1\\\ddot{x}_2\end{Bmatrix}+\begin{bmatrix}3 & -0.5\\-0.5 & 0.5\end{bmatrix}\begin{Bmatrix}\dot{x}_1\\\dot{x}_2\end{Bmatrix}+\begin{bmatrix}3 & -1\\-1 & 1\end{bmatrix}\begin{Bmatrix}x_1\\x_2\end{Bmatrix}=\begin{bmatrix}1\\1\end{bmatrix}\sin 2t$$

with the initial conditions $x_0=\begin{Bmatrix}0\\0.1\end{Bmatrix},\ \dot{x}_0=\begin{Bmatrix}1\\0\end{Bmatrix}$ m/s.

❍ ❍ ❍

CHAPTER 7

ENGINEERING MECHANICS

7.1 INTRODUCTION

Engineering mechanics is a science that considers the motion of bodies under the action of forces and the effects of forces on that motion. Mechanics includes *statics* and *dynamics*. Statics deals with the special case of a body at rest or a body that moves with constant velocity. A body at rest or moving with constant velocity is said to be in *equilibrium*. This is sometimes also called as static equilibrium. When the body moves with finite velocity or acceleration, the principles of statics are no longer applicable. The mechanics of such a system is called *dynamics*. When the body has no rotational motion, it is called as particle. Each point on a rigid body is always at a constant distance from any other point in the body. Dynamics is further divided into *kinematics* and *kinetics*. *Kinematics* defines the relationships among displacement, velocity and acceleration of a moving body. *Kinetics* defines the relationship between the forces that act on a body and the motion of the body. Analysis of the bodies can either be conducted in plane or in three-dimensions. A rigid body in space has six degree of freedom. This chapter provides a brief review of various topics in mechanics.

7.2 NEWTONIAN MECHANICS

Collectively, the study of statics and dynamics is called *classical mechanics*. Classical mechanics treats the motion of bodies of ordinary size that move at speeds that are small compared to the speed of light. Newton (1642–1727) formulated the law of universal gravitation and introduced the concepts of force and mass. Newton formulated the three laws of motion that are the basis of applications in mechanics. The classical mechanics is often called *Newtonian mechanics*.

7.3 NEWTON S LAWS OF MOTION

Newton's laws are fundamentally applicable directly to a particle that is a body which may be treated as having point mass. Newton's laws may be stated in terms of a particle parameters as follows:

First Law: In the absence of applied forces, a particle originally at rest or moving with constant speed in a straight line will remain at rest or continue to move with constant speed in a straight line.

Second Law: If a particle is subjected to a force, the particle will accelerate. The acceleration of the particle will be in the direction of the force, and the magnitude of the acceleration will be proportional to the force and inversely proportional to the mass of the particle.

Newton's second law can be expressed in the form

$$a = \frac{F}{m} \quad \text{...(7.1)}$$

where F = force

m = mass

a = acceleration

Newton's second law is the basis for the study of kinetics of a particle.

Third Law: For every action, there is an equal and opposite reaction, or the mutual forces exerted by two particles on each other are always equal and oppositely directed.

7.4 RESULTANTS OF COPLANAR FORCE SYSTEMS

In statics, it is often necessary to find the state of equilibrium or the resultant of several forces acting in plane. In coplanar system, the resultant R for a concurrent forces is given by

$$R = \sqrt{(\Sigma F_x)^2 + (\Sigma F_y)^2}$$

and

$$\theta_x = \tan^{-1}\left[\frac{\Sigma F_y}{\Sigma F_x}\right] \quad \text{...(7.2)}$$

where $\Sigma F_x, \Sigma F_y$ = algebraic sums of the x and y components of the forces of the system respectively.

θ_x = the angle that the resultant R makes with the x-axis.

For a parallel system, the resultant R is given by

$$R = \Sigma F$$

and

$$R\bar{a} = \Sigma M_O \quad \text{...(7.3)}$$

where ΣF = algebraic sum of the forces of the system

O = any moment center in the plane

$\bar{a}$ = perpendicular distance from the moment center O to the resultant R

$R\bar{a}$ = moment of R with respect to O

ΣM_O = algebraic sum of the moments of the forces of the system with respect to O

The resultant R for a non-concurrent and non-parallel system is given by

$$R = \sqrt{(\Sigma F_x)^2 + (\Sigma F_y)^2}$$

and $\theta_x = \tan^{-1}\left[\dfrac{\Sigma F_y}{\Sigma F_x}\right]$ ...(7.4)

where ΣF_x, ΣF_y = algebraic sums of the x and y components of the forces of the system respectively

θ_x = the angle that the resultant R makes with the x-axis.

The action of the line of the resultant force is given by

$$R\bar{a} = \Sigma M_o \quad ...(7.5)$$

where O = any moment center in the plane

$\bar{a}$ = perpendicular distance from the moment center O to the resultant R

$R\bar{a}$ = moment of R with respect to O

ΣM_o = algebraic sum of the moments of the forces of the system with respect to O.

7.5 RESULTANTS OF NON-COPLANAR FORCE SYSTEMS

In non-coplanar force systems, the forces are neither all concurrent nor in parallel. The resultant R for a concurrent system is given by

$$R = \sqrt{(\Sigma F_x)^2 + (\Sigma F_y)^2 + (\Sigma F_z)^2} \quad ...(7.6)$$

with the direction cosines

$$\cos\theta_x = \frac{\Sigma F_x}{R},\ \cos\theta_y = \frac{\Sigma F_y}{R} \text{ and } \cos\theta_z = \frac{\Sigma F_z}{R}$$

where ΣF_x, ΣF_y, ΣF_z = algebraic sums of the x, y and z components of the forces of the system respectively.

For a parallel system, the resultant R is given by

$$R = \Sigma F$$

$$R\bar{x} = \Sigma M_z \quad ...(7.7)$$

$$R\bar{z} = \Sigma M_x$$

where ΣF = algebraic sum of the forces of the system

$\bar{x}$ = perpendicular distance from the yz plane to the resultant

$\bar{z}$ = perpendicular distance from the xy plane to the resultant

ΣM_x, ΣM_z = algebraic sum of the moments of the forces of the system about the x and z axes respectively.

If $\Sigma F = 0$, thė resultant couple C when exists is given by

$$C = \sqrt{(\Sigma M_x)^2 + (\Sigma M_z)^2}$$

and $$\phi = \tan^{-1}\left[\frac{\Sigma M_z}{\Sigma M_x}\right] \qquad ...(7.8)$$

where ϕ is the angle that the vector representing the resultant couple makes with the x-axis.

The magnitude of the resultant R of the non-concurrent system at the origin (x, y and z axes is placed with their origin at the base point) is given by

$$R = \sqrt{(\Sigma F_x)^2 + (\Sigma F_y)^2 + (\Sigma F_z)^2} \qquad ...(7.9)$$

with the direction cosines

$$\cos\theta_x = \frac{\Sigma F_x}{R}, \cos\theta_y = \frac{\Sigma F_y}{R} \text{ and } \cos\theta_z = \frac{\Sigma F_z}{R} \qquad ...(7.10)$$

The magnitude of the resulting couple C is given by

$$C = \sqrt{(\Sigma M_x)^2 + (\Sigma M_y)^2 + (\Sigma M_z)^2} \qquad ...(7.11)$$

with the direction cosines

$$\cos\phi_x = \frac{\Sigma M_x}{C}, \cos\phi_y = \frac{\Sigma M_y}{C} \text{ and } \cos\phi_z = \frac{\Sigma M_z}{C} \qquad ...(7.12)$$

where ΣM_x, ΣM_y, ΣM_z = algebraic sums of the moments of the forces of the system about x, y and z axes respectively.

ϕ_x, ϕ_y, ϕ_z = angles which the vector representing the couple C makes with the x, y and z axes respectively.

7.6 EQUILIBRIUM OF COPLANAR FORCE SYSTEMS

The necessary and sufficient conditions for the equilibrium of a coplanar force system are:

$$R = \Sigma F = 0$$

and $$C = \Sigma M = 0 \qquad ...(7.13)$$

where ΣF = vector sum of all forces of the system

ΣM = vector sum of the moments of all the forces of the system.

For concurrent system, any of the following sets of equations ensures equilibrium (the resultant is zero). The concurrency is assumed at the origin.

Set 1: $\Sigma F_x = 0$

$\Sigma F_y = 0$

Set 2: $\Sigma F_x = 0$

$\Sigma M_A = 0 \qquad ...(7.14)$

(A may be chosen any place in the plane except on the y-axis)

Set 3: $\Sigma M_A = 0$

$\Sigma M_B = 0$

(A and B may be chosen any place in the plane except A, B and the origin do not lie on the same straight line)

where ΣF_x, ΣF_y = algebraic sum of the x and y components of the forces of the system respectively.

ΣM_A, ΣM_B = algebraic sum of the moments of the forces of the system about A and B respectively.

For parallel system, any of the following sets of equations ensures equilibrium (the resultant is neither a force nor a couple).

Set 1: $\Sigma F = 0$

$$\Sigma M_A = 0 \qquad \text{...(7.15)}$$

Set 2: $\Sigma M_A = 0$

$\Sigma M_B = 0$

(A and B may be chosen any place in the plane provided in the line joining A and B is not parallel to the forces of the system)

where ΣF = algebraic sum of the forces of the system parallel to the action lines of the forces

ΣM_A, ΣM_B = algebraic sum of the moments of the forces of the system about A and B respectively.

For non-concurrent and non-parallel system, any of the following sets of equations ensures equilibrium (the resultant is neither a force nor a couple).

Set 1: $\Sigma F_x = 0$

$\Sigma F_y = 0$

$$\Sigma M_A = 0 \qquad \text{...(7.16)}$$

Set 2: $\Sigma F_x = 0$

$\Sigma M_A = 0$

$$\Sigma M_B = 0 \qquad \text{...(7.17)}$$

(Provided that the line joining A and B is not perpendicular to the x-axis)

Set 3: $\Sigma M_A = 0$

$\Sigma M_B = 0$

$$\Sigma M_C = 0 \qquad \text{...(7.18)}$$

(Provided that A, B and C do not lie on the same straight line)

where ΣF_x, ΣF_y, ΣF_z = algebraic sum of the x; y and z components of the forces respectively

ΣM_A, ΣM_B, ΣM_C = algebraic sum of the moments of the forces of the system about any three points A, B and C in the plane respectively.

7.7 EQUILIBRIUM OF NON-COPLANAR FORCE SYSTEM

The necessary and sufficient conditions that R and C be zero vectors are given by

$$R = \Sigma F = 0$$

and $$C = \Sigma M = 0 \qquad ...(7.19)$$

where ΣF = vector sum of all the forces of the system

ΣM = vector sum of the moments of all the forces of the system relative to any point.

For a concurrent and non-coplanar system, the following set of equations must be satisfied:

$$\Sigma F_x = 0$$
$$\Sigma F_y = 0 \qquad ...(7.20)$$
$$\Sigma F_z = 0$$

where ΣF_x, ΣF_y, ΣF_z = algebraic sums of the x, y and z components of the forces of the system respectively.

For a parallel non-coplanar system, the set of equations to be satisfied for equilibrium are:

$$\Sigma F_y = 0$$
$$\Sigma M_x = 0 \qquad ...(7.21)$$
$$\Sigma M_z = 0$$

where ΣF_y = algebraic sum of the forces of the system along the y-axis which is selected parallel to the system.

ΣM_x, ΣM_z = algebraic sums of the moments of the forces of the system about the x and z axes respectively.

The necessary and sufficient conditions required for equilibrium for a non-concurrent non-coplanar system are given by

$$\Sigma F_x = 0$$
$$\Sigma F_y = 0$$
$$\Sigma F_z = 0$$
$$\Sigma M_x = 0$$
$$\Sigma M_y = 0$$
$$\Sigma M_z = 0 \qquad ...(7.22)$$

where ΣF_x, ΣF_y, ΣF_z = algebraic sums of the x, y and z components of the forces of the system respectively.

ΣM_x, ΣM_y, ΣM_z = algebraic sums of the components of the forces of the system about the x, y and z axes respectively.

7.8 TRUSSES

A *truss* is a system of slender members that are pinned together. The members are free to rotate at the pinned joints and carry forces only. All the external forces act at the joints.

Trusses are examples of coplanar force systems in equilibrium. Trusses are assumed to be rigid members all located in one plane. The weights of the truss members are neglected. Forces are transmitted from one member to another through pin joints. These members are called two-force members. A two-force member is in equilibrium under the effect of two resultant forces one at each end. The two-force members will be either in tension or compression. There are two methods available for the analysis of trusses.

For a stable planar truss, the following condition applies:

$$2n = m + p \qquad \text{...(7.23)}$$

where n = number of joints

m = number of members

p = number of unknown external forces

In a stable three-dimensional truss, the condition that holds is

$$3n = m + p \qquad \text{...(7.24)}$$

Method of Joints:

In this method, a free-body diagram of any pin in the truss is drawn. Maximum of two unknown forces act on that pin. Proceed from one pin to another until all unknowns have been obtained.

Method of Sections:

A free-body diagram of a section of the truss is drawn. The forces in the members can act as external forces. The system is a non-concurrent and non-parallel one. In any one section, not more than three unknown forces are to be found.

7.9 ANALYSIS OF BEAMS

A *beam* is a long member that is subjected to external lateral forces, F and external lateral moments, T. These cause internal lateral forces V called *shear forces* and internal lateral moments M known as *bending moments*. The shear forces and the bending moments induce lateral deformations, also called *bending*.

Shear and Moment Diagrams:

Shear and moment diagrams show the variation of V and M across a beam. Summation of the forces and moments of forces are used to plot V and M directly for the beams.

The slope of the shear diagram at any section along the beam is the negative of the load per unit length at that point. The change in shear between two sections of a beam carrying a distributed load equals the negative area of the load diagram between the two sections. The slope of the moment diagram at any section along the beam is the value of the shear at that section. The change in the moment between two sections of a beam equals the area of the shear diagram between the two sections.

7.10 FRICTION

The tangential force that opposes the sliding of one body relative to the other is the *static friction* between the two bodies. *Kinetic friction* is the tangential force between two bodies after motion begins. The body begins to slide only when the applied force exceeds the static frictional force at the floor. Referring to Fig. 7.1, the following terms are defined:

Limiting friction F' is the maximum value of static friction that occurs when motion is impending.

Coefficient of static friction is the ratio of the limiting friction F' to the normal force N, or $\mu = \left(\frac{F'}{N}\right)$. *Coefficient of kinetic friction* is the ratio of the kinetic friction to the normal force. *Angle of repose*, α is the angle to which an inclined plane may be raised before an object resting on it will move under the action of the force of gravity and the reaction of the plane. In Fig. 7.1, R is the resultant of F' and N and $\alpha = \phi$.

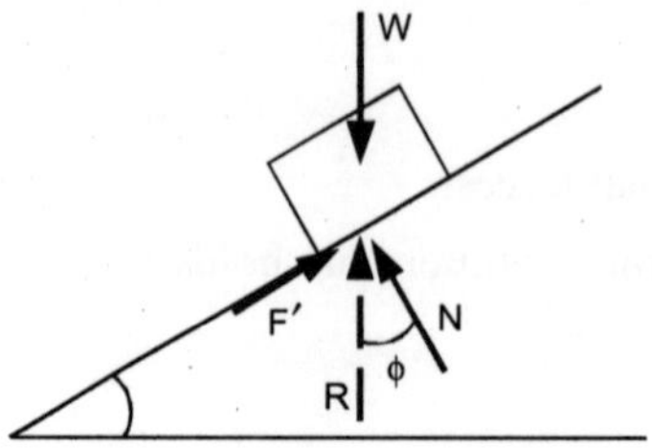

Fig. 7.1 Sliding friction

Belt Friction: When a belt passes over a pulley, the tensions in the belt on the two sides of the pulley will differ. When slip is about to occur, the tensions T_1 and T_2 are given by

$$T_1 = T_2 e^{\mu\beta} \quad \text{...(7.25)}$$

where T_1 = larger tension

T_2 = smaller tension

μ = coefficient of friction

β = angle of wrap (radians)

e = 2.718 (base of natural logarithms)

Screw frictional force occurs when a nut is screwed over a bolt.

7.11 FIRST MOMENTS AND CENTROIDS

The centroidal position vector $\bar{\mathbf{r}}$ of a geometry composed of n areas $d_1, d_2, d_3, ..., d_n$ located at points $P_1, P_2, P_3, ..., P_n$ represented by position vectors $\mathbf{r}_1, \mathbf{r}_2, \mathbf{r}_3, ..., \mathbf{r}_n$ respectively is defined as

$$\bar{\mathbf{r}} = \frac{\sum_{i=1}^{n} \mathbf{r}_i d_i}{\sum_{i=1}^{n} d_i}$$

where d_i = area of ith element

$\mathbf{r}_i$ = position vector of the ith element

$\sum_{i=1}^{n} d_i$ = total area of all n elements

$\sum_{i=1}^{n} \mathbf{r}_i d_i$ = first moment of area of all elements relative to selected point O.

The centroid can be written in terms of x, y and z coordinates as

$$\bar{x} = \frac{\sum_{i=1}^{n} x_i d_i}{\sum_{i=1}^{n} d_i}$$

$$\bar{y} = \frac{\sum_{i=1}^{n} y_i d_i}{\sum_{i=1}^{n} d_i}$$

$$\bar{z} = \frac{\sum_{i=1}^{n} z_i d_i}{\sum_{i=1}^{n} d_i}$$

where d_i = magnitude of area of the ith element

$\bar{x}, \bar{y}, \bar{z}$ = coordinates of centroid of the assemblage

x_i, y_i, z_i = coordinates of P_i at which d_i is concentrated.

The centroid of a continuous quantity of mass m is given by

$$\bar{\mathbf{r}} = \frac{\int \mathbf{r} dm}{\int dm}$$

or

$$\bar{x} = \frac{\int x dm}{\int dm} = \frac{Q_{yz}}{m}$$

$$\bar{y} = \frac{\int y dm}{\int dm} = \frac{Q_{xz}}{m}$$

$$\bar{z} = \frac{\int z dm}{\int dm} = \frac{Q_{xy}}{m}$$

where Q_{xy}, Q_{yz}, Q_{xz} = first moments with respect to xy, yz and xz planes respectively.

7.12 VIRTUAL WORK

A *virtual displacement* δs of a particle is defined as any infinitesimal change in the position of the particle consistent with the constraints imposed on the particle. *Virtual work* δU done by a force, F_t is defined as $F_t\,\delta s$, where F_t is the magnitude of the component of the force along the virtual displacement δs. Similarly, virtual work δU done by a couple of moment M is defined as $M\delta\theta$, where $\delta\theta$ is the virtual angular displacement.

Equilibrium: The necessary and sufficient condition for the *equilibrium of a particle* is zero *i.e.*, virtual work done by all the forces acting on the particle during any virtual displacement δs. The necessary and sufficient condition for the *equilibrium of a rigid body* is zero *i.e.*, virtual work done by all the external forces acting on the body during any virtual displacement consistent with the constraints imposed on the body. The *equilibrium* of a system of rigid bodies exists if the potential energy V has a stationary value. *Stable equilibrium* occurs if the potential energy V is a minimum. *Unstable equilibrium* occurs if the potential energy V is a maximum. *Neutral equilibrium* exists if a system remains in any position in which it is placed.

If x is the variable and V the potential energy of the system, then we have

$$\frac{d^2V}{dx^2} > 0 \quad \text{(stable equilibrium)}$$

$$\frac{d^2V}{dx^2} < 0 \quad \text{(unstable equilibrium)}$$

$$\frac{d^2V}{dx^2} = 0 \quad \text{(neutral equilibrium)}$$

7.13 KINEMATICS OF A PARTICLE

Kinematics is the study of motion without considering the forces or other factors that influence the motion.

Rectilinear motion: The general expression for displacement(s), velocity(v) and acceleration(a) are derived from the following three differential relations:

$$a = dv/dt$$

$$v = ds/dt$$

$$ads = vdv$$

For motion of a point along a straight line, the following formulas are valid for constant acceleration $a = k$:

$$v = v_0 + kt$$

$$v^2 = v_0^2 + 2ks$$

$$s = v_0 t + \frac{1}{2}kt^2 \qquad \text{...(7.25a)}$$

$$s = \frac{1}{2}(v + v_0)t$$

where v_0 = initial velocity

v = final velocity

k = constant acceleration

t = time

s = displacement.

Curvilinear motion: In a plane, curvilinear motion is motion along a plane curve (path). The velocity and acceleration of a point on such a curve can be expressed either as:

(a) Rectangular components

(b) Tangential and normal components

(c) Radial and transverse components

(a) Rectangular components

The position vector $\mathbf{r}(t)$, the velocity vector $\mathbf{v}(t)$ and the acceleration vector $\mathbf{a}(t)$ are given by

$$\mathbf{r}(t) = x(t)\mathbf{i} + y(t)\mathbf{j} + z(t)\mathbf{k}$$

$$\mathbf{v}(t) = v_x(t)\mathbf{i} + v_y(t)\mathbf{j} + z_z(t)\mathbf{k} = \dot{x}(t)\mathbf{i} + \dot{y}(t)\mathbf{j} + \dot{z}(t)\mathbf{k}$$

$$\mathbf{a}(t) = a_x(t)\mathbf{i} + a_y(t)\mathbf{j} + a_z(t)\mathbf{k} = \ddot{x}(t)\mathbf{i} + \ddot{y}(t)\mathbf{j} + \ddot{z}(t)\mathbf{k} \quad ...(7.26)$$

where the over-dot represents time differentiation.

The rectangular components of velocity and acceleration are given by

$$\mathbf{v}(t) = \dot{x}(t), \mathbf{v}_y(t) = \dot{y}(t), \mathbf{v}_z(t) = \dot{z}(t)$$

$$\mathbf{a}(t) = \ddot{x}(t), \mathbf{a}_y(t) = \ddot{y}(t),\ \mathbf{a}_z(t) = \ddot{z}(t) \quad ...(7.27)$$

The components of position are given by

$$\mathbf{x}(t) = x(t_1) + \int_{t_1}^{t} v_x(s)\,ds$$

$$\mathbf{y}(t) = y(t_1) + \int_{t_1}^{t} v_y(s)\,ds$$

$$\mathbf{z}(t) = z(t_1) + \int_{t_1}^{t} v_z(s)\,ds \quad ...(7.28)$$

The components of velocity are given by

$$\mathbf{v}_x(t) = v_x(t_1) + \int_{t_1}^{t} a_x(s)\,ds$$

$$\mathbf{v}_y(t) = v_y(t_1) + \int_{t_1}^{t} a_y(s)\,ds$$

$$\mathbf{v}_z(t) = v_z(t_1) + \int_{t_1}^{t} a_z(s)\,ds \quad ...(7.29)$$

Also $$v_x^2 x = v_x^2(x_1) + 2\int_{x_1}^{x} a_x(x)\,dx \quad ...(7.30)$$

(b) Tangential and normal components

Referring to Fig. 7.2, the velocity vector $\boldsymbol{v}$ can be written as

$$\mathbf{v} = u\mathbf{n}_t \quad ...(7.31)$$

where v = magnitude of the velocity vector

$\mathbf{n}_t$ = tangential unit vector directed along the velocity vector.

Also $$\dot{\mathbf{n}}_t = \dot{\theta}\mathbf{n}_n \qquad \text{...(7.32)}$$

and $$\dot{\mathbf{n}}_n = -\dot{\theta}\mathbf{n}_t$$

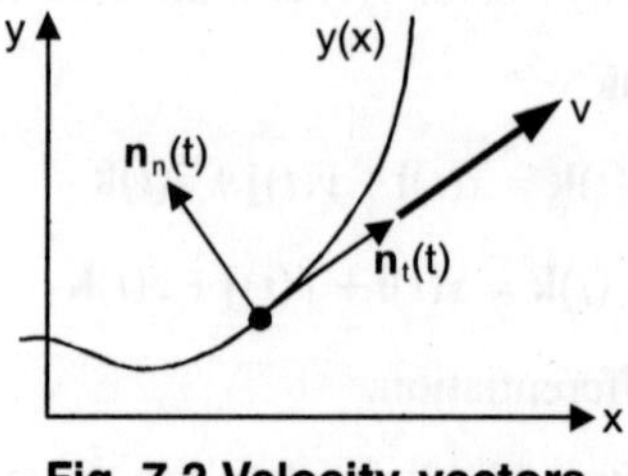

Fig. 7.2 Velocity vectors

where $\mathbf{n}_n$ = the normal unit vector defined to be perpendicular to the tangential unit vector.

In Fig. 7.3, the radius of curvature ρ of the path at time t is shown which is obtained by the intersection of the lines extending from $\mathbf{n}_t(t)$ and $\mathbf{n}_t(t + \Delta t)$ where Δt is time increment. The angle θ changes an incremental amount Δθ and the point moves an incremental amount Δs.

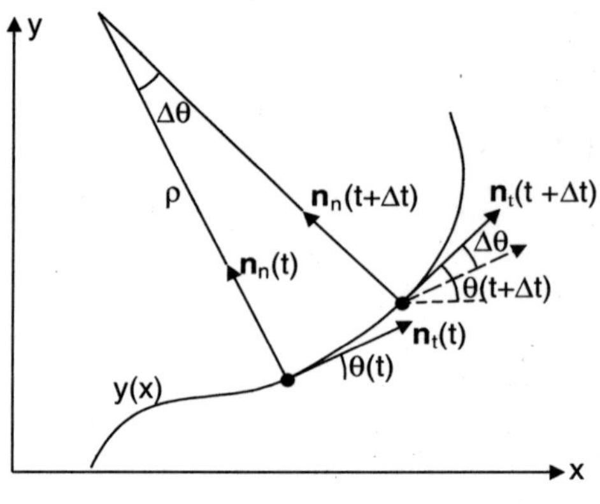

Fig. 7.3 Radius of curvature of path

Now $\rho\Delta\theta = \Delta s$

or $$\rho\dot{\theta} = v \qquad \text{...(7.33)}$$

where $$\dot{\theta} = \frac{d\theta}{dt}$$

$$v = \frac{ds}{dt}$$

Differentiating Eq. (7.31) with respect to time gives

$$\mathbf{a} = a_t\mathbf{n}_t + a_n\mathbf{n}_n \qquad \text{...(7.34)}$$

where $a_t = \dot{v}$

$$a_n = \frac{v^2}{\rho} \quad ...(7.35)$$

(c) Radial and transverse components

The polar form of a position vector is

$$\mathbf{r} = r\mathbf{n}_r \quad ...(7.36)$$

where $r = |\mathbf{r}|$ is the magnitude of r

$\mathbf{n}_r$ = unit vector in the direction of $\mathbf{r}$

$\mathbf{n}_r$ = the radial unit vector

$\mathbf{n}_\theta$ = the circumferential unit vector

The circumferential unit vector is perpendicular to $\mathbf{n}_r$. Hence, $\mathbf{n}_r$ and $\mathbf{n}_\theta$ are related to $\mathbf{i}$ and $\mathbf{j}$ in Fig. 7.4 as

$$\mathbf{n}_r(t) = \cos\theta(t)\mathbf{i} + \sin\theta(t)\mathbf{j}$$

$$\mathbf{n}_\theta(t) = -\sin\theta(t)\mathbf{i} + \cos\theta(t)\mathbf{j} \quad ...(7.37)$$

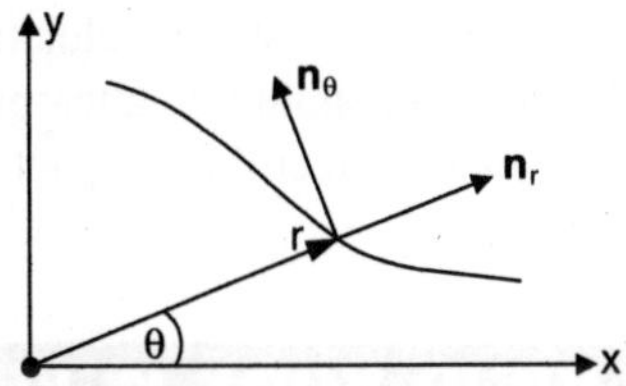

Fig. 7.4 Radial and transverse components

Differentiating Eq. (7.37) with respect to time gives

$$\dot{\mathbf{n}}_r = -\dot{\theta}\sin\theta\mathbf{i} + \dot{\theta}\cos\theta\mathbf{j} = \dot{\theta}(-\sin\theta\mathbf{i} + \cos\theta\mathbf{j}) = \dot{\theta}\mathbf{n}_\theta \quad ...(7.38)$$

and $\dot{\mathbf{n}}_\theta(t) = -\dot{\theta}\mathbf{n}_r$ ...(7.39)

Hence, the derivatives of the unit vectors are given by

$$\dot{\mathbf{n}}_r = \dot{\theta}\mathbf{n}_\theta$$

$$\dot{\mathbf{n}}_\theta = -\dot{\theta}\mathbf{n}_r \quad ...(7.40)$$

Similarly, from Eqs. (7.36) and (7.40), we get

$$\mathbf{v} = v_r\mathbf{n}_r + v_\theta\mathbf{n}_\theta \quad ...(7.41)$$

where $v_r = \dot{r}$

$v_\theta = r\dot{\theta}$

Differentiating Eq. (7.41) with respect to time gives

$$\mathbf{a} = a_r\mathbf{n}_r + a_\theta\mathbf{n}_\theta \quad ...(7.42)$$

where $a_r = \ddot{r} - r\dot{\theta}^2$

$$a_\theta = r\ddot{\theta} + 2\dot{r}\dot{\theta} \quad ...(7.43)$$

7.14 D' ALEMBERT'S PRINCIPLE

Kinetics of particles begins with Newton's second law, which relates forces, accelerations and time. The second form of writing Newton's law is called d' Alembert's principle which gives the condition for dynamic equilibrium. It states that

$$\Sigma F - ma = 0 \quad ...(7.44)$$

where ΣF = vector sum of all the forces acting on the particle

m = mass of the particle

a = acceleration of the particle.

Hence, an imaginary force (also known as inertia force) which is collinear with ΣF but opposite in sense and of magnitude ma would cause it to be in equilibrium if applied to the particle. All the equations of equilibrium are then applicable. Kinetics of particles can also be attempted with work-energy principle and impulse-momentum principle, just as a rigid body. When velocities and displacements are given instead of acceleration as in spring problems, the problem should be attempted with work-energy principle. On the other hand when velocity and time are given as in recoil or impact problems, the equations of motion are formulated from impulse-momentum relations.

7.15 KINEMATICS OF A RIGID BODY IN PLANE MOTION

A rigid-body is configured by specified dimensions and rotational motion should be considered in addition to translation. In plane motion of a rigid body, every point in the body remains at a constant distance from a fixed plane. As shown in Fig. 7.5, B is an arbitrary point in the body and x-y-z is a non-rotating reference frame.

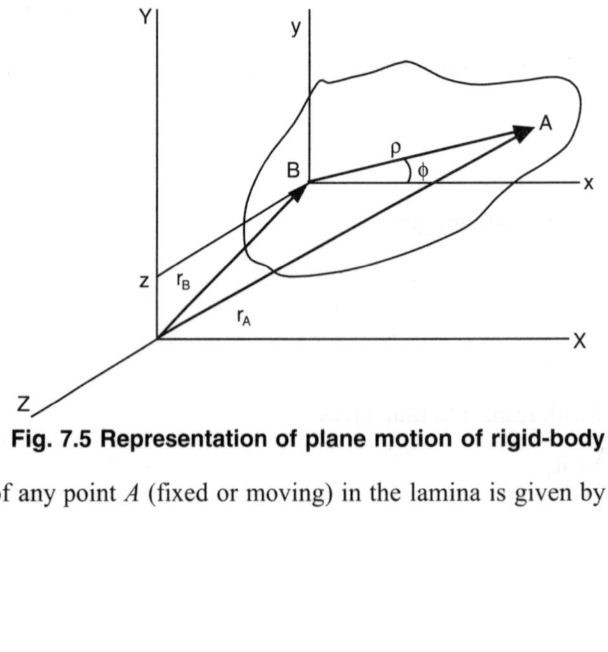

Fig. 7.5 Representation of plane motion of rigid-body

The position vector $\mathbf{r}_A$ of any point A (fixed or moving) in the lamina is given by

$$\mathbf{r}_A = \mathbf{r}_B + \rho \qquad ...(7.45)$$

where $\mathbf{r}_B$ = position vector of B

ρ = vector BA

Differentiating Eq. (7.45) gives

$$\mathbf{v}_A = \dot{\mathbf{r}}_A = \dot{\mathbf{r}}_B + \dot{\rho} = \dot{\mathbf{r}}_B + \rho\omega\mathbf{e}_\phi \qquad ...(7.46)$$

where $\dot{\mathbf{r}}_B$ = linear velocity of B relative to the fixed axes X, Y and Z

ω = angular velocity (magnitude) of ρ about any line parallel to Z-axis

$\mathbf{e}_\phi$ = unit vector perpendicular to ρ (in the direction of increasing ϕ)

The acceleration $\mathbf{a}_A$ is given by

$$a_A = \dot{v}_A = \ddot{r}_A = \ddot{r}_B - \rho\omega^2 e_\rho + \rho\alpha e_\phi \qquad ...(7.47)$$

where $\ddot{\mathbf{r}}_B$ = acceleration of B relative to fixed axes X, Y and Z

e_ρ = unit vector along ρ directed from B towards A

e_ϕ = unit vector perpendicular to ρ (in the direction of increasing ϕ)

α = angular acceleration (magnitude) of ρ about any line parallel to the Z-axis.

Equations (7.46) and (7.47) can also be written in vector form as follows:

$$\mathbf{v}_A = \mathbf{v}_B + \omega \times \rho$$

or $$\mathbf{v}_A = \mathbf{v}_B + \mathbf{v}_{A/B} \qquad ...(7.48)$$

and $$\mathbf{a}_A = \mathbf{a}_B + \omega \times (\omega \times \rho) + \alpha \times \rho$$

$$\mathbf{a}_A = \mathbf{a}_B + \mathbf{a}_{A/B} \qquad ...(7.49)$$

Here $\times$ is a vector (cross) product.

Also $$\omega = \dot{\phi}_k = \omega_k$$

$$\alpha = \ddot{\phi}_k = \dot{\omega}_k = \alpha_k \qquad ...(7.50)$$

$$\rho\alpha e_\rho = \omega \times \rho$$

$$\rho\alpha e_\phi = \alpha \times \rho$$

$$-\rho\omega^2 e_\rho = \omega \times (\omega \times \rho)$$

in which $\mathbf{v}_{A/B}$ = relative velocity of A as it rotates around B.

$\mathbf{a}_{A/B}$ = relative acceleration of A as it rotates around B.

Thus in plane motion the term '$\omega\times(\omega\times\rho)$' becomes $-\rho\omega^2$.

Another method of computing velocities and accelerations in rigid bodies is to draw the vector diagrams. These are drawn based on the concept that relative velocity is always perpendicular to the line joining the two points and the two components of relative acceleration are perpendicular to each other. Sometimes a rotating frame of reference is used to represent the motion of a body translating with velocity **v** and acceleration **a** on another rotating body as in case of a crank and slotted lever linkage. Here, the acceleration expression becomes

$$\mathbf{v}_A = \mathbf{v}_B + (\omega\times\rho) + \mathbf{v}$$

and $$\mathbf{a}_A = \mathbf{a}_B + \omega\times(\omega\times\rho) + \alpha\times\rho + 2\omega\times\mathbf{v}_{AB} + \mathbf{a}$$

Here, the term '$2\omega\times\mathbf{v}_{AB}$' is called Coriolis component of acceleration.

7.16 MOMENTS OF INERTIA

The axial moment of inertia or the second moment of inertia I, of an element of area about an axis in its plane (Fig. 7.6) is given by

$$dI_x = y^2 dA$$

$$dI_y = x^2 dA \qquad ...(7.51)$$

The polar moment of inertia J, of an element about an axis perpendicular to its plane is the product of the area of the element and square of its distance from the axis. Referring to Fig. 7.6, the polar moment of inertia is

$$dJ = \rho^2 dA = (x^2 + y^2)dA = dI_y + dI_x \qquad ...(7.52)$$

The product of inertia of an element of area in Fig. 7.6 is given by

$$dI_{xy} = xydA \qquad ...(7.53)$$

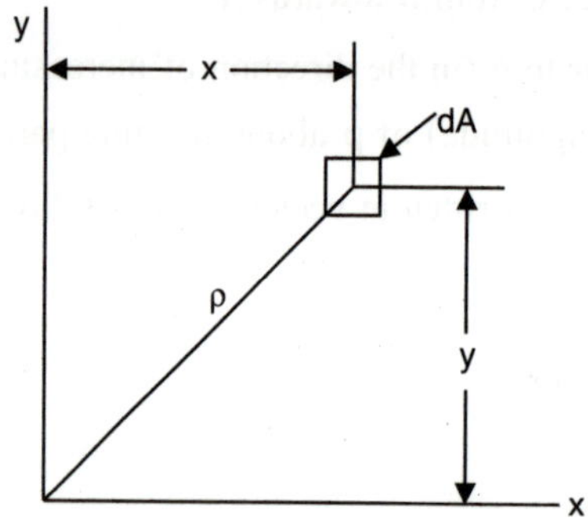

Fig. 7.6 Definition of product of inertia

The axial moment of inertia of an area is the sum of the axial moments of inertia of its elements

$$I_x = \int y^2 dA$$

$$I_y = \int x^2 dA \qquad ...(7.54)$$

The radius of gyration of an area with respect to an axis is given by

$$k = \sqrt{I/A} \qquad ...(7.55)$$

The polar moment of inertia of an area is the sum of the polar moments of inertia of its elements

$$J = \int \rho^2 dA \qquad ...(7.56)$$

The product of inertia of an area is the sum of the products of inertia of its elements

$$I_{xy} = \int xydA \qquad ...(7.57)$$

The parallel-axis theorem states that the axial or polar moment of inertia of an area about any axis equals the axial or polar moment of inertia of the area about a parallel axis through the centroid of the area plus the product of the area and the square of the distance between the two parallel axes. Referring to Fig. 7.7, we have

$$I_x = I_{x'} + Am^2$$
$$I_y = I_{y'} + An^2$$
$$I_z = J + Ar^2$$
$$I_{xy} = I_{x'y'} + Amn \qquad ...(7.58)$$

where A = area

I_{xy} = product of inertia of the area with respect to x and y axes

$I_{x'y'}$ = product of inertia about two parallel centroid axes x' and y'

m, n = coordinates of G relative to the (x, y) axes through O or the coordinates of O relative to the (x', y') axes through G.

x, y = any axes through O

x', y' = coplanar parallel axes through the centroid G.

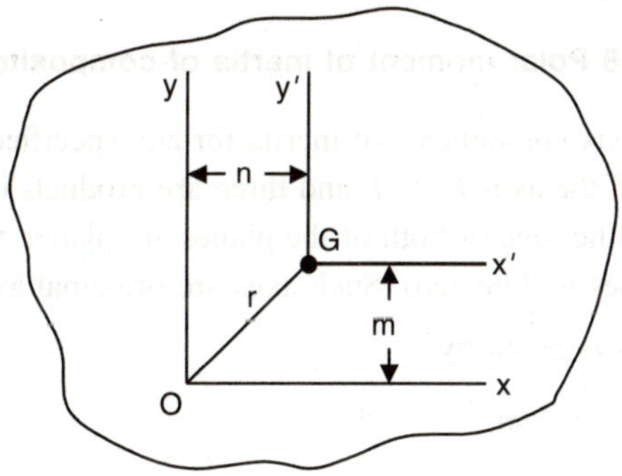

Fig. 7.7 Parallel-axis theorem

The axial or polar moment of inertia or product of inertia of a composite area is the sum of the axial or polar moments of inertia, or products of inertia, of the component areas of the whole area.

Mass moment of inertia of a rigid body is defined as: $I = \int r^2\, dm$, where r is perpendicular distance from the z-axis to the arbitrary element dm. Thus, the value of I differs for each axis about which it is computed. Usually in planar kinetics, the axis which is generally chosen for analysis passes through body's mass center G and is always perpendicular to the plane of motion. Its units are kgm^2. Sometimes, I is given as radius of gyration about center G. The radius of gyration k of a body with respect to an axis is given by

$$k = \sqrt{I/m} \qquad ...(7.59)$$

Consider Fig. 7.8, the axial moment of inertia of a mass dm is given by

$$I_{xx} = I_x = \int (y^2 + z^2)\, dm \text{ and } I_{xy} = I_{yx} = \int xy\, dm$$
$$I_{yy} = I_y = \int (x^2 + z^2)\, dm \text{ and } I_{yz} = I_{zy} = \int yz\, dm$$
$$I_{zz} = I_z = \int (x^2 + y^2)\, dm \text{ and } I_{zx} = I_{xz} = \int xz\, dm \qquad ...(7.60)$$

where dm = mass of element

I_x, I_y, I_z = axial moments of inertia with respect to the x, y and z axes respectively.

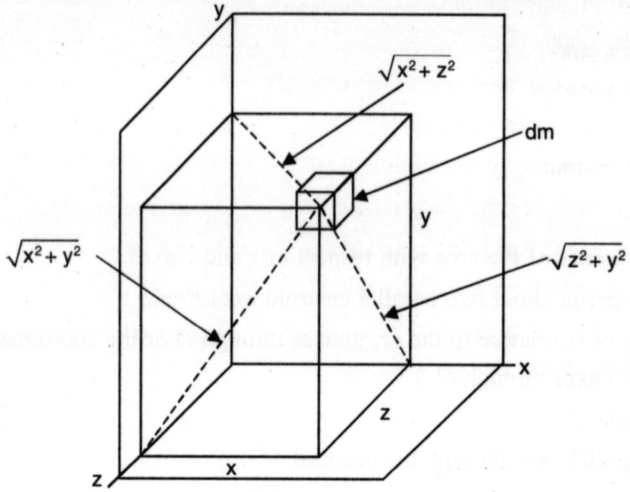

Fig. 7.8 Polar moment of inertia of composite area

In three dimensions, a body has six components of inertia for any specified x, y, z axes. Three of these are moments of inertia about each of the axes I_x, I_y, I_z and three are products of inertia each defined from two orthogonal planes I_{xy}, I_{yz}, I_{xz}. If either one or both of the planes are planes of symmetry, then the product of inertia with respect to these planes will be zero. Such axes are principal axes of inertia.

The product of inertia of a mass is given by

$$I_{xy} = \int xydm$$

The parallel axis theorem states that the moment of inertia of a body about an axis is equal to the moment of inertia I about a parallel axis through the center of gravity of the body plus the product of the mass of the body and the square of the distance between the two parallel axes. For example, moment of inertia of slender rod about one end can be computed in terms of moment of inertia about mass center G according to the following relation: $I_C = I_G + m\left(\frac{\ell}{2}\right)^2$.

7.17 DYNAMICS OF A RIGID BODY IN PLANE MOTION

When the motion is specified in terms of acceleration and forces, Newton's second law or d' Alembert's principle can be directly used. For a rigid body in plane motion, there are three equations describing dynamic equilibrium: Two force relations for translation along x and y direction and one moment equation about a point usually the center of mass G. In vector form, the equations of plane motion are given by

$$\Sigma \mathbf{F} = m\,\bar{\mathbf{a}} \qquad ...(7.61)$$

$$\Sigma \mathbf{M}_O = I_O\alpha\mathbf{k} + m\mathbf{r}_{G/O} \times \mathbf{a}_O = \left(I_O\alpha + m\bar{x}a_{Oy} - m\bar{y}a_{Ox}\right)\mathbf{k} \qquad ...(7.62)$$

where $\Sigma \mathbf{F}$ = resultant of the external forces acting on the body

$\Sigma \mathbf{M}_O$ = resultant of the external moments acting on the body

m = mass of the body

$\bar{\mathbf{a}}$ = acceleration of the mass center of the body

$\mathbf{a}_O$ = acceleration of reference point O

α = angular acceleration of the body

I_O = moment of inertia of the body relative to the reference point O

$\bar{x}, \bar{y}$ = coordinates of the mass center relative to the reference point O

$\mathbf{r}_{G/O}$ = position vector of the mass center relative to the reference point O

a_{Ox}, a_{Oy} = magnitude of the components of the acceleration of the reference point O along the x and y axes.

The scalar equations of the plane motion are given by

$$\Sigma F_x = m\bar{a}_x$$

$$\Sigma F_y = m\bar{a}_y$$

$$\Sigma \bar{M} = \bar{I}\alpha \qquad \text{...(7.62a)}$$

where $\Sigma F_x, \Sigma F_y$ = algebraic sums of the magnitudes of the components of the external forces along the x and y axes respectively.

m = mass of the body

$\bar{a}_x, \bar{a}_y$ = components of the linear acceleration of the mass center in x and y directions respectively.

$\Sigma \bar{M}$ = algebraic sum of the moments of the external forces about the mass center.

$\bar{I}$ = moment of inertia of the body about the mass center.

α = magnitude of the angular acceleration of the body.

The scalar equations for translation of a rigid body are given by

$$\Sigma F_x = ma_x$$

$$\Sigma F_y = ma_y \qquad \text{...(7.63)}$$

and

$$\Sigma M = 0$$

where $\Sigma F_x, \Sigma F_y$ = algebraic sums of the components of the external forces in the x and y directions respectively.

m = mass of the body.

a_x, a_y = acceleration components in the x and y directions respectively.

ΣM = sum of the moments of the external forces about the mass center of the body.

The scalar equations of motion of a rigid body under the action of an unbalanced force system for a body with a plane of symmetry and rotates about a fixed axis perpendicular to the plane are given by

$$\Sigma F_n = m\bar{r}\omega^2$$

$$\Sigma F_t = m\bar{r}\alpha \qquad \text{...(7.64)}$$

$$\Sigma M_O = I_O\alpha$$

where ΣF_n = algebraic sum of the components of all external forces (which are the applied forces F_1, F_2, F_3, etc., the gravitational force on the body, and the reaction R of the axis on the body) along the n axis, which is the line drawn between the center of rotation O and the mass center G; note that the positive sense is from G towards O because $\bar{a}_n = \bar{r}\omega^2$ has that sense

ΣF_t = algebraic sum of the components of the external forces along the t axis, which is perpendicular to the n axis at O; note that the positive sense along this axis agrees with that of $\bar{a}_t = \bar{r}\alpha$

ΣM_O = algebraic sum of the moments of the external forces about the axis of rotation through O; note that positive sense agrees with the assumed sense of the angular acceleration α

m = mass of the body

G = center of mass of the body

$\bar{r}$ = distance from the center of rotation O to the mass center G

I_O = moment of inertia of the body about the axis of rotation

ω = angular speed of the body

α = magnitude of the angular acceleration of the body

This type of rotation is called *non-centroidal rotation*. Example: A lever oscillating about a point of suspension.

When G and O coincide (rotation about a fixed axis through G) and $F = 0$, the equations of motion are given by

$$\Sigma F_x = 0, \Sigma F_y = 0, \Sigma \bar{M} = \bar{I}\alpha \qquad \text{...(7.65)}$$

where ΣF_x = algebraic sum of the components of the external forces along any axis chosen as the x-axis.

ΣF_y = algebraic sum of the components of the external forces along the y-axis

$\Sigma \bar{M}$ = algebraic sum of the moments of the external forces about the axis of rotation through the mass center G (axis of symmetry)

$\bar{I}$ = moment of inertia of the body about the axis of rotation through the mass center G

α = magnitude of the angular acceleration of the body

This type of rotation is called *centroidal rotation*.

7.18 WORK AND ENERGY

The work done to move particle or a body from point 1 to point 2 by the resultant force F acting on the particle is given by

$$U_{1-2} = \int_1^2 \mathbf{F} \bullet dr \qquad \text{...(7.66)}$$

The kinetic energy T of a particle with mass m and moving with speed v is defined as $\frac{1}{2}mv^2$. In connected rigid bodies the total kinetic energy of all the bodies at a configuration is computed.

The work done on a particle by the resultant force as it moves from point 1 to point 2 is equal to the change in kinetic energy.

$$U_{1-2} = T_2 - T_1 \qquad ...(7.67)$$

where T_1, T_2 = initial and final kinetic energy respectively at points 1 and 2.

The kinetic energy T of a rigid-body in translation is

$$T = \frac{1}{2}mv^2.$$

The kinetic energy T of a rigid body in rotation is

$$T = \frac{1}{2}I_O\omega^2 \qquad ...(7.68)$$

where I_o = mass moment of inertia of the body about the axis of rotation

ω = angular speed

The kinetic energy T of a body in plane motion is given by

$$T = \frac{1}{2}\bar{I}\omega^2 \qquad ...(7.69)$$

where ω = angular speed

$\bar{I}$ = moment of inertia about an axis through the mass center parallel to the z-axis.

The change in potential energy may be defined as the negative of the work done by the conservative force acting on the body in bringing it from the datum to a final position. The selection of the datum is arbitrary. The principle of work and energy states that 'the work done by thc cxternal forces acting on a rigid zbody during a displacement is equal to the change in kinetic energy of the body during the same displacement'. The sum of the work done by the non-conservative external forces such as friction and the work done by the internal forces acting on a system of particles is equal to the change in the total (kinetic and potential) energy of the system of the particles over the time interval of the action

or $$E = T + V \qquad ...(7.70)$$

where E = total energy (kinetic and potential) of conservative system.

T = kinetic energy

V = potential energy

The law of conservation of energy states that if a particle (or body) is acted upon by a conservation force system, the sum of the kinetic energy and potential energy is a constant. Thus for non-conservative system, principle of work and energy is used and for conservative system, principle of conservation of energy can be employed.

7.19 IMPULSE AND MOMENTUM

In particles, there is only linear momentum since it has no angular motion.

The *linear momentum* of the *i*th particle is defined as

$$\mathbf{L}_i = m_i\mathbf{v}_i \qquad ...(7.71)$$

where m_i = mass of the ith particle

$\mathbf{v}_i$ = ith particle's velocity.

The linear momentum of the system of particles is the sum of the linear momenta of the particles.

or $$\mathbf{L} = \sum_{i=1}^{n} \mathbf{L}_i \qquad ...(7.72)$$

The linear impulse acting on the system imparted over a time interval is given by

$$\mathbf{G}_{1-2} = \int_{t_1}^{t_2} \mathbf{F} dt \qquad ...(7.73)$$

Then the principle of impulse and momentum can be written as:

$$\mathbf{G}_{1-2} = \mathbf{L}_2 - \mathbf{L}_1 \qquad ...(7.74)$$

where $\mathbf{L_p}$ = linear momentum of the system at a state p.

Equation (7.74) states that the linear impulse acting on the system is equal to the change in the system's linear momentum over the time interval.

For a rigid body, there is angular momentum and angular impulse in addition to linear counterparts. Angular impulse is created by a moment of a force while the angular momentum is due to inertia of the body and angular velocity of rotation. Angular momentum sometimes called as the moment of the linear momentum is defined as:

$$\mathbf{H}_o = \mathbf{r} \times \mathbf{L} \qquad ...(7.75)$$

where $\mathbf{H}_o$ is the angular momentum about the point O.

The angular momentum of a system of n rigid bodies about a point A is given by

$$\mathbf{H}_A = \sum_{i=1}^{n} \mathbf{H}_{Ai} = \sum_{i=1}^{n} \mathbf{r}_{i/A} \times \mathbf{L}_i = \sum_{i=1}^{n} \mathbf{r}_{i/A} \times m_i \mathbf{v}_i \qquad ...(7.76)$$

where A is any point.

The resultant external moment about the point A is given by

$$\mathbf{M}_A = \sum_{i=1}^{n} M_{Ai} = \sum_{i=1}^{n} \mathbf{r}_{i/A} \times \mathbf{F}_i \qquad ...(7.77)$$

Differentiating Eq. (7.76) with respect to time yields

$$\dot{\mathbf{H}}_A = -\mathbf{v}_A \times \mathbf{L} + \mathbf{M}_A \qquad ...(7.78)$$

If the point A is fixed then $\mathbf{v}_A = 0$ and if the point A is the mass center C then $\mathbf{v}_A \times \mathbf{L} = \mathbf{v}_C \times m\mathbf{v}_C = 0$. Thus, whether the point A represents a fixed point O or the mass center C:

$$\dot{\mathbf{H}}_A = \mathbf{M}_A \qquad ...(7.79)$$

Equation (7.79) states that the time derivative of the angular momentum about a fixed point O (or the mass center O) is equal to the resultant external moment about the fixed point O (or the mass center C). Integrating Eq. (7.79) yields

$$\mathbf{N}_{A1-2} = \int_{t_1}^{t_2} \mathbf{M}_A dt = \int_{t_1}^{t_2} \dot{\mathbf{H}}_A dt = \mathbf{H}_A(t_2) - \mathbf{H}_A(t_1) = \mathbf{H}_{A2} - \mathbf{H}_{A1} \quad \text{...(7.80)}$$

where $\mathbf{N}_{A1-2} = \int_{t_1}^{t_2} \mathbf{M}_A dt$ angular impulse imparted over the time interval

Hence $\mathbf{N}_{A1-2} = \mathbf{H}_{A2} - \mathbf{H}_{A1}$ ...(7.81)

Equation (7.81) states that the angular impulse acting on the system about the fixed point *O* (or the mass center *G*) is equal to the change in the system's angular momentum about the point *O* (or the mass center *G*) over the time interval. This is illustrated in Fig. 7.9, where initial and final velocities are taken at mass center *G*.

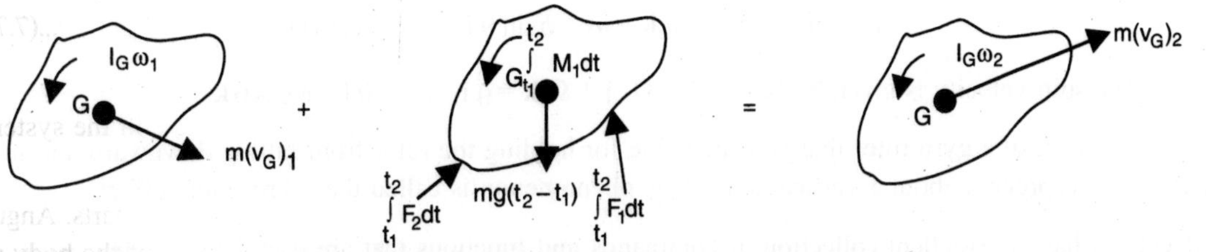

Fig. 7.9 Principle of impulse-momentum of rigid body

Conservation of linear momentum in a given direction occurs if the sum of the external forces in that direction is zero. For examples in case of two balls (particles) colliding head-on with each other either centrally or obliquely, the linear momentum is conserved along the line of collision. Mathematically, it is written as $\Sigma L_p = 0$. Conservation of angular momentum about an axis occurs if the sum of the moments of the external forces about that axis is zero. Mathematically, it is written as: $\Sigma H_p = 0$. This occurs in cases where the rotating or oscillating body suffers different speeds when the point of suspension changes. As an example, a diver jumping from a height into water maintains the constant angular momentum during his motion.

7.20 THREE-DIMENSIONAL MECHANICS

In three-dimensional motion, the angular velocity and acceleration vector has components in more than one axis, unlike in plane motion where for example $\omega = \omega\hat{k}a$ a single component parallel to *z*-axis. Similar to two-dimensional motion the motion of two points *A* and *B* on a body, or a series of connected bodies can be related using relative motion analysis with rotating and translating axes at *B*. If a body undergoes general motion, then the motion of a point *A* in the body can be related to the motion of another point *B* using a relative motion analysis along with translating axes at *B*:

$$\mathbf{v}_A = \mathbf{v}_B + \omega \times \mathbf{r}_{AB}$$

$$\mathbf{a}_A = \mathbf{a}_B + \alpha \times \mathbf{r}_{AB} + \omega \times (\omega \times \mathbf{r}_{AB})$$

There are three scalar equations of translational motion for a rigid body that moves in three dimensions.

$$\Sigma F_x = m(a_{Gx})$$

$$\Sigma F_y = m(a_{Gy})$$

$$\Sigma F_z = m(a_{Gz})$$

The three scalar equations of rotational motion depend upon the location of the x, y, z reference.

$$\Sigma M_x = I_x\dot{\omega}_x - (I_y - I_z)\omega_y\omega_z$$

$$\Sigma M_y = I_y\dot{\omega}_y - (I_z - I_x)\omega_z\omega_x$$

$$\Sigma M_z = I_z\dot{\omega}_z - (I_x - I_y)\omega_x\omega_y$$

Most often, these axes are oriented so that they are the principal axes of inertia. If the axes are fixed in and move with the rotation ω of the body, then the equations are referred to as Euler equations of motion.

The angular motion of a gyroscope is best described using the changes in motion of the three Euler angles. These angular velocity components are the precision ϕ, nutation $\dot{\theta}$ and spin ψ. If $\psi = 0$ and ϕ and θ are constant then the motion is referred to as steady precision. The angular velocity of the body is specified only in terms of Euler angle θ as:

$$\omega = \omega_x\mathbf{i} + \omega_y\mathbf{j} + \omega_z\mathbf{k} = \dot{\theta}\mathbf{i} + \dot{\phi}\sin\theta\,\mathbf{j} + (\dot{\phi}\cos\theta + \dot{\psi})\mathbf{k}$$

The spin velocity is given by $\Omega = \Omega_x\mathbf{i} + \Omega_y\mathbf{j} + \Omega_z\mathbf{k} = \dot{\theta}\,\mathbf{i} + \dot{\phi}\sin\theta\,\mathbf{j} + \dot{\phi}\cos\theta\,\mathbf{k}$

It is spin of a gyro rotor that is responsible for holding the rotor from falling downward and instead causing it to precess about a vertical axis. This phenomenon is called the 'gyroscopic effect'.

MATLAB has an excellent collection of commands and functions that are useful for solving engineering mechanics problems. The problems presented in this chapter are basic and are normally presented in introductory mechanics courses. The application of MATLAB to the problems in the analysis and design of engineering mechanics is presented in this chapter with a number of illustrative examples. These examples cover different topics of Mechanics. Each solution begins with a problem formulation followed by a corresponding MATLAB code with simple explanations wherever possible. The background required for solving mechanics problems is the knowledge of differentiation, integration, trigonometry along with basic physical laws. Table 7.1 summarizes some of the important mathematical relations often used for computations in statics and dynamics.

Table 7.1 Some mathematical expressions

S.No.	Mathematical entity
1.	If $ax^2 + bx + c = 0$, then $x = \dfrac{-b \pm \sqrt{b^2 - 4ac}}{2a}$ is root.
2.	If sin θ = *A* and cos θ = *B* then (*i*) $A^2 + B^2 = 1$, (*ii*) $\sin 2\theta = 2AB$, (*iii*) $\cos 2\theta = B^2 - A^2$ (*iv*) $\tan\theta = \dfrac{A}{B}$, (*v*) $\sin(\theta \pm \phi) = \sin\theta\cos\phi \pm \cos\theta\sin\phi$ In a triangle: (*a*) **Sine rule** $a/\sin(\theta) = b/\sin(\phi)$, where *a* is side opposite to angle ϕ and *b* is side opposite to angle θ. (*b*) **Cosine rule**: $c^2 = a^2 + b^2 - 2ab\cos(\theta)$, where θ is angle opposite to side *c*.
3.	Important derivatives: (*i*) $\dfrac{d}{dx}(u^n) = nu^{n-1}\dfrac{du}{dx}$ (*ii*) $\dfrac{d}{dx}(uv) = u\dfrac{dv}{dx} + v\dfrac{du}{dx}$ (*iii*) $\dfrac{d}{dx}\left(\dfrac{u}{v}\right) = \dfrac{v\dfrac{du}{dx} - u\dfrac{dv}{dx}}{v^2}$

Contd...

	(iv) $\frac{d}{dx}(\sin\theta) = \cos\theta\frac{d\theta}{dx}$ (v) $\frac{d}{dx}(\cos\theta) = -\sin\theta\frac{d\theta}{dx}$ (vi) $\frac{d}{dx}(\tan\theta) = \sec^2\theta\frac{d\theta}{dx}$
4.	Important integrals (here c is a constant) (i) $\int x^p dx = \frac{x^{p+1}}{p+1} + c, p \neq -1$ (ii) $\int \frac{dx}{p+qx} = \frac{1}{q}\log_e(p+qx) + c$ (iii) $\int \frac{dx}{p+qx^2} = \frac{1}{2\sqrt{-pq}}\log_e\frac{p+x\sqrt{-pq}}{p-x\sqrt{-pq}} + c$, where $pq < 0$ (iv) $\int \sin x\, dx = -\cos x + c$, (v) $\int \cos x\, dx = \sin x + c$, (vi) $\int e^{ax}\, dx = \frac{1}{a}e^{ax} + c$

7.21 EXAMPLE PROBLEMS AND SOLUTIONS

In all the examples solved in this chapter, a script is written in the form of '*m*' files and the program is executed by typing the *m* file name with extension at the command prompt. It is emphasized to develop each program with different commands to learn MATLAB with perfection.

7.21.1 Statics

Problems in statics are presented on the following common topics: forces on a particle, rigid bodies and equivalent forces, equilibrium of rigid bodies, truss analysis, beams, friction and distributed forces (centroids).

Example ES7.1: Write a MATLAB program to determine the magnitude and direction of the resultant of 3-coplanar forces applied at point *A* in Fig. ES7.1. Use the following values:

$$F_1 = 20 \text{ kN}, \; F_2 = 40 \text{ kN}, \; F_3 = 200 \text{ kN}, \; \alpha_1 = 40°, \; \alpha_2 = 25° \text{ and } \alpha_3 = 58°.$$

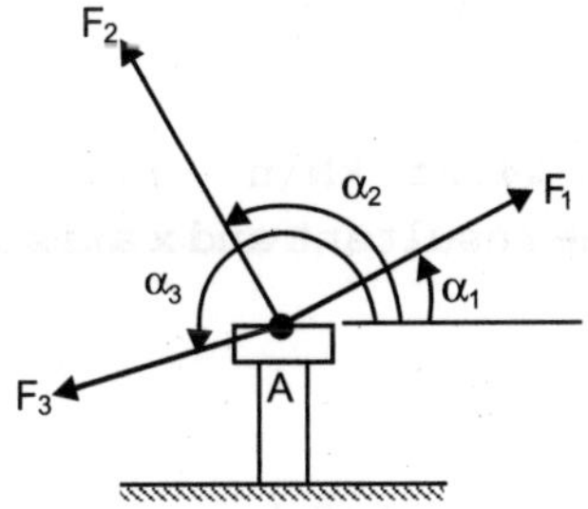

Fig. ES7.1

Solution: We know that for a coplanar force system

$$R_x = \sum_{i=1}^{n} F_i \cos\alpha_i, \qquad R_y = \sum_{i=1}^{n} F_i \sin\alpha_i \qquad ...(1)$$

Therefore $$R = \sqrt{R_x^2 + R_y^2} \qquad ...(2)$$

and $$\alpha_R = \tan^{-1}\frac{R_y}{R_x} \qquad ...(3)$$

Let α_R^* be the value defined by Eq. (3) and such that $-90° \le \alpha_R^* \le 90°$. Then, we have

If $R_x \ge 0$ and $R_y \ge 0$: $\alpha_R = \alpha_R^*$ ...(4)

If $R_x \ge 0$ and $R_y < 0$: $\alpha_R = 360° + \alpha_R^*$ ...(5)

If $R_x < 0$: $\alpha_R = 180° + \alpha_R^*$ ...(6)

MATLAB Solution:

```
n=3; % Number of forces
alpha= [40 25 58];
alpha1=alpha*pi/180;
force= [20 40 200];
sumx=0;
sumy=0;
for i=1: n
  sumx=sumx + force (i)*cos (alpha1 (i));
  sumy=sumy + force (i)*sin (alpha1(i));
end
 r=sqrt (sumx^2+sumy^2);
 alphar = atan2 (sumy, sumx);
 alphar=alphar*180/pi;
 if alphar < 0
 alphar = alphar + 360;
end
fprintf ('The resultant R is %4.2f  kN\n', r);
fprintf ('The angle between the resultant and x axis is % 4.2f degrees\n', alphar);
```

Output is given below:

The resultant *R* is 254.11kN.

The angle between the resultant and *x* axis is 51.68 degrees.

Example ES7.2: Figure ES7.2 shows two forces, one 500 N and the other *P* applied by cables on each side of the obstruction *A* in order to remove the spike. Write a MATLAB program to determine:

(*a*) the magnitude of *P* necessary to such that the resultant *T* is directed along the spike

(*b*) the magnitude of *T*

(*c*) plot *P* and *T* as a function of *d*. (Range of *d* between 1 and 20 mm).

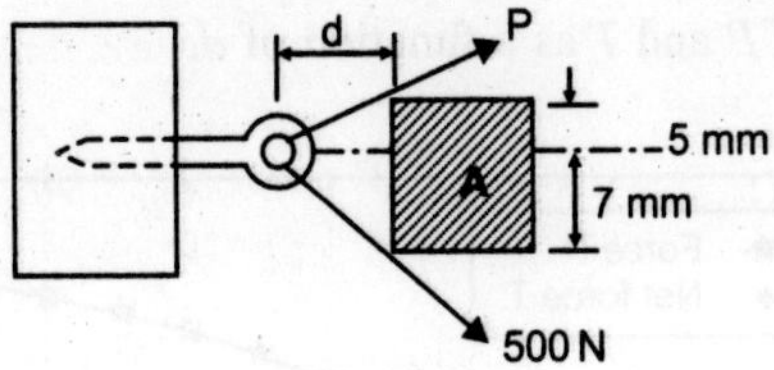

Fig. ES7.2

Solution: Free-body diagram of the system is shown in Fig. ES7.2 (*a*).

From equilibrium equations, resolving the forces along positive *x* and *y* directions:

$$T = \Sigma F_x = P\cos\alpha + 500\cos\beta$$

$$0 = \Sigma F_y = P\sin\alpha - 500\sin\beta$$

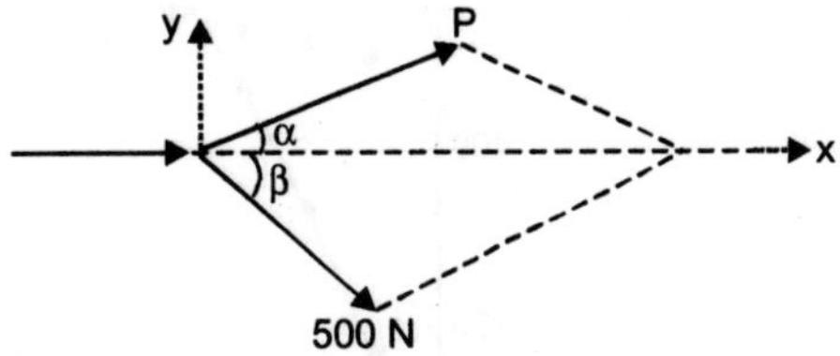

Fig. ES7.2 (a)

Solving the above two equations, we obtain

$$P = \frac{500\sin\beta}{\sin\alpha}$$

and $$T = 500\,(\sin\beta\cot\alpha + \cos\beta)$$

From the geometry

$$\alpha = \tan^{-1}(5/d) \text{ and } \beta = \tan^{-1}(7/d)$$

Complete MATLAB program is given below:

```
% Range of d
d = 1:1:20;
% Define alpha
alpha = atan (5./d);
%Define beta
beta = atan(7./d);
% Compute force P
P = 500*sin(beta)./sin(alpha);
% Define force T
T=500*(sin (beta).*cot (alpha) +cos (beta));
plot (d, P,'-*', d, T,'-p')
xlabel ('d (mm)');
ylabel ('Force (N)');
legend('Force P', 'Net force T');
grid on;
```

Figure ES7.2 (*b*) shows the plot of *P* and *T* as a function of *d*.

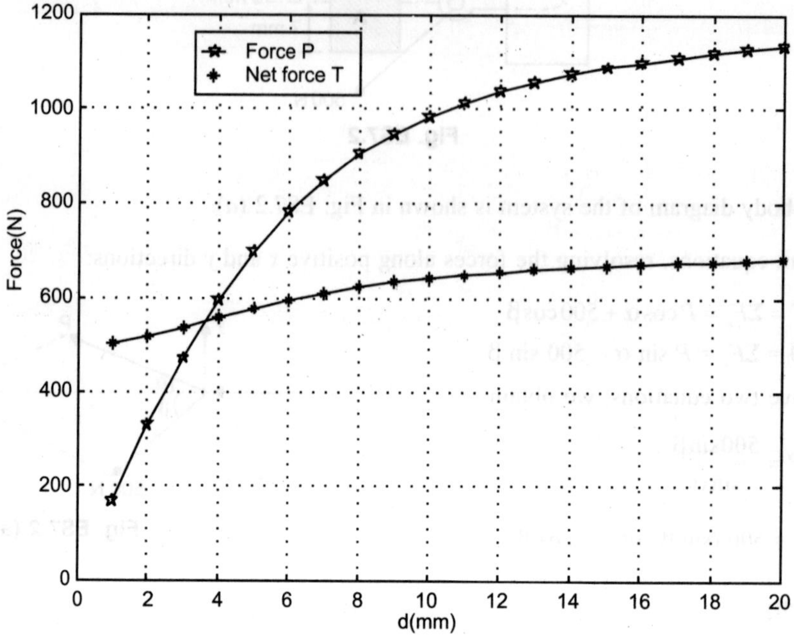

Fig. ES7.2(b)

Example ES7.3: Figure ES7.3 shows the two cables *MO* and *NO* tied together at *O* and the loadings are also shown. The magnitude of *F* is 150 N.

(*a*) Derive the expressions relating the tension in each cable as a function of α.

(*b*) Write a MATLAB program to plot the tension in each cable for 0° ≤ α ≤ 90°.

(*c*) Determine the smallest value of α for which both cables are in tension.

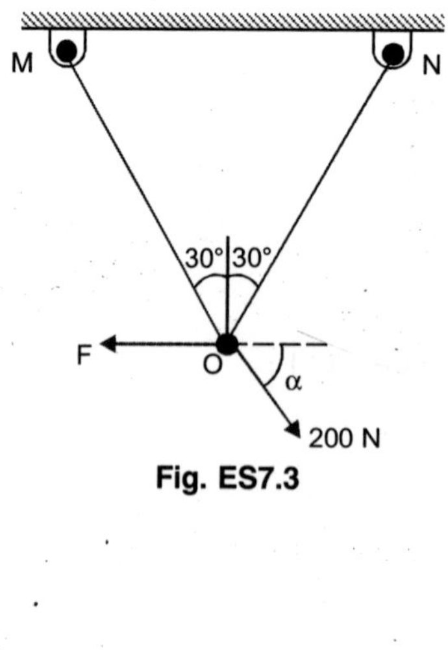

Fig. ES7.3

Solution: Free-body diagram is shown in Fig. ES7.3 (*a*).
Applying the equations of equilibrium:

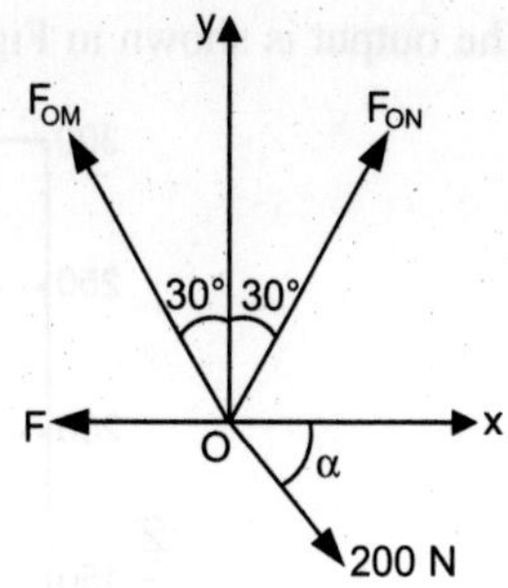

Fig. ES 7.3 (a)

(a) $\Sigma F_x = 0 \Rightarrow (F_{ON} - F_{OM}) \sin 30° - F + 200 \cos \alpha = 0$

or $(F_{ON} - F_{OM}) = 2F - 400 \cos \alpha$

Substituting $F = 150$ N

$$(F_{ON} - F_{OM}) = 300 - 400 \cos \alpha \quad (1)$$

$$\Sigma F_y = 0 \Rightarrow (F_{OM} + F_{ON}) \cos 30° - 200 \sin \alpha = 0$$

or $$(F_{OM} + F_{ON}) = 200 \times \frac{2}{\sqrt{3}} \cdot \sin \alpha = 230.94 \sin \alpha \quad (2)$$

Solving eqn. (1) and (2),

$$F_{ON} = 150 - 200 \cos \alpha + 115.47 \sin \alpha$$

$$F_{OM} = 115.47 \sin \alpha + 200 \cos \alpha - 150$$

For finding range of α, at which tensions are positive equate $F_{ON} = 0$ and $F_{OM} = 0$ and find α.

(b) **MATLAB Program:**

```
Alpha= [0:2:90];
alpha=Alpha*pi/180;
fon =150-200*cos (alpha) +115.47*sin (alpha);
fom=-150+115.47*sin (alpha) +200*cos (alpha);
ton=abs (fon);
tom=abs (fom);
[ton_min, i]=min (ton);
[tom_min, j]=min (tom);
Ang1_min=Alpha (i);
Ang2_min=Alpha (j);
plot (Alpha, fon, Alpha, fom);
legend ('Fon', 'Fom', 2)
xlabel ('Alpha (degree)')
ylabel ('Cable tension (N)')
grid on
fprintf ('(c)\n')
fprintf ('Smallest value of Alpha for which the tensions are positive is from
%g to %g degrees\n', Ang1_min, Ang2_min)
```

The output is shown in Fig. ES7.3 (*b*).

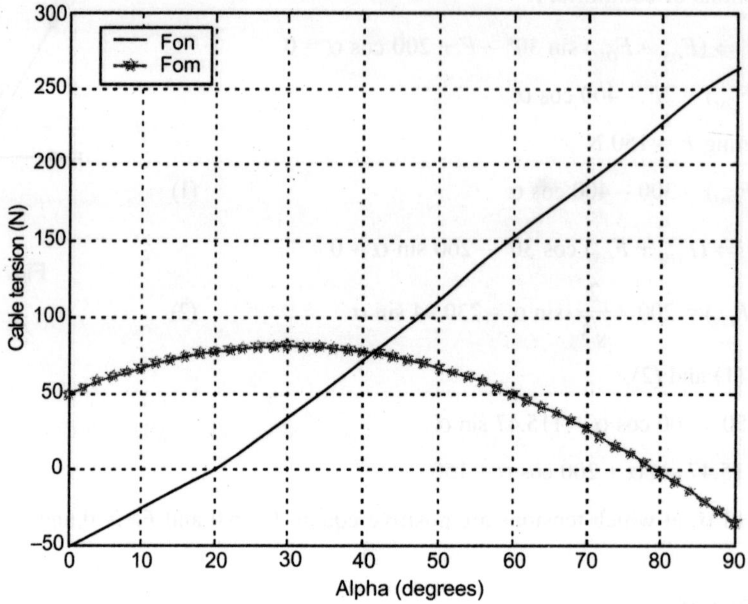

Fig. ES7.3 (b)

(*c*) Smallest value of alpha for which the tensions are positive is from 20 to 80 degrees.

Example ES7.4: Figure ES7.4 shows a weight *W* hung from the end of a horizontal pole of negligible weight.

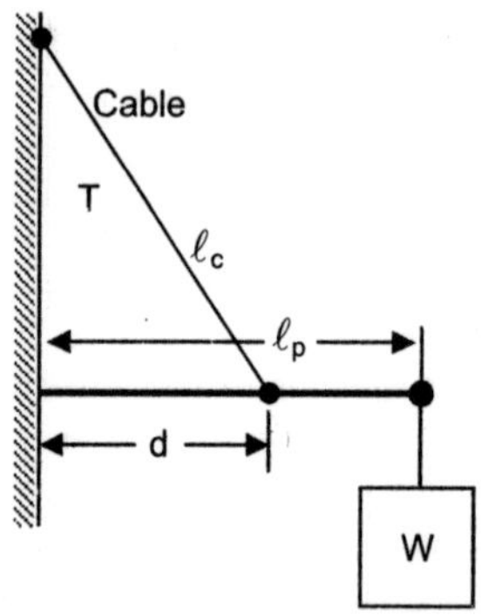

Fig. ES7.4

The pole is attached to the wall by a pivot and is supported by a cable attached to the wall at a higher point. The tension *T*, in the cable is given by

$$T = \frac{W \ell_c \ell_p}{d\sqrt{\ell_p^2 - d^2}}$$

where T = tension in the cable, W = weight of the object, ℓ_c = length of the cable, ℓ_p = length of the pole and d = distance along the pole at which the cable is attached.

Write a MATLAB program to (*a*) determine the distance (*d*) at which the cable can be attached to the pole in order to minimize the tension in the cable, (*b*) plot the tension in the cable as *a* function of *d*.

Given: $W = 250$ N, $\ell_p = 50$ cm, $\ell_c = 40$ cm.

Solution: The free-body diagram of the system is shown in Fig. ES7.4 (*a*).

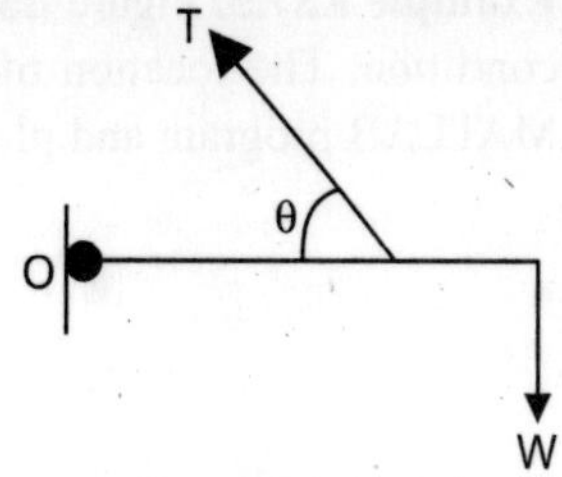

Fig. ES7.4 (a)

MATLAB program is given below:

```
lc=0.40;
lp=0.50;
W=250;
d=0.05:0.05:lp;
% Calculate tension
T=W *lc *lp./(d.*sqrt(lp^2-d.^2));
plot(d*100,T,'-p');
xlabel('Distance d in cm);
ylabel('Tension in string in N');
grid on;
[Tmin, I]=min(T);
fprintf('Minimum tension is %g N at %g cm',Tmin,d(I)*100)
```

The output is given in Fig. ES7.4(*b*).

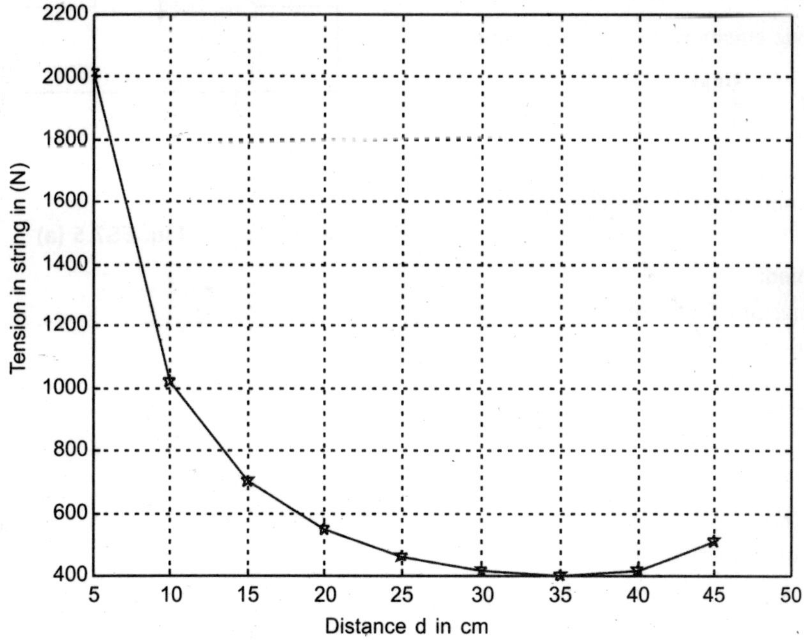

Fig. ES7.4 (b)

At the command prompt following output is obtained:

>> Minimum tension is 400.08 N at 35 cm.

Example ES7.5: Figure ES7.5 shows the location of the center of gravity of a 5000 N truck for the unloaded condition. The location of the added load W_L is at a distance of x inches behind the rear axle. Write a MATLAB program and plot W_L as a function of x for x ranging from 0 to 60 mm.

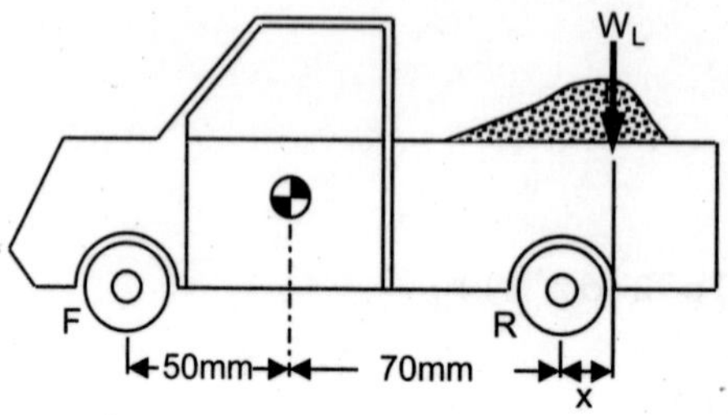

Fig. ES7.5

Solution: Free-body diagram of the system is shown in Fig. ES7.5(*a*).

The equilibrium equations can be written as

Moment about rear wheel axle:

$$\Sigma M_R = 0 = 5000(70) - N(120) - W_L x = 0$$

$$\Sigma F_y = 0 = N + N - 5000 - W_L = 0$$

Solving the above equations for W_L, we obtain

$$W_L = \frac{5000}{(60 + x)}$$

The plot of W_L as a function of x is shown in Fig. ES7.5 (*b*) from the following program.

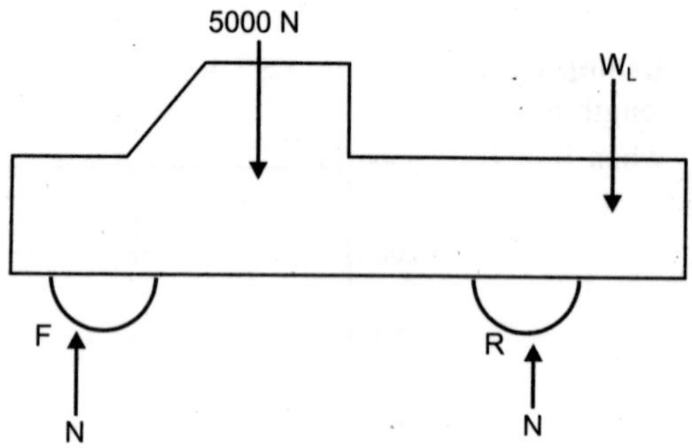

Fig. ES7.5 (a)

MATLAB Solution:

```
% Define the range of x for the plot
x = 0:0.05:60;
% Define Wl
Wl=5000/(60 + x);
plot(x, Wl)
% Labels
xlabel ('x (mm)')
ylabel ('Load weight (N)')
grid on;
```

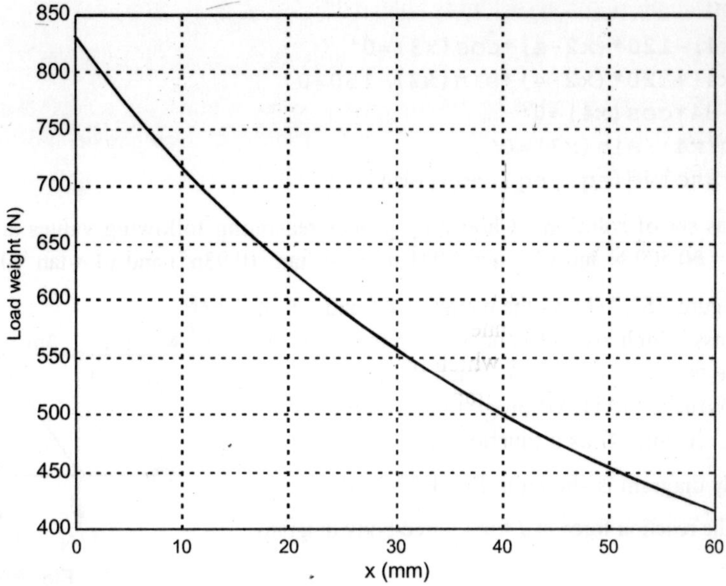

Fig. ES7.5 (b)

Example ES7.6: Figure ES7.6 shows a container of weight W suspended from ring C to which cable CB of length 6 m and spring AC are attached. Write a MATLAB program to determine the tension in the cable when $W = 150$ N. Given: The spring constant as 120 N/m, and its unstreched length as 4 m.

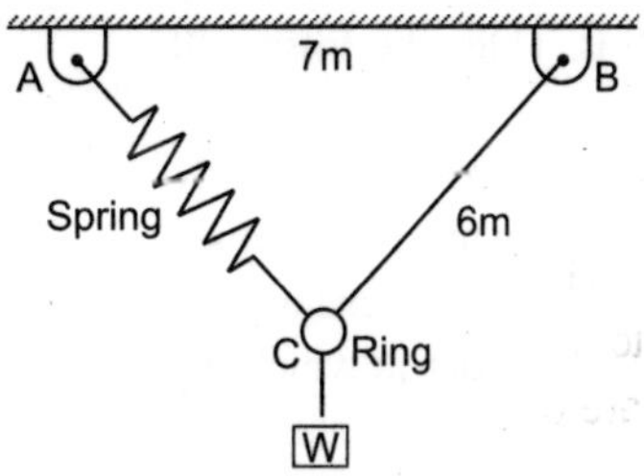

Fig. ES7.6

Solution: Free-body diagram of the system is shown in Fig. ES7.6 (*a*).

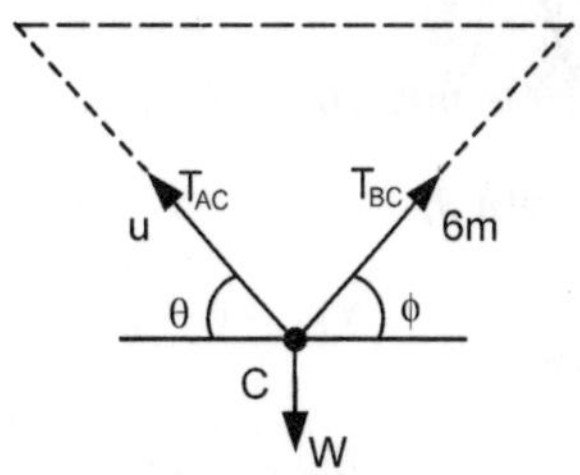

Fig. ES7.6 (a)

$$\Sigma F_x = 0 \Rightarrow T_{BC} \cdot \cos\phi - T_{AC}\cos\theta = 0 \quad ...(1)$$

$$\Sigma F_y = 0 \Rightarrow T_{BC} \cdot \sin\phi + T_{AC}\sin\theta - W = 0 \quad ...(2)$$

Geometry:

$$u^2 = 6^2 + 7^2 - 2(6)(7)\cos\phi = 78 - 84\cos\phi \quad ...(3)$$

$$\frac{u}{\sin\phi} = \frac{6}{\sin\theta} \quad ...(4)$$

Stiffness:

$$T_{AC} = k(u - u_0) = 120(u - 4) \quad ...(5)$$

Replacing T_{AC} in terms of u, the problem reduces to find four unknowns, T_{BC}, u, θ and ϕ.

Calling them respectively as $x1$, $x2$, $x3$, $x4$ following MATLAB program is developed to solve the equations.

MATLAB Program:

```
eq1='x1*cos(x4)-120*(x2-4)*cos(x3)=0'
eq2='x1*sin(x4)+120*(x2-4)*sin(x3)-150=0'
eq3='x2^2-78+84*cos(x4)=0'
eq4='x2-6*sin(x4)/sin(x3)=0';
[x1,x2,x3,x4]=solve(eq1,eq2,eq3,eq4)
```

This gives output as set of solutions. Choose by proper reasoning following values are obtained. Output is $x1 = T_{BC} = 60.509$ N and $x2 = u = 4.921$ m, $x3 = \tan^{-1}(0.9365)$ and $x4 = \tan^{-1}(0.7681)$.

Example ES7.7: Figure ES7.7 shows the members *CJ* and *CF* of the loaded truss cross which are not connected to members *BI* and *DG*. Determine the values of α for which the truss cannot be in equilibrium. Write a MATLAB program to plot the forces in members *BC*, *JC*, *IC* and *IG* as a function of α.

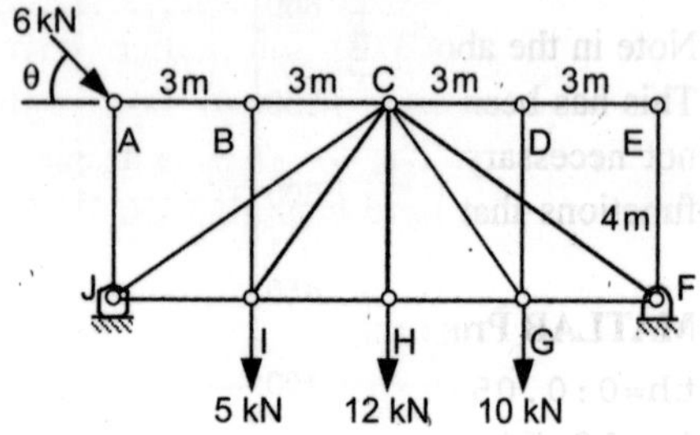

Fig. ES7.7

Solution: Free-body diagram is shown in Fig. ES7.7 (*a*).

First we determine the reaction force at *J* from a free-body diagram for the entire truss.

$$\circlearrowleft \Sigma M_F = 0 = 6\sin\theta(12) - 6\cos\theta(4) + 4(9) + 10(6) + 8(3) - J_y(12)$$

$$J_y = 10 + 6\sin\theta - 2\cos\theta$$

Note that the rocker can only exert an upward force at *A*. Thus, to be in equilibrium, J_y must be positive. Since sin θ and cos θ vary between plus and minus one, the above equation indicates that J_y will be positive for all θ. Thus, the truss will be in equilibrium for all values of θ.

To obtain the required forces we now consider free-body diagrams for joints *A*, *J* and *I*. Note that each member is assumed to be in tension. Thus, positive answers will imply tension and negative answers compression. Also note the order in which the joints are analysed. In each case there are only two unknown forces.

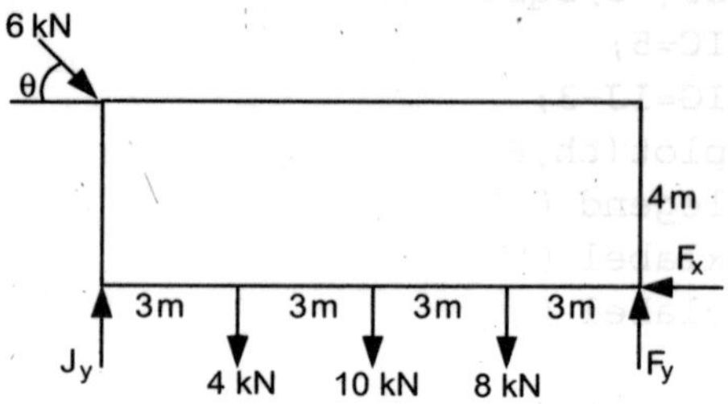

Fig. ES7.7 (a)

Joint *A*:

$$\Sigma F_x = 0 = AB + 6\cos\theta,\ \Sigma F_y = 0 = -6\sin\theta - AJ$$

$$AJ = -6\sin\theta,\quad AB = -6\cos\theta$$

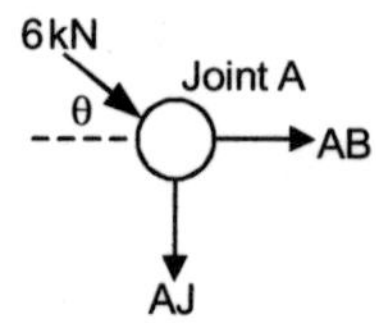

Note that *AB* = *BC* since *BI* is a zero-force member.

Joint *J*:

$$\Sigma F_x = 0 = IJ + \frac{3}{\sqrt{13}}JC,\ \Sigma F_y = 0 = AJ + J_y + \frac{2}{\sqrt{13}}JC$$

$$JC = -\frac{\sqrt{13}}{2}(AJ + J_y) = -\frac{\sqrt{13}}{2}(10 - 2\cos\theta)$$

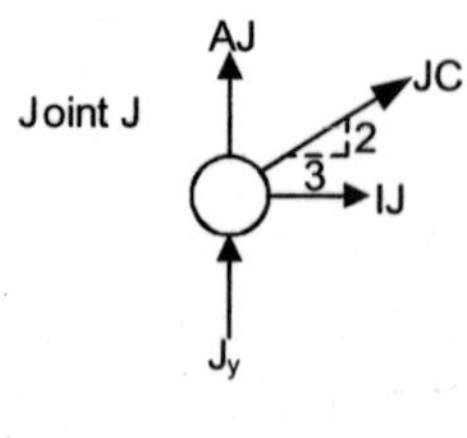

$$IJ = -\frac{3}{\sqrt{13}} JC = 15 - 3\cos\theta$$

Joint *I*:

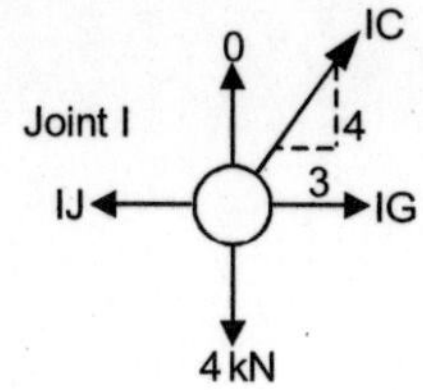

$$\Sigma F_x = 0 = GI - IJ + \frac{3}{5} IC,\ \Sigma F_y = 0 = \frac{4}{5} IC - 4$$

$$IC = 5 \text{ kN},\ \ IG = IJ - \frac{3}{5} 5 = 12 - 3\cos\theta$$

Note in the above that substitutions have been made in order to express each force explicitly in terms of θ. This has been done primarily for completeness. The program below shows that the explicit substitution is not necessary. The computer will substitute automatically provided each force is expressed in terms of functions that have been previously defined.

MATLAB Program:

```
th=0:0.05:2*pi;
Jy=10+6*sin (th)-2*cos (th);
AJ=-6*sin (th);
BC=-6*cos (th);
JC=sqrt (13)/2*(AJ + Jy);
IJ=-3/sqrt (13)*JC;
IC=5;
IG=IJ-3;
plot(th,BC,th,JC,th,IC,th,IG)
legend ('BC','JC','IC','IG')
xlabel ('Theta (rads)')
ylabel ('Force (kN)')
```

Output is shown in Fig. ES7.7(*b*).

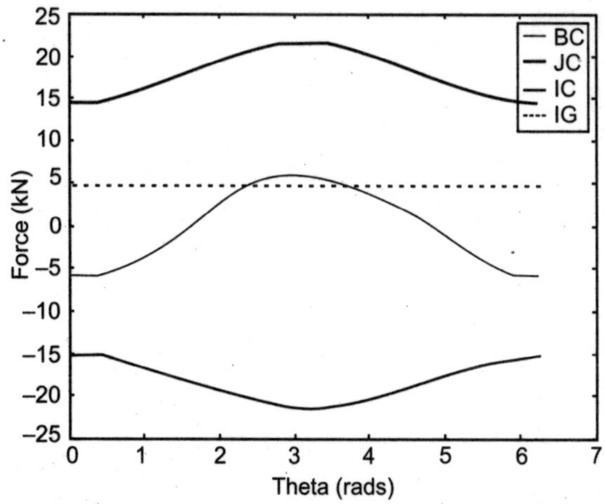

Fig. ES7.7 (b)

Example ES7.8: In Fig. ES7.8 rod *CB* is held by a cord *AC* which has a tension *T*.

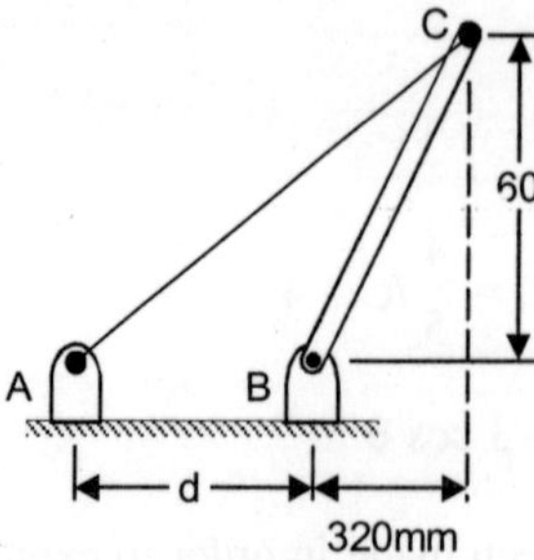

Fig. ES7.8

Write a MATLAB program to determine,

(*a*) the moment about *B* of the force exerted by the cord at point *C* as a function of the tension *T* and the distance *d*.

(*b*) plot the moment about *B* for 300 mm ≤ *d* ≤ 1000 mm when (*i*) *T* = 60 N, (*ii*) *T* = 80 N, (*iii*) *T* = 110 N.

Solution: Free-body diagram is shown in Fig. ES7.8 (*a*).

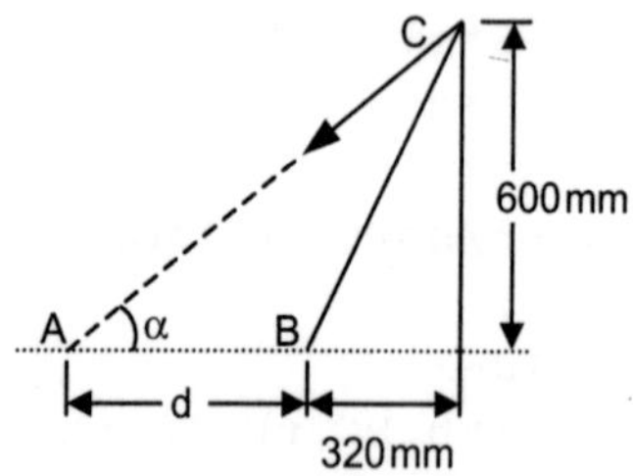

Fig. ES7.8 (a)

The length of *AC* is from the figure,

$$AC = \sqrt{(600)^2 + (320+c)^2}$$

For the angle α we have

$$\cos\alpha = \frac{320+c}{AC}$$

$$\sin\alpha = \frac{600}{AC}$$

The tension **T** is given by

$$\mathbf{T} = -T\cos\alpha\mathbf{i} - T\sin\mathbf{j}$$

and the position vector from point *B* as

$$\mathbf{r} = 320\mathbf{i} + 600\mathbf{j}$$

The moment about point *B* is

$$\mathbf{M}_B = \mathbf{r}\times\mathbf{T} = (320\mathbf{i} + 600\mathbf{j})\times(-\cos\alpha\mathbf{i} - \sin\alpha\mathbf{j})\,T$$

$$= T\,(600\cos\alpha - 320\sin\alpha)\,\mathbf{k}$$

The magnitude of the moment is

$$M_B = \frac{600Tc}{\sqrt{c^2 + 640c + 462400}}$$

$$M_B = \frac{T}{AC}[600(320+c) - 320(600)]$$

$$M_B = \frac{600Tc}{\sqrt{(600)^2 + (320+c)^2}}$$

or $$M_B = \frac{600Tc}{\sqrt{c^2 + 640c + 4624000}}$$

MATLAB Program:

```
c=[320:1:960];
Mb1=600*60*c./(sqrt(c.^2+640*c+462400));
Mb2=600*80*c./(sqrt(c.^2+640*c+462400));
Mb3=600*110*c./(sqrt(c.^2+640*c+462400));
plot(c,Mb1,c,Mb2,c,Mb3)
legend('T=60 N','T=80 N','T=110 N',2)
xlabel('c(mm)')
ylabel('Moment(N mm)')
grid on
```

Output is shown in Fig. ES7.8(*b*).

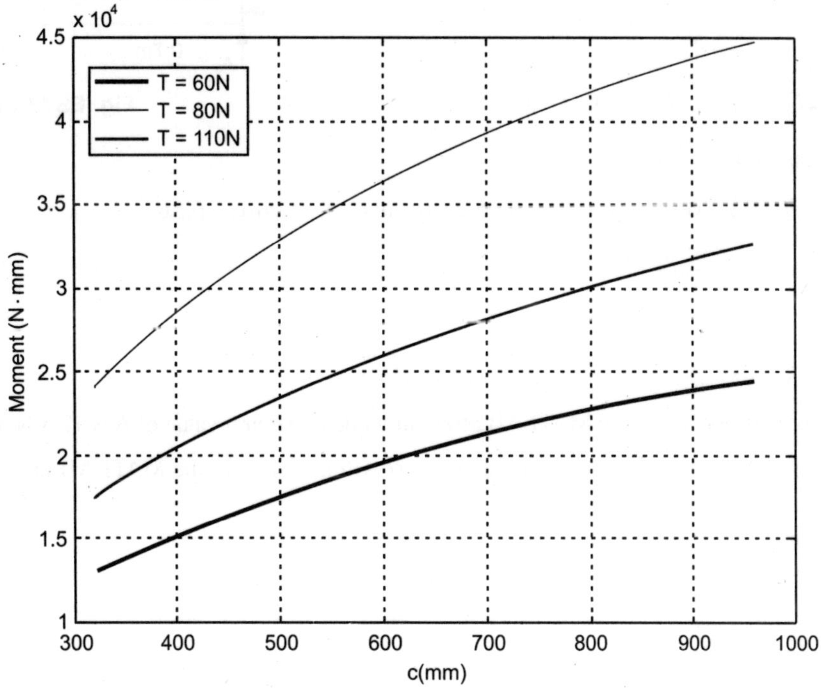

Fig. ES7.8 (b)

Example ES7.9: Figure ES7.9 shows a frame in which the structural members support the 5 kN load. The load may be applied at any angle α (–90° to + 90°). The pins at *A* and *B* need to be designed to support the maximum force transmitted to them. Write a MATLAB program to plot the forces at *A* and *B* as a function of α and find their maximum values and corresponding angles α.

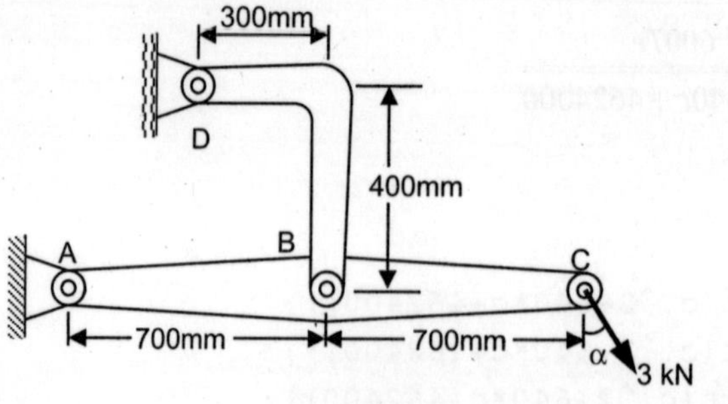

Fig. ES7.9

Solution: Free-body diagram of *ABC* is shown in Fig. ES7.9(*a*).

Note that member *BD* is a two-force member, thus the direction of the force ***B*** is from *B* to *D*. The equilibrium equations are,

$$\Sigma M_A = \frac{4}{5} B\,(0.6) - 5\cos\alpha(1.4) = 0$$

$$\Sigma F_x = A_x - \frac{3}{5} B + 5\sin\alpha = 0$$

$$\Sigma F_y = A_y + \frac{4}{5} B - 5\cos\alpha = 0$$

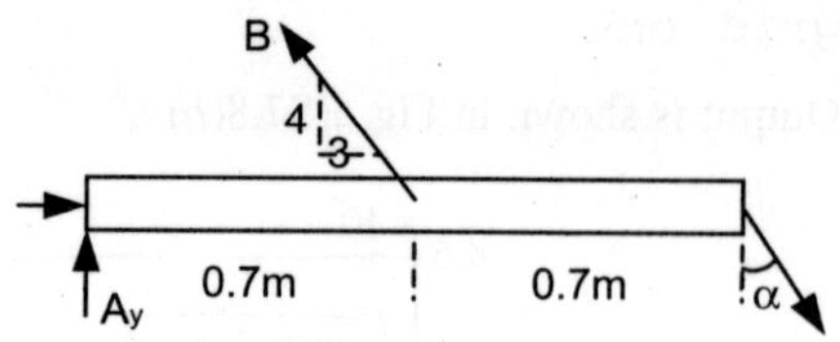

Fig. ES7.9 (a)

Solving these equations yields,

$$B = 12.5\cos\alpha,\quad A_x = 0.6\ \ B - 5\cos\alpha\quad \text{and}\quad A_y = 5\cos\alpha - 0.8B$$

$$A = \sqrt{A_x^2 + A_y^2}$$

Substitution and simplification yields

$$A = \sqrt{81.25\cos^2\alpha + 25\sin^2\alpha - 75\cos\alpha\sin\alpha}$$

Maximum value of *A* is obtained from MATLAB program while maximum value of *B* is 12.5 N at $\alpha = 0$.

The maximum value of *A* and the corresponding angle α will be found in the MATLAB program.

MATLAB Program:

```
al=-pi/2:0.01:pi/2;
B=12.5*cos(al);
Ax=0.6*B-5*sin(al);
Ay=5*cos(al)-0.8*B;
A=sqrt(Ax.^2+Ay.^2);
[Amax,K]=max(A);
plot(al,B,al,A)
legend('A','B')
xlabel('Alpha (rad)')
ylabel('Force (kN)')
fprintf('Maximum value of A=%f and corresponding angle =%f\n',Amax,al(K)*180/
pi);
```

Output is shown in Fig. ES7.9 (*b*).

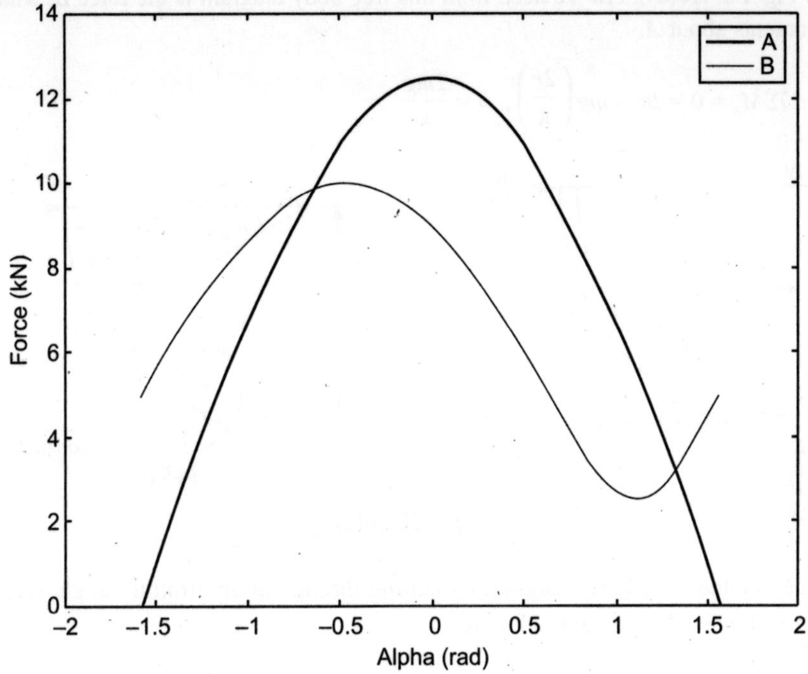

Fig. ES7.9 (b)

Example ES7.10: Figure ES7.10 shows a uniform quarter-circular member of mass *m* lying in the vertical plane and hinged at *A* and supported against the vertical wall by a small roller at *B*.

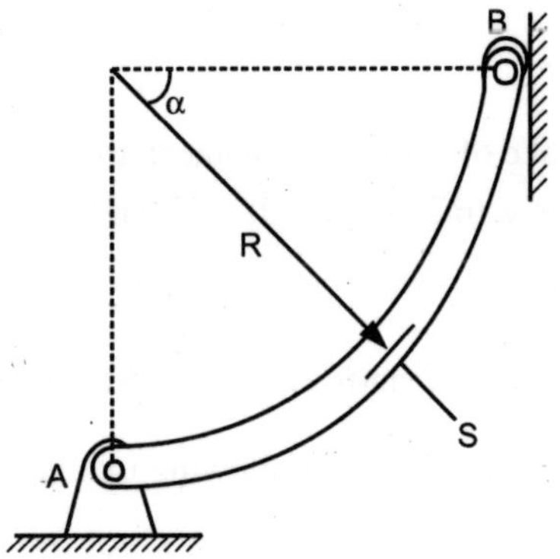

Fig. ES7.10

(*a*) Derive expressions for the shear force *V*, the compressive force *C*, and the bending moment *M* due to the weight of the member.

(*b*) Write a MATLAB program to plot the non-dimensional forces and moment (V/mg, C/mg and M/mgR) as a function of the section orientation angle α.

(*c*) Determine the maximum bending moment and its location angle α.

Solution: First consider the free-body diagram for the entire member. The centroid for a quarter-circular arc is $2r/\pi$. (see the Fig. ES7.10(*a*)). All we need from this free-body diagram is the force *B*, which we can find by summing moments about *A*.

$$\circlearrowleft \Sigma M_A = 0 = Br - mg\left(\frac{2r}{\pi}\right); \; B = \frac{2mg}{k}$$

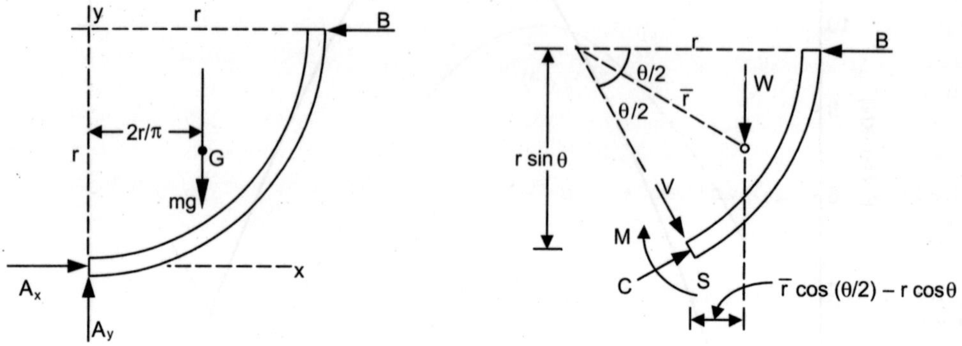

Fig. ES7.10(a)

Now we construct another free-body diagram by cutting through at an arbitrary angle θ as shown to the figure above. From Table *D*/3, the centroid $\bar{r}$ is,

$$\bar{r} = \frac{r\sin(\theta/2)}{\theta/2} = \frac{2r\sin(\theta/2)}{\theta}$$

The weight *W* of the section in the diagram will be *mg* (the total weight of the member) times the ratio of the length of the section $(r\theta)$ to the total length of the member $(r\pi/2)$. Thus,

$$W = \frac{r\theta}{r\pi/2}mg = \frac{2\theta}{\pi}mg$$

Now we sum moment about *S*. For sake of clarity, the moment arms for *W* and *B* are shown in the diagram.

$$\Sigma M_S = 0 = M + W(\bar{r}\cos(\theta/2) - r\cos\theta) - Br\sin\theta$$

Substitution and simplification yields,

$$M = \frac{2mgr}{\pi}(\theta\cos\theta + \sin\theta - 2\sin(\theta/2)) = \frac{2mgr}{\pi}\theta\cos\theta$$

Summing forces in the *x* and *y* directions gives the following two equations,

$$\Sigma F_x = 0 = C\sin\theta + V\cos\theta - B, \; \Sigma F_y = 0 = C\cos\theta - V\sin\theta - W$$

Solving these two equations followed by substitution and simplification yields,

$$C = \frac{2mg}{\pi}(\theta\cos\theta + \sin\theta); \quad V = \frac{2mg}{\pi}(\cos\theta - \theta\sin\theta)$$

In non-dimensional form we have,

$$\frac{M}{mgr} = \frac{2}{\pi}\theta\cos\theta; \quad \frac{C}{mg} = \frac{2}{\pi}(\theta\cos\theta + \sin\theta); \quad \frac{V}{mg} = \frac{2}{\pi}(\cos\theta - \theta\sin\theta)$$

The maximum moment and where it occurs will be found in the worksheet below. The results are,

$M_{max} = 0.357\ mgr$ at $\theta = 0.860$ radians (49.3°).

Complete MATLAB program is given below:

MATLAB Program:

```
%%%%%%%%%%%%%%%%%%Script #1%%%%%%%%%%%%%%%%%%%%%%
%This script plots the non-dimensional forces C and V as % functions of theta.
theta=0:0.01:pi/2;
C=2/pi.*(theta.*cos(theta)+sin(theta));
V=2/pi.*(cos(theta)-theta.*sin(theta));
plot(theta*180/pi,C,theta*180/pi,V)
legend('C','V')
xlabel('Theta(deg)')
title('Non-dimensional Forces')
%%%%%%%%%%%%%%%%%%%%%%%%%%%%%%%%%%%%%%%%%%%%%%%%%%%
```

Output is shown in Fig. ES7.10(*b*).

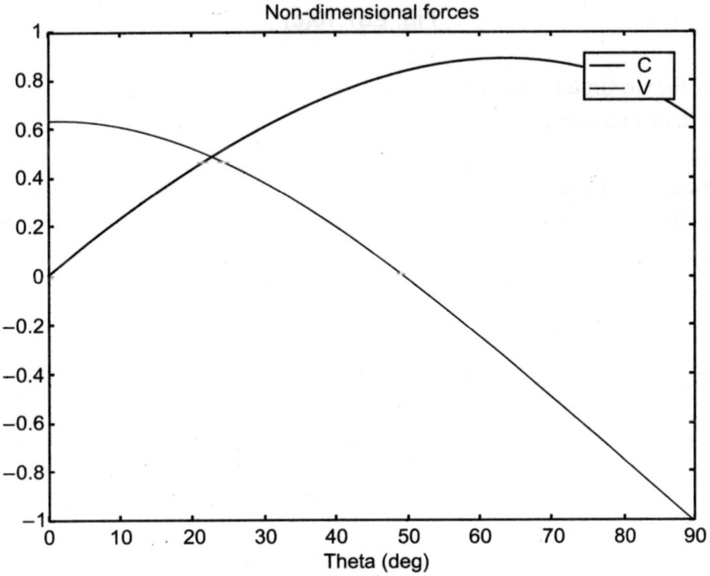

Fig. ES7.10 (b)

```
% This script plots the non-dimensional bending moment
% as a function of theta
theta = 0:0.01:pi/2;
M = 2/pi*theta.*cos (theta);
plot (theta*180/pi, M)
xlabel ('Theta  (deg)')
Title('Non-dimensional bending moment')
```

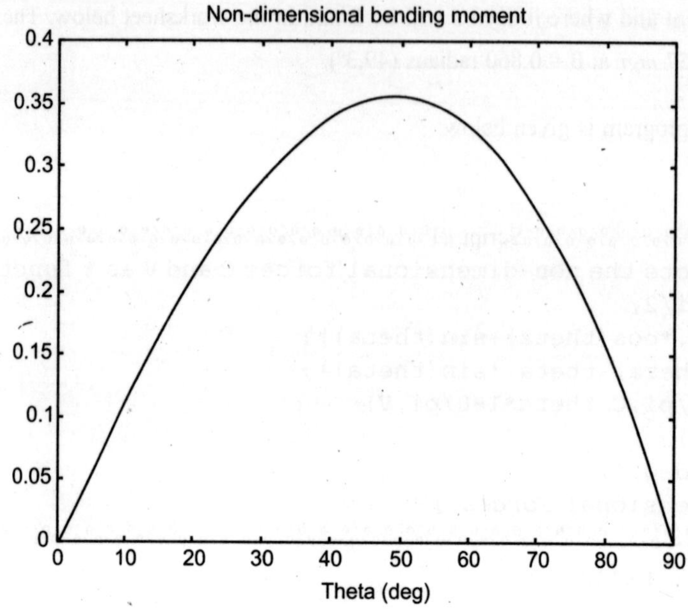

Fig. ES7.10(c)

```
% This program finds the maximum moment
% using MATLAB's max function
theta=0:0.01:pi/2;
M=2/pi*theta.*cos(theta);
[M_max, i]=max (M)
theta_max=theta (i)

Output is shown below:
M_max =
            0.3572
i =
    87
theta_max =
            0.8600

%This script plots y versus x using the values of T0
%found in the previous script

y = inline('T0./0.1177.*(cosh (0.1177.*x./T0)-1)');
x = -150:1:150;
y10 = 132.61./0.1177.*(cosh(0.1177.*x./132.61) -1);
y30 = 44.71./0.1177.*(cosh(0.1177.*x./44.71) -1);
y60 = 23.16./0.1177.*(cosh(0.1177.*x./23.16) -1);
plot (x, y10, x, y30, x, y60)
xlabel ('x (m)')
ylabel ('y (m)')
```

The output is shown in Fig. ES7.10 (*d*).

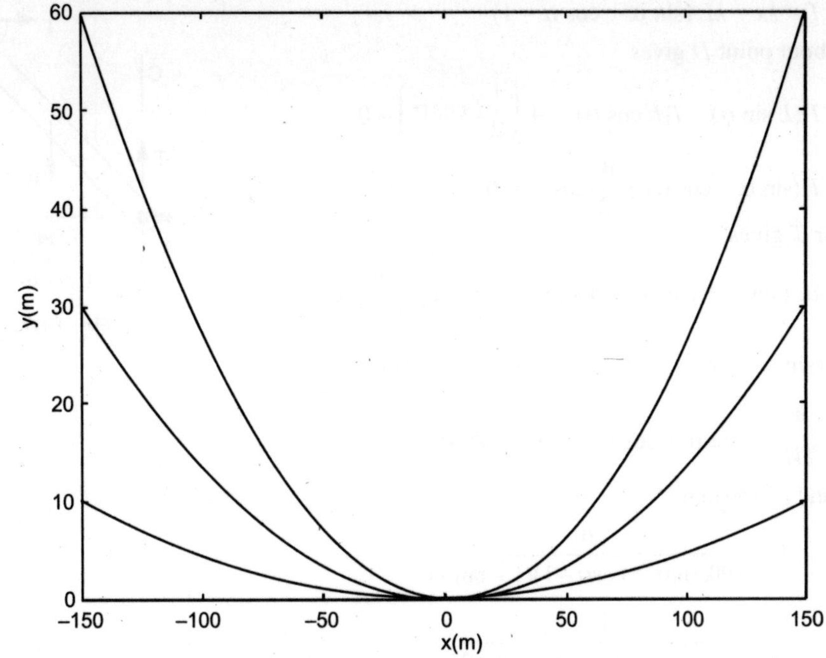

Fig. ES7.10(d)

Example ES7.11: Figure ES7.11 shows a slender rod *AB* of weight *W* attached to blocks at *A* and *B* which move freely in the guides.

(*a*) Derive a relationship between α, *W*, *L* and *k* that need to be satisfied for the rod to be in equilibrium. The spring constant is *k*, $W = 20$ N and $L = 50$ mm.

(*b*) Write a MATLAB program to compute and plot *k* as a function of α for $15° \leq \alpha \leq 40°$.

(*c*) Determine the two values of α corresponding to equilibrium when $k = 0.8$ N/mm.

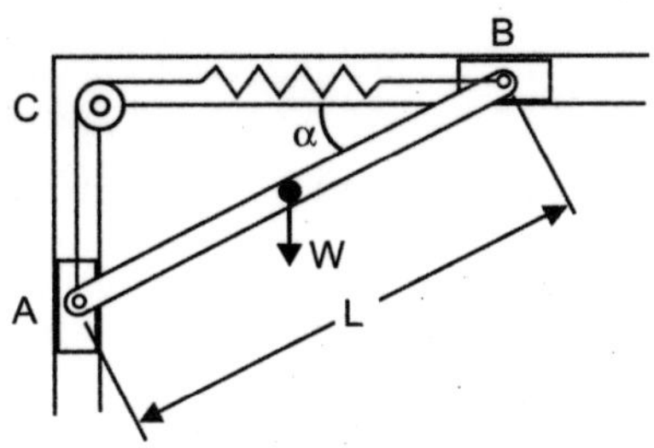

Fig. ES7.11

Solution: Refer to the free-body diagram shown in Fig. ES7.11(*a*).

If *x* is equal to the elongation of the spring, then

$$x = AC + BC - L$$
$$= L(\sin\alpha + \cos\alpha - 1)$$

The tension in the spring is given by

$$T = kx = kL\,(\sin\alpha + \cos\alpha - 1)$$

The moment about point D gives

$$\Sigma M_D = 0: T\,(L\sin\alpha) - T(L\cos\alpha) + W\left(\frac{1}{2}L\cos\alpha\right) = 0$$

or, $$T\,(\sin\alpha - \cos\alpha) + \frac{W}{2}\cos\alpha = 0$$

Substituting for T gives

$$kL\,(\sin\alpha + \cos\alpha - 1)\,(\sin\alpha - \cos\alpha) + \frac{W}{2}\cos\alpha = 0$$

$$(\sin\alpha + \cos\alpha - 1)\,(\tan\alpha - 1) + \frac{W}{2}\cos\alpha = 0$$

and $$\frac{W}{2kL} = (\sin\alpha + \cos\alpha - 1)\,(1 - \tan\alpha)$$

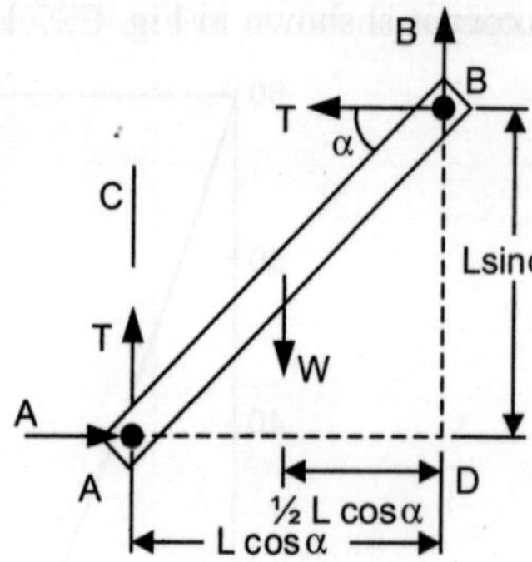

Fig. ES7.11(a)

For $W = 20$ N and $L = 50$ mm.

$$k = \frac{20}{100(\sin\alpha + \cos\alpha - 1)(1 - \tan\alpha)}$$

$$= \frac{1}{5(\sin\alpha + \cos\alpha - 1)(1 - \tan\alpha)}$$

MATLAB Program:

```
syms pt real % DEFINING pt and real as symbolic quantities
W=20;
L=50;
K=0.8;
rhs=W/(2*K*L);
Tha=[15:0.1:40];
t=Tha*pi/180;
k=1./(5*(sin(t)+cos(t)-1).*(1-tan(t)));
plot(Tha,k)
xlabel('Theta(deg)')
ylabel('Spring constant k (N/mm)')
grid on
eq1=(sin(pt)+cos(pt)-1)*(1-tan(pt))-rhs;
[pt]= solve(eq1);
Ang = real(double(pt));
Theta = Ang*180/pi;
fprintf('The calculated angles for Theta are:%8.2fdegrees\n',Theta)
```

Output is shown in Fig. ES7.11 (*b*).

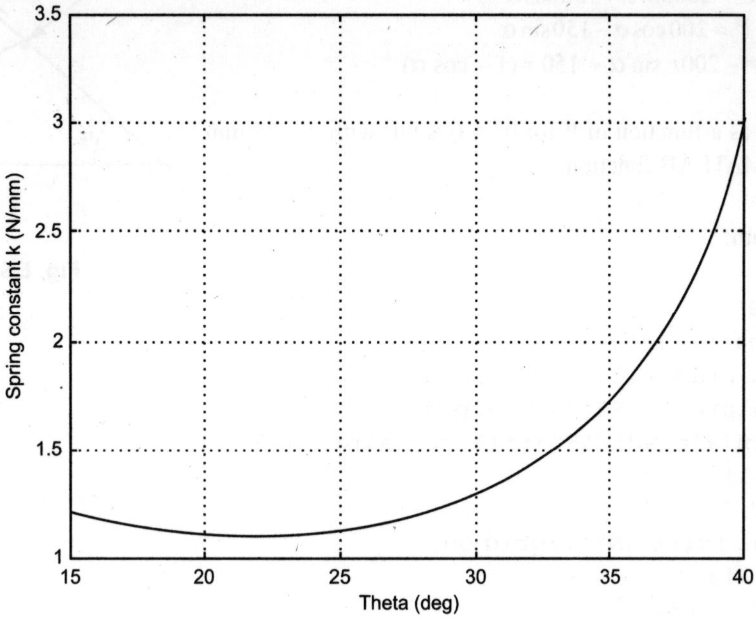

Fig. ES7.11(b)

The calculated angles for Theta are: –132.18 degrees
The calculated angles for Theta are: 21.09 degrees
The calculated angles for Theta are: 21.09 degrees.

Example ES7.12: Figure ES7.12 shows the loading on a semicircular member. The radius of the semicircular member is 25 mm. Write a MATLAB program to plot the internal forces, namely, the axial forces, shearing force and bending moment as functions of α for $0 < \alpha < 90°$.

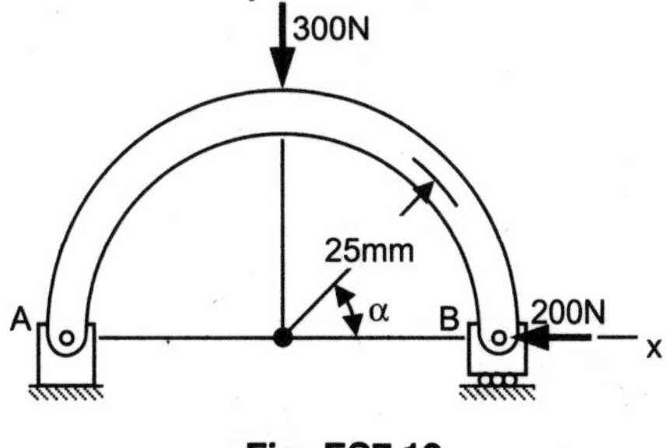

Fig. ES7.12

Solution: Figure ES7.12 (*a*) shows free-body diagram of the system.

For $0 \le \alpha \le 90^o$:

Axial force $C = 200\sin\alpha + 150\cos\alpha$

Shear force $V = 200\cos\alpha - 150\sin\alpha$

Moment $M = -200r\sin\alpha + 150r(1 - \cos\alpha)$

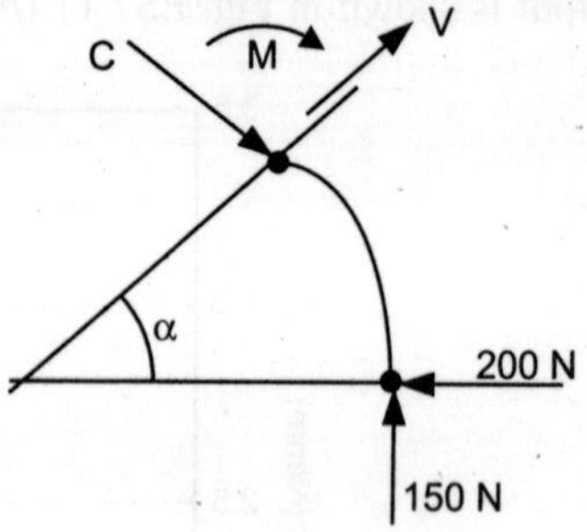

Fig. ES7.12(a)

Plot these values as a function of θ for $0° \le \theta \le 90°$ with $r = 25$ mm using following MATLAB function.

MATLAB Program:

```
r=25;
alpha = 0:5:90;
alprad = alpha*pi/180;
C=200.*sin(alprad)+150.*cos(alprad);
V=200.*cos(alprad)-150.*sin(alprad);
M=-200*r.*sin(alprad)+150*r*(1-cos(alprad));
subplot(3,1,1);
plot(alpha,C,'-p');
ylabel('Axial force (N)');grid on;
subplot(3,1,2);
plot(alpha,V, '-p');
ylabel('Shear force (N)');
grid on;
subplot(3,1,3);
plot(alpha,M,'-p');
ylabel('Moment(Nm)');
xlabel('Angle (degree)');
grid on;
```

Output is shown in Fig. ES7.12 (*b*).

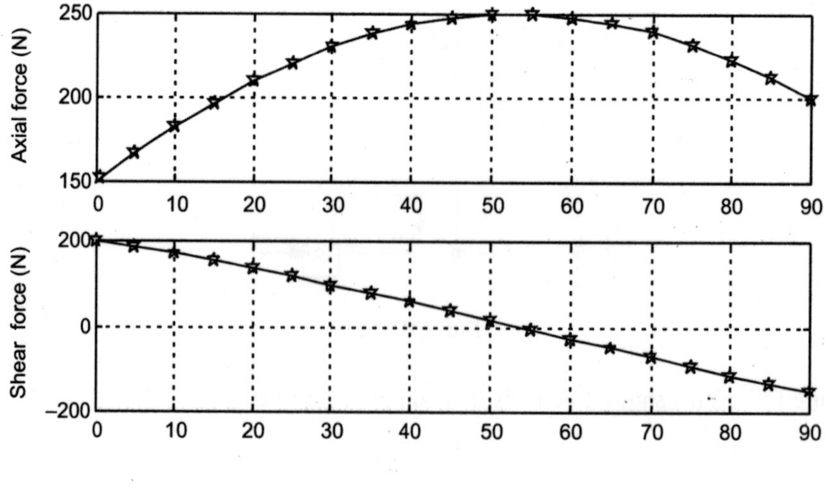

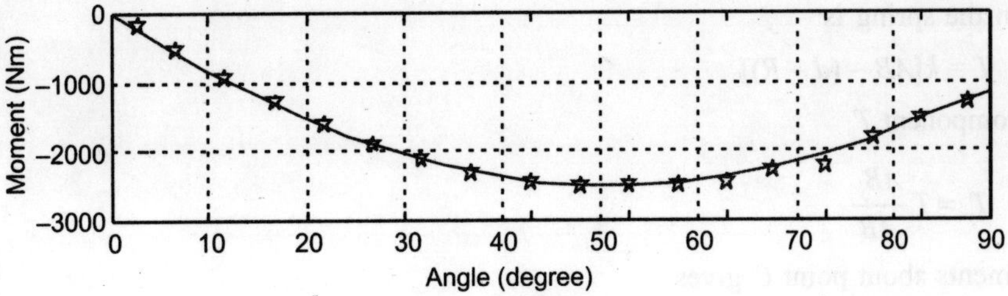

Fig. ES7.12(b)

Example ES7.13: In figure ES7.13, the spring is unstretched when $\alpha = 0$ and k is the spring constant. Write a MATLAB program to compute and plot the mass m corresponding to equilibrium as a function of α for values of α from 0° to 90°. Find the value of α corresponding to equilibrium $m = 2.5$ kg. Given $R = 210$ mm, $d = 50$ mm and $k = 1.2$ kN/m.

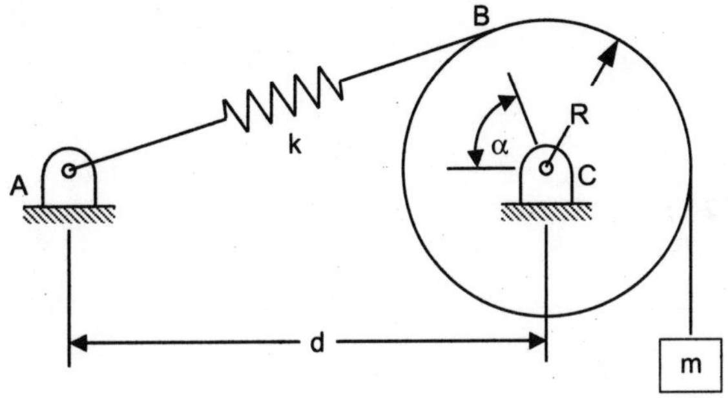

Fig. ES7.13

Solution: The free-body diagram is shown in Fig. ES7.13 (*a*).

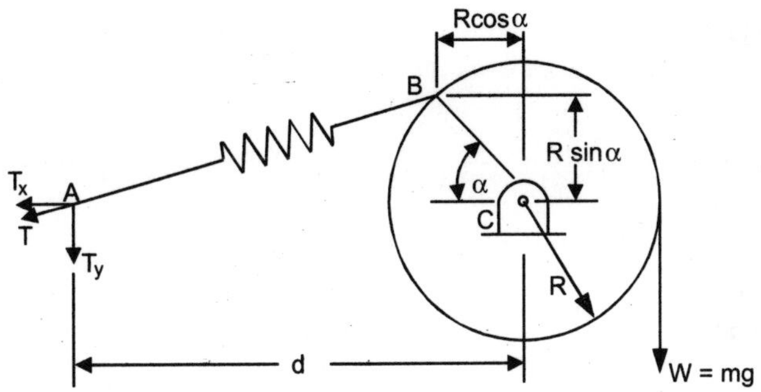

Fig. ES7.13 (a)

The length of spring AB is

$$AB_x = d - R\cos\alpha$$

$$AB_y = R\sin\alpha$$

$$AB = \sqrt{AB_x^2 + AB_y^2}$$

The tension in the spring is

$$T = k[AB - (d - R)]$$

The vertical component T_y

$$T_y = T\frac{AB_y}{AB}$$

Summing moments about point C gives

$$\Sigma M_C = 0:$$

$$T_y d - mgR = 0; \; m = T_y \frac{d}{Rg}$$

For this MATLAB program is as follows:

```
% Input Data
syms d R al g k real
ABx=d-R*cos(al);
ABy=R*sin(al);
AB=sqrt(ABx^2+ABy^2);
T=k*(AB-(d-R));
Ty=T*ABy/AB;
m=Ty*d/(R*g);
u=Ty*d-2*R*g;
u=subs(u,{R,g,d,k},{0.21,9.81,0.5,1200});
m=subs(m,{R,g,d,k},{0.21,9.81,0.5,1200});
th=solve(u,al);
Angle=th*180/pi;
Alpha=double(Angle)
td=[0:5:90];
ang=td*pi/180;
yd=subs(m,al,ang);
%
plot(td,yd)
xlabel('Alpha(deg)')
ylabel('Mass m,(kg)')
grid on
```

Output is as follows along with Fig. ES7.13 (*b*).

```
    Alpha =
              1.0e+002*
             -0.0957+0.1850i
              1.7683
             -0.0957-0.1850i
              0.2271
```

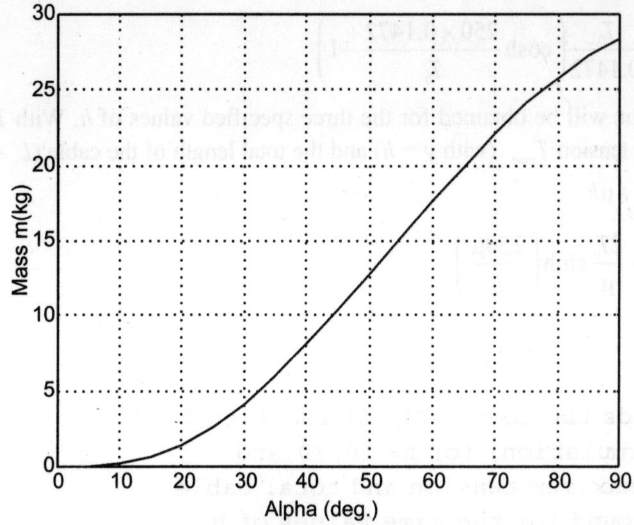

Fig. ES7.13 (b)

Example ES7.14: Figure ES7.14 shows a cable loaded uniformly along the horizontal, which has a mass of 15 kg per metre of its own length and supports its own weight only.

(*a*) Determine the tension at mid length, the maximum tension and the total length of the cable for $H = 10, 20, 30, 40, 50, 60, 70$ and 80 metres.

(*b*) Write a MATLAB program to plot y as a function of x for the above values of H.

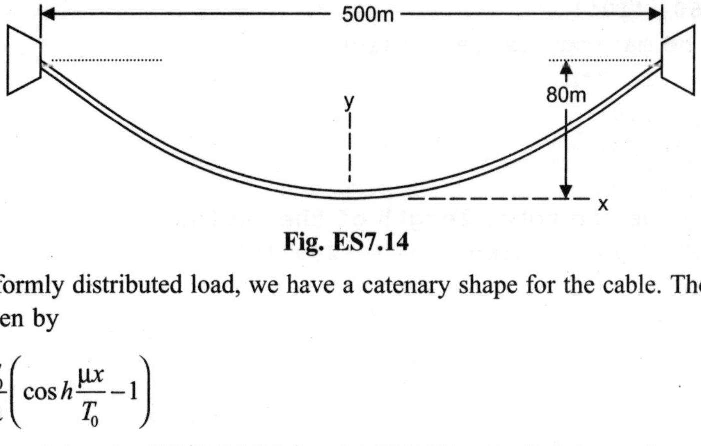

Fig. ES7.14

Solution: For a uniformly distributed load, we have a catenary shape for the cable. The curve assumed by the cable $y(x)$ is given by

$$y = \frac{T_0}{\mu}\left(\cos h\frac{\mu x}{T_0} - 1\right)$$

where μ = weight per unit length= $(15)(9.81)(10^{-3}) = 0.1472$ kN/m. To find the tension at mid length (T_0) we substitute $x = 250$ m and $y = h$, giving

$$h = \frac{T_0}{\mu}\left(\cos h\frac{250\mu}{T_0} - 1\right)$$

To use the solve function in MATLAB, we first need to re-write the above in terms of a function f whose root (zero) provides the solution to the original equation.

$$f = h - \frac{T_0}{0.1472}\left(\cosh\frac{250\times 0.1472}{T_0} - 1\right)$$

The roots of this equation will be obtained for the three specified values of h. With T_0 known we can easily find the maximum cable tension T_{max} (with $y = h$) and the total length of the cable ($L_c = 2s$) (with $x = 250$ m).

$$T_{max} = T_0 + \mu h$$

$$L_c = 2s = \frac{2T_0}{\mu}\sinh\left(\frac{250\mu}{T_0}\right)$$

MATLAB Program:

```
% This script finds the roots (T0) of function f
%(see problem formulation) for h= 10,30,and
% 60 meters. the maximum tension and total cable
%length is then found for the same values of h.

f='h-T0/0.1472*(cosh(0.1472*250/T0)-1)'
f10=subs(f,'h',10);
T0_10=solve(f10,'T0')
f30=subs(f,'h',30);
T0_30=solve(f30,'T0')
f60=subs(f,'h',60);
T0_60=solve(f60, 'T0')
% Now we find the maximum cable tension.
Tm=inline('T0+0.1472*h')
Tmax_10=Tm(T0_10,10)
Tmax_30=Tm(T0_30,30)
Tmax_60=Tm(T0_60,60)
% Next we determine the total length of the cable.
Lc=inline('2*T0/0.1472*(sinh(0.1472*250/T0))')
Lc_10=Lc(T0_10)
Lc_30=Lc(T0_30)
Lc_60=Lc(T0_60)
```

Output is:

```
f =
h-T0/0.1472*(cosh(0.1472*250/T0)-1)
T0_10 =
460.24512430858055194348798961110
T0_30 =
154.06375896035471416316009559463
```

```
T0_60 =
78.0958258286435987215366060353 24
Tm =
   Inline function:
    Tm(T0,h) = T0+0.1472*h
Tmax_10 =
461.717124308580551943487989611 10
Tmax_30 =
158.479758960354714163160095594 63
Tmax_60 =
86.9278258286435987215366060353 24
Lc =
    Inline function:
    Lc(T0) = 2*T0/0.1472*(sinh(0.1472*250/T0))
Lc_10 =
500.532935712450607775869277438 22
Lc_30 =
504.768175847491820921336322820 53
Lc_60 =
518.710228947860801431604899591 83
```

The results are summarized as follows:

h(m)	T_0 (kN)	T_{max} (kN)	L_c (m)
10	132.6	133.8	300.9
30	44.7	48.2	307.9
60	23.2	30.2	329.9

Example ES7.15: For the system shown in Fig. ES7.15, obtain the force in each member of the truss as a function of *d*. Write a MATLAB program to plot the force in each member for 30 mm ≤ *d* ≤ 250 mm.

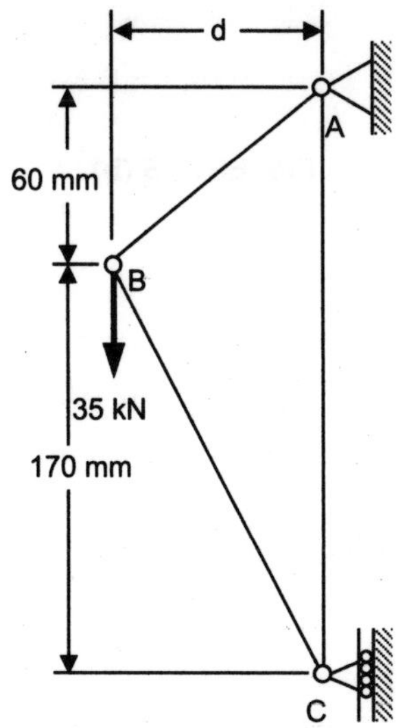

Fig. ES7.15

Solution: Free-body diagram is given in Fig. ES7.15(*a*).

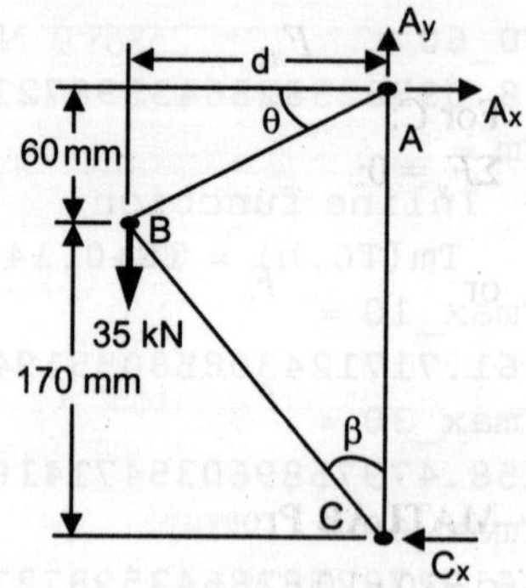

Fig. ES 7.15(a)

The length of *AB* and *BC* is given by

$$AB = \sqrt{d^2 + (60)^2}$$

$$BC = \sqrt{d^2 + (172)^2}$$

and the angles θ and β by

$$\sin\theta = \frac{60}{AB}, \quad \cos\theta = \frac{d}{AB}$$

$$\sin\beta = \frac{d}{BC}, \quad \cos\beta = \frac{170}{BC}$$

Reactions:

$\Sigma F_x = 0$: $\quad A_x - C_x = 0$

$\Sigma F_y = 0$: $\quad A_y - 35000 = 0, \quad A_y = 35000$

$\Sigma M_C = 0$: $\quad d(35000) - 230 \quad A_x = 0$

Thus $\quad A_x = \dfrac{35000}{230} d = 152.17d = C_x$

Joint *A* and *C*: (Fig. ES7.15 (*b*))

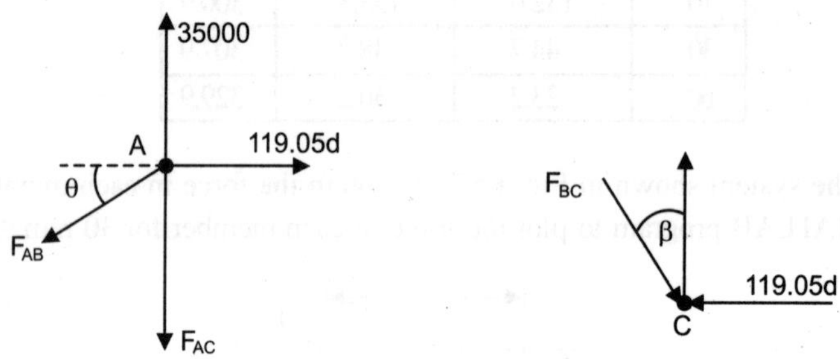

Fig. ES7.15 (b)

For *A*:

$\Sigma F_x = 0$: $\quad 152.17d - F_{AB}\cos\theta = 0$

or $\quad F_{AB} = \dfrac{AB}{d}(152.17d)$

$$F_{AB} = 152.17AB \text{ N(Tension)}$$

$\Sigma F_y = 0$: $\quad 35000 - F_{AC} - F_{AB}\sin\theta = 0$

or $\quad F_{AC} = 35000 - 152.17AB\left(\dfrac{60}{AB}\right)$

F_{AC} = 25868.9 N(Tension)

For *C*:

$\Sigma F_y = 0$: $\quad 25869 - F_{BC}\cos\beta = 0$

or $\quad F_{BC} = \dfrac{BC}{170}25868.9$

$F_{BC} = 152.17BC$ N(Compression)

MATLAB Program:

```
d=30:10:250;
AB=sqrt(d.^2+60^2);
BC=sqrt(d.^2+170^2);
Fab=152.17*AB;
Fac=25868.9+0*d;
Fbc=-152.17*BC;
plot(d,Fab,'-p',d,Fac,'-*',d,Fbc,'-o')
xlabel('d(mm)')
ylabel('Member force(N)')
legend('FAB','FAC','FBC')
grid on
```

Output is shown in Fig. ES7.15 (*c*).

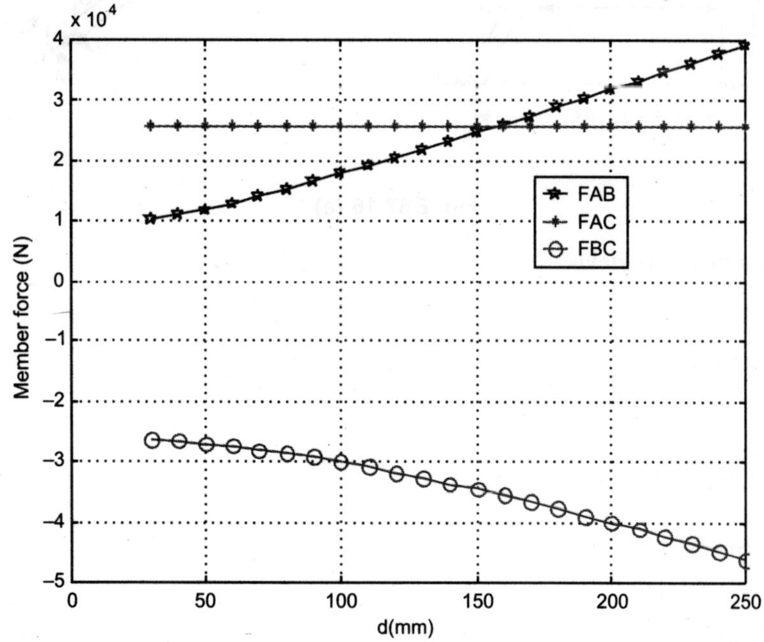

Fig. ES7.15 (c)

Example ES7.16: Figure ES7.16 shows a curved beam member *AB* which is a parabola and the vertex is at *A* and $\ell = nH$. Write a MATLAB program to determine,

(*a*) the internal forces and bending moment at an arbitrary point *C*.

(*b*) plot the internal forces and bending moment as a function of *x* for $0.1\ell \le x \le 0.9\ell$.

Given: The magnitude of the vertical load $F = 1.5$ kN, $\ell = 500$ mm and $n = 2, 3, 4$.

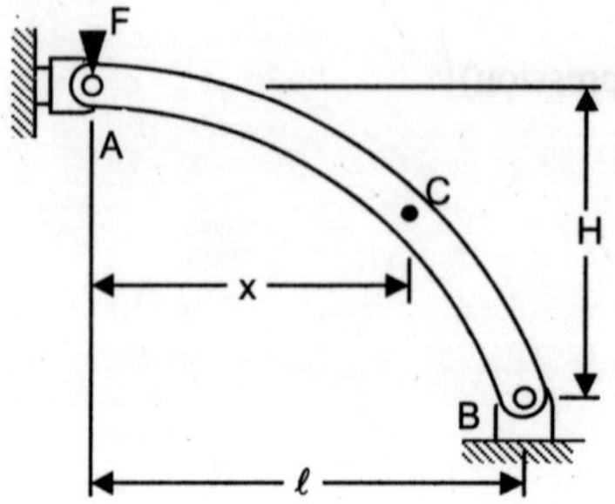

Fig. ES7.16

Solution: Free-body diagram is given in Fig. ES7.16(*a*).

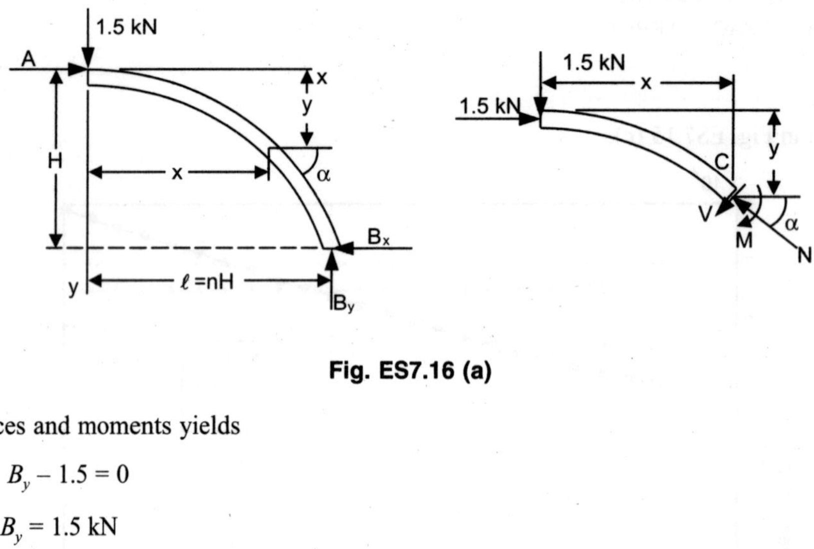

Fig. ES7.16 (a)

Summing forces and moments yields

$\Sigma F_y = 0$: $\quad B_y - 1.5 = 0$

or $\quad B_y = 1.5$ kN

$\Sigma M_B = 0$: $\quad 1.5(L) - A(H) = 0$

or $\quad A = 1.2\dfrac{\ell}{H} = 1.5n$ kN

For a parabola $y = kx^2$, then we have

$$h = k\ell^2 = k(nH)^2$$

and $\quad k = \dfrac{1}{Hn^2}$

Arbitrary section *AJ*:
At an arbitrary point *C*, we have

$$\text{slope} = \frac{dy}{dx} = \frac{2x}{Hn^2}$$

and $$\tan\alpha = \frac{2x}{Hn^2} \quad \text{or,} \quad \alpha = \tan^{-1}\left(\frac{2x}{Hn^2}\right)$$

At an arbitrary section *AC*:

$\Sigma M_J = 0$: $\quad 1.5(x) - 1.5n(y) - M = 0$

or $\quad M = 1.5(x - ny)$

$$= 1.5\left(x - \frac{nx^2}{Hn^2}\right)$$

$$M = 1.5x\left(1 - \frac{x}{Hn}\right)$$

Summing forces gives:

$\Sigma F_N = 0$: $\quad N - 1.5(\sin\alpha) - 1.5n(\cos\alpha) = 0$

or $\quad N = 1.5(\sin\alpha - n\cos\alpha)$

$\Sigma F_V = 0$: $\quad -V - 1.5(\cos\alpha) + 1.5n(\sin\alpha) = 0$

or $\quad V = 1.5(n\sin\alpha - \cos\alpha)$

With $\ell = 0.5\text{ m} = Hn$

$$M = 1.5x\left(1 - \frac{x}{0.5}\right)$$

where $\alpha = \tan^{-1}\left(\frac{2x}{\ell n}\right) = \tan^{-1}\left(\frac{x}{0.25n}\right)$

MATLAB program for this problem is given below:

```
syms n t real
L=0.5;
x1=0.1*L;
xf=0.9*L;
N= inline('1.5*(sin(atan(5*x/n))+n*cos(atan(5*x/n)))','x','n');
V= inline('1.5*(n*sin(atan(5*x/n))-cos(atan(5*x/n)))', 'x','n');
x=[x1:0.01:xf];
M=1.5*x.*(1-x./0.5);
figure(1)
plot(x,N(x,2),x,N(x,3),x,N(x,4));
```

```
xlabel('x(m)')
ylabel('Normal force(kN)')
legend('n=2','n=3','n=4',4)
grid on
figure(2)
plot(x,V(x,2),x,V(x,3),x,V(x,4));
xlabel('x(m)')
ylabel('Shear force(kN)')
legend('n=2','n=3','n=4',2)
grid on
figure(3)
plot(x,M)
xlabel('x(m)')
ylabel('Moment(kN.m)')
grid on
```

Output of the program is shown in Figures ES7.16 (*b*), (*c*) and (*d*).

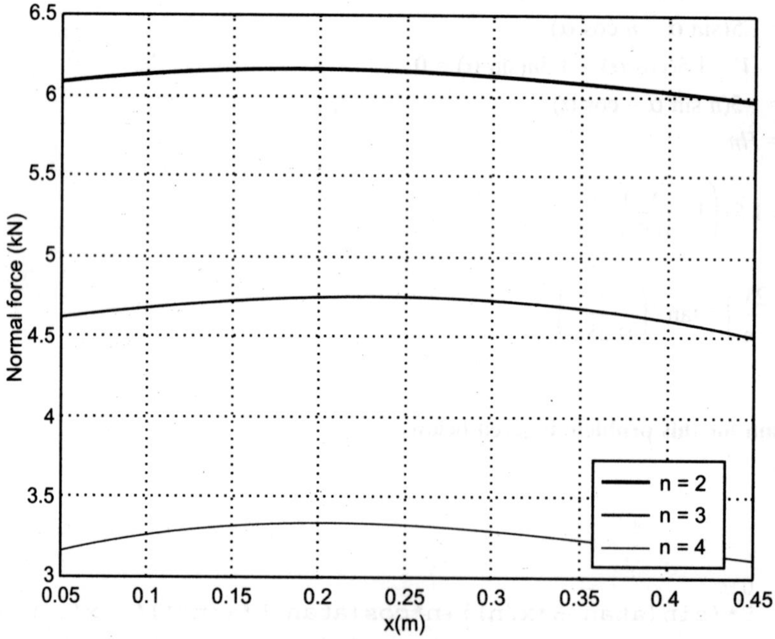

Fig. ES7.16(b)

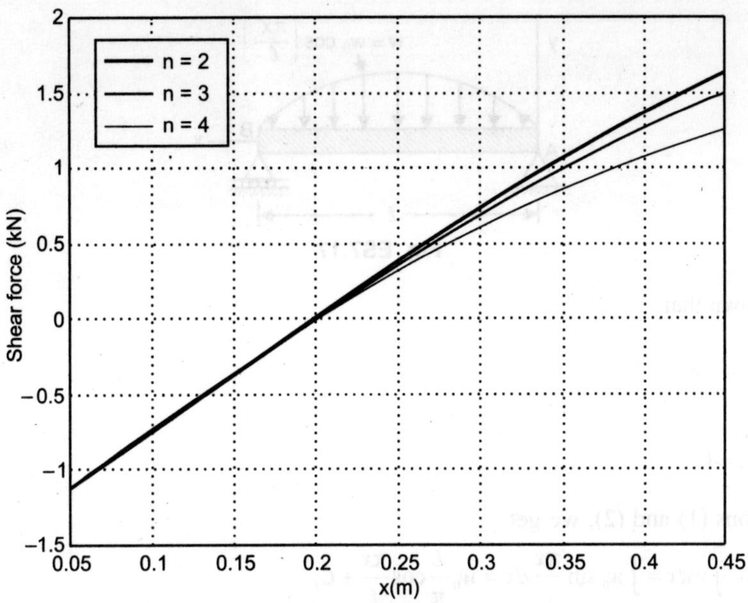

Fig. ES7.16(c)

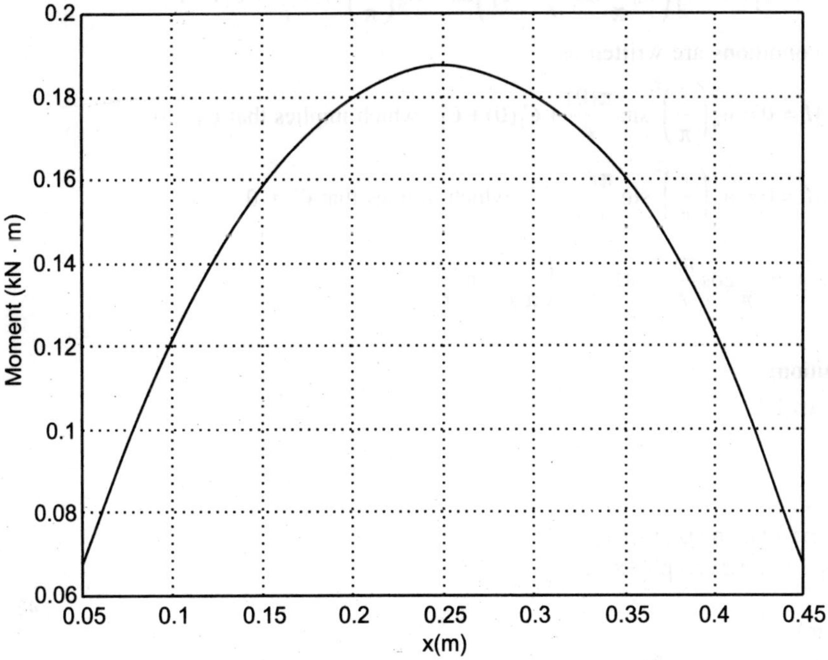

Fig. ES7.16(d)

Example ES7.17: Write a MATLAB program to plot the shear and bending moment diagrams for the beam shown in Fig. ES7.17. The length of the beam $\ell = 4$ m and $w_0 = 20$ kN/m.

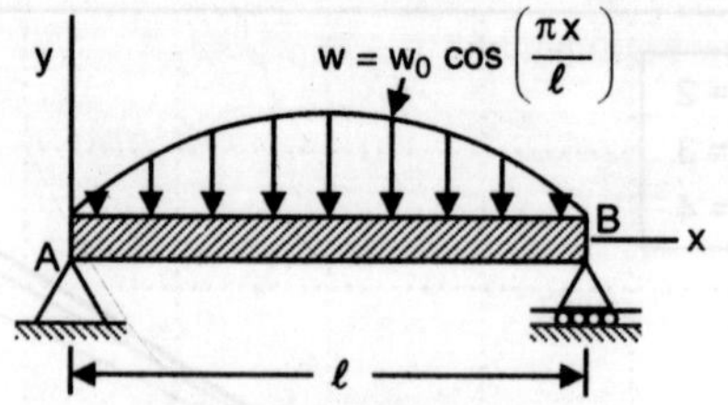

Fig. ES7.17

Solution: It is known that

$$\frac{dV}{dx} = -w \qquad ...(1)$$

$$\frac{dM}{dx} = V \qquad ...(2)$$

Integrating equations (1) and (2), we get

$$V = -\int w dx = \int w_0 \sin\frac{\pi x}{\ell} dx = w_0 \frac{L}{\pi}\cos\frac{\pi x}{\ell} + C_1$$

$$M = \int V dx = \int\left(w_0 \frac{\ell}{\pi}\cos\frac{\pi x}{\ell} + C_1\right)dx = w_0\left(\frac{\ell}{\pi}\right)^2 \sin\frac{\pi x}{\ell} + C_1 x + C_2$$

The boundary conditions are written as

At $x = 0$: $\quad M = 0 = w_0\left(\frac{\ell}{\pi}\right)^2 \sin\frac{\pi(0)}{\ell} + C_1(0) + C_2$, which implies that $C_2 = 0$.

At $x = \ell$: $\quad M = 0 = w_0\left(\frac{\ell}{\pi}\right)^2 \sin\frac{\pi\ell}{\ell} + C_1\ell$, which implies that $C_1 = 0$.

Hence, $\quad V = w_0\frac{\ell}{\pi}\cos\frac{\pi x}{\ell}, \quad M = w_0\left(\frac{\ell}{\pi}\right)^2 \sin\frac{\pi x}{\ell}.$

MATLAB Solution:

```
% Input w0 and l
w0=20;
l = 4;
x = [0:0.1:4];
v1 = w0*(l/pi)*cos(pi*x/l);
m1= w0*(l/pi)^2*sin(pi*x/l);
plot(x,v1)
xlabel('x(m)')
ylabel('Shear force (kN)')
grid on
plot(x,m1)
xlabel('x,(m)')
ylabel('Bending moment kN-m)')
```

Output for this program is shown in Figs. ES7.17 (*a*) and (*b*).

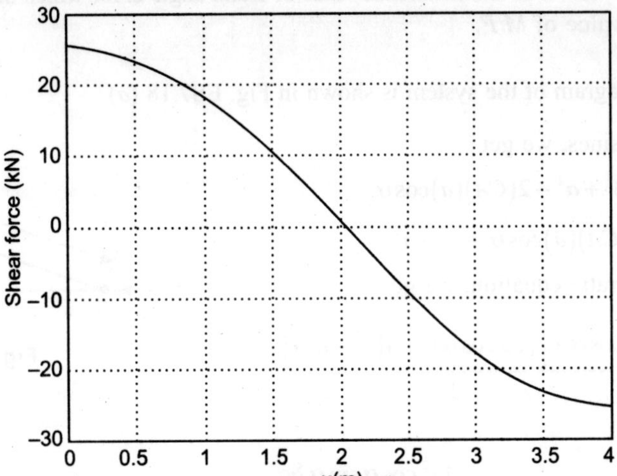

Fig. ES7.17(a)

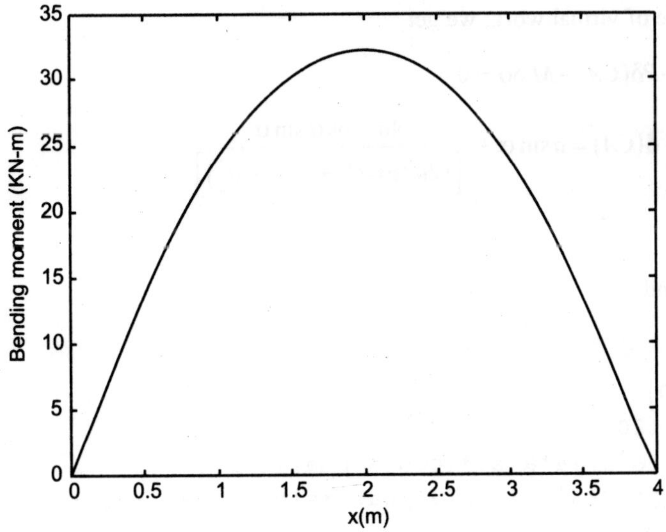

Fig. ES7.17(b)

Example ES7.18: Figure ES7.18 shows a crank shaft mechanism where a couple M is applied to the crank AB to maintain the equilibrium of the system. The force applied to the system is F.

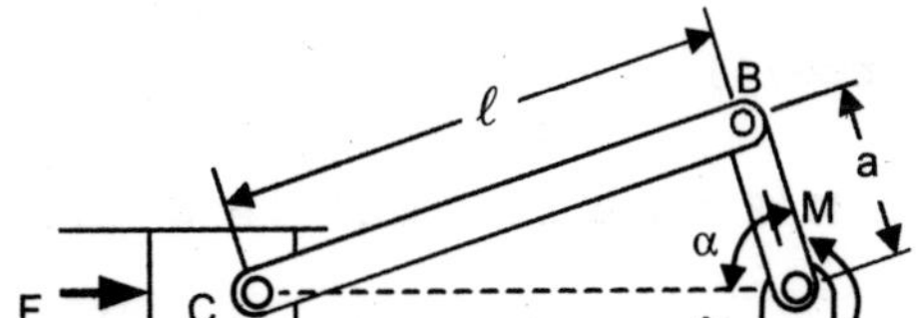

Fig. ES7.18

Write a MATLAB program to plot the ratio of *M*/*F* as a function of crank angle α from 0 to 180 degrees. Given $a = 50$ mm and $\ell = 150$ mm. Determine the value of crank angle α for which the ratio *M*/*F* is maximum and the corresponding value of *M*/*F*.

Solution: Free-body diagram of the system is shown in Fig. ES7.18 (*a*).

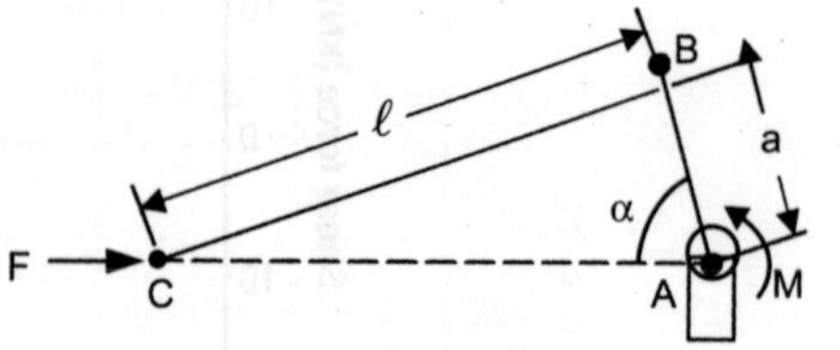

Fig. ES7.18(a)

Applying the law of cosines, we get

$$\ell^2 = (CA)^2 + a^2 - 2(CA)(a)\cos\alpha$$

or

$$(CA)^2 - 2(CA)(a)\cos\alpha = \ell^2 - a^2$$

Solving the above quadratic equation, we get

$$CA = \frac{2a\cos\alpha + \left[(2a\cos\alpha)^2 + 4(\ell^2 - a^2)\right]^{1/2}}{2}$$

Differentiating gives

$$\delta(CA) = -a\sin\alpha\,\delta\alpha - \frac{4a^2\cos\alpha\sin\alpha\,\delta\alpha}{\left[(2a\cos\alpha)^2 + 4(\ell^2 - a^2)\right]}$$

Applying the principle of virtual work, we get

$$\delta U = -P\delta(CA) - M\,\delta\alpha = 0$$

or

$$\frac{M}{P} = -\delta(CA) = a\sin\alpha + \frac{4a^2\cos\alpha\sin\alpha}{\left[(2a\cos\alpha)^2 + 4(\ell^2 - a^2)\right]}$$

MATLAB Solution:

```
% Program inputs: a and
a = 0.050;
l = 0.150;
alpha = Ho:1:180;
alpha=alpha*pi/180;
den=sqrt(4*(l^2-a^2)+4*a^2.*(cos(alpha)).^2);
mbf=a.*sin(alpha)-2*a^2.*cos(alpha).*sin(alpha)./den;
[mbfmax,i]=max(mbf);
vt=alpha(i);
mbfMax=mbfmax
plot(alpha,mbf)
grid on
xlabel('Angle alpha (degree)')
ylabel('M/F ( meter)')
fprintf('a) Alpha when M/F is a maximum is = %3.0f degrees and M/F =
%6.4f(m)\n',vt,mbfmax)
```

Output comes like this including Figure ES 7.18 (*b*).

(*a*) Alpha when *M*/*F* is a maximum is = 93 degrees and *M*/*F* = 0.0501(m)>> *vt* = alpha(i);

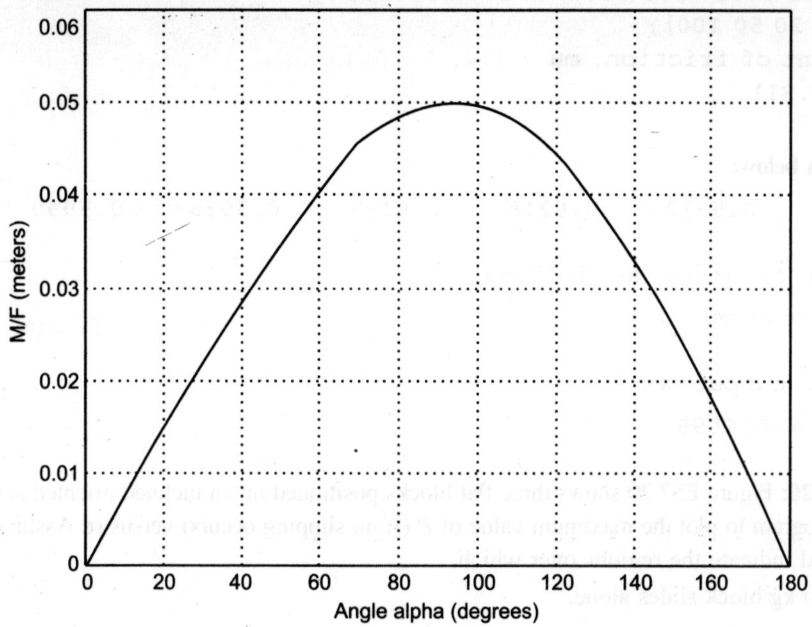

Fig. ES7.18 (b)

Example ES7.19: The coefficient of friction μ, can be determined by $\mu = F/mg$ where *F* is the measured force (N), *m* is the mass (kg) and *g* = acceleration due to gravity (9.81 m/s²). The following table gives the experimental data. Determine

(*a*) the coefficient of friction in each test

(*b*) the average from all tests.

Test #	1	2	3	4	5	6	7
Mass m (kg)	2	4	5	10	20	50	100
Force F (N)	12.4	23.2	30.5	60.8	116.5	293.8	597.3

Solution: System under equilibrium is shown in Fig. ES7.19.

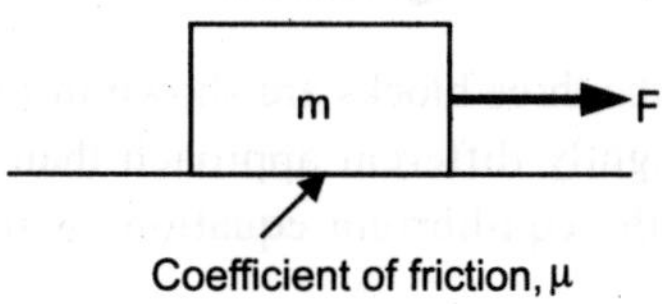

Fig. ES7.19

This is simple application of mathematics.

Program is given below:

```
% Force and mass values in vector form
F=[12.4 23.2 30.5 60.8 116.5 293.8 597.3];
m=[2 4 5 10 20 50 100];
%Coefficient of friction, mu
mu=F./(m*9.81)
```

Output is given below:

```
mu=0.6320    0.5912    0.6218    0.6198    0.5938    0.5990    0.6089
```

```
Average is obtained as follows:
averagemu=mean(mu)
```

```
This gives output as
averagemu = 0.6095
```

Example ES7.20: Figure ES7.20 shows three flat blocks positioned on an inclined oriented at angle α. Write a MATLAB program to plot the maximum value of *P* (if no slipping occurs) versus α. Assume only positive values of *P* and indicate the regions over which

(*i*) the 40 kg block slides alone,

(*ii*) the 40 kg and 30 kg blocks slide together.

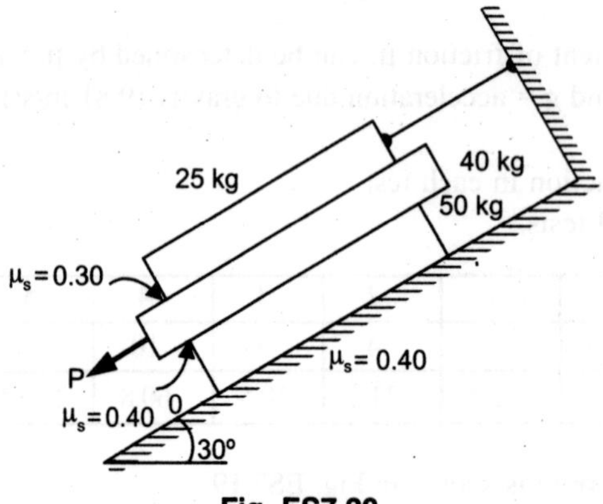

Fig. ES7.20

Solution: The free-body diagrams for the three blocks are shown in Fig. ES7.20 (*a*). To obtain the required plot it will be convenient to use a slightly different approach than that used in the sample problem in your text. We start by writing down the equilibrium equations without making any assumptions about where sliding occurs.

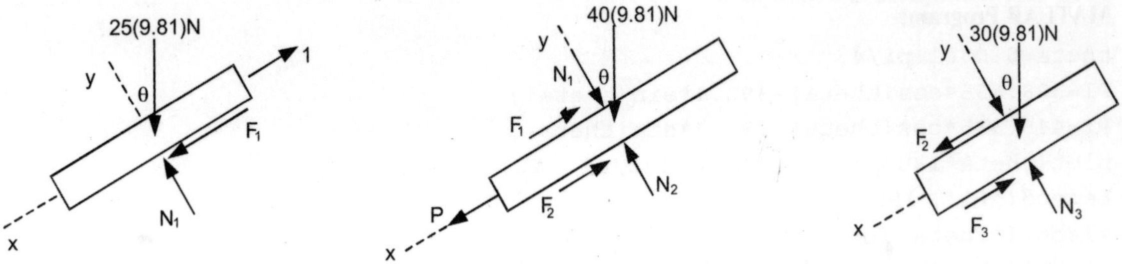

Fig. ES7.20 (a)

$[\Sigma F_y = 0]$: 25 kg ; $N_1 - 25(9.81)\cos\theta = 0$

40 kg ; $N_2 - N_1 - 40(9.81)\cos\theta = 0$

30 kg ; $N_3 - N_2 - 30(9.81)\cos\theta = 0$

These equations can be readily solved for the normal forces.

$$N_1 = 25(9.81)\cos\theta \; ; N_2 = 65(9.81)\cos\theta \; ; N_3 = 95(9.81)\cos\theta$$

$[\Sigma F_x = 0]$: 40 kg ; $P - F_1 - F_2 + 40(9.81)\sin\theta = 0$

30 kg ; $F_2 - F_3 + 30(9.81)\sin\theta = 0$

Now we have two equations with four unknowns P, F_1, F_2 and F_3. Note that we have not written the equation for the summation of forces in the x-direction for the 25 kg block. The reason is that this equation introduces an additional unknown (T) that we are not interested in determining.

The next step is to make assumptions about which block(s) slide. As will be seen, either of the two possible assumptions about impending motion will reduce two of the friction forces to functions of θ only. This will result in two equations that may be solved for P and the remaining friction force. The forces calculated will be designated P_1 or P_2 to distinguish the two cases for impending slip.

Case 1: Only the 40 kg block slips.

Impending slippage at both surface of the 40 kg block gives $F_1 = 0.3N_1 = 73.575\cos\theta$ and $F_2 = 0.4N_2 = 255.06\cos\theta$. Substituting these results into the equilibrium equations yields

$$P_1 = 328.635\cos\theta - 392.4\sin\theta$$

Case 2: The 30 and 40 kg blocks slide together.

Impending slippage at the upper surface of the 30 kg block and lower surface of the 40 kg block gives F_1=$0.3N_1$=$73.575\cos\theta$ and $F_3 = 0.4N_3 = 372.78\cos\theta$. Substitution of these results into the equilibrium equations gives,

$$P_2 = 446.355\cos\theta - 686.7\sin\theta$$

which of these two values of P represents the maximum load that can be applied without slippage on any surface is best illustrated by plotting the two expressions as a function of θ. This plot will be generated in the script below. The basic idea is that at any specified angle θ, the critical or maximum value of P will be the smaller of two values calculated.

MATLAB Program:

```
theta=0:0.01:pi/4;
P1=328.635*cos(theta)-392.4*sin(theta);
P2=446.335*cos(theta)-686.7*sin(theta);
plot(theta*180/pi, P1, theta*180/pi , P2)
Legend('P1', 'P2')
xlabel('Theta  (degree)')
ylabel('P  (N)')
```

Figure 3.20(*b*) shows P_1 and P_2 plotted as a function of θ. For each θ, the critical or maximum value of *P* will be the smaller of two values calculated. By setting $P_1 = P_2$ we find that the two curves intersect at $\theta = 0.503$ radian (28.8°). Thus, for $\theta \leq 28.8°$ *P* controls and the 50 kg block slides by itself while for $\theta \leq 28.8°$, P_2 controls and the 40 and 50 kg blocks slide together.

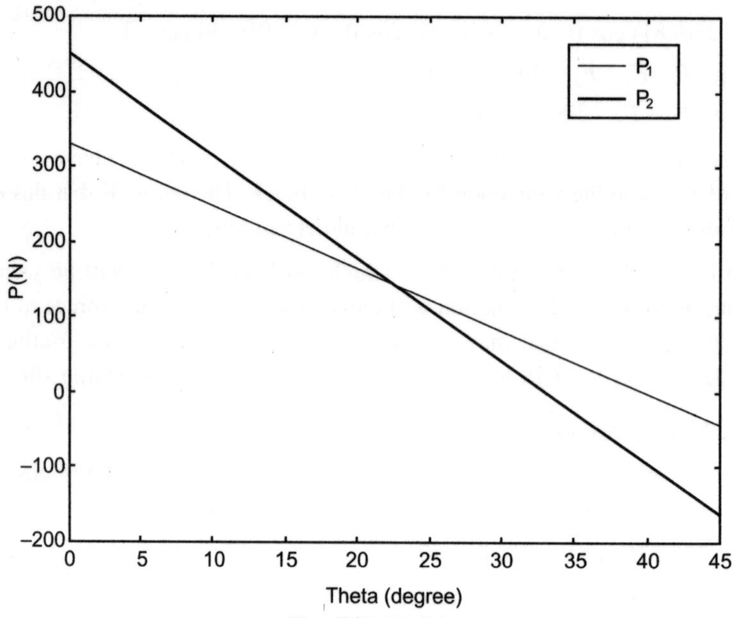

Fig. ES7.20 (b)

Example ES7.21: In Fig. ES7.21, the horizontal position of the rectangular block is adjusted by the wedge under the action of the force *P*. The wedge angle is α, μ_1 and μ_2 are the coefficient of the static friction at the two wedge surfaces and between the block and the horizontal surfaces respectively.

(*a*) Obtain a general expression for *P* (the least force required to move the block) in terms of α, μ_1 and μ_2.

(*b*) Write a MATLAB program to plot *P* as a function of μ_1 for $\alpha = 15°$, 20° and 25°; $\mu_2 = 0.5$.

(*c*) For $\alpha = 10°$, plot *P* as a function of μ_1 for $\mu_2 = 0.2$, 0.4, 0.6 and 0.8.

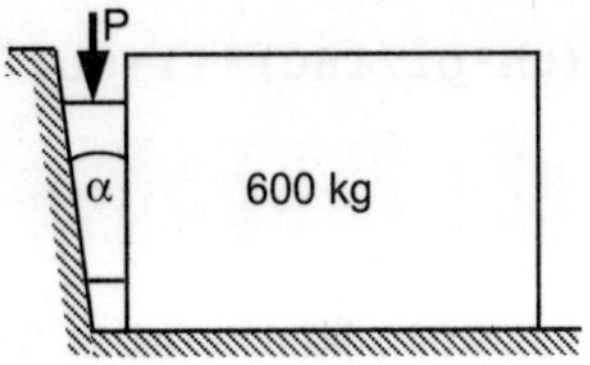

Fig. ES7.21

Solution: Free-body diagram of wedge and block is shown in Fig. ES7.21 (*a*).

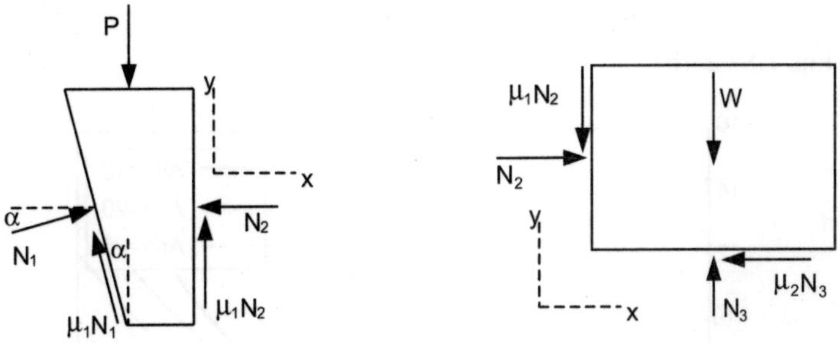

Fig. ES7.21(a)

(*a*) First we write the equilibrium equations from the free-body diagrams for the wedge and for the block.

For the Block:

$$\Sigma F_x = 0 = N_2 - \mu_2 N_3,\ \Sigma F_y = 0 = N_3 - mg - \mu_1 N_2$$

These two equations are readily solved for N_2 and N_3.

$$N_2 = \frac{\mu_2 mg}{1-\mu_1\mu_2}, \quad N_3 = \frac{mg}{1-\mu_1\mu_2}$$

For the Wedge:

$$\Sigma F_x = 0 = N_1 \cos\alpha - \mu_1 N_1 \sin\alpha - N_2$$
$$\Sigma F_y = 0 = N_1 \sin\alpha + \mu_1 N_1 \cos\alpha + \mu_1 N_2 - P$$

After substituting for N_2 we solve the first equation for N_1. Substituting this result into the second yields an expression for P.

$$P = \frac{\mu_2 mg(2\mu_1 + (1-\mu_1^2)\tan\alpha)}{(1-\mu_1\tan\alpha)(1-\mu_1\mu_2)}$$

This result is used to generate the plots for parts (*b*) and (*c*) in the worksheet below.

MATLAB Program:

```
% This script produces the plot for part(b)
% Note the conversion factor on theta in the following
% function. This allows us to use degrees rather than
% radians when we use P. Also note the division by 1000,
```

```
% converting to kN.
P=inline('.5*600*9.81*(tan(th*pi/180)*(1-mu1^2)+2*mu1)/(1-mu1*tan(th*pi/
180))/(1-mu1*.6)/1000');
P=vectorize(P);
mu1=0:0.01:0.8;
plot(mu1,P(mu1,15),mu1,P(mu1,20),mu1,P(mu1,25))
legend('mu_1=15','mu_1=20','mu_1=25')
xlabel('mu_1')
ylabel('P(kN)')
```

Output is shown in Fig. ES7.21(b).

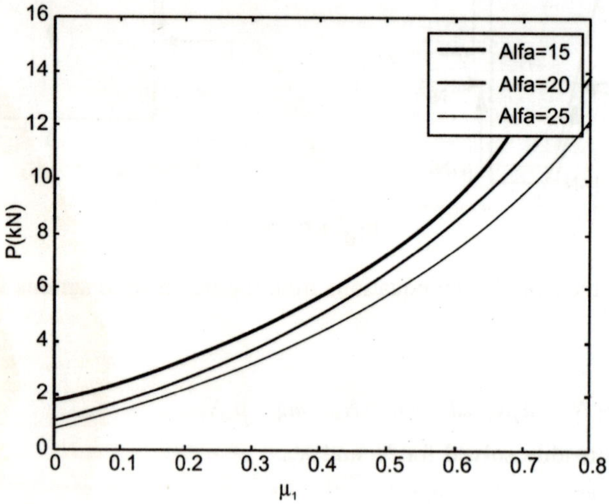

Fig. ES7.21 (b)

```
% This script produces the plot for part(c).
% Note that P is a function of mu1 and mu2 in this case.
% Also note that the division by 1000, converting to kN.
P=inline('mu2*600*9.81*(tan(10*pi/180)*(1-mu1^2)+2*mu1)/(1-mu1*tan(10*pi/
180))/ 1-mu1*mu2)/1000');
P=vectorize(P);
mu1=0:0.01:0.8;
plot(mu1,P(mu1,.2),mu1,P(mu1,.4),mu1,P(mu1,.6),mu1,P(mu1,.8))
legend('mu_2=0.2','mu_2=0.4','mu_2=0.6','mu_2=0.8')
xlabel('mu_1')
ylabel('P(kN)')
```

The output is shown in Fig. ES7.21 (*c*).

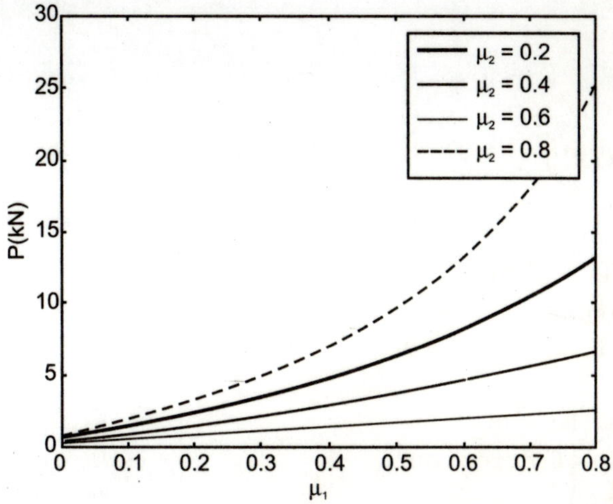

Fig. ES7.21 (c)

Example ES7.22: Figure ES7.22 shows a large turnbuckle which supports a cable tension of 12,000 N. The mean diameter of the two 1.0 mm screws is 1.15 mm and has five square threads per mm. Both screws have single start threads.

(*a*) Determine the moments M_T and M_L that must be applied to the body of the turnbuckle in order to tighten and loosen it respectively.

(*b*) Write a MATLAB program to plot the moments M_T and M_L as functions of μ for $0 \le \mu \le 1$, where μ is the coefficient of friction for the threads.

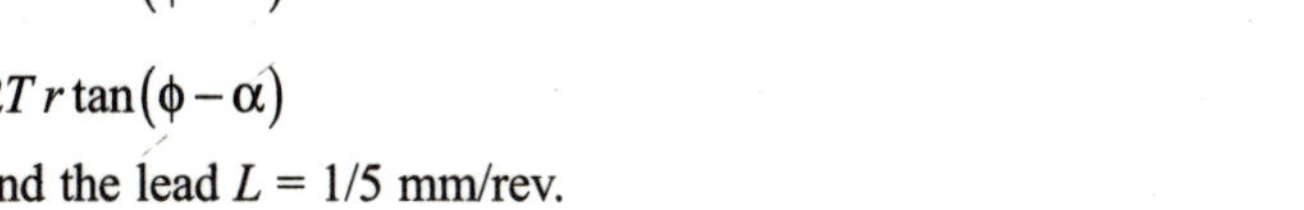

Fig. ES7.22

Solution: M_T and M_L can be obtained as

$$M_T = 2T\,r\tan(\phi+\alpha) \quad \text{...(1)}$$

and $$M_L = 2T\,r\tan(\phi-\alpha) \quad \text{...(2)}$$

where T = 12,000 N and the lead L = 1/5 mm/rev.

The mean radius is given by r = 1.15/2 = 0.575 mm

We also have

$$\alpha = \tan^{-1}\left(\frac{L}{2\pi r}\right) \text{ and } \phi = \tan^{-1}(\mu) \quad \text{...(3)}$$

From Eqs. (1), (2) and (3), we can compute M_L and M_T explicitly.

MATLAB Program:

```
% Input T,L, and r
T=12000;
L=1/5;
r=1.15/2;
alpha = atan(L/2/pi/r);
mu = 0:0.01:1;
phi = atan(mu);
MT = 2*T*r*tan(alpha + phi);
ML=2*T*r*tan(phi-alpha);
% Place a horizontal line at x = 0
M=0*mu;
plot(mu,MT,mu,ML,mu,M)
xlabel('Coefficient of friction')
ylabel('Moment (lb-in)')
text(0.5,5000,'To loosen')
text(0.3,8000,'To tighten')
```

The plot of moments M_T and M_L as functions of μ for $0 \le \mu \le 1$ is shown in Fig. ES7.22(*a*).

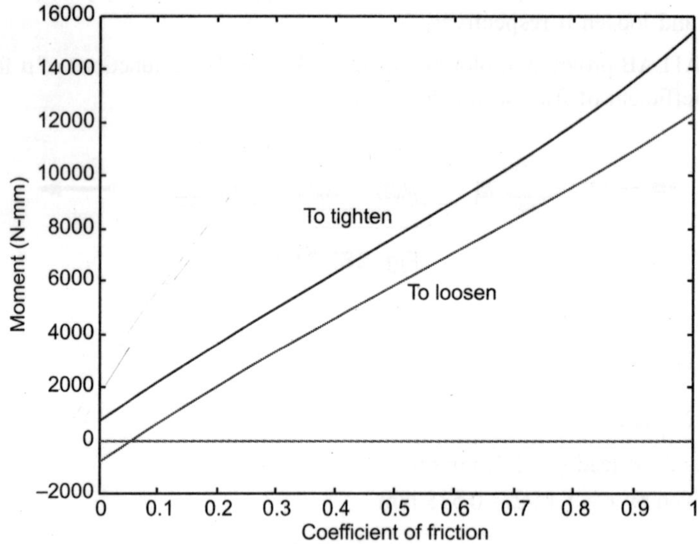

Fig. ES7.22 (a)

Example ES7.23: Figure ES7.23 shows a flexible cable which supports the 100 kg load and passes over a circular drum and is subjected to a force *P* to maintain equilibrium.

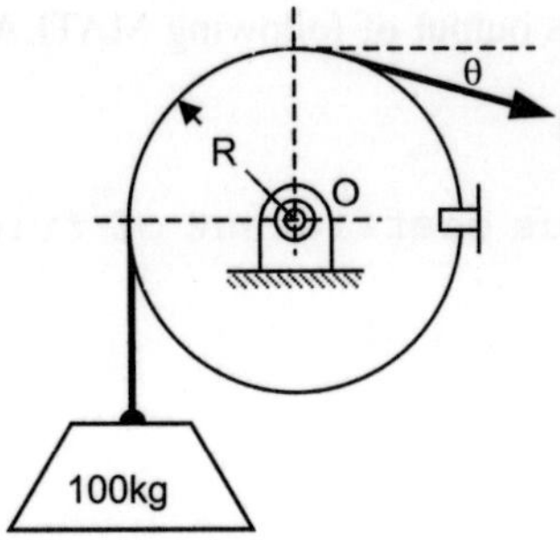

Fig. ES7.23

(*a*) For θ = 0, determine the maximum and minimum values of P may have in order to raise or lower the load.

(*b*) Write a MATLAB program to plot P_{max} and P_{min} versus μ for $0 \le \mu \le 1$, where μ is the coefficient of static friction between the cable and the fixed drum.

(*c*) For P = 550 N, determine the minimum value for which the angle θ may have before the load begins to slip.

(*d*) Plot θ_{min} versus μ for $0 \le \mu \le 1$.

Limit the variation of θ between –60° and 360°.

Solution: Free-body diagram of the circular drum is shown in Figures ES7.23 (*a*) and (*b*).

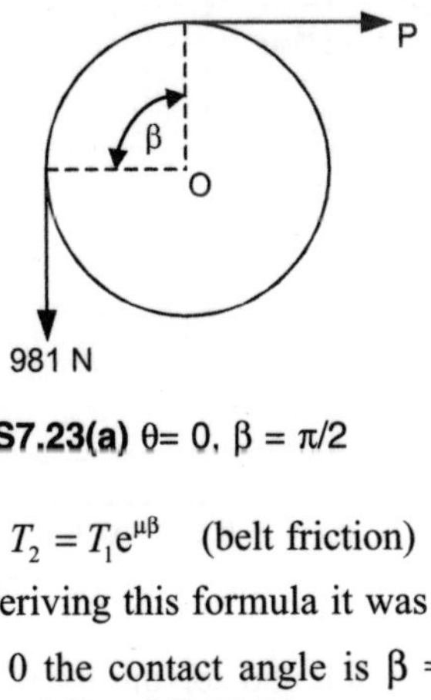

Fig. ES7.23(a) θ= 0, β = π/2

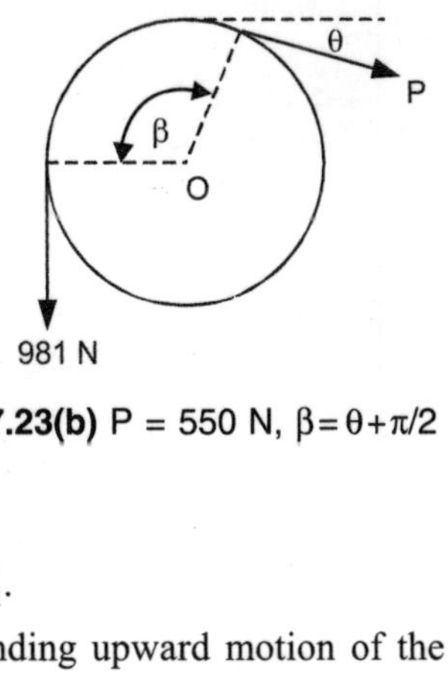

Fig. ES7.23(b) P = 550 N, β= θ+π/2

Here we have $T_2 = T_1 e^{\mu\beta}$ (belt friction)

Recall that in deriving this formula it was assumed that $T_2 > T_1$.

(*a*) With θ = 0 the contact angle is β = π/2 rad. For impending upward motion of the load we have $T_2 = T_{max}$ and T_1 = 981 N. Hence

$$P_{max} = 981 e^{\mu\pi/2}$$

For impending downward motion of the load we have T_2 = 981 N and $T_1 = P_{min}$.

$$981 = P_{min} e^{\mu\pi/2} \quad \text{or} \quad P_{min} = 981 e^{-\mu\pi/2}$$

(*b*) With P = 550 N we have β = π/2 +θ, T_2 = 981 N and $T_1 = P$ = 550 N. Therefore,

$$981/550 = e^{\mu(\theta+\pi/2)}$$

The plots are shown in Fig. ES7.23(*c*) as output of following MATLAB program.

MATLAB Solution:

```
% Plots of Pmax and Pmin versus coefficient of friction
mu=0:0.005:1;
pmax=981*exp(mu*pi/2)/1000;
pmin=981*exp(-mu*pi/2)/1000;
plot(mu,pmax,mu,pmin)
grid on
xlabel('Coefficient of friction')
ylabel('Force P (kN)')
text(0.7,2.5,'Pmax')
text(0.6,0.5,'Pmin')
```

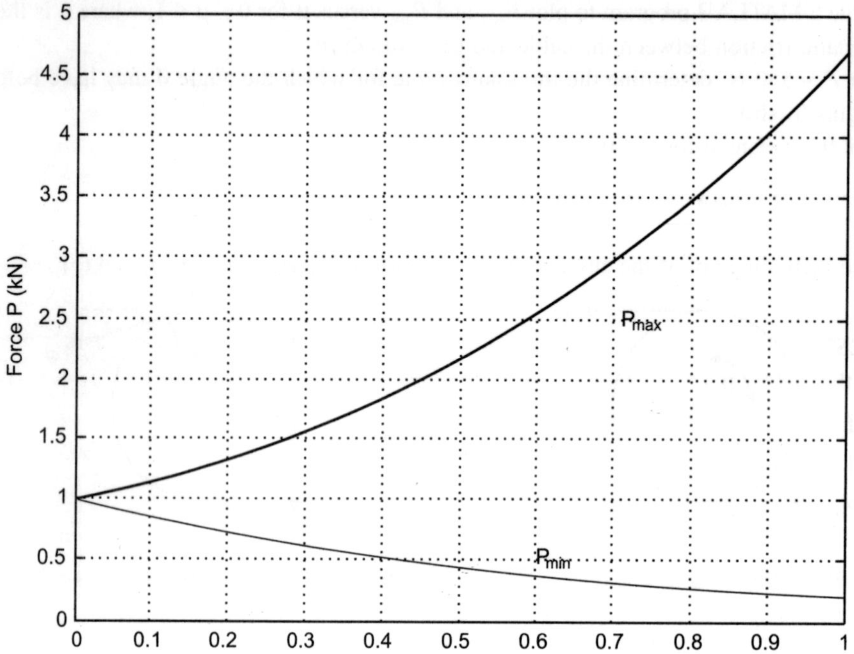

Fig. ES7.23 (c)

(*c*) Taking the natural logarithms on both sides of the above equation and solving for θ gives,

$$\theta = \frac{\ell n(981/550)}{\mu} - \frac{\pi}{2}$$

(*d*) Following program plots minimum value of θ versus μ.

```
% Plot of minimum angle theta versus mu
mu=0:0.005:1;
thet=log(981/550)./mu-pi/2
plot(mu,thet*180/pi)
```

```
axis([1 1 -60 360])
xlabel('Coefficient of friction')
ylabel('Theta (degree)')
```

Figure ES7.23 (*d*) shows the output.

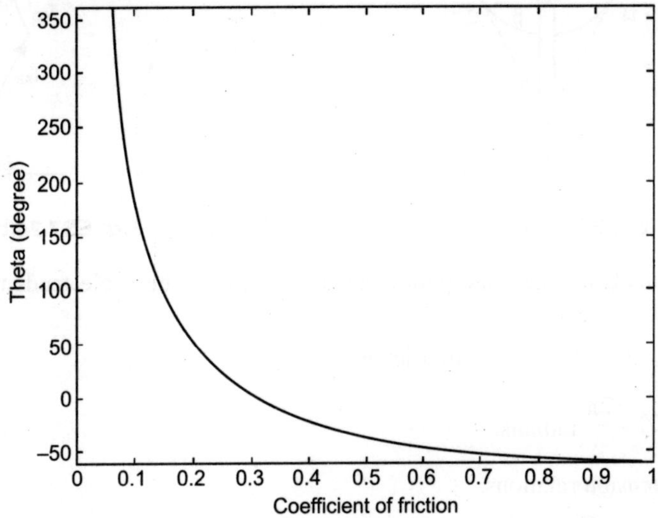

Fig. ES7.23(d)

Example ES7.24: Figure ES7.24 shows axle pulley system where the coefficient of friction between cable *ABCD* and the pulley varies between 0 and 0.60. Write a MATLAB program to determine,

(*a*) the values of α for the system to remain in equilibrium

(*b*) the reactions at *A* and *D*

(*c*) Plot α as a function of the coefficient of friction.

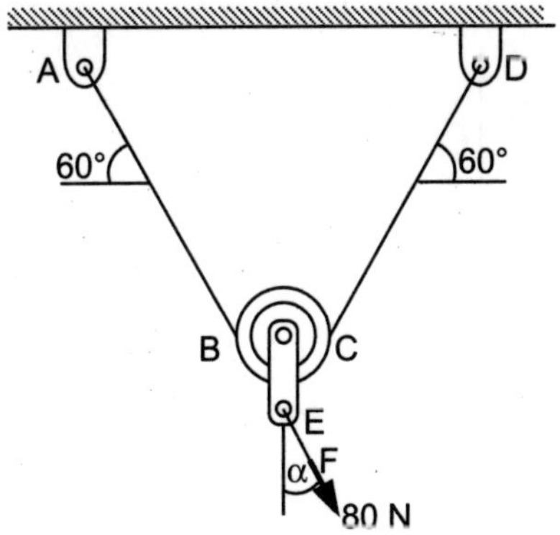

Fig. ES7.24

Solution: Free-body diagram and force triangle are given in Figs. ES7.24 (*a*) and (*b*).

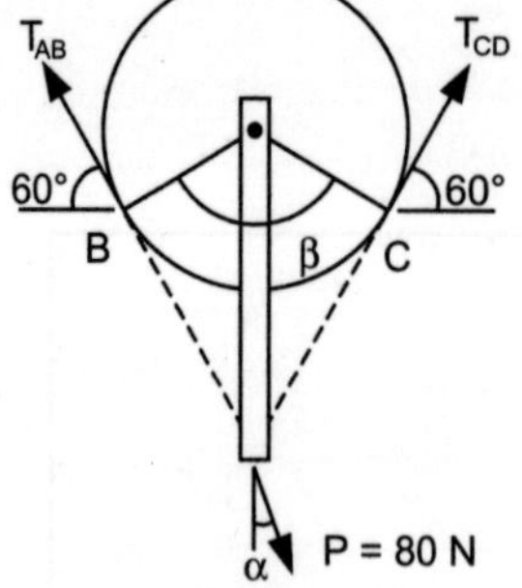

Fig. ES7.24(a)

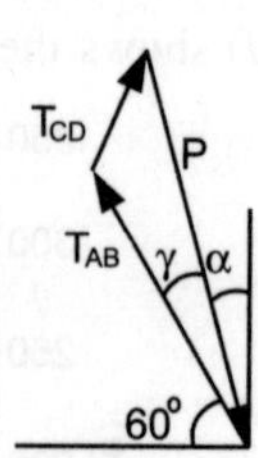

Fig. ES7.24(b)

Since the 80 N force tends to rotate the pulley counterclockwise, the cable tends to slip relative to the pulley clockwise and we have

$$T_1 = T_{CD},\ T_2 = T_{AB},\ \mu_s = \text{static friction}$$

$$\beta = 120^\circ = \frac{2\pi}{3} \text{ radians.}$$

From the ratio of belt-tension relations:

$$\frac{T_2}{T_1} = e^{\mu_s \beta} \Rightarrow \frac{T_{AB}}{T_{CD}} = e^{\frac{2\pi}{3}\mu_s}$$

or $$T_{AB} = e^{\frac{2\pi}{3}\mu_s} T_{CD} \qquad \text{...(1)}$$

From the force triangle, we have using the law of cosines

$$P^2 = T_{AB}^2 + T_{CD}^2 - 2T_{AB}T_{CD}\cos\beta$$

$$= \left(e^{\frac{2\pi}{3}\mu_s} T_{CD}\right) + T_{CD}^2 - 2\left(e^{\frac{2\pi}{3}\mu_s} T_{CD}\right) T_{CD}\left(-\frac{1}{2}\right)$$

$$= \left[\left(e^{\frac{2\pi}{3}\mu_s}\right)^2 + 1 + e^{\frac{2\pi}{3}\mu_s}\right] T_{CD}^2$$

$$P^2 = FT_{CD}^2$$

where $$F = \left[\left(e^{\frac{2\pi}{3}\mu_s}\right)^2 + 1 + e^{\frac{2\pi}{3}\mu_s}\right]$$

Hence, we have that

$$T_{CD} = \frac{1}{\sqrt{F}} P \qquad \text{...(2)}$$

(*a*) The corresponding values of α for the system to remain in equilibrium. Using the law of sines we have

$$\frac{\sin\gamma}{T_{CD}} = \frac{\sin\beta}{P}, \qquad \sin\gamma = \frac{T_{CD}}{P}\sin\beta$$

$$\sin\gamma = \frac{1}{\sqrt{F}}\sin\beta, \qquad \gamma = \sin^{-1}\left(\frac{1}{\sqrt{F}}\sin\beta\right)$$

$$\alpha = 90^\circ - (60^\circ + \gamma)$$

(*b*) The reactions at *A* and *D* are as follows:
Substituting $P = 80$ N in Eq.(2), then

$$D = T_{CD} = \frac{1}{\sqrt{F}}(80)\,\text{N}$$

and from Eq.(1), $A = T_{AB} = e^{\frac{2\pi}{3}\mu_s}\left(\frac{1}{\sqrt{F}}\right)(50)\,\text{N}$

MATLAB program for this problem is given below:

```
mu=0;
%Output Headings
fprintf('Friction Angle\n')
fprintf('\n')
ang=120.*pi/180.;
N=1;
while mu<0.60
  Y(N)=mu;
  a=exp(pi*ang*mu);
  E=sqrt(a^2+1.+a);
  ooe=1./E;
  sgamma=ooe*sin(ang);
  Gamma=asin(sgamma);
  alpha(N)=pi/2.-(1.0472+Gamma);
  X(N)=alpha(N)*180/pi;
  D(N)=ooe*80.;
  A(N)=a*D(N);
  fprintf('%5.3f    %5.3f\n',Y(N),X(N))
  mu=mu+.05;
  N=N+1;
end%while
fprintf('\n')
fprintf('\n')
fprintf('Friction    Reac.A    Reac.D\n')
fprintf('\n')
for I=1:N-1
fprintf('%5.3f    %5.3f    %5.3f\n',Y(I),A(I),D(I))
```

```
end
figure(1)
plot(Y,X)
xlabel('Coefficient of friction')
ylabel('Angle alpha')
grid on
figure(2)
plot(Y,D,Y,A)
xlabel('Coefficient of friction')
ylabel('Reactions')
legend('Reaction at A','Reaction at D',2)
grid on
```

Output is as follows:

Friction	Angle
0.000	0.000
0.050	5.377
0.100	10.391
0.150	14.780
0.200	18.425
0.250	21.332
0.300	23.582
0.350	25.286
0.400	26.558
0.450	27.497
0.500	28.186
0.550	28.687

Friction	Reac.A	Reac.D
0.000	46.188	46.188
0.050	53.481	38.488
0.100	59.860	31.001
0.150	65.068	24.251
0.200	69.105	18.535
0.250	72.125	13.922
0.300	74.336	10.326
0.350	75.934	7.591
0.400	77.083	5.546
0.450	77.907	4.033
0.500	78.498	2.925
0.550	78.921	2.116

Also following Figs. ES7.24(*c*) and (*d*) are obtained.

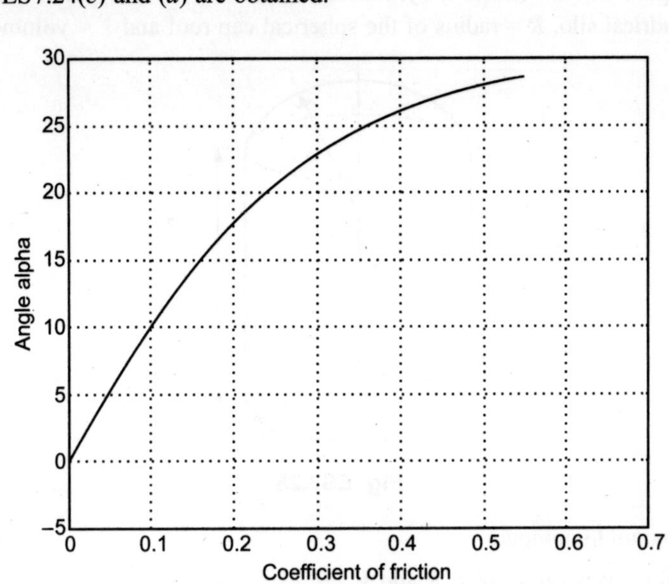

Fig. ES7.24(c)

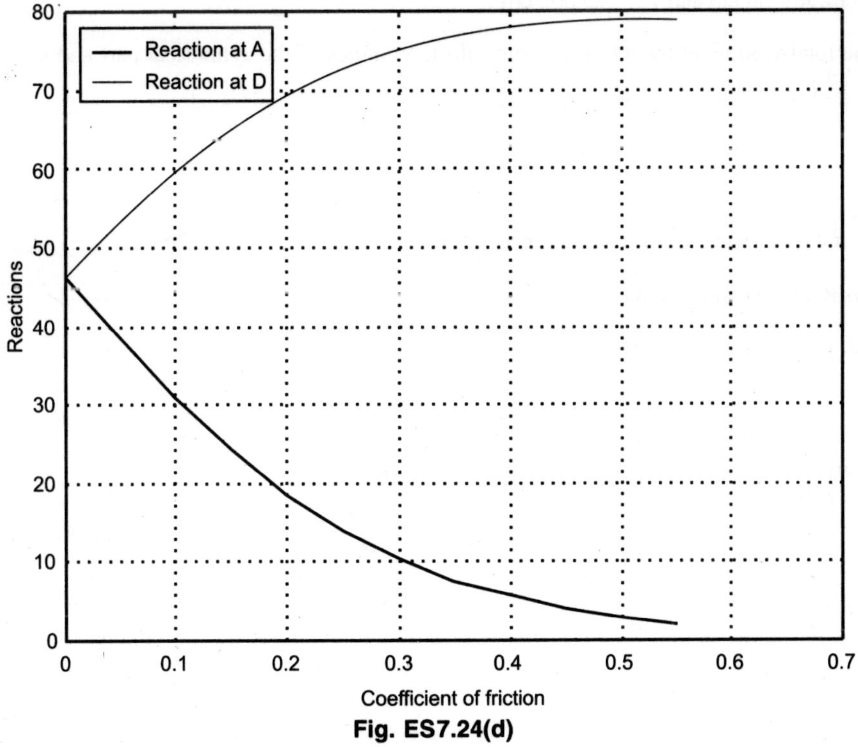

Fig. ES7.24(d)

Example ES7.25: Figure ES7.25 shows a cylindrical silo where H = height of the cylindrical portion, r = radius of the cylindrical silo, R = radius of the spherical cap roof and V = volume of the silo.

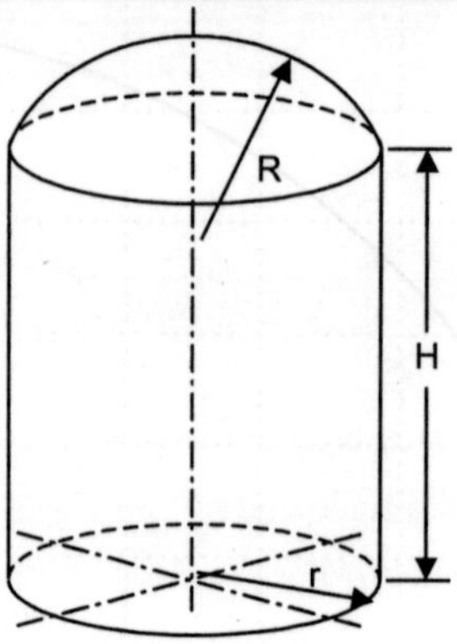

Fig. ES7.25

Write a MATLAB program to compute

(*a*) the height for given values of r, R and V

(*b*) the surface area of the silo, S

Use the program to determine the height and surface area of a silo, given r = 32 cm, R = 50 cm and V = 125,000 cm^3.

Solution: The total volume of the silo is the sum of the volumes of the cylindrical part and the spherical cap.

$$V_{\text{total}} = V_{\text{cyl}} + V_{\text{cap}}$$

$$= \pi r^2 H + \frac{1}{3}\pi h^2 (3R - h)$$

where,

$$h = R - R\cos\theta = R(1-\cos\theta) \text{ (see Fig. ES7.25(a))}$$

and $r = R\sin\theta$ or $\theta = \sin^{-1}(r/R)$

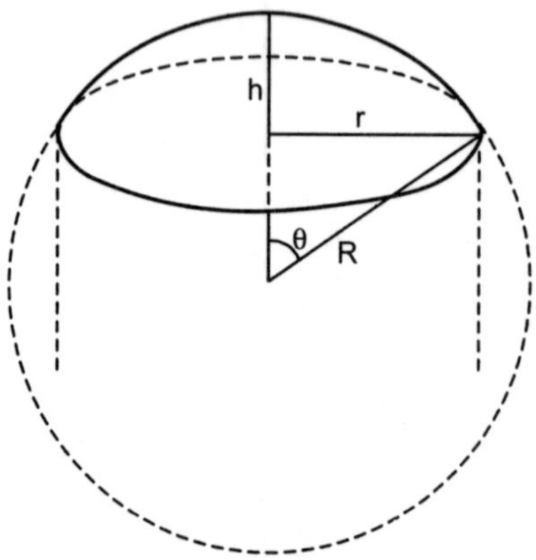

Fig. ES7.25 (a)

The height H, of the cylindrical part is given by

$$H = \frac{V - V_{\text{cap}}}{\pi r^2}$$

The surface area of the silo is the sum of the surface areas of the cylindrical part and the spherical cap.

$$S = S_{\text{cyl}} + S_{\text{cap}} = 2\pi rH + 2\pi RH.$$

%MATLAB Solution:

```
r=32;
R=50;
V=125000;
```

```
Theta=asin(r/R);
h = R*(1-cos(Theta));
Vcap=pi*h^2*(3*R-h)/3;
H=(V-Vcap)/(pi*r^2);
S=2*pi*(r*H+R*h);
fprintf('The height H = %f cm',H);
fprintf('The surface area of the silo S = %f square cm.',S);
```

Output comes as follows:
The height $H = 32.812738$ cm. The surface area of the silo $S = 10235.750764$ square cm.

Example ES7.26: Figure ES7.26 shows a trapezoid.

(*a*) Obtain the *x* and *y* coordinates of the centroid when $H_1 = a/n^2$ and $H_2 = a/n$.

(*b*) Write a MATLAB program to plot the values of $\bar{x}$ and $\bar{y}$ for $1 \le n \le 5$ and $a = 9$ mm.

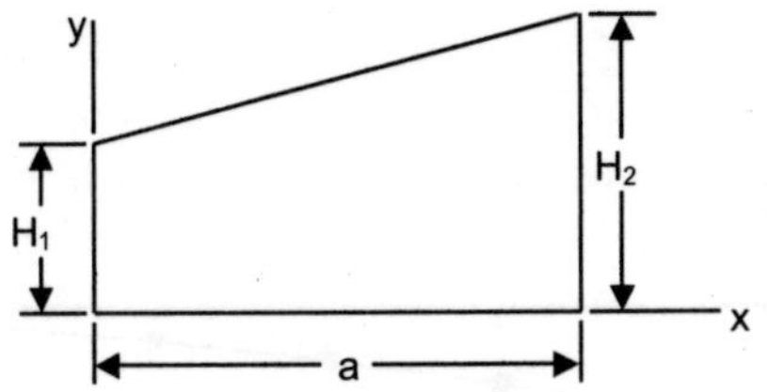

Fig. ES7.26

Solution: Entire trapezoid is divided into two triangles 1 and 2 as shown in Fig. ES7.26 (*a*).

Following table gives the area, centroid information of each area and total area.

#	Area	$\bar{x}$	$\overline{Ax}$	$\bar{y}$	$\overline{Ay}$
1.	aH_1	$\frac{a}{2}$	$\frac{1}{2}a^2H_1$	$\frac{1}{2}H_1$	$\frac{1}{2}aH_1^2$
2.	$\frac{1}{2}a(H_2-H_1)$	$\frac{2}{3}a$	$\frac{1}{3}a^2(H_2-H_1)$	$H_1+\frac{1}{3}(H_2-H_1)$ $=\frac{1}{3}(2H_1+H_2)$	$\frac{a}{6}\left(H_2^2+H_1H_2-2H_1^2\right)$
Σ	$\frac{a}{2}(H_1+H_2)$		$\frac{a^2}{6}(H_1+2H_2)$		$\frac{a}{6}\left(H_2^2+H_1H_2-2H_1^2\right)$

Hence, $$\bar{x} = \frac{a}{3}\left(\frac{H_1+2H_2}{H_1+H_2}\right); \quad \bar{y} = \frac{1}{3}\left(\frac{H_2^2+H_1H_2+H_1^2}{H_1+H_2}\right)$$

Substituting $H_1 = a/n^2$, $H_2 = a/n$ and $a = 9$ mm yields

$$\bar{x} = \frac{a}{3}\left(\frac{1+2n}{1+n}\right) = 3\left(\frac{1+2n}{1+n}\right)$$

$$\bar{y} = \frac{a}{3n^2}\left(\frac{n^2+n+1}{1+n}\right) = \frac{3}{n^2\left(\frac{n^2+n+1}{1+n}\right)}.$$

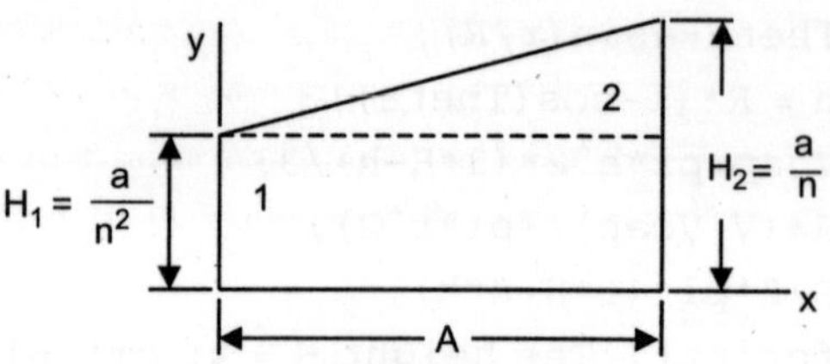

Fig. ES7.26 (a)

MATLAB Solution:

```
n=[1:.5:5];
xbar=3*(1+2*n)./(1+n);
ybar=(3./n.^2).*(n.^2+n+1)./(n+1);
plot(n,xbar,'-p',n,ybar,'-*')
text(3,5,'xbar')
text(3,1.4,'ybar')
xlabel('n')
ylabel('Centroid (mm)')
grid on
```

Output is shown in Fig. ES7.26(*b*).

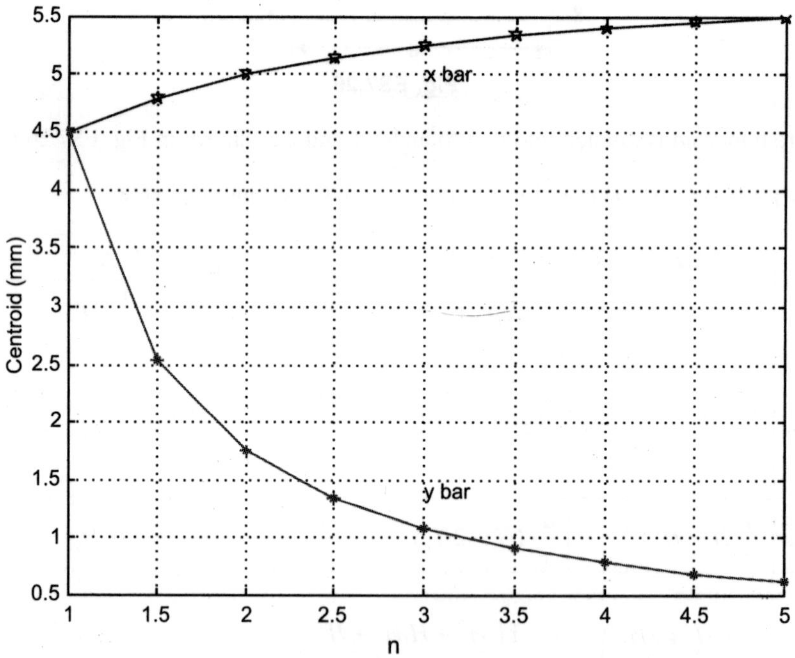

Fig. ES7.26(b)

Example ES7.27: Determine the *y* coordinate of the centroid of the body shown in Fig. ES7.27 when $h = nb$ and $h = n^2b$.

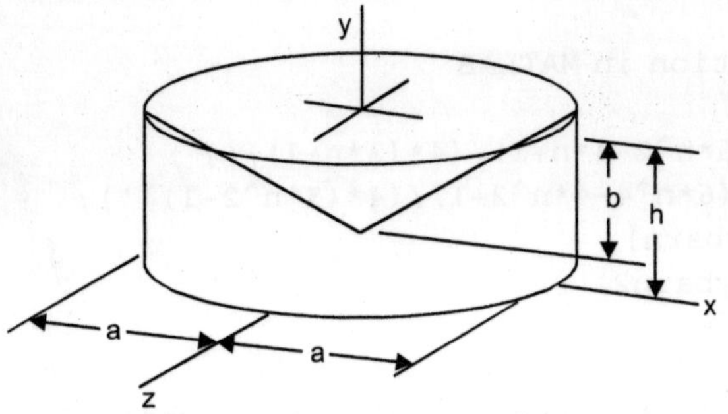

Fig. ES7.27

Write a MATLAB program to plot $\bar{y}$ as a function of n for both cases using $1 \le n \le 12$ and

(*i*) $b = 5$ mm, (*ii*) $b = 7$ mm and (*iii*) $b = 9$ mm.

Solution: This contains two parts as shown in Figures ES7.27 (*a*), (*b*) and (*c*).

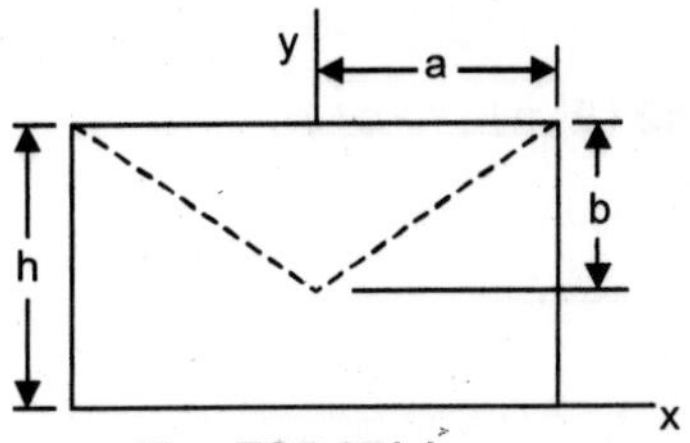

Fig. ES7.27(a)

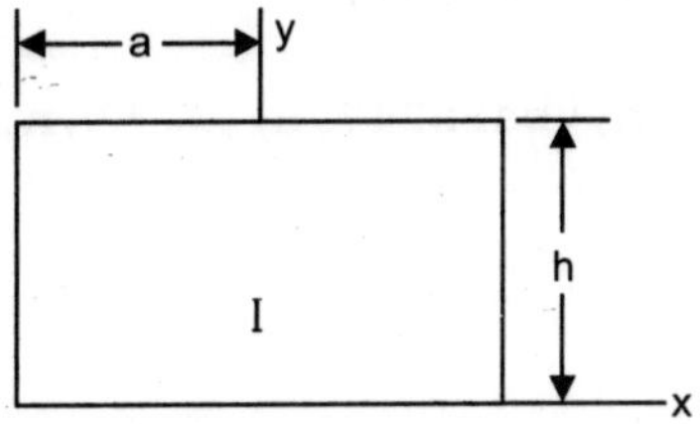

Fig. ES7.27(b)

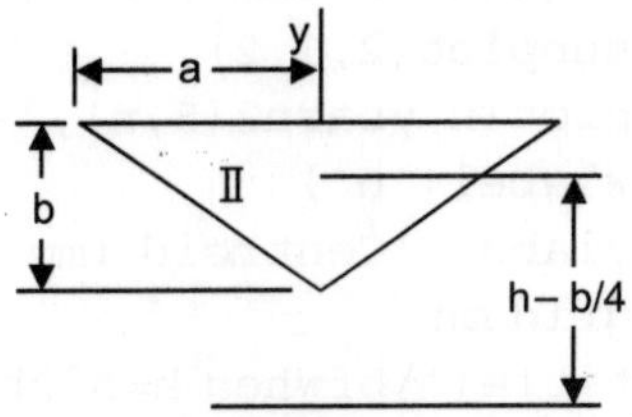

Fig. ES7.27(c)

Based on the Fig. ES7.27(*a*), the following table is constructed.

	V	$\bar{y}$	$\bar{y}V$
I	$\pi a^2 h$	$\frac{1}{2}h$	$\frac{1}{2}\pi a^2 h^2$
II	$-\frac{1}{3}\pi a^2 b$	$h-\frac{1}{4}b$	$-\frac{\pi}{3}a^2 bh + \frac{\pi}{12}a^2 b^2$

$\bar{y}\Sigma V = \Sigma \bar{y} V$ gives

$$\bar{y}\left(\pi a^2 h - \frac{\pi}{3}a^2 b\right) = \frac{\pi}{12}a^2 b^2 + \frac{\pi}{2}a^2 h^2 - \frac{\pi}{3}a^2 bh$$

and
$$\bar{y} = \frac{6h^2 - 4hb + b^2}{4(3h-b)}$$

For $h = nb$

$$\bar{y} = \frac{b\left(6n^2 - 4n + 1\right)}{4(3n-1)}$$

For $h = n^2 b$

$$\bar{y} = \frac{b\left(6n^2 - 4n^2 + 1\right)}{4\left(3n^2 - 1\right)}$$

The plot of $\bar{y}$ as a function of n for $1 \le n \le 12$ for the cases is shown in Figs. ES7.27(*d*) and (*e*).

MATLAB Solution:

```
% Use symbolic notation in MATLAB
syms b n
 ybarn=inline('b*(6*n^2-4*n+1)/(4*(3*n-1))') ;
 ybarn2=inline('b*(6*n^4-4*n^2+1)/(4*(3*n^2-1))');
  ybarn=vectorize(ybarn)
 ybarn2=vectorize(ybarn2)
 n=[1:1:12];
 subplot(2,1,1)
 plot(n,ybarn(5,n),'-p',n,ybarn(7,n),'-*',n,ybarn(9,n),'-o')
 xlabel('n')
 ylabel('Centroid  (mm)')
 grid on
 title('\bfwhen h=nb')
 legend('b=5mm','b=7mm','b=9mm',2);
 subplot(2,1,2)
 plot(n,ybarn2(5,n),'-p',n,ybarn2(7,n),'-*',n,ybarn2(9,n),'-o')
 xlabel('n')
 ylabel('Centroid (mm)')
 grid on
 title('\bfwhen h=n^2b')
```

Output of the program is shown in Fig. ES7.27(*d*).

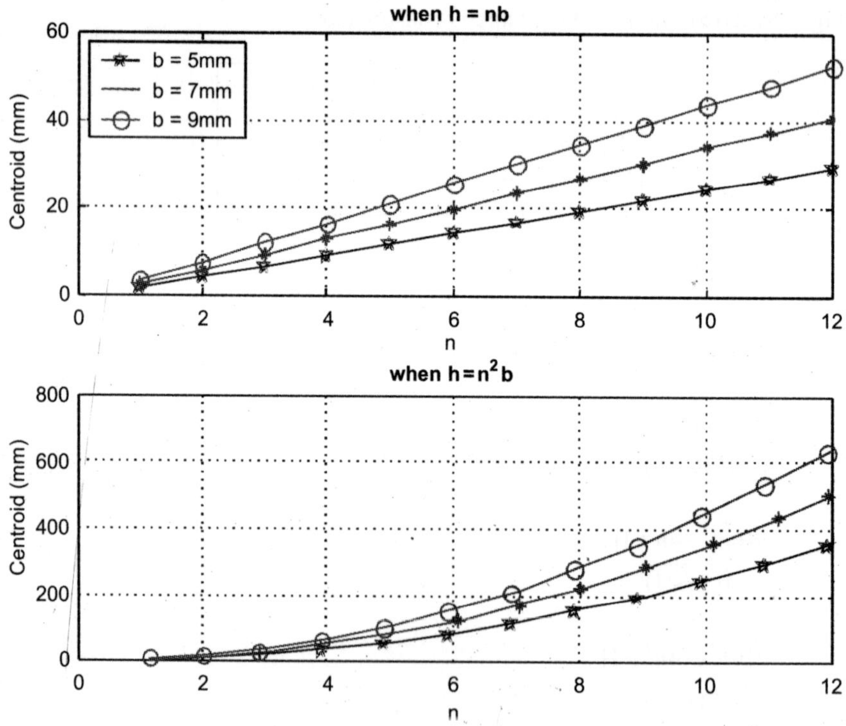

Fig. ES7.27(d) MATLAB output

Example ES7.28: For the area shown in Fig. ES7.28, write a MATLAB program to plot I_{xy} as a function of N for values of N from 1 to 12 knowing that A = 100 mm and B = 80 mm.

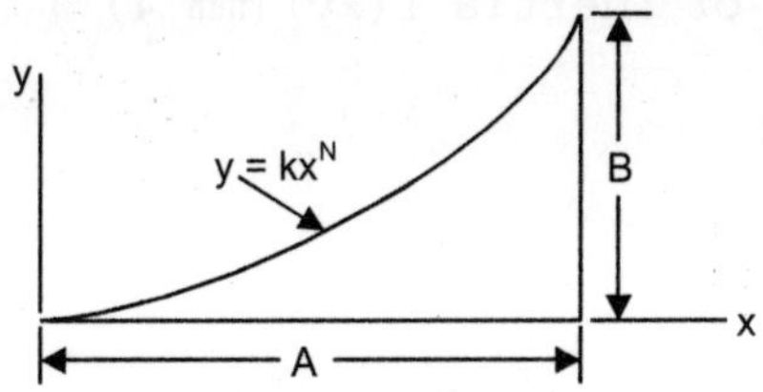

Fig. ES7.28

Solution: Consider an elemental length dx as shown in Fig. ES7.28 (a).

When $x = A$, $B = ka^N$

Therefore, $k = \dfrac{B}{A''}$

and $y = \dfrac{B}{A^N} x^N$

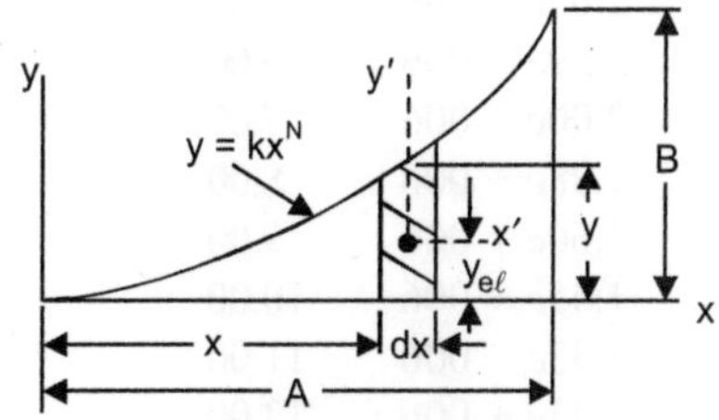

Fig. ES7.28(a)

Also $dI_{xy} = \overline{dI}_{x'y'} + \overline{x}_{el}\overline{y}_{el}dA$

But due to symmetry

$$\overline{dI}_{x'y'} = 0$$

Since $\overline{x}_{el} = x$, $\overline{y}_{el} = 1/2y$ and $dA = ydx$, we have

$$I_{xy} = \int dI_{xy} = \int_0^a x\left(\frac{1}{2}y\right)ydx = \frac{1}{2}\int_0^A x\left(\frac{B}{A^N}x^N\right)^2 dx$$

$$I_{xy} = \frac{1}{2}\frac{B^N}{A^{2N}}\int_0^A x^{2n+1}dx = \frac{1}{2}\frac{B^N}{A^{2N}}\frac{A^{2N+2}}{2N+2}$$

$$I_{xy} = \frac{A^2B^2}{4(N+1)}$$

MATLAB Solution:

```
% Input A and B [in mm]
A=100;
B=80;
fprintf('Enter A and B\n');
fprintf('A=%g mm, and B=%gmm\n',A,B);
fprintf('I(xy) N\n')
for N=1:15
  Ixy(N)=A^2*B^2/(4.*(N+1));
 NN(N)=N;
 fprintf('%5.2e %5.2f\n',Ixy(N),NN(N))
end
```

```
plot(NN, Ixy)
xlabel('N')
ylabel('Computed moment of inertia I(xy)(mm^4)')
grid on
```

Output comes like this:

Enter *A* and *B*

A = 100 mm, and *B* = 80 mm

I(*xy*)	*N*
8.00*e* + 006	1.00
5.33*e* + 006	2.00
4.00*e* + 006	3.00
3.20*e* + 006	4.00
2.67*e* + 006	5.00
2.29*e* + 006	6.00
2.00*e* + 006	7.00
1.78*e* + 006	8.00
1.60*e* + 006	9.00
1.45*e* + 006	10.00
1.33*e* + 006	11.00
1.23*e* + 006	12.00
1.14*e* + 006	13.00
1.07*e* + 006	14.00
1.00*e* + 006	15.00

Plot is shown in Fig. ES7.28(*b*).

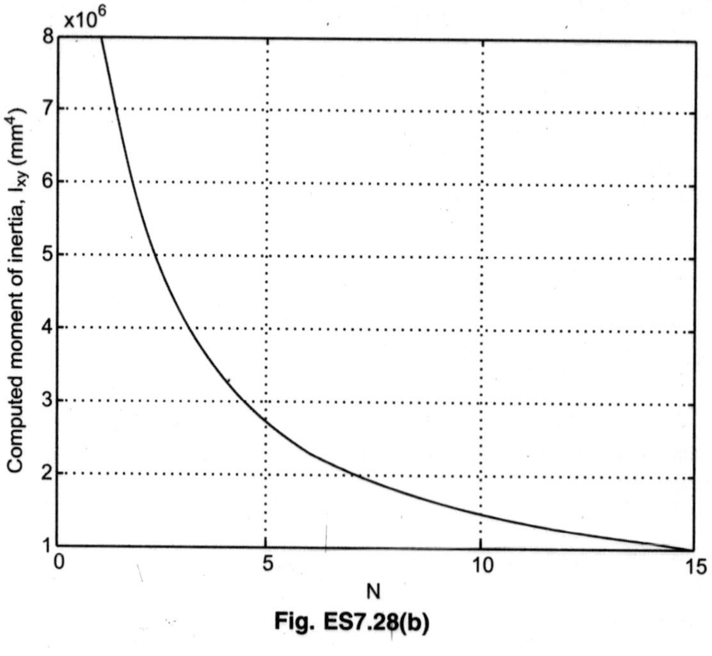

Fig. ES7.28(b)

7.21.2 Dynamics

Particle Kinematics

Example ED7.1: The motion of a particle is defined by the equation

$$x = 35t^2 - 110t$$

and $$y = 115t^2 - 42t^3$$

where x and y = displacement of the particle (mm)

t = time (sec.) for the time interval $0 \le t \le 25s$

Write a MATLAB program to plot:

(*a*) the path of the particle in the *x-y* plane,
(*b*) the components of the velocity v_x and v_y and the magnitude of the velocity v,
(*c*) the components of the acceleration a_x and a_y and the magnitude of the acceleration a.

Solution:

Given $x = 35t^2 - 110t;$ $y = 115t^2 - 42t^3$ as the position vector of the particle.

Hence, $v_x = \dot{x} = 70t - 110;$ $v_y = \dot{y} = 230t - 126t^2$ are component of velocities and

$a_x = \ddot{x} = 70;$ $a_y = \ddot{y} = 230 - 252t$ are components of accelerations.

Here particle path refers to the plot of x and y positions at various instants of time.
So first x and y are found by varying t from 0 to 25 seconds.

MATLAB Program is given below:

```
t=[0:0.5:25];% Vary the time from 0 to 25 in steps of 0.5
x=35*t.^2-110*t; % compute x
y=115*t.^2-42*t.^3; % compute y
v_x=70*t-110; % compute vx
v_y=230*t-126*t.^2; % compute vy
v=sqrt(v_x.^2+v_y.^2); % compute v
a_x=70;% compute ax
a_y=230-252*t; % compute ay
a=sqrt(a_x.^2+a_y.^2); % compute a
PLOTING THE CALCULATED DATA%%%%%%%%%%%%%%%
figure(1)
plot(x,y);
xlabel('x(mm)')
ylabel('y(mm)')
legend('Trajectory')
grid on
axis([0 10000 -2.5e5 0])
figure(2)
plot(t,v_x,t,v_y,t,v)
```

```
xlabel('t(sec)')
ylabel('v_x,v_y,v(mmps)')
legend('v_x','v_y','v',2)
grid on
figure(3)
plot(t,a_x,t,a_y,t,a)
xlabel('t(sec)')
ylabel('a_x,a_y,a(mmps^2)')
legend('a_x','a_y','a',2)
grid on
```

The plots are shown in Figs. ED7.1(*a*), (*b*) and (*c*) respectively.

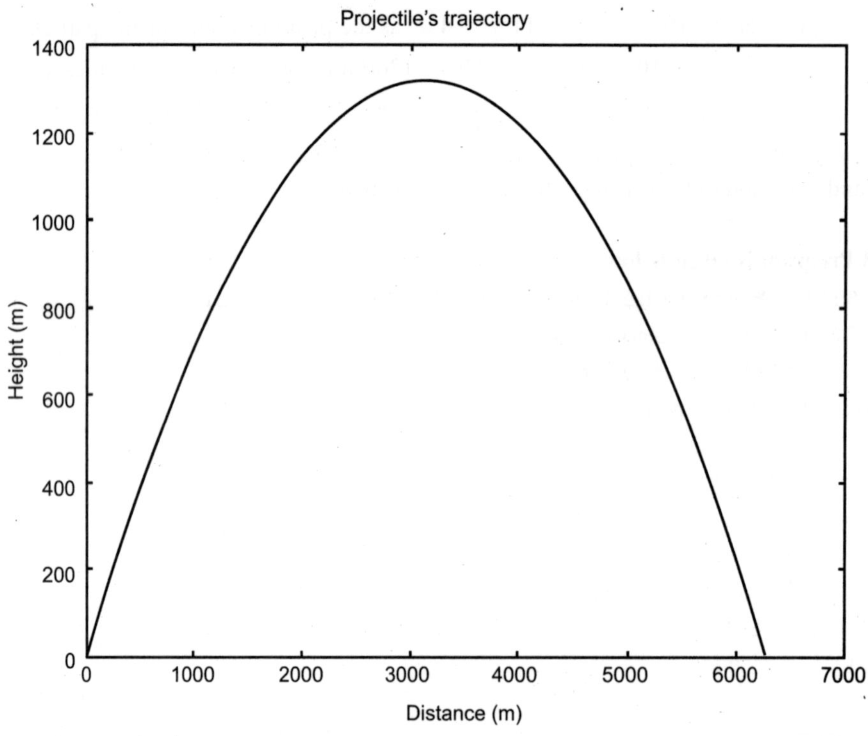

Fig. ED7.1 (a) Position

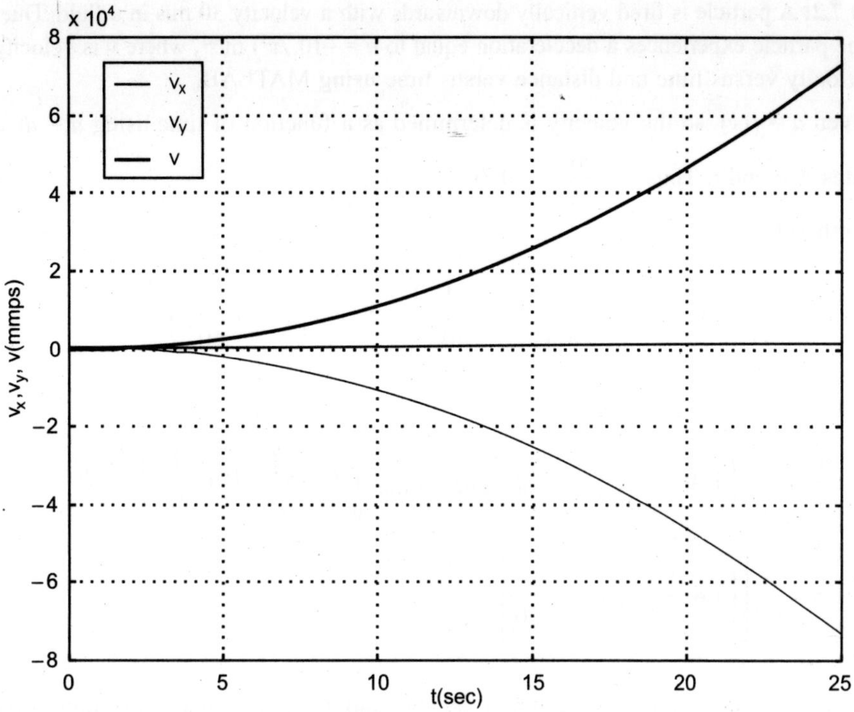

Fig. ED7.1 (b) Velocities

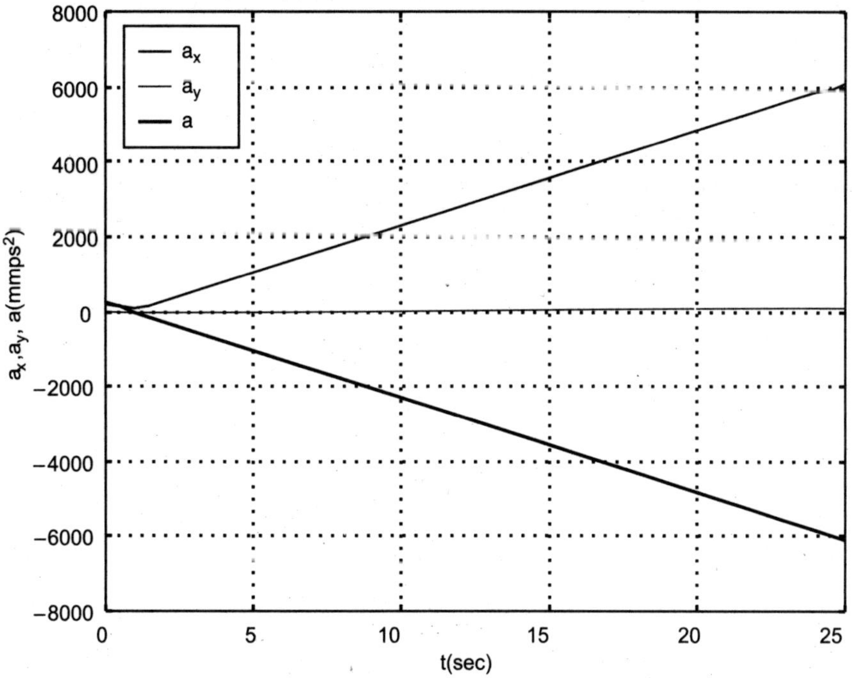

Fig. ED7.1 (c) Accelerations

Example ED 7.2: A particle is fired vertically downwards with a velocity 30 m/s in a fluid. Due to resistance of the fluid the particle experiences a deceleration equal to $a = -(0.7v^3)$ m/s^2, where v is velocity in m/s. Plot a graph of velocity versus time and distance versus time using MATLAB.

Solution: Given $a = f(v)$, so the velocity is determined as a function of time using $a = dv/dt$, since this equation relates v, a and t. Thus $a = \dfrac{dv}{dt} = -0.7v^3$.

Integrating both sides

$$-\int_{30}^{v} \frac{dv}{0.7v^3} = \int_{0}^{t} dt \quad \text{or} \quad t = \frac{1}{1.4}\left[\frac{1}{v^2} - \frac{1}{30^2}\right] \quad \text{or} \quad v = \left(1.4t + \frac{1}{30^2}\right)^{-0.5}$$

Position s is given by

$$\frac{ds}{dt} = v = \left(1.4t + \frac{1}{30^2}\right)^{-0.5} \quad \text{or integrating} \quad \int_{0}^{s} ds = \int_{0}^{t} \left(1.4t + \frac{1}{30^2}\right)^{-0.5} dt$$

or

$$s = \frac{2}{1.4}\left[\left(1.4t + \frac{1}{30^2}\right)^{0.5} - \frac{1}{30}\right]$$

Using MATLAB, the graphical representation of velocity and displacement as a function of time t is given with following simple program.

MATLAB Program:

```
t=0:0.05:1.5;
v0=30; %INITIAL VELOCITY
v=(1.4*t+1/v0^2).^-0.5;
s=2/1.4*(sqrt(1.4*t+1/v0^2)-1/30);
figure(1)
plot(t,v);
xlabel('t(sec)')
ylabel('v(mps)')
grid on
figure(2)
plot(t,s)
xlabel('t(sec)')
ylabel('s(m)')
grid on
```

The output of the program is shown in Figs. ED7.2 (*a*) and (*b*).

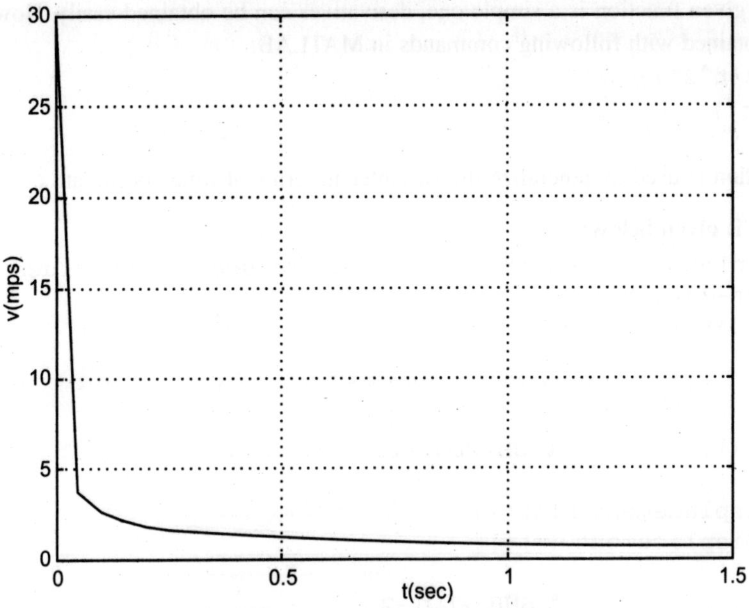

Fig. ED7.2 (a) Velocity variation

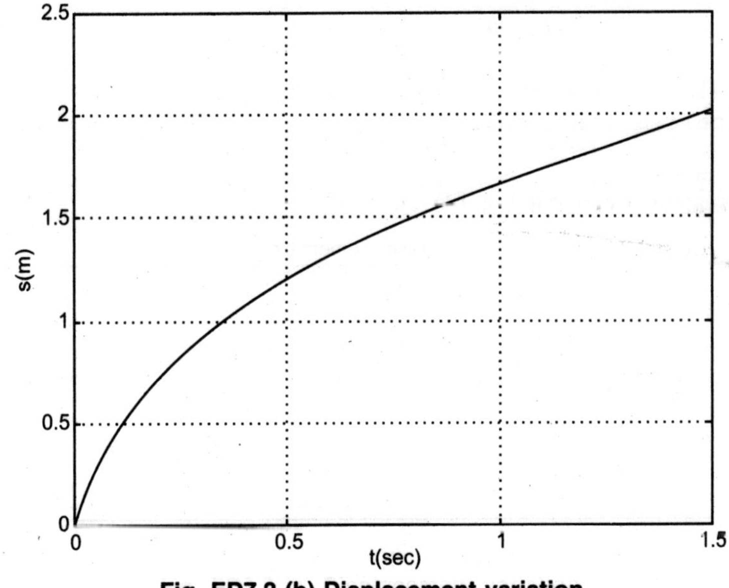

Fig. ED7.2 (b) Displacement variation

Example ED 7.3: If position of a car is defined as $s = (5t - 3t^2)$, construct $s - t$, $v - t$ and $a - t$ graphs over the interval $0 < t < 10$ sec.

Solution: As the given function is a simple one, derivatives can be obtained easily. However, initially the derivatives are obtained with following commands in MATLAB.

```
s=sym('5*t-3*t^2');
v= diff(s, 't')
a=diff(v,'t')
```

The 'inline' function is used to generalize the variables in terms of time coordinate t.

The entire script is given below:

```
% The script plots s-t, v-t and a-t curves for specified values of t
s=inline('5*t-3*t.^2');
v=inline('5-6*t');
a=inline('-6');
t=0:0.5:10;
figure(1);
subplot(3,1,1);            %SUB-PLOT-1
plot(t,s(t));
title('\bfDisplacement Plot');
ylabel('\bfDisplacement (m)');
grid on;
subplot(3,1,2);            % SUB-PLOT-2
plot(t,v(t));
title('\bfVelocity Plot');
ylabel('\bfVelocity (mps)');
grid on;
subplot(3,1,3);            % SUB-PLOT-3
plot(t,a(t),'*');
title('\bfAcceleration Plot');
ylabel('\bfAcceleration (mps^2)');
grid on;
```

The output of the program is shown in Fig. ED7.3.

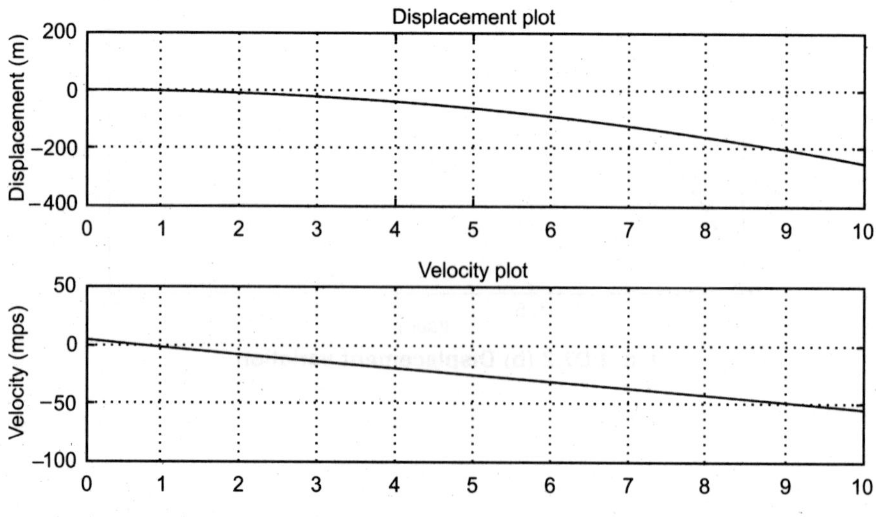

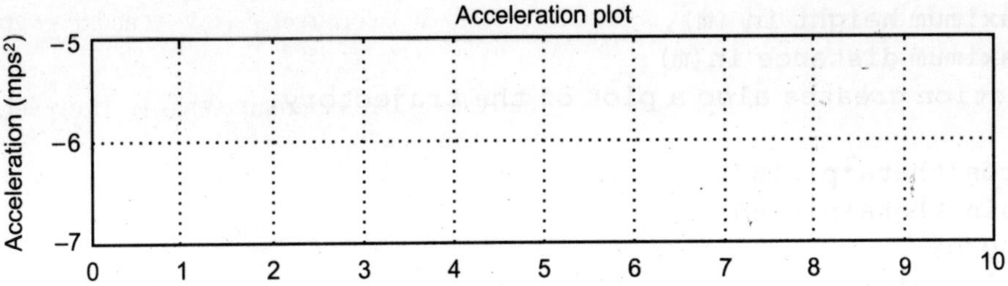

Fig. ED7.3 MATLAB output

Example ED 7.4: Figure ED7.4 shows the motion of a particle. The initial velocity and the angle at which the projectile is fired are known. Write a MATLAB program to calcualte and plot the maximum height and distance. Use the program to calculate and plot the trajectory of a projectile that is fired at a velocity of 250 m/s at an angle of 40º.

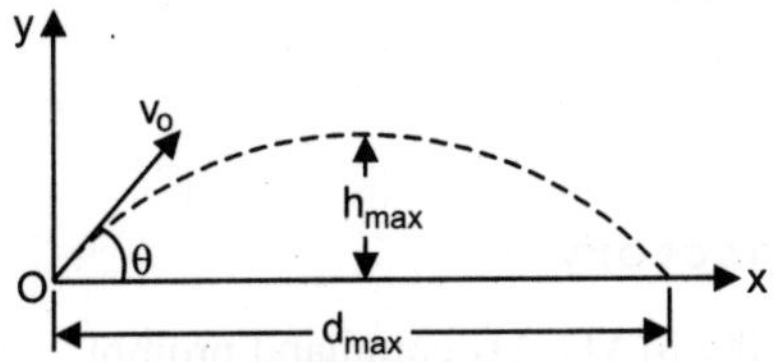

Fig. ED7.4

Solution: Components of velocity $v_{ox} = v_o \cdot \cos\theta$ and $v_{oy} = v_o \cdot \sin\theta$.

Height $$h_{max} = \frac{v_{oy}^2}{2g}$$

and corresponding time

$$t_{max} = \frac{v_{oy}}{g}$$

But to draw trajectory as a function of distance(x), use

$$y = v_{oy}t - \frac{1}{2}gt^2 \text{ and } x = v_{ox}t$$

MATLAB script is shown below:

Open the file "trajectory.m" and type the following

```
function[hmax,dmax]=trajectory(v0,theta)
% Trajectory calculates the max height and distance of a projectile,
% makes a plot of the trajectory.
% Input arguments are:
%v0=initial velocity in(m/s).
%theta=angle in degrees.
%Output arguments are:
```

```
%hmax=maximum height in (m).
%dmax=maximum distance in(m).
%The function creates also a plot of the trajectory.
g=9.81;
v0x=v0*cos(theta*pi/180);
v0y=v0*sin(theta*pi/180);
thmax=v0y/g;
hmax=v0y^2/(2*g);
ttot=2*thmax;
dmax=v0x*ttot;

%Creating a trajectory plot
tplot=linspace(0,ttot,200);
x=v0x*tplot;
y=v0y*tplot-0.5*g*tplot.^2;
plot(x,y)
xlabel('Distance(m)')
ylabel('Height(m)')
title('Projectile's  Trajectory')
```

To execute it type the following at the MATLAB command prompt

>> [*h* *d*] = trajectory(250,40)

Then the output comes as:

$h =$

$1.3162e + 003$

$d =$

$6.2743e + 003$

Followed by the Fig. ED7.4 (*a*).

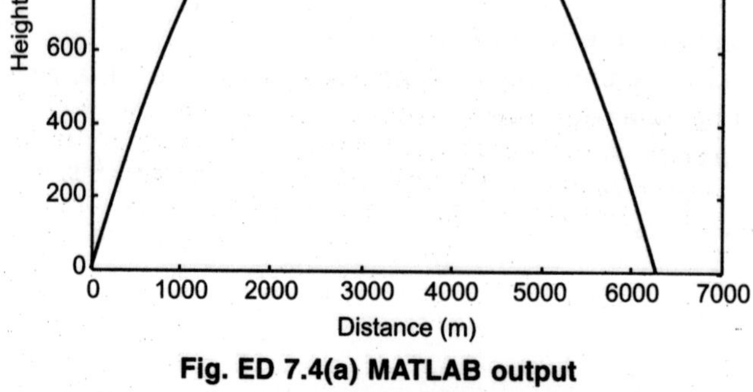

Fig. ED 7.4(a) MATLAB output

Example ED7.5: A jet plane is going in a parabolic path described by $y=0.05x^2$. At a point in the path, it has a velocity of 200 m/s, which is increasing at the rate of 0.8 m/s^2 . Find the resultant acceleration and plot the variation of acceleration as a function of its horizontal position x.

Solution: The motion of the plane is described in Fig. ED7.5.

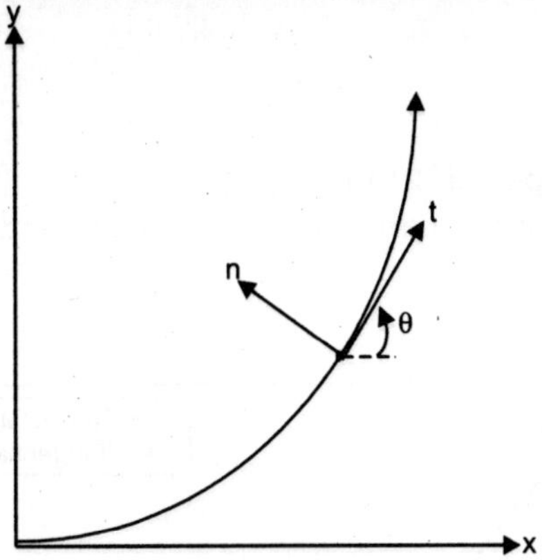

Fig. ED7.5

The components of acceleration along n and t directions are as follows:

$$a_t = dv/dt = 0.8 \text{ m/s}^2, \quad a_n = v^2/(\rho g) = 200^2/(\rho g), \text{ with } \rho = \frac{\left[1+\left(\dfrac{dy}{dx}\right)^2\right]^{3/2}}{\left|\dfrac{d^2y}{dx^2}\right|}$$

So, it requires computation of differentials as a function of x. Then using these differentials, the resultant acceleration $a=\sqrt{a_r^2+a_n^2}$ is plotted as a function of x in MATLAB.

As usual first define

y = sym('0.05**x*^2');
yd = diff(*y*, '*x*'); %% first derivative
ydd = diff(*yd*, '*x*');%% second derivative

They give *yd*=0.10**x* and *ydd*=0.10
Now use the following program to plot variation of acceleration with x.

MATLAB Program:

```
ac=0.8;
v=200;vs=v*v;
y=inline('0.05*x.^2');
yd=inline('0.1*x');
```

```
ydd=inline('0.1');
x=0.1:0.1:20;
rho=((1+yd(x).*yd(x)).^1.5)/abs(ydd(x));
an=vs./rho;
at=ac./x.*x;
a=sqrt(at.^2+an.^2);
plot(x,an,x,at,'*')
xlabel('x-position');
ylabel('Acceleration in m per s^2');
legend('Normal acceleration','tangential acceleration')
```

The output is shown in Fig. ED7.5 (*a*).

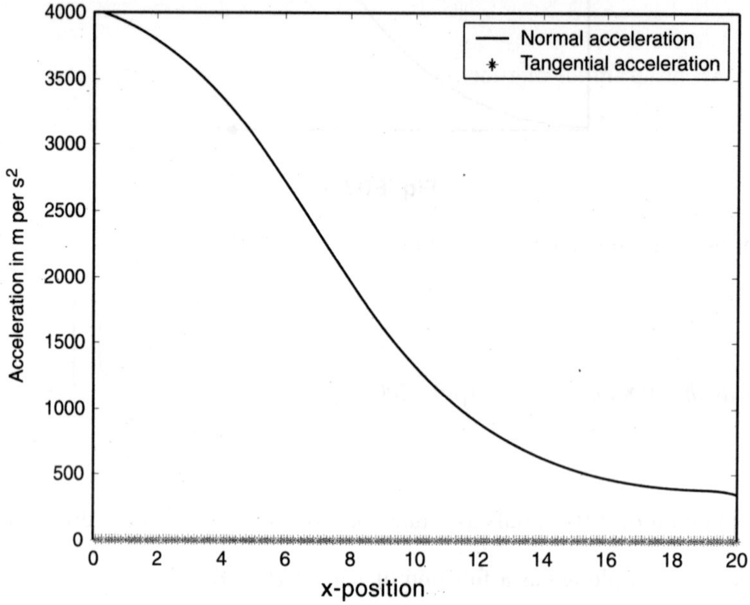

Fig. ED7.5 (a) MATLAB output

Example ED7.6: Path of a particle *P* is ellipse defines with $r = 1.75/(1 - 0.75\cos\pi t)$ and $\theta = \pi t$. Derive expressions for velocity and acceleration. Plot the components of velocities and accelerations as a function of time.

Solution: This problem should be solved in cylindrical coordinate system. Thus

Radial velocity $v_r = \dot{r}$ and transverse velocity $v_\theta = r\dot{\theta}$,

where $\dot{\theta} = \pi$ and $\dot{r} = 1.75 \times 0.75 \times \pi \sin\pi t/(1 - 0.75\cos\pi t)^2$

Radial acceleration $a_r = \ddot{r} - r\dot{\theta}^2$ and transverse acceleration $a_\theta = r\ddot{\theta} + 2\dot{r}\dot{\theta}$. Here $\ddot{\theta} = 0$, but $\ddot{r}$ should be found from the MATLAB's diff command. This is done as follows:

```
y=sym('1.75/(1-0.75*cos(3.14*t))')
yd= diff(y, 't');
ydd=diff(yd,'t');
```

Output:

```
y =1.75/(1-0.75*cos(3.14*t))
 yd=-4.121250/(1-.75*cos(3.14*t))^2*sin(3.14*t)
 ydd=
19.4110875000/(1-.75*cos(3.14*t)).^3*sin(3.14*t)^2-12.94072500/
(1-.75*cos(3.14*t))^2*cos(3.14*t)
```

This defines the differentials $\dot{r}$ and $\ddot{r}$ as follows:

$$\dot{r} = -4.121\ \sin\pi t/(1-0.75\cos\pi t)^2 \text{ and}$$

$$\ddot{r} = \frac{19.4\sin^2 \pi t}{(1-0.75\cos \pi t)^3} - \frac{12.94\cos \pi t}{(1-0.75\cos \pi t)^2}$$

The complete MATLAB program for plotting the velocities and acceleration is given below:

```
pi=3.14;
r =inline('1.75./(1-0.75*cos(3.14*t))');
rd=inline('-4.121*sin(3.14*t)./(1-0.75*cos(3.14*t)).^2');
rdd=inline('19.4*sin(3.14*t).^2/(1-0.75*cos(3.14*t)).^3-12.94*cos(3.14*t)./
(1-.75*cos(3.14*t)).^2');
theta=inline('3.14*t');
thetad=inline('3.14*t./t');
t=0.5:0.1:2;
vr=rd(t);vt=r(t).*theta(t);
ar=(rdd(t)-r(t).*thetad(t).^2);
at=2*rd(t).*thetad(t);
figure(1);
subplot(2,1,1); %SUB-PLOT-1
plot(t,vr,t,vt,'-p');
title('\bfVelocity Plot');
ylabel('Velocity (m per s)');
legend('radial velocity','transverse velocity');
grid on;
subplot(2,1,2); % SUB-PLOT-2
plot(t,ar,t,at,'-p');
title('\bfAcceleration Plot');
ylabel('Acceleration (mps^2)');
xlabel('Time in s');
legend('radial acceleration','transverse acceleration');
grid on;
```

The output plot is shown in Fig. ED7.6.

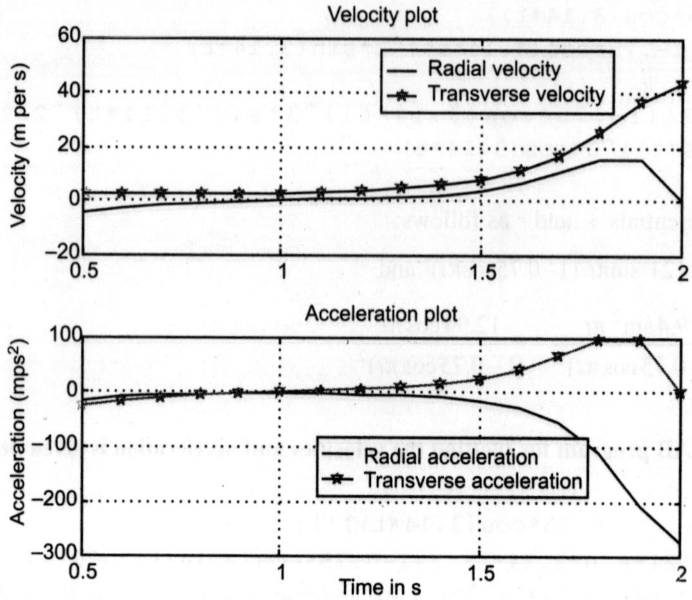

Fig. ED7.6 Velocity and acceleration of particle in ellipse

Example ED7.7: Two planes A and B are flying at a speed of 600 km/h with A in a straight line path while B is along a circular path of radius ρ. If A is accelerating at 50 km/h², while B decelerates at 100 km/h², plot the resultant acceleration of B with respect to A as a function of radius of curvature ρ.

Solution: The motion of two planes A and B are given in Fig. ED7.7.

Acceleration of B is

$$a_B = a_{Bt}\hat{u}_t + a_{Bn}\hat{u}_n,$$

where $a_{Bt} = -100$ km/h², $a_{Bn} = 600^2/\rho$

Likewise for A $a_{At} = 50$ km/h² and $a_{An} = 0$

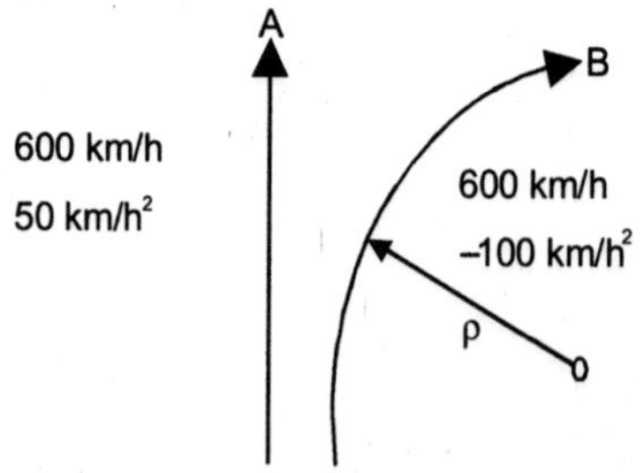

Fig. ED7.7

The relative velocity is then given by $a_{BA} = a_B - a_A = (a_{Bt} - a_{At})\,\hat{u}_t + (a_{Bn} - a_{An})\,\hat{u}_n$

$$= (a_{Bt} - a_{At})\,\hat{u}_t + (a_{Bn})\,\hat{u}_n$$

Its magnitude is given by $\sqrt{(a_{Bt} - a_{At})^2 + a_{Bn}^2}$

Following MATLAB code can be readily employed for this problem:

```
v0=600;
aA=50;
aBt=-100;
r=100:20:600;
aB=sqrt((aBt-aA).^2+(v0*v0./r).^2);
plot(r,aB);
xlabel('Radius of curvature');
ylabel('Relative acceleration of plane B');
grid on;
```

The output of the program is presented in Fig. ED7.7 (*a*).

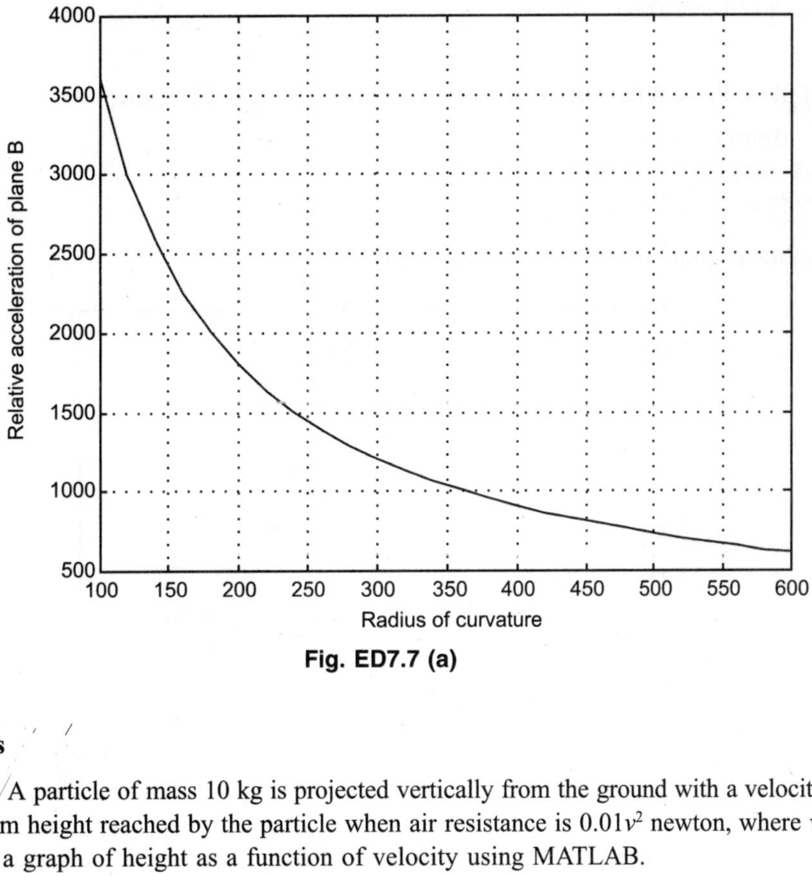

Fig. ED7.7 (a)

Particle Kinetics

Example ED7.8: A particle of mass 10 kg is projected vertically from the ground with a velocity of 50 m/s. Find the maximum height reached by the particle when air resistance is $0.01v^2$ newton, where v is speed at any instant. Plot a graph of height as a function of velocity using MATLAB.

Solution: Here the particle is under the influence of forces shown in Fig. ED7.8.

Fig. ED7.8

Applying Newton's second law along *y*-direction: $\Sigma F_y = ma_y$,
where $\Sigma F_y = -F - mg = (-0.01v^2 - mg)$
Thus $\quad ma_y = (-0.01v^2 - mg)$ or $a_y = (-0.01v^2 - mg)/m$
As the distance Vs velocity plot is required use the relation $vdv = ads$

i.e., $$ds = \frac{-mvdv}{0.01v^2 + mg} \text{ or } \frac{ds}{dv} = -\frac{mv}{0.01v^2 + mg}$$

This differential equation is solved with initial conditions at $s = 0$, $v = 50$ m/s with the following program.

```
s0=0;
v0=50;
vspan=[v0:-1:0];% a vector that specifies the interval of the solution
[v s]=ode45('resist',vspan,s0);% Solving the ODE
plot(s,v)
xlabel('x(m)');ylabel('Velocity(m/s)')
grid on;
```

The function file with the differential equation named 'resist.m' is listed below:

```
function dsdv=resist(v,s)
m=10; g=9.81;
dsdv=-m*v/(0.01*v^2+m*g);
```

The output of the program is shown in Fig. ED7.8(*a*).

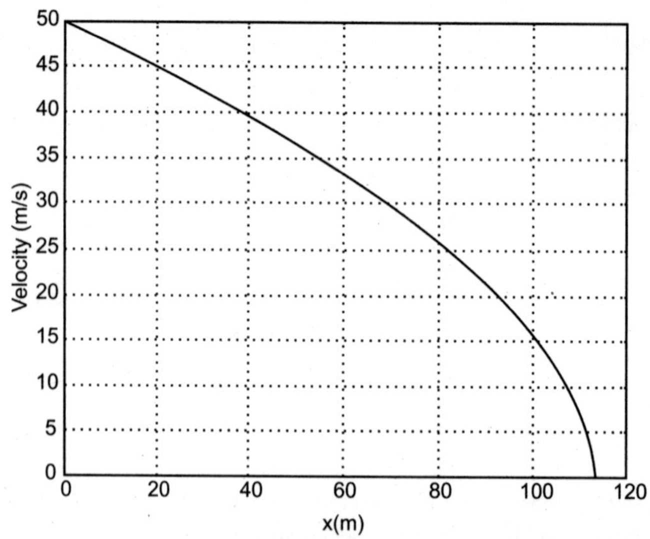

Fig. ED7.8 (a)

Example ED7.9: Figure ED7.9 shows a safety bumper placed at the end of a racetrack to stop out-of-control vehicles. The force that the bumper applies to the vehicle is given by

$$F = Kv^3(x + 1)^3$$

where K = 32 kg-s/m^5 (a constant)

x = displacement of the front edge of the bumper

v = velocity of the front edge of the bumper.

A vehicle of mass 2000 kg hits the bumper at a speed of 100 km/h. Write a MATLAB program to determine and plot the velocity of the vehicle as a function of x for $0 \le x \le 5$m.

Fig. ED7.9

Solution: The deceleration of the car once it hits the bumper can be calculated from Newton's second law of motion.

$$ma = -Kv^3(x + 1)^3$$

which can be solved for the acceleration a as a function of v and x:

$$a = \frac{-Kv^3(x+1)^3}{m}$$

The velocity as a function of x can be calculated by substituting the acceleration in the equation:

$$vdv = adx$$

which gives:

$$\frac{dv}{dx} = \frac{-Kv^2(x+1)^3}{m}$$

The last equation is a first order ODE that needs to be solved for the interval $0 \le x \le 3$ with the initial condition:

$$v = 90 \text{ km/h at } x = 0.$$

Numerical solution of differential equation is shown in the following program written in a script file (*m*-file), which should be executed by typing the file name in command prompt.

MATLAB Program:

```
global k m
k=32;m=2000;v0=100;
xspan=[0:0.2:5];% a vector that specifies the interval of the solution
v0mps=v0*1000/3600; % changing velocity in m/s
[x v]=ode45('bumper',xspan,v0mps);% Solving the ODE
table=[x,v];
disp('disp velocity')
disp(table);
```

```
plot(x,v)
xlabel('x(m)');
ylabel('velocity(m/s)')
grid on;
```

The function file with the differential equation named bumper.m is listed below:

```
function dvdx=bumper(x,v)
global k m
dvdx=-(k*v^2*(x+1)^3)/m;
```

The output of the above program is the vectors *x* and *v* as follows along with plot.

disp	velocity
0	27.7778
0.2000	24.8173
0.4000	21.1176
0.6000	17.1814
0.8000	13.5109
1.0000	10.4127
1.2000	7.9665
1.4000	6.0685
1.6000	4.6826
1.8000	3.6212
2.0000	2.8257
2.2000	2.2268
2.4000	1.7734
2.6000	1.4268
2.8000	1.1588
3.0000	0.9505
3.2000	0.7855
3.4000	0.6552
3.6000	0.5501
3.8000	0.4651
4.0000	0.3959
4.2000	0.3389
4.4000	0.2919
4.6000	0.2526
4.8000	0.2197
5.0000	0.1920

Output is given in Fig. ED7.9(*a*).

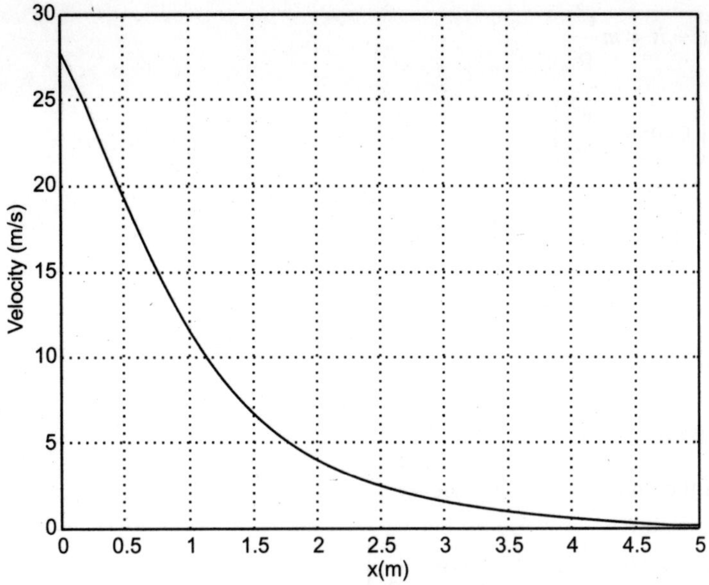

Fig. ED7.9(a)

Example ED7.10: Figure ED7.10 shows a block of mass m which is at rest on the top of a cylindrical surface. When an initial velocity v_0 is given to the block towards right, it starts to slide on the cylindrical surface. Write a MATLAB program to plot the variation of velocity of block and α as a function of time at a friction coefficient $\mu_k = 0.2$. Also find the angle at which the block leaves the surface. Assume mass of the block = 0.60 kg and initial velocity of the block, $v_0 = 4$ m/s.

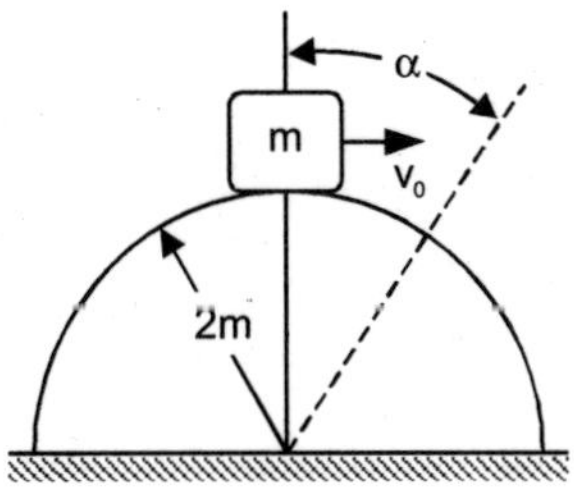

Fig. ED7.10

Solution: The free-body diagram of block when moved at an angle α is given in Fig. ED7.10(*a*).

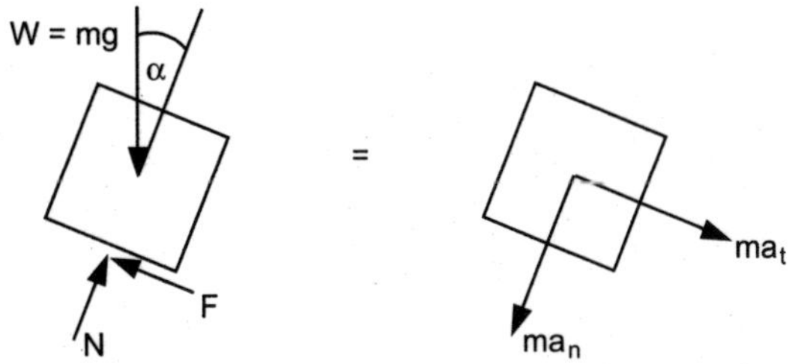

Fig. ED7.10(a) Free-body diagram

Summing forces in the normal direction gives $\Sigma F_n = ma_n$:

i.e., $$W\cos\alpha - N = m\frac{v^2}{\rho}$$

or $$N = m\left(g\cos\alpha - \frac{v^2}{\rho}\right)$$

Hence frictional force $(F) = \mu_k N = \mu_k m\left(g\cos\alpha - \frac{v^2}{\rho}\right)$

Summing forces in the tangential direction gives

$$\Sigma F_t = ma_t:$$

or $$W\sin\alpha - F = ma_t$$

or $$a_t = g\sin\alpha - \frac{1}{m}F$$

Substituting for F in the above expression yields

$$a_t = g\sin\alpha - \frac{1}{m}\mu_k m\left(g\cos\alpha - \frac{v^2}{\rho}\right)$$

$$= g\sin\alpha - \mu_k g\cos\alpha + \frac{\mu_k v^2}{\rho}$$

Now $$a_t = \frac{dv}{dt},$$

Thus $$\frac{dv}{dt} = g(\sin\alpha - \mu_k\cos\alpha) + \mu_k\frac{v^2}{\rho} \quad ...(1)$$

Also, we have that

$$v = r\dot{\alpha}$$

where $r = \rho$, (in polar coordinates)

or $$\frac{d\alpha}{dt} = \frac{1}{\rho}v \quad ...(2)$$

Thus, differential equations (1) and (2) define the motion of the block.

As the block leaves the surface, $N = 0$. Hence $\left(g\cos\alpha - \frac{v^2}{\rho}\right) = 0$, which defines the value of α at which the block leaves the surface.

The MATLAB program for this problem is given as follows:

```
global g rho mk
vo=4; % initial velocity
g=9.81;  % acceleration due to gravity
rho=2.0;% radius of curvature
```

```
mk=0.2;% coefficient of kinetic friction
tspan=[0:0.01:0.35]; % initial and final times
x0=[vo,0]'; % Initial velocity and angle
[t,x]=ode45('f3',tspan,x0); % solving two differential eqs.
figure(1);
subplot(2,1,1)
plot(t,x(:,1),'-o');
xlabel('time (sec');ylabel('velocity (m/s)');
title('Coefficient friction between surface and block is 0.2')
grid on;
subplot(2,1,2)
plot(t,x(:,2)*180/pi,'-p');
xlabel('time (sec)');ylabel('angle (degree)';
grid on;
eq1=g*cos(x(:,2))-x(:,1).^2/rho; % Expression for Normal reaction
[y,k]=min(abs(eq1)); % Minimum value and corresponding index of this function
theta=x(k,2)*180/pi; % Finding theta
fprintf('Minimum angle in degrees it leaves the surface at friction mu=%3.2f
is %4.2f\n',mk, theta);
```

Here the subfunction $f3(\ )$ is defined in separate *m* file as follows:

```
function vdot = f3(t,x)
global g rho mk;
vdot=[g*(sin(x(2))-mk*cos(x(2)))+mk*x(1)^2/rho;x(1)/rho];
```

Ouput is shown in Fig. ED7.10 (*b*).

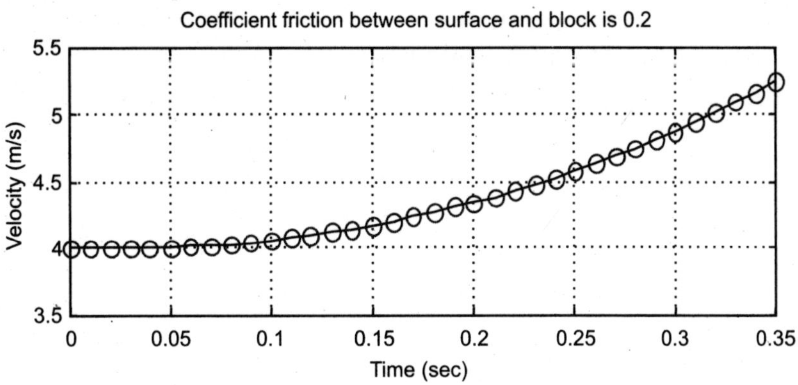

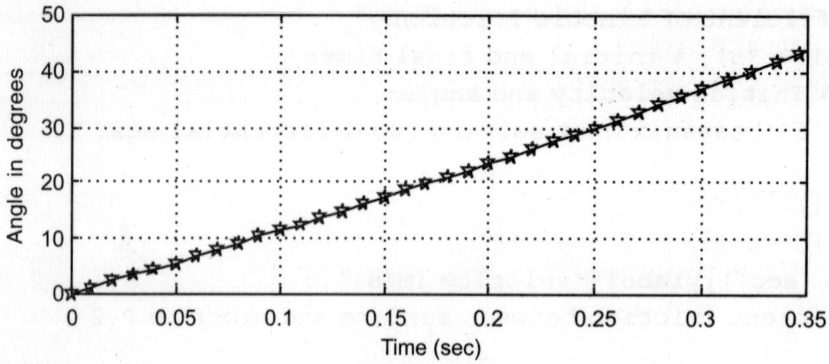

Fig. ED7.10 (b)

>> Minimum angle in degrees it leaves the surface at friction mu = 0.2 is 21.03.

Example ED7.11: The acceleration due to gravity due to earth at any height *h* above the surface of the earth is given by

$$g = \frac{-GM}{(R+h)^2} \text{ m/s}^2$$

where G = the gravitational constant (6.67×10^{-11} Nm²/kg²)

M = mass of the earth (5.99×10^{24} kg)

R = mean radius of the earth (6372 km)

h = height above the surface of the earth (m).

Write a MATLAB program to calculate and plot the acceleration due to earth's gravity for $0 \leq h \leq 45{,}000$ km in 5000 km increments.

Solution: This problem is an application of central force motion and space mechanics. MATLAB code presented with explanations is given as follows:

```
G=6.67E-11; % Gravitational constant
m_earth=5.99e24; % Mass of earth (kg)
r_earth=6372.e3; % Radius of the earth(m)

disp('This program displays the acceleration due to gravity');
disp('as a function of height above the Earth's surface:');
fprintf('\n\n Height Acceleration\n');
fprintf(   ' (km)    (m/sec**2)   \n');
fprintf(   ' =======        ============\n');

% Now calculate values
jj=0;
for ii=0:5000000:45000000
  % Increment counter
   jj=jj+1;
  %Get height
   height(jj)=ii;
 % Calculate acceleration
```

```
 grav(jj)=-G*m_earth/(r_earth+height(jj))^2;
% Write out results
 fprintf('%7d %8.3f\n',height(jj)/1000,grav(jj));
  end
% Now plot the acceleration due to gravity vs height
figure(1);
plot(height/1000,grav,'LineWidth',2);
title('\bfAcceleration due to gravity vs height');
xlabel('\bfHeight above Earth's surface (km)');
ylabel('\bfAcceleration (m/s^{2})');
```

Program output:

This program displays the acceleration due to gravity as a function of height above the Earth's surface:

Height (km)	Acceleration (m/sec**2)
0	– 9.840
5000	– 3.089
10000	– 1.491
15000	– 0.875
20000	– 0.574
25000	– 0.406
30000	– 0.302
35000	– 0.233
40000	– 0.186
45000	– 0.151

Figure ED7.11 shows the plot of acceleration due to gravity as a function of height.

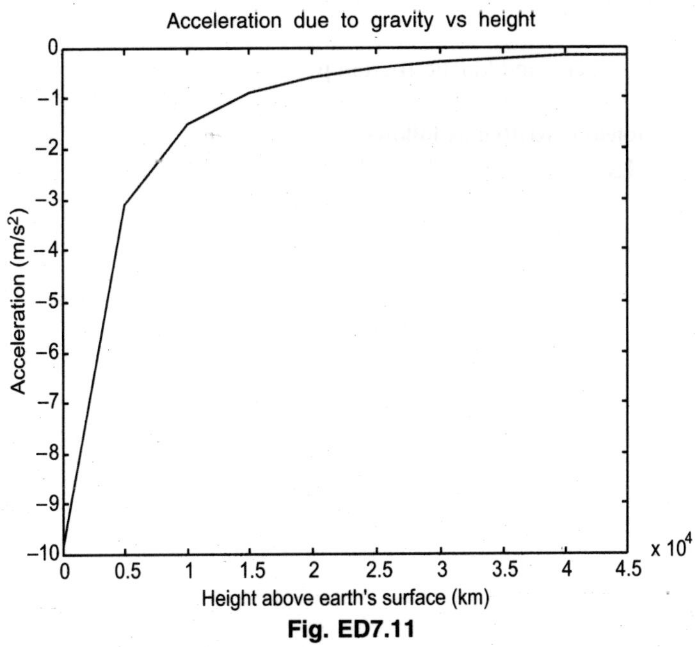

Fig. ED7.11

Example ED7.12: A 3 kg block is subjected to two forces as shown in Fig. ED7.12. If block starts from rest, determine the distance it has moved when it attains a velocity of 10 m/s. Plot its distance as a function of coefficient of kinetic-friction between the block and floor.

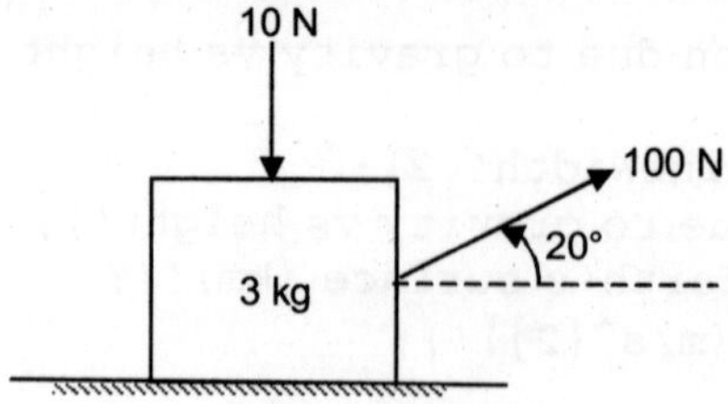

Fig. ED7.12

Solution: This is an application of work-energy principle on the motion of a particle. The work-energy principle is

$$T_1 + \Sigma U = T_2,$$

where T_1 = Initial kinetic energy and

T_2 = Final kinetic energy of the particle.

Here, $T_1 = 0$ and $T_2 = \frac{1}{2}mv^2$.

The forces doing the work on the particle are horizontal component of external force 100 N and friction acting on the floor. Work-done by the forces are

$$\Sigma U = (100 \cos 20° - \mu N) \times s,$$

where $N = (10 + W - 100 \sin 10°)$,

W = 3g, the weight of block.

Thus $\frac{1}{2}mv^2 = \Sigma U$, relates velocity and kinetic friction μ.

The program for this problem is written as follows:

```
% DEFINE ALL VARIABLES
m=3;
v=10;
g=9.81;
F1=100;
F2=10;
T=0.5*m*v^2;
mu=0:0.05:0.5;
s=150./(F1*cos(20*pi/180)-mu*(F2+m*g-F1*sin(20*pi/180)));
plot(mu,s,'-p')
xlabel('Kinetic friction');
ylabel('Distance (m)');
grid on;
```

Output is given in Fig. ED7.12 (*a*).

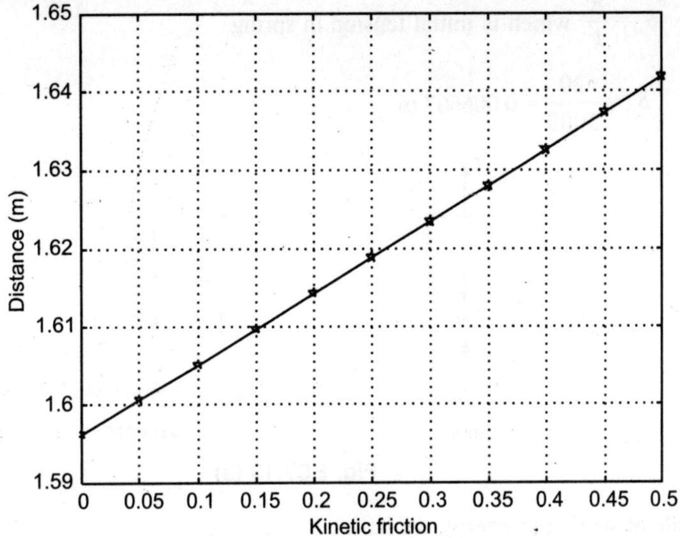

Fig. ED7.12 (a)

Example ED7.13: A 5 kg block is attached to a cable and to a spring as shown in Fig. ED7.13.

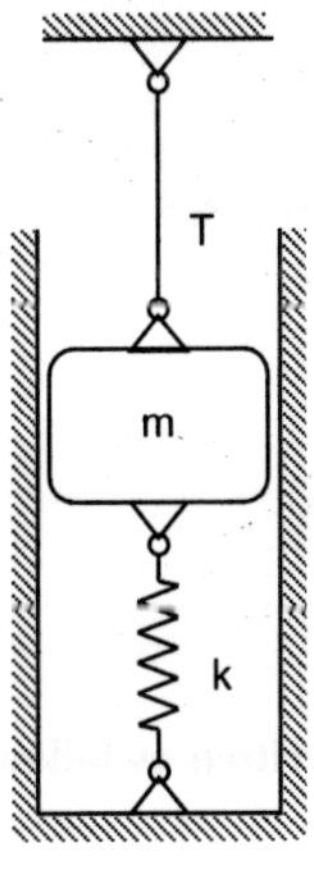

Fig. ED7.13

The constant of the spring is $k = 3$ kN/m and the tension in the cable is 30 N. When the cable is cut, (*a*) derive an expression for the velocity of the block as a function of its displacement x, (*b*) determine the maximum displacement x_m and the maximum speed v_m, (*c*) plot the speed of the block as a function of x for $0 \le x \le x_m$.

Solution: Free-body diagram of the block before and after the cable is cut is shown in Fig. ED7.13 (*a*). For the static case we have entire forces are in equilibrium.

$\therefore \quad T + R - W = 0$ with $T = 30$ N, $W = mg = 50$ N from which $R = 20$ N

But,

$$R = k\delta_{st} \text{ or } \delta_{st} = \frac{R}{k} \text{ which is initial tension in spring.}$$

$$\delta_{st} = \frac{20}{3000} = 0.006667 \text{ m}$$

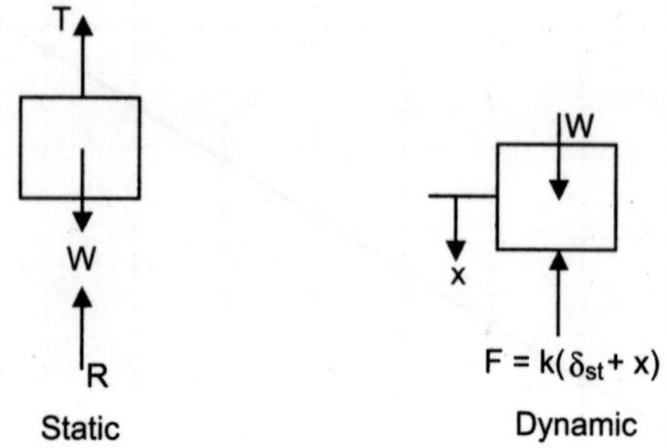

Fig. ED7.13 (a)

Using the principle of work and energy we have

$$T_1 + U_{1\to2} = T_2$$

or

$$\int_0^x [W - k(\delta_{st} + x)]\, dx = \frac{1}{2} mv^2$$

Substituting yields

$$\int_0^x [50 - 3000(0.006667 + x)]dx = 2.5v^2$$

$$\Rightarrow \quad 50x - 20x - 1500x^2 = 2.5v^2$$

$$v^2 = 12x - 600x^2$$

At maximum displacement, the velocity is zero.

$$\therefore \quad 12x - 600x^2 = 0 \text{ or } x = 0.02 \text{ m.}$$

The MATLAB program for plotting can be written as follows:

```
xmax=0.02;
x=[0:.001:xmax];
v=sqrt(12.*x-600.*x.^2);% Expression for velocity for given values
[vmax,i]=max(v); % finding minimum value of velocity and corresponding
index
fprintf('The maximum velocity is %5.4fm/s and the maximum displacement is
%5.4fm\n',vmax,xmax);
figure(1)
plot(x,v,'-o')
xlabel('x,(m)')
ylabel('Velocity(m/s)')
grid on
```

Output is shown in Fig. ED7.13(*b*).

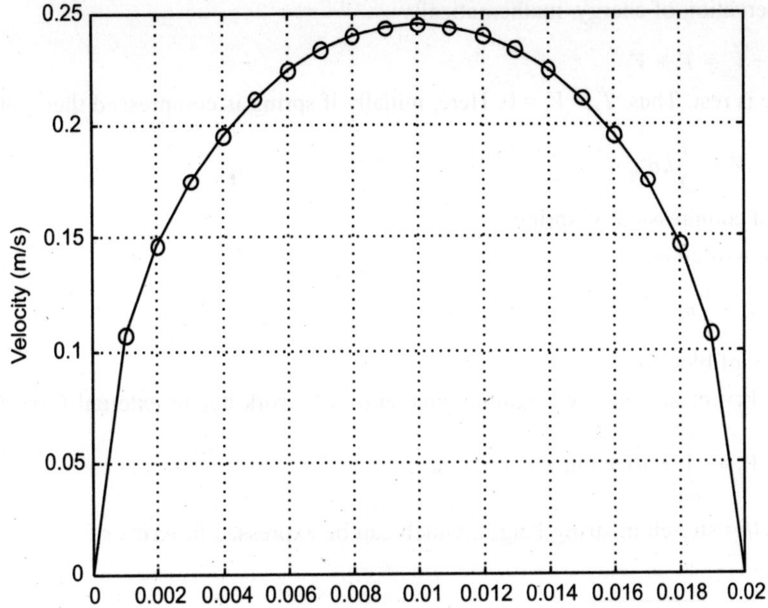

Fig. ED7.13(b)

>> The maximum velocity is 0.2449m/s and the maximum displacement is 0.0200m.

Example ED7.14: A block of 0.8 kg mass moves within the smooth vertical slot as shown in Fig. ED7.14. If it starts from rest when the attached spring is in unstretched position at *A*, plot a graph of velocity of block as a function of distanced moved by the block. Assume $F = 100$ N, $k = 100$ N/m, $0 \le s \le 0.4$.

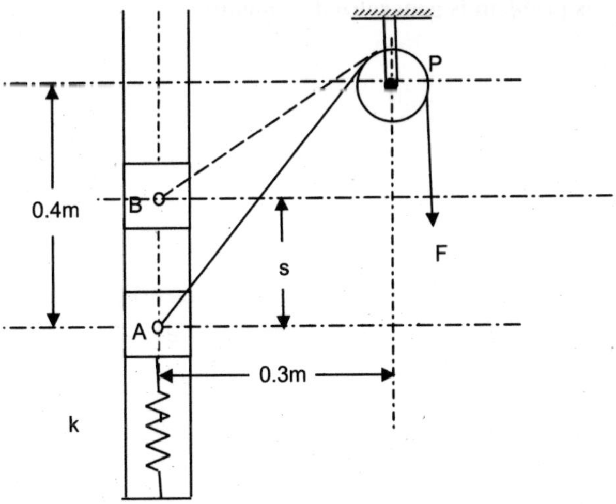

Fig. ED7.14

Solution: This is an application of work-energy principle. As surfaces are smooth, no frictional force is possible. Thus, there are no non-conservative forces in the system. So work-energy principle reduces to principle of conservation of energy, mathematically

$$T_1 + V_1 = T_2 + V_2$$

where initial state is rest. Thus, $T_1 = V_1 = 0$. Here, initially if spring is compressed then potential energy

$$V_1 = \frac{1}{2}k\partial_{ini}^2$$

where ∂_{ini} is initial compression of spring.
Final energies are written as

$$T_2 = \frac{1}{2}mv^2,$$

where v is velocity of block

and V_2 = elastic energy + gravitational energy + work due to external force F.

Thus $$V_2 = \int_{x=0}^{\partial} kxdx + \text{mg} \times s - F \times \Delta f$$

where $\Delta f = AP - BP$ = stretch in string length, which can be expressed in terms of s.
From geometry,

$$AP = \sqrt{0.4^2 + 0.3^2} = 0.5 \text{ m}$$

and $$BP = \sqrt{(0.4 - s)^2 + 0.3^2}.$$

Now the principle of conservation of energy can be applied to relate velocity v and distance s.

i.e., $V_2 + T_2 = 0$

MATLAB program for this problem is generalized as follows:

% Set of default values

```
g=9.81;
m=0.8;
k=100;
F=100;
W=m*g;% weight of block
s=0:0.05:0.4;
df= 0.5-sqrt((0.4-s).^2+0.3^2); % distance moved by string
V2= (W.*s+0.5*k*s.^2-F.*df); % potential energy of block
v=sqrt((2/m).*(-V2)); % Velocity of block
plot(s,v);
xlabel('Distance moved along slot (m)');
ylabel('Velocity of block (m/s)')
grid on;
```

The output is shown in Fig. ED7.14(*a*).

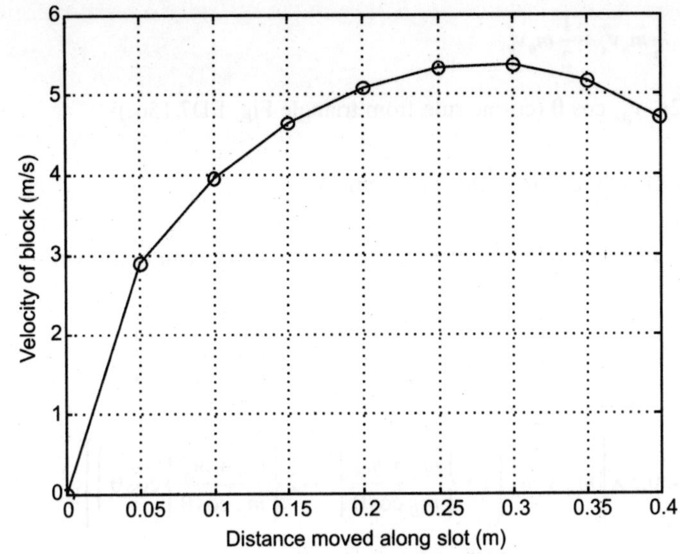

Fig. ED7.14(a) Output

Example ED7.15: Figure ED7.15 shows a block *B* of mass m_B starts from rest and slides down an inclined plane of a wedge of mass m_A which is supported by a horizontal surface. (*a*) Obtain an expression for the speed of block *B* relative to wedge *A*. (*b*) The speed of wedge *A*, (*c*) Write a MATLAB program to plot the speed of *B* relative to *A* and the speed of *A* as function of *s*, where '*s*' is the distance traveled by the block *B* down the surface of the wedge for $0 \le s \le 1.0$ m. Neglect friction between all the surfaces. Given: $m_B = 10$ kg and $m_A = 16$ kg.

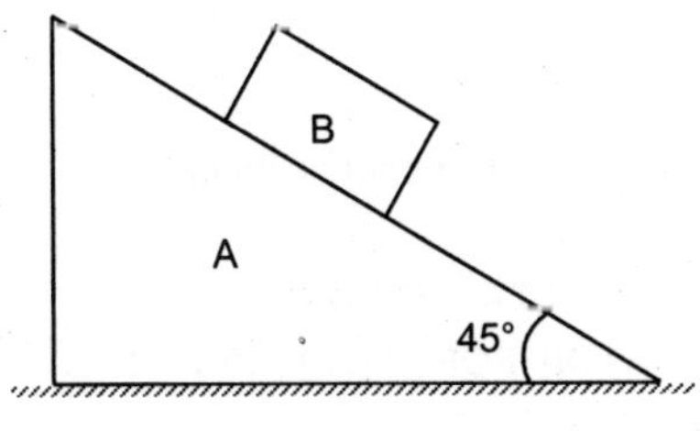

Fig. ED7.15

Solution: Drawing velocity triangle as shown in Fig. ED7.15 (*a*).

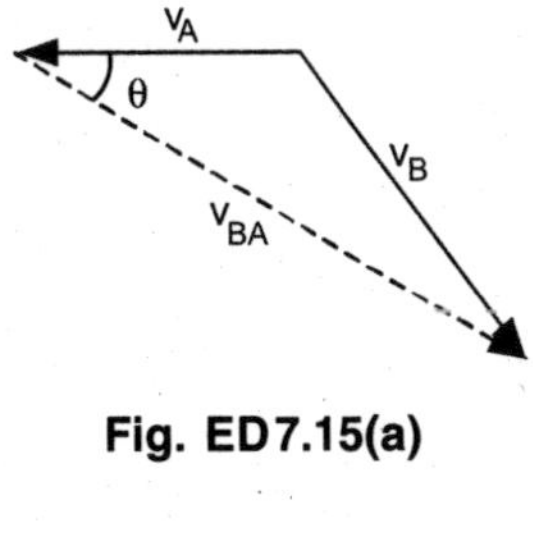

Fig. ED7.15(a)

Applying principle of conservation of momentum to the particles *A* and *B*

$$m_B\, v_{BA} \cos\theta - (m_A + m_B)\, v_A = 0$$

Therefore, speed of block *B* relative to wedge *A*:

$$v_{BA} = \frac{(m_A + m_B)\, v_A}{m_B \cos\theta}$$

Applying conservation of energy rule (as there is no friction)

$$m_B gh = \frac{1}{2} m_A v_A^2 + \frac{1}{2} m_B v_B^2$$

where $v_B^2 = v_A^2 + v_{BA}^2 - 2v_A\, v_{BA} \cos\theta$ (cosine rule from triangle Fig. ED7.15(*a*))

$$\Rightarrow \qquad 10 \times 9.81 \times s \cos\theta = \frac{1}{2} m_A v_A^2 + \frac{1}{2} m_B v_B^2$$

Here v_B and v_{BA} can be replaced in terms of v_A and plot of v_A and s can be drawn.

i.e., $$m_B g{\cdot}s \cos\theta = \frac{1}{2} m_A v_A^2 + \frac{1}{2} m_B v_A^2 \left(1 + \frac{(m_A + m_B)^2}{m_B^2 \cos^2\theta} - 2\frac{(m_A + m_B)}{m_B}\right)$$

$$= 0.5 \times \left[m_A + m_B \left(1 + \left\{ \frac{m_A + m_B}{m_B \cos\theta} \right\}^2 - 2\left\{ \frac{m_A + m_B}{m_B \cos\theta} \right\} \cos\theta \right) \right] v_A^2$$

Now speed of wedge v_A and relative velocity v_{BA} are plotted as a function of s. Complete MATLAB program is given below:

MATLAB Program:

```
% DEFAULT DATA GIVEN
g=9.81;
ma=16;
mb=10;
theta=45*pi/180; % ANGLE OF WEDGE
mul=(ma+mb)/(mb*cos(theta)); % MULTIPLICATION FACTOR
den=0.5*ma+0.5*mb*(1+mul^2-2*mul*cos(theta)));
s=[0:0.02:1];
pe=mb*s*cos(theta)*g; % POTENTIAL ENERGY
va=sqrt(pe./den); % EXPRESSION FOR VELOCITY OF A
vba=mul*va; % RELATIVE VELOCITY
plot(s,va,'-*',s,vba,'-p')
xlabel('s(m)')
ylabel('Velocity (m/s)')
legend('Velocity of A','Velocity of B relative to A',2);
grid on
```

Output is shown in Fig. ED7.15(*b*).

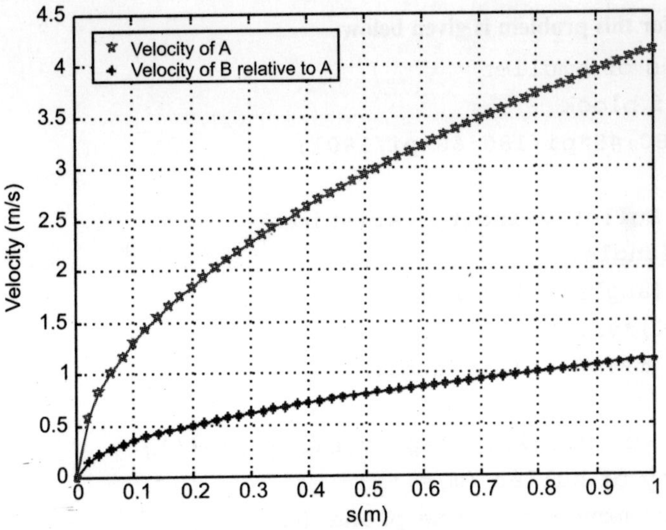

Fig. ED7.15 (b)

Example ED7.16: A 10 kg block is held at rest on the smooth inclined plane by the stop block at *A* (see Fig. ED7.16). If a 10 gm bullet traveling at velocity *v* strikes and embedded in the block, plot the distance moved-up by the block along the plane as a function of velocity before it comes to momentary stop.

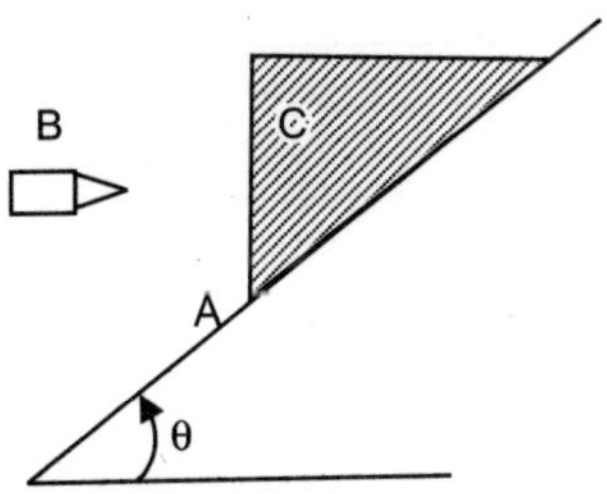

Fig. ED7.16

Solution: If block (*C*) and bullet (*B*) are considered as a system, the impulsive force *F*, caused by impact is internal to the system. Therefore, it will cancel out. Also weight of block and bullet are non-impulsive forces. Hence the principle of conservation of linear momentum can be applicable.

$$m_B \times v_{Bx} = (m_B + m_C) \times v_2$$

where *x* is in upward direction parallel to the inclined plane.

Here $v_{Bx} = v \cos \theta$, the component of bullet velocity along the positive *x*-direction. Here the datum is set as block's initial position as shown in Fig. ED7.16 (*a*).

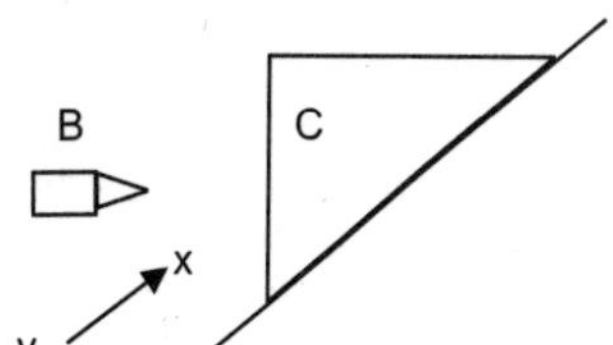

Fig. ED7.16(a)

To find the distance moved by the block, apply the work-energy principle.

i.e., $$\Sigma U = -s \times (m_B + m_C) g \sin \alpha = T_2 - T_1 = -\frac{1}{2}(m_B + m_C) v_2^2 .$$

Thus s can be plotted as a function of velocity.

MATLAB program for this problem is given below:

```
mB=10e-3; % Mass of bmullet
mC=10; % Mass of block
angle=[30*pi/180;45*pi/180;60*pi/180];
g=9.81;
v=50:50:500; % Bullet velocity variation
for k=1:length(angle)
   v2=mB.*v*cos(angle(k))/(mB+mC);
   dT=0.5*(mB+mC)*v2.^2;
   s(k,:)=dT./((mB+mC)*g*sin(angle(k)));
end
plot(v,s(1,:),'-o',v,s(2,:),'-p',v,s(3,:),'-*');
xlabel('Velocity of bullet (m/s)');
ylabel('Distance moved over the plane (m)');
grid on;
legend('angle=30deg','angle=45deg','angle=60deg')
```

The output of this program is shown in Fig. ED7.16 (*b*).

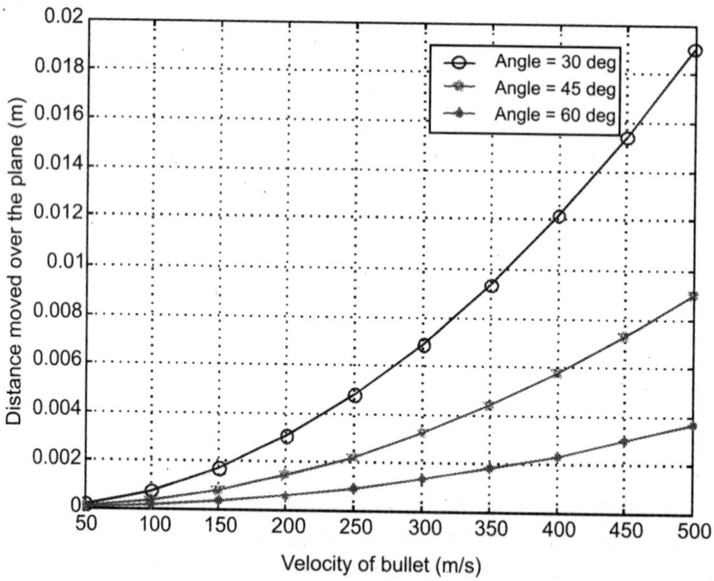

Fig. ED7.16 (b) Output of MATLAB

Example ED7.17: A system consists of n particles A_i of mass m_i and coordinates x_i, y_i and z_i having velocity components $(v_x)_i$, $(v_y)_i$ and $(v_z)_i$. Derive expression for components of angular momentum about origin O of coordinates. Use MATLAB to solve the following system:

Particle	*Mass (kg)*	*Position (m)*	*Velocity (m/s)*
A_1	3	$3\hat{j}$	$4\hat{i}+2\hat{j}+2\hat{k}$
A_2	2	$1.2\hat{i}+2.4\hat{j}+3\hat{k}$	$4\hat{i}+3\hat{j}$
A_3	4	$3.6\hat{i}$	$-2\hat{i}+4\hat{j}+2\hat{k}$

Solution: Angular momentum (H_O) about O of system of n-particles is defined as:

$$H_O = \sum_{i=1}^{n} r_i \times m_i v_i \text{. This is a vector cross-product.}$$

$$= r_1 \times m_1 v_1 + r_2 \times m_2 v_2 + r_3 \times m_3 v_3$$

$$= \left[m_1 \begin{vmatrix} r_{1y} & r_{1z} \\ v_{1y} & v_{1z} \end{vmatrix} + m_2 \begin{vmatrix} r_{2y} & r_{2z} \\ v_{2y} & v_{2z} \end{vmatrix} + \cdots\cdots \right] \hat{i} - \left[m_1 \begin{vmatrix} r_{1x} & r_{1z} \\ v_{1x} & v_{1z} \end{vmatrix} + m_2 \begin{vmatrix} r_{2x} & r_{2z} \\ v_{2x} & v_{2z} \end{vmatrix} + \cdots\cdots \right] \hat{j}$$

$$+ \left[m_1 \begin{vmatrix} r_{1x} & r_{1y} \\ v_{1x} & v_{1y} \end{vmatrix} + m_2 \begin{vmatrix} r_{2x} & r_{2y} \\ v_{2x} & v_{2y} \end{vmatrix} + \cdots\cdots \right] \hat{k}$$

MATLAB program for this problem is written as follows:

```
n=3; % NUMBER OF PARTICLES
m=[3 2 4]; % MASSES OF THREE PARTICLES
Hx=0;Hy=0;Hz=0; % INITIAL ANGULAR MOMENTA
r=[0 3 0;1.2 2.4 3;3.6 0 0]; % POSITION VECTORS OF PARTICLES
% HERE COLUMNS SHOW THE X, Y AND Z coordinate & rows the points
v=[4 2 2;4 3 0;-2 4 2]; % VELOCITY VECTORS
for k=1:n
 P=[r(k,2) r(k,3);v(k,2) v(k,3)];
 Q=[r(k,1) r(k,3);v(k,1) v(k,3)];
 R=[r(k,1) r(k,2);v(k,1) v(k,2)];
 Hx=Hx+m(k)*det(P);
 Hy=Hy-m(k)*det(Q);
 Hz=Hz+m(k)*det(R);
end
disp('Total angular momentum is');
fprintf('%5.2f i+%5.2f j+%5.2f k\n' ,Hx,Hy,Hz);
```

Output of the program:
Total angular momentum is

0.00 *i* + – 4.80 *j* + 9.60 *k*

Example ED7.18: A rocket has a mass 960 kg including 800 kg of fuel, which is consumed at the rate of 10 kg/s and ejected with a relative velocity of 3600 m/s. Plot the magnitude of velocity of rocket as a function of time, neglect air resistance.

Solution: This is an example of systems of particles with variable mass flow. Rocket is an example of a system loosing the mass. Only external force acting on the system is its weight $W = mg$, but here m reduces as a function of time.
Figure ED7.18 shows the initial and final states of the rocket in a short time 'dt'.

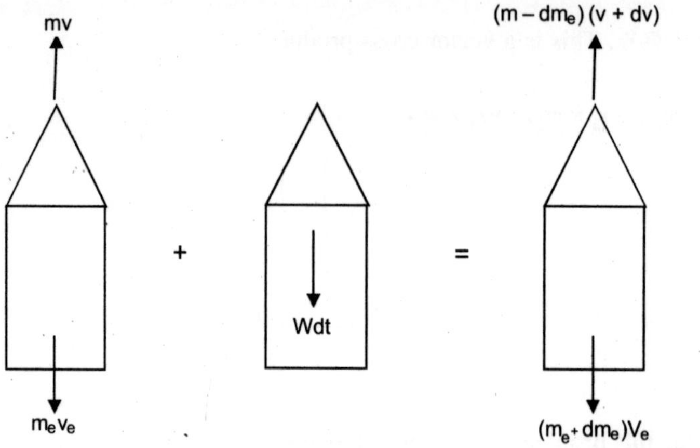

Fig. ED7.18 Initial momentum + Impulse = Final momentum

Applying principle of impulse and momentum to this system gives:

$$mv - m_e v_e - mg\,dt = (m - dm_e)(v + dv) - (m_e + dm_e)v_e$$

or $$-mg = m\,(dv/dt) - u\,(dm_e/dt) \quad ...(1)$$

where $u = v + v_e$ is relative velocity of exhaust.

Substituting the given values:

$$-mg = m\,(dv/dt) - 3600\,(10)$$

Here m = mass of rocket at an instant of time t during flight

$$= m_o - (dm/dt)t = 960 - 10t \quad ...(2)$$

Substituting (2) in (1) we obtain

$$-(960 - 10t)g = (960 - 10t)(dv/dt) - 36000$$

At $t = 0$, $v = 0$. This gives initial conditions for the problem.

So it requires to solve the differential equation:

$$(dv/dt) = \frac{36000}{960 - 10t} - g$$

Time required to consume all the fuel is given by $(960 - 10t) = 0$ or $t = 96$ seconds.

MATLAB program for plotting the variation of velocity of rocket as a function of time is given below:

```
v0=0;
    tspan=[0:5:95];% a vector that specifies the interval of the solution
    [t v]=ode45('rock',tspan,v0);% Solving the ODE
    plot(t,v,'-p')
    xlabel('t(sec)');
    ylabel('velocity(m/s)')
    grid on;
```

The function file with the differential equation named rock.m is listed below:

```
function dvdt=rock(t,v)
m0=960;g=9.81;mr=10; u=3600;
dvdt=-g+mr*u/(m0-mr*t);
```

The output is shown in Fig. ED7.18(*a*), below:

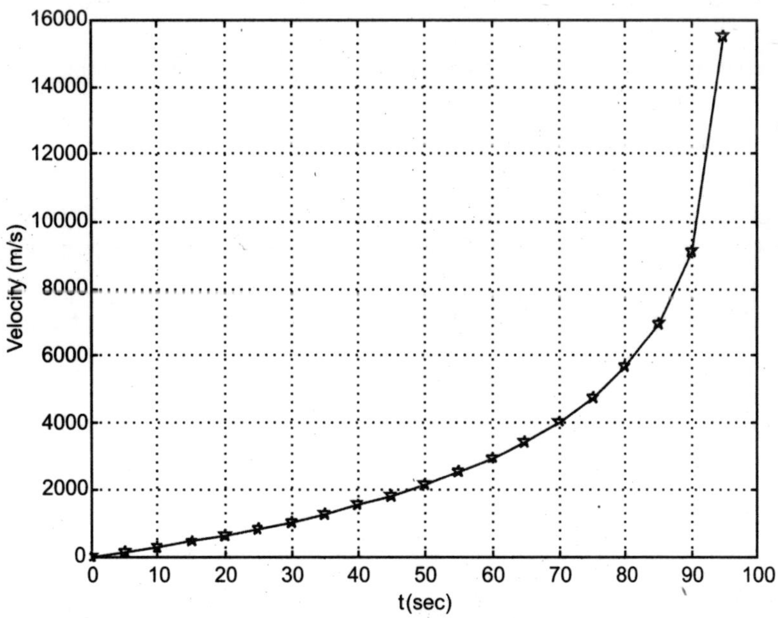

Fig. ED7.18(a) MATLAB output

Plane Kinematics of Rigid Bodies

Example ED7.19: Motion of an oscillating flywheel is defined by the relation $\theta = \theta_0\, e^{3\pi t} \cos 4\pi t$ with $\theta_0 = 0.5$ radians. Plot the angular velocity and acceleration of flywheel as a function of time. Take $0 \le t \le 0.5$s.

Solution: As θ is defined explicitly as a function of time it is easy to find ω and α from their definitions. The derivatives are evaluated in the worksheet below.

```
syms t
theta=0.5*exp(-3*pi*t)*cos(4*pi*t);
omega=diff(theta,t);
alpha=diff(omega,t);
th=vectorize(theta)
om=vectorize(omega)
al=vectorize(alpha)
```

Output of this program will be as follows:

```
th =
1./2.*exp(-3.*pi.*t).*cos(4.*pi.*t)

om =
-3./2.*pi.*exp(-3.*pi.*t).*cos(4.*pi.*t)-2.*exp(-3.*pi.*t).*sin(4.*pi.*t)
.*pi
al =
-7./2.*pi.^2.*exp(-3.*pi.*t).*cos(4.*pi.*t)+12.*pi.^2.*exp(-3.*pi.*t).*sin
(4.*pi.*t)
```

These results are used further for plotting. They can be pasted in the final program.

MATLAB code of plotting is written as follows:

```
t=0:0.05:0.5;
th =1./2.*exp(-3.*pi.*t).*cos(4.*pi.*t);
om=-3./2.*pi.*exp(-3.*pi.*t).*cos(4.*pi.*t)-2.*exp(-3.*pi.*t).*sin
(4.*pi. *t).*pi;
al =-7./2.*pi.^2.*exp(-3.*pi.*t).*cos(4.*pi.*t)+12.*pi.^2.*exp(-3.*pi.*t).
*sin(4.*pi.*t);
subplot(3,1,1);
plot(t,th,'-p');
ylabel('Theta (rad)');
grid on;
subplot(3,1,2);
plot(t,om,'-*');
ylabel('Omega (rad/s)');
grid on;
subplot(3,1,3);
```

```
plot(t,al,'-o');
ylabel('Alpha (rad/s^2)');
grid on;
xlabel('Time (s)');
```

Output is shown in Fig. ED7.19.

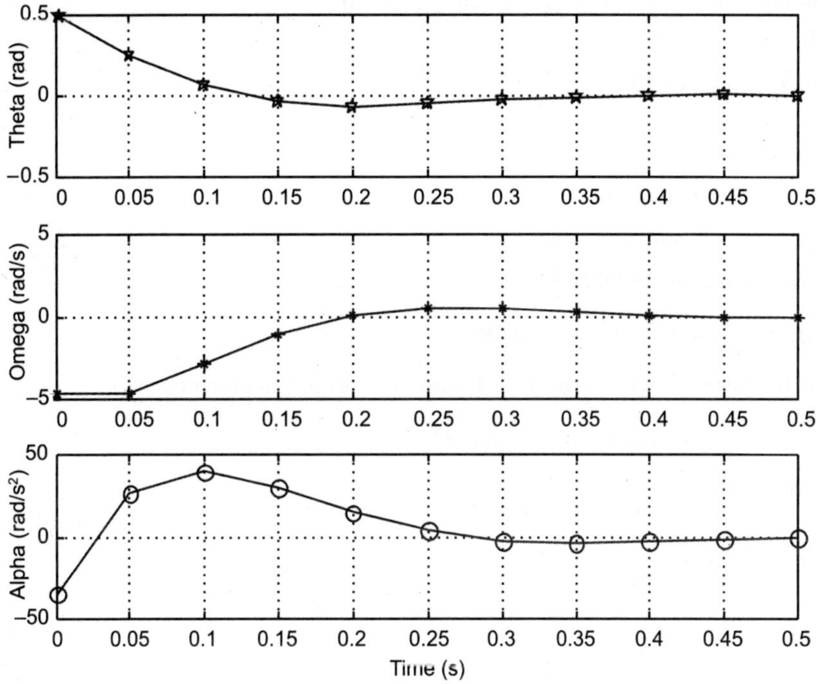

Fig. ED7.19 MATLAB output

Example ED7.20: Figure ED7.20 shows the slider crank mechanism. Write a MATLAB program that calculates and plots the position, velocity and acceleration of the piston for one full revolution of the crank. Assume that the crank is rotating at a constant speed of 550 rpm. Given radius of crank = 125 mm and radius of crank shaft = 250 mm.

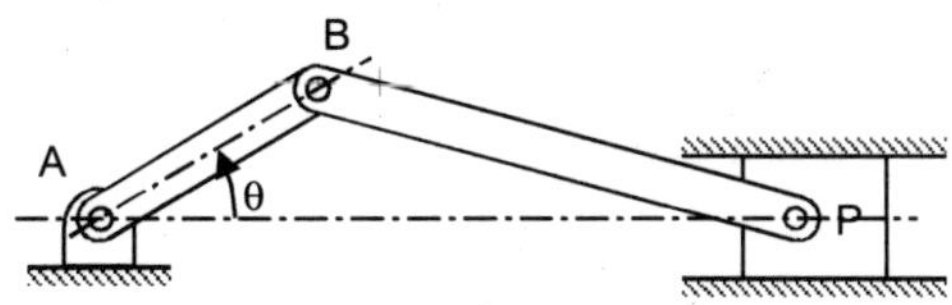

Fig. ED7.20

Solution: This problem can be done with either absolute motion analysis or relative motion analysis. Let us do it with absolute motion analysis, where the coordinates of points *B* and *P* are defined first with common origin *A* and then differentiated with respect to time to obtain velocities.
Figure ED7.20 (*a*) shows the line diagram of the mechanism.

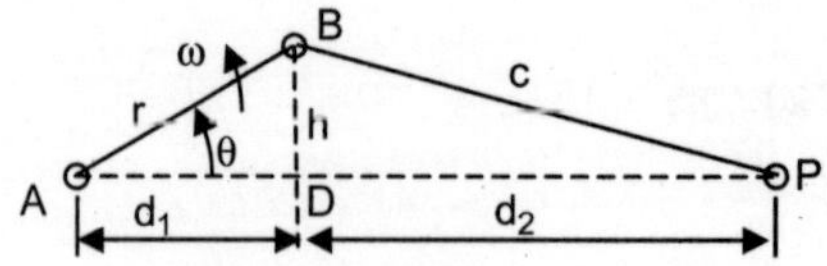

Fig. ED7.20(a)

The crank is rotating with a constant angular velocity $\omega = \dot{\theta}$.

When $t = 0$, $\theta = 0°$.

At time t, the angle θ is given by

$$\theta = \omega t = \dot{\theta} t \text{, and}$$

that $\ddot{\theta} = 0$ at all times.

The distances d_1 and h are given by

$$d_1 = r\cos\theta \text{ and } h = r\sin\theta$$

Knowing h, the distance d_2 is obtained as:

$$d_2 = \left(c^2 - h^2\right)^{1/2} = \left(c^2 - r^2\sin^2\theta\right)^{1/2}$$

The position x of the piston P with respect to A (common origin) is given by

$$x = d_1 + d_2 = r\cos\theta + \left(c^2 - r^2\sin^2\theta\right)^{1/2}$$

The velocity of the piston is given by

$$\dot{x} = -r\dot{\theta}\sin\theta - \frac{r^2}{2\left(c^2 - r^2\sin^2\theta\right)^{1/2}}$$

The acceleration of the piston is given by

$$\ddot{x} = -r\dot{\theta}^2\cos\theta - \frac{4r^2\dot{\theta}^2\cos 2\theta\left(c^2 - r^2\sin^2\theta\right) + \left(r^2\dot{\theta}\sin 2\theta\right)^2}{4\left(c^2 - r^2\sin\theta\right)^{3/2}}$$

Complete MATLAB program for this problem is given below:

% MATLAB Solution:

```
% Define TD, r, and c
N=550; % Speed in rpm
TD=N*2*pi/60; % Speed in radians/sec
tf=2*pi/TD;
r=0.125; % radius of crank in meters
c=0.250; % length of connecting rod in meters
t=linspace(0,tf,200); % Create a vector with 200 elements
TH=TD*t; % Compute Theta for each t
d2s=c^2-r^2*sin(TH).^2; % d2 squared
x=r*cos(TH)+sqrt(d2s);   % Calculate x for each Theta
xd=-r*TD*sin(TH)-(r^2*TD*sin(2*TH))./(2*sqrt(d2s)); % Velocity
```

```
% Acceleration
xdd=-r*TD^2*cos(TH)-(4*r^2*TD^2*cos(2*TH).*d2s+(r^2*sin(2*TH)*TD).^2)./
(4*d2s.^(3/2));
subplot(3,1,1)
plot(t, x)% Plot x versus t
grid
xlabel('Time (s)')
ylabel(' Position (m)')
subplot(3,1,2)
plot(t, xd) % Plot Velocity vs. t
grid
xlabel(' Time (s)')
ylabel('Velocity (m/s)')
subplot(3,1,3)
plot(t, xdd) % Plot Acceleration Vs. t
grid
xlabel('Time (s)')
ylabel('Acceleration  (m/s^2)')
```

Output of the program is shown in Fig. ED7.20(*b*).

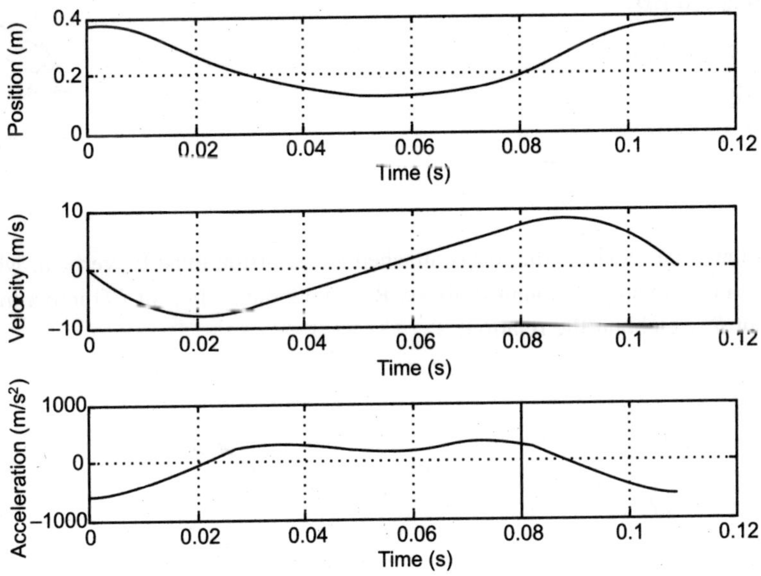

Fig. ED7.20(b) MATLAB output

Example ED7.21: Figure ED7.21 shows an engine system where the crank AB rotates with a constant angular velocity ω_{AB} clockwise. Write a MATLAB program to determine the plot for values of θ from 0 to 180° (*a*) the angular velocity and angular acceleration of connecting rod BD, (*b*) the velocity and acceleration of piston P. The length of the connecting rod, ℓ = 10 cm, crank length, AB = 3.5 cm and ω_{AB} = 1000 rpm.

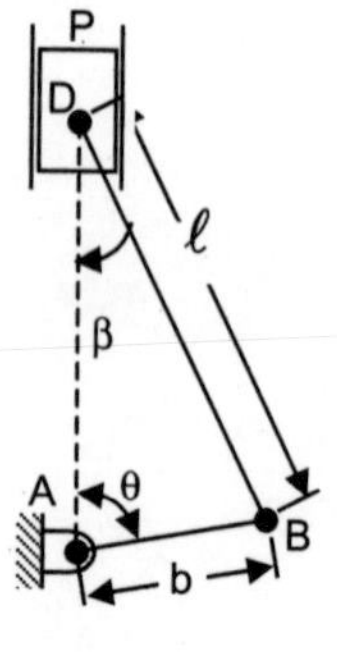

Fig. ED7.21

Solution: This problem is attempted with relative motion analysis method.

Motion of Crank:

Kinematic diagram showing the motion of crank is illustrated in Fig. ED7.21(*a*).

The velocity for the rod AB: $v_B = b\omega_{AB}$

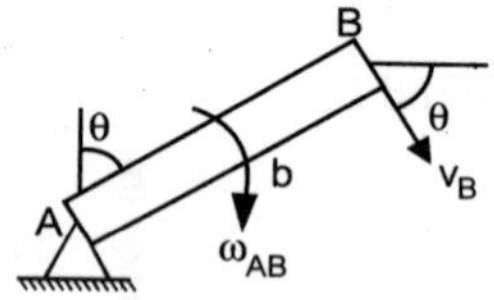

Fig. ED7.21(a)

Motion of connecting rod BD:

From the law of sines, we have

$$\frac{\sin\beta}{b} = \frac{\sin\theta}{\ell}$$

$$\sin\beta = \frac{b}{\ell}\sin\theta = \frac{\sin\theta}{n} \quad \text{where, } n = \ell/b.$$

The velocity v_D of the point D where the rod is attached to the piston must be vertical, while the velocity of point B is equal to the velocity v_B obtained above. Resolving the motion of BD into a translation with B and a rotation about B, we obtain the relation:

$$v_D = v_B + v_{DB}$$

Figure ED7.21(*b*), shows this motion.

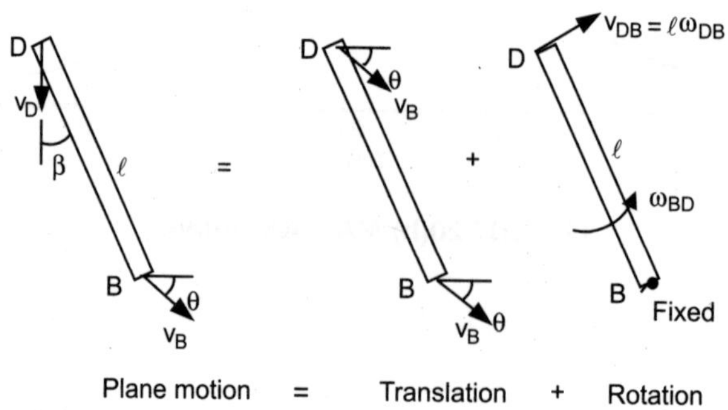

Fig. ED7.21(b)

The vector diagram corresponding to this equation is presented in Fig. ED7.21(*c*).

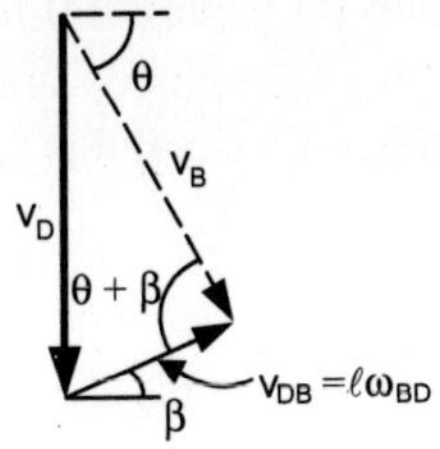

Fig. ED7.21 (c)

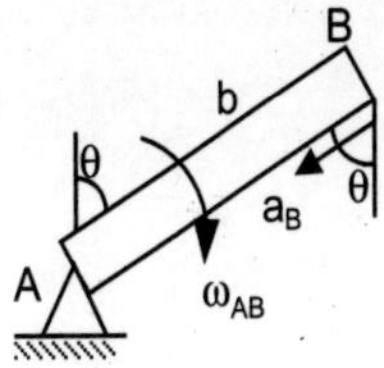

Fig. ED7.21 (d)

Using the law of sines in this triangle:

$$\frac{v_D}{\sin(\theta+\beta)} = \frac{v_B}{\sin(90°-\beta)} = \frac{\ell\omega_{BD}}{\sin(90°-\theta)}$$

$$v_D = v_B \frac{\sin(\theta+\beta)}{\sin(90°-\beta)} = v_B \frac{\sin(\theta+\beta)}{\cos\beta}$$

$$\omega_{BD} = \frac{v_B}{\ell} \frac{\sin(90°-\theta)}{\sin(90°-\beta)} = \frac{v_B}{\ell} \frac{\cos\theta}{\cos\beta}$$

For the acceleration we have for rod *AB*

$a_B = b\omega^2_{AB}$ (parallel to *AB* towards *A*) (see Fig. ED7.21 (*d*))

For rod *BD*:

$$(a_{D/B})_t = \ell\alpha BD$$

$$(a_{D/B})_n = \ell\omega^2_{BD}$$

For the acceleration we again look at plane motion with the translation of *B* plus a rotation about *B*. For *B* we have

$$a_D = a_B + a_{DB}$$

$$a_D = a_B + (a_{DB})_t + (a_{DB})_n$$

Figure ED7.21(*e*) shows the plane motion comprising of translation and rotation.

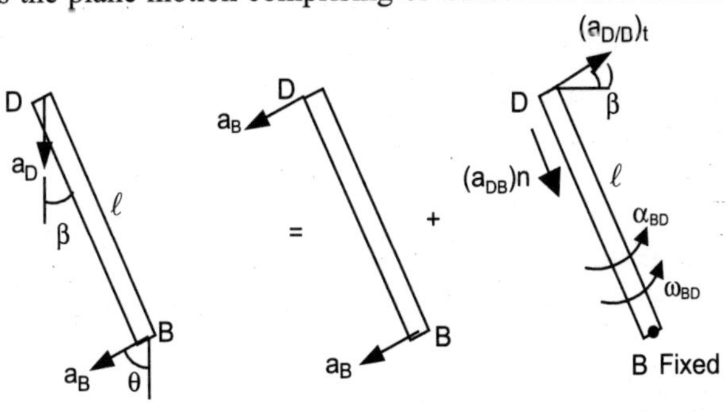

Fig. ED7.21(e)

Using the acceleration vector diagram (Fig. ED7.21(*f*)) :

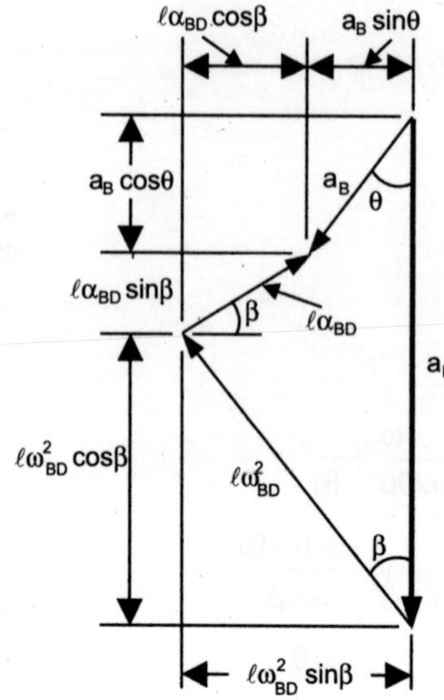

Fig. ED7.21(f)

We obtain $a_B \sin\theta = \ell\omega_{BD}^2 \sin\beta - \ell\alpha_{BD} \cos\beta$

$$\alpha_{BD} = \frac{\ell\omega_{BD}^2 \sin\beta - a_B \sin\theta}{\ell \cos\beta}$$

$$a_B \cos\theta = a_D - \ell\omega_{BD}^2 \cos\beta - \ell\alpha_{BD} \sin\beta$$

$$a_D = a_B \cos\theta + \ell\omega_{BD}^2 \cos\beta + \ell\alpha_{BD} \sin\beta$$

Based on this formulation, following MATLAB script is used to obtain variation of velocities and accelerations as a function of angle θ.

MATLAB Program :

```
L=10; % Length of connecting rod in cm
b=3.5; % crank radius in cm
N=1000; % speed in rpm
%Velocity
omega_AB=N*2*pi/60; % angular velocity in rad/s
v_B=b*omega_AB; % linear velocity of crank pin in cm/s
Theta=[0:20:180];
t=Theta*pi/180;
beta=asin((b/L)*sin(t));% inclination of connecting rod with axis of piston
v_D=v_B*sin(t+beta)./cos(beta);% velocity of piston in cm/sec
omega_BD=v_B*cos(t)./(L*cos(beta));% angular velocity of connecting rod
% acceleration
a_B=b*omega_AB^2; % acceleration of point B
```

```
alpha_BD=(L.*omega_BD.^2.*sin(beta)-a_B.*cos(t))./(L.*cos(beta));
a_D=a_B.*cos(t)+L.*omega_BD.^2.*cos(beta)+L.*alpha_BD.*sin(beta);
% Determine and plot values
z=[Theta;omega_BD;alpha_BD;v_D;a_D];
fprintf('Theta    Angular      Angular      Piston      Piston\n')
fprintf('  velocity   acceleration      velocity    acceleration\n')
fprintf('(deg)    (rad/s)      (rad/s^2)   (cm/s)      (cm/s^2)\n')
fprintf('\n');
fprintf('%5.3f    %6.3f %6.3f %6.3f %6.3f\n',z);
fprintf('\n');
%fprintf('The two values of theta for zero collar speed are %5.3f and %5.3f
degrees\n',a1,a2)
figure(1)
plot(Theta,omega_BD,'-p')
xlabel('Theta(degree)')
ylabel('Angular Velocity Rod BD (rad/s)')
grid on
figure(2)
plot(Theta,alpha_BD, '-*')
xlabel('Theta (degree)')
ylabel('Angular acceleration rod BD(rad/s^2)')
grid on
figure(3)
plot(Theta,v_D, '-p')
xlabel('Theta(degree)')
ylabel('Piston Velocity (cm/s)')
grid on
figure(4)
plot(Theta,a_D,'-*')
xlabel('Theta(degree)')
ylabel('Piston Acceleration D (cm/s^2)')
grid on
```

Output is as follows:

Theta (deg)	Angular velocity (rad/s)	Angular acceleration (rad/s^2)	Piston velocity (cm/s)	Piston acceleration (cm/s^2)
0.000	36.652	–3838.179	0.000	51815.423
20.000	34.691	–3487.725	166.884	43840.145
40.000	28.816	–2825.851	300.422	31135.267
60.000	19.231	–1896.200	375.705	16967.547
80.000	6.780	– 693.123	384.320	4707.369
100.000	–6.780	726.881	337.581	–3727.977
120.000	–19.231	2131.457	259.125	–9206.061
140.000	–28.816	3209.296	170.766	–14091.443
160.000	–34.691	3777.938	83.829	–19596.523
180.000	–36.652	3838.179	0.000	–24948.167

Figure ED7.21(g)–(j) shows the variations of angular and linear velocities.

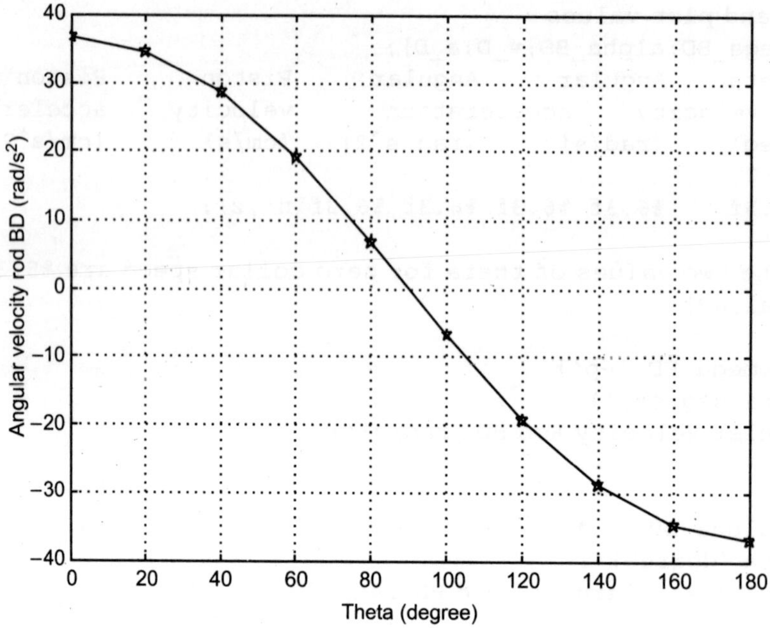

Fig. ED7.21(g) Angular velocity of connecting rod

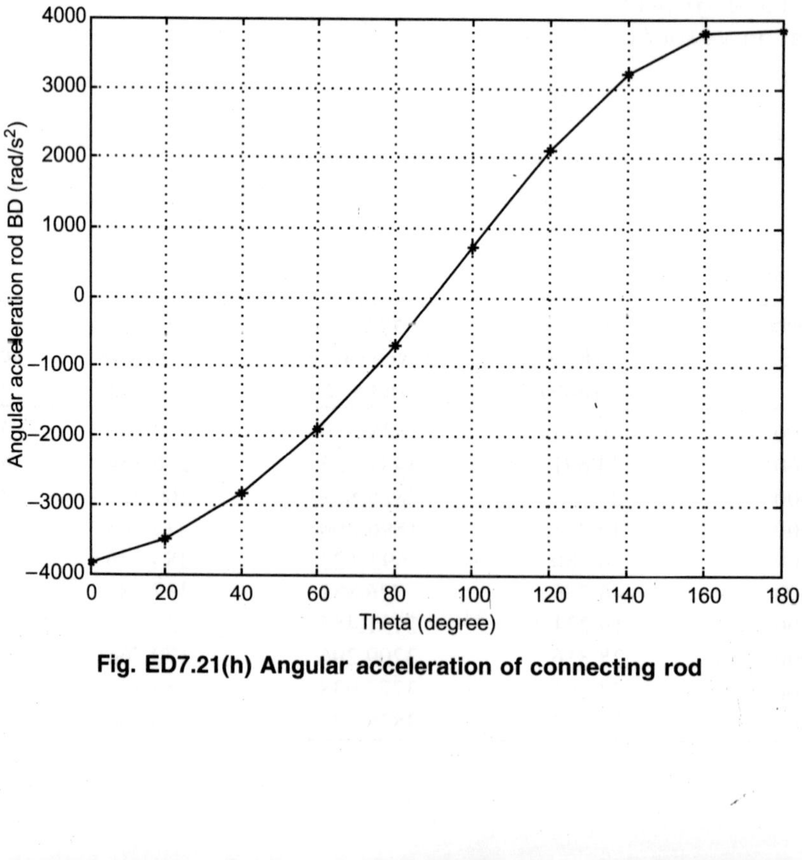

Fig. ED7.21(h) Angular acceleration of connecting rod

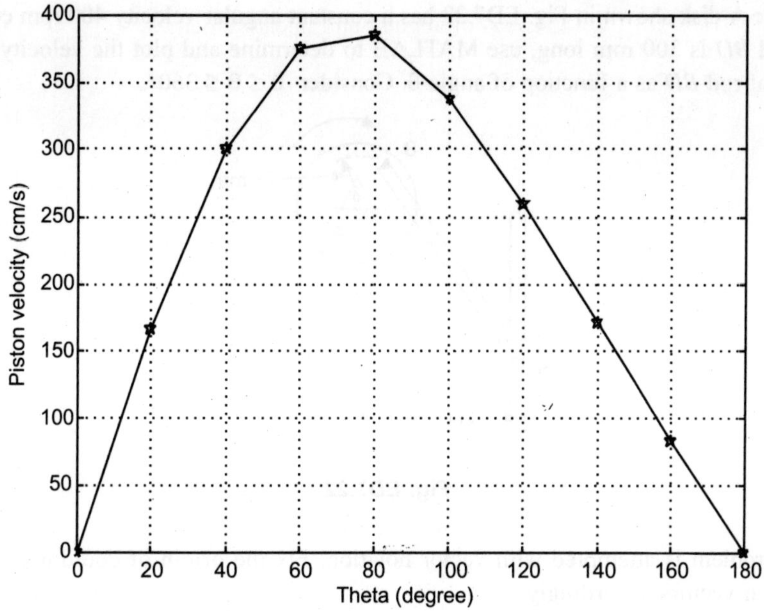

Fig. ED7.21(i) Piston velocity

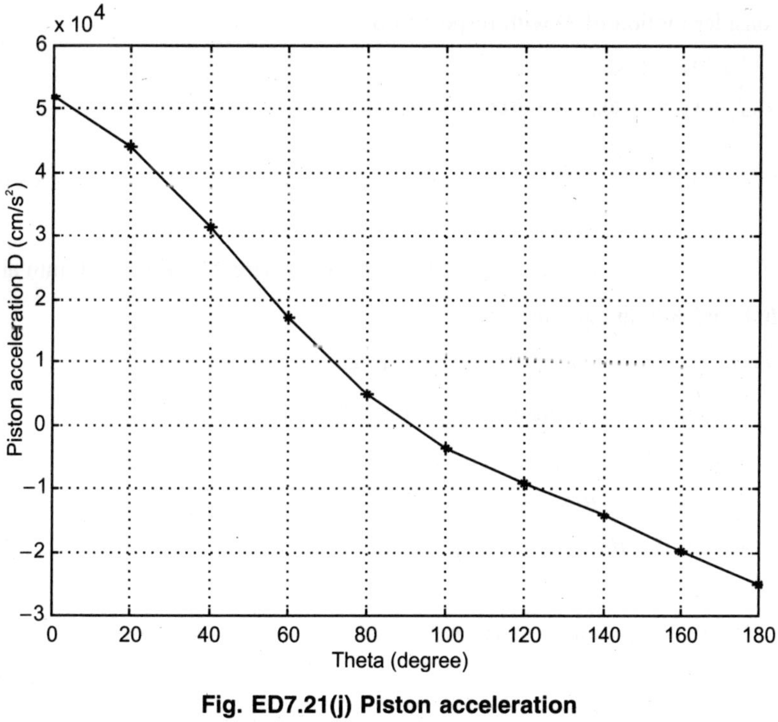

Fig. ED7.21(j) Piston acceleration

Example ED7.22: A disk shown in Fig. ED7.22 has a constant angular velocity 400 rpm counterclockwise. Knowing that rod *BD* is 300 mm long, use MATLAB to determine and plot the velocity of collar *D* and angular velocity of rod *BD* as a function of angle θ. Consider $0 \le \theta \le 360°$.

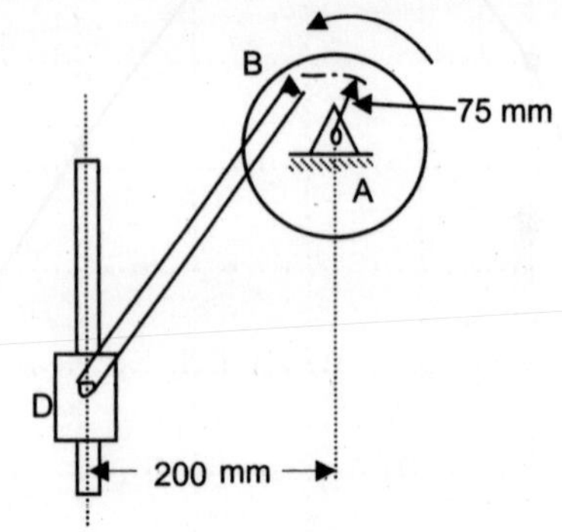

Fig. ED7.22

Solution: This problem is attempted with vector notation. Fix the origin of coordinate system at *A* and define the position vectors accordingly.

Motion of *BA*:

$$v_B = (+\,\omega\hat{k}) \times AB = \omega\hat{k} \times (r\cos\theta\,\hat{j} - r\sin\theta\,\hat{i}) = (-\,\omega r\cos\theta\,\hat{i} - \omega r\sin\theta\,\hat{j}) \quad ...(1)$$

Motion of *BD*: Consider motion of *D* with respect to *B*.

$$v_D = v_B + v_{DB}$$

i.e., $$-\,v_D\,\hat{j} = v_B + (+\,\omega_{DB}\hat{k}) \times BD \quad ...(2)$$

Here $BD = -\,BD_x\hat{i} - BD_y\hat{j}$, where BD_x is horizontal distance from *B* to *D* and BD_y is vertical distance. From geometry,

$$BD_x = (200 - r\sin\theta) \text{ and } BD_y = \sqrt{\ell^2 - (BD_x)^2}, \text{ where } \ell = BD = 300 \text{ mm and } r = 75 \text{ mm}$$

Substituting v_B, BD_x and BD_y in equation (2)

$$-\,v_D\,\hat{j} = (-\,\omega r\cos\theta\,\hat{i} - \omega r\sin\theta\,\hat{j}) + (+\,\omega_{DB}\hat{k}) \times (-\,BD_x\hat{i} - BD_y\hat{j})$$

$$= (-\,\omega r\cos\theta\,\hat{i} - \omega r\sin\theta\,\hat{j}) + (\omega_{DB}\,BD_y\hat{i} - \omega_{DB}\,BD_x\hat{j})$$

Equating $\hat{i}$ and $\hat{j}$ terms independently on both sides:

$$-\,\omega r\cos\theta + \omega_{DB}\,BD_y = 0$$

$\Rightarrow$ $$\omega_{DB} = \omega r\cos\theta\,/\,(BD_y) \quad ...(3)$$

and $$v_D = \omega r\sin\theta + \omega_{DB}\,BD_x \quad ...(4)$$

Based on the eqs.(3) and (4), complete MATLAB program is written as follows:

```
% Initialization of constants
L=300; %Length of BD in mm
r=75; % radius AB
N=400; % Speed in rpm
```

```
w =2*pi*N/60; % angular velocity of BA
%variation of theta in steps of 20 degrees
th=0:20:360;
thr=th.*pi/180; % theta in radians
BDx=200-r.*sin(thr);
BDy=sqrt(L^2-BDx.^2);
wDB= w*r*cos(thr)./BDy;
vD=w*r.*sin(thr)+wDB.*BDx
subplot(2,1,1);
plot(th,wDB,'-p');
ylabel('Angular velocity of rod BD in rad/s)');
grid on;
subplot(2,1,2);
plot(th,vD,'-*');
ylabel('Linear velocity of D in (mm/s)');
xlabel('Angle theta (degree)');
grid on;
```

The output of the program is shown below in Fig. ED7.22 (*a*).

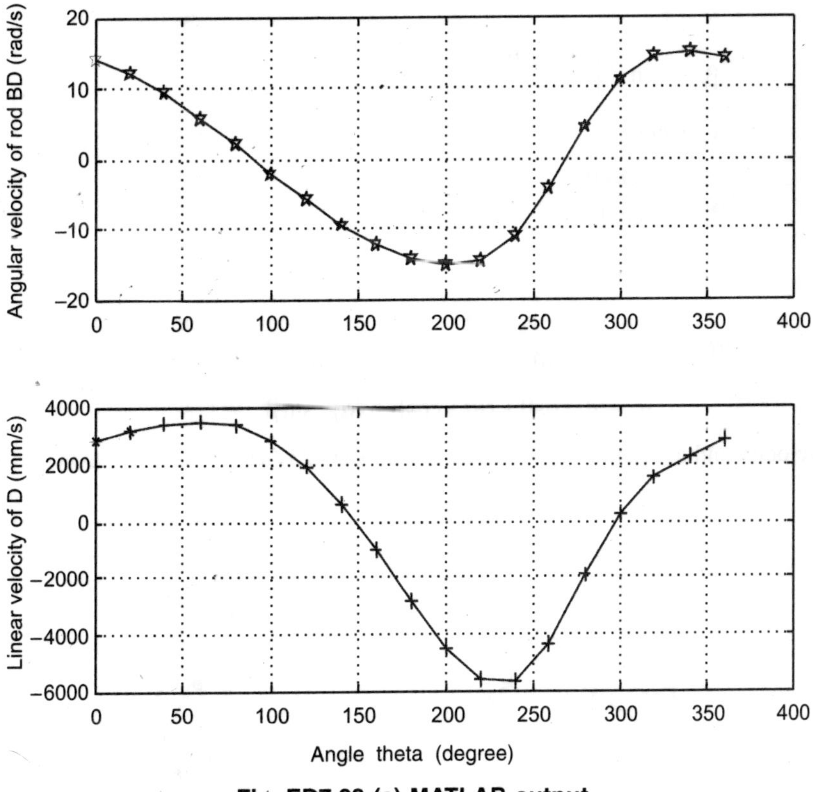

Fig. ED7.22 (a) MATLAB output

$$\overset{+}{\rightarrow}\sum F_x = \sum (F_x)_{\text{eff}}:$$

$$B_x - D_x = m_{BD}\bar{a}_x$$

$$B_x = m_{BD}\bar{a}_x + D_x \quad \text{...(12)}$$

$$+\downarrow \sum F_x = \sum (F_x)_{\text{eff}}:$$

$$B_y + D_y = m_{BD}\bar{a}_y$$

$$B_y = m_{BD}\bar{a}_y - D_y \quad \text{...(13)}$$

Complete MATLAB program to find these reactions as a function of angle θ is given below:

MATLAB Program:

```
g=9.81; % Acceleration due to gravity
Wbd=5.5; % Weight of the connecting rod in N
Wp=6.3; % Weight of the piston in N
mp=Wp/g; % Mass of the piston
mbd=Wbd/g;
Lcm=10; % Length of connecting rod in cm
L=0.1; % Length of connecting rod in m
b=3.5/100; % crank radius in m
I_bar=(1/12)*mbd*L^2; % mass moment of inertia in kg-m^2
omega_AB=1000*(2*pi)/60;
v_B=b*omega_AB;
Theta=[0:10:180];
t=Theta*pi/180;
beta=asin(b*sin(t)/L);
omega_BD=v_B*cos(t)./(L*cos(beta));
%acceleration
a_B=b*omega_AB^2;
alpha_BD=(L.*omega_BD.^2.*sin(beta)-a_B.*sin(t))./(L.*cos(beta));
a_D=a_B.*cos(t)+L.*omega_BD.^2.*cos(beta)+L.*alpha_BD.*sin(beta);
%
ax_bar=-0.5*a_B*sin(t);
ay_bar=0.5*a_B*cos(t)+0.5*a_D;
Dy=-mp*a_D;
Dx=-Dy.*tan(beta)+(I_bar*alpha_BD)./(L*cos(beta))-mbd*ax_bar./
2+mbd*ay_bar.*tan(beta)./2;
Bx=mbd*ax_bar+Dx;
By=mbd*ay_bar–Dy;
%Determine and plot values
z=[Theta;Bx;By;Dx;Dy];
fprintf('Theta      Bx             By Dx   Dy\n')
fprintf('(deg)      (N)     (N)     (N)    N)\n')
```

```
fprintf('\n');
fprintf('%5.0f  %8.3f   %8.3f %7.3f   %8.3f\n',z);
fprintf('\n');
figure(1)
plot(Theta,Bx,'-+',Theta,By,'-p')
xlabel('Theta(degree)')
ylabel('Dynamic Reactions(N)')
legend('Bx','By')
grid on
figure(2)
plot(Theta,Dx,'-+',Theta,Dy,'-p')
xlabel('Theta(degrees)')
ylabel('Dynamic Reactions(N)')
legend('Dx','Dy',2)
grid on
```

The output of the program is given below:

Theta (deg)	B_x (N)	B_y (N)	D_x (N)	D_y (N)
0	0.000	– 79.913	0.000	– 332.760
10	15.186	– 76.766	33.869	– 324.273
20	26.121	– 67.551	62.920	– 299.305
30	29.169	– 52.964	82.966	– 259.353
40	21.931	– 34.202	91.091	– 206.966
50	3.837	– 12.972	86.259	– 145.755
60	– 23.455	8.566	69.725	– 80.269
70	– 56.109	27.998	44.997	– 15.620
80	– 88.824	43.018	17.136	43.185
90	– 116.153	51.895	– 8.559	92.096
100	– 133.977	53.888	– 28.018	128.789
110	– 140.462	49.408	– 39.356	152.989
120	– 136.079	39.866	– 42.899	166.220
130	– 122.848	27.267	– 40.426	171.124
140	– 103.327	13.753	– 34.166	170.676
150	– 79.839	1.249	– 26.042	167.578
160	– 54.116	– 8.726	– 17.317	163.942
170	– 27.279	– 15.116	– 8.596	161.215
180	– 0.000	– 17.313	– 0.000	160.218

Figure ED7.23 (*c*) shows the output plots.

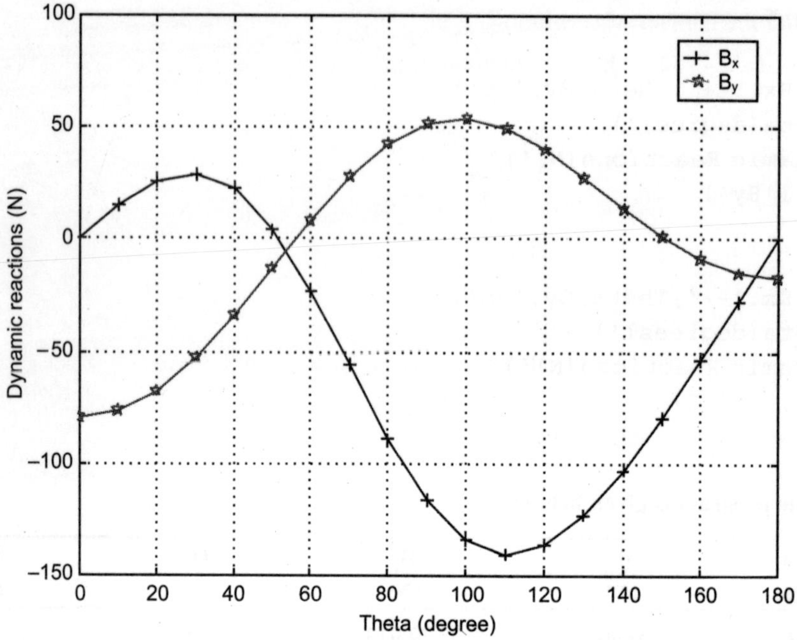

(i)

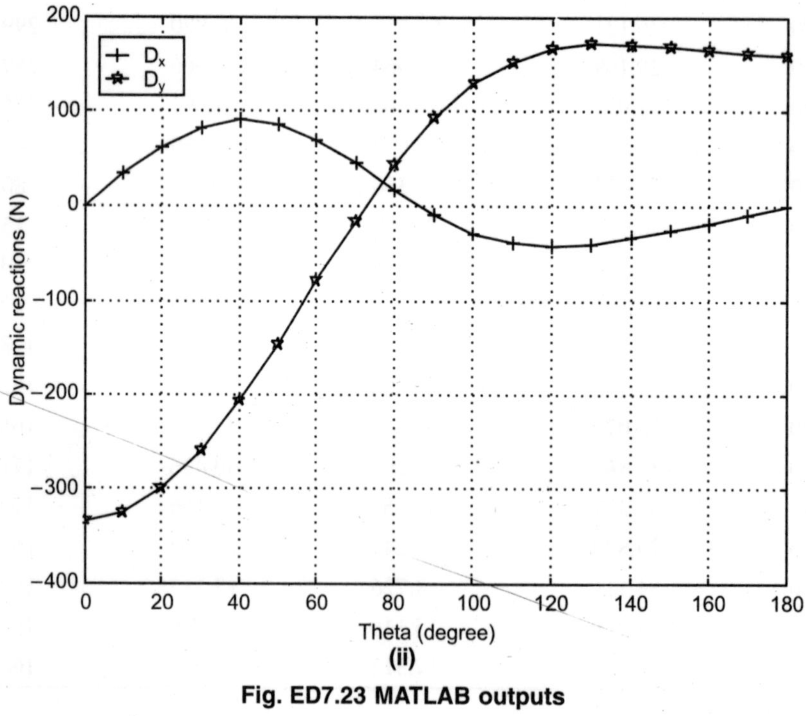

(ii)

Fig. ED7.23 MATLAB outputs

Example ED7.24: A 30 kg disk is pin-supported at its center. It is acted upon by a constant force F =10 N which is applied to a cord wrapped around its periphery and a constant couple 5 Nm. Plot the variation of angular speed with the number of revolutions it makes. Assume the system started from rest.

Solution: Figure ED7.24 shows the configuration of the system.

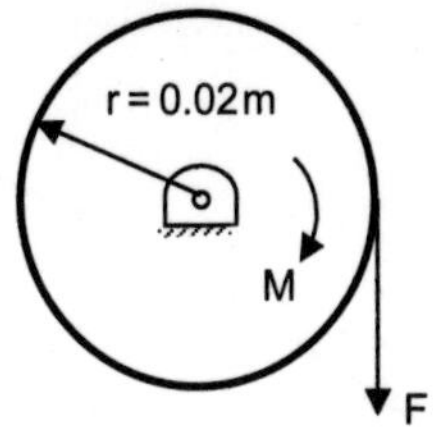

Fig. ED7.24 Configuration of the system

Here as angular speed and displacement are involved, one can apply work-energy principle. But remember that it is rigid-body motion.

i.e., $T_1 + \Sigma\, U_{1\text{-}2} = T_2$

Here T_1 = initial kinetic energy of the system =0

T_2 = final kinetic energy $= \dfrac{1}{2} I\omega^2$, where $I = \dfrac{1}{2} mr^2$

$\Sigma U_{1\text{-}2}$ = work done by force and moment = $M\theta + Fs = (M + Fr)\theta$

Hence $(M + Fr)\,\theta = \dfrac{1}{2} I\omega^2 = \dfrac{1}{2}\left(\dfrac{1}{2} mr^2\right)\omega^2 = \dfrac{1}{4} mr^2\omega^2$

A simple program that relates ω and θ is given below:

```
% Initialize values
F=10;
M=5;
m=30;
r=0.02;
theta=0:10;
omega=2*sqrt((M+F*r).*theta/(m*r^2));
plot (theta,omega,'-p');
xlabel('Number of revolutions');
ylabel('Angular speed (rad/s)');
grid on;
```

Output is shown in Fig. ED7.24 (*a*)

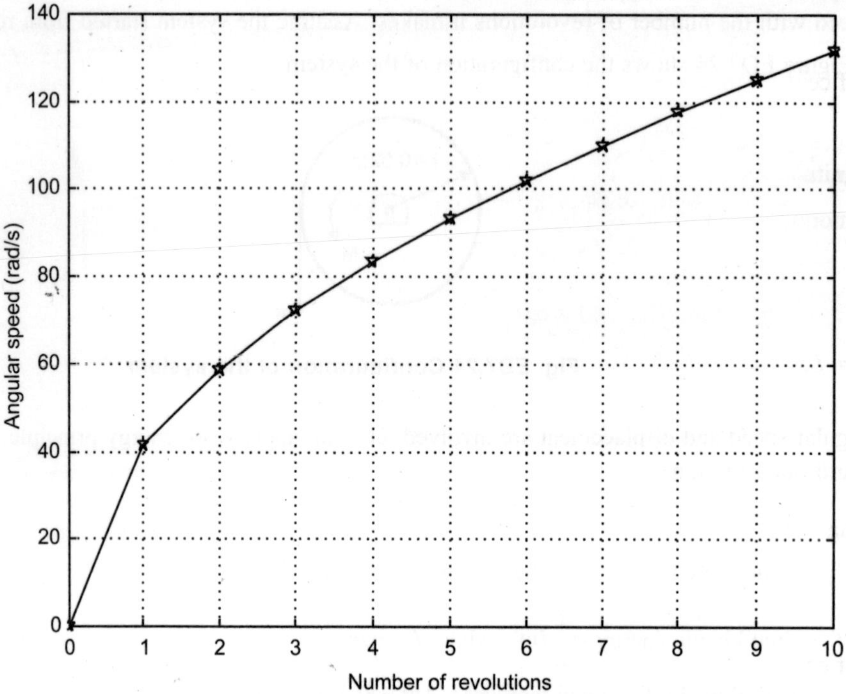

Fig. ED7.24(a) MATLAB output

Example ED7.25: Two identical slender rods are pin connected as shown in Fig. ED7.25 have lengths $L = 600$ mm. If the system is released from rest when $\beta = 60°$. Use MATLAB to plot angular velocity of rod *AB* and velocity of point *D* for various values of β ranging from 0° to 60°.

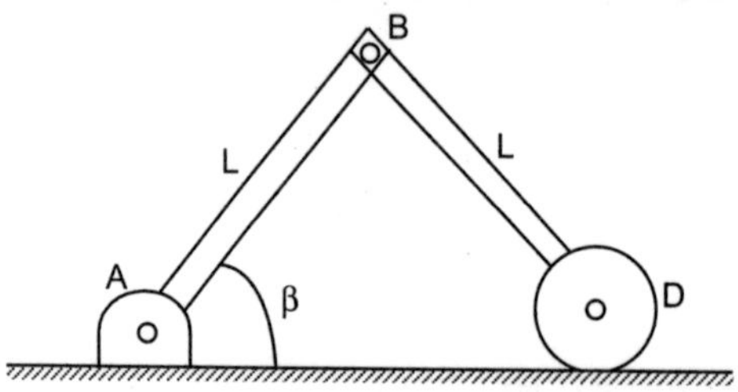

Fig. ED7.25

Solution: Here as there is no friction given, principle of conservation of energy can be applied.

Thus $T_1 + V_1 = T_2 + V_2$

where T_1 = initial kinetic energy = 0

T_2 = final kinetic energy = $\frac{1}{2}mv_{AB}^2 + \frac{1}{2}I_{AB}\omega_{AB}^2 + \frac{1}{2}mv_{BD}^2 + \frac{1}{2}I_{BD}\omega_{BD}^2$

V_1 = initial potential energy = $2mg\, y_1 = 2mg\,(L\sin 60°) = \sqrt{3}\, mg\, L$

V_2 = final potential energy = $2mg\, y_2 = 2mg\,(L\sin\beta)$

The angular velocity ω_{BD} is obtained in terms of $\omega_{AB}= \omega$ from the kinematics of the linkage at any angle β. Taking A as the fixed frame of reference, the velocity of B is

$$v_B= (-\omega\hat{k}) \times AB = -\omega\hat{k} \times (L \sin\beta\,\hat{j} + L\cos\beta\,\hat{i}) = (\omega L \sin\beta\,\hat{i} - \omega L\cos\beta\,\hat{j})$$

Velocity of center of mass of AB is

$$v_{AB}= (\omega(L/2)\sin\beta\,\hat{i} - \omega(L/2)\cos\beta\,\hat{j}). \qquad ...(1)$$

It has magnitude = $\omega(L/2)$

Consider motion of D with respect to B.

$$v_D = v_B + v_{DB}$$

i.e., $$v_D\hat{i} = v_B + (\omega_{DB}\hat{k}) \times BD$$

Here $BD = L\cos\beta\,\hat{i} - L\sin\beta\,\hat{j}$

$$\therefore \quad v_D\hat{i} = v_B + (\omega_{DB}\hat{k}) \times (L\cos\beta\,\hat{i} - L\sin\beta\,\hat{j})$$

$$= v_B + \omega_{DB}(L\cos\beta\,\hat{j} + L\sin\beta\,\hat{i})$$

So equating $\hat{i}$ and $\hat{j}$ terms independently

$$v_D= \omega L\sin\beta + L\,\omega_{DB}\sin\beta,$$

and $$\omega_{DB} = \omega L\cos\beta / L\cos\beta = \omega$$

Velocity of center of gravity of BD is

$$v_{BD}= v_B + \omega_{DB}((L/2)\cos\beta\,\hat{j} + (L/2)\sin\beta\,\hat{i})$$

$$= (\omega L\sin\beta\,\hat{i} - \omega L\cos\beta\,\hat{j}) + \omega_{DB}(L/2)\cos\beta\,\hat{j} + \omega_{DB}(L/2)\sin\beta\,\hat{i}$$

$$= (\omega L + \omega_{DB}(L/2))\sin\beta\,\hat{i} + (-\omega L + \omega_{DB}(L/2))\cos\beta\,\hat{j} \qquad ...(2)$$

$$= (3\omega L/2)\sin\beta\,\hat{i} + (-\omega L/2)\cos\beta\,\hat{j}$$

It has magnitude $$= \sqrt{\left(\frac{3\omega L\sin\beta}{2}\right)^2 + \left(\frac{-\omega L\cos\beta}{2}\right)^2} = \omega L/2\sqrt{9\sin^2\beta + \cos^2\beta}$$

Substituting all the terms in T_2,

$$T_2 = \frac{1}{2}m\left(\frac{\omega L}{2}\right)^2 + \frac{1}{2}\left(\frac{1}{12}mL^2\right)\omega^2 + \frac{1}{2}m\frac{\omega^2L^2}{4}(9\sin^2\beta+\cos^2\beta) + \frac{1}{2}\left(\frac{1}{12}mL^2\right)\omega^2$$

$$= \frac{5}{24}mL^2\omega^2 + \frac{1}{8}mL^2\omega^2(9\sin^2\beta + \cos^2\beta)$$

Thus $$T_2 = V_1 - V_2 \Rightarrow \frac{5}{24}mL^2\omega^2 + \frac{1}{8}mL^2\omega^2(9\sin^2\beta+\cos^2\beta) = \sqrt{3}mgL - 2mg\,(L\sin\beta)$$

or $$\omega = \sqrt{\frac{g\sqrt{3} - 2g\sin\beta}{\left(\frac{5}{24}L + \frac{1}{8}L(9\sin^2\beta + \cos^2\beta)\right)}} \text{ and } v_D = 2L\omega\sin\beta$$

Complete MATLAB program for computing ω and v_D is presented below:

% Initial values

```
g=9.81; % Acceleration due to gravity
L=0.600 % Length of rod in m
beta=60:-5:0; % angle beta decrement
betar=beta*pi/180;
num=g*(3^0.5)-2*g*sin(betar);
den=(5/24)*L+((1/8)*L*(9*sin(betar).^2+cos(betar).^2))
omega=sqrt(num./den);
vD=2*L*omega.*sin(betar);
subplot(2,1,1);
plot(beta,omega,'-p');
ylabel('Angular velocity (rad/s)');
grid on;
subplot(2,1,2);
plot(beta,vD,'-*');
ylabel('Linear velocity of D (m/s)');
xlabel('Angle beta degree');
grid on;
```

Output of the program is shown in Fig. ED7.25 (*a*).

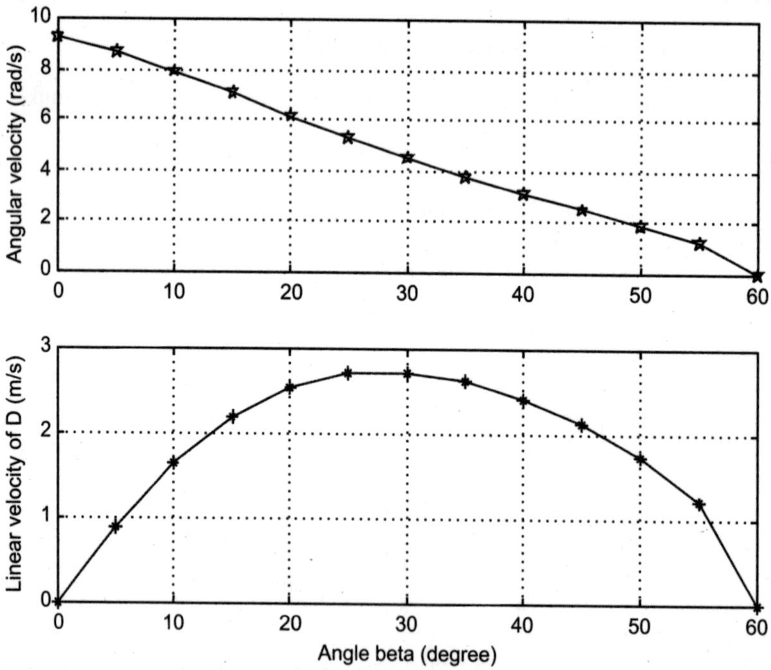

Fig. ED7.25 (a) MATLAB output

Example ED7.26: Figure ED7.26 shows the 3-D projectile trajectory where a projectile is fired with an initial velocity of v_0 at an angle of θ relative to the ground.

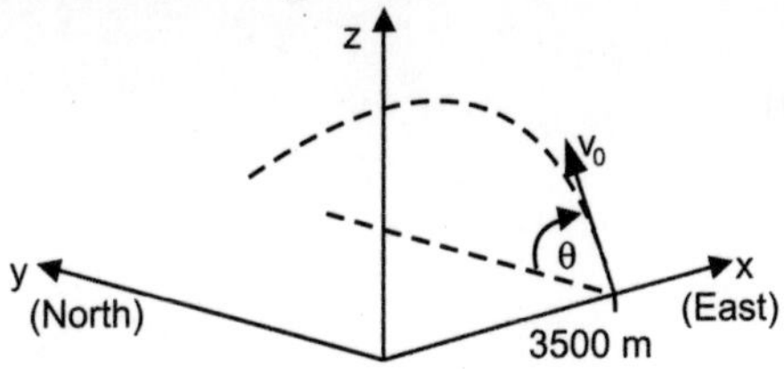

Fig. ED7.26

The projectile is aimed directly north. The projectile also moves in the western direction at a constant speed of 25 m/s. Write a MATLAB program to (*a*) determine and plot the trajectory of the projectile until it hits the ground, (*b*) plot the trajectory that the projectile would have had if the projectile does not move in the western direction. Given $v_0 = 300$ m/s and $\theta = 60°$.

Solution: *x* and *y* axes represent East and North directions. Consider vertical direction as *z*. As projectile is fired in north, the initial velocity v_0 can be resolved into *y* and *z* direction as:

$$v_{0y} = v_0 \cdot \cos\theta \quad \text{and} \quad v_{0z} = v_0 \cdot \sin\theta$$

Time taken by projectile to reach highest point ($v_z = 0$) is

$$t_h = \frac{v_{0z}}{g}$$

Total flying time, $t_t = 2 \cdot t_h$

Due to wind, projectile has a constant velocity in the negative *x* direction, $v_x = -25$.

∴ Position of projectile is given by

$$x - x_0 + v_x t \quad \text{and} \quad y = y_0 + v_{oy} t$$

$$z = z_0 + v_{0z} t - \frac{1}{2} g t^2$$

Start with initial point $(x_0, y_0, z_0) = (3000, 0, 0)$. Complete MATLAB program is given below:

MATLAB Program:

```
v0=300;g=9.81;theta=60;
x0=3000;vx=-25;
v0z=v0*sin(theta*pi/180);
v0y=v0*cos(theta*pi/180);
t=2*v0z/g;
tplot=linspace(0,t,100); % CREATING A TIME VECTOR WITH 100 ELEMENTS
z=v0z*tplot-0.5*g*tplot.^2;
y=v0y*tplot;
x=x0+vx*tplot;
 % CALCULATING X,Y,Z COORDINATES OF THE PROJECTILE AT EACH TIME
xnowind(1:length(y))=x0; % CONSTANT X-COORDINATE WHEN NO WIND
plot3(x,y,z,'k-',xnowind,y,z,'k–') % TWO 3-D LINE PLOTS
grid on
```

```
xlabel('x(m)');
ylabel('y(m)');
zlabel('z(m)')
```

Output is shown in Fig. ED7.26 (*a*).

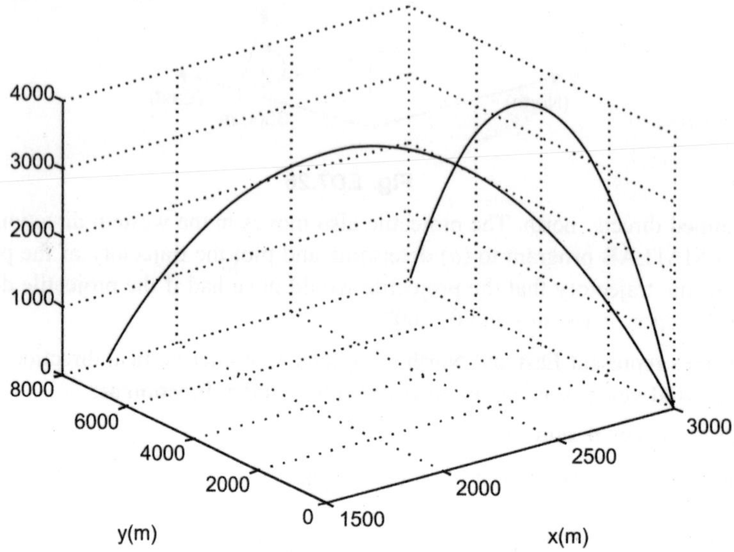

Fig. ED7.26(a) MATLAB output

REFERENCES

Bedford, A. and Fowler, W., *Engineering Mechanics: Statics & Dynamics*, 4th ed., Prentice-Hall, New Jersey, 2005.

Beer, F.B., Russell Johnston, E. and Eisenberg, E.R., *Vector Mechanics for Engineers—Statics and Dynamics,* 8th ed., McGraw-Hill, New York, 2007.

Beer, F.B., Russell Johnston, E. and DeWolf, J.T., *Mechanics of Materials,* 3rd ed., McGraw-Hill, New York, 2001.

Boresi, A. and Schmidt, R.J., *Engineering Mechanics: Statics,* 2nd ed., Brooks/Cole Publishing Company, New York, 2001.

Cernica, J.N., *Strength of Materials*, Holt, Rinehart and Winston, Inc., New York, 1966.

Hibbler, R.C., *Engineering Mechanics: Statics & Dynamics,* Prentice-Hall, Englewood Cliffs, NJ, 1995.

Meriam, J.L. and Kraige, L.G., *Engineering Mechanics: Dynamics*, 5th ed., Wiley, New York, 2002.

Nash, W., *Schaum's Outlines: Statics and Mechanics of Materials,* McGraw-Hill, New York, 1992.

Nash, W., *Schaum's Outlines: Strength of Materials,* 4th ed., McGraw-Hill, New York, 1998.

Nelson, E.W., Best, C.L. and McLean, W.G., *Schaum's Outlines: Engineering Mechanics—Statics and Dynamics,* 5th ed., McGraw-Hill, New York, 1998.

Pytel, A. and Kiusalaas, J., *Engineering Mechanics: Statics*, 2nd ed., Brooks/Cole Publishing Company, New York, 1999.

Riley, W., Sturges, L. and Morris, D., *Mechanics of Materials*, Wiley, New York, 2007.

Shelley, J.F., *Vector Mechanics for Engineers* (Vol. I)*: Statics*, Schaum's Solved Problems Series, McGraw-Hill, New York, 1990.

PROBLEMS

ES7.1: Determine the resultant or equivalent force applied to the bracket for the system shown in Fig. ES7.1

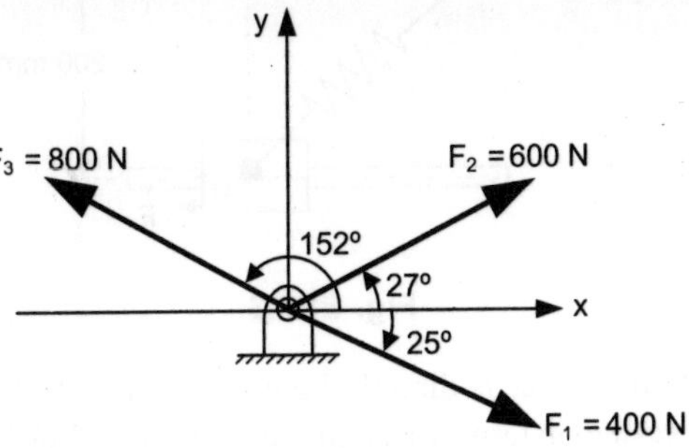

Fig. ES7.1

ES7.2: Figure ES7.2 shows a load W supported by two cables AC and BC.

Use the following three sets of values:

(*i*) $\alpha = 30°, \beta = 80°, W = 1.5$ kN

(*ii*) $\alpha = 60°, \beta = 40°, W = 2.5$ kN

(*iii*) $\alpha = 35°, \beta = 65°, W = 1.2$ kN

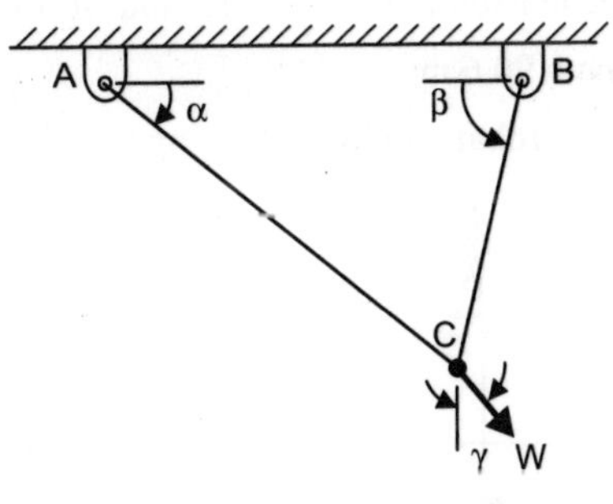

Fig. ES7.2

(*a*) Determine the tension in AC and BC as a function of W and γ.

(*b*) Write a MATLAB program to plot the tensions T_{AC} and T_{BC} for values of γ ranging from $(\beta - 90°)$ to $(90° - \alpha)$.

(*c*) Determine from the plots the value of γ for which the tension in the cables T_{AC} and T_{BC} is as small as possible and the respective values of T_{AC} and T_{BC}.

ES7.3: A collar P sliding freely on the horizontal frictionless rod as shown in Fig. ES7.3, is attached with a spring (spring constant k).

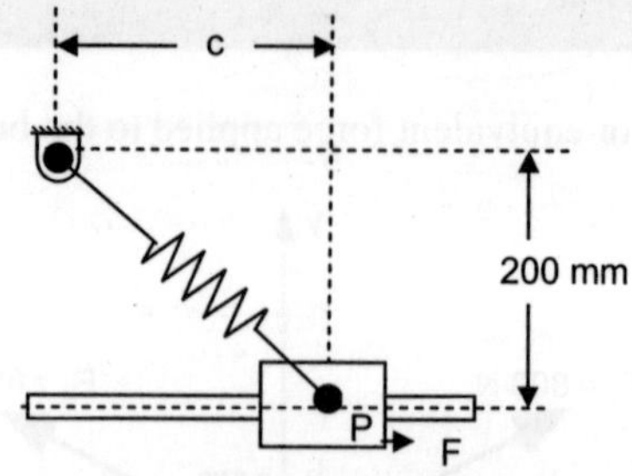

Fig. ES7.3

The spring is undeformed when the collar is directly below the support *Q*. Express the force *F* required to maintain the equilibrium of the system in terms of *k* and the distance *c*. Plot *F* as a function of *c* for values of *c* from 0 to 400 mm when (*i*) $k = 1$ N/mm, (*ii*) $k = 2$ N/mm and (*iii*) $k = 3$ N/mm

ES7.4: Figure ES7.4 shows an acrobat walking on a tight rope attached to support at *A* and *B*. The friction between his shoes and the rope is high enough to prevent him from slipping. The weight of the rope and elastic deformation may be neglected. Write a MATLAB program to determine the deflection *y* and the tension in *AC* and *BC* of the rope for values of *x* ranging from 0.2 m to 50 m using 0.5 m increments. Determine also

(*a*) the maximum deflection of the rope

(*b*) the maximum tension in the rope

(*c*) the minimum values of the tension in portions *AC* and *BC* of the rope.

The length of the tight rope = 90.6 m

The combined mass of the acrobat and his balancing pole is 80 kg.

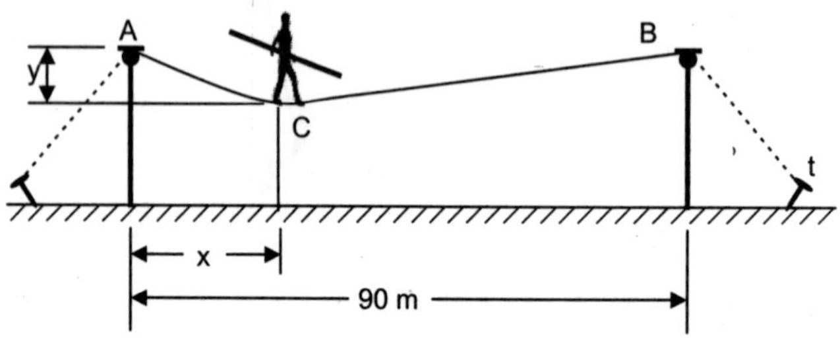

Fig. ES7.4

ES7.5: A barge is pulled by two tug boats as shown in Fig. ES7.5. To move the barge along the water properly, the tug-boats must exert a resultant force of 3 kN along the direction of motion of the barge. Supposing that tug-2 can move anywhere such that $0 \le \beta \le 90°$, determine angle β at which a minimum tension in the rope connected to tug-2 is obtained.

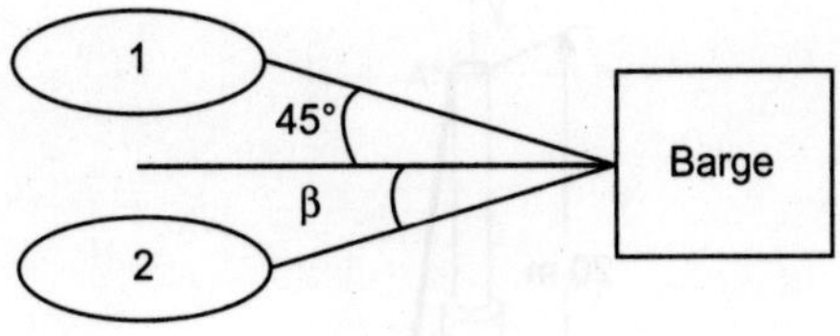

Fig. ES7.5

ES7.6: A 50 kg crate is held in equilibrium as it rests on a frictionless inclined plane making an angle θ with the horizontal as shown in Fig. ES7.6. Compute the tension in the cable T and the normal force at the surface for θ at 2° increments, increments increasing from 0 to 90°. Is there some value of θ for which T = N? If cable is replaced by a spring of stiffness 100 N/m, plot the deflection of the cable as a function of θ.

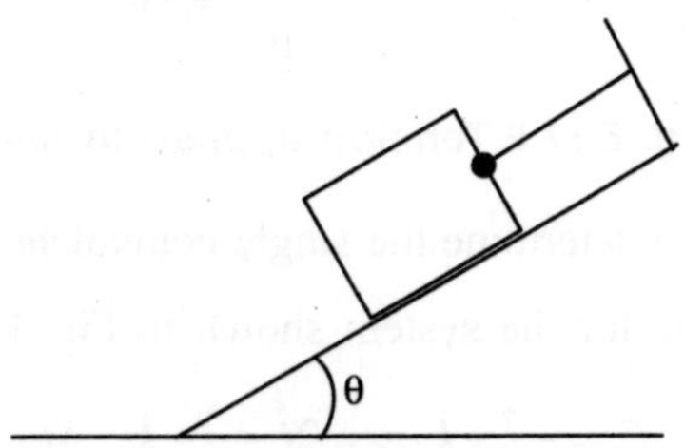

Fig. ES7.6

ES7.7: Write a generalized MATLAB script to find the perpendicular distance between the line of a force $F = 6\hat{i} + 10\hat{j} + 18\hat{k}$ acting at point A(1, 2, 3) and the line OB shown in Fig. ES7.7 having direction angles (60°, 100° and acute angle).

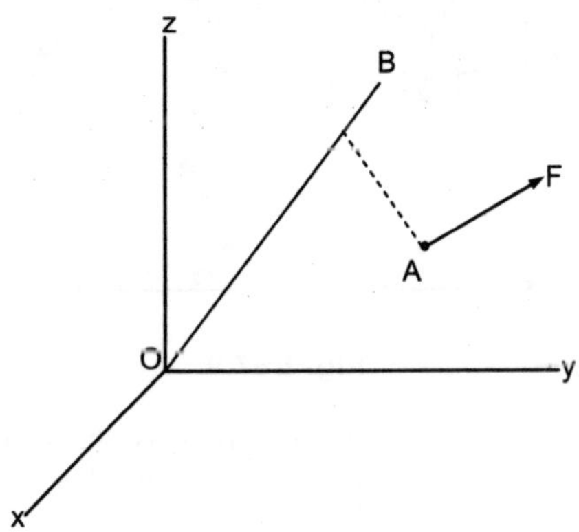

Fig. ES7.7

ES7.8: A tension T is applied to the cable attached to the top A of the rigid mast and secured to the ground at B as shown in Fig. ES7.8.

(*a*) Obtain a general expression for the moment of T about the base O (*i.e.*, M_O) as a function of x_B and z_B.

(*b*) Write a MATLAB program to plot the magnitude of M_O and its components about the x and z axes as a function of x_B for z_B=12 m.

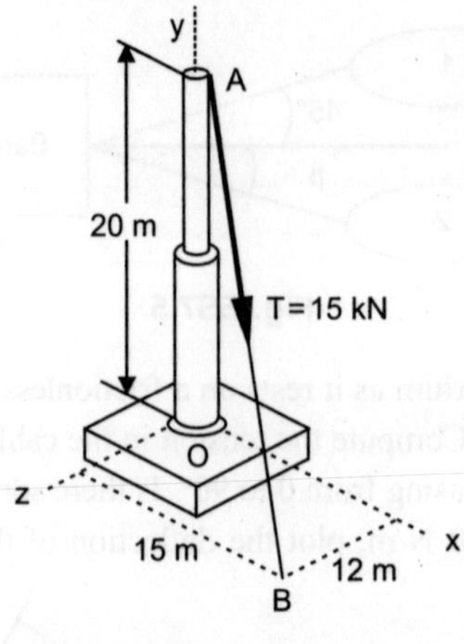

Fig. ES7.8 Tension applied to mast

ES7.9: Write a MATLAB program to determine the single equivalent force R and the point where the line of action of R intersects the yz plane for the system shown in Fig. ES7.9. Take $F_1 = \hat{i} + \hat{j}$,

$r_1 = \hat{i} + \hat{j} - \hat{k}$, $M_1 = \hat{j} - 2\hat{k}$, $F_2 = -\hat{i} + \hat{k}$, $r_2 = 2\hat{i} - \hat{j} + \hat{k}$, $M_2 = \hat{j}$ and $F_3 = \hat{i} + 4\hat{j} - \hat{k}$,

$r_3 = 2\hat{i} - \hat{j} - \hat{k}$, $M_3 = \hat{i} - \hat{k}$.

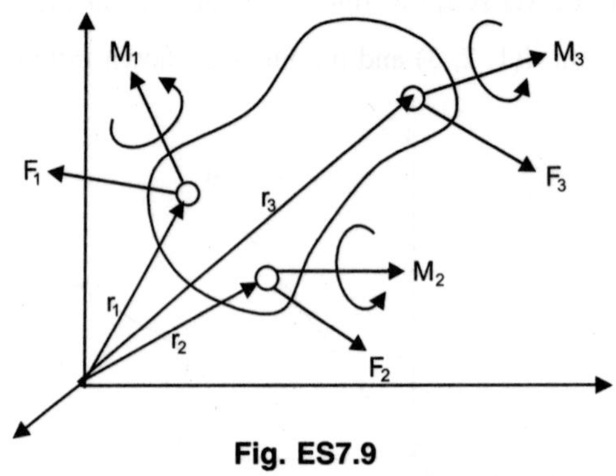

Fig. ES7.9

ES7.10: A beam AB is subjected to several vertical forces as shown in Fig. ES7.10. Using MATLAB, determine the magnitude of the resultant of the forces and the distance x_C, where the line of action of resultant intersects AB.

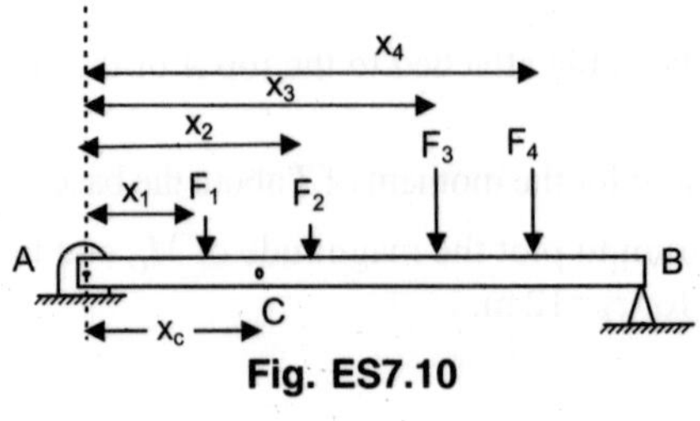

Fig. ES7.10

Take $F_1 = 10$ N, $F_2 = 20$ N, $F_3 = 30$ N, $F_4 = 40$ N and $X_1 = 0.3$ m, $X_2 = 1.2$ m, $X_3 = 2$ m, $X_4 = 2.2$ m.

ES7.11: Figure ES7.11 shows a uniform circular plate supported by three vertical wires that are equally spaced around its edge.

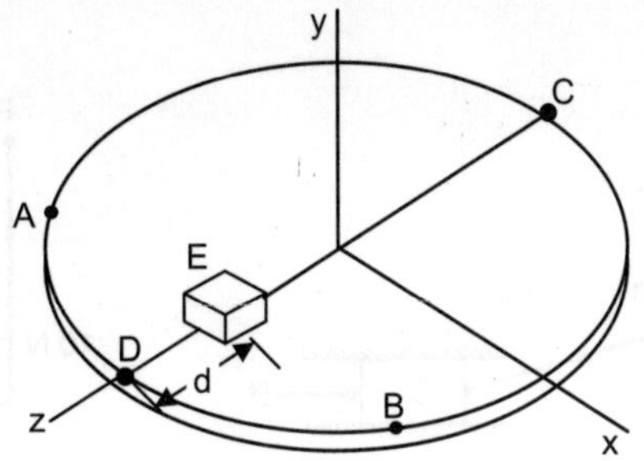

Fig. ES7.11

A small block E is placed on the plate at D and is then slowly moved along the diameter CD until it reaches C. Write a MATLAB program to plot the tension in the wires A and C as a function of d, where d is the distance of the block from D. Find the value of d for which the tension in wires A and C is minimum. Take radius of the circular plate = 310 mm, mass of the plate = 30 kg and mass of the block E = 3.5 kg.

ES7.12: Figure ES7.12 shows a slender rod AB attached to blocks A and B.

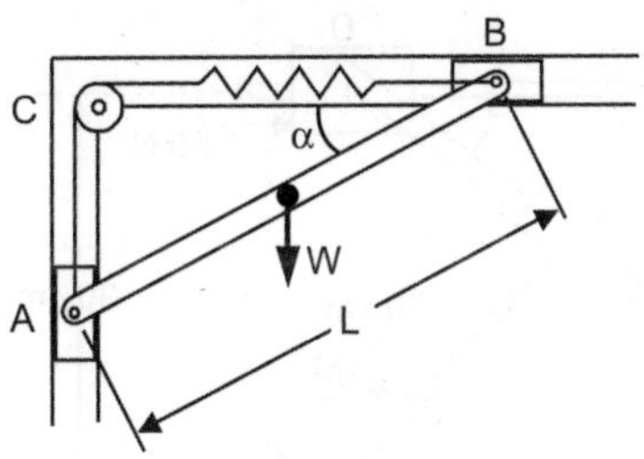

Fig. ES7.12

The weight of the rod AB is W and the blocks A and B move freely in the guides. The spring constant is k and the spring is unstretched when AB is horizontal. Write a MATLAB program to determine the three values of the angle α corresponding to equilibrium for values of W from 1 to 10 N in 2 N increments and ℓ = 25 cm, and k = 1.5 N/cm.

ES7.13: Figure ES7.13 shows a two-rod mechanism where the rods AC and BD are connected by a slider block D. Write a MATLAB program to compute and plot the couple M_A required to hold the rods in equilibrium for values of α from 0 to 120°. Also plot the magnitude of the force F exerted by rod AC on the slider-block for values of α ranging from 0 to 120°. Neglect the effect of friction.

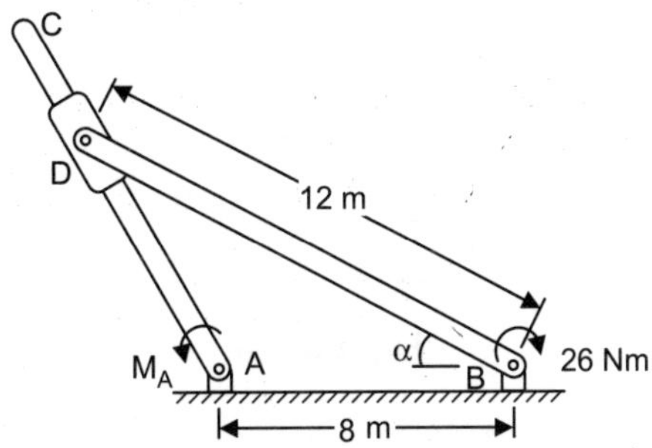

Fig. ES7.13

ES7.14: The magnitude of the force *P* applied to the piston of an engine system during one revolution of crank *AB* is shown in Fig. ES7.14. Plot the magnitude of the couple *M* required to hold the system in equilibrium as a function of θ for $0 \le \theta \le 2\pi$.

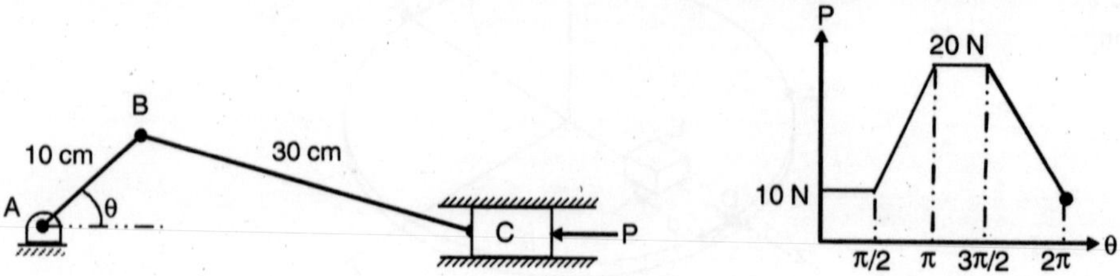

(i) Engine mechanism

(ii) Variation of P

Fig. ES7.14 (i) and (ii)

ES7.15: Figure ES7.15 shows a rod *CD* attached to collar *D* and passes through another collar welded to the end *B* of lever *AB*. As an initial step in the design of lever *AB*, use MATLAB to plot the magnitude of couple *M* required to hold the system in equilibrium as a function of θ for $10° \le \theta \le 90°$. Also determine the value of θ at which *M* becomes minimum and corresponding value of *M*.

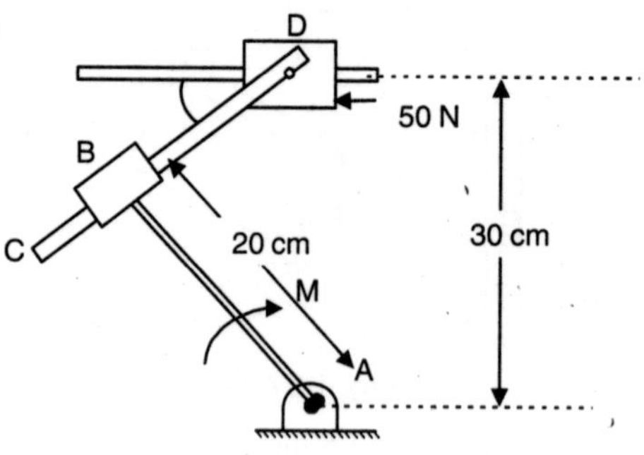

Fig. ES7.15

ES7.16: A 100 N force is pushing a 50 kg block as shown in Fig. ES7.16. The angle of inclination of the plane is α which varies from 0 to 45° in increments of 5°. The coefficient of static friction between the block and the incline is $\mu_s = 0.75$ and the coefficient of kinetic friction is $\mu_k = 0.65$. Will the block slide on the plane? If it does, will it slide up or down the plane? What is the friction force between the block and the plane?

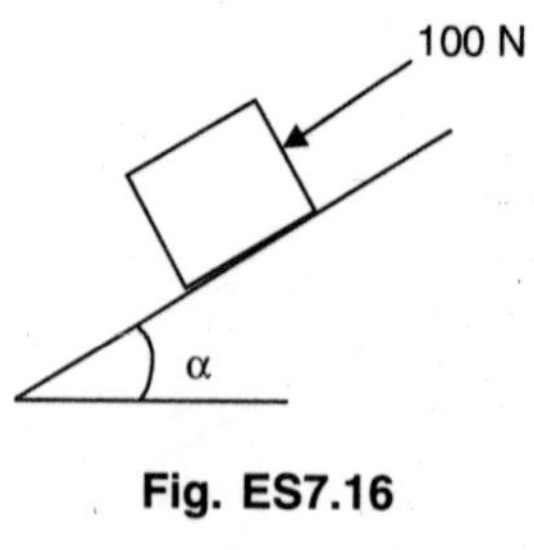

Fig. ES7.16

ES7.17: Figure ES7.17 shows the position of the rod *AB* controlled by the block which is slowly moved to the left by the force *P*. The weight of the rod *AB* is 30 N and that of the block is 5 N. The coefficient of kinetic friction between all surfaces contact is 0.3. Write a MATLAB program to plot the magnitude *P* of the force as a function of *x* for values of *x* from 55 into 5 cm. Find the maximum value of *P* and the corresponding values of *x*.

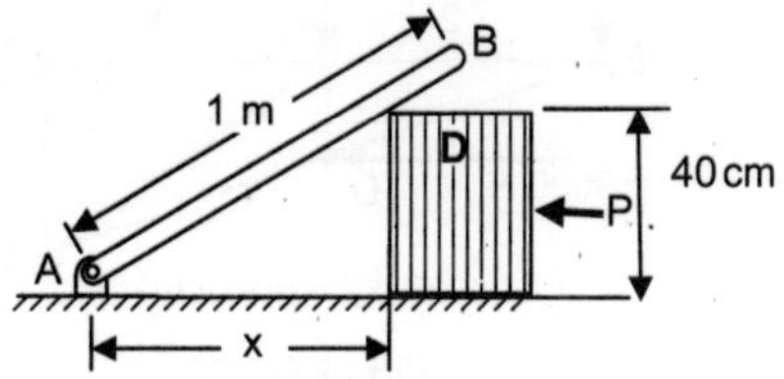

Fig. ES7.17

ES7.18: Figure ES7.18 shows a truss supporting a ramp (shown as a dashed line).

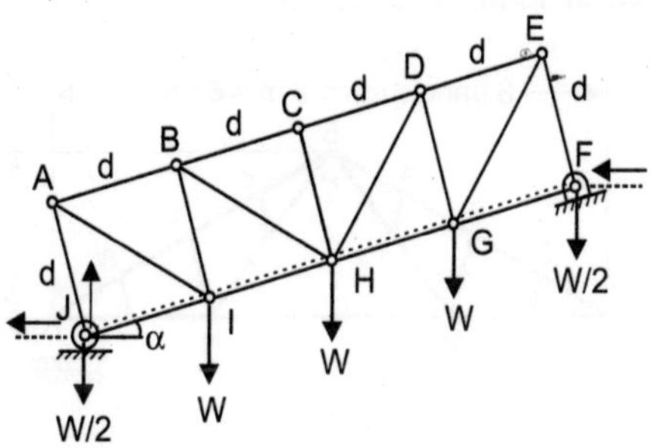

Fig. ES7.18

The ramp extends from a fixed approach level at joint *F* to a fixed exit level at joint *J*. The loads shown in figure represent the weight of the ramp.

(*a*) Determine the forces in members *CD*, *BH* and *IH* as a function of α and *W*.

(*b*) Write a MATLAB program to plot the non-dimensional forces in *CD*, *BH* and *IH* as a function of α for the values of α ranging between 0° and 45°. Take *W* = 1 Newton.

ES7.19: For the truss shown in Fig. ES7.19, determine the forces in the members F_1 to F_7 by writing the equilibrium equations and solve them using MATLAB.

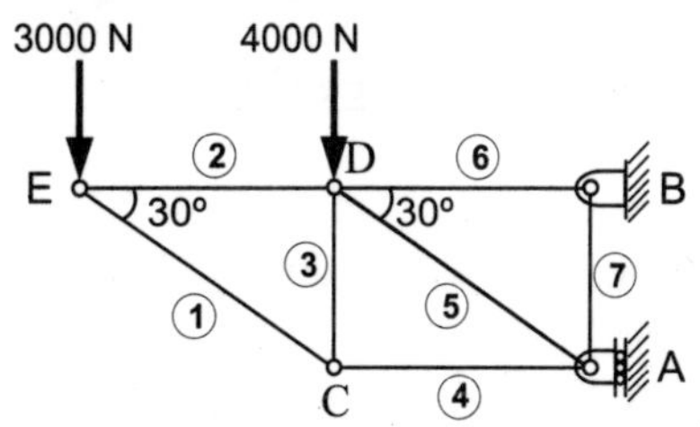

Fig. ES7.19

ES7.20: Consider the cantilever truss shown in Fig. ES7.20. Calculate the forces in each member if a wind load of 3000 N is added at the joint *D*. Vary the length of *CE* from 2 to 10 m and plot the corresponding forces in member *CD*.

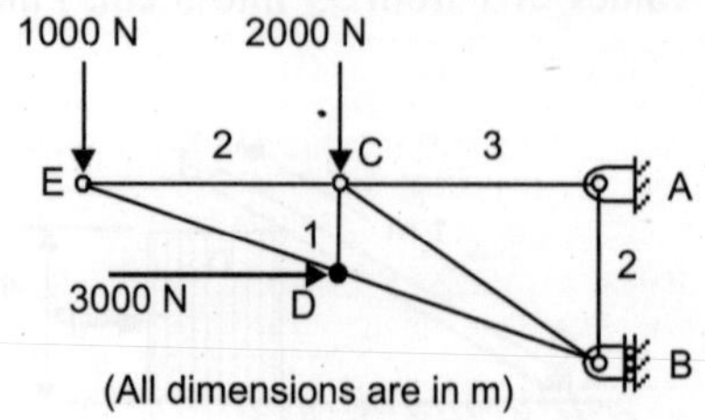

Fig. ES7.20

ES7.21: Figure ES7.21 shows the Fink truss. A single point load of 4 kN is to be applied to the top chord of the truss at one of the joints 1, 2, ..., 9. Write a MATLAB program to calculate the force in member *MN* as the load is successively applied at joints 1, 2, ..., 9.

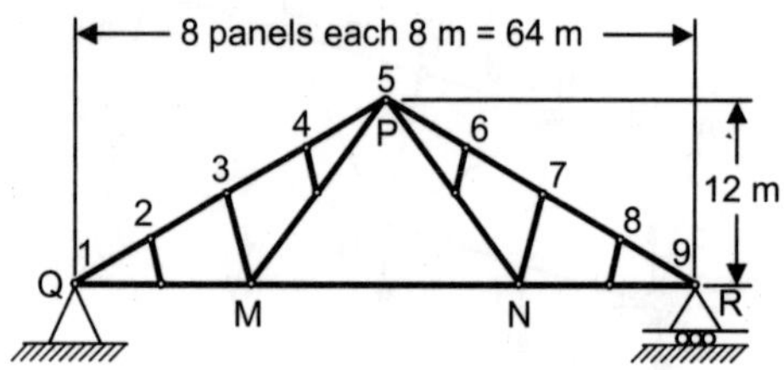

Fig. ES7.21

ES7.22: Figure ES7.22 shows the loading on a beam. At $x = 0$, the load is increasing at the rate of 80 N/m per m.

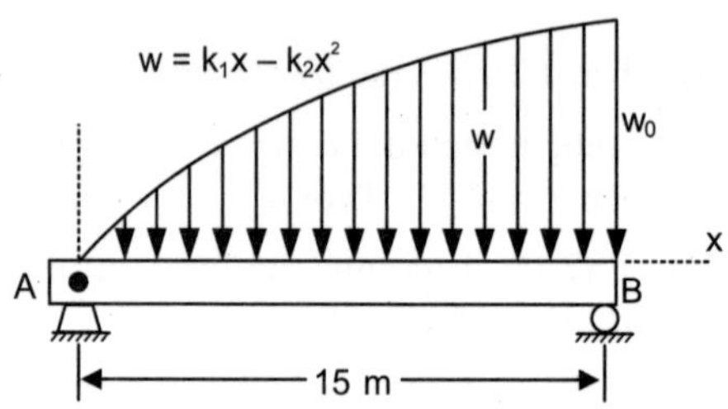

Fig. ES7.22

Write a MATLAB program to plot

(*a*) the distributed load $w(x)$ for $w_0 = 0, 100, 200, 300$ and 400 N/m.

(*b*) the reactions at the two supports as a function of w_0 for $0 \le w_0 \le 400$ N/m.

ES7.23: Figure ES7.23 shows a beam subjected to distributed and varying loads. Write a MATLAB program to plot the magnitude of the vertical reactions at supports *A* and *B* as functions of distance *d* over $0 \le d \le 4$m.

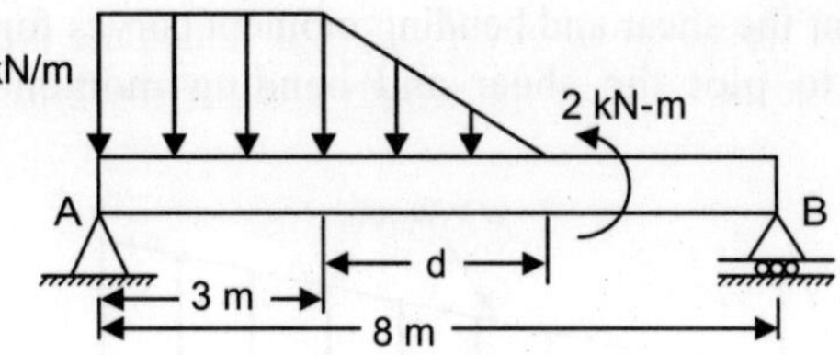

Fig. ES7.23

ES7.24: Figure ES7.24 shows a cantilever loaded with uniformly distributed load.

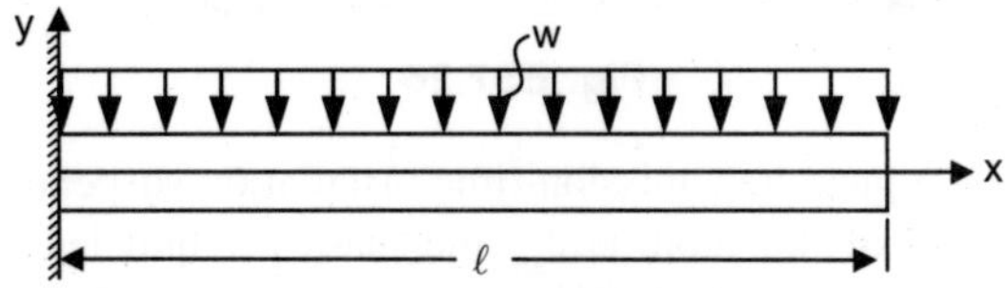

Fig. ES7.24

The deflection y at any point located at a distance x with a uniformly distributed load w is given by:

$$y = -\frac{wx^2}{24EI}\left(6\ell^2 - 4x\ell + x^2\right)$$

where, E is the Young's modulus of elasticity, I is the area moment of inertia and l is the length of the beam. Write a MATLAB program to plot the deflection y of the beam as a function of x. Take $l = 10$ m, $E = 70 \times 10^9$ Pa, $I = 10 \times 10^{-6}$ m^4, and $w = 1000$ N/m. Also plot the deflection of a simply supported beam under same conditions by considering the deflection relation as: $y = \frac{wx}{24EI}(2\ell x^2 - x^3 - \ell^3)$

ES7.25: Figure ES7.25 shows a simply supported beam with a constant distributed load w over half of its length.

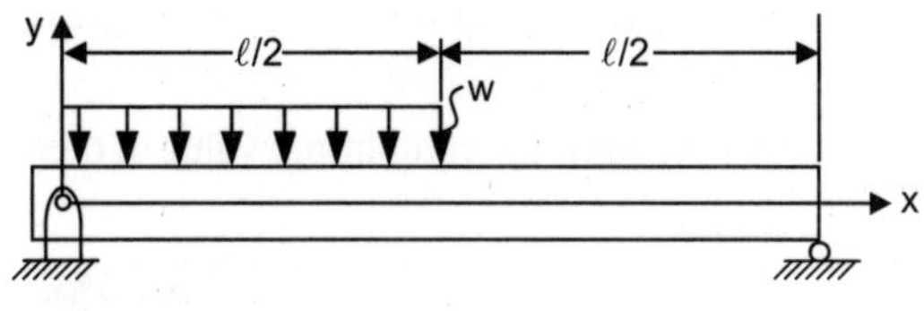

Fig. ES7.25

The deflection y as a function of x is given by

$$y = \frac{-wx}{384EI}(16x^3 - 24\ell x^2 + 9\ell^3) \text{ for } 0 \le x \le \frac{\ell}{2}$$

$$y = \frac{-wx}{384EI}(8x^3 - 24\ell x^2 + 17\ell^2 x - \ell^3) \text{ for } \frac{\ell}{2} \le x \le \ell$$

where E = Young's modulus of elasticity, I = moment of inertia and ℓ = length of the beam.
Write a MATLAB program to plot the deflection of the beam y as a function of x.
Given $\ell = 25$ m, $E = 200 \times 10^9$ Pa, $I = 350 \times 10^{-6}$ m^4 and $w = 6 \times 10^3$ N/m.

ES7.26: Derive the equations for the shear and bending moment curves for the beam shown in Fig. ES7.26. Write a MATLAB program to plot the shear and bending moment diagrams for the beam with $w_0 = 20$ kN/m and $\ell = 4$ m.

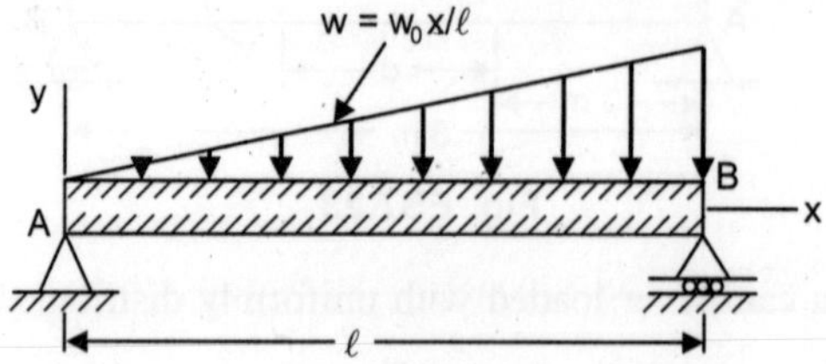

Fig. ES7.26

ES7.27: Figure ES7.27 shows a typical transmission-time installation suspended between two points lying at the same elevation. The length of the cable is ℓ_{AB} and mass per unit length is m'. Write a MATLAB program to plot the dimensionless quantities: H/ℓ, ℓ_{AB}/ℓ, $T_0/m'g\ell$ and $T_{max}/m'g\ell$ for values of c/ℓ from 0.1 to 0.6 using 0.01 increments and from 0.6 to 5 using 0.2 increments. Here c is deflection of cable.

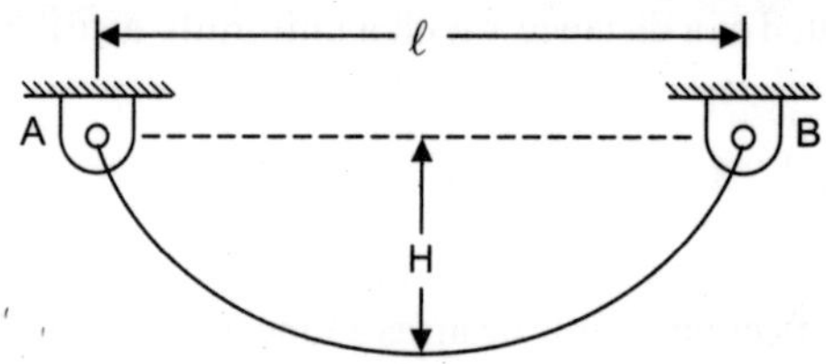

Fig. ES7.27

ES7.28: Figure ES7.28 shows a planar mechanism with two uniform links OQ and OP each of mass m are connected and constrained as shown. When a horizontal force F is applied, the angle α between the links increases, the light rod connected at M and passing through a pivoted collar at N compresses the spring. The stiffness of the spring is k N/m.

(*a*) Determine the force F which will produce equilibrium at the angle α if the spring is uncompressed in the position when $\alpha = 0$

(*b*) Write a MATLAB program for determine the equilibrium value of α corresponding to a given force F.

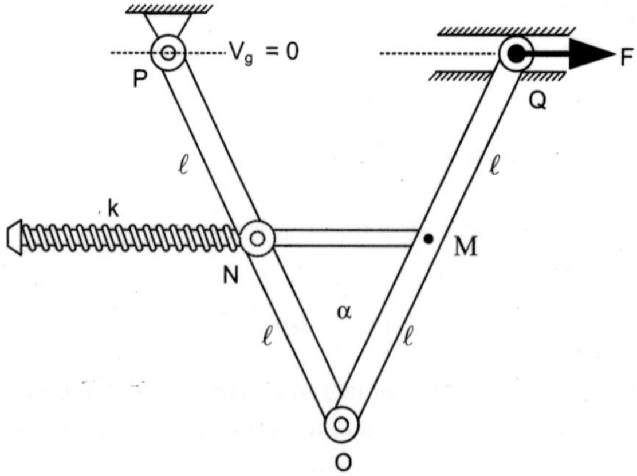

Fig. ES7.28

ES7.29: A mechanism is shown in Fig. ES7.29. Use MATLAB to plot the force in member *BD* as a function of θ for values of θ ranging from 20 to 120°.

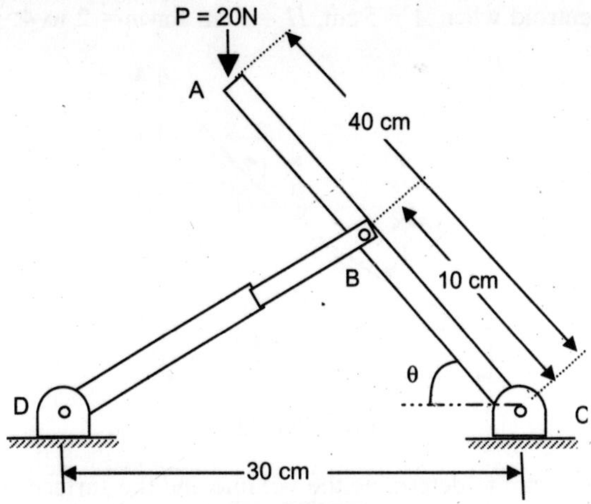

Fig. ES7.29

ES7.30: An 10 kg block is hung from the midpoint *C* of the cable *AB* which is attached to two springs as shown in Fig. ES7.30. Knowing that the springs are unstretched when $y = 0$, plot the distance y corresponding to equilibrium, as a function of the spring constant k_1 ranging from 500 N/m to 800 N/m. Take $k_2 = 1000$ N/m.

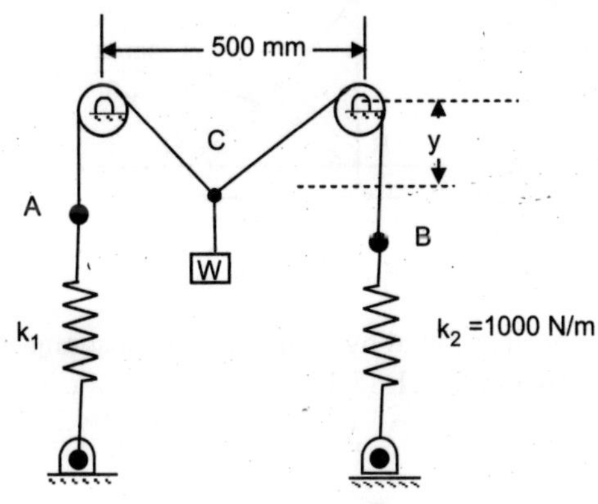

Fig. ES7.30

ES7.31: Determine the distance *H* for which the centroid of the shaded area in Fig. ES7.31 is as high above *BB′* as possible. Write a MATLAB program to plot the ratio *H*/*B* as a function of *k* for $0.1 \leq k \leq 0.9$.

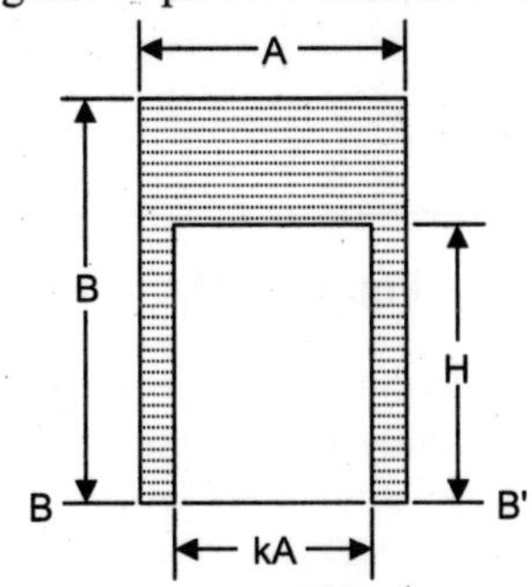

Fig. ES7.31

ES7.32: Figure ES7.32 shows an approximating the general spandrel using a series of n rectangles, each of width ΔA and of the form bcc′b'. Write MATLAB program to calculate the coordinates of the centroid of the area. Determine the centroid when A = 5 cm, H = 5 cm for m = 2 to 4.

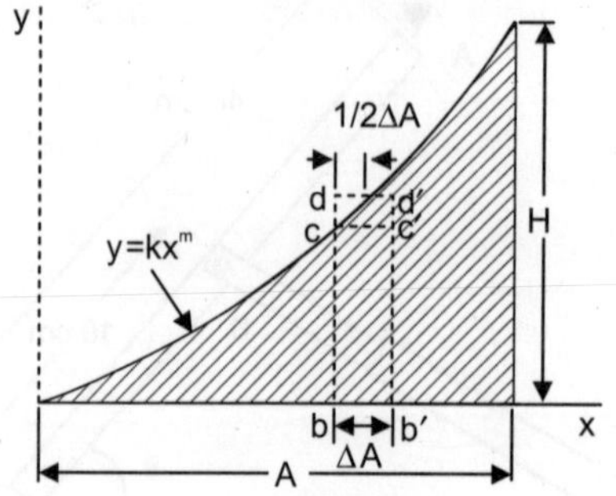

Fig. ES7.32

ES7.33: Write a MATLAB program to determine the volume and the surface area of the solid obtained by rotating the area shown in Fig. ES7.33 about the y-axis when A = 100 mm and n = 1.

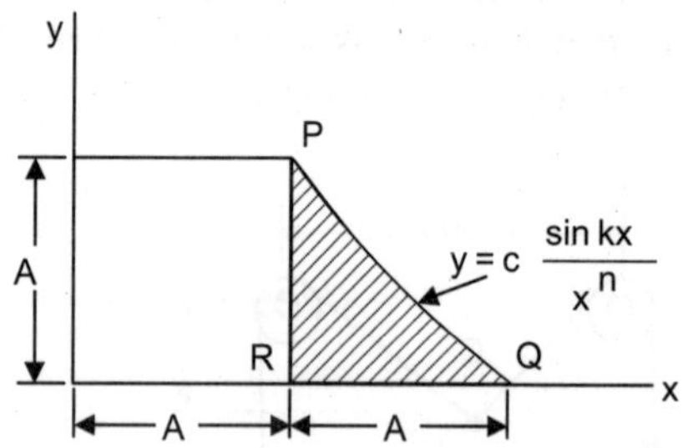

Fig. ES7.33

ES7.34: Calculate the centroid of the area found by deducting the quadrant of an ellipse from the rectangle of dimensions 10 cm × 5 cm as shown in Fig. ES7.34.

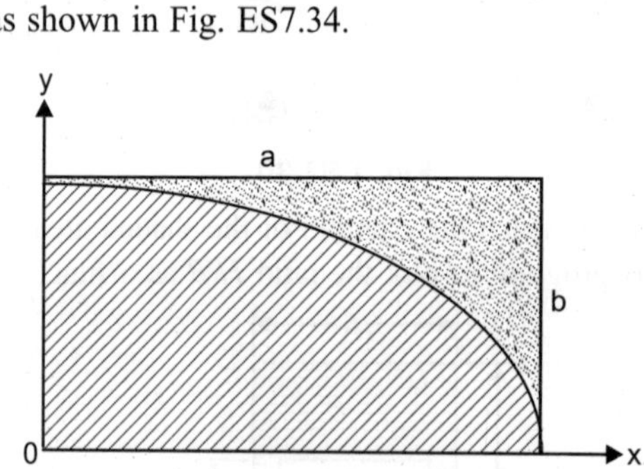

Fig. ES7.34

ES7.35: A 3-dimensional structure is fabricated during a project work from four steel-rods of equal diameter as shown in Fig. ES7.35. Using MATLAB, study the variation of center of gravity of the structure as a function of h and R.

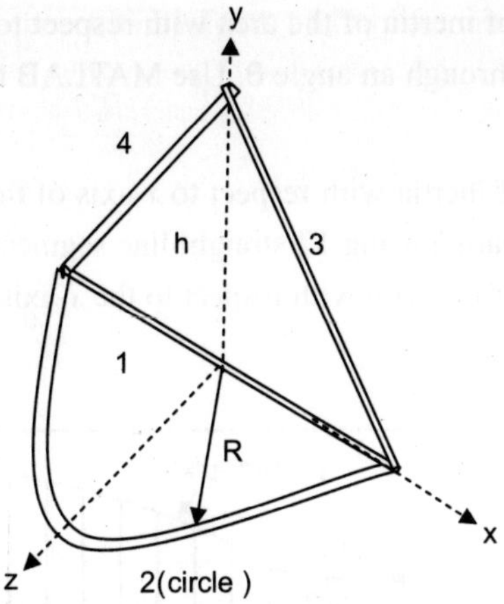

Fig. ES7.35 Three-dimensional structure

ES7.36: Many cross-sections can be approximated by a series of rectangles as shown in Fig. ES7.36. Using MATLAB, calculate the moment of inertia and the radii of gyration of the cross-section with respect to horizontal and vertical centroidal axes. Take b_1 = 3 cm, h_1 =1 cm, b_2 = 1 cm, h_2 = 4 cm, b_3 = 5 cm and h_3 = 1 cm. The centroids are: (0, –2.5), (0,0), (2.5,0)

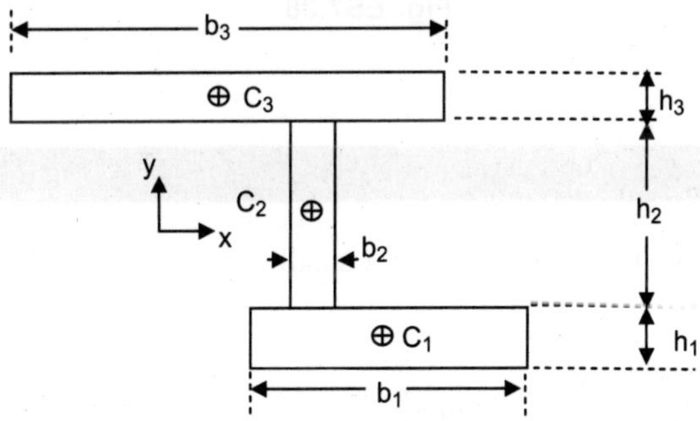

Fig. ES7.36

ES7.37: Figure ES7.37 shows an area with known moments of inertia I_x, I_y and product of inertia I_{xy} .

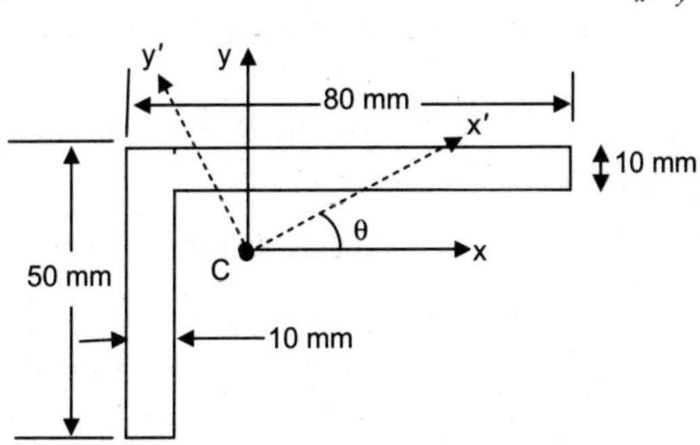

Fig. ES7.37

Calculate the moment and product of inertia of the area with respect to axes x' and y' obtained by rotating the original axes counterclockwise through an angle θ. Use MATLAB to plot Ix', Iy' and $IxIy'$ as a function of θ for $0 \leq \theta \leq 90°$.

ES7.38: Obtain the mass moment of inertia with respect to x-axis of the homogeneous wire with mass per unit length as 0.1 kg/m by approximating using 12 straight line segments as shown in Fig. ES7.38. Write a MATLAB program to determine I_x of the wire with respect to the x-axis when p = 25 mm, l = 250 mm, and H = 100 mm.

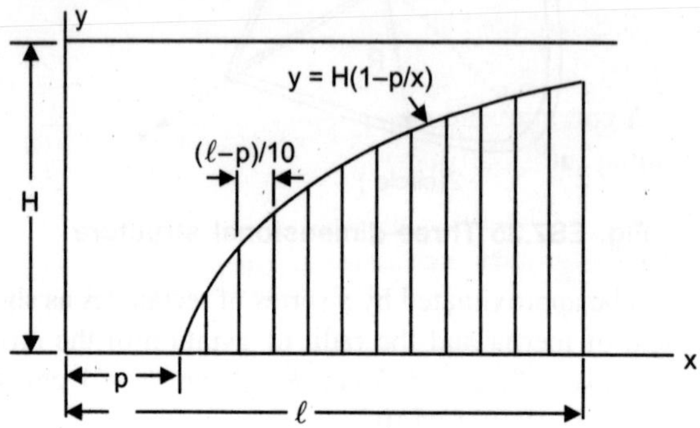

Fig. ES7.38

DYNAMICS

ED7.1: The total acceleration y of the nose cone of a small experimental rocket as it moves up and down is given by

$$\begin{aligned} \ddot{y} &= -g - 0.00016v^2 \text{ up} \\ &= -g + 0.00016v^2 \text{ down} \end{aligned} \quad \text{in m/s}^2$$

where v = velocity in m/s.

(*a*) Derive an expression for the speed of the cone as a function of height as the cone moves up to its maximum height and as it returns to the ground. The nose cone is projected vertically from the ground with an initial velocity of 400 m/s.

(*b*) Write a MATLAB program to plot the speed of the cone as a function of the height for the upward motion and for the downward motion.

ED7.2: The position x as a function of time of a particle that moves along a straight line is given by

$$x(t) = 0.5t^3 - 2.5t^2 - 6t + 15$$

(*a*) Derive expressions for the velocity and acceleration of the particle.

(*b*) Write a MATLAB program to plot the position, velocity and acceleration as a function of time for $0 \leq t \leq 10$ seconds.

ED7.3: The height of the ball at any time t after it is thrown is given by $y(t) = y_0 + v_{y0}t - \frac{1}{2}gt^2$

where y_0 = the initial height of the object above the ground

v_{y_0} = the initial vertical velocity of the object

g = acceleration due to gravity

The horizontal distance traveled by the ball after it is thrown is given by

$$x(t) = x_0 + v_{x_0} t$$

where x_0 = the initial horizontal position of the ball on the ground and v_{x_0} = the initial horizontal velocity of the ball.

In the above, air friction and earth's curvature are neglected. Assume that the ball is initially thrown from $(x_0, y_0) = (0,0)$ with 25 m/s at an initial angle of θ degrees.

(*a*) Write a MATLAB program to plot the trajectory of the ball and obtain the horizontal distance traveled before it touches the ground, by taking the range of θ as: $0 \le \theta \le 90°$.

(*b*) Determine the angle θ that maximizes the range of the ball and plot the trajectory.

ED7.4: A motorcycle is moving along a circular path having a radius of 6 m such that its position as a function of time is given by $\theta = \sin 3t$, find the acceleration of particle as a function of time t and plot the components of acceleration.

ED7.5: The height, h, horizontal distance, x and speed of a projectile, v, launched with a speed, v at an angle θ to the horizontal axis are given by

$$h(t) = vt\sin\theta - \frac{1}{2}gt^2$$

$$x(t) = vt\cos\theta$$

$$v(t) = \sqrt{v^2 - 2vgt\sin\theta + g^2t^2}$$

The projectile will strike the ground when $h(t) = 0$, and the time of the hit is given by

$$t_{hit} - 2\frac{v}{g}\sin\theta$$

Assuming $\theta = 35°$, $v = 50$ m/s, and $g = 9.81$ m/s², write a MATLAB program using logical operators to find (a) the height is no less than 16 m, (b) the height is no less than 16 m and the speed is no greater than 45 m/sec.

ED7.6: The gravitational force F between two bodies of masses m_1 and m_2 is given by

$$F = \frac{Gm_1 m_2}{r^2}$$

where,

G = gravitational constant (6.67×10^{-11} Nm²/kg²)

m_1, m_2 = masses of the bodies (kg)

r = distance between the two bodies (m).

Write a MATLAB program to calculate the gravitational force between two bodies given their masses and distance between them. Determine the force on an 1,000 kg satellite in orbit 40,000 km above the earth's surface. The mass of the earth is 5.98×10^{24} kg.

ED7.7: A cameraman standing at *A* (see Fig. ED7.7) is following the movement of a race car *B* which is traveling along a straight track at a constant speed *v*. Plot the variation of angular velocity (with which he must turn in order to keep the camera directed on the car) as a function of angle θ shown in the figure. Given: $v = 24$ m/s and $a = 30$ m.

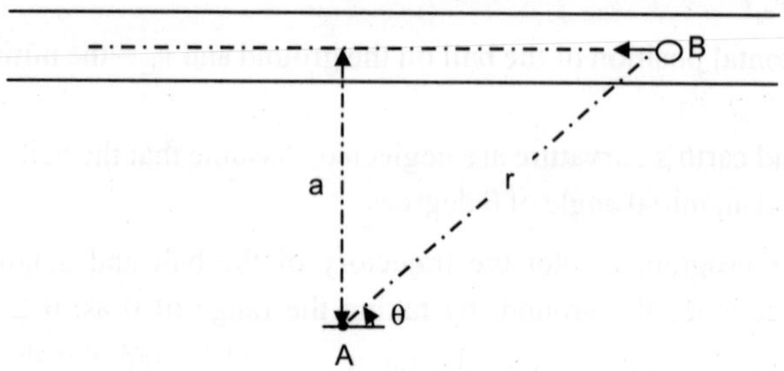

Fig. ED7.7

ED7.8: The satellite's orbit in polar coordinates is given by

$$r = \frac{p}{1 - \varepsilon \cos \theta}$$

where r = distance of the satellite from the center of the earth

θ = angle of the satellite from the center of the earth

p = a parameter specifying the size of the orbit

ε = a parameter specifying the eccentricity of the orbit

Note that when a satellite orbits the earth, the satellite's orbit will form an ellipse with the earth located at one of the focal points of the ellipse. Write a MATLAB program to plot the orbit of a satellite for (*a*) $\varepsilon = 0$, (*b*) $\varepsilon = 0.25$ and (*c*) $\varepsilon = 0.5$. The size parameter, $p = 1100$ km.

ED7.9: Figure ED7.9 shows a block of mass attached to a spring of spring constant *k*. The block is released from rest when the spring is in a horizontal and undeformed position. Write (*a*) MATLAB program to determine and plot the length of the spring, the magnitude and direction of velocity of the block as the block passes directly under the point of suspension of the spring for $k/m = 14s^{-2}$, $22s^{-2}$ and $25s^{-2}$ (*b*) the value of k/m for which that velocity is horizontal. Assume $r_0 = 2$ m.

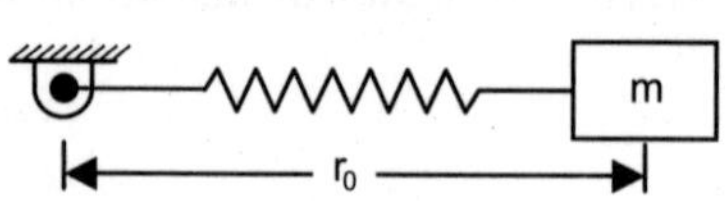

Fig. ED7.9

ED7.10: Figure ED7.10 shows a block of mass *m* initially at rest acted upon by a force *P* which varies in magnitude with time as shown in Fig. ED7.10(*a*). Write a MATLAB program to determine and plot the speed of the block as a function of time *t* for $0 \le t \le 20$ s. Determine the maximum velocity of the block and the corresponding value of t. The coefficient of static and kinetic friction between the block and the horizontal surface are $\mu_s = 0.45$ and $\mu_k = 0.25$. The mass of the block $m = 30$ kg.

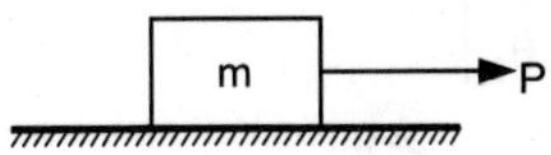

Fig. ED7.10

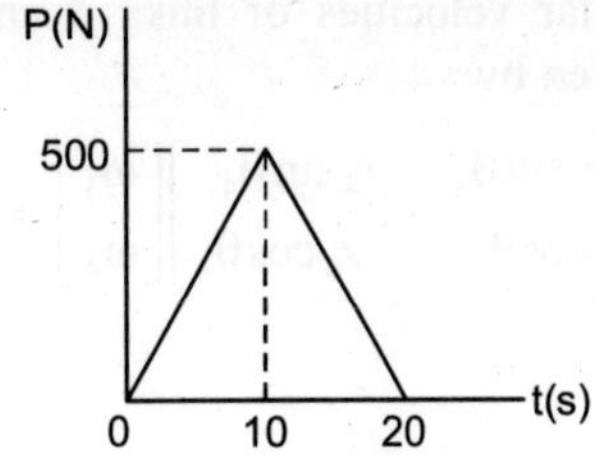

Fig. ED7.10 (a)

ED7.11: Figure ED7.11 shows two hemispheres held together by a cord only which maintain the spring under compression. Write a MATLAB program to calculate and plot the magnitude of the resulting velocity of each hemisphere as a function of θ for 10° ≤ θ ≤ 150° knowing that the cord is severed causing the hemispheres to fly apart. The potential energy of the compressed spring is 120 J and the assembly has an initial velocity of magnitude $v_0 = 8$ m/s.

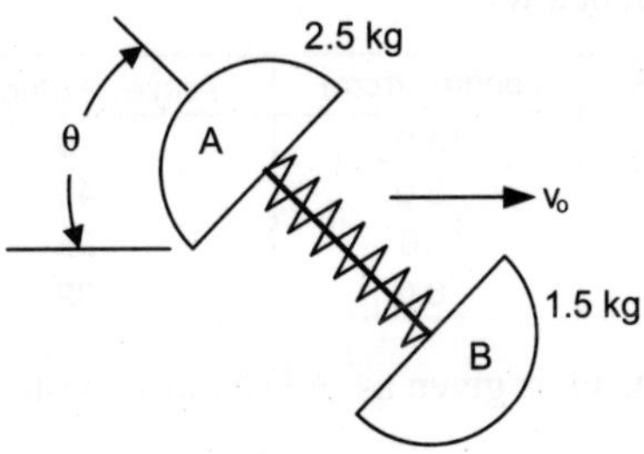

Fig. ED7.11

ED7.12: A freely rolling base (*B*) has 60 kg mass. A box (*A*) of 40 kg is sliding over it from rest, 5 m down the base as shown in Fig. ED7.12. Determine base speed, when the box reaches bottom of the crate assuming it as smooth surface.

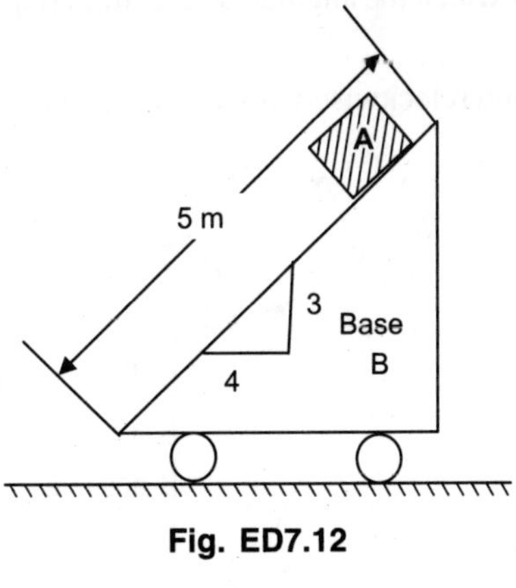

Fig. ED7.12

ED7.13: A chain has a mass per unit length 0.2 kg/m. If it is raised with a constant speed 5 cm/s starting from rest, plot the force required to raise it as a function of height.

ED7.14: The angular velocities of links 3 and 4 of the four-bar mechanism at an instant shown in Fig. ED7.14 are given by

$$\begin{bmatrix} -r_3\sin\theta_3 & r_4\sin\theta_4 \\ r_3\cos\theta_3 & -r_4\cos\theta_4 \end{bmatrix}\begin{bmatrix}\omega_3\\ \omega_4\end{bmatrix} = \begin{bmatrix}\omega_2 r_2\sin\theta_2 \\ -\omega_2 r_2\cos\theta_2\end{bmatrix}$$

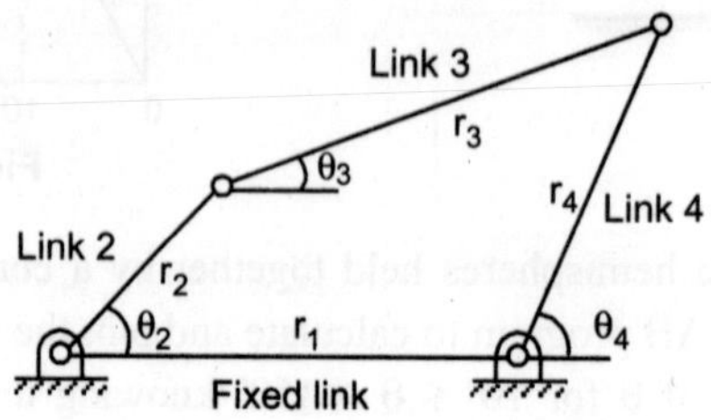

Fig. ED7.14 Four-bar mechanism

The link lengths and angles are given below:

Link	Length, r(cm)	Angle, θ (degree)
1	13.0	0
2	5.0	45
3	11.0	25
4	8.0	89

The angular velocity of the input link, ω_2 is given as + 110 rad/s. Write a MATLAB program to solve for the angular velocities of links 3 and 4.

ED7.15: Figure ED7.15 shows two rotating rods connected by a slider *P*. Write a MATLAB program to determine and plot for values of θ from 0 to 180°,

(*a*) the angular velocity and angular acceleration of rod *AE*

(*b*) determine the value of θ for which the angular acceleration α_{AE} of rod *AE* is maximum and the corresponding value of α_{AE}.

Assume that the rod *BP* rotates counterclockwise with a constant angular velocity of 10 rad/s.

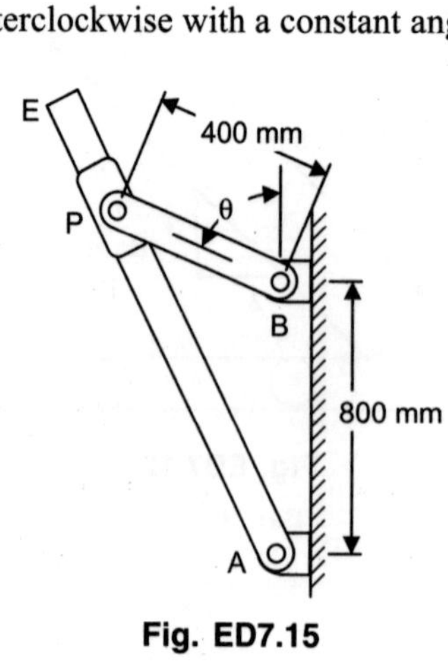

Fig. ED7.15

ED7.16: A mechanism used to convert the constant circular motion ω of the rod AB into translating motion of the rod CD is shown in Fig. ED7.16. Plot the velocity and acceleration of CD as a function of angle θ of AB. Take $AB = 100$ mm and $\omega = 10$ rad/s.

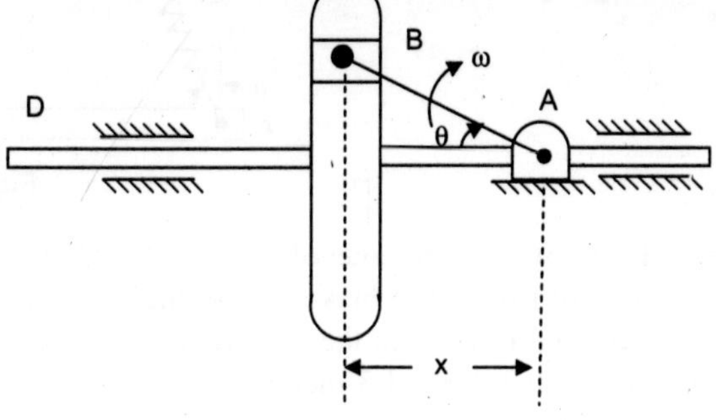

Fig. ED7.16

ED7.17: A rod AB shown in Fig. ED7.17 is confined to move along the inclined paths. If point A has an acceleration 3 m/s^2 and velocity of 2 m/s at any instant θ, study the variation of angular acceleration of rod as function of angle θ, using MATLAB. Take $AB = 10$ m.

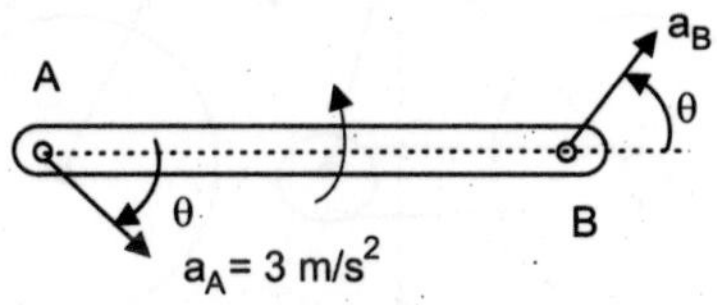

Fig. ED7.17

ED7.18: Figure ED7.18 shows that the end A of the rod AB moved to the left with a constant speed v_A. Write a MATLAB program to calculate and plot the normal reactions at ends A and B of the rod for values of θ from 0° to 50°. Determine the value of θ at which end B of the rod loses contact with the wall.

The mass of the rod $AB = 12$ kg.

The constant speed of end $A = 70$ cm/s.

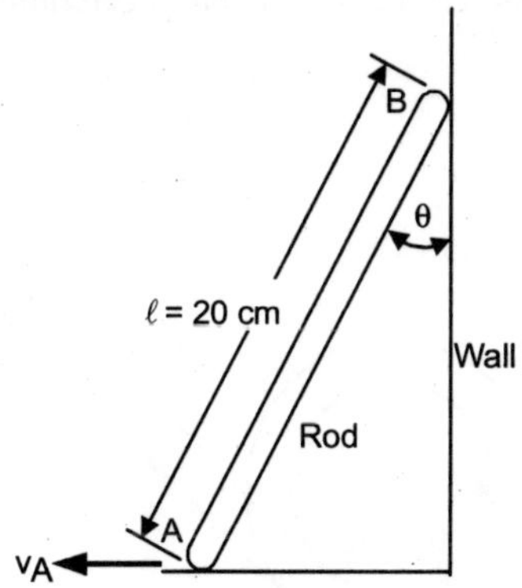

Fig. ED7.18

ED7.19: Figure ED7.19 shows a uniform slender bar *AB* of weight *W* suspended from springs *AC* and *BD*. Write a MATLAB program to calculate and plot the accelerations of ends *A* and *B* immediately after spring *AC* has broken for values of θ from 0° to 90°.

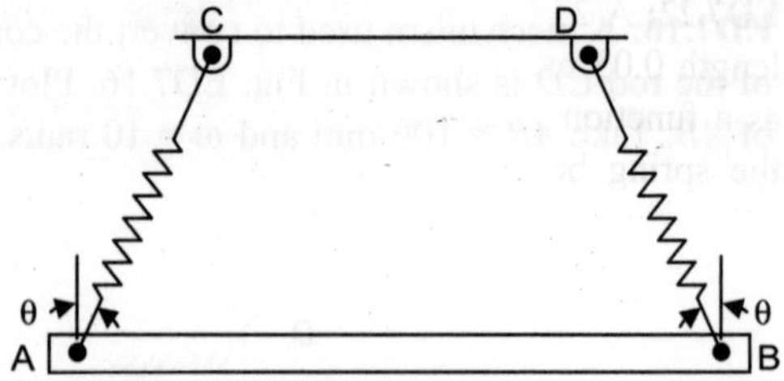

Fig. ED7.19

ED7.20: A bicycle and rider of total mass 80 kg with center of mass located *G*. If coefficient of kinetic friction at rear tire is 0.8, plot the deceleration of rider when brakes are applied as a function of height of *G* from ground. Also show the variation of normal reaction at the rear wheel. Assume *G* lies between two wheels separated by a distance 150 cm. Choose $0.9 \leq h \leq 1.3$ metres.

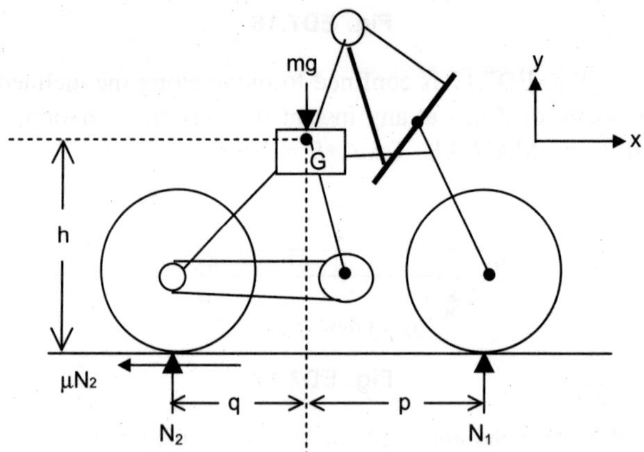

Fig. ED7.20 Free-body diagram of the cycle

ED7.21: A spool has a mass of 75 kg and a radius of gyration $k_G = 0.38$ m. It rests on the inclined surface (Fig. ED7.21) for which coefficient of kinetic friction is $\mu_k = 0.15$. If the spool is released from rest and slips at *A*, plot the initial tension in the cord and angular acceleration of the spool as a function of angle of incline θ.

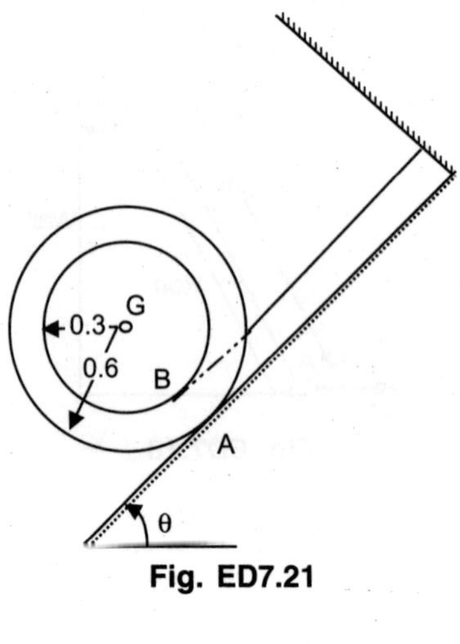

Fig. ED7.21

ED7.22: A 25 kg slender rod AB of 0.4 m long is attached to a spring BC (Fig. ED7.22) having unstretched length 0.05 m. If the rod is released from rest at $\theta = 40^o$, plot the variation of angular velocity of the rod as a function of angle θ. Consider $CA=AB$ and spring stiffness as 500 N/m. Also find the angle at which the spring becomes unstretched.

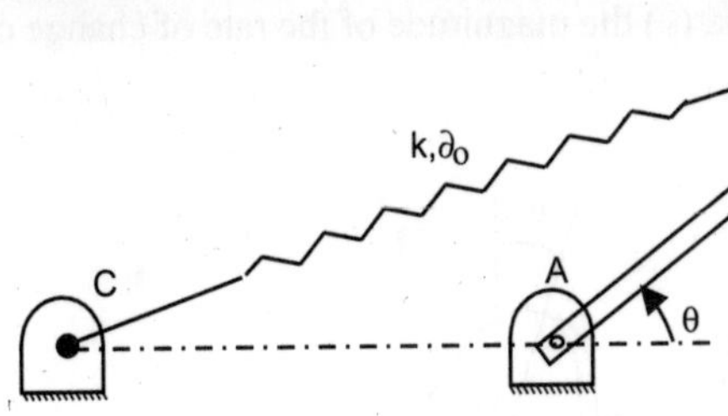

Fig. ED7.22

ED7.23: A 100 kg spool has a radius of gyration $k_G = 0.35$ m. A cable is wrapped around hub of the spool (see Fig. ED7.23) and horizontal force $P = (2 + e^{-3t})$ is applied. Determine its angular velocity as a function of time $0 \le t \le 10$s, if spool starts from rest initially. Assume that there is no slipping at the floor during rolling.

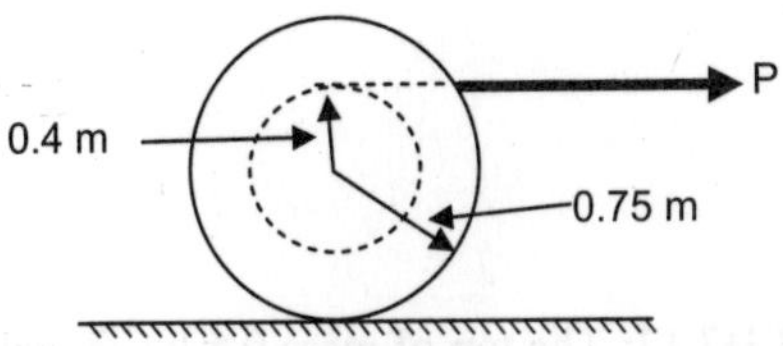

Fig. ED7.23

ED7.24: Figure ED7.24 shows a box of mass m pulled by a rope. The force required to move the box is

given by $$F = \frac{\mu mg}{\cos\theta + \mu \sin\theta}$$

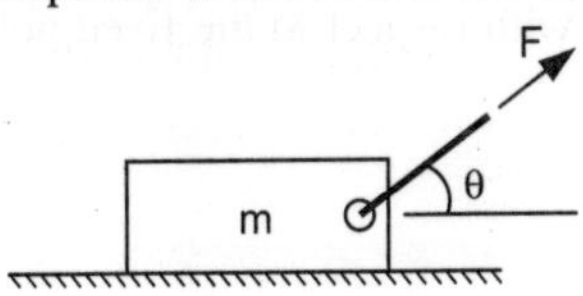

Fig. ED7.24

where μ = coefficient of friction

m = mass of the box

g = acceleration due to gravity (9.81 m/s^2)

θ = angle with horizontal.

If mass of box, m = 25 kg and coefficient of friction, μ = 0.40, write a MATLAB program to determine the angle θ when the pulling force F is 100 N. Also write a MATLAB program to determine (*a*) the angle θ at which the force required to pull the box is the smallest, (*b*) the magnitude of the force in (*a*).

ED7.25: In Fig. ED7.25 shown, the rod BD is rotating about vertical axis with an angular velocity of 7 rad/s and acceleration 4 rad/s^2. If the limb AC is rotating downwards, such that its angular speed $\dot{\theta}$ = 2 rad/s and acceleration $\ddot{\theta}$ = 3 rad/s^2 in clockwise sense. Plot the variation of velocity and acceleration of point A on the limb as a function of angle θ. Given length of AC = 0.8 m.

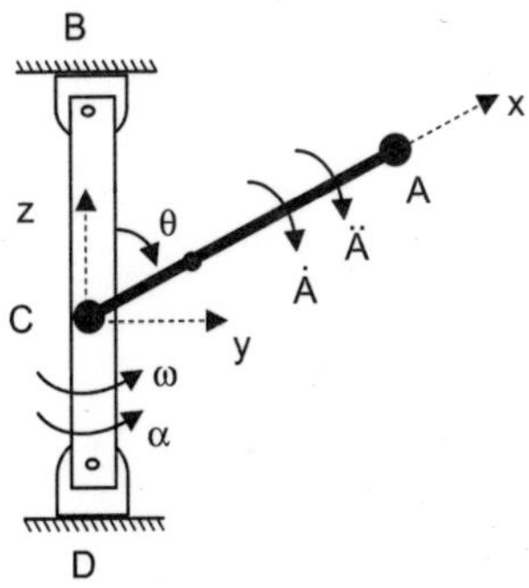

Fig. ED7.25

ED7.26: Figure ED7.26 shows a thin homogeneous disk of mass 10 kg and radius 0.3 m mounted centrally on the horizontal axle *AB*. The constant angular velocity of the axle is 30 rad/s. The disk is laid at an angle θ with the plane normal to the rotating axle. If the axle has negligible mass, write a MATLAB program (for $0° \leq \theta \leq 90°$) to (*a*) determine and plot θ formed by the axle as a function of angular momentum of the disk about *C*, (*b*) the kinetic energy of the disk, (*c*) the magnitude of the rate of change of the angular momentum of the disk about *C*.

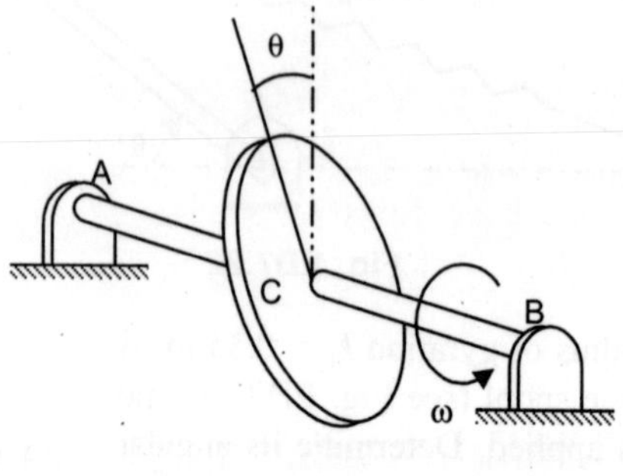

Fig. ED7.26

ED7.27: The top of mass 0.5 kg shown in Fig. ED7.27 precessing about the vertical axis at a constant angle θ. If it spins with an angular velocity ω_s = 100 rad/s, plot the precessional velocity ω_p as a function of angle θ. Take the axial and transverse moments of inertia of the top as 0.45 mg-m² and 1.2 mg-m² respectively measured with respect to the fixed point *O*. Take *OG* = 5 cm.

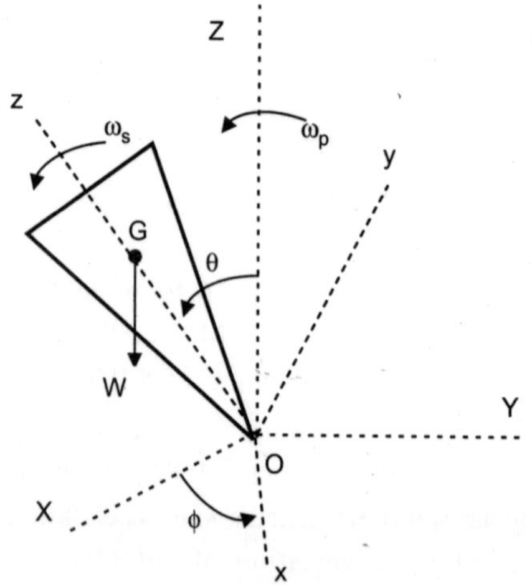

Fig. ED7.27

❍ ❍ ❍

CHAPTER 8

MECHANICAL VIBRATIONS

8.1 INTRODUCTION

Vibration is the motion of a particle or a body or system of connected bodies displaced from a position of equilibrium. Most vibrations are undesirable in machines and structures because they produce increased stresses, energy losses, cause added wear, increase bearing loads, induce fatigue, create passenger discomfort in vehicles, and absorb energy from the system. Rotating machine parts need careful balancing in order to prevent damage from vibrations.

Vibration occurs when a system is displaced from position of stable equilibrium. The system tends to return to this equilibrium position under the action of restoring forces (such as the elastic forces, as for a mass attached to a spring, or gravitational forces, as for a simple pendulum). The system keeps moving back and forth across its position of equilibrium. A *system* is a combination of elements intended to act together to accomplish an objective. For example, an automobile is a system whose elements are the wheels, suspension, car body and so forth. A *static* element is one whose output at any given time depends only on the input at that time while a *dynamic* element is one whose present output depends on past *inputs*. In the same way, we also speak of *static* and *dynamic systems*. A *static system* contains all elements while a *dynamic system* contains at least one dynamic element.

A physical system undergoing a time-varying interchange or dissipation of energy among or within its elementary storage or dissipative devices is said to be in a *dynamic state*. All of the elements in general are called *passive*, *i.e.*, they are incapable of generating net energy. A dynamic system composed of a finite number of storage elements is said to be *lumped* or *discrete*, while a system containing elements, which are dense in physical space, is called *continuous*. The analytical description of the dynamics of the discrete case is a set of ordinary differential equations, while for the continuous case it is a set of partial differential equations. The analytical formation of a dynamic system depends upon the kinematic or geometric constraints and the physical laws governing the behaviour of the system.

8.2 CLASSIFICATION OF VIBRATIONS

Vibrations can be classified into three categories: *free, forced* and *self-excited. Free vibration* of a system is vibration that occurs in the absence of external force. An external force that acts on the system causes forced vibrations. In this case, the exciting force continuously supplies energy to the system. Forced vibrations may be either deterministic or random (see Fig. 8.1a). *Self-excited vibrations* are periodic and deterministic oscillations. Under certain conditions, the equilibrium state in such a vibration system becomes unstable, and any disturbance causes the perturbations to grow until some effect limits any further growth. In contrast to forced vibrations, the exciting force is independent of the vibrations and can still persist even when the system is prevented from vibrating.

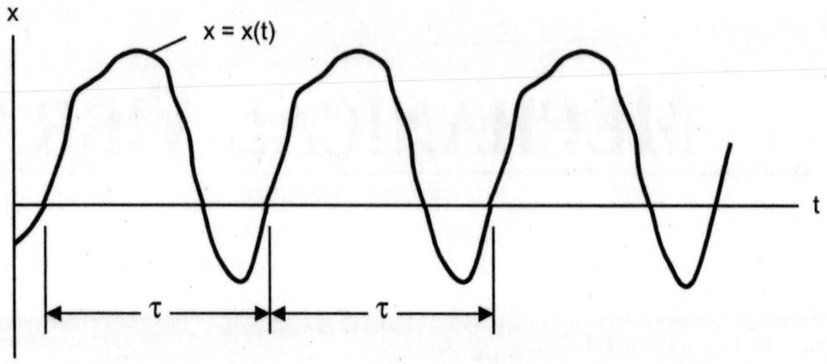

Fig. 8.1(a) A deterministic (periodic) excitation

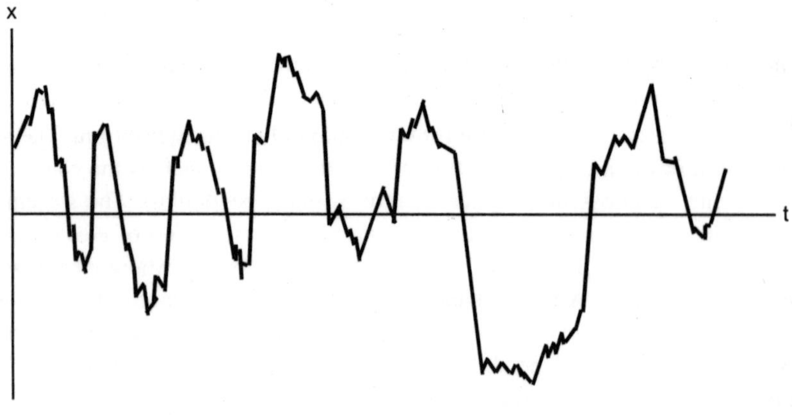

Fig. 8.1(b) Random excitation

8.3 ELEMENTARY PARTS OF VIBRATING SYSTEMS

In general, a vibrating system consists of a spring (a means for storing potential energy), a mass or inertia (a means for storing kinetic energy), and a damper (a means by which energy is gradually lost) as shown in Fig. 8.2. An undamped vibrating system involves the transfer of its potential energy to kinetic energy and kinetic energy to potential energy, alternatively. In a damped vibrating system, some energy is dissipated in each cycle of vibration and should be replaced by an external source if a steady state of vibration is to be maintained.

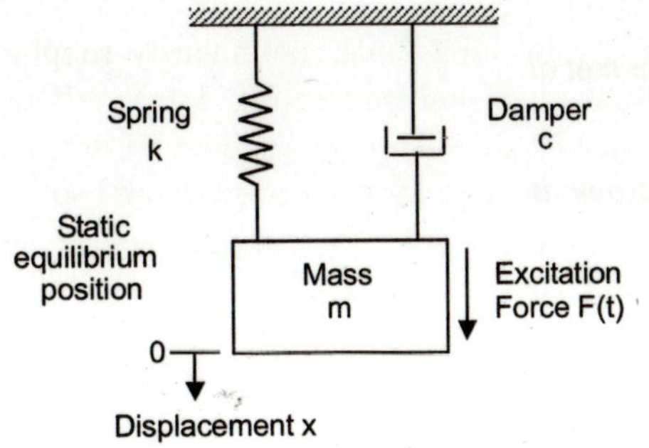

Fig. 8.2 Elementary parts of vibrating systems

PERIODIC MOTION

When the motion is repeated in equal intervals of time, it is known as *periodic motion.* Simple harmonic motion is the simplest form of periodic motion. If $x(t)$ represents the displacement of a mass in a vibratory system, the motion can be expressed by the equation

$$x = A\cos\omega t = A\cos 2\pi\frac{t}{\tau}$$

where A is the amplitude of oscillation measured from the equilibrium position of the mass. The repetition time τ is called the *period of the oscillation*, and its reciprocal, $f = \frac{1}{\tau}$, is called the *frequency.* Any periodic motion satisfies the relationship

$$x(t) = x(t+\tau)$$

i.e., Period $\tau = \frac{2\pi}{\omega}$ s/cycle

Frequency $f = \frac{1}{t} = \frac{\omega}{2\pi}$ cycles/s or Hz

ω is called the *circular frequency* measured in rad/sec.

The velocity and acceleration of a harmonic displacement are also harmonic of the same frequency, but lead the displacement by $\pi/2$ and π radians, respectively. When the acceleration $\ddot{x}$ of a particle with rectilinear motion is always proportional to its displacement from a fixed point on the path and is directed towards the fixed point, the particle is said to have *simple harmonic motion.*

The motion of many vibrating systems in general is not harmonic. In many cases the vibrations are periodic as in the impact force generated by a forging hammer. If $x(t)$ is a periodic function with period τ, its Fourier series representation is given by

$$x(t) = \frac{a_0}{2} + \sum_{n=1}^{\infty}(a_n\cos n\omega t + b_n\sin n\omega t)$$

where $\omega = 2\pi/\tau$ is the fundamental frequency and $a_0, a_1, a_2, \ldots, b_1, b_2, \ldots$ are constant coefficients, which are given by:

$$a_0 = \frac{2}{\tau}\int_0^{\tau} x(t)\,dt$$

$$a_n = \frac{2}{\tau}\int_0^{\tau} x(t)\cos n\omega t\, dt$$

$$b_n = \frac{2}{\tau}\int_0^{\tau} x(t)\sin n\omega t\, dt$$

The exponential form of $x(t)$ is given by:

$$x(t) = \sum_{n=-\infty}^{\infty} c_n e^{in\omega t}$$

The Fourier coefficients c_n can be determined, using

$$c_n = \frac{1}{\tau}\int_0^{\tau} x(t)\, e^{-in\omega t} dt$$

The harmonic functions a_n cos $n\omega t$ or b_n sin $n\omega t$ are known as the *harmonics of order n* of the periodic function $x(t)$. The harmonic of order n has a period τ/n. These harmonics can be plotted as vertical lines in a diagram of amplitude (a_n and b_n) versus frequency ($n\omega$) and is called *frequency spectrum*.

8.4 DISCRETE AND CONTINUOUS SYSTEMS

Most of the mechanical and structural systems can be described using a finite number of degrees of freedom. However, there are some systems, especially those include continuous elastic members, have an infinite number of degree of freedom. Most mechanical and structural systems have elastic (deformable) elements or components as members and hence have an infinite number of degrees of freedom. Systems which have a finite number of degrees of freedom are known as *discrete* or *lumped parameter systems*, and those systems with an infinite number of degrees of freedom are called *continuous* or *distributed systems*.

8.5 VIBRATION ANALYSIS

The outputs of a vibrating system, in general, depend upon the initial conditions and external excitations. The vibration analysis of a physical system may be summarized by the following steps:

1. Mathematical Modeling of a Physical System
2. Formulation of Governing Equations
3. Mathematical Solution of the Governing Equations
4. Physical Interpretation of the Results

1. Mathematical Modeling of a Physical System

The purpose of the mathematical modeling is to determine the existence and nature of the system, its features and aspects, and the physical elements or components involved in the physical system. Necessary assumptions are made to simplify the modeling. Implicit assumptions are used that include:

(*a*) A physical system can be treated as a continuous piece of matter

(*b*) Newton's laws of motion can be applied by assuming that the earth is an internal frame

(*c*) Ignore or neglect the relativistic effects

All components or elements of the physical system are linear. The resulting mathematical model may be linear or non-linear, depending on the given physical system. Generally speaking, all physical systems exhibit non-linear behaviour. Accurate mathematical modeling of any physical system will lead to non-linear differential equations governing the behaviour of the system. Often, these non-linear differential equations have either no solution or difficult to find a solution. Assumptions are made to linearise a system, which permits quick solutions for practical purposes. The advantages of linear models are the following:

(1) their response is proportional to input

(2) superposition is applicable

(3) they closely approximate the behaviour of many dynamic systems,

(4) their response characteristics can be obtained from the form of system equations without a detailed solution

(5) a closed-form solution is often possible

(6) numerical analysis techniques are well developed, and

(7) they serve as a basis for understanding more complex non-linear system behaviours.

It should, however, be noted that in most non-linear problems it is not possible to obtain closed-form analytic solutions for the equations of motion. Therefore, a computer simulation is often used for the response analysis.

When analysing the results obtained from the mathematical model, one should realize that the mathematical model is only an approximation to the true or real physical system and therefore the actual behaviour of the system may be different.

2. Formulation of Governing Equations

Once the mathematical model is developed, we can apply the basic laws of nature and the principles of dynamics and obtain the differential equations that govern the behaviour of the system. A basic law of nature is a physical law that is applicable to all physical systems irrespective of the material from which the system is constructed. Different materials behave differently under different operating conditions. Constitutive equations provide information about the materials of which a system is made. Application of geometric constraints such as the kinematic relationship between displacement, velocity and acceleration is often necessary to complete the mathematical modeling of the physical system. The application of geometric constraints is necessary in order to formulate the required boundary and/or initial conditions.

The resulting mathematical model may be linear or non-linear, depending upon the behaviour of the elements or components of the dynamic system.

3. Mathematical Solution of the Governing Equations

The mathematical modeling of a physical vibrating system results in the formulation of the governing equations of motion. Mathematical modeling of typical systems leads to a system of differential equations of motion. The governing equations of motion of a system are solved to find the response of the system. There are many techniques available for finding the solution, namely, the standard methods for the solution of ordinary differential equations, Laplace transformation methods, matrix methods and numerical methods. In general, exact analytical solutions are available for many linear dynamic systems, but for only a few non-linear systems. Of course, exact analytical solutions are always preferable to numerical or approximate solutions.

4. Physical Interpretation of the Results

The solution of the governing equations of motion for the physical system generally gives the performance. To verify the validity of the model, the predicted performance is compared with the experimental results. The model may have to be refined or a new model is developed and a new prediction compared with the experimental results. Physical interpretation of the results is an important and final step in the analysis procedure. In some situations, this may involve (*a*) drawing general inferences from the mathematical solution, (*b*) development of design curves, (*c*) arrive at a simple arithmetic to arrive at a conclusion (for a typical or specific problem), and (*d*) recommendations regarding the significance of the results and any changes (if any) required or desirable in the system involved.

8.6 COMPONENTS OF VIBRATING SYSTEMS

(a) Stiffness elements

Sometimes, it requires finding out the equivalent spring stiffness values when a continuous system is attached to a discrete system or when there are a number of spring elements in the system. Stiffness of continuous elastic elements such as rods, beams and shafts, which produce restoring elastic forces, is obtained from deflection considerations.

The stiffness coefficient of the rod (Fig. 8.3) is given by $k = \frac{EA}{l}$

The cantilever beam (Fig. 8.4) stiffness is $k = \frac{3EI}{l^3}$

The torsional stiffness of the shaft (Fig. 8.5) is $K = \frac{GJ}{l}$

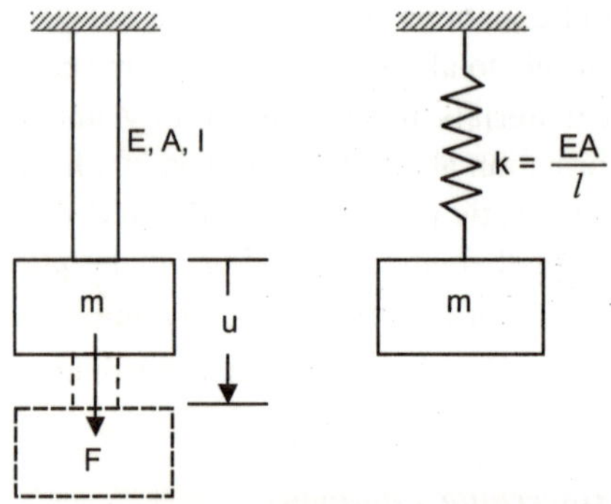

Fig. 8.3 Longitudinal vibration of rods

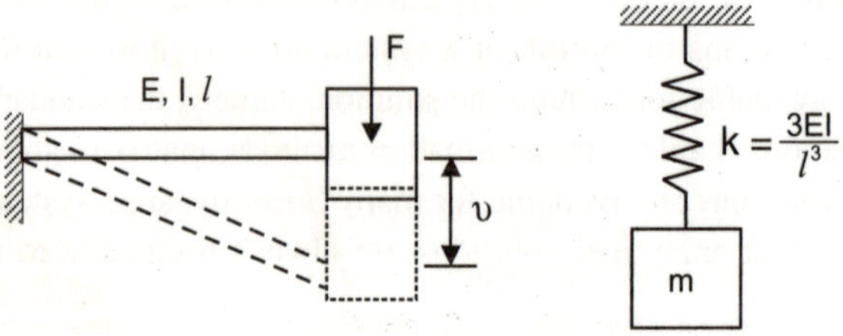

Fig. 8.4 Transverse vibration of cantilever beams

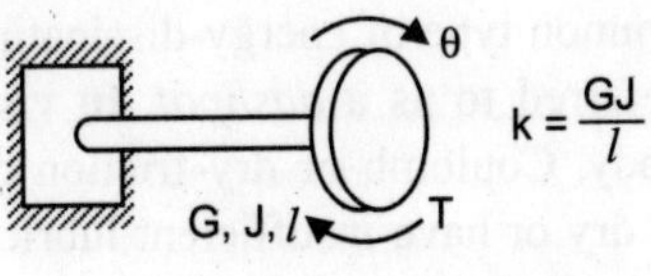

Fig. 8.5 Torsional system

When there are several springs arranged in parallel as shown in Fig. 8.6, the equivalent spring constant is given by algebraic sum of the stiffness of individual springs. Mathematically,

$$k_{eq} = \sum_{i=1}^{n} k_i$$

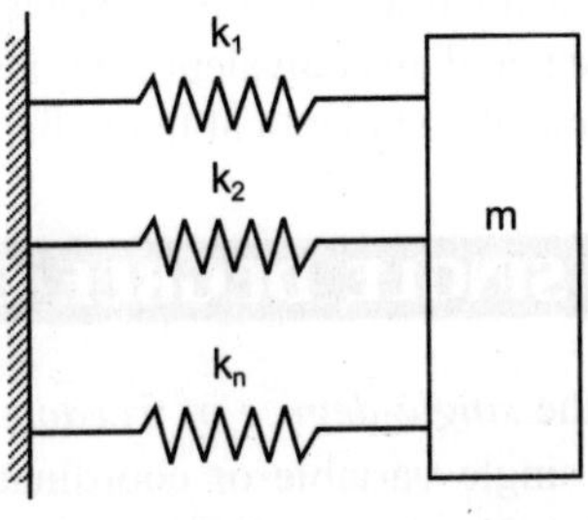

Fig. 8.6 Springs in parallel

When the springs are arranged in series as shown in Fig. 8.7, the same force is developed in each spring and is equal to the force acting on the mass.

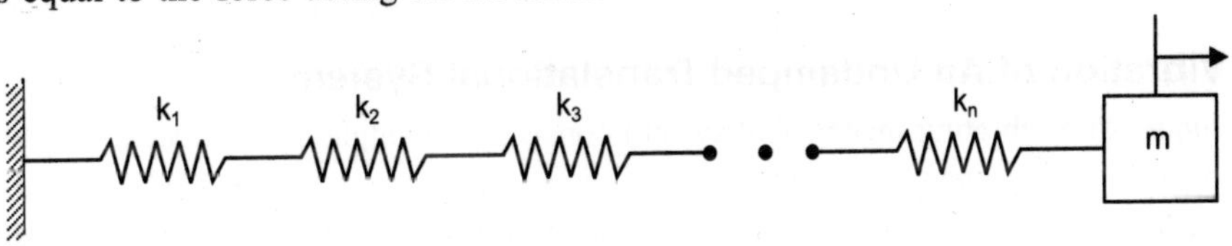

Fig. 8.7 Springs in series

The equivalent stiffness k_{eq} is given by:

$$1/k_{eq} = \frac{1}{\sum_{i=1}^{n} \frac{1}{k_i}}$$

Hence, when elastic elements are in series, the reciprocal of the equivalent elastic constant is equal to the reciprocals of the elastic constants of the elements in the original system.

(b) Mass or Inertia elements

The mass or inertia element is assumed to be a rigid body. Once the mathematical model of the physical vibrating system is developed, the mass or inertia elements of the system can be easily identified.

(c) Damping elements

In real mechanical systems, there is always energy dissipation in one form or another. The process of energy dissipation is referred to in the study of vibration as *damping*. A damper is considered to have neither mass nor elasticity. The three main forms of damping are *viscous damping,Coulomb* or *dry-friction damping* and *hysteresis damping*. The most common type of energy-dissipating element used in vibrations study is the *viscous damper*, which is also referred to as a *dashpot*. In viscous damping, the damping force is proportional to the velocity of the body. Coulomb or dry-friction damping occurs when sliding contact exists between surfaces in contact are dry or have insufficient lubrication. In this case, the damping force is constant in magnitude but opposite in direction to that of the motion. In dry-friction damping energy is dissipated as heat.

Solid materials are not perfectly elastic and when they are deformed, energy is absorbed and dissipated by the material. The effect is due to the internal friction due to the relative motion between the internal planes of the material during the deformation process. Such materials are known as viscoelastic solids and the type of damping which they exhibit is called as *structural* or *hysteretic damping*, or *material* or *solid damping*.

In many practical applications, several dashpots are used in combination. It is quite possible to replace these combinations of dashpots by a single dashpot of an equivalent damping coefficient so that the behaviour of the system with the equivalent dashpot is considered identical to the behaviour of the actual system.

8.7 FREE VIBRATION OF SINGLE DEGREE OF FREEDOM SYSTEMS

The most basic mechanical system is the *single-degree of freedom system*, which is characterized by the fact that its motion is described by a single variable or coordinates. Such a model is often used as an approximation for a generally more complex system. Excitations can be broadly divided into two types, initial excitations and externally applied forces. The behaviour of a system characterized by the motion caused by these excitations is called as the *system response*. The motion is generally described by displacements.

8.7.1 Free Vibration of An Undamped Translational System

The simplest model of a vibrating mechanical system consists of a single mass element which is connected to a rigid support through a linearly elastic massless spring as shown in Fig. 8.8. The mass is constrained to move only in the vertical direction. The motion of the system is described by a single coordinate $x(t)$ and hence it has one degree of freedom (DOF).

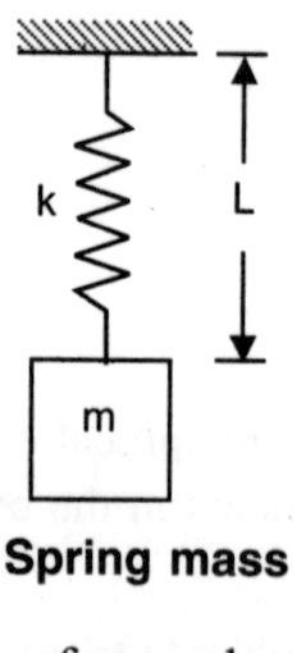

Fig. 8.8 Spring mass system

The equation of motion for the free vibration of an undamped single degree of freedom system can be rewritten as

$$m\ddot{x}(t) + k\,x(t) = 0$$

Dividing through by m, the equation can be written in the form

$$\ddot{x}(t) + \omega_n^2\,x(t) = 0$$

in which $\omega_n = \sqrt{k/m}$ is a real constant. The solution of this equation is obtained from the initial conditions

$$x(0) = x_0, \dot{x}(0) = \upsilon_0$$

where x_0 and υ_0 are the initial displacement and initial velocity, respectively.

The general solution can be written as

$$x(t) = A_1 e^{i\omega_n t} + A_2 e^{-i\omega_n t}$$

in which A_1 and A_2 are constants of integration, both complex quantities. It can be finally simplified as:

$$x(t) = \frac{X}{2}\left[e^{i(\omega_n t - \phi)} + e^{-i(\omega_n t - \phi)}\right] = X \cos(\omega_n t - \phi)$$

so that now the constants of integration are X and ϕ.

This equation represents harmonic oscillation, for which reason such a system is called a *harmonic oscillator*. There are three quantities defining the response, the *amplitude* X, the *phase angle* ϕ and the *frequency* ω_n, the first two depending on external factors, namely, the initial excitations, and the third depending on internal factors, namely, the system parameters. On the other hand, for a given system, the frequency of the response is a characteristic of the system that stays always the same, independently of the initial excitations. For this reason, ω_n is called the *natural frequency* of the harmonic oscillator.

The constants X and ϕ are obtained from the initial conditions of the system as follows:

$$X = \sqrt{x_0^2 + \left(\frac{\upsilon_0}{\omega_n}\right)^2}$$

and
$$\phi = \tan^{-1}\left[\frac{\upsilon_0}{x_0\omega_n}\right]$$

The *time period* τ, is defined as the time necessary for the system to complete one vibration cycle, or as the time between two consecutive peaks. It is related to the natural frequency by

$$\tau = \frac{2\pi}{\omega_n} = 2\pi\sqrt{\frac{m}{k}}$$

Note that the natural frequency can also be defined as the reciprocal of the period, or

$$f_n = \frac{1}{\tau} = \frac{1}{2\pi}\sqrt{\frac{k}{m}}$$

in which case it has units of cycles per second (cps), where one cycle per second is known as one Hertz (Hz).

8.7.2 Free Vibration of An Undamped Torsional System

A mass attached to the end of the shaft is a simple torsional system (Fig. 8.9). The mass of the shaft is considered to be small in comparison to the mass of the disk and is therefore neglected.

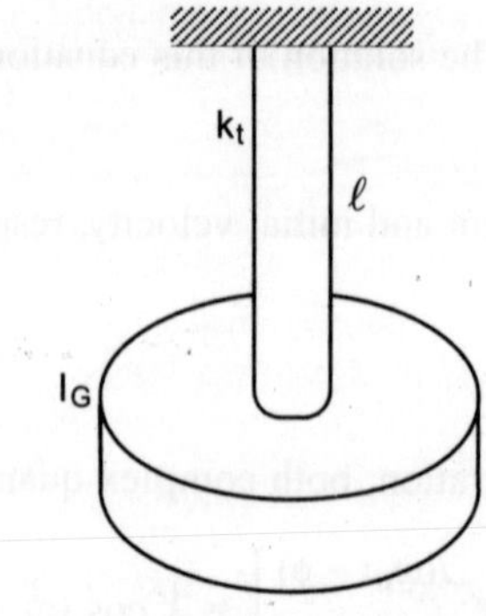

Fig. 8.9 Torsional system

The torque that produces the twist M_t is given by

$$M_t = \frac{GJ}{\ell}$$

where J = the polar mass moment of inertia of the shaft ($J = \frac{\pi d^4}{32}$ for a circular shaft of diameter d)

G = shear modulus of the material of the shaft.

ℓ = length of the shaft.

The torsional spring constant k_t is defined as

$$k_t = \frac{T}{\theta} = \frac{GJ}{\ell}$$

The equation of motion of the system can be written as:

$$I_G\ddot{\theta} + k_t\theta = 0$$

The natural circular frequency of such a torsional system is $\omega_n = \left(\frac{k_t}{I_G}\right)^{1/2}$

The general solution of equation of motion is given by

$$\theta(t) = \theta_0 \cos\omega_n t + \frac{\dot{\theta}_0}{\omega_n}\sin\omega_n t\,.$$

8.7.3 Energy Method

Free vibration of systems involves the cyclic interchange of kinetic and potential energy. In undamped free vibrating systems, no energy is dissipated or removed from the system. The kinetic energy T is stored in the mass by virtue of its velocity and the potential energy U is stored in the form of strain energy in elastic deformation. Since the total energy in the system is constant, the principle of conservation of mechanical energy applies. Since the mechanical energy is conserved, the sum of the kinetic energy and potential energy is constant and its rate of change is zero. This principle can be expressed as

$$T + U = \text{constant}$$

or

$$\frac{d}{dt}(T + U) = 0$$

where T and U denote the kinetic and potential energy, respectively. The principle of conservation of energy can be restated by

$$T_1 + U_1 = T_2 + U_2$$

where the subscripts 1 and 2 denote two different instances of time when the mass is passing through its static equilibrium position and select $U_1 = 0$ as reference for the potential energy. Subscript 2 indicates the time corresponding to the maximum displacement of the mass at this position, we have then

$$T_2 = 0$$

and $$T_1 + 0 = 0 + U_2$$

If the system is undergoing harmonic motion, then T_1 and U_2 denote the maximum values of T and U, respectively and therefore last equation becomes

$$T_{max} = U_{max}$$

It is quite useful in calculating the natural frequency directly.

8.7.4 Stability of Undamped Linear Systems

The mass/inertia and stiffness parameters have an affect on the stability of an undamped single degree of freedom vibratory system. The mass and stiffness coefficients enter into the characteristic equation which defines the response of the system. Hence, any changes in these coefficients will lead to changes in the system behaviour or response. In this section, the effects of the system inertia and stiffness parameters on the stability of the motion of an undamped single degree of freedom system are examined. It can be shown that by a proper selection of the inertia and stiffness coefficients, the instability of the motion of the system can be avoided. A stable system is one which executes bounded oscillations about the equilibrium position.

8.7.5 Free Vibration with Viscous Damping

Viscous damping force is proportional to the velocity $\dot{x}$ of the mass and acting in the direction opposite to the velocity of the mass and can be expressed as

$$F = c\dot{x}$$

where c is the damping constant or coefficient of viscous damping. The differential equation of motion for free vibration of a damped spring-mass system (Fig. 8.10) is written as:

$$\ddot{x} + \frac{c}{m}\dot{x} + \frac{k}{m}x = 0$$

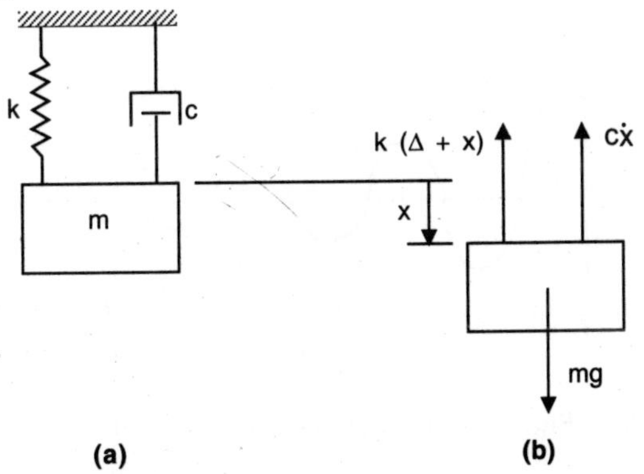

Fig. 8.10 Damped spring-mass system

By assuming $x(t) = Ce^{st}$ as the solution, the auxiliary equation obtained is

$$s^2 + \frac{c}{m}s + \frac{k}{m} = 0$$

which has the roots

$$s_{1,2} = -\frac{c}{2m} \pm \sqrt{\left(\frac{c}{2m}\right)^2 - \frac{k}{m}}$$

The solution takes one of three forms, depending on whether the quantity $(c/2m)^2 - k/m$ is zero, positive or negative. If this quantity is zero,

$$c = 2m\omega_n$$

This results in repeated roots $s_1 = s_2 = -c/2m$, and the solution is

$$x(t) = (A + Bt)e^{-(c/2m)t}$$

As the case in which repeated roots occur has special significance, we shall refer to the corresponding value of the damping constant as the *critical damping constant*, denoted by $C_c = 2m\omega_n$. The roots can be written as:

$$s_{1,2} = (-\zeta \pm \sqrt{\zeta^2 - 1})\omega_n$$

where $\omega_n = (k/m)^{1/2}$ is the circular frequency of the corresponding undamped system, and

$$\zeta = \frac{c}{C_c} = \frac{c}{2m\omega_n}$$

is known as the *damping factor*.

If $\zeta < 1$, the roots are both imaginary and the solution for the motion is

$$x(t) = Xe^{-\zeta\omega_n t}\sin(\omega_d t + \phi)$$

where $\quad \omega_d = \sqrt{1-\zeta^2}\,\omega_n$

is called the damped circular frequency which is always less than ω, and ϕ is the phase angle of the damped oscillations. The general form of the motion is shown in Fig. 8.11. For motion of this type, the system is said to be *underdamped*.

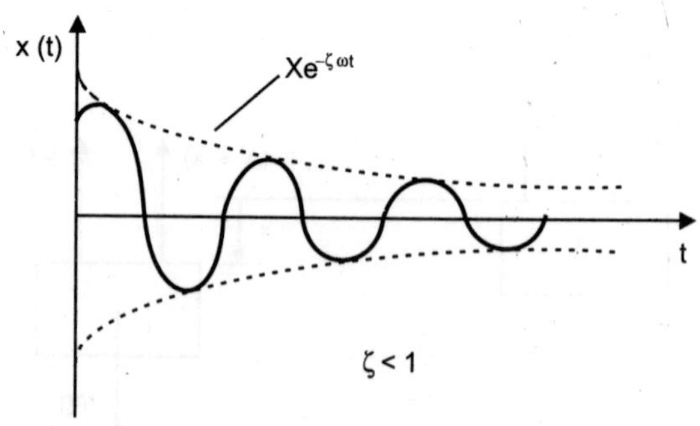

Fig. 8.11 The general form of motion

If $\zeta = 1$, the damping constant is equal to the critical damping constant, and the system is said to be *critically damped*. The displacement is given by

$$x(t) = (A + Bt)\, e^{-\omega_n t}$$

The solution is the product of a linear function of time and a decaying exponential. Depending on the values of A and B, many forms of motion are possible, but each form is characterized by amplitude which decays without oscillations, such as is shown in Fig. 8.12.

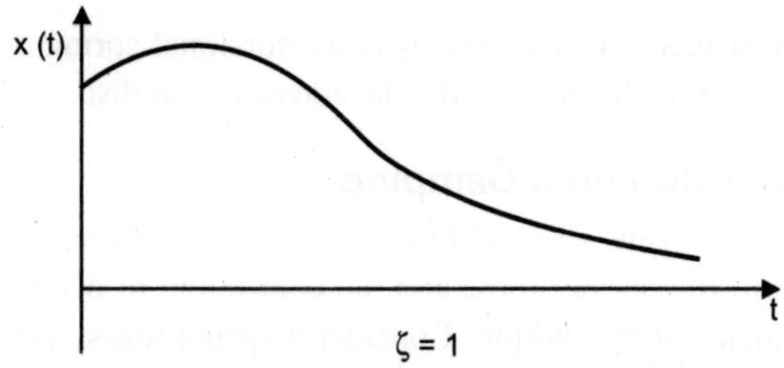

Fig. 8.12 Amplitude decaying without oscillations

In this case $\zeta > 1$, and the system is said to be *overdamped*. The solution is given by:

$$x(t) = C_1\, e^{(-\zeta+\sqrt{\zeta^2-1})\omega_n t} + C_2\, e^{(-\zeta-\sqrt{\zeta^2-1})\omega_n t}$$

The motion will be non-oscillatory and will be similar to that shown in Fig. 8.13.

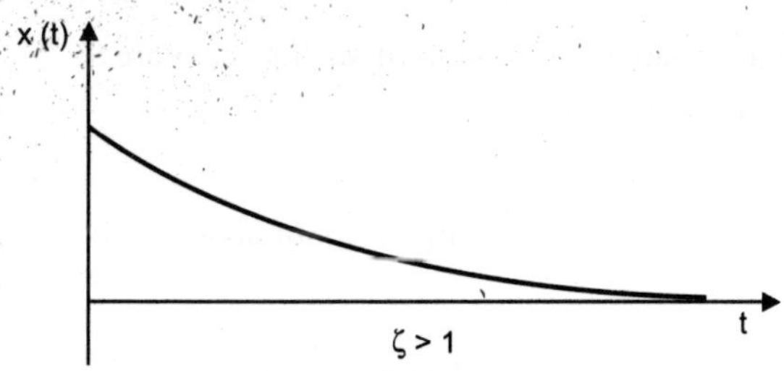

Fig. 8.13 Non-oscillatory motion

8.7.6 Logarithmic Decrement

The logarithmic decrement represents the rate at which the amplitude of a free damped vibration decreases. It is defined as the natural logarithm of the ratio of any two successive amplitudes.

The ratio of successive amplitudes is

$$\frac{x_i}{x_{i+1}} = \frac{Xe^{-\zeta\omega_n t_i}}{Xe^{-\zeta\omega_n (t_i+\tau_d)}} = e^{\zeta\omega_n \tau_d} = \text{constant}$$

The logarithmic decrement

$$\delta = \ln \frac{x_i}{x_{i+1}} = \ln e^{\zeta\omega_n \tau_d} = \zeta\omega_{n\tau d}$$

Substituting $\tau_d = 2\pi/\omega_d = 2\pi/\omega_n\sqrt{1-\zeta^2}$ gives

$$\delta = \frac{2\pi\zeta}{\sqrt{1-\zeta^2}}$$

8.7.7 Torsional System with Viscous Damping

The equation of motion for such a system can be written as

$$I\ddot{\theta} + c_t\dot{\theta} + k_t\theta = 0$$

where I is the mass moment of inertia of the disc, k_t is the torsional spring constant (restoring torque for unit angular displacement), and θ is the angular displacement of the disc.

8.7.8 Free Vibration with Coulomb Damping

Coulomb or dry-friction damping results when sliding contact exists between two dry surfaces. The damping force is equal to the product of the normal force and the coefficient of dry friction. The damping force is quite independent of the velocity of the motion. Consider a spring-mass system in which the mass slides on a horizontal surface having coefficient of friction *f*, as in Fig. 8.14.

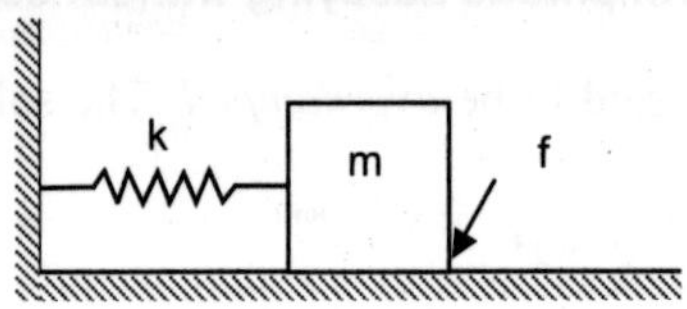

Fig. 8.14 Free vibration with coulomb damping

The corresponding differential equations of motion of such system are

$$m\ddot{x} = -kx - F_d \quad \text{if } \dot{x} > 0$$

$$m\ddot{x} = -kx + F_d \quad \text{if } \dot{x} < 0$$

These differential equations and their solutions are discontinuous at the end points of their motion.

The general solution is then

$$x = A\sin\omega t + B\cos\omega t + \frac{F_d}{k} \quad (\dot{x} < 0)$$

for motion toward the left. For the initial conditions of $x = x_0$ and $\dot{x} = 0$ at $t = 0$ for the extreme position at the right, the solution becomes

$$x = \left(x_0 - \frac{F_d}{k}\right)\cos\omega t + \frac{F_d}{k} \quad (\dot{x} < 0)$$

This holds for motion toward the left, or until $\dot{x}$ again becomes zero.

Hence, the displacement is negative, or to the left of the neutral position, and has a magnitude $2F_d/k$ less than the initial displacement x_0.

A constant amplitude loss of $4F_d/k$ occurs for each cycle of motion as shown in Fig. 8.15. The motion is a linearly decaying harmonic function of time, consisting of one-half sine wave parts which are offset successively up or down by F_d/k depending on whether the motion is to the left or to the right.

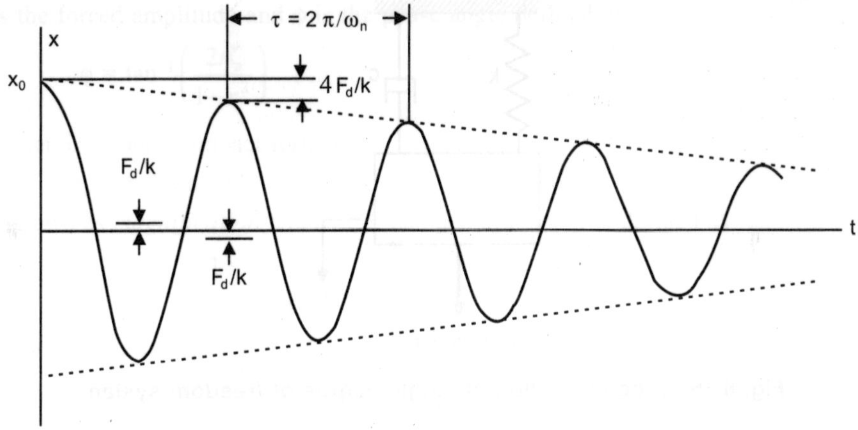

Fig. 8.15 Response of system subjected to Coulomb damping

8.7.9 Free Vibration with Hysteretic Damping

In general, solid materials are not perfectly elastic solid materials, in particular, metals exhibit what is commonly referred to as *hysteretic* or *structural damping*. The hysteresis effect is due to the friction between internal planes which slip or slide as the deformations takes place. The enclosed area in the hysteresis loop is the energy loss per loading cycle. The energy loss ΔU can then be written as

$$\Delta U = \pi\beta\, kX^2$$

where β is a dimensionless *structural damping coefficient*, k is the equivalent spring constant, X is the displacement amplitude, and the factor π is included for convenience. The energy loss is a non-linear function of the displacement.

The equivalent viscous damping constant is given by

$$c_e = \frac{\beta k}{\omega} = \beta\sqrt{mk}.$$

8.8 FORCED VIBRATION OF SINGLE-DEGREE OF FREEDOM SYSTEMS

A mechanical or structural system is often subjected to an external forces or external excitations. The external forces may be harmonic, non-harmonic but periodic, non-periodic but having a defined form or random. The response of the system to such excitations or forces is called *forced response*. The response of a system to a harmonic excitation is called *harmonic response*. The non-periodic excitations may have a long or short duration. The response of a system to suddenly applied non-periodic excitations is called *transient response*. The sources of harmonic excitations are unbalanced in rotating machines, forces generated by reciprocating machines, and the motion of the machine itself in certain cases.

8.8.1 Forced Vibrations of Damped System

Consider a viscously damped single degree of freedom spring mass system shown in Fig. 8.16, subjected to a harmonic function $F(t) = F_0 \sin \omega t$, where F_0 is the force amplitude and ω is the circular frequency of the forcing function.

In the undamped systems, the particular solution is reduced to

$$x_p(t) = \frac{\frac{F_0}{k}}{\left[1-\left(\frac{\omega}{\omega_n}\right)^2\right]} \sin \omega t$$

The maximum amplitude can also be expressed as

$$\frac{X}{\delta_{st}} = \frac{1}{1-\left(\frac{\omega}{\omega_n}\right)^2}$$

where $\delta_{st} = F_0/k$ denotes the static deflection of the mass under a force F_0 and is sometimes known as *static deflection* since F_0 is a constant static force. The quantity X/δ_{st} represents the ratio of the dynamic to the static amplitude of motion and is called the *magnification factor, amplification factor*, or *amplitude ratio.*

8.8.2 Resonance

The case $r = \frac{\omega}{\omega_n} = 1$, that is when the circular frequency of the forcing function is equal to the circular frequency of the spring-mass system is referred to as *resonance.* In this case, the displacement $x(t)$ goes to infinity for any value of time t.

The amplitude of the forced response grows with time as in Fig. 8.19 and will eventually become infinite at which point the spring in the mass-spring system fails in an undesirable manner.

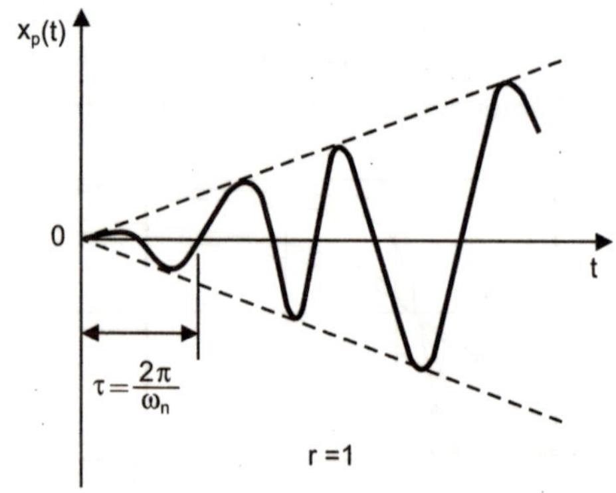

Fig. 8.19 Resonance response

8.8.3 Beats

The phenomenon of *beating* occurs for an undamped forced single degree of freedom spring-mass system when the forcing frequency ω is close, but not equal, to the system circular frequency ω_n. In this case, the amplitude builds up and then diminishes in a regular pattern. The phenomenon of beating can be noticed in cases of audio or sound vibration and in electric power generation when a generator is started.

8.8.4 Transmissibility

The forces associated with the vibrations of a machine or a structure will be transmitted to its support structure. These transmitted forces in most instances produce undesirable effects such as noise. Machines and structures are generally mounted on designed flexible supports known as *vibration isolators* or *isolators*. In general, the amplitude of vibration reduces with the increasing values of the spring stiffness k and the damping coefficient c. In order to reduce the force transmitted to the support structure, a proper selection of the stiffness and damping coefficients must be made.

From regular spring-mass-damper model, force transmitted to the support can be written as

$$F_T = k\, x_p + c\,\dot{x}_p = X_0\beta\sqrt{k^2 + (c\omega)^2}\,\sin(\omega t - \bar{\phi})$$

where $\bar{\phi} = \phi - \phi_t$

and ϕ_t is the phase angle defined as

$$\phi_t = \tan^{-1}\left(\frac{c\omega}{k}\right) = \tan^{-1}(2r\zeta)$$

Transmitted force can also be written as:

$$F_T = F_0\beta_t\,\sin(\omega t - \bar{\phi})$$

where $$\beta_t = \frac{\sqrt{1+(2r\zeta)^2}}{\sqrt{(1-r^2)^2+(2r\zeta)^2}}$$

The *transmissibility* β_t is defined as the ratio of the maximum transmitted force to the amplitude of the applied force. Figure 8.20 shows a plot of β_t versus the frequency ratio r for different values of the damping factor ζ.

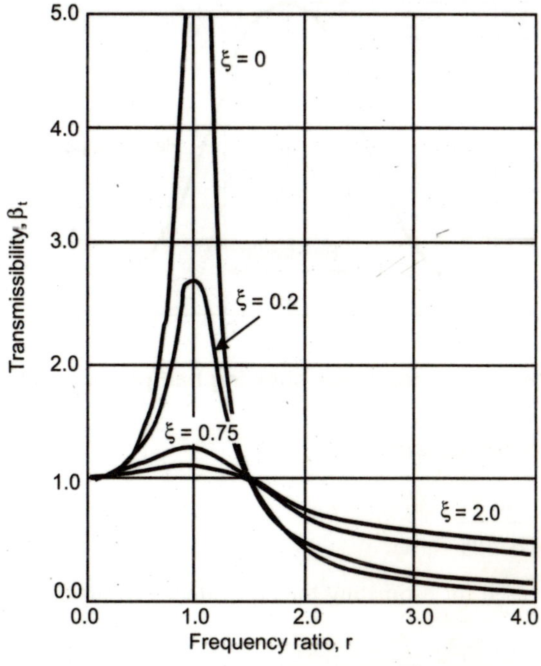

Fig. 8.20 Non-dimensional force transmitted *vs* frequency ratio

It can be observed from Fig. 8.20, that $\beta > 1$ for $r < \sqrt{2}$ which means that in this region the amplitude of the transmitted force is greater than the amplitude of the applied force. Also, the $r < \sqrt{2}$, the transmitted force to the support can be reduced by increasing the damping factor ζ. For $r = \sqrt{2}$, every curve passes through the point $\beta_t = 1$ and becomes asymptotic to zero as the frequency ratio is increased. Similarly, for $r > \sqrt{2}$, $\beta_t < 1$, hence, in this region the amplitude of the transmitted force is less than the amplitude of the applied force. Therefore, the amplitude of the transmitted force increases by increasing the damping factor ζ. Thus, vibration isolation is best accomplished by an isolator composed only of spring-elements for which $r > \sqrt{2}$ with no damping element used in the system.

8.8.5 Quality Factor and Bandwidth

The value of the amplitude ratio at resonance is also known as the *Q-factor* or *Quality factor* of the system in analogy with the term used in electrical engineering applications. That is,

$$Q = \frac{1}{2\zeta}$$

The points R_1 and R_2, whereby the amplification factor falls to $Q/\sqrt{2}$, are known as *half power points*, since the power absorbed by the damper responding harmonically at a given forcing frequency is given by

$$\Delta W = \pi c \omega X^2$$

The *bandwidth* of the system is defined as the difference between the frequencies associated with the half power points R_1 and R_2 as depicted in Fig. 8.21.

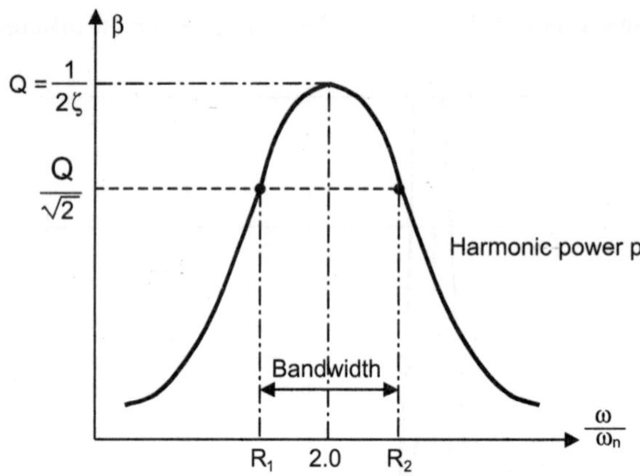

Fig. 8.21 Harmonic response curve showing half power points and bandwidth

It can be shown that Q-factor can be written as:

$$Q = \frac{1}{2\zeta} = \frac{\omega_n}{\omega_2 - \omega_1}$$

The quality factor Q can be used for estimating the equivalent viscous damping in a vibrating system.

8.8.6 Rotating Unbalance

Unbalance in many rotating mechanical systems is a common source of vibration excitation which may often lead to unbalance forces. If M is the total mass of the machine including an eccentric mass m rotating with an angular velocity ω at an eccentricity e, it can be shown that the particular solution takes the form:

$$x_p(t) = \left(\frac{me}{M}\right)\beta_r \sin(\omega t - \phi)$$

where β_r is the magnification factor which is given by

$$\beta_r = \frac{r^2}{\sqrt{(1-r^2)^2 + (2r\zeta)^2}}$$

The steady state vibration due to unbalance in rotating component is proportional to the amount of unbalance m and its distance e from the center of the rotation and increases as the square of the rotating speed. The maximum displacement of the system lags the maximum value of the forcing function by the phase angle ϕ.

8.8.7 Base Excitation

In many mechanical systems such as vehicles mounted on a moving support or base, the forced vibration of the system is due to the moving support or base. The motion of the support or base causes the forces being transmitted to the mounted equipment. Figure 8.22 shows a damped single degree of freedom mass-spring system with a moving support or base.

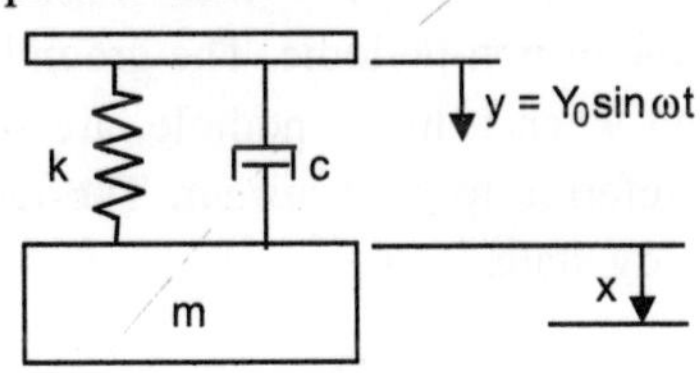

Fig. 8.22 Harmonically excited base

The steady state solution can be written as:

$$x_p(t) = Y_0\beta_b \sin(\omega t - \phi + \phi_b),$$

where phase angle ϕ is given by $\phi = \tan^{-1}\left(\frac{2r\zeta}{1-r^2}\right)$ and β_b is known as the displacement transmissibility given by:

$$\beta_b = \frac{\sqrt{1+(2r\zeta)^2}}{\sqrt{(1-r^2)^2 + (2r\zeta)^2}}$$

The motion of the mass relative to the support denoted by z can be written as

$$z = x - y$$

$$= \frac{Y_0 r^2}{\sqrt{(1-r^2)^2 + (2r\zeta)^2}} \sin(\omega t - \phi)$$

8.8.8 Response under Coulomb Damping

When a single degree of freedom with Coulomb damping subjected to a harmonic forcing conditions, the amplitude relationship is written as:

$$X = \frac{X_0}{\sqrt{(1-r^2)^2 + (4F/\pi X k)^2}}$$

which gives $X = X_0 \dfrac{\sqrt{1-(4F/\pi F_0)^2}}{1-r^2}$

This expression for X has a real value, provided that

$$4F < \pi F_0 \qquad \text{or} \qquad F < \frac{\pi}{4} F_0$$

8.8.9 Response under Hysteresis Damping

The steady-state motion of a single degree of freedom forced harmonically with hysteresis damping is also harmonic. The steady-state amplitude can then be determined by defining an equivalent viscous damping constant based on equating the energies.

The amplitude is given in terms of hysteresis damping coefficient β as follows

$$X = \frac{X_0}{\sqrt{(1-r^2)^2 + \beta^2}}$$

8.8.10 General Forcing Conditions and Response

A general forcing function may be periodic or non-periodic. The ground vibrations of a building structure during an earthquake, the vehicle motion when it hits a pothole, are some examples of general forcing functions. Non-periodic excitations are referred to as *transient*. The term *transient* is used in the sense that non-periodic excitations are not steady state.

8.8.11 Fourier Series and Harmonic Analysis

The Fourier series expression of a given periodic function $F(t)$ with period T can be expressed in terms of harmonic functions as

$$F(t) = \frac{a_0}{2} + \sum_{n=1}^{\infty} a_n \cos n\omega t + \sum_{n=1}^{\infty} b_n \sin n\omega t$$

where $\omega = \dfrac{2\pi}{T}$ and a_0, a_n and b_n are constants.

$F(t)$ can also be written as follows:

$$F(t) = F_0 + \sum_{n=1}^{\infty} F_n \sin(\omega_n t + \phi_n)$$

where $F_0 = a_0/2$, $F_n = \sqrt{a_n^2 + b_n^2}$, with $\omega_n = n\omega$ and $\phi_n = \tan^{-1}\left(\dfrac{a_n}{b_n}\right)$.

8.9 HARMONIC FUNCTIONS

Harmonic functions are periodic functions in which all the Fourier coefficients are zeros except one coefficient.

8.9.1 Even Functions

A periodic function $F(t)$ is said to be even if $F(t) = F(-t)$. A cosine function is an even function since $\cos\theta = \cos(-\theta)$. If the function $F(t)$ is an even function, then the coefficients b_m are all zeros.

8.9.2 Odd Functions

A periodic function $F(t)$ is said to be odd if $F(t) = -F(-t)$. The sine function is an odd function since $\sin\theta = -\sin(-\theta)$. For an odd function, the Fourier coefficients a_0 and a_n are identically zero.

8.9.3 Response under A Periodic Force of Irregular Form

Usually, the values of periodic functions at discrete points in time are available in graphical form or tabulated form. In such cases, no analytical expression can be found or the direct integration of the periodic functions in a closed analytical form may not be practical. In such cases, one can find the Fourier coefficients by using a numerical integration procedure. If one divides the period of the function T into N equal intervals, then length of each such interval is $\Delta t = T/N$.

The coefficients are given by

$$a_0 = \frac{2}{N}\sum_{i=1}^{N} F(t_i)$$

$$a_n = \frac{2}{N}\sum_{i=1}^{N} F(t_i)\cos n\omega t_i$$

$$b_n = \frac{2}{N}\sum_{i=1}^{N} F(t_i)\sin n\omega t_i$$

8.9.4 Response under A General Periodic Force

To find the response of a system under general periodic force consider, a single degree of freedom system shown in Fig. 8.23.

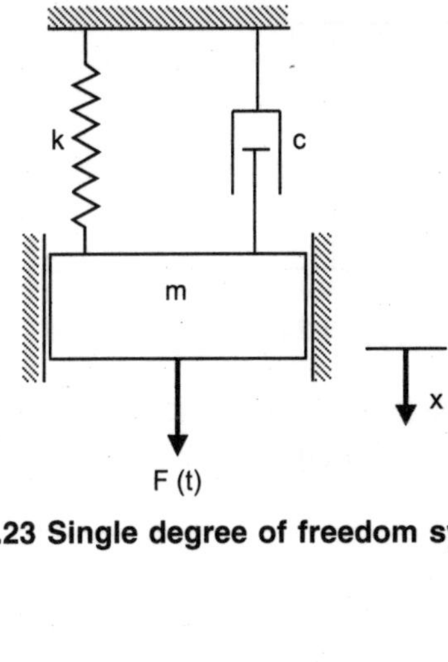

Fig. 8.23 Single degree of freedom system

Let the periodic force F(t) can be expressed in terms of harmonic functions by the use of Fourier series as follows.

$$F(t) = \frac{a_0}{2} + \sum_{n=1}^{\infty} (a_n + \cos n\omega t + b_n \sin n\omega t)$$

Then steady-state solution can be written as

$$x_p(t) = \frac{a_0}{2k} + \sum_{n=1}^{\infty} \frac{a_n / k}{\sqrt{(1-r_n^2)^2 + (2\xi r_n)^2}} \cos(n\omega t - \psi_n)$$

$$+ \sum_{n=1}^{\infty} \frac{b_n / k}{\sqrt{(1-r_n^2)^2 + (2\xi r_n)^2}} \sin(n\omega t - \psi_n)$$

In most cases, the first two or three terms of this series are sufficient to describe the response of the system. If one of the harmonic frequencies $n\omega$ is close to or equal to ω, then $r \approx 1$, and the corresponding amplitude ratio can become large and resonance can occur.

8.9.5 Transient Vibration

When a mechanical or structural system is excited by a suddenly applied non-periodic excitation $F(t)$, the response to such excitation is called *transient response*, as the steady-state oscillations are generally not produced.

8.9.6 Unit Impulse

Impulse is time integral of the force which is finite and is written as

$$\hat{F} = \int F(t)\, dt$$

where $\hat{F}$ is the linear impulse (in pound seconds or newton seconds) of the force.

Figure 8.24 shows an impulsive force of magnitude $F = \hat{F}/\epsilon$ acting at $t = a$ over the time interval ϵ. As ϵ approaches zero, the magnitude of the force becomes infinite but the linear impulse $\hat{F}$ is well defined.

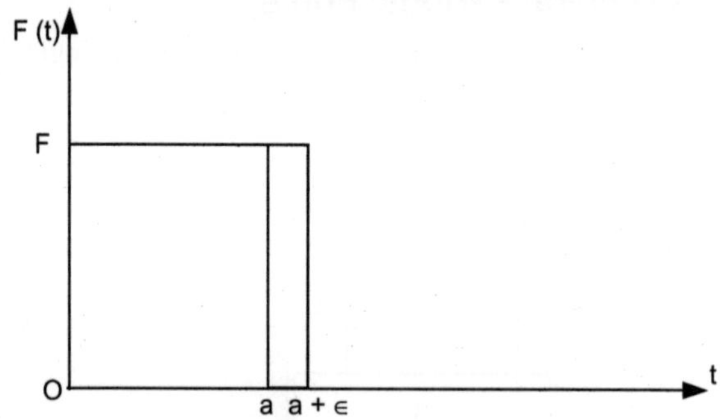

Fig. 8.24 Impulsive force

When $\hat{F}$ is equal to unity, such a force in the limiting case ($\epsilon \to 0$) is called the *unit impulse*, or the *Direct delta function* $\delta(t - a)$, which has the following properties:

$$\delta(t - a) = 0 \quad \text{for } t \neq a$$

$$\int_0^{\infty} \delta(t-a)dt = 1$$

$$\int_0^{\infty} \delta(t-a)\ F(t)\ dt = F(a)$$

where $0 < a < \infty$. By using these properties, an impulsive force $F(t)$ acting at $t = a$ to produce a linear impulsive $\hat{F}$ of arbitrary magnitude can be expressed as

$$F(t) = \hat{F}\ \delta(t-a).$$

8.9.7 Impulsive Response of a System

The response of a damped spring-mass system to an impulsive force is given by

$$x(t) = \hat{F}\ H(t)$$

where $H(t)$ is called the *impulse response function* can be written as

$$H(t) = \frac{1}{m\omega_d}\ e^{-\zeta\omega_n t} \sin \omega_d t, \text{ where } \omega_d \text{ is damped natural frequency}$$

If the force applied at a time $t = \tau$, this can be written as:

$$H(t-\tau) = \frac{1}{m\omega_d}\ e^{-\zeta\omega_n (t-\tau)} \sin \omega_d(t-\tau)$$

8.9.8 Response to an Arbitrary Input

The total response is obtained by finding the integration

$$x(t) = \int_0^t F(\tau)\ H(t-\tau)\ d\tau$$

This is called the Convolution integral or Duhamel's integral and is sometimes referred as the superposition integral.

8.9.9 Laplace Transformation Method

The Laplace transformation method can be used for calculating the response of a system to a variety of force excitations, including periodic and non-periodic. The Laplace transformation method can treat discontinuous functions with no difficulty and it automatically takes into account the initial conditions. The usefulness of the method lies in the availability of tabulated Laplace transform pairs. From the equations of motion of a single degree of freedom system subjected to a general forcing function $F(t)$, the Laplace transform of the solution $x(t)$ is given by:

$$\overline{x}\ (s) = \frac{\overline{F}(s) + (ms + c)x(0) + m\dot{x}(0)}{ms^2 + cs + k}$$

The method of determining $x(t)$ given $\overline{x}\ (s)$ can be considered as an inverse transformation which can be expressed as

$$x(t) = L^{-1}\{\overline{x}\ (s)\}$$

8.10 TWO-DEGREE OF FREEDOM SYSTEMS

Systems that require two independent coordinates to describe their motion are called *two degree of freedom systems.* Some examples of two-degree of freedom models of vibrating systems are shown in Fig. 8.25(*a*) and (*b*).

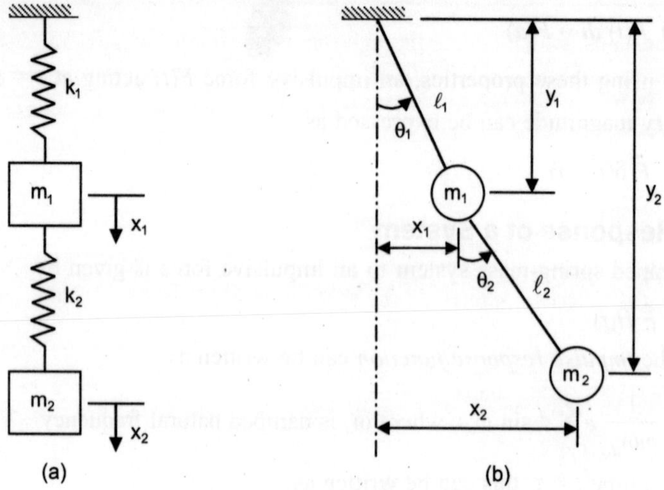

Fig. 8.25 Two-degree of freedom systems

8.10.1 Equations of Motion

Consider the viscously damped two-degree of freedom spring mass system shown in Fig. 8.26.

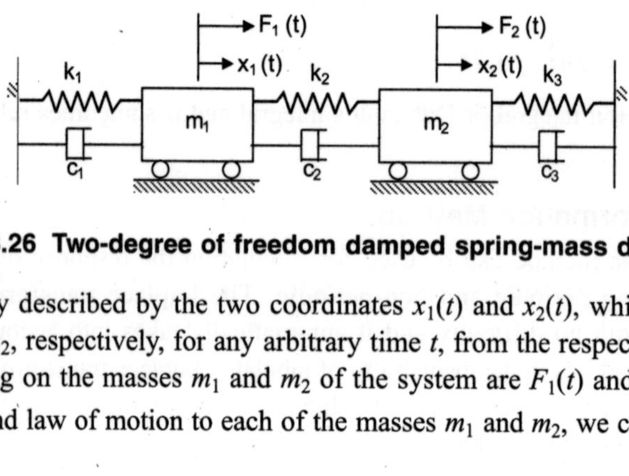

Fig. 8.26 Two-degree of freedom damped spring-mass damper

The system is completely described by the two coordinates $x_1(t)$ and $x_2(t)$, which define the positions of the two masses m_1 and m_2, respectively, for any arbitrary time t, from the respective equilibrium positions. The external forces acting on the masses m_1 and m_2 of the system are $F_1(t)$ and $F_2(t)$ respectively.

Applying Newton's second law of motion to each of the masses m_1 and m_2, we can write the two equations of motion as:

$$m_1 \ddot{x}_1 (t) + (c_1 + c_2) \dot{x}_1 (t) - c_2 \dot{x}_2 (t) + (k_1 + k_2)x_1(t) - k_2x_2(t) = F_1(t)$$

$$m_2 \ddot{x}_2 (t) - c_2 \dot{x}_1 (t) + (c_2 + c_3) \dot{x}_2 (t) - k_2x_1(t) + (k_2 + k_3)x_2(t) = F_2(t)$$

These equations reveal that the motion of m_1 will influence the motion of mass, m_2 and vice versa.

8.10.2 Free Vibration Analysis

Let the free vibration solution of the equations of motion be

$$x_1(t) = X_1 \cos (\omega t + \phi)$$
$$x_2(t) = X_2 \cos (\omega t + \phi)$$

where X_1 and X_2 are constants, which denote the maximum amplitudes of $x_1(t)$ and $x_2(t)$, and ϕ is the phase angle. Substituting these expressions in equations of motion leads to a characteristic determinant

$$\det\begin{bmatrix} \{-m_1\omega^2 + (k_1 + k_2)\} & -k_2 \\ -k_2 & \{m_2\omega^2 + (k_2 + k_3)\} \end{bmatrix}$$ which should be zero for consistency.

or $$(m_1m_2)\omega^4 - \{(k_1 + k_2)\, m_2 + (k_2 + k_3)\, m_1\}\omega^2 + \{(k_1 + k_2)\,(k_2 + k_3) - k_2^2\} = 0$$

This equation is known as the *frequency or characteristic equation.* The solution of this equation yields the frequencies or the characteristic values of the system.

$$\omega_1^2, \omega_2^2 = \frac{1}{2}\left\{\frac{(k_1 + k_2)m_2 + (k_2 + k_3)m_1}{m_1m_2}\right\}$$

$$\mp \frac{1}{2}\left[\left\{\frac{(k_1 + k_2)m_2 + (k_2 + k_3)m_1}{m_1m_2}\right\}\right]^2$$

$$-4\left\{\frac{(k_1 + k_2)(k_2 + k_3) - k_2^2}{m_1m_2}\right\}^{1/2}$$

ω_1 and ω_2 are called the *natural frequencies* of the system.

The values of X_1 and X_2 depend on the natural frequencies ω_1 and $\omega_{1.3.}$ By denoting the values of X_1 and X_2 corresponding to ω_1 as $X_1^{(1)}$ and $X_2^{(1)}$ and those corresponding to ω_2 as $X_1^{(2)}$ and $X_2^{(2)}$:

$$r_1 = \frac{X_2^{(1)}}{X_1^{(1)}} = \frac{-m_1\omega_1^2 + (k_1 + k_2)}{k_2} = \frac{k_2}{-m_2\omega_1^2 + (k_2 + k_3)}$$

$$r_2 = \frac{X_2^{(2)}}{X_1^{(2)}} = \frac{-m_1\omega_2^2 + (k_1 + k_2)}{k_2} = \frac{k_2}{-m_2\omega_2^2 + (k_2 + k_3)}$$

The normal modes of vibration corresponding to ω_1^2 and ω_2^2 can be expressed, respectively, as

$$\{X^{(1)}\} = \begin{Bmatrix} X_1^{(1)} \\ X_2^{(1)} \end{Bmatrix} = \begin{Bmatrix} X_1^{(1)} \\ r_1X_1^{(1)} \end{Bmatrix}$$

and $$\{X^{(2)}\} = \begin{Bmatrix} X_1^{(2)} \\ X_2^{(2)} \end{Bmatrix} = \begin{Bmatrix} X_1^{(2)} \\ r_2X_1^{(2)} \end{Bmatrix}$$

The vectors $\{X^{(1)}\}$ and $\{X^{(2)}\}$, which denote the normal modes of vibration, are known as the *modal vectors* of the system.

8.10.3 Torsional System

Consider the torsional system shown in Fig. 8.27, consisting of two disks on a shaft supported in frictionless bearings at the ends.

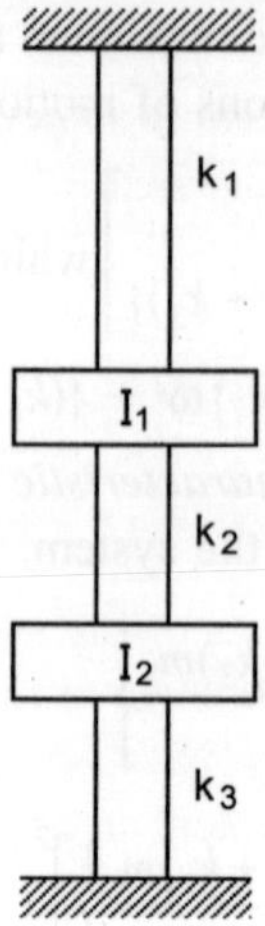

Fig. 8.27 Torsional system

The differential equations of motion as

$$I_1 \ddot{\theta}_1 + (k_1 + k_2)\theta_1 - k_2\theta_2 = 0$$

$$I_2 \ddot{\theta}_2 + (k_2 + k_3)\theta_2 - k_2\theta_1 = 0$$

where k_i is the torsional stiffness of shaft i, $i = 1, 2, 3$, defined as

$$k_i = \frac{G_i J_i}{\ell_i}$$

where G_i is the modulus of rigidity, J_i is the polar moment of inertia, and ℓ_i is the length of the shaft. By using the matrix notation, the differential equations of motion can be written in matrix form as

$$\begin{bmatrix} I_1 & 0 \\ 0 & I_2 \end{bmatrix} \begin{bmatrix} \ddot{\theta}_1 \\ \ddot{\theta}_2 \end{bmatrix} + \begin{bmatrix} k_1 + k_2 & -k_2 \\ -k_2 & k_2 + k_3 \end{bmatrix} \begin{bmatrix} \theta_1 \\ \theta_2 \end{bmatrix} = \begin{bmatrix} 0 \\ 0 \end{bmatrix}$$

8.10.4 Coordinate Coupling and Principal Coordinates

The term *coupling* is used in vibration analysis to indicate a connection between equations of motion. In general an n degree of freedom vibration system requires n independent coordinates to describe completely its configuration. Often, it is quite possible to find some other set of n coordinates to describe the same configuration of the system completely. Each of these sets of n coordinates is called the *generalized coordinates*.

In the dynamic equations of motion, if the mass matrix [M] is non-diagonal, then mass or *dynamic coupling* exists and if the stiffness matrix [K] is non-diagonal then *static* or *stiffness* or *static coupling* exists. In general, it is possible to find a coordinate system that has neither *mass* or *dynamic coupling* nor *stiffness* or *static coupling*. Then the equations are decoupled into two independent equations and can be solved independently of the other. Such coordinates are called *principal coordinates* or *normal coordinates*.

8.10.5 Forced Vibrations

When a two degree of freedom undamped system is subjected to the harmonic forces, $F_1(t) = F_1 \sin\omega t$ and $F_2(t) = F_2 \sin \omega t$, then the amplitudes of displacement of masses is given by

$$X_1 = \frac{a_{22}F_1 - a_{12}F_2}{a_{11}a_{22} - a_{12}a_{21}}$$

and
$$X_2 = \frac{a_{11}F_2 - a_{21}F_1}{a_{11}a_{22} - a_{12}a_{21}}$$

The denominator defines the natural frequencies of the system ω_1 and ω_3. The motions of the system are coupled and hence each mass will exhibit resonance even if the resonant force acts on only one mass of the system.

For a damped two-degree of spring-mass system under external forces the solution is obtained from mechanical impedance concept.

The mechanical impedance $Z_{rs}(i\omega)$ is defined as

$$Z_{rs}(i\omega) = -\omega^2 m_{rs} + i\omega c_{rs} + k_{rs}, \quad (r, s = 1, 2)$$

8.10.6 Orthogonality Principle

If ω_1 and ω_2 are two eigenvalues (natural frequencies) and $X^{(1)}$ and $X^{(2)}$ are the corresponding eigenvectors (natural modes) they must satisfy

$$\omega_1^2 [M] X^{(1)} = [K] X^{(1)}$$
$$\omega_2^2 [M] X^{(2)} = [K] X^{(2)}$$

Then it can be shown that

For $\omega_1 \neq \omega_2$, $[X^{(2)}]^T [M] X^{(1)} = 0$

This property is very useful, as for example to check the accuracy of computation of normal modes by its application.

8.11 MULTI-DEGREE OF FREEDOM SYSTEMS

A *multi-degree of freedom system* is defined as a system whose motion is described by more than one generalized coordinate. In general, *n* coordinates are needed in order to describe the motion of an *n*-degree of freedom system. Figure 8.28 shows some examples of multi-degree of freedom systems.

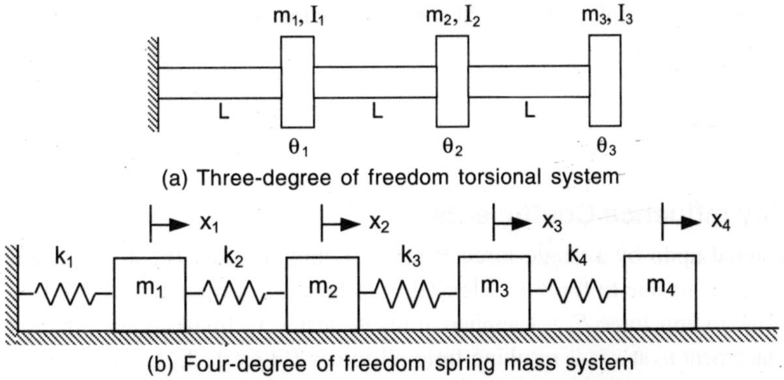

Fig. 8.28 Multi-degree of freedom systems

An n degree of freedom system is governed by n coupled differential equations and has n natural frequencies. The solution of coupled differential equations can be written as the sum of a homogeneous solution and a particular solution. The free-vibration properties of the system are represented by the homogeneous solution while the particular solution represents the forced response.

8.11.1 Equations of Motion

Consider the motion of an n-degree of freedom system whose motion is described by the generalized coordinates, $x_1, x_2, \ldots, x_n$ as shown in Fig. 8.29.

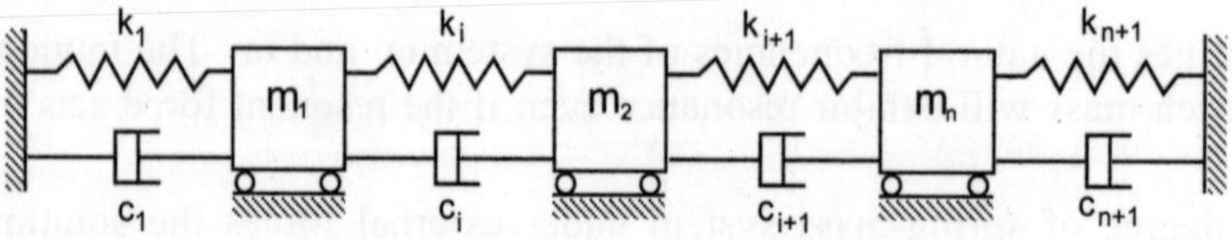

Fig. 8.29 Multi-degree of freedom system

Applying the Newton's second law to mass m_i ($i = 1, 2, \ldots, n$), one can write the differential equation of motion as:

$$m_i\, \ddot{x}_i(t) - c_{i+1}\, \dot{x}_{i+1} + (c_i + c_{i+1})\, \dot{x}_i - c_i\, \dot{x}_{i-1} - k_{i+1}x_{i+1} + (k_i + k_{i+1})\, x_i - k_i x_{i-1} = 0$$

For general use, it is convenient to write this equation as in the following matrix form

$$[M]\, \ddot{x}\,(t) + [C]\, \dot{x}\,(t) + [K]x(t) = 0$$

with $[M]$, $[C]$ and $[K]$ being square matrices containing the coefficients m_{ij}, c_{ij} and k_{ij} respectively.

In this particular case, the mass-matrix is diagonal. For a different set of coordinates, $[M]$ is not necessarily diagonal.

8.11.2 Stiffness Influence Coefficients

For a linear system, inertial, damping and stiffness properties enter explicitly in the differential equations through the mass-coefficients m_{ij}, damping-coefficients c_{ij} and stiffness coefficients k_{ij} ($i, j = 1, 2,\ldots, n$) respectively. Of the three, stiffness coefficients are the elastic properties causing a dynamic system to vibrate, e.g., restoring-forces. *Stiffness coefficients* are also known as *stiffness influence coefficients*. Stiffness influence coefficients k_{ij} is defined as the force required at $x = x_i$ to produce a unit displacement $u_j = 1$ at point $x = x_j$ and also the displacements at all other points for which $x \neq x_j$ are zero. In other words, they define a relation between the displacement at a point and the forces acting at various other points of system. Invoking the superposition principle, the force at $x = x_i$ producing displacements u_j at $x = x_j$ ($j =1, 2,\ldots, n$) is

$$F_i = \sum_{j=1}^{n} k_{ij} u_j$$

8.11.3 Flexibility Influence Coefficients

Let the system be acted upon by a single-force F_j at $x = x_j$ and consider the displacement of any arbitrary point $x = x_i$ ($i = 1, 2, \ldots, n$) due to force F_j. Flexibility influence coefficient is defined as the *displacement of the point* $x = x_i$ due to unit force $F_j = 1$ applied at the point $x = x_j$. Invoking the principle of superposition and obtaining displacement u_i at $x = x_i$ resulting from all forces F_j ($j = 1, 2, \ldots, n$) by simply summing up the individual contributions.

$$U_i = \sum_{j=1}^{n} a_{ij} F_j$$

Note that the units of a_{ij} are m/N.

For a single degree of freedom system with only one spring, the stiffness influence coefficient is merely the spring-constant, where as the flexibility influence coefficient is its reciprocal.

8.11.4 Matrix Formulation

For multi-degree of freedom systems, a more general formulation is employed. Arranging the flexibility and stiffness influence coefficients in the square matrices as

$$[a_{ij}] = [A], \text{ and } [k_{ij}] = [K]$$

where $[A]$ is the flexibility matrix and $[K]$ is the stiffness matrix.

The flexibility and stiffness matrices are the inverse of one another. Often the stiffness coefficients are easier to evaluate than the flexibility coefficients. When the stiffness matrix is singular, the flexibility matrix does not exist. This implies that the system admits rigid-body motions, in which the system undergoes no elastic deformations. This can happen when supports do not fully restrain the system from moving. Thus in the absence of adequate supports, the definition of flexibility coefficients cannot be applied, so that the coefficients are not defined.

8.11.5 Inertia Influence Coefficients

The mass-matrix is associated with the kinetic energy. For a multi-degree of freedom system with $\dot{x}_i$ as the velocity of mass m_i ($i = 1, 2, \ldots, n.$), the kinetic energy is given by

$$T = \frac{1}{2}\dot{x}^T [M]\dot{x}$$

where $[M]$ is the mass-matrix or inertia matrix.

The elements of the mass-matrix m_{ij} are known as the inertia influence coefficients. The coefficients m_{ij} can be obtained using the impulse-momentum relations. The inertia influence coefficients $m_{1j}, m_{2j}, \ldots, m_{nj}$ are defined as the set of impulses applied at points $1, 2, \ldots, n$ respectively, to produce a unit velocity at points $1, 2, \ldots, n$ respectively to produce a unit velocity at point j and zero velocity at every other point. Thus, for a multi degree of freedom system, the total impulse at point i, can be found by summing up the impulses causing the velocities $\dot{x}_j$ ($j = 1, 2, \ldots, n$) as

$$\tilde{F} = [M]\dot{X}$$

where $[M]$ is the mass matrix, $\dot{X}$ and $\tilde{F}$ are the velocity and impulse vectors of size $n \times 1$ respectively.

8.11.6 Normal Mode Solution

The general formulation of the differential equations governing the free-vibrations of a linear-undamped n-degree of freedom system can be written as

$$[M]\ddot{x} + [K]x = 0$$

where $[M]$ and $[K]$ are symmetric $n \times n$ mass and stiffness matrices respectively and x is the n-dimensional column-vector of generalized coordinates.

The matrix triple products possessing orthogonality properties, is written as

$$[U]^T[M][U]\{\ddot{P}\} + [U]^T(\alpha[K] + \beta[M])\,[U]\{\dot{P}\} + [U]^T[K][U]\{P\} = 0$$

The orthogonality of modes with respect to mass and stiffness permits the following substitutions:

$$[U]^T\,[M]\,[U] = [I]$$

and $$[U]^T\,[K]\,[U] = [\text{diag }\omega^2] = [\Omega]$$

The equations can now be decoupled into governing equations for each degree of freedom. Mathematically,

$$\ddot{p}_i + (\alpha\,\omega_i^2 + \beta)\,\dot{p}_i + \omega_i^2\,p_i = 0$$

In this connection, modal damping ratio is defined as $\xi_i = \dfrac{1}{2}\left(\alpha\omega_i + \dfrac{\beta}{\omega_i}\right)$

The general solution for free vibration problem under $\xi_i < 1$ is given by

$$p_i(t) = A_i\,e^{-\xi_i\omega_i t}\,\sin\left(\omega_i\sqrt{1-\xi_i^2}\;t - \phi_i\right)$$

where A_i and ϕ_i are constants determined from the initial conditions. Finally, the solution is obtained in terms of generalized coordinates.

8.14 GENERAL VISCOUS DAMPING

The differential equations governing the free-vibrations of a multi-degree of freedom system with viscous damping are given by

$$[M]\ddot{X} + [C]\dot{X} + [K]X = 0$$

If the damping is arbitrary, then the principal coordinates of the undamped system do not uncouple the above equation. The equation can be reformulated as $2n$ first-order differential equations by writing

$$[\tilde{M}]\dot{y} + [\tilde{K}]y = 0$$

where $[\tilde{M}] = \begin{bmatrix} O & [M] \\ [M] & [C] \end{bmatrix}, [\tilde{K}] = \begin{bmatrix} -[M] & O \\ O & [K] \end{bmatrix}, y = \begin{bmatrix} \dot{X} \\ X \end{bmatrix}$

If the values of γ are complex-conjugate eigenvalues of $[\tilde{M}]^{-1}[\tilde{K}]$ and ϕ is a corresponding eigenvector, then solution takes the form as

$$y = \phi\,e^{-\gamma t}$$

8.15 HARMONIC EXCITATIONS

Differential equations governing the motion of an n-degree of freedom undamped system subject to a single-frequency excitation with all excitation terms at the same phase can be written as:

$$[M]\ddot{x} + [K]x = F\sin\omega t$$

where F is an n-dimensional vector of constant forces. A particular solution of the form is assumed as follows:

$$x(t) = U\sin\omega t$$

where U is an n-dimensional vector of undetermined coefficients.

It results in by usual method as a solution

$$U = (-\omega^2[M] + i\omega[C] + [K])^{-1}F$$

Alternative to this method of undetermined coefficients, Laplace transform method can also be employed.

8.16 MODAL ANALYSIS FOR UNDAMPED SYSTEMS

The differential equations governing the forced vibration motion of an undamped linear *n*-degree of freedom system are

$$M\ddot{X} + KX = F$$

The method of modal analysis uses the principal coordinates of the system to uncouple this equation as follows:

$$\sum_{i=1}^{n} \ddot{p}_i(X_j \cdot MX_i) + \sum_{i=1}^{n} p_i(X_j KX_i) = X_j F$$

Application of mode shape orthogonality leads to only one non-zero term in each summation, *i.e.*, the term corresponding to $i = j$. Since the mode shapes are normalized, following set of equations are obtained

$$\ddot{p}_j + \omega_j^2 p_j = g_j(t)$$

where $g_j(t) = X_j F$

If the initial conditions for p_i are both zero, then the convolution integral solution is given by

$$p_i(t) = \frac{1}{\omega_i}\int_0^t g_i(\tau)\sin[\omega_i(t-\tau)]\,d\tau$$

Once the solution for each p_i is obtained, the original generalized coordinates can be determined.

The same methodology can be applied to systems having proportional damping.

Here it leads to the differential equations for the principal coordinates as

$$\ddot{p}_i + 2\xi_i\omega_i\dot{p}_i + \omega_i^2 p_i = g_i(t)$$

where ξ_i is modal damping-ratio

In this case, the convolution-integral solution is given by

$$p_i(t) = \frac{1}{\omega_{d_i}}\int_0^t g_i(\tau)e^{-\xi_i\omega_i(t-\tau)}\sin\omega_{d_i}(t-\tau)d\tau$$

where $\omega_{d_i} = \omega_i\sqrt{1-\xi_i^2}$.

8.17 LAGRANGE S EQUATION

There are two general approaches to classical dynamics: *vectorial dynamics* and *analytical dynamics*. *Vectorial dynamics* is based directly on the application of Newton's second law of motion, concentrating on forces and motions. *Analytical dynamics* treats the system as a whole dealing with scalar quantities such as the kinetic and potential energies of the system. Lagrange proposed an approach, which provides a powerful and versatile method for the formulation of the equations of motion for any dynamical system. *Lagrange's equation* obtains the equation of motion in generalized coordinates approaching the system from the analytical dynamics point of view. Lagrange's equations are differential equations in which one considers the energies of the system and the work done instantaneously in time.

8.17.1 Generalized Coordinates

The coordinates used to describe the motion in each degree of freedom of a system are termed as *generalized coordinates*. They may be Cartesian, polar, cylindrical or spherical coordinates provided any one of them can be used to describe the configuration of the system where the motion along any one coordinate direction is independent of others. But, sometimes they may not have such simple physical or geometrical meaning. For example, the deflections of a string, stretched between two points, can be expressed in the form of trigonometric Fourier series, and the coefficients of all the terms in the series can be considered as a generalized coordinate set. This is because each trigonometric function in the series may be considered as a unique degree of freedom and the coefficients describe the extent of deflection in each degree of freedom.

It is possible to transform the coordinates from any one system to the generalized coordinate system or vice versa, through coordinate transformation. Consider a mechanical system consisting of N particles whose positions are (x_i, y_i, z_i), $i = 1, 2,\ldots, N$, in a Cartesian coordinate system. The motion of the mechanical system is completely defined if the variation with time of these positions *i.e.*, $x_i = x_i(t)$, $y_i = y_i(t)$, $z_i = z_i(t)$, are known. These $3N$ coordinates completely define a representative space. If it is possible to find another set of generalized coordinates, q_i, $i = 1, 2,\ldots.n$, where $n = 3N$, then these two coordinate systems are related by the following:

$$x_i(t) = x_i(q_1, q_2, \ldots, q_n, t)$$
$$y_i(t) = y_i(q_1, q_2, \ldots, q_n, t)$$
$$z_i(t) = z_i(q_1, q_2, \ldots, q_n, t)$$

8.18 PRINCIPLE OF VIRTUAL WORK

The principle of virtual work is essentially a statement of the static or dynamic equilibrium of a mechanical system. A *virtual displacement*, denoted by δr, is an imaginary displacement and it occurs without the passage of time. The virtual displacement being infinitesimal obeys the rules of differential calculus.

Consider a mechanical system with N particles in a three-dimensional space whose Cartesian coordinates are $(x_1, y_1, z_1,\ldots, z_n)$. Suppose the system is subjected to k constraints $\phi_j(x_1, y_1, z_1,\ldots, z_n, t) = 0, j = 1, 2,\ldots, k$. The virtual displacements $\delta x_1, \delta y_1, \delta z_1$, etc., are said to be *consistent* with the system constraints if the constraint equations are still satisfied.

The virtual work performed by the resultant force vector $\overline{F}_i$ over the virtual displacement vector δr_i of particle i is

$$\delta W = \sum_{i=1}^{N} \overline{F}_i \cdot \delta \overline{r}_i$$

When the system is in equilibrium, the resultant force acting on each particle is zero. The resultant force is the sum of the applied force and the reaction force or the constraint force. The virtual work done by all the forces in moving through an arbitrary virtual displacement consistent with the constraints is zero.

8.19 D ALEMBERT S PRINCIPLE

The principle of virtual work is extended to dynamics, in which form it is known as d'Alembert's principle. The principle of virtual work is extended to the dynamic case by considering the inertia forces and considering the systems to be in dynamic equilibrium.

The generalized principle of d'Alembert states that *the virtual work performed by the effective forces through infinitesimal virtual displacements compatible with the system constraints is zero.*

8.20 LAGRANGE S EQUATIONS OF MOTION

If Q_i is called the *generalized force* in the direction of the ith generalized coordinate, T is the kinetic energy and V is potential energy, then Lagrange's equation is given by

$$\frac{d}{dt}\left(\frac{\partial T}{\partial \dot{q}_i}\right)-\frac{\partial T}{\partial q_i}+\frac{\partial V}{\partial q_i}=Q_i$$

Expressing $T - V = L$, called the *Lagrangian*, the equation can be written as

$$\frac{d}{dt}\left(\frac{\partial L}{\partial \dot{q}_i}\right)-\frac{\partial L}{\partial q_i}=Q_i$$

8.21 VARIATIONAL PRINCIPLES

An alternative approach to the study of motion is the use of variational principle, which views the motion as a whole from the beginning to the end. This involves a search for the path in the configuration space, which yields a stationary value for a certain integral. Unlike as in the case of differential equations, the initial and final points in the configuration space are fixed in this approach. The most celebrated variational principle in dynamics is the *Hamilton's principle.*

8.22 HAMILTON S PRINCIPLE

Hamilton's principle is the most important and powerful variational principle in dynamics. It is derived from the generalized d'Alembert's principle. The generalized version of Hamilton's principle can be written as

$$\int_{t_0}^{t_1}(\delta T+\delta W)dt=0 \text{ or } \int_{t_0}^{t_1}\delta(T-V)dt=0, \delta\int_{t_0}^{t_1}Ldt=0$$

where $L = T - V$.

The usual form of Hamilton's principle applies to a more restricted class of systems, which are called *conservative systems*. In these systems, all the applied forces are derivable from a potential function $V(q, t)$.

The usual form of Hamilton's principle states that: The actual path in the configuration space followed by a holonomic system from t_0 and t_1 is such that the integral

$$I=\int_{t_0}^{t_1}Ldt$$

is stationary with respect to any path variations, which vanish at the end points.

8.23 EXAMPLE PROBLEMS AND SOLUTIONS

Example E8.1: Write a MATLAB script for plotting

(*a*) the non-dimensional response magnitude for a system with harmonically moving base shown in Fig. E 8.1.

(*b*) the response phase angle for system with harmonically moving base.

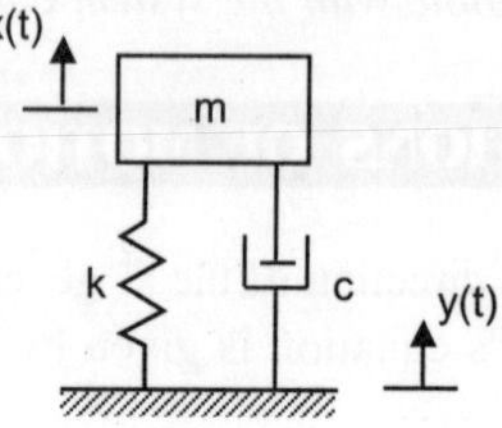

Fig. E8.1 Single degree of freedom system with moving base

Solution: The magnitude of the frequency response is given as

$$|G(i\omega)| = \frac{1}{\left[\left[\left(1-\left(\frac{\omega}{\omega_n}\right)^2\right]^2 + \left(2\zeta\frac{\omega}{\omega_n}\right)^2\right]^{1/2}}$$

The magnitude of $X(i\omega)$ is given as

$$|X(i\omega)| = \left[1+\left(\frac{2\zeta\omega}{\omega_n}\right)^2\right]^{1/2} |G(i\omega)|\, A$$

where $y(t) = Re\, A^{i\omega t}$

$$x(t) = X(i\omega)\, e^{i\omega t}$$

The phase angle ϕ is given as

$$\phi(\omega) = \tan^{-1}\left[\frac{2\zeta\left(\frac{\omega}{\omega_n}\right)^3}{1-\left(\frac{\omega}{\omega_n}\right)^2+\left(\frac{2\zeta\omega}{\omega_n}\right)^2}\right]$$

The frequency ratio

$$r = \frac{\omega}{\omega_n}$$

The non-dimensional response magnitude is given as the transmissibility

$$\frac{|X(i\omega)|}{A} = \left[\frac{1+\left(\frac{2\zeta\omega}{\omega_n}\right)^2}{1-\left(\frac{\omega}{\omega_n}\right)^2+\left(\frac{2\zeta\omega}{\omega_n}\right)^2}\right]$$

Based on these equations MATLAB script is written as follows:

```
zeta= [0.05; 0.1; 0.15; 0.25; 0.5; 1.25; 1.5]; % damping factors
r= [0:0.01:3]; %frequency ratio
for k=1: length (zeta)
  G(k,:)=sqrt((1+(2*zeta(k)*r).^2)./((1-r.^2).^2+(2*zeta(k)*r).^2));
  phi(k,:)=atan2(2*zeta(k)*r.^3,1-r.^2+(2*zeta(k)*r).^2);
end
figure (1)
plot(r, G)
xlabel ('\omega/\omega_n')
ylabel ('|x (i\omega)|/A')
grid
legend('\zeta_1=0.05','\zeta_2=0.1','\zeta_3=0.15','\zeta_4=0.25','\zeta_5=0.5',
  '\zeta_6=1.25','\zeta_7=1.5')
figure (2)
plot(r, phi)
xlabel ('\omega/\omega_n')
ylabel ('\phi (\omega)')
grid
ha=gca;
set (ha,'ytick',[0:pi/2:pi])
set(ha,'yticklabel',{[];'pi/2';'p'})
legend('\zeta_1=0.05','\zeta_2=0.1','\zeta_3=0.15','\zeta_4=0.25','\zeta_5=0.5',
  '\zeta_6=1.25', '\zeta_7=1.5')
```

The output of this program is shown in Fig. E8.1(a) and (b).

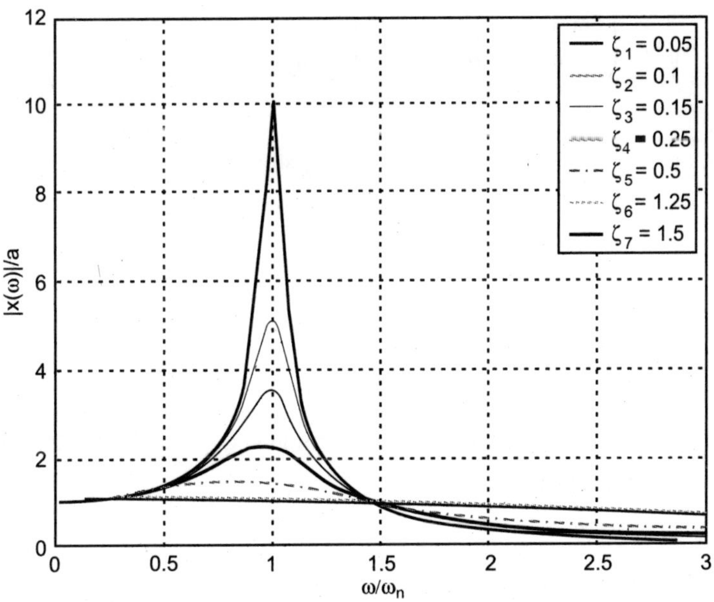

(a)

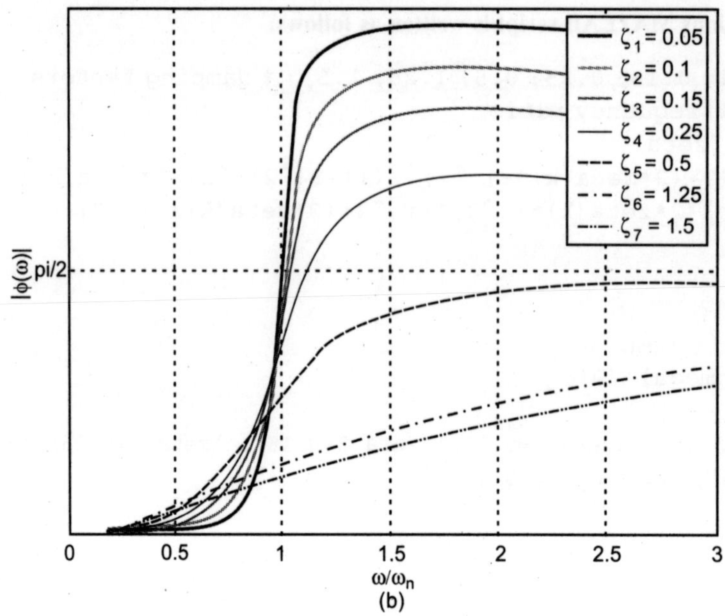

Fig. E8.1

Example E8.2: An analytical expression for the response of a damped single degree of freedom system (Fig. E8.2) to given initial displacement and velocity is given by

$$x(t) = Ce^{-\zeta\omega_n t}\cos(\omega_d t - \phi)$$

where C and ϕ represent the amplitude and phase angle of the response, respectively having the values

$$C = \sqrt{x_0^2 + \left(\frac{\zeta\omega_n x_0 + v_0}{\omega_d}\right)^2}, \phi = \tan^{-1}\left(\frac{\zeta\omega_n x_0 + v_0}{\omega_d x_0}\right)$$

and $\omega_d = \sqrt{1-\zeta^2}\,\omega_n$

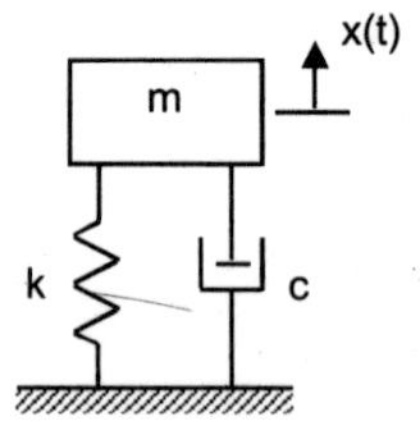

Fig. E8.2

Plot the response of the system using MATLAB for ω_n=5rad/s, ζ = 0.05, 0.1, 0.2 subjected to the initial conditions $x(0) = 0$, $\dot{x}(0) = v_0 = 60$ cm/s.

Solution:

```
clear
clf
wn=5; % Natural frequency
zeta=[0.05;0.1;0.2]; % Damping ratio
x0=0; % Initial displacement
v0=60; % Initial velocity
t0=0; % Initial time
deltat=0.01; % Time step
tf=6; % Final time
t=[t0:deltat:tf];
for i=1:length(zeta),
  wd=sqrt(1-zeta(i)^2)*wn; % Damped frequency
  x=exp(-zeta(i)*wn*t).*(((zeta(i)*wn*x0+v0)/wd)*sin(wd*t)
    + x0*cos(wd*t));
  plot(t,x)
      hold on
end
title('Response to initial excitations')
xlabel('t[s]')
ylabel('x(t)')
grid
```

The output of this program is as follows:

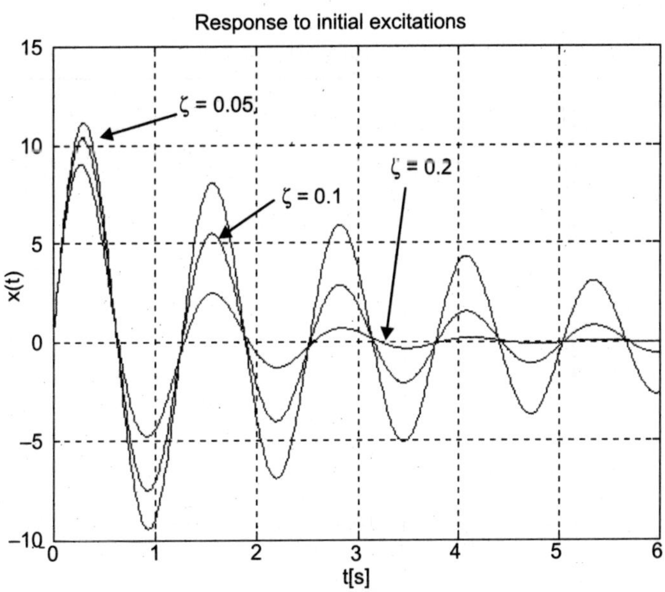

Fig. E8.2(a)

Example E8.3: Plot the response of the system in Example E8.2 using MATLAB for $\omega_n = 5$ rad/sec, $\zeta = 1.3$, 1.5, 2.0 subjected to the initial conditions $x(0) = 0$, $\dot{x}(0) = v_0 = 60$ cm/s.

Solution: Changing the program slightly, with zeta = [1.3, 1.5, 2.0] in E8.2, we obtain Fig. E8.3.

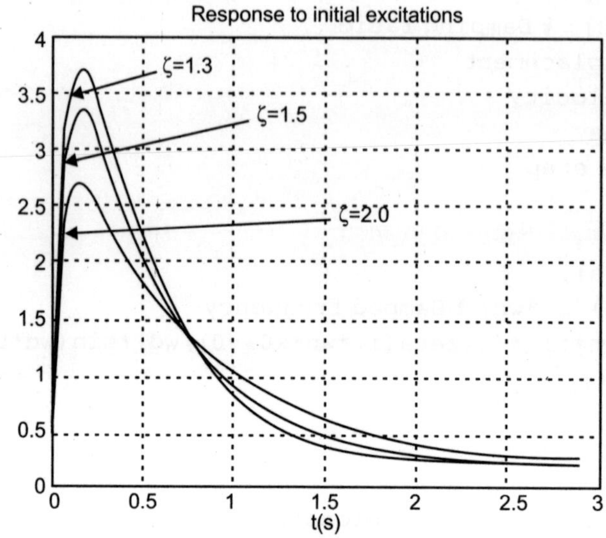

Fig. E8.3

Example E8.4: Plot the response of the system in Example E8.2 using MATLAB for $\omega_n = 5$ rad/sec and $\zeta = 1.0$ subjected to the initial conditions $x(0) = 0$, $\dot{x}(0) = v_0 = 60$ cm/s.

Solution: The solution obtained is shown in Fig. E8.4.

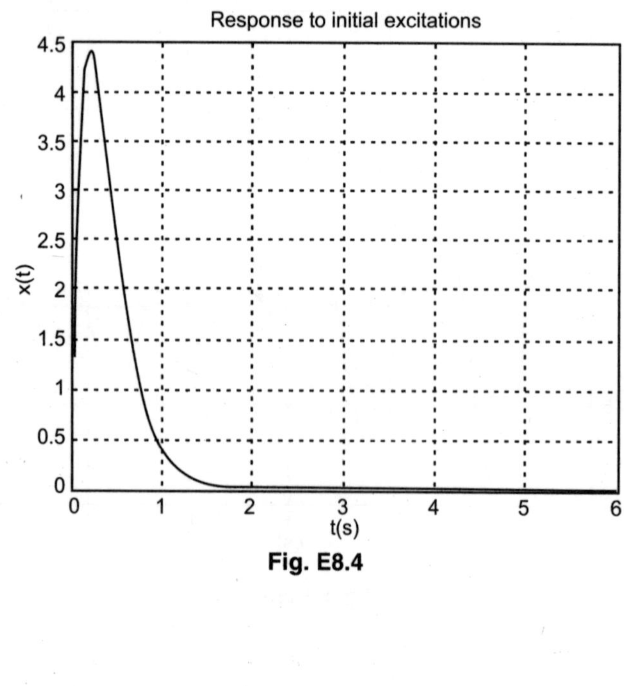

Fig. E8.4

Example E8.5: Write MATLAB script for plotting the magnitude of the frequency response of a system with rotating unbalanced masses as shown in Fig. E8.5.

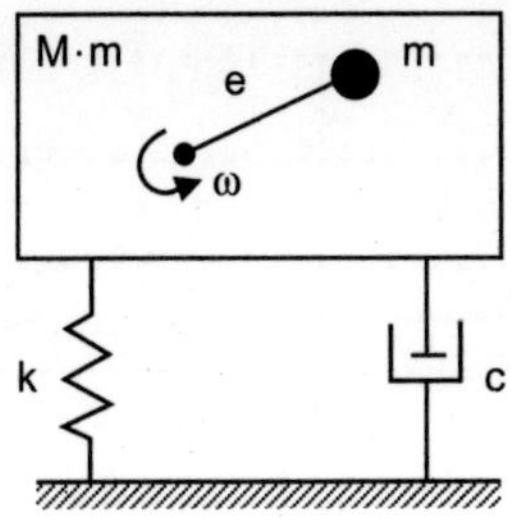

Fig. E8.5 Single degree of freedom system with rotating eccentric mass

Hint: The magnitude of the frequency response is given as

$$|G(i\omega)| = \frac{1}{\left[\left(1-\left(\frac{\omega}{\omega_n}\right)^2\right)^2 + \left(2\zeta\frac{\omega}{\omega_n}\right)^2\right]^{1/2}},$$

Solution: The magnitude of the frequency response is given as

$$|G(i\omega)| = \frac{1}{\left[\left(1-\left(\frac{\omega}{\omega_n}\right)^2\right)^2 + \left(2\zeta\frac{\omega}{\omega_n}\right)^2\right]^{1/2}}$$

for $\xi = 0.05, 0.01, 0.15, 0.20, 0.20, 0.25, 0.5, 0.75, 1.0, 1.25, 1.5.$
$r = \omega/\omega_n = 0$ to 3 in steps of 0.01.

MATLAB Program:

```
zeta=[0.05;0.1;0.15;0.25;0.5;1;1.25;1.5]; % Damping factors
r=[0:0.01:3]; % Frequency ratios
for k=1:length(zeta),
  G=(r.^2)./sqrt((1-r.^2).^2+(2*zeta(k)*r).^2);
  plot(r,G)
  hold on
end
xlabel('\omega/\omega_n')
ylabel('({\omega/\omega_n})^2|G(I\omega)|')
grid
```

Figure E8.5 (a) shows the output of the program

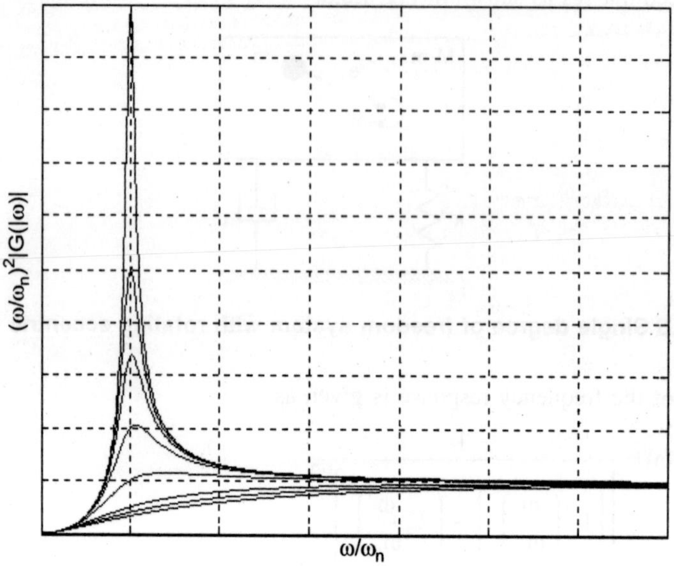

Fig. E8.5(a)

For showing legends on the curves, gtext command can be employed.

Example E8.6: A single degree of freedom spring-mass system subjected to coulomb damping is shown in Fig. E8.6.

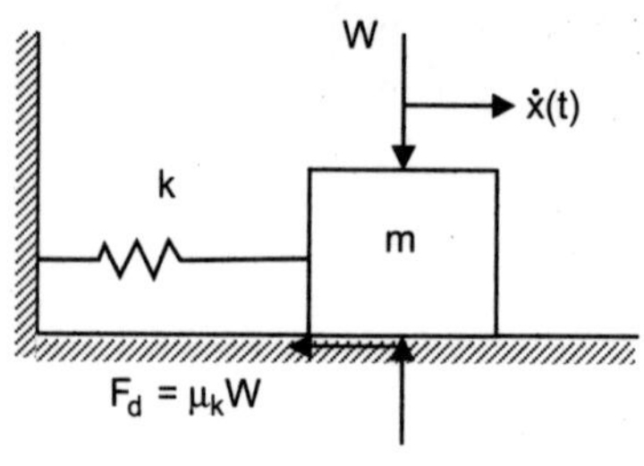

Fig. E8.6

The parameters of the system have the values m = 600 kg, k = 20×10⁴ N/m, μ_s = 0.15 and μ_k = 0.10. The initial conditions are $x(0) = x_0$ =1.5 cm, $\dot{x}(0) = 0$. Plot the response $x(t)$ versus t using MATLAB.

The magnitude of the average response value f_d is given as

$$f_d = \frac{F_d}{k} = \frac{\mu_k mg}{k}$$

If n denotes the half-cycle just prior to the cessation of motion, then n is the smallest integer satisfying the inequality

$$x_0 - (2n-1) f_d < \left(1 + \frac{\mu_s}{\mu_f}\right) f_d$$

where μ_s = static coefficient of friction

μ_k = kinetic coefficient of friction

Solution: The following MATLAB program can be developed:

```
m=600; % Mass
k=200000; % Stiffness
mus=0.15; % Static friction coefficient
muk=0.10; % Kinetic friction coefficient
x0=1.5; % Initial displacement
t0=0;
deltat=0.005; % Time increment
wn=sqrt(k/m); % Natural frequency
fd=100*muk*m*9.81/k;
N=ceil(0.5*((x0-(1+mus/muk)*fd)/fd+1)); % Half cycles
t=[];
x=[];
if N>0
  for n=1:N,
    t1=[t0:deltat:t0+pi/wn];
    x1=(x0-(2*n-1)*fd)*cos(wn*t1)+fd*(-1)^(n+1);
    t=[t t1];
    x=[x x1];
    t0=t0+pi/wn;
  end
end
plot(t,x,t,fd*ones(length(t)),'--',t,-fd*ones(length(t)),'--')
title('Response to initial excitations')
xlabel('t[s]')
ylabel('x(t) [cm]')
grid
```

The output is shown in Fig. E8.6(a).

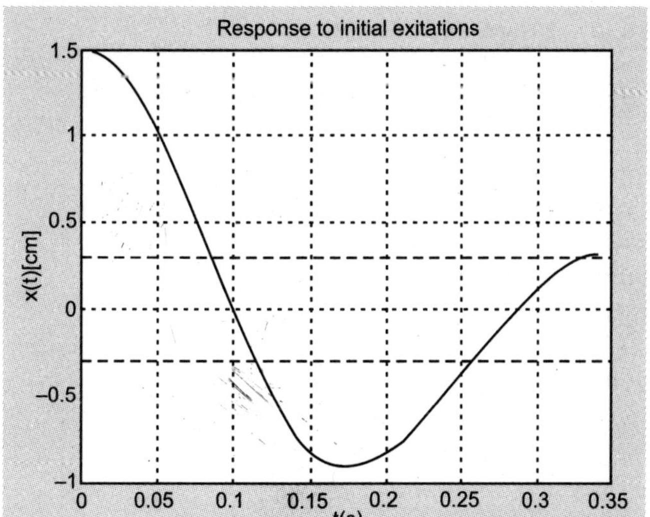

Fig. E8.6(a)

Example E8.7: Write a MATLAB script for obtaining the response of a viscosity damped single degree of freedom system to the force $F(t) = F_0\, e^{-\alpha t}\, u(t)$ by means of the convolution integral. The pulse is rectangular as shown in Fig. E8.7 with $T = 0.1$ seconds.

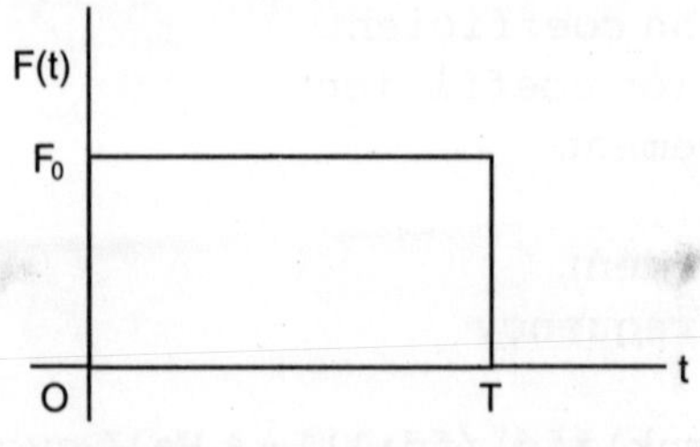

Fig. E8.7 Rectangular pulse

Use the sampling period of $T = 0.001$ s and the number of sampling times $n = 300$. The parameters of the system are given as $m = 25$ kg, $c = 30$ Ns/m, $k = 6000$ N/m, $F_0 = 300$ N, and $\alpha = 1$. The impulse response of a mass-damper spring system is given by

$$g(t) = \frac{1}{m\omega_d} e^{-\zeta\omega_n t} \sin \omega_d t\, u(t)$$

Solution:

```
m=25; % mass
c=30;% damping
k=6000; % stiffness
F0=300; % Force amplitude
T=0.1;
wn=sqrt(k/m);% Natural frequency
zeta=c/(2*sqrt(m*k));%damping factor
Ts=0.001;% sampling period
N=301;% sampling times
wd=wn*sqrt(1-zeta^2);% damped frequency
for n=1:N,
 if n<=T/Ts+1; F(n)=F0; else F(n)=0; end   %force
end
n=[1:N];
g=Ts*exp(-(n-1)*zeta*wn*Ts).*sin((n-1)*wd*Ts)/(m*wd);
% discrete-time impulse response
c0=conv(F,g);%convolution sum
c=c0(1:N); % plot to N samples
n=[0:N-1];
axes('position',[0.1 0.2 0.8 0.7])
plot(n,c,'.')
title('Response to Rectangular pulse')
xlabel('n')
ylabel('x(n) m');
grid
```

The output is shown in Fig. E8.7(a)

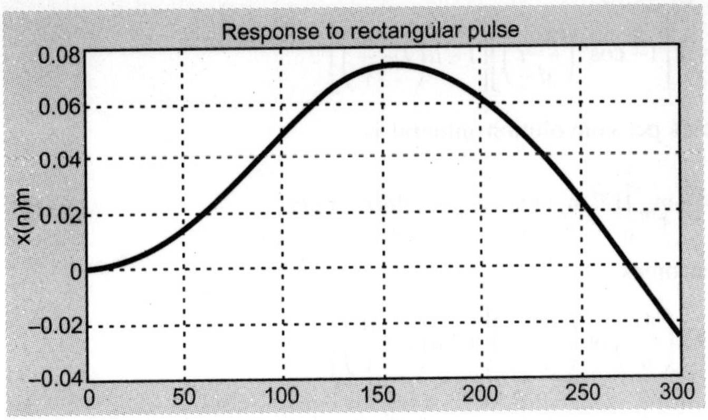

Fig. E8.7(a)

Example E8.8: A simplified single degree of freedom model of an automobile suspension system is shown in Fig. E8.8. The automobile is travelling over a rough road at a constant horizontal speed when it encounters a bump in the road of the shape shown in Fig. E8.8(a), (b). The velocity of the automobile is 20 m/s, m = 1500 kg, k = 150,000 N/m, and ζ = 0.10. Determine the response of the automobile.

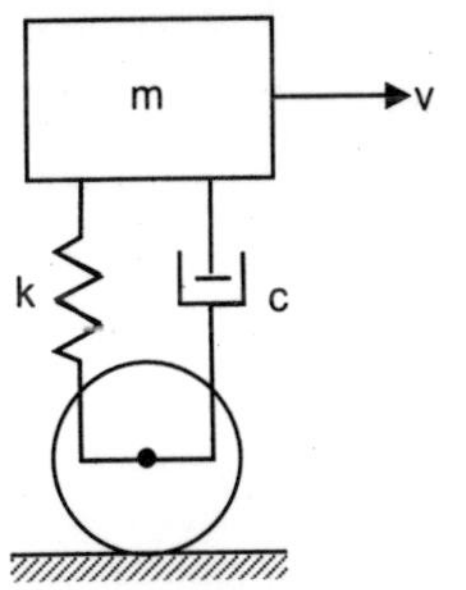

Fig. E8.8 Simplified single degree of pulse model for bump

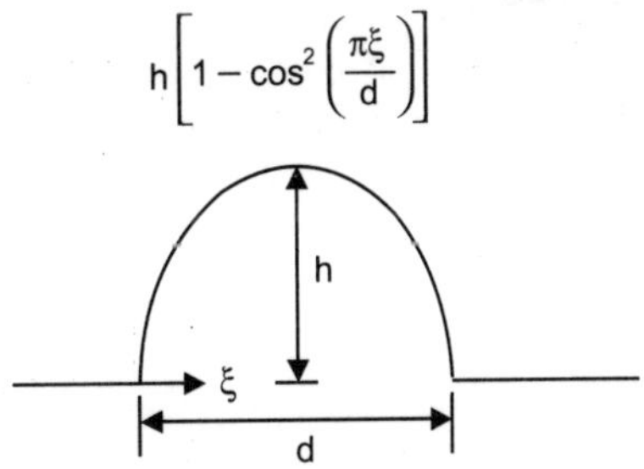

Fig. E8.8(a) Versed sine freedom automobile model

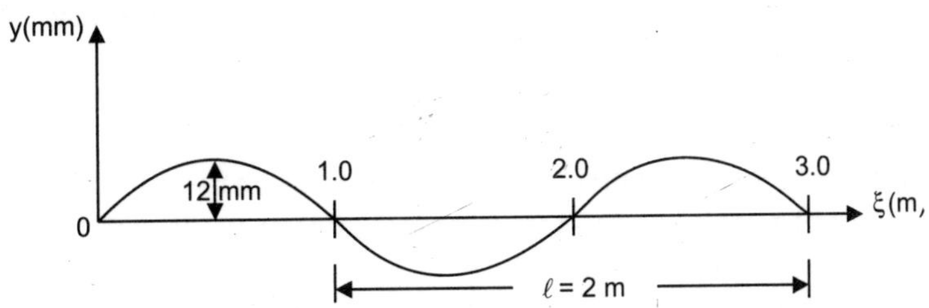

Fig. E8.8(b) Road contour

$$y(\zeta) = h\left[1-\cos^2\left(\frac{\pi\xi}{d}\right)\right][1-u(\xi-d)]$$

Here $h = 0.012$ m, $d = 1.0$ m and for constants automobile speed, $\xi = vt$. The vertical displacement of the automobile wheels is given by

$$y(t) = h\left[1-\cos^2\left(\frac{\pi v}{d}t\right)\right]\left[1-u\left(t-\frac{d}{v}\right)\right]$$

The system response as per convolution integral is

$$x(t) = -m_{eq}\int_0^t [2\zeta\omega_n\dot{y}(\tau)+\omega_n^2 y(\tau)]h(t-\tau)d\tau$$

The wheel velocity becomes

$$\dot{y}(t) = 2\left(\frac{\pi v}{d}\right)\sin\left(\frac{2\pi v}{d}t\right)\left[1-u\left(t-\frac{d}{v}\right)\right]$$

Solution: MATLAB program for this is given below:

```
% Simplified one-degree-of-freedom model of vehicle suspension system
% Vehicle encounters bump in road modeled as a versed sinusoidal pulse
% y(t)=h(1-(cos(pi*v*t/ t0))^2)*(u(t)-u(t-d/v))
%convolution integral is used to evaluate system response
syms t tau
% input parameters
digits(10)
format short e
m=1500;
k=150000;
zeta=0.10;
hb=0.012;
d=1.0;
v=20;
% system parameters and constants
omega_n=sqrt(k/m); % Natural frequency
omega_d=omega_n*sqrt(1-zeta^2); % damped natural frequency
c1=pi/d;
% wheel displacement and velocity
% MATLAB 'Heaviside' for the unit step function
y=hb*(1-cos(c1*v*t)^2)*(1-sym('Heaviside(t-0.04)'));
ydot=hb*c1*sin(2*c1*v*tau)*(1-sym('Heaviside(tau-0.04)'))
%convolution integral evaluation
h=exp(-zeta*omega_n*(t-tau)).*sin(omega_d*(t-tau))/(m*omega_d);
g1=-2*zeta*m*omega_n*ydot*h;
g2=-omega_n^2*m*y*h;
g1a=vpa(g1,5);
g2a=vpa(g2,5);
I1=int(g1a,tau,0,t);
```

```
I1a=vpa(I1,5);
I2=int(g2a,tau,0,t);
I2a=vpa(I2,5);
x1=I1a+I2a;
x=vpa(x1,5);
vel=diff(x);
acc=diff(vel);
time=linspace(0,0.3,50);
for i=1:50
 x1=subs(x,t,time(i));
 xa(i)=vpa(x1);
end
xp=double(xa);
plot(time,xp,'-');
grid;
xlabel('time(sec)')
ylabel('x(t) [m]')
```

The output of this MATLAB program is given in Fig. E8.8(c)

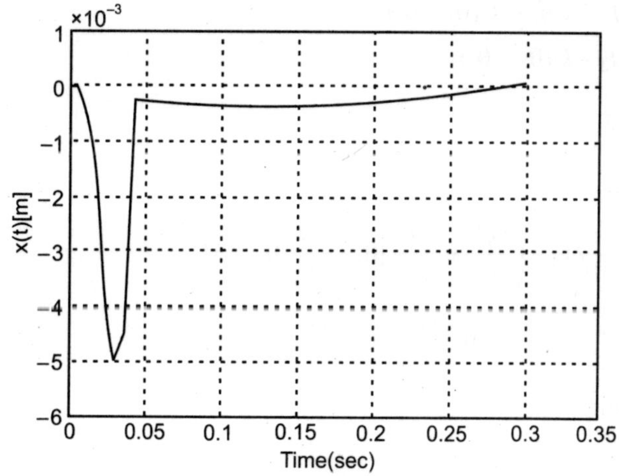

Fig. E8.8(c)

Example E8.9: Figure E8.9 shows two disks of mass polar moments of inertia I_1 and I_2 mounted on a circular shaft with torsional stiffnesses G_{J1} and G_{J2}. Neglect the mass of the shaft.

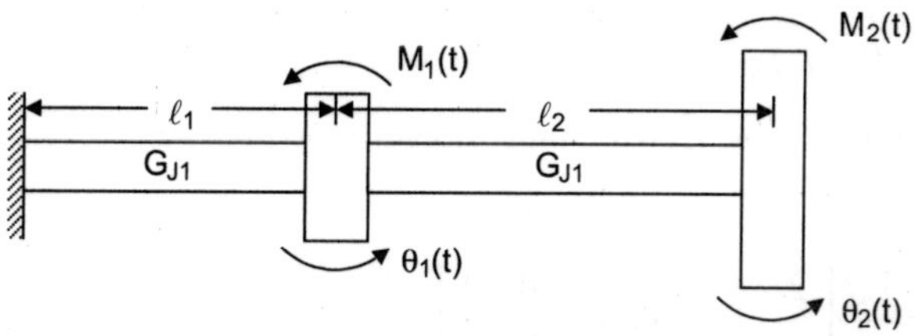

Fig. E8.9

(*a*) Obtain the differential equations of motion for the angular displacements of the disks

(*b*) Determine the natural frequencies and natural modes of the system if $I_1 = I_2 = I$, $G_{J1} = G_{J2} = G_J$, and $\ell_1 = \ell_2 = \ell$

(*c*) Obtain the response of the system to the torques $M_1(t) = 0$, and $M_2(t) = M_2e^{-\alpha t}$ in discrete time

(*d*) Obtain the response of the system to the torques $M_1(t) = 0$, and $M_2(t) = M_2e^{-\alpha t}$

(*e*) Obtain in discrete time the response of the system to the torques $M_1(t) = 0$, and $M_2(t) = M_2e^{-\alpha t}$ using MATLAB.

Solution:

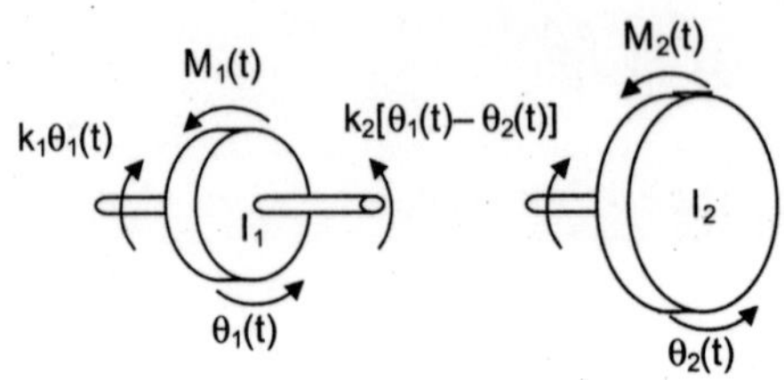

Fig. E8.9(a)

(*a*) The equations of motion are given by

$$I_1\ddot{\theta}_1 = M_1 - k_1\theta_1 + k_2(\theta_2 - \theta_1)$$
$$I_2\ddot{\theta}_2 = M_2 - k_2(\theta_2 - \theta_1) \quad \text{...(1)}$$

where $k_i = \dfrac{GJ_i}{L_i}, i = 1, 2$

Rearranging Eq.(1), we get

$$I_i\ddot{\theta}_1 + \left(\frac{GJ_1}{L_1} + \frac{GJ_2}{L_2}\right)\theta_1 - \frac{GJ_2}{L_2}\theta_2 = M_1$$

$$I_2\ddot{\theta}_2 - \frac{GJ_2}{L_2}\theta_1 + \frac{GJ_2}{L_2}\theta_2 = M_2 \quad \text{...(2)}$$

In matrix form, we can write

$$\begin{bmatrix} I_1 & 0 \\ 0 & I_2 \end{bmatrix}\begin{bmatrix} \ddot{\theta}_1 \\ \ddot{\theta}_2 \end{bmatrix} + \begin{bmatrix} \dfrac{GJ_1}{L_1} + \dfrac{GJ_2}{L_2} & -\dfrac{GJ_2}{L_2} \\ -\dfrac{GJ_2}{L_2} & \dfrac{GJ_2}{L_2} \end{bmatrix}\begin{bmatrix} \theta_1 \\ \theta_2 \end{bmatrix} = \begin{bmatrix} M_1 \\ M_2 \end{bmatrix} \quad \text{...(3)}$$

(*b*) Denoting

$GJ_1 = GJ_2 = GJ, I_1 = I_2 = I, L_1 = L_2 = L$ ...(4)

The equations of motion of the system [Eq.(3)] can be written as

$M\ddot{\theta}(t) + K\theta(t) = 0$ ...(5)

where $M = 1\begin{bmatrix} 1 & 0 \\ 0 & 1 \end{bmatrix}, K = \dfrac{GJ}{L}\begin{bmatrix} 2 & -1 \\ -1 & 1 \end{bmatrix}, \theta(t) = \begin{bmatrix} \theta_1(t) \\ \theta_2(t) \end{bmatrix}$ ...(6)

are the mass matrix, stiffness matrix and configuration vector, respectively. The free vibration solution can be written as

$$\theta_i(t) = \Theta_i e^{i\omega t}, i = 1, 2 \quad \text{...(7)}$$

where ω is the frequency of oscillation and $\Theta = [\Theta_1 \;\; \Theta_2]^T$ is a vector of constants, we have

$$\begin{bmatrix} 2 & -1 \\ -1 & 1 \end{bmatrix}\begin{bmatrix} \Theta_1 \\ \Theta_2 \end{bmatrix} = \lambda \begin{bmatrix} \Theta_1 \\ \Theta_2 \end{bmatrix}, \lambda = \omega^2 \frac{IL}{GJ} \quad \text{...(8)}$$

The characteristic equation can be written as

$$\begin{vmatrix} 2-\lambda & -1 \\ -1 & 1-\lambda \end{vmatrix} = \lambda^2 - 3\lambda + 1 = 0 \quad \text{...(9)}$$

The eigenvalues are given by

$$\begin{matrix} \lambda_1 \\ \lambda_2 \end{matrix} = \frac{3}{2} \mp \frac{\sqrt{5}}{2} \quad \text{...(10)}$$

The natural frequencies are given by

$$\omega_1 = 0.6180\sqrt{GJ/IL}\,, \omega_2 = 1.6180\sqrt{GJ/IL} \quad \text{...(11)}$$

Denote the modal vector corresponding to λ_1 by $\Theta_1 = [\Theta_{11} \;\; \Theta_{21}]^T$, the modal vector is from the matrix equation as

$$\begin{bmatrix} 2 & -1 \\ -1 & 1 \end{bmatrix}\begin{bmatrix} \Theta_{11} \\ \Theta_{21} \end{bmatrix} = \lambda_1 \begin{bmatrix} \Theta_{11} \\ \Theta_{21} \end{bmatrix} = \frac{3-\sqrt{5}}{2}\begin{bmatrix} \Theta_{11} \\ \Theta_{21} \end{bmatrix} \quad \text{...(12)}$$

or $$\Theta_1 = \Theta_{11}\begin{bmatrix} 1 \\ 1.6180 \end{bmatrix} \quad \text{...(13)}$$

In a similar way by letting $\Theta_2 = [\Theta_{12} \;\; \Theta_{22}]^T$, we have

$$\begin{bmatrix} 2 & -1 \\ -1 & 1 \end{bmatrix}\begin{bmatrix} \Theta_{12} \\ \Theta_{22} \end{bmatrix} = \lambda_2 \begin{bmatrix} \Theta_{12} \\ \Theta_{22} \end{bmatrix} = \frac{3+\sqrt{5}}{2}\begin{bmatrix} \Theta_{12} \\ \Theta_{22} \end{bmatrix} \quad \text{...(14)}$$

or $$\Theta_2 = \Theta_{12}\begin{bmatrix} 1 \\ 1.6180 \end{bmatrix} \quad \text{...(15)}$$

The modal vectors are shown below

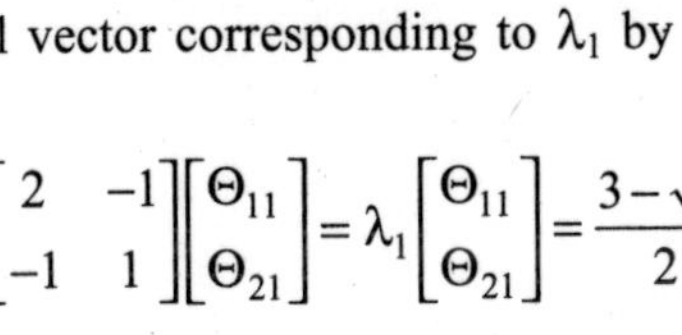

Fig. E8.9(b)

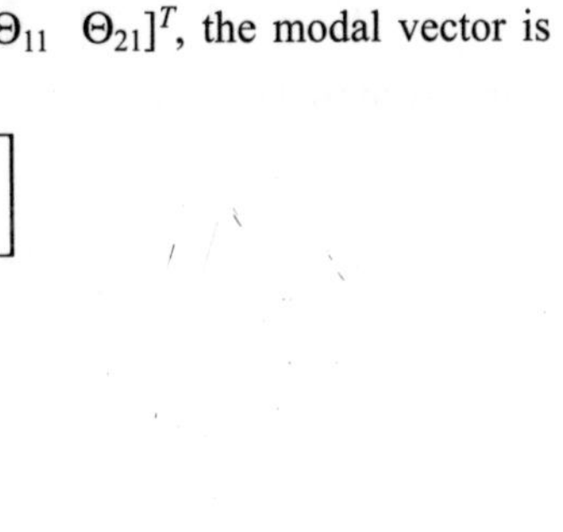

Fig. E8.9(c)

(*c*) The equations of motion are

$$M\ddot{\theta}(t)+K\theta(t)=M(t) \qquad ...(16)$$

$$\text{where } M=I\begin{bmatrix}1&0\\0&1\end{bmatrix}, K=\frac{GJ}{L}\begin{bmatrix}2&-1\\-1&1\end{bmatrix}, \theta(t)=\begin{bmatrix}\theta_1(t)\\\theta_2(t)\end{bmatrix} M(t)=\begin{bmatrix}M_1(t)\\M_2(t)\end{bmatrix} \qquad ...(17)$$

The solution $\theta(t)$ is given by

$$\theta(t)=\eta_1(t)\,\Theta_1+\eta_2(t)\,\Theta_2 \qquad ...(18)$$

where $\eta_1(t)$ and $\eta_2(t)$ are modal coordinates and Θ_1 and Θ_2 are modal vectors. The modal equations can be written as

$$m'_{11}\ddot{\eta}_1(t)+m'_{11}\omega_1^2\eta_1(t)=N_1(t), m'_{22}\ddot{\eta}_2(t)+m'_{22}\omega_2^2\eta_2(t)=N_2(t) \qquad ...(19)$$

$$\text{where } \omega_1=\sqrt{\frac{3-\sqrt{5}}{2}\frac{GJ}{IL}}, \omega_2=\sqrt{\frac{3+\sqrt{5}}{2}\frac{GJ}{IL}} \qquad ...(20)$$

The natural frequencies are given by Eq.(20).

$$\Theta_1=\begin{bmatrix}1\\\frac{1+\sqrt{5}}{2}\end{bmatrix}, \Theta_2=\begin{bmatrix}1\\\frac{1-\sqrt{5}}{2}\end{bmatrix} \qquad ...(21)$$

The modal vectors are given by Eq.(21).

$$m'_{11}=\Theta_1^T M\Theta_1=\begin{bmatrix}1\\\frac{1+\sqrt{5}}{2}\end{bmatrix}^T\begin{bmatrix}I&0\\0&I\end{bmatrix}\begin{bmatrix}1\\\frac{1+\sqrt{5}}{2}\end{bmatrix}=\frac{5+\sqrt{5}}{2}I$$

$$m'_{22}=\Theta_2^T M\Theta_2=\begin{bmatrix}1\\\frac{1+\sqrt{5}}{2}\end{bmatrix}^T\begin{bmatrix}I&0\\0&I\end{bmatrix}\begin{bmatrix}1\\\frac{1-\sqrt{5}}{2}\end{bmatrix}=\frac{5-\sqrt{5}}{2}I \qquad ...(22)$$

The modal mass coefficients are given by Eq. (22).

$$N_1(t)=\Theta_1^T M(t)=\begin{bmatrix}1\\\frac{1+\sqrt{5}}{2}\end{bmatrix}^T\begin{bmatrix}0\\M_2e^{-\alpha t}\end{bmatrix}=\frac{1+\sqrt{5}}{2}M_2e^{-\alpha t}$$

$$N_2(t)=\Theta_2^T M(t)=\begin{bmatrix}1\\\frac{1-\sqrt{5}}{2}\end{bmatrix}^T\begin{bmatrix}0\\M_2e^{-\alpha t}\end{bmatrix}=\frac{1+\sqrt{5}}{2}M_2e^{-\alpha t} \qquad ...(23)$$

The modal forces are given by Eq.(23). The solutions $\eta_1(t)$ and $\eta_2(t)$ of the modal equations are written in the form of the convolution integrals

$$\eta_1(t)=\frac{1}{m'_{11}\omega_1}\int_0^t N_1(t-\tau)\sin\omega_1\tau\,d\tau$$

$$= \frac{1+\sqrt{5}}{(5+\sqrt{5})(\alpha^2+\omega_1^2)} \frac{M_2}{I}\left[e^{-\alpha t} - \left(\cos\omega_1 t - \frac{\alpha}{\omega_1}\sin\omega_1 t\right)\right]$$

$$\eta_2(t) = \frac{1-\sqrt{5}}{(5-\sqrt{5})(\alpha^2+\omega_2^2)} \frac{M_2}{I}\left[e^{-\alpha t} - \left(\cos\omega_2 t - \frac{\alpha}{\omega_2}\sin\omega_2 t\right)\right] \quad ...(24)$$

where ω_1 and ω_2 are given above. Hence, the response can be written as

$$\theta_1(t) = \eta_1(t) + \eta_2(t), \theta_2(t) = \frac{1+\sqrt{5}}{2}\eta_1(t) + \frac{1-\sqrt{5}}{2}\eta_2(t) \quad ...(25)$$

(*d*) The equations of motion are

$$M\ddot{\theta}(t) + K\theta(t) = M(t) \quad ...(26)$$

where $M = I\begin{bmatrix} 1 & 0 \\ 0 & 1 \end{bmatrix}, K = \frac{GJ}{L}\begin{bmatrix} 2 & -1 \\ -1 & 1 \end{bmatrix}, \theta(t) = \begin{bmatrix} \theta_1(t) \\ \theta_2(t) \end{bmatrix}, M(t) = \begin{bmatrix} 0 \\ M_2 e^{-\alpha t} \end{bmatrix}$ ...(27)

Assuming a solution of the form

$$\theta(t) = \eta_1(t)\Theta_1 + \eta_2(t)\Theta_2 \quad ...(28)$$

in which $\eta_1(t)$ and $\eta_2(t)$ are modal coordinates and

$$\Theta_1 = \begin{bmatrix} 1 \\ \frac{1+\sqrt{5}}{2} \end{bmatrix}, \Theta_2 = \begin{bmatrix} 1 \\ \frac{1-\sqrt{5}}{2} \end{bmatrix} \quad ...(29)$$

are the modal vectors. The modal equations are given by

$$m'_{11}\ddot{\eta}_1(t) + m'_{11}\omega_1^2\eta_1(t) = N_1(t)$$

$$m'_{22}\ddot{\eta}_2(t) + m'_{22}\omega_2^2\eta_2(t) = N_2(t) \quad ...(30)$$

in which $\omega_1 = \sqrt{\frac{3-\sqrt{5}}{2}\frac{GJ}{IL}}, \omega_2 = \sqrt{\frac{3+\sqrt{5}}{2}\frac{GJ}{IL}}$ ...(31)

are the natural frequencies

$$m'_{11} = \frac{5+\sqrt{5}}{2}I, m'_{22} = \frac{5-\sqrt{5}}{2}I \quad ...(32)$$

are modal mass coefficients.

The modal forces are given by

$$N_1(t) = \frac{1+\sqrt{5}}{2}M_2 e^{-\alpha t}, N_2(t) = \frac{1-\sqrt{5}}{2}M_2 e^{-\alpha t} \quad ...(33)$$

The response is given by

$$\theta(n) = \eta_1(n)\Theta_1 + \eta_2(n)\Theta_2, n = 1, 2, ... \quad ...(34)$$

where $\eta_1(n)=\sum_{k=0}^{n} N_1(k)g_1(n-k),$

$$\eta_2(n)=\sum_{k=0}^{n} N_2(k), g_2(n-k), n=1,2,... \quad ...(35)$$

are the discrete-time modal coordinates given in the form of convolution sums, in which the discrete time impulse responses are given by

$$g_1(n)=\frac{T}{m'_{ii}\omega_i}\sin n\omega_i T, i=1,2 \quad ...(36)$$

where T is the sampling period. The discrete-time response is given by

$$\theta(n)=T\sum_{k=0}^{n}\left\{\left[\frac{N_1(k)}{m'_{11}\omega_1}\sin(n-k)\omega_1 T\right]\Theta_1+\left[\frac{N_2(k)}{m'_{22}\omega_2}\sin(n-k)\omega_2 T\right]\Theta_2\right\}$$

$$=\frac{TM_2}{1\sqrt{GJ/IL}}\sum_{k=0}^{n}\left\{e^{-\alpha kT}\sin(n-k)0.618034\sqrt{\frac{GJ}{IL}}T\begin{bmatrix}0.723607\\1.17082\end{bmatrix}\right.$$

$$\left.+e^{-\alpha kt}\sin(n-k)1.618034\sqrt{GJ/IL}\,T\begin{bmatrix}-0.276393\\0.17082\end{bmatrix}\right\} \quad ...(37)$$

Denoting $\sqrt{GJ/IL}=1$, $M_2/I=1$, $\alpha=1$ and $T=0.01$ s, the response is given by

$$\theta(n)=0.01\sum_{k=0}^{n}e^{-0.01k}\left\{\sin 0.618034(n-k)\begin{bmatrix}0.723607\\1.170820\end{bmatrix}\right.$$

$$\left.+\sin 1.618034(n-k)T\begin{bmatrix}-0.276393\\0.170820\end{bmatrix}\right\} \quad ...(38)$$

The discrete-time response sequence is given by

$$\theta(0)=\begin{bmatrix}0\\0\end{bmatrix}$$

$$\theta(1)=0.01\left\{\sin 0.00618034\begin{bmatrix}0.723607\\1.170820\end{bmatrix}\right.$$

$$\left.+\sin 0.0161803\begin{bmatrix}-0.276393\\0.170820\end{bmatrix}\right\}=\begin{bmatrix}1.82291\times10^{-9}\\9.999\times10^{-5}\end{bmatrix}$$

$$\theta(2)=0.01\left\{[\sin(0.00618034\times 2)+e^{-0.01}\sin 0.00618034]\begin{bmatrix}0.723607\\1.170820\end{bmatrix}\right.$$

$$\left.+[\sin(0.0161803\times 2)+e^{-0.01}\sin 0.0161803]\begin{bmatrix}-0.276393\\0.170820\end{bmatrix}\right\}$$

$$=\begin{bmatrix}1.54497\times10^{-8}\\2.990\times10^{-4}\end{bmatrix} \quad ...(39)$$

(*e*) The response $\theta_i(n)$ (i = 1, 2) is plotted in Fig. E8.9(d) obtained from the following MATLAB program.

```
% Response of 2-degree of freedom system
clear
clf
I=1; % mass
k=1;%=GJ/L torsional stiffness
M=I*[1 0;0 1];% mass matrix
K=k*[2 -1;-1 1];% stiffness matrix
[u,W]=eig(K,M);% eigenvalue problem
% W= eigenvalues
u(:,1)=u(:,1)/max(u(:,1)); % normalization
u(:,2)=u(:,2)/max(u(:,2));
[w(1),I1]=min(max(W)); % relabeling of the eigenvalues
[w(2),I2]=max(max(W));
w(1)=sqrt(w(1)); % lowest natural frequency
w(2)=sqrt(w(2)); % highest natural frequency
U(:,1)=u(:,I1); % relabeling of the eigenvectors
U(:,2)=u(:,I2);
m1=U(:,1)'*M*U(:,1); % mass quantities
m2=U(:,2)'*M*U(:,2);
T=0.01; % sampling period
N=2000; % sampling times
M2=1; % second disk torque amplitude
alpha=1;
n=[1:N];
N1=U(:,1)'*[zeros(1,N);M2*exp(-alpha*n*T)]; % modal forces
N2=U(:,2)'*[zeros(1,N);M2*exp(-alpha*n*T)];
g1=T*sin((n-1)*w(1)*T)/(m1*w(1)); %discrete time impulse responses
g2=T*sin((n-1)*w(2)*T)/(m2*w(2));
c1=conv(N1,g1); %convolution sum
c2=conv(N2,g2);
theta=U(:,1)*c1(1:N)+U(:,2)*c2(1:N); % N samples for plotting
n=[0:N-1];
axes('position',[0.1 0.2 0.8 0.7])
plot(n,theta(1,:),'.',n,theta(2,:),'.')
h=title('Response by the convolution sum');
set(h,'FontName', 'Times','FontSize',12)
h=xlabel('n')
set(h,'FontName','Times','FontSize',12)
h=ylabel('\theta_1(n),\theta_2(n)');
set(h,'FontName','Times','FontSize',12)
grid
```

Its output is shown in Fig. E8.9(d).

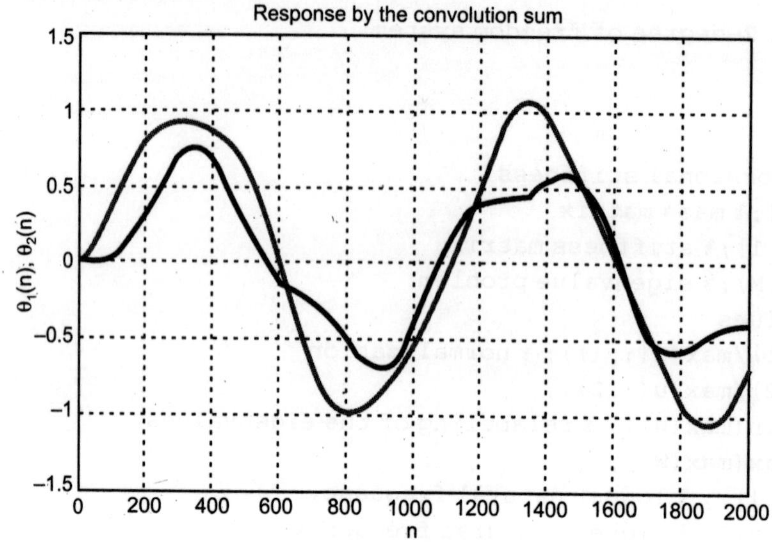

Fig. E8.9(d)

Example E8.10: Obtain the response of the system of Problem E8.9 to the initial excitation $\theta_1(0) = 0$, $\theta_2(0) = 1.5$, $\dot{\theta}_1(0) = 1.8\sqrt{GJ/I\ell}$, and $\dot{\theta}_2(0) = 0$. Plot the response of the system using MATLAB.

Solution: The initial conditions are given as

$$\theta_1(0) = 0,\ \theta_2(0) = 1.5,\ \dot{\theta}_1(0) = 1.8\sqrt{\frac{GJ}{IL}},\ \dot{\theta}_2(0) = 0 \qquad ...(1)$$

From Problem E8.9, we have

$$\omega_1 = 0.6180\sqrt{\frac{GJ}{IL}},\ \Theta_1 = \begin{bmatrix}\Theta_{11}\\ \Theta_{21}\end{bmatrix} = \Theta_{11}\begin{bmatrix}1\\ 1.6180\end{bmatrix}$$

$$\omega_2 = 0.6180\sqrt{\frac{GJ}{IL}},\ \Theta_2 = \begin{bmatrix}\Theta_{12}\\ \Theta_{22}\end{bmatrix} = \Theta_{12}\begin{bmatrix}1\\ 1.6180\end{bmatrix} \qquad ...(2)$$

The response to the initial excitation is a superposition of the natural modes. Hence

$$\theta(t) = C_1 \cos(\omega_1 t - \phi_1)\Theta_1 + C_2 \cos(\omega_2 t - \phi_2)\Theta_2$$

or

$$\theta(t) = C_1(\cos \omega_1 t \cos \phi_1 + \sin \omega_1 t \sin \phi_1)\Theta_1 + C_2(\cos \omega_2 t \cos \phi_2 + \sin \omega_2 t \sin \phi_2)\Theta_2 \qquad ...(3)$$

and

$$\theta(t) = C_1\omega_1(\sin \omega_1 t \cos \phi_1 - \cos \omega_1 t \sin \phi_1)\Theta_1 - C_2\omega_2(\sin \omega_2 t \cos \phi_2 - \cos \omega_2 t \sin \phi_2)\Theta_2$$

If $t = 0$, then Eq.(3) become

$$\theta(0) = \begin{bmatrix}\theta_1(0)\\ \theta_2(0)\end{bmatrix} = C_1 \cos\phi_1\begin{bmatrix}\Theta_{11}\\ \Theta_{21}\end{bmatrix} + C_2 \cos\phi_2\begin{bmatrix}\Theta_{12}\\ \Theta_{22}\end{bmatrix}$$

$$\dot{\theta}(0) = \begin{bmatrix} \dot{\theta}_1(0) \\ \dot{\theta}_2(0) \end{bmatrix} = C_1\omega_1 \sin\phi_1 \begin{bmatrix} \Theta_{11} \\ \Theta_{21} \end{bmatrix} + C_2\omega_2 \sin\phi_2 \begin{bmatrix} \Theta_{12} \\ \Theta_{22} \end{bmatrix} \quad ...(4)$$

From Eq.(4), we have

$$C_1 \cos\phi_1 = \frac{\Theta_{22}\theta_{10} - \Theta_{12}\theta_{20}}{|\Theta|}, C_2 \cos\phi_2 = \frac{\Theta_{11}\theta_{20} - \Theta_{21}\theta_{10}}{|\Theta|}$$

$$C_1 \sin\phi_1 = \frac{\Theta_{22}\dot{\theta}_{10} - \Theta_{12}\dot{\theta}_{20}}{\omega_1 |\Theta|}, C_2 \sin\phi_2 = \frac{\Theta_{11}\dot{\theta}_{20} - \Theta_{21}\dot{\theta}_{10}}{\omega_2 |\Theta|} \quad ...(5)$$

where $\theta_{10} = \theta_1(0)$, $\theta_{20} = \theta_2(0)$, $\dot{\theta}_{10} = \dot{\theta}_1(0)$, $\dot{\theta}_{20} = \dot{\theta}_2(0)$ and $|\Theta|$ is the determinant of the matrix

$$\Theta = \begin{bmatrix} \Theta_{11} & \Theta_{12} \\ \Theta_{21} & \Theta_{22} \end{bmatrix} \quad ...(6)$$

Letting $\Theta_{11} = \Theta_{12} = 1$,

$$C_1 \cos\phi_1 = \frac{1.5}{|\Theta|},\ C_2 \cos\phi_2 = \frac{1.5}{|\Theta|}$$

$$C_1 \sin\phi_1 = \frac{1.8}{|\Theta|},\ C_2 \sin\phi_2 = \frac{1.8}{|\Theta|}$$

$$|\Theta| = \begin{vmatrix} 1 & 1 \\ 1.6180 & -0.6180 \end{vmatrix} = -2.2360 \quad ...(7)$$

The response to the given initial excitation is given by

$$\theta(t) = \begin{bmatrix} \theta_1(t) \\ \theta_2(t) \end{bmatrix} = \frac{1}{2.2360}\left[(1.5\cos\omega_1 t + 1.8\cos\omega_1 t) \begin{bmatrix} 1 \\ 1.6180 \end{bmatrix} \right.$$

$$\left. + (-1.5 \cos \omega_2 t + 1.8 \sin \omega_2 t) \begin{bmatrix} 1 \\ -0.6180 \end{bmatrix} \right]$$

or by components

$$\theta_1(t) = 0.6708\left(\cos 0.6180\sqrt{\frac{GJ}{IL}}\, t - \cos 1.6180\sqrt{\frac{GJ}{IL}} t \right)$$

$$+0.8060\left(\sin 0.6180\sqrt{\frac{GJ}{IL}} t + \sin 1.6180\sqrt{\frac{GJ}{IL}} t \right)$$

$$\theta_2(t) = 1.0854 \cos 0.6180\sqrt{\frac{GJ}{IL}} t + 1.3025 \sin 0.6180\sqrt{\frac{GJ}{IL}} t$$

$$+ 0.4146 \cos 1.6180 \sqrt{\frac{GJ}{IL}}\, t - 0.4975 \sin 106180\sqrt{\frac{GJ}{IL}} t \quad ...(8)$$

The MATLAB program listed as follows:

```
% response of a two-degree of freedom system to initial excitations
clear
clf
I=1; % inertia
k=1;%=GJ/L stiffness
M=I*[1 0;0 1];% mass
K=k*[2 -1;-1 1];%stiffness
[u,W]=eig(K,M);% eigenvalue problem
% W=matrix of eigenvalues
u(:,1)=u(:,1)/max(u(:,1)); % normalization
u(:,2)=u(:,2)/max(u(:,2));
[w(1),I1]=min(max(W)); % relabeling
[w(2),I2]=max(max(W));
w(1)=sqrt(w(1)); % lowest natural frequency
w(2)=sqrt(w(2)); % highest natural frequency
U(:,1)=u(:,I1); % relabeling
U(:,2)=u(:,I2);
x0=[0;2];% Initial displacement
v0=[2*sqrt(k/I);0]; % initial velocity
t=[0:0.1:20]; % initial time, time increment, final time
% displacement
x1=(((U(2,2)*x0(1)-U(1,2)*x0(2))*cos(w(1)*t)+(U(2,2)*v0(1)
-U(1,2)*v0(2))*sin(w(1)*t)/w(1))*U(1,1)+((U(1,1)*x0(2)
-U(2,1)*x0(1))*cos(w(2)*t)+(U(1,1)*v0(2)-U(2,1)*v0(1))*sin(w(2)*t)/
w(2))*U(1,2))/det(U);
x2=(((U(2,2)*x0(1)-U(1,2)*x0(2))*cos(w(1)*t)+(U(2,2)*v0(1)-
U(1,2)*v0(2))*sin(w(1)*t)/w(1))*U(2,1)+((U(1,1)*x0(2)-
U(2,1)*x0(1))*cos(w(2)*t)+(U(1,1)*v0(2)-U(2,1)*v0(1))*sin(w(2)*t)/
w(2))*U(2,2))/det(U);
axes('position',[0.2 0.3 0.6 0.5])
plot(t,x1,t,x2)
title('Response to initial excitation')
ylabel('\theta_1(t),\theta_2(t)')
xlabel('t[s]')
legend('\theta_1(t)','\theta_2(t)',1)
grid
```

The corresponding output obtained is shown in Fig. E8.10(a).

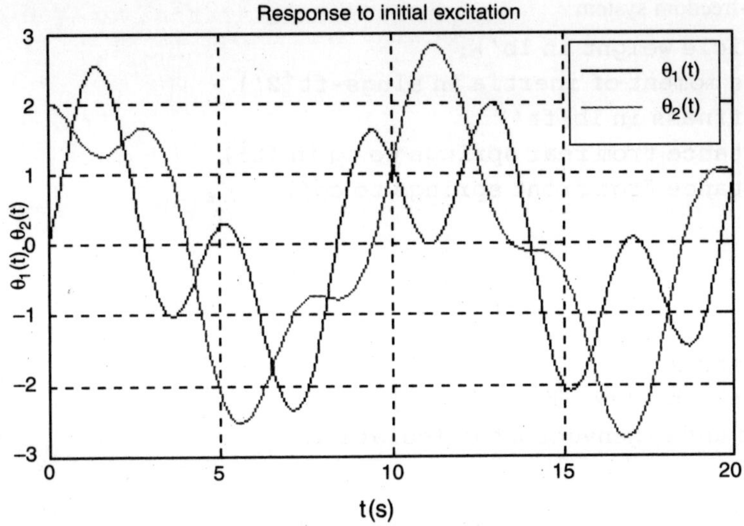

Fig. E8.10(a)

Example E8.11: A simplified model of an automobile suspension system is shown in Fig. E8.11 as a two degree of freedom system. Write a MATLAB script to determine the natural frequencies of this model.

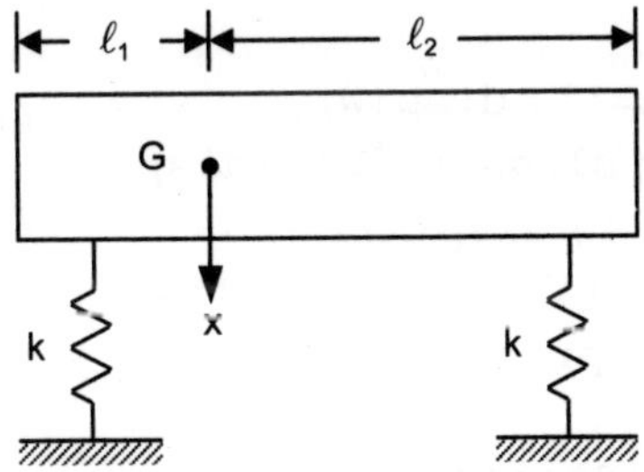

Fig. E8.11 Simplified model of an automobile

The differential equations governing the motion of the system are given as

$$\begin{bmatrix} m & 0 \\ 0 & I \end{bmatrix}\begin{bmatrix} \ddot{x} \\ \ddot{\theta} \end{bmatrix} + \begin{bmatrix} 2k & (\ell_2-\ell_1)k \\ (\ell_2-\ell_1)k & (\ell_2^2-\ell_1^2)k \end{bmatrix}\begin{bmatrix} x \\ \theta \end{bmatrix} = \begin{bmatrix} 0 \\ 0 \end{bmatrix}$$

where x is the displacement of the mass center and θ is the angular rotation of the body from its horizontal position.

The parameters are given as

Automobile weight, $W = 5000$ lb

Centroidal moment of inertia, $I = 400$ slug-ft^2

Spring stiffness, $k = 2500$ lb/ft

$\ell_1 = 3.4$ ft

$\ell_2 = 4.6$ ft

Solution: The MATLAB program is given as follows:

```
% Two-degree-of-freedom system
W=input('Vehicle weight in lb');
I=input('Mass moment of inertia in slugs-ft^2')
k=input('Stiffness in lb/ft')
a=input('Distance from rear springs to cg in ft')
b=input('Distance from front springs to cg')
% mass matrix
g=32.2;
m=W/g;
M=[m,0;0,I];
% stiffness matrix
K=[2*k,(b-a)*k;(b-a)*k,(b^2+a^2)*k];
% eigenvalues and eigenvectors calculation
C=inv(M)*K;
[V,D]=eig(C);
om_1=sqrt(D(1,1));
om_2=sqrt(D(2,2));
X1=[V(1,1);V(2,1)];
X2=[V(1,2);V(2,2)];
% Output
disp('Vehicle weight in lb='); disp(W)
disp('moment of inertia in slugs-ft^2');disp(I)
disp('Stiffness in lb/ft='); disp(k)
disp('Distance from rear springs to cg in ft='); disp(a)
disp('Distance from front springs to cg in ft=');disp(b)
disp('Mass-matrix');disp(M)
disp('Stiffness-matrix');disp(K)
disp('Natural frequencies in rad/s=');
disp(om_1)
disp(om_2)
disp('Mode shape vectors'); disp(X1)
disp(X2)
```

The output of this program is as follows:

Vehicle weight in lb 5000
    $W = 5000$
Mass moment of inertia in slugs-ft^2 400
    $I = 400$
Stiffness in lb/ft 2500
    $k = 2500$

Distance from rear springs to cg gravity in ft 3.4
$a = 3.4000$
Distance from front springs to cg 4.6
$b = 4.6000$
Vehicle weight in lb = 5000
Moment of inertia in slugs-ft^2 400
Stiffness in lb/ft = 2500
Distance from rear springs to cg in ft = 3.4000
Distance from front springs to cg in ft = 4.6000
Mass-matrix

```
155.2795    0
  0       400.0000
```

Stiffness-matrix

```
1.0e + 004 *
0.5000   0.3000
0.3000   8.1800
```

Natural frequencies in rad/s=

```
5.6003
14.3296
```

Mode shape vectors

```
-0.9991
 0.0433

-0.1109
-0.9938
```

Example E8.12: Determine the free-vibration response of a two-degree of freedom system shown in Fig. E8.12 with the initial conditions $x_1(0) = 0$, $x_2(0) = 0.005$ m, $\dot{x}_1(0) = 0$, $\dot{x}_2(0) = 0$. The parameters of the system are given as $m = 30$ kg, $k = 20{,}000$ N/m, and $c = 150$ N.s/m.

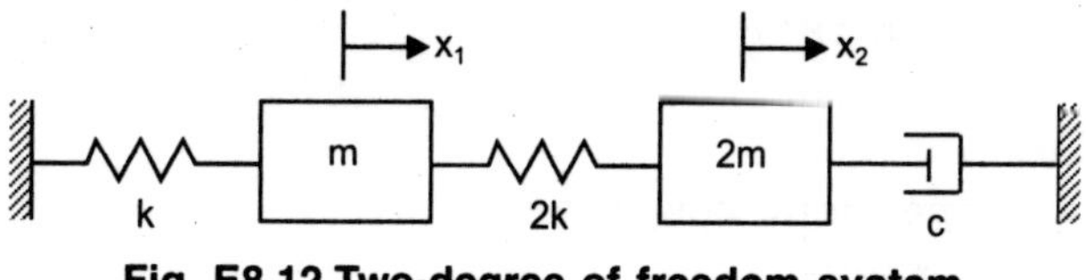

Fig. E8.12 Two-degree of freedom system

The differential equations governing the motion of the system are:

$$\begin{bmatrix} m & 0 \\ 0 & 2m \end{bmatrix}\begin{bmatrix} \ddot{x}_1 \\ \ddot{x}_2 \end{bmatrix} + \begin{bmatrix} 0 & 0 \\ 0 & c \end{bmatrix}\begin{bmatrix} \dot{x}_1 \\ \dot{x}_2 \end{bmatrix} + \begin{bmatrix} 3k & -2k \\ -2k & 2k \end{bmatrix}\begin{bmatrix} x_1 \\ x_2 \end{bmatrix} = \begin{bmatrix} 0 \\ 0 \end{bmatrix}$$

or $\quad M\dot{y} + Ky = 0$

where $\quad M = \begin{bmatrix} 0 & M \\ M & c \end{bmatrix}; K = \begin{bmatrix} -M & 0 \\ 0 & K \end{bmatrix}; Y = \begin{bmatrix} \dot{x} \\ x \end{bmatrix}$

The solution is assumed as

$$y = \phi e^{-\gamma t}$$

where γ are the eigenvalues of $M^{-1}K$ and ϕ are the eigenvectors. The general solution is a linear combination over all solutions, that is,

$$y = \sum_{j=1}^{4} c_j \, \phi_j \, e^{-\gamma_j t}$$

and application of initial conditions gives

$$y_0 = \sum_{j=1}^{4} c_j \, \phi_j = VC$$

and $C = V^{-1} y_0$

Solution: The MATLAB program is given as follows:

```
m=30; % Mass
k=20000; % Stiffness
c=150; % Damping
% 4 x 4 matrices
disp('4 x 4 Mass matrix');
mt=[0,0,m,0;0,0,0,2*m;m,0,0,0;0,2*m,0,c];
disp('4 x 4 stiffness matrix');
kt=[-m,0,0,0;0,-2*m,0,0;0,0,3*k,-2*k;0,0,-2*k,2*k];
Z=inv(mt)*kt;
[V,D]=eig(Z);
disp('Eigenvalues');
V
disp('Initial conditions');
x0=[0;0;0.005;0]
disp('Integration constants');
S=inv(V)*x0
tk=linspace(0,2,101);
% Evaluation of time dependent response
% Recall that x1=y3 and x2=y4
for k=1:101
  t=tk(k);
  for i=3:4
    x(k,i-2)=0;
    for j=1:4
          x(k,i-2)=x(k,i-2)+(real(S(j))*real(V(i,j))-imag(S(j))*imag(V(i,j)))
*cos(imag(D(j,j))*t);
          x(k,i-2)=x(k,i-2)+(imag(S(j))*real(V(i,j))-real(S(j))*imag(V(i,j)))
*sin(imag(V(i,j))*t);
      x(k,i-2)=x(k,i-2)*exp(-real(D(j,j))*t);
```

```
    end
  end
end
plot(tk,x(:,1),'-',tk,x(:,2),':')
title('Solution of problem E8.12')
xlabel('t[sec]')
ylabel('x(m)')
legend('x1(t)','x2(t)')
```

The output of this program is given below. See also Fig. E8.12(a).

$V=$

-0.9390	-0.9390	$0.5886-0.0085i$	$0.5886+0.0085i$
$0.3428-0.0185i$	$0.3428+0.0185i$	0.8050	0.8050
$0.0001-0.0188i$	$0.0001+0.0188i$	$-0.0026+0.0440i$	$-0.0026-0.0440i$
$0.0003+0.0069i$	$0.0003-0.0069i$	$-0.0044+0.0601i$	$-0.0044-0.0601i$

Initial conditions

$x0=$

0
0
0.0050
0

Integration constants

$S=$

$-0.0013 + 0.1048i$
$-0.0013 - 0.1048i$
$-0.0019 - 0.0119i$
$-0.0019 + 0.0119i$

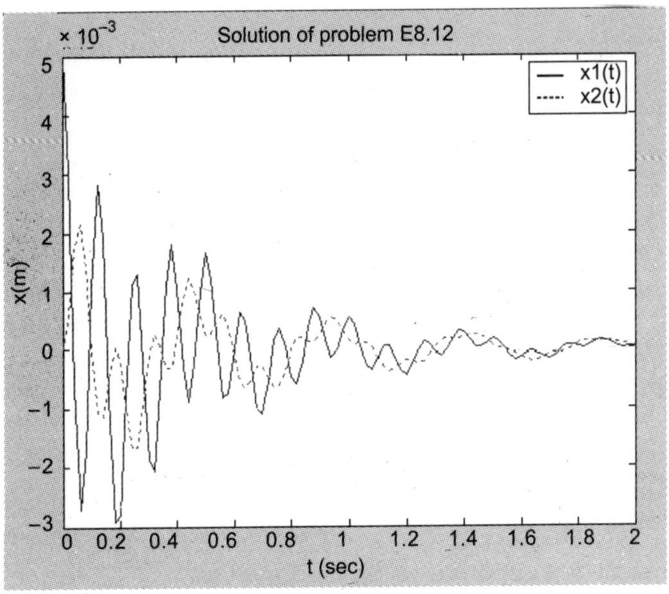

Fig. E8.12(a)

Example E8.13: For systems with arbitrary viscous-damping, the response must be obtained in the state-space, which implies the use of the transition-matrix. If the response is to be evaluated on a computer, then the state-equations must be transformed to discrete time. Determine the free-vibration response of a 2-degree of freedom damped system with initial conditions $X(0) = \{0, 0.01\}$ and $\dot{X}(0) = \{0, 0\}$. Given

$$M = \begin{bmatrix} 0 & 0 & 30 & 0 \\ 0 & 0 & 0 & 50 \\ 30 & 0 & 0 & 0 \\ 0 & 50 & 0 & 80 \end{bmatrix}$$

$$[K] = \begin{bmatrix} -40 & 0 & 0 & 0 \\ 0 & -50 & 0 & 0 \\ 0 & 0 & 35000 & -25000 \\ 0 & 0 & -25000 & 4000 \end{bmatrix}$$

Solution: The solution is similar to the problem E8.12, and the MATLAB program is written as follows:

```
mt=[0 0 30 0;0,0,0,50;30,0,0,0;0,50,0,80];
kt=[-40,0,0,0;0,-50,0,0;0,0,35000,-25000;0,0,-25000, 4000];
Z=inv(mt)*kt;
[V,D]=eig(Z);
disp('Eigenvalues')
DS=[D(1,1),D(2,2),D(3,3),D(4,4)]
disp('Eigenvectors')
V
x0=[0;0;0.01;0];
S=inv(V)*x0;
tk=linspace(0,2,101);
for k=1:101
 t=tk(k);
 for i=3:4
 x(k,i-2)=0;
 for j=1:4
 x(k,i-2)=x(k,i-2)+(real(S(j))*real(V(i,j))-imag(S(j))*imag(V(i,j)))*cos
(imag(D(j,j))*t);
  x(k,i-2)=x(k,i-2)+(imag(S(j))*real(V(i,j))-imag(S(j))*imag(V(i,j)))
*sin(imag(V(i,j))*t);
 x(k,i-2)=x(k,i-2)*exp(-real(D(j,j))*t);
 end
 end
end
plot(tk,x(:,1),'-',tk,x(:,2),':')
title('Free Vibration response of damped system')
```

```
xlabel('t (sec)')
ylabel('x (m)')
legend('x1(t)','x2(t)')
```

The output obtained is given as follows:

Eigenvalues

DS =

Columns 1 through 2

1.1082e – 001 + 4.4615e + 001i 1.1082e – 001 – 4.4615e + 001i

Columns 3 through 4

–1.5162e + 001 1.6541e + 001

Eigenvectors

V =

Columns 1 through 2

9.5465e – 001 9.5465e – 001

– 2.9638e – 001 + 9.4404e – 003i – 2.9638e – 001 – 9.4404e – 003i

– 6.3783e – 005 + 2.5677e – 002i – 6.3783e – 005 – 2.5677e – 002i

– 1.9510e – 004 – 6.6437e – 003i – 1.9510e – 004 + 6.6437e – 003i

Columns 3 through 4

4.6275e – 001 – 4.5475e – 001

8.8381e – 001 – 8.8839e – 001

3.6624e – 002 3.2991e – 002

5.8290e – 002 5.3710e – 002

Figure E8.13 shows the response in time-domain obtained from the output of the MATLAB program.

Note: Here $M = \begin{bmatrix} 25 & 0 \\ 0 & 50 \end{bmatrix}, C = \begin{bmatrix} 0 & 0 \\ 0 & 80 \end{bmatrix}$ and

$$K = \begin{bmatrix} 35000 & -25000 \\ -25000 & 3000 \end{bmatrix}$$

and state matrices are respectively

$$M^T = \begin{bmatrix} 0 & 0 & 25 & 0 \\ 0 & 0 & 0 & 50 \\ 25 & 0 & 0 & 0 \\ 0 & 50 & 0 & 80 \end{bmatrix}$$

and $$K^T = \begin{bmatrix} -30 & 0 & 0 & 0 \\ 0 & -50 & 0 & 0 \\ 0 & 0 & 35000 & -25000 \\ 0 & 0 & -25000 & 3000 \end{bmatrix}$$

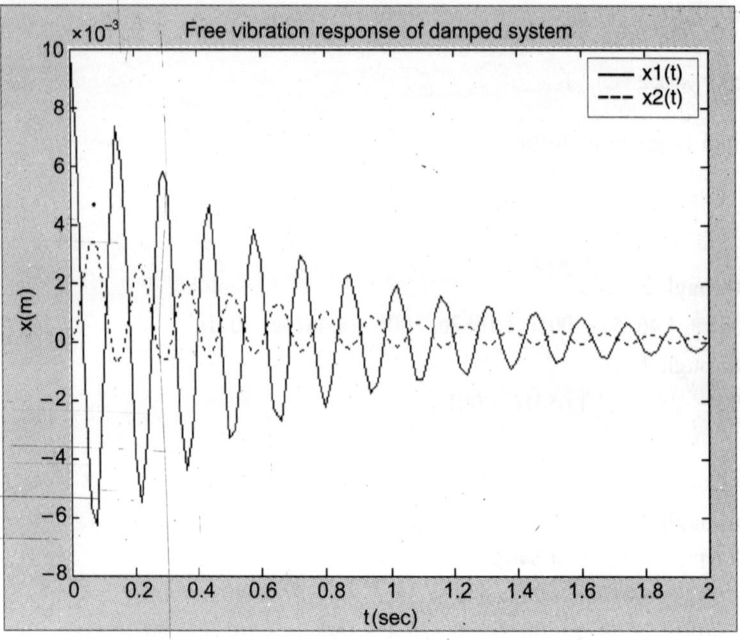

Fig. E8.13

Example E8.14: In the Example E8.13, if a force $F_0\exp(-\alpha t)$ acts on the system, find the forced vibration response using the MATLAB program. Given $F_0 = 60$.

Solution: Here first few steps are common as in free-vibration response problem.

```
syms t tau
m=25;
k=12500;
c=80;
F0=60;
alpha=1.5;
mt=[0,0,m,0;0,0,0,2*m;m,0,0,0;0,2*m,0,c];
kt=[-m,0,0,0;0,-2*m,0,0;0,0,3*k,-2*k;0,0,-2*k,2*k];
z=inv(mt)*kt;
[V,D]=eig(z);
L=conj(V)'*mt*V;
for j=1:4
 ss=1/sqrt(L(j,j));
 for i=1:4
 P(i,j)=V(i,j)*ss;
 end
end
F=[0;0;0;F0*exp(-alpha*tau)];
G=P'*F;
```

```
G=vpa(G);
%Convolution integral solution
for i=1:4
 f(i)=G(i)*exp(-D(i,i)*(t-tau));
 p(i)=int(f(i),tau,0,t);
end
disp('solution for modal coordinates')
p=[p(1);p(2);p(3);p(4)]; disp(p)
y=P*p;
disp('response')
disp('x1=y3, x2=y4')
y=vpa(y);
% Plotting the system response
time=linspace(0,1.5,101);
for k=1:101
 x1a=subs(y(3),t,time(k));
 x2a=subs(y(4),t,time(k));
 x1b(k)=vpa(real(x1a));
 x2b(k)=vpa(real(x2a));
end
x1=double(x1b);
x2=double(x2b);
plot(time,x1,'-',time,x2,':')
xlabel('t(seconds)')
ylabel('response(m)')
legend('x1(t)', 'x2(t)')
```

The output of the program is shown as the forced vibration response in Fig. E8.14.

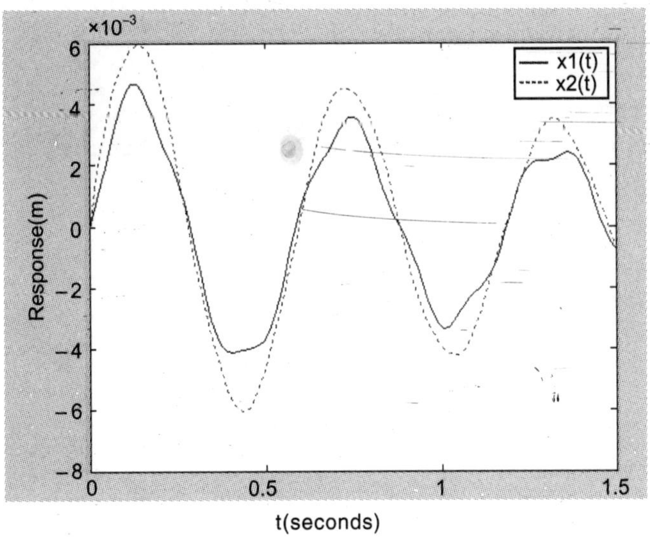

Fig. E8.14

Example E8.15: Two gears A and B in mesh are mounted on two uniform circular shafts of equal stiffness $\frac{GJ}{L}$. If the gear A is subjected to a torque $M_0 \cos \omega t$, derive an expression for angular motion of B. Assume the radius ratio as: $\frac{R_A}{R_B} = n$. Here L is length of each shaft. Write a MATLAB script to plot the response.

Solution: Here the equation of motion is given by

$$I_{eq}\ddot{\theta}_A + k_{eq} \cdot \theta_A = M_A = M_0 \cos \omega t \qquad \text{...(1)}$$

where the equivalent stiffness of the gears $k_{eq} = \frac{GJ}{L}(1+n^2)$ and equivalent moment of inertia of gears $I_{eq} = I_A + n^2 I_B$.

Simplifying the above equation of motion we get:

$$\ddot{\theta}_A + \omega_n^2 \theta_A = \frac{M_0}{I_A + n^2 I_B} \cos \omega t, \text{ and } \omega_n^2 = \frac{GJ(1+n^2)}{L(I_A + n^2 I_B)} \qquad \text{...(2)}$$

Since $\theta_B = n\,\theta_A$, the solution is given by

$$\theta_B = \frac{M_0 L n}{GJ(1+n^2)[1-(\omega/\omega_n)^2]} \cos \omega t$$

The MATLAB program to plot the values of amplitude of θ_B for various values of ω is given as follows:

```
M0=1;% amplitude of the moment
L=1; % length of shaft
GJ=1;% torsional stiffness
n=3;% gear ratio
r=[0:0.01:3];% frequency ratio
thetab=(M0*L*n)./(GJ*(1+(n.^n))*(1-r.^2)); % amplitude
plot(r,thetab)
title('Response to torque')
ylabel('\theta_b')
xlabel('\omega/\omega_n')
grid
```

The output is shown in Fig. E8.15 (a).

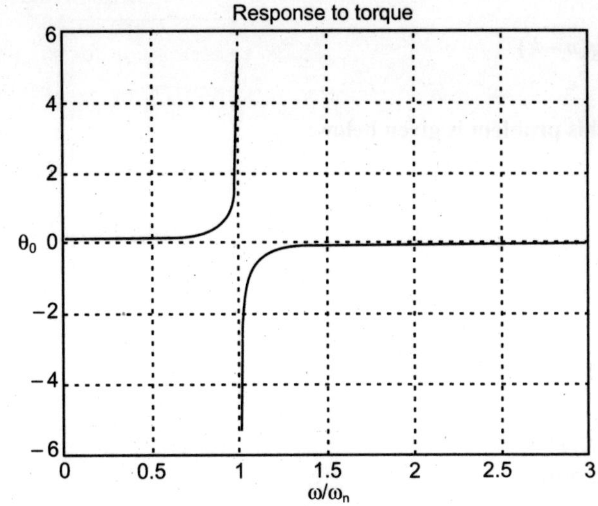

Fig. E8.15(a)

Example E8.16: Derive the response of a viscously damped single-degree of freedom system to the trapezoidal pulse shown in Fig. E8.16. Plot response for system parameters, m = 15 kg, c = 25 Ns/m and k = 5000 N/m. Use convolution sum

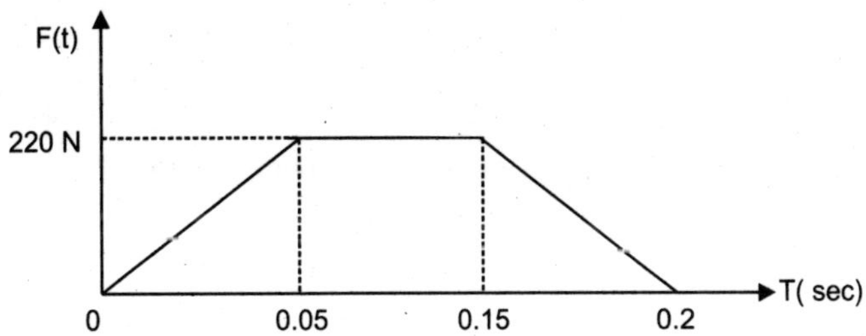

Fig. E8.16

Solution: The system is described by:

$$\ddot{x}+2\xi\omega_n\dot{x}+\omega_n^2 x=\frac{F(t)}{m}$$

$$F(t)=\begin{cases}\dfrac{2F_0}{T}t, \ 0<t<\dfrac{T}{2}\\ F_0, \dfrac{T}{2}<t<\dfrac{3T}{2}\\ 2F_0(2-\dfrac{t}{T}), \dfrac{3T}{2}<t<2T\\ 0, t>2T\end{cases}$$

where T = 0.2 sec in Fig. E8.16

The discrete time response by convolution sum is:

$$x(n) = \sum_{k=0}^{n} F(k)g(n-k)$$

The MATLAB script for this problem is given below:

```
m=15; % mass
c=25; % damping
k=5000; % stiffness
F0=220;
T=0.2;
wn=sqrt(k/m); % Natural frequency
zeta=c/(2*sqrt(m*k));
Ts=0.003; % Sampling period
N=201; % sampling times
wd=wn*sqrt(1-zeta^2); % frequency
% force
for n=1:N,
if n<=(T/2)/Ts+1;F(n)=2*F0*(n-1)*Ts/T; else;F(n)=F0;end
if n>(3*T/2)/Ts+1;F(n)=2*F0*(2-(n-1)*Ts/T);end
if n>2*T/Ts+1;F(n)=0;end
end
n=[1:N];
g=Ts*exp(-(n-1)*zeta*wn*Ts).*sin((n-1)*wd*Ts)/(m*wd);
% discrete-time impulse response
c0=conv(F,g); % Convolution sum
c=c0(1:N); % plot to N samples
n=[0:N-1];
axes('position',[0.1 0.2 0.8 0.7])
plot(n,c,'.');
title('Response to the Trapezodial pulse');
xlabel('n')
ylabel('x(n) [m]')
grid
```

Output of this program is the Fig. E8.16(a).

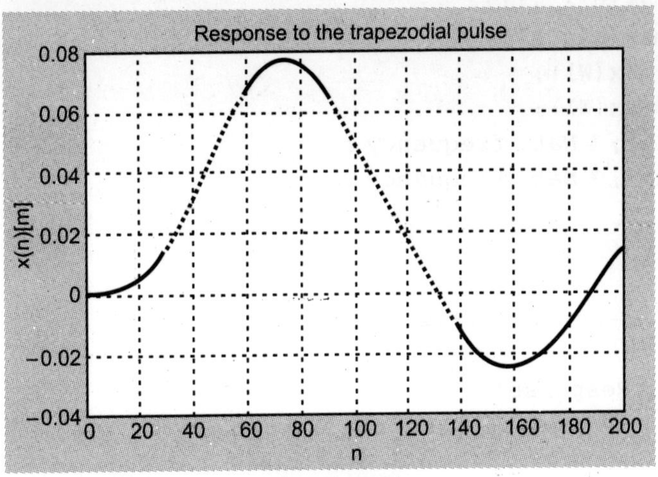

Fig. E8.16(a)

Example E8.17: A two storey building is undergoing a horizontal motion $y(t) = Y_0 \cdot \sin\omega t$. Derive expression for displacement of second floor. Write MATLAB script to plot the response. Assume appropriate values of stiffness and mass of the system.

Equations of motion for building can be written as:

$$\begin{bmatrix} 2 & 0 \\ 0 & 2 \end{bmatrix} \begin{Bmatrix} \ddot{x}_1 \\ \ddot{x}_2 \end{Bmatrix}_{+\alpha 2} \begin{bmatrix} 4 & -2 \\ -2 & 2 \end{bmatrix} \begin{Bmatrix} x_1 \\ x_2 \end{Bmatrix}_{=\alpha 2} \begin{Bmatrix} Y_0 \sin \omega t \\ 0 \end{Bmatrix}$$

where $\quad \alpha^2 = \dfrac{12EI}{mH^3} = \dfrac{12}{m} = 6$

Solving for steady-state response we get:

$$X_1 = \frac{(\alpha^2 - \omega^2)\alpha^2}{(\omega^2 - \omega_1^2)(\omega^2 - \omega_2^2)} Y_0$$

$$X_2 = \frac{\alpha^4}{(\omega^2 - \omega_1^2)(\omega^2 - \omega_2^2)} Y_0$$

These values are to be plotted against various values of ω.

Solution: The MATLAB script for this problem is given as follows:

```
m=20;% mass
k=200; % k=12EI/H³ stiffness
w0=k/m;
M=[m 0;0 m]; %mass matrix
K=[2*k -k;-k k]; % stiffness matrix
%eigenvalues
```

```
[u,W]=eig(K,M);
u(:,1)=u(:,1)/max(u(:,1));
u(:,2)=u(:,2)/max(u(:,2));
[wn(1),I1]=min(max(W));
[wn(2),I2]=max(max(W));
wn(1)=sqrt(wn(1)); % Nat. frequency 1
wn(2)=sqrt(wn(2)); % Nat. frequency 2
U(:,1)=u(:,I1);
U(:,2)=u(:,I2);
w=[0:0.002:6];
T2=(w0^2)./((w.^2-wn(1)^2).*(w.^2-wn(2)^2));
plot(w,T2)
title('Frequency Response')
ylabel('{\it{X}}_2(\omega)/{\it{Y}}_0')
xlabel('\omega')
axis([0 8 -5 5])
grid
```

The MATLAB output is shown in Fig. E8.17(a).

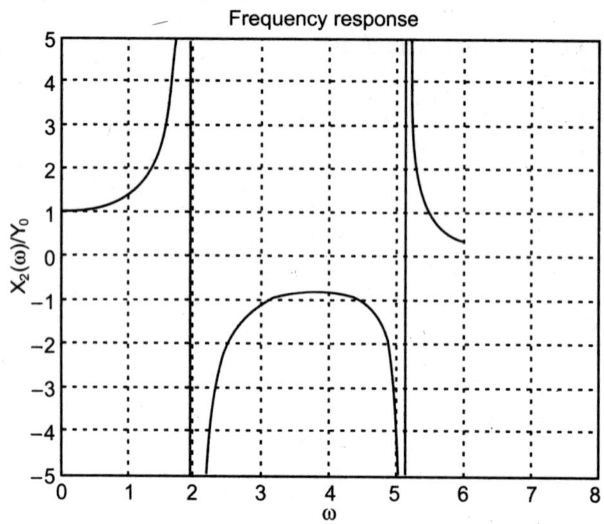

Fig. E8.17(a)

Example E8.18: A 3-degree of freedom system shown in Fig. E8.18. Obtain the natural frequencies and mode shapes using MATLAB script. Assume $k = m = 1$.

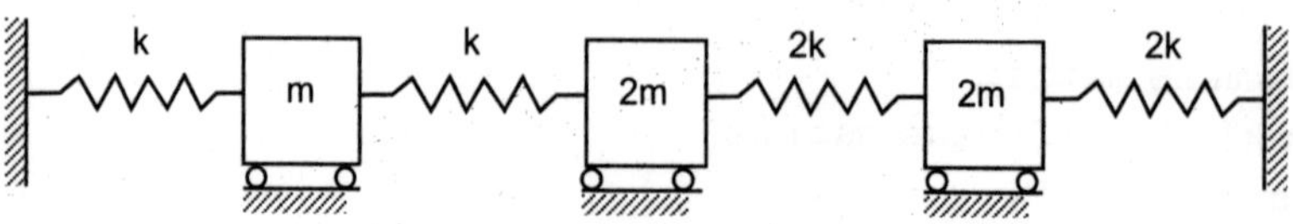

Fig. E8.18

The equations of motion can be written as:

$$M\ddot{x}(t) + Kx(t) = 0$$

with $x(t) = [x_1(t)\ x_2(t)\ x_3(t)]$; T as the displacement vector

$$M = \begin{bmatrix} m & 0 & 0 \\ 0 & 2m & 0 \\ 0 & 0 & 2m \end{bmatrix} \text{and } K = \begin{bmatrix} 2k & -k & 0 \\ -k & 3k & -2k \\ 0 & -2k & 4k \end{bmatrix}$$

as the mass and stiffness matrices.

Solution:

The MATLAB script for finding the natural frequencies and mode shapes is given as follows:

```
k=1; % stiffness
m=1; % mass
M=m*[1 0 0;0 2 0;0 0 2]; % mass matrix
K=k*[2 -1 0;-1 3 -2;0 -2 4]; % stiffness matrix
N=3;
R=chol(M); % Cholesky decomposition technique
L=R';
A=inv(L)*K*inv(L');
[x,W]=eig(A);
v=inv(L')*x;
for i=1:N,
 w1(i)=sqrt(W(i,i));
end
[w,I]=sort(w1);
disp('The first three natural frequencies are')
disp(w(1))
disp(w(2))
disp(w(3))
n=[1:N];
disp('The corresponding mass-orthonormalized mode shapes are')
for j=1:N,
 U(:,j)=v(:,I(j));
 U(:,j)=U(:,j)/(U(:,j)'*M*U(:,j));
 disp('mode-')
 disp(j)
 disp(U(:,j))
end
```

The outputs are as follows:

The first three natural frequencies are

0.7071
1.4142
1.7321

The corresponding mass-orthonormalized mode shapes are

mode–

1
–0.3651
–0.5477
–0.3651

mode–

2
0.8165
–0.0000
–0.4082

mode–

3
–0.4472
0.4472
–0.4472

Example E8.19: In Fig. E8.18, if mass *m* is subjected to unit step function *u*(*t*), determine the response using modal analysis. Write a MATLAB script to plot the displacement response of all the masses.

Solution: The MATLAB program is given as follows:

```
M=[1 0 0;0 2 0;0 0 2]; % mass matrix
C=[0 0 0;0 0 0;0 0 0]; % damping matrix
K=[2 -1 0;-1 3 -2;0 -2 4]; % stiffness
A=[zeros(size(M)) eye(size(M));-inv(M)*K -inv(M)*C];
B=[zeros(size(M)); inv(M)];
TO=10; %RISE TIME OF FORCE
N=200;
T=0.1; % SAMPLING PERIOD
NO=TO/T;
phi=eye(size(A))+T*A+T^2*A^2/2+T^3*A^3/6;
gamma=inv(A)*(phi-eye(size(A)))*B;
x(:,1)=zeros(2*length(M),1);
for k=1:N,
 f(k)=1;
F(:,k)=[1;0;0]*f(k); % Force is only applied to mass m
x(:,k+1)=phi*x(:,k)+gamma*F(:,k);
end
k=[0:N];
plot(k,x(1,:),'o',k,x(2,:),'s',k,x(3,:),'.')
title('system response for unit step at first mass E8.19')
ylabel('x_1(k),x_2(k),x_3(k)')
xlabel('k')
legend('x_1(k)','x_2(k)','x_3(k)')
grid
```

The output obtained is shown in Fig. E8.19(a).

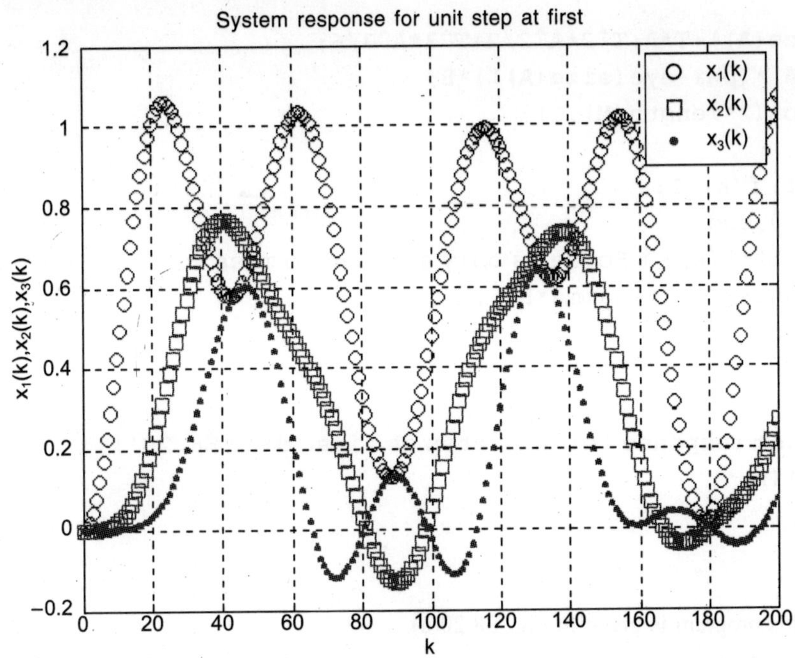

Fig. E8.19(a)

Example E8.20: (*a*) A two-degree of freedom torsional system shown in Fig. E8.20 and is subjected to a torque of unit pulse nature $[u(t) - u(t-4)]$ at the disc B.

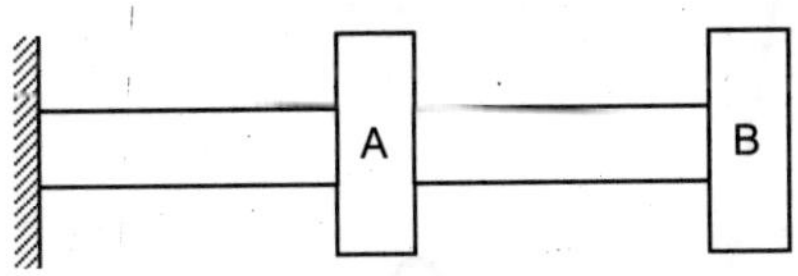

Fig. E8.20

The mass, stiffness and damping matrices are

$$M = \begin{bmatrix} 3 & 0 \\ 0 & 5 \end{bmatrix}, K = \begin{bmatrix} 5 & -4 \\ -4 & 4 \end{bmatrix} \text{and } C = \begin{bmatrix} 1.6 & -0.8 \\ -0.8 & 0.8 \end{bmatrix}$$

(*b*) Plot the response of disc A using MATLAB.

Solution: The MATLAB script is given as follows:

```
M=[1 0;0 2]; % mass matrix
C=[1.6 -0.8; -0.8 0.8]; % damping matrix
K=[5 -4;-4 4]; % stiffness matrix
A=[zeros(size(M)) eye(size(M));-inv(M)*K -inv(M)*C];
B=[zeros(size(M)); inv(M)];
TO=4; %RISE TIME OF FORCE
N=600;
```

```
T=0.1; % SAMPLING PERIOD
NO=TO/T;
phi=eye(size(A))+T*A+T^2*A^2/2+T^3*A^3/6;
gamma=inv(A)*(phi-eye(size(A)))*B;
x(:,1)=zeros(2*length(M),1);
for k=1:N,
 if k<=NO +1; f(k)=1;
 else;f(k)=0;end
 F(:,k)=[0;1]*f(k); % Force is only applied to mass m
 x(:,k+1)=phi*x(:,k)+gamma*F(:,k);
end
k=[0:N];
plot(k,x(1,:),'.')
title('system response for unit step at first disc E8.20')
ylabel('x_1(k)')
xlabel('k')
grid
```

The output of this program is given in Fig. E8.20(a).

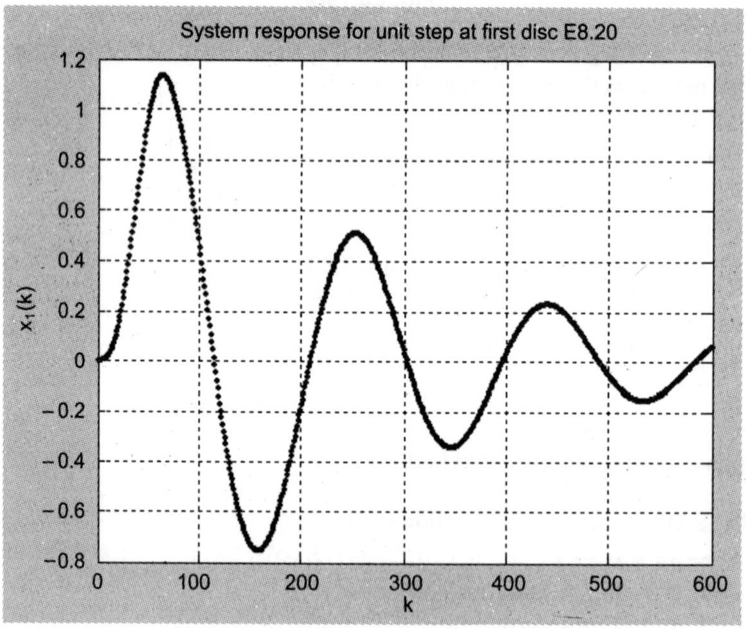

Fig. E8.20(a)

Example E8.21: For the single degree of freedom vibrating system shown in Fig. E8.21, determine the motion of the mass subjected to the initial conditions $x(0) = 0.15$ m and $\dot{x}(0) = 0.04$ m/s. (Given: $m = 1$ kg, $c = 5$ N-s/m, and $k = 5$ N/m.)

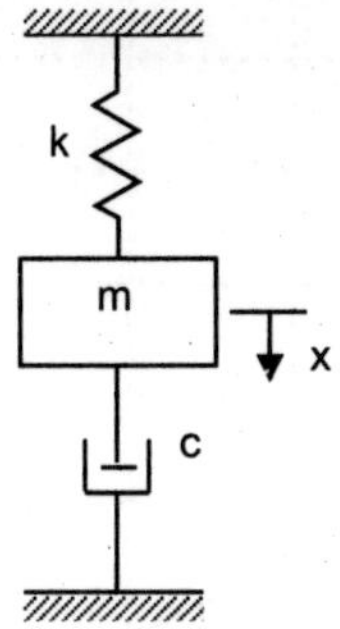

Fig. E8.21

Solution:

The system equation is

$$m\,\ddot{x} + c\,\ddot{x} + kx = 0$$

with the initial conditions $x(0) = 0.15$ m and $\dot{x}(0) = 0.04$ m/s. The Laplace transform of the system equation gives

$$m[s^2X(s) - sx(0) - \dot{x}(0)] + c[sX(s) - x(0)] + kX(s) = 0$$

or $$(ms^2 + cs + k)X(s) = mx(0)s + m\,\dot{x}(0) + cx(0)$$

Solving this last equation for $X(s)$ and substituting the given numerical values, we obtain

$$X(s) = \frac{mx(0)s + m\dot{x}(0) + cx(0)}{ms^2 + cs + k} = \frac{0.15s + 0.79}{s^2 + 5s + 5}$$

This equation can be written as

$$X(s) = \frac{0.15s^2 + 0.79s}{s^2 + 5s + 5}\,\frac{1}{s}$$

Hence, the motion of the mass m may be obtained as the unit-step response of the following system:

$$G(s) = \frac{0.15s + 0.79}{s^2 + 5s + 5}$$

MATLAB program will give a plot of the motion of the mass. The plot is shown in Fig. E8.21(a).

```
num = [0.15  0.79  0];
den = [1  5  5];
step(num,den)
grid
title('Response of spring mass-damper system to initial condition')
```

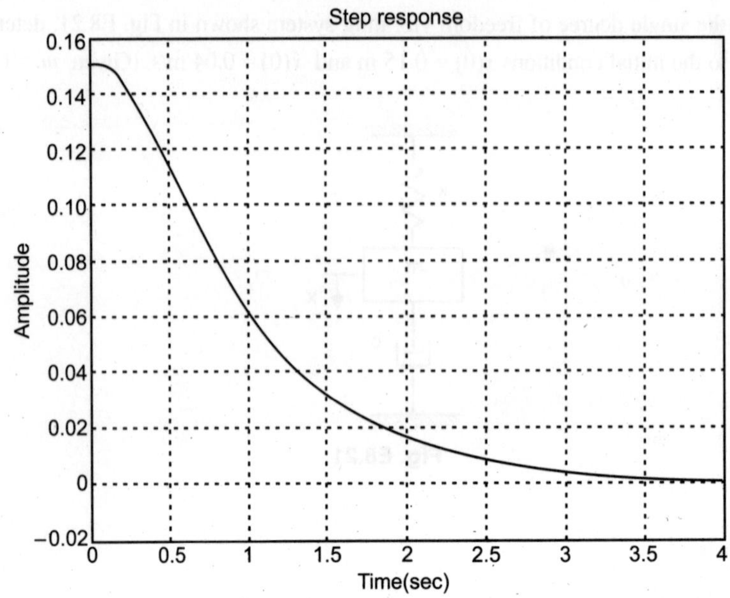

Fig. E8.21(a)

Example E8.22: For the vibrating single degree of freedom shown in Fig. E8.22, determine the response of the system when 12 N of free (step input) is applied to the mass m and plot the response using MATLAB. Given that the system is at rest initially and the displacement x is measured from the equilibrium position. Assume that $m = 2$ kg, $c = 10$ N-s/m, and $k = 80$ N/m.

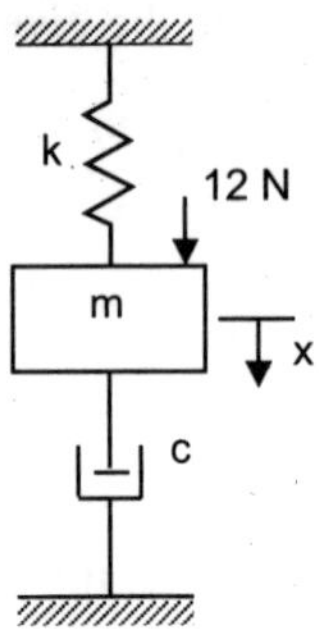

Fig. E8.22

Solution: The equation of motion for the system is

$$m\dot{x} + c\dot{x} + kx = P$$

By substituting the numerical values into this last equation, we get

$$2\ddot{x} + 10\dot{x} + 80x = 12$$

By taking the Laplace transform of this last equation and substituting the initial conditions [$x(0) = 0$ and $\dot{x}(0) = 0$], the result is

$$(s_2 + 5s + 40)X(s) = \frac{6}{s}$$

Solving for $X(s)$, we obtain

$$X(s) = \frac{6}{s(s^2 + 5s + 40)}$$

The response exhibits damped vibrations.

MATLAB program is used to a plot of the response curve, which is shown in Fig. E8.22(a).

```
num = [0  0  6];
den = [1  5 40];
step(num,den)
grid
```

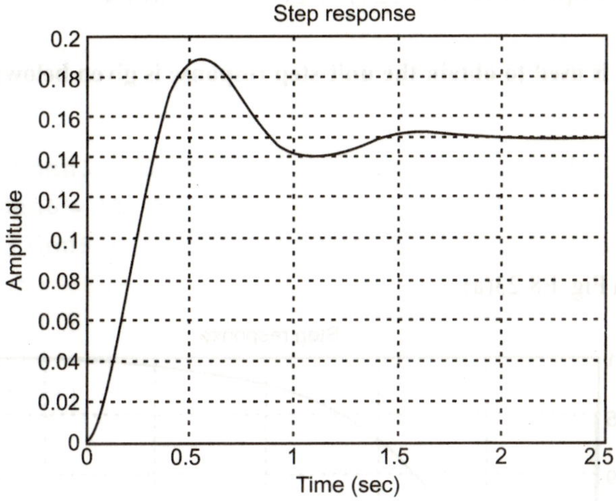

Fig. E8.22(a)

Example E8.23: For the mechanical system shown in Fig. E8.23, obtain the response $x_0(t)$ when $x_i(t)$ is a unit step displacement input. Assume that $k_1 = 2$ N/m, $k_2 = 4$ N/m, $c_1 = 1$ N-s/m, and $c_2 = 2$ N-s/m.

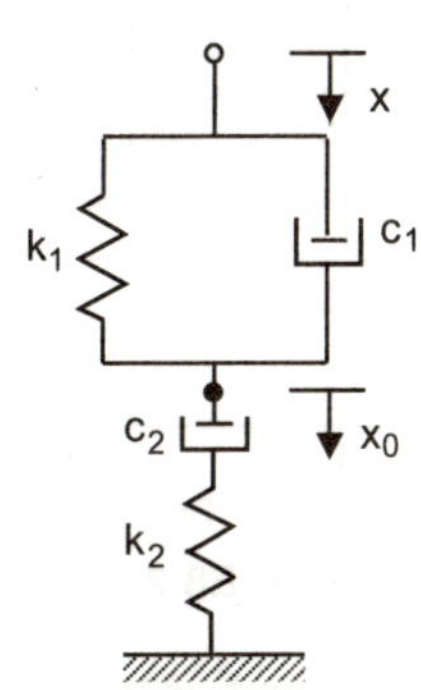

Fig. E8.23

The output is shown in Fig. E8.24 (a).

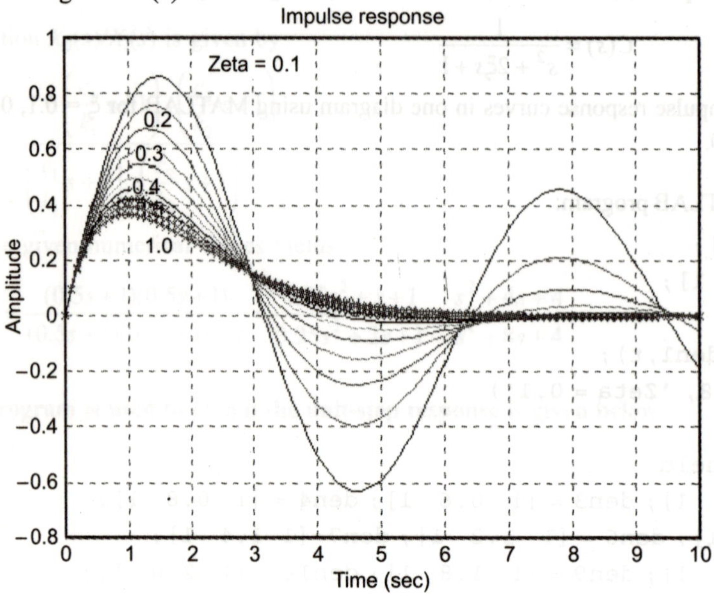

Fig. E8.24(a) Unit-impulse response curves

Example E8.25: For the mechanical system shown in Fig. E8.25, assume that $m = 1$ kg, $m_1 = 2$ kg, $k_1 = 15$ N/m, and $k_2 = 60$ N/m. Determine the vibration when the initial conditions are given as: $x(0) = 0.23$ m, $\dot{x}(0) = 0$ m/s, $y(0) = 1$ m, $\dot{y}(0) = 0$ m/s. Write a MATLAB program to plot curves $x(t)$ versus t and $y(t)$ versus t for the initial conditions.

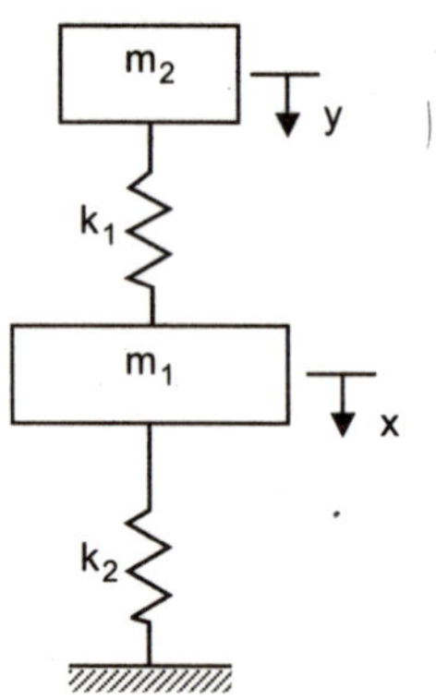

Fig. E8.25

Solution:

The equations for the system are

$$(2s^2 + 75)X(s) = 2sx(0) + 15Y(s) \quad \text{...(1)}$$

$$(s^2 + 15)Y(s) = sy(0) + 15X(s) \quad \text{...(2)}$$

Solving we obtain

$$X(s) = \frac{2(s^2 + 15)sx(0) + 15sy(0)}{2s^4 + 105s^2 + 900} \quad \text{...(3)}$$

For the initial conditions

$$x(0) = 0.23 \text{ m}, \dot{x}(0) = 0 \text{ m/s}, y(0) = 1 \text{ m}, \dot{y}(0) = 0 \text{ m/s}$$

Equation (3) becomes as follows:

$$X(s) = \frac{0.46s^3 + 21.9s}{2s^4 + 105s^2 + 900}$$

$$= \frac{0.46s^4 + 21.9s^2}{2s^4 + 105s^2 + 900}\frac{1}{s} \quad \text{...(4)}$$

By substituting Eq.(4) into Eq.(2) and solving for $Y(s)$, we obtain

$$Y(s) = \frac{1}{s^2 + 15}sy(0) + 15X(s)$$

Substituting $y(0) = 1$ into the last equation and simplifying, we get

$$Y(s) = \frac{1}{s^2 + 15}\frac{24s^5 + 105s^3 + 900s + 6.9s^3 + 328.5s}{2s^4 + 105s^2 + 900}$$

To obtain plot of $x(t)$ versus t, we may enter the following MATLAB program into the computer. The resulting plots are shown in Fig. E8.25(a). Likewise $y(t)$ versus t can be also plotted.

```
num1 = [0.46 0 21.9 0 0];
den = [2  0 105 0 900];   % see equation (4)
t=0:0.01:20;
x=step(num1,den,t)
plot(t,x)
title('Responses mass m1- x(t) due to initial conditions')
xlabel('t sec')
ylabel('x(t)')
grid
```

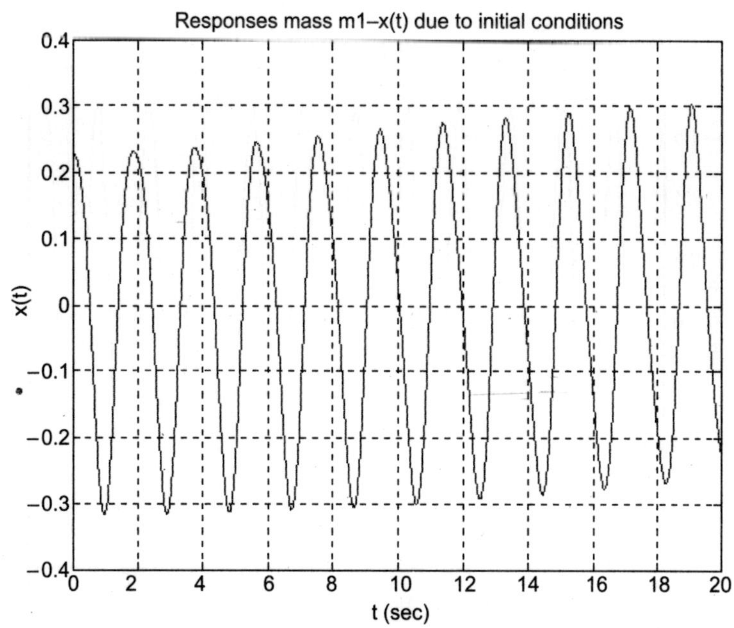

Fig. E8.25(a)

Example E8.26: For the mechanical system shown in Fig. E8.25, assume that $m = 1$ kg, $m_1 = 2$ kg, $k_1 = 15$ N/m, and $k_2 = 60$ N/m. Determine the vibration when the initial conditions are given as: $x(0) = 1.75$ m, $\dot{x}(0) = 0$ m/s, $y(0) = -1$ m, $\dot{y}(0) = 0$ m/s. Write a MATLAB program to plot curves $x(t)$ versus t and $y(t)$ versus t for the initial conditions.

Solution:

$$X(s) = \frac{2(s^2+15)sx(0)+15sy(0)}{2s^4+105s^2+900}$$

$$Y(s) = \frac{1}{s^2+15}sy(0)+15X(s)$$

For the initial conditions

$$x(0) = 1.75 \text{ m},\ \dot{x}(0) = 0 \text{ m/s},\ y(0) = -1 \text{ m},\ \dot{y}(0) = 0 \text{ m/s}$$

we obtain the following expressions for $X(s)$ and $Y(s)$:

$$X(s) = \frac{3.5s^3+37.5s}{2s^4+105s^2+900} = \frac{3.5s^4+37.5s^2}{2s^4+105s^2+900}\frac{1}{s}$$

$$Y(s) = \frac{1}{s^2+15} - s + 15X(s)$$

A MATLAB program for obtaining plots of $x(t)$ versus t given below. The resulting plot is shown in Fig. E8.26.

```
num1 = [3.5  0 37.5 0  0];
den = [2  0  105 0 900];
step(num1,den)
```

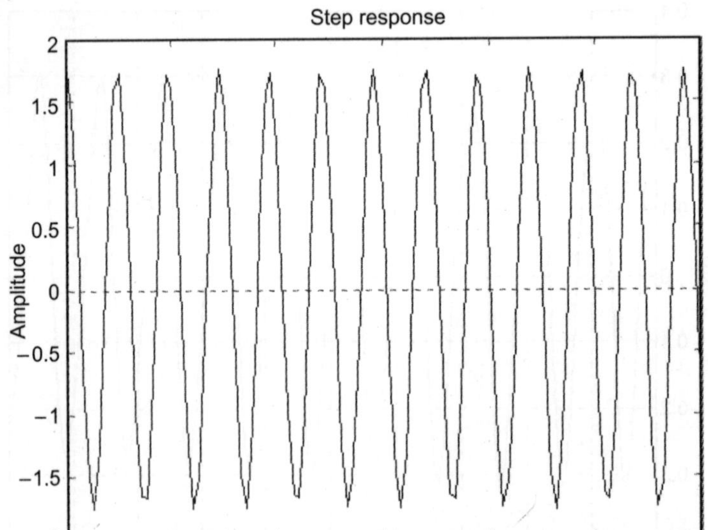

Fig. E8.26 Plot of motion of mass m_1

Example E8.27: For the mechanical system shown in Fig. E8.25, assume that m = 1 kg, $m_1 = 2$ kg, $k_1 = 15$ N/m, and $k_2 = 60$ N/m. Determine the vibration when the initial conditions are given as: $x(0) = 0.5\ m$, $\dot{x}(0) = 0$ m/s, $y(0) = -0.5$ m, $\dot{y}(0) = 0$ m/s. Write a MATLAB program to plot curves $x(t)$ versus t and $y(t)$ versus t for the initial conditions.

Solution:

$$X(s) = \frac{2(s^2+15)sx(0)+15sy(0)}{2s^4+105s^2+900}$$

$$Y(s) = \frac{1}{s^2+15}sy(0)+15X(s)$$

For the initial conditions

$$x(0) = 0.5 \text{ m},\ \dot{x}(0) = 0 \text{ m/s},\ y(0) = -0.5 \text{ m},\ \dot{y}(0) = 0 \text{ m/s}$$

we obtain the following expressions for $X(s)$ and $Y(s)$:

$$X(s) = \frac{s^4+7.5s^2}{2s^4+105s^2+900}\frac{1}{s}$$

$$Y(s) = \frac{-0.5s}{s^2+15}+\frac{15X(s)}{s^2+15}$$

A MATLAB program for obtaining plots of $x(t)$ versus t given below. The resulting plots are shown in Fig. E8.27. Likewise $y(t)$ can also be plotted.

```
num1 = [1 0 7.5  0  0];
den = [2  0  105  0 900];
t = 0:0.02:5;
x = step(num1,den,t)
plot(t, x, 'o')
title('Responses x(t) due to initial conditions ')
xlabel('t sec')
ylabel('x(t)')
grid
```

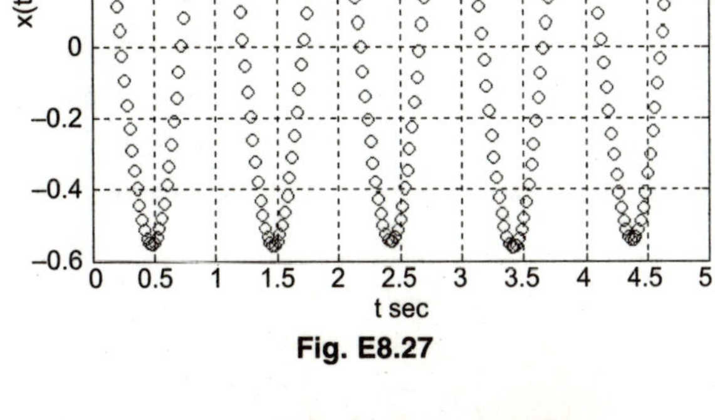

Fig. E8.27

REFERENCES

Adams, M.L., *Rotating Machinery Vibration*, Marcel Dekker, New York, NY, 2002.

Anderson, J.F. and Anderson, M.B., *Solution of Problems in Vibrations,* Longman Scientific and Technical, Essex, UK, 1987.

Anderson, R.A., *Fundamentals of Vibrations*, Macmillan, New York, NY, 1967.

Balachandran, B. and Magrab, E.B., *Vibrations*, Brooks/Cole, Pacific Grove, CA, 2004.

Barker, J.R., *Mechanical and Electrical Vibrations*, Wiley, New York, NY, 1964.

Beards, C.F., *Structural Vibration Analysis,* Ellis Harwood, U.K., 1983.

Beards, G.F., *Vibrations and Control System,* Ellis Horwood, UK, 1988.

Benaroya, H., *Mechanical Vibrations*, Prentice-Hall, Upper Saddle River, NJ, 1998.

Bendat, J.S. and Piersol, A.G., *Engineering Applications of Correlation and Spectral Analysis*, Wiley, New York, 1980.

Bendat, J.S. and Piersol, A.G., *Measurement and Analysis of Random Vibration Data*, Wiley, New York, NY, 1965.

Bendat, J.S. and Piersol, A.G., *Random Data*, Wiley, New York, NY, 1986.

Bendat, J.S. and Piersol, A.G., *Random Data: Analysis and Measurement Procedures*, Wiley, New York, NY, 1971.

Beranek, L.L., *Noise and Vibration Control*, McGraw-Hill, New York, NY, 1971.

Beranek, L.L. and Ver, I.L., *Noise and Vibration Control Engineering: Principles and Applications*, Wiley, New York, NY, 1992.

Berg, G.V., *Elements of Structural Dynamics*, Prentice-Hall, Englewood Cliffs, NJ, 1989.

Bernhard, R.K., *Mechanical Vibrations*, Pitman Publishing, 1943.

Bhat, R.B. and Dukkipati, R.V., *Advanced Dynamics,* Narosa Publishing House, New Delhi, India, 2001.

Bickley, W.G., and Talbot, A., *Vibrating Systems*, Oxford University Press, Oxford, 1961.

Bishop, R.E.D., *Vibration,* Cambridge University Press, Cambridge, England, 1979.

Bishop, R.E.D. and Gladwell, G.M.L., *The Matrix Analysis of Vibration*, Cambridge University Press, Cambridge, England, 1965.

Bishop, R.E.D. and Johnson, D.C., *Vibration Analysis Tables*, Cambridge University Press, Cambridge, England, 1956.

Bishop, R.E.D. and Johnson, D.C., *The Mechanics of Vibration*, Cambridge University Press, New York, NY, 1960.

Blevins, R.D., *Formulas for Natural Frequencies and Mode Shapes*, R.E. Krieger, Melbourne, FL, 1987.

Broch, J.F., *Mechanical Vibrations and Shock Measurements*, Larson & Sons, Copenhagen, Denmark, 1980.

Brommundt, E., *Vibration of Continuous Systems*, CISM, Udine, Italy, 1969.

Burton, R., *Vibration and Impact,* Dover Publications, New York, NY, 1958.

Bykhovsky, I., *Fundamentals of Vibration Engineering*, MIR Publications, 1972.

Centa, G., *Vibration of Structures and Machines,* Springer-Verlag, New York NY, 1993.

Chen, Y., *Vibrations*: *Theoretical Methods*, Addison-Wesley, Reading, MA, 1966.

Church, A.H., *Mechanical Vibrations,* 2nd ed., Wiley, New York, NY, 1963.

Cole, E.B., *The Theory of Vibrations for Engineers*, Crosby Lockwood, 1950.

Crafton, P.A., *Shock and Vibration in Linear Systems,* Harper & Row, New York, NY, 1961.

Crandall, S.H., *Random Vibration*, MIT Press, Cambridge, MA, 1963.

Crandall, S.H. and Mark, W.D., *Random Vibration in Mechanical Systems*, Academic Press, New York, NY, 1963.

De Silva, C.W., *Vibration: Fundamentals and Practice*, CRC Press, Boca Raton, FL, 2000.

Del Pedro, M. and Pahud, P., *Vibration Mechanics,* Kluwer Academic Publishers, Dordrecht, Netherlands, 1989.

Den Hartog. J.P., *Mechanical Vibrations*, 4th ed., McGraw-Hill, New York, NY, 1956.

Dimarogonas, A.D., *Vibration for Engineers,* 2nd ed., Prentice-Hall, Englewood Cliffs, NJ, 1996.

Dimarogonas, A.D. and Haddad, S.D., *Vibration for Engineers,* Prentice-Hall, Englewood Cliffs, NJ, 1992.

Dukkipati, R.V., *Vehicle Dynamics,* Narosa Publishing House, New Delhi, India, 2000.

Dukkipati, R.V. and Amyot, J.R., *Computer Aided Simulation in Railway Vehicle Dynamics*, Marcel-Dekker, New York, NY, 1988.

Fertis, D.G., *Mechanical and Structural Vibrations*, Wiley, New York, NY, 1995.

Garg, V.K. and Dukkipati, R.V., *Dynamics of Railway Vehicle Systems*, Academic Press, New York, NY, 1984.

Genta, G., *Vibration of Structures and Machines,* Springer-Verlag, New York, NY, 1992.

Ginsberg, J.H., *Mechanical and Structural Vibrations*, Wiley, New York, NY, 2001.

Gorman, D.J., *Free Vibration Analysis of Beams and Shafts*, Wiley, New York, NY, 1975.

Gorman, D.J., *Free Vibration Analysis of Rectangular Plates*, Elsevier, 1982.

Gough, W., Richards, J.P.G., and Williams, R.P., *Vibrations and Waves,* Wiley, New York, NY, 1983.

Gross, E.E., *Measurement of Vibration*, General Radio, 1955.

Grover, G.K., *Mechanical Vibration*, Nem Chand and Bros, Roorkee, 1972.

Haberman, C.M., *Vibration Analysis*, Merril, Columbus, OH, 1968.

Hansen, H.M. and Chenea, P.F., *Mechanics of Vibration*, Wiley, New York, NY, 1952.

Harris, C.M. and Crede, C.E., *Shock and Vibration Handbook*, 4th ed., McGraw-Hill, New York, NY, 1996.

Hatter, D.H., *Matrix Computer Methods of Vibration Analysis*, Wiley, New York, NY, 1973.

Hayashi, C., *Nonlinear Oscillations in Physical Systems*, McGraw-Hill, New York, NY, 1964.

Hurty, W.C. and Rubenstein, M.F., *Dynamics of Structures*, Prentice-Hall, NJ, 1964.

Huston, R. and Joseph, H., *Dynamics of Mechanical Systems*, CRC Press, Boca Raton, FL, 2002.

Inman, D.J., *Vibration with Control Measurement and Stability*, Prentice-Hall, Englewood Cliffs, NJ, 1989.

Jackson, C., *The Practical Vibration Primer*, Gulf Publishing, Houston, TX, 1979.

Jacobsen, L.S. and Ayre, R.S., *Engineering Vibrations*, McGraw-Hill, New York, 1958.

James, M.L. Smith, G.M., Wolford, J.C. and Whaley, P.W., *Vibration of Mechanical and Structural Systems*, Harper and Row, 1989.

Jones, D.S., *Electrical and Mechanical Oscillations,* Routledge and Kegan, London, 1961.

Karnopp, D.C., Margolis, D.L. and Rosenberg, R.C., *System Dynamics*, 3rd ed., Wiley Interscience, New York, NY, 2000.

Kelly, S.G., *Fundamentals of Mechanical Vibration*, McGraw-Hill, New York, NY, 1993.

Kelly, S.G., *Theory and Problems of Mechanical Vibrations*, Schaum's Outline Series, McGraw-Hill, New York, NY, 1996.

Kimball, A.L., *Vibration Prevention in Engineering*, Wiley, New York, NY, 1932.

Lalanne, M., Berthier, P. and Der Hagopian, J., *Mechanical Vibrations for Engineers,* Wiley, New York, NY, 1983.

Lancaster, P., *Lambda-Matrices and Vibrating Systems*, Pergamon, 1966.

Loewy, R.G. and Piarulli, V.J., *Dynamics of Rotating Shafts*, Naval Publication, 1969.

Manley, R.G., *Fundamentals of Vibration Study*, Wiley, New York, NY, 1942.

Marguerre, K. and Wolfel, H., *Mechanics of Vibration,* Sitjthoff and Noordhoff, 1979.

Mclachlan, N.W., *Theory of Vibration*, Dover Publications, 1951.

Meirovitch, L., *Analytical Methods in Vibrations*, Macmillan, New York, NY, 1967.

Meirovitch, L., *Elements of Vibration Analysis*, 2nd ed., McGraw-Hill, New York, NY, 1986.

Meirovitch, L., *Introduction to Dynamics and Control*, Wiley, New York, NY, 1985.

Meirovitch, L., *Methods of Analytical Dynamics,* McGraw-Hill, New York, NY, 1970.

Meirovitch, L., *Principles and Techniques of Vibrations*, Prentice-Hall, Upper Saddle River, NJ, 1997.

Minorosky, M., *Nonlinear Oscillations*, Van Nostrand, Princeton, NJ, 1962.

Moretti, P.M., *Modern Vibrations Primer*, CRC Press, Boca Raton, FL, 2002.

Morrill, B., *Mechanical Vibration*, The Ronald Press, 1937.

Morrow, C.T., *Shock and Vibration Engineering,* Wiley, New York, NY, 1963.

Morse, P.M., *Vibration and Sound*, McGraw-Hill, New York, NY, 1948.

Muller, P.C. and Schiehlen, W.O., *Linear Vibrations*, Martinus Nighoff, 1985.

Myklestad, N.O., *Fundamentals of Vibration Analysis,* McGraw-Hill, New York, NY, 1956.

Nakra, B.C., Yadava, G.S. and Thurestadt, L., *Vibration Measurement and Analysis,* NPC, New Delhi, India, 1989.

Nashif, A.D., Jonés, D.I.G. and Henderson, J.P., *Vibration Damping,* Wiley, New York, NY, 1985.

Nayfeh, A.H. and Mook, D.T., *Nonlinear Oscillations*, Wiley, New York, NY, 1979.

Newland, D.E., *An Introduction to Random Vibrations and Spectral Analysis*, 2nd ed., Longman, 1984.

Newland, D.E., *Mechanical Vibration Analysis and Computation,* Longman, 1989.

Newland, D.E., *Random Vibrations and Spectral Analysis*, 2nd ed., Longman, London, 1984.

Nigam, N.C., *Introduction to Random Vibrations*, MIT Press, 1983.

Norton, M.P., *Fundamentals of Noise and Vibration Analysis for Engineers*, Cambridge University Press, Cambridge, 1989.

Pain, H.J., *The Physics of Vibrations and Waves*, Wiley, New York, NY, 1983.

Pippard, A.B., *The Physics of Vibration*, Cambridge University Press, Cambridge, 1978.

Piszek, K. and Niziol, J., *Random Vibrations of Mechanical Systems*, Ellis Horwood, 1986.

Prentis, J.M. and Leckie, F.A., *Mechanical Vibrations: An Introduction to Matrix Methods,* Longman, 1963.

Ramamurti, V., *Mechanical Vibration Practice with Basic Theory*, CRC Press, Boca Raton, FL, 2000.

Rao, J.S., *Advanced Theory of Vibration*, Wiley, New York, NY, 1991.

Rao, J.S., and Dukkipati, R.V., *Mechanism and Machine Theory*, 2nd ed., Wiley Eastern, New Delhi, India, 1992.

Rao, J.S., and Gupta, K., *Introductory Course on Theory and Practice of Mechanical Vibrations,* Wiley Eastern, New Delhi, India, 1984.

Rao, S.S., *Mechanical Vibrations*, 3rd ed., Addison-Wesley, Reading, MA, 1995.

Rocard, V., *General Dynamics of Vibrations*, Unger, New York, NY, 1960.

Seto, W.W., *Theory and Problems of Mechanical Vibrations*, Schaum's Outline Series, McGraw-Hill, New York, NY, 1964.

Shabana, A.A., *Theory of Vibration: An Introduction*, Springer-Verlag, New York, NY, 1991.

Shabana, A.A., *Theory of Vibration: Discrete and Continuous Systems*, Springer, New York, NY, 1991.

Smith, J.D., *Vibration Measurement and Analysis,* Butterworths, 1989.

Snowdon, J.C., *Vibration and Shock in Damped Mechanical Systems,* Wiley, New York, NY, 1968.

Srinivasan, P., *Mechanical Vibration Analysis*, Tata-McGraw-Hill, New Delhi, India, 1982.

Steidel, R.F., *An Introduction to Mechanical Vibrations*, 3rd ed., Wiley, New York, NY, 1981.

Stoker, J.J., *Nonlinear Vibrations*, Interscience, New York, NY, 1950.

Thompson, J.M.T. and Stewart, H.B., *Nonlinear Dynamics and Chaos*, Wiley, New York NY, 1986.

Thomson, W.T. and Dahleh, M.D., *Theory of Vibrations with Applications,* 5th ed., Prentice-Hall, Englewood Cliffs, NJ.

Thornson, D.L., *Mechanics Applied to Vibrations and Balancing*, Wiley, New York, NY, 1940.

Timoshenko, S., Young, D.H. and Weaver, W., *Vibration Problems in Engineering*, 5th ed., Wiley, New York, NY 1990.

Timoshenko, S.P. and Young, D.H., *Advanced Dynamics*, McGraw-Hill New York, NY, 1948.

Timoshenko, S.P., *Vibrations in Engineering*, D. Van Nostrand, New York, NY, 1955.

Tong, K.N., *Theory of Mechanical Vibration*, Wiley, New York, NY, 1960.

Tse, F.S., Morse, I.E. and Hinkle, R.T., *Mechanical Vibrations,* Allyn and Bacon, Boston, MA, 1963.

Tuplin, W.A., *Torsional Vibration*, Wiley, New York, NY, 1934.

Van Santen, G.W., *Mechanical Vibration*, Macmillan, New York, NY, 1998.

Vernon, J.B., *Linear Vibration Theory*, Wiley, New York, NY, 1967.

Vierck, R.K., *Vibration Analysis,* 2nd ed., Harper & Row, New York, NY, 1979.

Volterra, E. and Zachmanoglon, E.C., *Dynamics of Vibrations*, Merrill, 1965.

Wallace, R.H., *Understanding and Measuring Vibrations*, Springer, New York, NY, 1970.

Walshaw, A.C., *Mechanical Vibrations with Applications*, Ellis Hardwood, 1984.

Weaver, W., Timoshenko, S.P. and Young, D.H., *Vibration Problems in Engineering*, 5th ed., Wiley, New York, NY, 1990.

Wilson, W.K., *Practical Solution of Torsional Vibration Problems*, Vol.1, Wiley, New York, NY, 1949.

Wilson, W.K., *Practical Solution of Torsional Vibration Problems*, Vol.2, Wiley, New York, NY, 1949.

Wowk, V., *Machinery Vibration: Measurement and Analysis*, McGraw-Hill, New York, NY, 1991.

PROBLEMS

P8.1: A safety bumper placed at the end of a race track to stop out-of-control cars as shown in Fig. P8.1. The bumper is designed such that the force that the bumper applies to the car is a function of the velocity v and the displacement x of the front end of the bumper given by the equation:

$$F = Kv^3(x+1)^3$$

where $K = 35$ kg-s/m^5 (a constant).

A car with a mass of 2000 kg hits the bumper at a speed of 100 km/h. Determine and plot the velocity of the car as a function of its position for $0 \le x \le 5$ m.

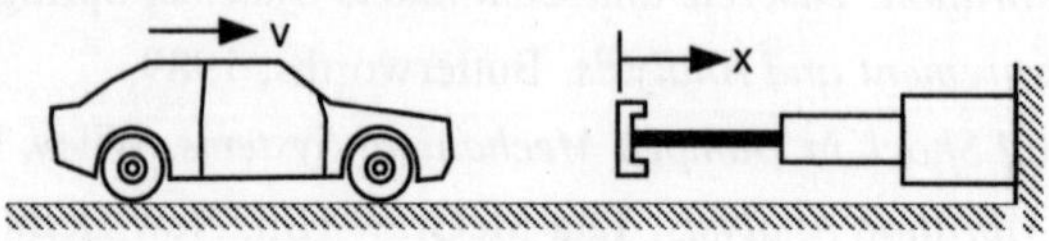

Fig. P8.1

P8.2: The 10 kg body is moved 0.25 m to the right of the equilibrium position and released from rest at $t = 0$ as shown in Fig. P8.2. Plot the displacement as a function of time for four cases: $c = 10$, 40, 50 and 60 N.s/m. The stiffness of the spring is 40 N/m.

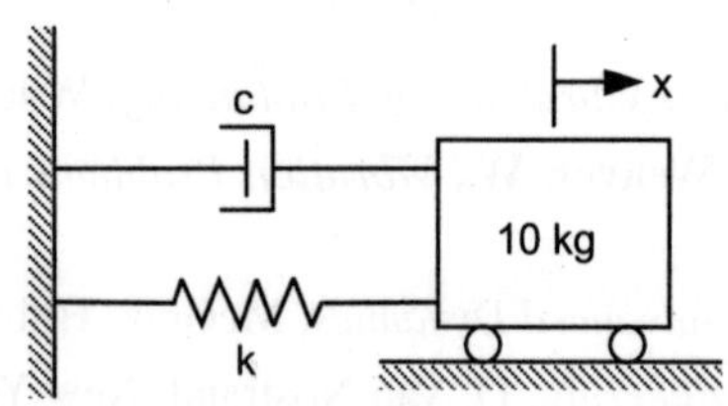

Fig. P8.2

P8.3: An airplane uses a parachute (see Fig. P8.3) and other means of braking as it slow down on the runway after landing. The acceleration of the airplane is given by $a = -0.005v^2 - 4$m/s^2

Consider an airplane with a velocity of 500 km/h that opens its parachute and starts decelerating at $t = 0$ s.

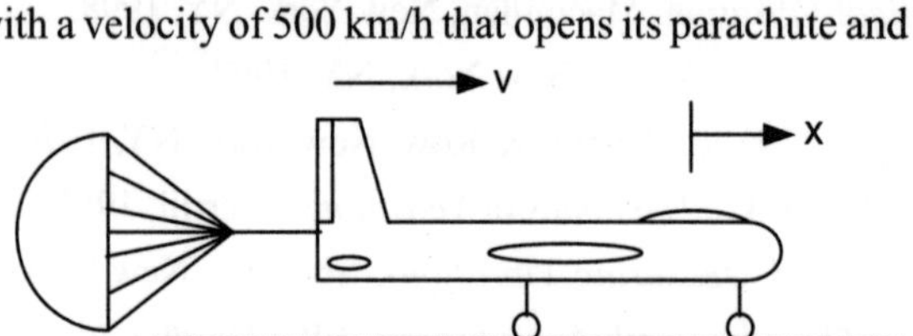

Fig. P8.3

P8.4: The piston of 150 lb is supported by a spring of modulus $k = 250$ lb/in. A dashpot of damping coefficient $c = 100$ lb.sec/ft acts in parallel with the spring. A fluctuating pressure $p = 0.75 \sin 30t$ (psi) acts on the piston, whose top surface area is 100 in^2. Plot the response of the system for initial conditions $x_0 = 0.06$ ft and $\dot{x}_0 = 6$, 0, and -6 ft./sec.

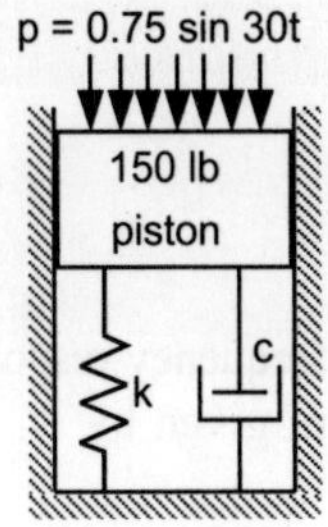

Fig. P8.4

P8.5: The 15 kg oscillator contains an unbalanced motor whose speed is *N* rpm as shown in Fig. P8.5. The stiffness of the spring $k = 1100$ N/m. The oscillator is also restrained by a viscous damper whose piston is resisted by a force of 50 *N* when moving at a speed of 0.6 m/s. Determine:

(*a*) the viscous damping factor

(*b*) plot the magnification factor for motor speeds from 0 to 350 rpm

(*c*) the maximum value of the magnification factor and the corresponding motor speed.

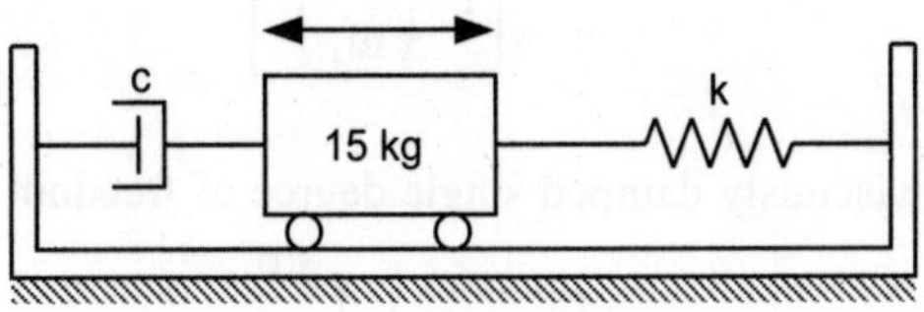

Fig. P8.5

P8.6: Write a MATLAB script file that computes the response of a single degree of freedom under damped system shown in Fig. P8.6 to initial excitations. Use the program to determine and plot the response for the following data:

Initial conditions:

$$x(0) = 0,\ \dot{x}(0) = v_0 = 30 \text{ cm/sec},$$

$$\omega_n = 6 \text{ rad/s, and } \xi = 0.05, 0.1, 0.2, 0.30.$$

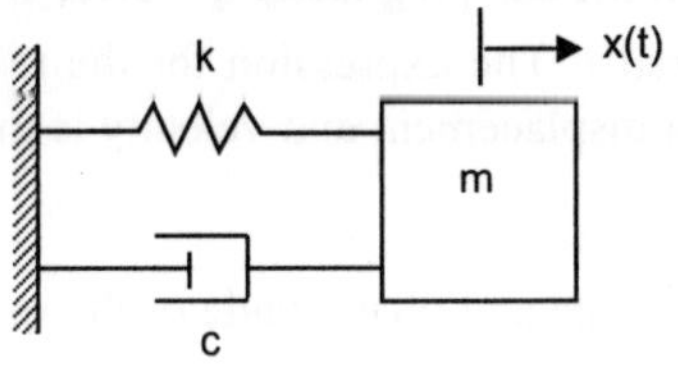

Fig. P8.6 Damped single degree of freedom system

The response of the under damped single degree of freedom system is given by

$$x(t) = A\,e^{-\xi\omega_n t}\cos(\omega_t^d - \phi)$$

where *A* and ϕ represent the amplitude and phase angle of the response respectively. These are

$$A = \sqrt{x_0^2 + \left(\frac{\zeta\omega_n x_0 + v_0}{\omega_d}\right)^2}$$

$$\omega_d = \sqrt{1-\zeta^2}\,\omega_n$$

and $$\phi = \tan^{-1}\left(\frac{\zeta\omega_n x_0 + v_0}{\omega_d x_0}\right)$$

P8.7: Write a MATLAB script for plotting the frequency response magnitude and phase angle using complex notation for a single degree of freedom system given by

$$G(i\omega) = \frac{1-\left(\frac{\omega}{\omega_n}\right)^2 - i2\zeta\left(\frac{\omega}{\omega_n}\right)}{\left[1-\left(\frac{\omega}{\omega_n}\right)^2\right]^2 + \left(2\zeta\frac{\omega}{\omega_n}\right)^2}$$

and $$\phi(\omega) = \tan^{-1}\left[\frac{-Im\,G(i\omega)}{Re\,G(i\omega)}\right] = \tan^{-1}\left[\frac{2\zeta\frac{\omega}{\omega_n}}{1-\left(\frac{\omega}{\omega_n}\right)^2}\right]$$

P8.8: Consider the force-free, viscously damped single degree of freedom system shown in Fig. P8.8.

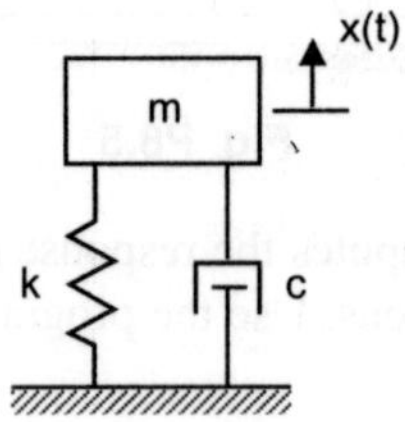

Fig. P8.8

Plot the response of the system using MATLAB over the interval $0 \le t \le 10$s to the initial conditions $x(0) = 3$ cm, $\dot{x}(0) = 0$ for the values of the damping factor $\zeta = 0.05, 0.1, 0.5$. The frequency of the undamped oscillation have the values $\omega_n = 15$ rad/s. The expression for the response of a damped single degree of freedom system in Fig. P8.3 to initial displacement and velocity is given by

$$x(t) = Ce^{-\zeta\omega_n t}\cos(\omega_d t - \phi)$$

where C and ϕ represent the amplitude and phase angle of the response, respectively having the values

$$C = \sqrt{x_0^2 + \left(\frac{\zeta\omega_n x_0 + v_0}{\omega_d}\right)^2}$$

$$\phi = \tan^{-1}\left(\frac{\zeta\omega_n x_0 + v_0}{\omega_d x_0}\right)$$

and $$\omega_d = \sqrt{1-\zeta^2}\,\omega_n$$

P8.9: Write a MATLAB script to obtain the motion of the mass subjected to the initial condition. There is no external forcing function acting on the system. The single degree of freedom system is shown in Fig. P8.9 and the parameters are given as $m = 3$ kg, $k = 6$ N/m, and $C = 5$ N-s/m. The displacement of the mass is measured from the equilibrium position and at $t = 0$, $x(0) = 0.04$m and $\dot{x}(0) = 0.10$ m/s.

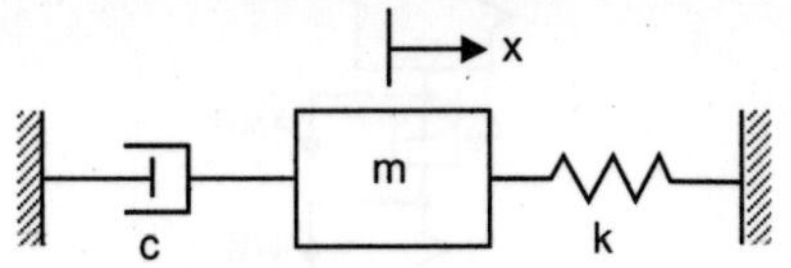

Fig. P8.9 Single degree of freedom system

P8.10: Determine and plot the response of the single degree of freedom system shown in Fig. P8.10 using MATLAB when 25 N of force (step input) is applied to the mass m. The system is at rest initially and the displacement of the mass m is measured from equilibrium position. The parameters of the system are given as $m = 3$ kg, $c = 25$ N-s/m, and $k = 200$ N/m. The initial conditions are $x(0) = \dot{x}(0) = 0$.

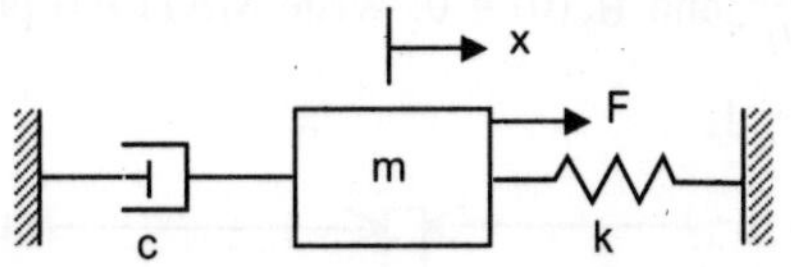

Fig. P8.10 Single degree of freedom system

P8.11: Write a MATLAB script for determining the response of a single degree of freedom system with viscous damping to an exponential excitation $F(t) = e^{-\alpha t}$.

P8.12: A single degree of freedom spring-mass-damper model has following properties: $m = 15$ kg, $c = 25$ Ns/m and $k = 3500$ N/m. If it is subjected a triangular pulse of amplitude 1000 N for 0.1 seconds, compute the time-domain response and plot the same in MATLAB. The excitation function is shown in Fig. P8.12.

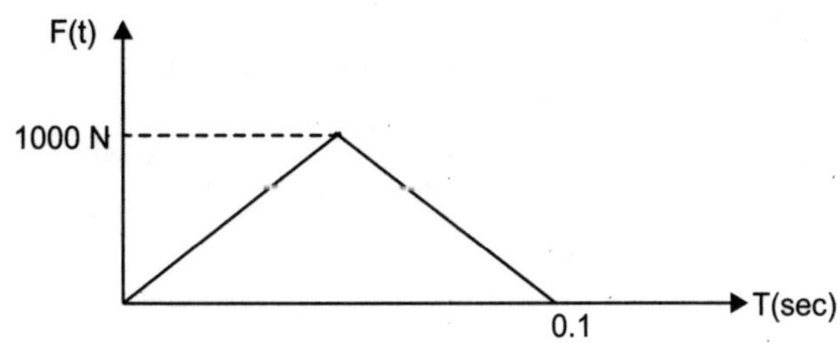

Fig. P8.12

P8.13: Determine and plot the response of the system shown in Fig. P8.13 using MATLAB. The response is $x_0(t)$ when the input $x_i(t)$ is a unit step displacement input. The parameters of the system are $k_1 = 15$ N/m, $k_2 = 25$ N/m, $c_1 = 7$ N-s/m, $c_2 = 15$ N-s/m.

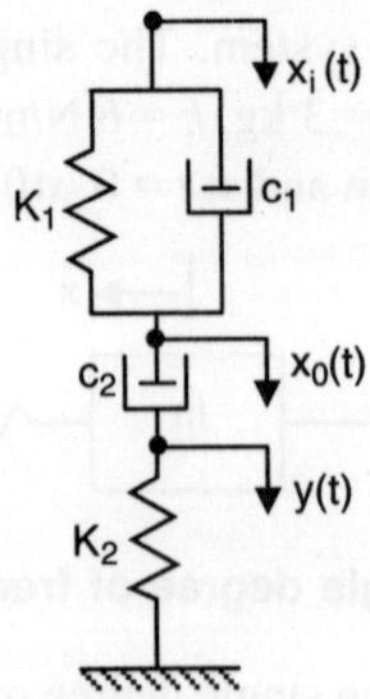

Fig. P8.13

P8.14: A two-degree of freedom torsional system shown in Fig. P8.14 is subjected to initial excitation $\theta_1(0) = 0$, $\theta_2(0) = 2$, $\dot{\theta}_1(0) = 2\sqrt{\dfrac{GJ}{IL}}$ and $\dot{\theta}_2(0) = 0$. Write MATLAB program and plot the response of the system. Assume $I = 1$ and $GJ = l = 1$.

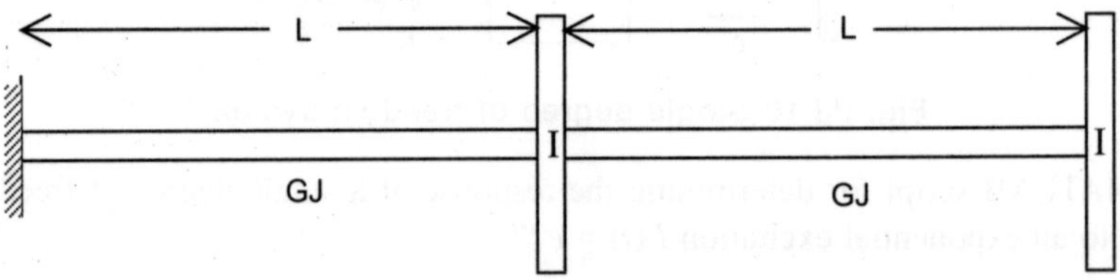

Fig. P8.14

P8.15: The mass m_2 in a 2-degree of freedom system shown in Fig. P8.15 is subjected to a force in the form of saw-tooth pulse of amplitude 1.5 N for duration of 1.5 second. Obtain the response in terms of two coordinates $x_1(t)$ and $x_2(t)$. Assume $k_1 = k_2 = 15$ N/m and $m_1 = m_2 = 2$ kg.

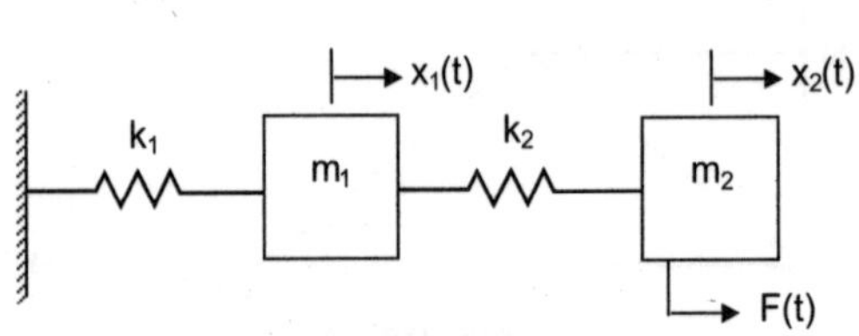

Fig. P8.15

The mass and stiffness matrices of the system for given system are given as

$$M = \begin{bmatrix} m_1 & 0 \\ 0 & m_2 \end{bmatrix} \text{ and } K = \begin{bmatrix} k_1 + k_2 & -k_2 \\ -k_2 & k_2 \end{bmatrix}$$

Force vector is:

$$F = \begin{Bmatrix} F(t) \\ 0 \end{Bmatrix}$$

The saw-tooth pulse takes the form as shown in Fig. P8.15(a).

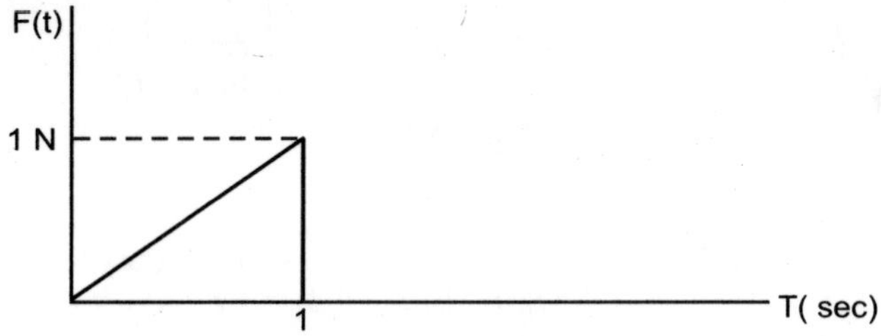

Fig. P8.15(a)

P8.16: A two-storey building (Fig. P8.16) is undergoing a horizontal motion $y(t) = Y_0 \sin \omega t$.

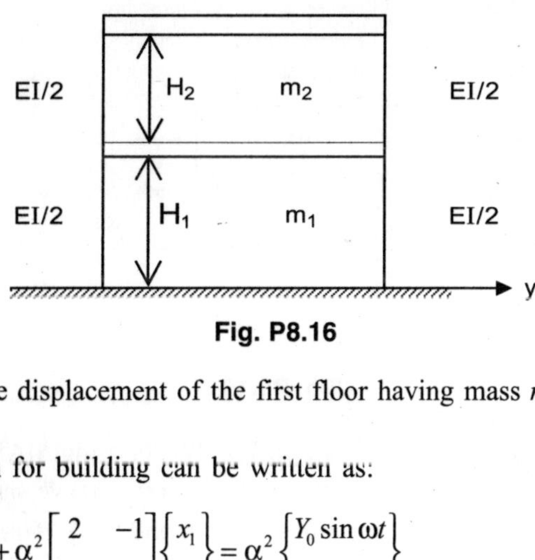

Fig. P8.16

Derive expression for the displacement of the first floor having mass m_1. Assume $m_1 = m_2 = 4$, $EI = 2$ and $H = 1$m.

The equations of motion for building can be written as:

$$\begin{bmatrix} 4 & 0 \\ 0 & 4 \end{bmatrix} \begin{Bmatrix} \ddot{x}_1 \\ \ddot{x}_2 \end{Bmatrix} + \alpha^2 \begin{bmatrix} 2 & -1 \\ -1 & 1 \end{bmatrix} \begin{Bmatrix} x_1 \\ x_2 \end{Bmatrix} = \alpha^2 \begin{Bmatrix} Y_0 \sin \omega t \\ 0 \end{Bmatrix}$$

where $$\alpha^2 = \frac{12EI}{mH^3} = \frac{12 \times 2}{m} = 6$$

Solving for steady-state response we get:

$$X_1 = \frac{(\alpha^2 - \omega^2)\alpha^2}{(\omega^2 - \omega_1^2)(\omega^2 - \omega_2^{2)}} Y_0$$

$$X_2 = \frac{\alpha^4}{(\omega^2 - \omega_1^2)(\omega^2 - \omega_2^{2)}} Y_0$$

These values are to be plotted against various values of ω.

P8.17: Derive the response of the system shown in Fig. P8.17 in discrete time and plot the response. Given $F(t) = e^{-\alpha t}$.

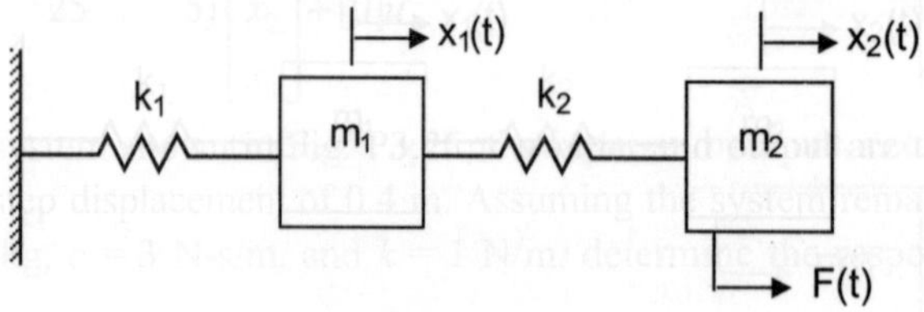

Fig. P8.17

P8.18: Consider the system with $M = \begin{bmatrix} 3 & 0 \\ 0 & 2 \end{bmatrix}, K = \begin{bmatrix} 6 & -4 \\ -4 & 5 \end{bmatrix}$ with arbitrary viscous damping. Find the eigenvalues and normalized eigenvectors.

P8.19: For the vibrating system shown in Fig. P8.19, a mass of 5 kg is placed on mass m at $t = 0$ and the system is at rest initially (at $t = 0$). Given that $m = 20$ kg, $k = 600$ N/m, and $c = 60$ Ns/m. Plot the response curve $x(t)$ versus t using MATLAB.

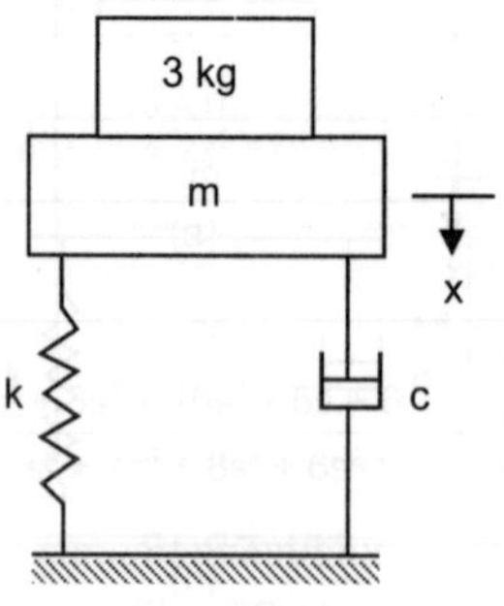

Fig. P8.19

P8.20: For the mechanical vibrating system shown in Fig. P8.20, using MATLAB assume that $m = 3$ kg, $k_1 = 15$ N/m, $k = 25$ N/m, and $c = 10$ N-s/m. Plot the response curve $x(t)$ versus t when the mass m is pulled slightly downward and the initial conditions are $x(0) = 0.05$ m and $\dot{x}(0) = 0.8$ m/s.

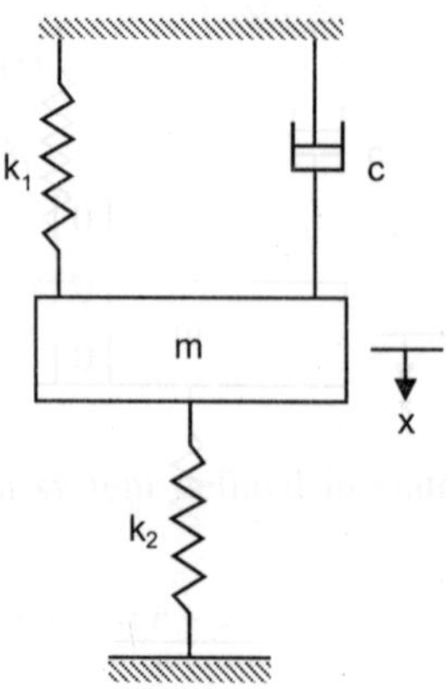

Fig. P8.20

P8.21: For the mechanical vibrating system shown in Fig. P8.21, k_1 = 10 N/m, k_2 = 30 N/m, c_1 = 3 N-s/m, and c_2 = 25 N-s/m.

(*a*) Determine the displacement $x_2(t)$ when *F* is a step force input of 4 N.

(*b*) Plot the response curve $x_2(t)$ versus *t* using MATLAB.

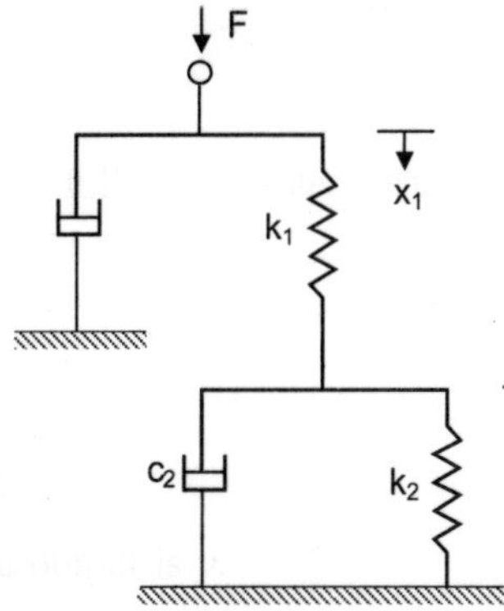

Fig. P8.21

P8.22: For the electrical system shown in Fig. E8.22, assume that R_1 = 2Ω, R_2 = 1 MΩ, C_1 = 0.75 μF, and C_2 = 0.25 μF and the capacitors are not charged initially and e_0 (0) = 0 and $\dot{e}_0$ (0) = 0.

(*a*) Find the response $e_0(t)$ where $e_i(t)$ = 5V (stop input) is applied to the system.

(*b*) Plot the response curve $e_0(t)$ versus *t* using MATLAB.

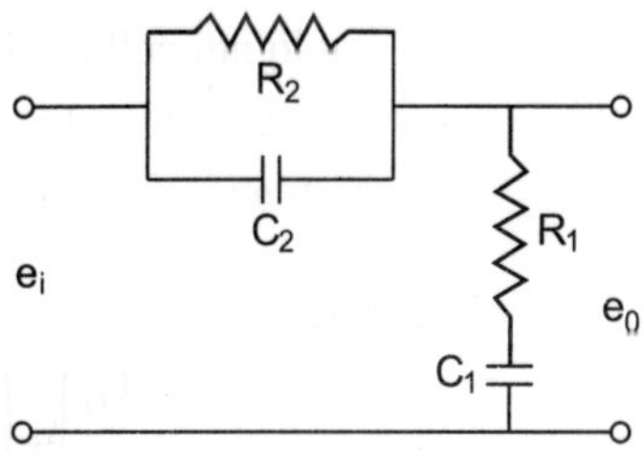

Fig. P8.22

P8.23: For the mechanical system shown in Fig. P8.23, assume *m* = 3 kg, *M* = 25 kg, k_1= 25 N/m, and k_2 = 300 N/m. Determine

(*a*) the natural frequencies and modes of vibration

(*b*) the vibration when the initial conditions are: $x(0)$ = 0.05 *m*, $\dot{x}(0)$ = 0 m/s, $y(0)$ = 0 m/s, and $\dot{y}(0)$ = 0 m/s.

Use MATLAB program to plot curves $x(t)$ versus *t* and $y(t)$ versus *t*.

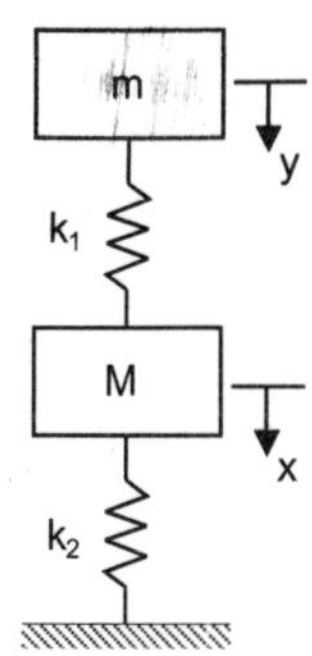

Fig. P8.23

❍ ❍ ❍

BIBLIOGRAPHY

There are several outstanding text and reference books on MATLAB that merit consultation for those readers who wish to pursue these topics further. The following list is but a representative sample of the many excellent references.

Chapman, S.J., *MATLAB Programming for Engineers,* 2nd ed., Brooks/Cole, Thomson Learning, Pacific Grove, CA, 2002.

Chapra, S.C., *Applied Numerical Methods with MATLAB*, 2nd ed., McGraw-Hill, New York, 2008.

Dabney, J.B. and Harman, T.L., *Mastering SIMULINK 4,* Prentice-Hall, Upper Saddle River, NJ, 2001.

Daku, B.L.F., *MATLAB Tutor CD-Learning MATLAB Superfast*, Wiley, New York, 2006.

Djaferis, T.E., *Automatic Control—The Power of Feedback using MATLAB*, Brooks/Cole, Thomson Learning, Pacific Grove, CA, 2000.

Dukkipati, R.V., *Analysis and Design of Control Systems using MATLAB*, New Age International Publishers, New Delhi, India, 2006.

Dukkipati, R.V. and Srinivas, J., *Solving Engineering Mechanics Problems with MATLAB*, New Age International Publishers, New Delhi, India, 2007.

Dukkipati, R.V., *Solving Engineering System Dynamics Problems with MATLAB*, New Age International Publishers, New Delhi, India, 2006.

Dukkipati, R.V., *Solving Vibration Analysis Problems with MATLAB*, New Age International Publishers, New Delhi, India, 2006.

Dukkipati, R.V., *MATLAB for Mechanical Engineers*, New Age International Publishers, New Delhi, India, 2008.

Dukkipati, R.V., *MATLAB for Electrical Engineers*, New Age International Publishers, New Delhi, India, 2008.

Etter, D.M., *Engineering Problem Solving with MATLAB,* Prentice-Hall, Englewood Cliffs, NJ, 1993.

Gardner, J.F., *Simulation of Machines using MATLAB and SIMULINK*, Brooks/Cole, Thomson Learning, Pacific Grove, CA, 2001.

Hahn, B.D. and Valentine, D.T., *Essential MATLAB for Engineers and Scientists*, 3rd ed., Elsevier, Burlington, MA, 2007.

Hanselman, D. and Littlefield, B., *Mastering MATLAB 7*, Prentice-Hall, Upper Saddle River, NJ, 2005.

Harper, B. D., *Solving Dynamics Problems in MATLAB*, 5th ed., Wiley, New York, 2002.

Herniter, M.E., *Programming in MATLAB*, Brooks/Cole, Pacific Grove, CA, 2001.

Hunt, B.R., Lipsman, R.L. and Rosenberg, J.M., *A Guide to MATLAB—for Beginners and Experienced Users,* 2nd ed., Cambridge University Press, Cambridge, UK, 2006.

Karris, S.T., *Signals and Systems with MATLAB Applications*, Orchard Publications, Fremont, CA, 2001.

Kiusalaas, J., *Numerical Methods in Engineering with MATLAB,* Cambridge University Press, Cambridge, UK, 2005.

Leonard, N.E. and Levine, W.S., *Using MATLAB to Analyze and Design Control Systems*, Addison-Wesley, Redwood City, CA, 1995.

Lyshevski, S.E., *Engineering and Scientific Computations using MATLAB*, Wiley, New York, 2003.

Moore, H., *MATLAB for Engineers*, Prentice-Hall, Upper Saddle River, NJ, 2007.

Ogata, K., *Designing Linear Control Systems with MATLAB*, Prentice-Hall, Upper Saddle River, NJ, 1994.

Ogata, K., *Solving Control Engineering Problems with MATLAB*, Prentice-Hall, Upper Saddle River, NJ, 1994.

Palm, W.J. III., *Introduction to MATLAB 7 for Engineers,* McGraw-Hill, New York, 2005.

Pratap, Rudra, *Getting started with MATLAB—A Quick Introduction for Scientists and Engineers,* Oxford University Press, New York, NY, 2002.

Recktenwald, G., *Numerical Methods with MATLAB*, Prentice-Hall, Upper Saddle River, NJ, 2000.

Saadat, Hadi, *Computational Aids in Control Systems using MATLAB*, McGraw-Hill, New York, NY, 1993.

Sigman, K. and Davis, T.A., *MATLAB Primer*, 6th ed., Chapman & Hall/CRC Press, Boca Raton, FL, 2002.

The MathWorks, Inc., *SIMULINK, Version 3*, The MathWorks, Inc., Natick, MA, 1999.

The MathWorks, Inc., *MATLAB: Application Program Interface Reference Version 6*, The MathWorks, Inc., Natick, 2000.

The MathWorks, Inc., *MATLAB: Control System Toolbox User's Guide, Version 4*, The MathWorks, Inc., Natick, 1992–1998.

The MathWorks, Inc., *MATLAB: Function Reference,* The MathWorks, Inc., Natick, 2000.

The MathWorks, Inc., *MATLAB: Symbolic Math Toolbox User's Guide, Version 2*, The MathWorks, Inc., Natick, 1993–1997.

The MathWorks, Inc., MATLAB: *Using MATLAB Graphics, Version 6*, The MathWorks, Inc., Natick, 2000.

The MathWorks, Inc., *MATLAB: Using MATLAB, Version 6*, The MathWorks, Inc., Natick, 2000.

INDEX

B

C

G

H

I

S

U

V

W

Y

Z